A Dictionary of Research Methodology and Statistics in Applied Linguistics

A Dictionary of Research Methodology and Statistics in Applied Linguistics

Hossein Tavakoli

سرشناسه:	توکلی، حسین، ۱۳۵۵- Tavakoli, Hossein
عنوان و نام پدیدآور:	A Dictionary of Research Methodology and Statistics in Applied Linguistics / Hossein Tavakoli
مشخصات نشر:	تهران: رهنما، ۱۳۹۰ = ۲۰۱۲م.
مشخصات ظاهری:	۷۶۱ ص.
شابک:	۰-۵۰۸-۳۶۷-۹۶۴-۹۷۸
یادداشت:	انگلیسی.
آوانویسی عنوان:	دیکشنری آو...
موضوع:	زبان شناسی کاربردی - - واژه‌نامه‌ها
رده‌بندی کنگره:	P۱۲۹/ت۹د۹ ۱۳۹۰
رده‌بندی دیویی:	۴۱۸/۰۰۳
شماره کتابشناسی ملی:	۲۶۶۳۵۰۶

All rights reserved. No part of this book may be reproduced in any form or by any means without the permission, in writing, from the Publisher.
RAHNAMA PRESS
Copyright © 2012
No. 112, Shohadaye Zhandarmerie St. (Moshtagh St.), Between Farvardin & Fakhre Razi, Enghelab Ave., Oppo. Tehran University, Tehran, Iran.
P.O. Box: 13145/1845 - Tel: (021) 66416604 & 66400927
E-mail: info@rahnamapress.com
http://www.rahnamapress.com
ISBN-13: 978-9643675080
IISBN-10: 9643675084

A Dictionary of Research Methodology and Statistics in Applied Linguistics، مؤلف: حسین توکلی، لیتوگرافی: رهنما، چاپ: چاپخانه نقره‌فام، چاپ اول: زمستان ۱۳۹۰، تیراژ: ۱۵۰۰ نسخه، ناشر: انتشارات رهنما، آدرس: مقابل دانشگاه تهران، خیابان فروردین، نبش خیابان شهدای ژاندارمری، پلاک ۱۱۲، تلفن: ۶۶۴۰۰۹۲۷، ۶۶۴۱۶۶۰۴، ۶۶۴۸۱۶۶۲، فاکس: ۶۶۴۶۷۴۲۴ فروشگاه رهنما، سعادت‌آباد، خیابان علامه طباطبایی جنوبی، بین ۴۰ و ۴۲ شرقی پلاک ۲۹، تلفن: ۸۸۶۹۴۱۰۲، آدرس فروشگاه شماره ۴: خیابان پیروزی نبش خیابان سوم نیروی هوایی، تلفن: ۷۷۴۸۲۵۰۵، نمایشگاه کتاب رهنما، مقابل دانشگاه تهران پاساژ فروزنده، تلفن: ۶۶۹۵۰۹۵۷، شابک: ۰-۵۰۸-۳۶۷-۹۶۴-۹۷۸

حق چاپ برای ناشر محفوظ است

To my mother

Introduction

'*A dictionary of research methodology and statistics in applied linguistics*' is a reference guide which offers an authoritative and comprehensive overview of key terms and concepts in the areas of research and statistics as concerns the field of applied linguistics. The volume is intended as a resource to delineate the meaning and use of various concepts, approaches, methods, designs, techniques, tools, types, and processes of applied linguistics research in an efficient and accessible style. Some entries relating to statistical aspects of research are also used so as to help the researcher in the successful formulation, analysis, and execution of the research design and carry the same towards its logical end. This book makes use of approximately 2000 entries on the key concepts and issues of research with cross references where necessary. Cross-referencing is achieved in several ways. Within the text, there are terms which have their own alphabetical entries and are printed in SMALL CAPITAL LETTERS. There are also in-text entries that are defined within the body of the paragraph and are printed in **bold letters**. Other entries that are related to the term at issue that might be of interest and further investigation are either provided in the main text or listed at the end of each entry under 'see' and 'see also' respectively. In this volume, the sign 📖 has also been used for representing the resources from which the materials have been reproduced or adapted.

This volume is designed to appeal to undergraduate and graduate students, teachers, lecturers, practitioners, researchers, consultants, and consumers of information across the field of applied linguistics and other related disciplines. I hope that this dictionary succeeds in fulfilling its intent as a resource that can convey essential information about research issues, practices, and procedures across the whole gamut of the applied linguistics.

I would very much welcome reactions and comments from readers, especially relating to points where I may have lapsed or strayed from accuracy of meaning, consistency of style, etc., in the interests of improving coverage and treatment for future editions.

Hossein Tavakoli 2012

A

ABA design
see EQUIVALENT TIME-SAMPLES DESIGN. See also SINGLE-SUBJECT REVERSAL DESIGN

ABAB design
see EQUIVALENT TIME-SAMPLES DESIGN. See also SINGLE-SUBJECT REVERSAL DESIGN

ABABA design
see EQUIVALENT TIME-SAMPLES DESIGN. See also SINGLE-SUBJECT REVERSAL DESIGN

ABACA design
see MULTIPLE-I DESIGN

ABCDEFG design
see MULTIPLE-I DESIGN

abduction
the least familiar mode of reasoning and the mode that was systematized most recently. In conjunction with deduction and induction (see INDUCTIVE REASONING, DEDUCTIVE REASONING), abduction is used to make logical inferences about the world. It is an interpretivist research strategy (see NORMATIVE PARADIGM). Whereas positivists (see POSITIVISM) and variable analysts marginalize the meaning-making activities of social actors, interpretivists focus on these activities, and in particular, individuals' intentions, reasons, and motives. This is an insider's perspective, and therefore outsider or external accounts of social actors' beliefs and intentions are considered to give a partial view of reality. It is the beliefs and practices of individuals that constitute the subject matter of research. The abductive process comprises the way educational researchers go beyond the accounts given by social actors about their plans, intentions, and actions in the real world. This process is multi-layered, with the first stage being the collection of data that reports how individuals understand reality, using methods such as semi-structured and auto-biographical interviews. At the second stage the researcher moves from reporting lay accounts to constructing social scientific theories about human relations. Some types of interpretivists argue that this constitutes an illegitimate step, and for them, concepts, ideas, and constructs have to be embedded in lay accounts, and their task is to report them.

There are a number of problems with this approach: the process of collecting data about these accounts is likely to influence them; and analyzing and reporting such constitute a going beyond the original account.
📖 Scott & Morrison 2005

abscissa
another term for HORIZONTAL AXIS

abstract
a brief summary of research that includes the research questions, the methods used and the results. The structure may vary but a well-written abstract should summarize five essential things to help the reader know what the study is about: (a) purpose of the study, (b) source(s) from where the data are drawn (usually referred to as PARTICIPANTS), (c) the method(s) used for collecting data, (d) the general results, and (e) general interpretation of the results.

A well-prepared abstract can be the most important single paragraph in an article. Most people have their first contact with an article by seeing just the abstract, usually in comparison with several other abstracts, as they are doing a literature search. Readers frequently decide on the basis of the abstract whether to read the entire article. The abstract needs to be dense with information. By embedding key words in your abstract, you enhance the user's ability to find it. A good abstract is:

- *Accurate*: You should ensure that the abstract correctly reflects the purpose and content of the manuscript. Do not include information that does not appear in the body of the manuscript. If the study extends or replicates previous research, note this in the abstract and cite the author's last name and the year of the relevant report. Comparing an abstract with an outline of the manuscript's headings is a useful way to verify its accuracy.
- *Nonevaluative*: You should report rather than evaluate; do not add to or comment on what is in the body of the manuscript.
- *Coherent and readable*: You should write in clear and concise language. You should use verbs rather than their noun equivalents and the active rather than the passive voice (e.g., *investigated* rather than *an investigation of; The authors presented the results* instead of *Results were presented*). Also, you should use the present tense to describe conclusions drawn or results with continuing applicability; use the past tense to describe specific variables manipulated or outcomes measured.
- *Concise*: You should be brief, and make each sentence maximally informative, especially the lead sentence. Begin the abstract with the most important points. Do not waste space by repeating the title. In-

clude in the abstract only the four or five most important concepts, findings, or implications. You should use the specific words in your abstract that you think your audience will use in their electronic searches.
see also RESEARCH REPORT
📖 American Psychological Association 2010; Mackey & Gass 2005; Perry 2011

ACASI
an abbreviation for AUDIO COMPUTER-ASSISTED SELF-INTERVIEWING

accelerated longitudinal design
a type of LONGITUDINAL MIXED DESIGN which is used in obtaining perspective-like data in less time; in such a design multiple COHORTs of different ages are observed longitudinally for shorter period of time. The idea is that if the cohorts are slightly overlapping, the researcher can statistically combine the cohorts and estimate a single growth path, extending from the youngest age observed to the oldest.
see also ROTATING PANELS, SPLIT PANELS, LINKED PANELS, COHORT STUDY, DIARY STUDY
📖 Dörnyei 2007

acceptability judgment
an ELICITATION tool in which a list of grammatical and ungrammatical sentences is presented to learners who are then asked to indicate whether they consider them acceptable in the second language or not.
📖 Mackey & Gass 2005

accessible population
see POPULATION

accidental sampling
another term for OPPORTUNISTIC SAMPLING

accommodation
a strategy employed when a researcher has reservations about removal or inclusion of OUTLIERs. Accommodation involves the use of a procedure which utilizes all the data, but at the same time minimizes the influence of outliers. Two obvious options within the framework of accommodation that reduce the impact of outliers are: a) use of the MEDIAN in lieu of the MEAN as a measure of central tendency; b) employing an inferential STATISTICAL TEST that uses rank-orders instead of *interval/ratio* data. Accommodation is often described within the context of employing a ROBUST statistical procedure (e.g., a procedure that assigns weights to the different observations when calculating the sample mean). Two commonly used methods for dealing with outliers (which are sometimes

discussed within the context of accommodation) are TRIMMING and WIN-SORIZATION.
📖 Sheskin 2011

accumulative treatment effect
another term for ORDER EFFECT

achievement test
a test which is designed to measure the knowledge and skills that individuals learn in a relatively well-defined area through formal or informal educational experiences. Achievement tests include tests designed by teachers for use in the classroom and standardized tests developed by school districts, states, national and international organizations, and commercial test publishers.
Achievement tests have been used for:

a) *summative purposes* (see SUMMATIVE EVALUATION) such as measuring student achievement, assigning grades, grade promotion and evaluation of competency, comparing student achievement across states and nations, and evaluating the effectiveness of teachers, programs, districts, and states in accountability programs;
b) *formative purposes* such as identifying student strengths and weaknesses, motivating students, teachers, and administrators to seek higher levels of performance, and informing educational policy; and
c) *placement and diagnostic purposes* such as selecting and placing students, and diagnosing learning disabilities, giftedness, and other special needs.

see also PROFICIENCY TEST
📖 Fernandez-Ballesteros 2003

acquiescence bias
also **acquiescence response bias**
a common threat inherent to QUESTIONNAIRE which refers to the tendency that respondents may have to say *yes*, regardless of the question or, indeed, regardless of what they really feel or think. Acquiescent people include yeasayers, who are ready to go along with anything that sounds good and the term also covers those who are reluctant to look at the negative side of any issue and are unwilling to provide strong negative responses. There are a number of strategies researchers may use to avoid or control for acquiescence response bias. One such strategy is to include multiple items to measure a construct of interest, approximately half of which are worded so that the 'agree' response indicates one position and the other half worded so that the 'agree' response indicates the opposite position. For example, respondents might be asked whether they agree or

disagree with the statement, 'It is important for the teacher to be a person of high moral character', and then later asked whether they agree or disagree with the statement, 'It is not important for the teacher to be a person of high moral character'. If respondents exhibit acquiescence response bias and agree with both statements, their answers to these two questions cancel each other out.

Another strategy for dealing with acquiescence response bias in agree-disagree questions involves rewriting all questions so that each question requires respondents to report directly about the dimension of interest. For example, the previous question about the importance of the teacher's moral character could be rewritten to read, 'How important do you believe it is for the teacher to have a strong moral character: extremely important, very important, somewhat important, a little important, or not at all important?' This strategy also allows researchers to avoid agree-disagree questions.

see also SOCIAL DESIRABILITY BIAS

📖 Cohen et al. 2011; Dörnyei 2003

acquiescence response bias
another term for ACQUIESCENCE BIAS

action research
also **practitioner research, teacher research, teacher-as-researcher**
a research approach which is an on-the-spot procedure designed to deal with a concrete problem located in an immediate situation. This means that a step-by-step process is constantly monitored over varying periods of time and by a variety of mechanisms (e.g., OBSERVATION, INTERVIEW, QUESTIONNAIRE, DIARY STUDY, and DISCOURSE ANALYSIS) so that ensuing feedback may be translated into modifications, adjustments, directional changes, redefinitions, as necessary, so as to bring about lasting benefit to the ongoing process itself. Action research involves *action* in that it seeks to bring about change, specifically in local educational contexts. It is usually associated with identifying and exploring an issue, question, dilemma, gap, or puzzle in your own context of work. It is also *research* because it entails the processes of systematically collecting, documenting, and analyzing data and it is participatory and collaborative in that teachers work together to examine their own classrooms.

Action research is a generic term for a family of related methods that share some important common principles. The most important tenet concerns the close link between research and teaching as well as the researcher and the teacher. It is conducted by or in cooperation with teachers for the purpose of gaining a better understanding of their educational environment and improving the effectiveness of their teaching. Thus, the enhancement of practice and the introduction of change into the social enterprise are central characteristics of action research. Traditionally, the teacher-researcher link was taken so seriously in this area that only research done by the teacher him/herself was considered action research proper. However, after it was realized that it is often unrealistic to expect teachers to have the expertise to conduct rigorous research, scholars started to emphasize the collaboration between teachers and researchers. This collaboration can take several forms, from the researcher owning the project and co-opting a participating teacher to real collaboration where researchers and teachers participate equally in the research agenda. The language teachers might reflect on their treatment of new students and decide that intervention (i.e., the INDEPENDENT VARIABLE or TREATMENT) would be appropriate. The nature of appropriate intervention might be apparent to the teacher, or it may be necessary to wait for a new intake, keep a JOURNAL and record lessons in order to build up a picture of the ways in which induction is handled in class. Analysis of this might reveal very prescriptive teacher-centered approaches that are not conducive to building a classroom community, so the teacher might develop a set of more appropriate strategies for achieving this end. These strategies could then be implemented with the next intake and their success evaluated on the basis of journals, recordings, and perhaps interviews.

There are two main types of action research, although variations and combinations of the two are possible: PRACTICAL ACTION RESEARCH and PARTICIPATORY ACTION RESEARCH.

 Cohen et al. 2011; Dörnyei 2007; McKay 2006; Richards 2003

adjacency pairs
see CONVERSATION ANALYSIS

adjusted R^2
another term for ADJUSTED R SQUARE

adjusted means
also **least squares means, adjusted treatment means**
statistical averages that have been corrected to compensate for data imbalances. OUTLIERs, present in data sets will often be removed as they have a large impact on the calculated MEANs of small POPULATIONs; an adjusted mean can be determined by removing these outlier figures. Adjusted means are calculated using a MULTIPLE REGRESSION equation. Adjusted means are frequently used in EXPERIMENTAL DESIGN when an increase in precision is desired and a concomitant observation is used. The overall objective is to adjust the average response so that it reflects the true effect of the treatment. For example, in studying both men and women who participate in a particular behavior or activity, it may be necessary

to adjust the data to account for the impact of gender on the results. Without using adjusted means, results that might at first seem attributable to participating in a certain activity or behavior could be skewed by the impact of participants' gender. In this example, men and women would be considered COVARIATEs, a type of VARIABLE that the researcher cannot control but that affects an experiment's results. Using adjusted means compensates for the covariates to see what the effect of the activity or behavior would be if there were no differences between the genders.
  Sahai & Khurshid 2001

adjusted R square
also **adjusted R^2**
a modified estimate of R SQUARE (R^2) in the POPULATION which takes into account the SAMPLE SIZE and the number of INDEPENDENT VARIABLEs (IVs). When a small sample is involved, the R square value in the sample tends to be a rather optimistic overestimation of the true value in the population. The adjusted R square statistic corrects this value to provide a better estimate of the true population value. The smaller the sample and the larger the number of IVs the larger the adjustment.
  Clark-Carter 2010; Pallant 2010

adjusted treatment means
another term for ADJUSTED MEANS

administrative panels
another term for LINKED PANELS

agency
a term used by researchers to describe the active and intentional role of the individual in the construction and reconstruction of social life. It is frequently aligned with, and even contrasted with, *structure*(s). Furthermore, some research methodologies, strategies, and methods prioritize agency, whereas others prioritize structures. If research is understood as the examination of persistent relational patterns of human conduct, which are sometimes institutionalized, then the methodology, strategy, or method that is adopted is likely to marginalize individual human intention or agency.
On the other hand, if researchers are concerned with human intentions and the reasons individuals give for their actions, then they are more likely to focus on methods and strategies that allow those individuals to give expression to these inner states. What is being suggested here is that methodologies that prioritize agency and do not seek to reduce the individual to a mere appendage of external structures require the application of certain types of data-collection processes, such as SEMI-STRUCTURED

INTERVIEWs, because only these are appropriate in the circumstances. However, there is a danger with some of these approaches, i.e., PHENOMENOLOGY or ETHNOMETHODOLOGY. First, persistent patterns of human relations or structures, whether institutional or discursive, are ignored; and second, descriptions of educational activities are reduced to individual actions with social influences being marginalized.
 Scott & Morrison 2005

agreement coefficient
also **percentage agreement**
a measure of INTERRATER RELIABILITY that provides an estimate of the proportion of subjects who have been consistently classified as masters and nonmasters on two administrations. Using a pre-determined CUT POINT, the subjects are classified on the basis of their scores into the master and non-master groups on each test administrations. A major disadvantage of simple percentage agreement is that a high degree of agreement may be obtained simply by chance, and thus it is impossible to compare percentage agreement across different situations where the distribution of data differs. This shortcoming can be overcome by using another common measure of agreement, COHEN'S KAPPA.
 Boslaugh & Watters 2008; Brown 2005

AH
an abbreviation for ALTERNATIVE HYPOTHESIS

alpha (α)
another term for SIGNIFICANCE LEVEL

alpha coefficient of reliability
another term for CRONBACH'S ALPHA

alpha (α) error
another term for TYPE I ERROR

alpha (α) level
another term for SIGNIFICANCE LEVEL

alpha (α) reliability
another term for CRONBACH'S ALPHA

alternate-form reliability
another term for PARALLEL-FORM RELIABILITY

alternative-form reliability
another term for PARALLEL-FORM RELIABILITY

alternative hypothesis
see NULL HYPOTHESIS

ANACOVA
an abbreviation for ANALYSIS OF COVARIANCE

analyses
a subsection in the METHOD section of a RESEARCH REPORT (sometimes headed *data analysis, statistical procedures,* or *design*) in which you describe how the data were arranged and analyzed in the study. The analyses should be explained just as they were planned, step by step. Were subjects placed into CONDITIONs that were manipulated, or were they observed naturalistically? If multiple conditions were created, how were participants assigned to conditions, through RANDOM ASSIGNMENT or some other selection mechanism? Was the study conducted as a BETWEEN-SUBJECTS or a WITHIN-SUBJECTS DESIGN? Usually, such analyses also have certain ASSUMPTIPONS, or preconditions, that must be met for the mathematical calculations to be accurate and appropriate.
see also PARTICIPANTS, MATERIALS, PROCEDURES
📖 American Psychological Association 2010; Brown 1988

analysis of covariance
also **ANCOVA, ANACOVA**
a statistical procedure which allows us to assess whether there are significant group differences on a single *continuous* DEPENDENT VARIABLE (DV), after statistically controlling for the effects of one or more continuous INDEPENDENT VARIABLEs (IVs) (i.e., COVARIATEs). Analysis of covariance (ANCOVA) allows one or more *categorical* IVs and one continuous DV, plus one or more covariate(s). Thus, ANCOVA always has at least two IVs (i.e., one or more categorical, grouping IVs, and one or more continuous covariates). To be sure that it is the IV that is doing the influencing, ANCOVA statistically removes the effect of the covariate(s). By removing the influence of these additional variables, ANCOVA can increase the power or sensitivity of the F VALUE. That is, it may increase the likelihood that you will be able to detect differences between your groups.
ANCOVA is similar to and an extension of ANALYSIS OF VARIANCE (ANOVA) in that they both examine group differences with the same kinds of IVs and DV. ANCOVA, however, has greater capability to fine-tune the nature of the group differences by including other possible confounding IVs or covariates (such as a pretest score or subject variables

such as intelligence, anxiety, aptitude scores). In essence, we are examining how much groups differ on a DV that is separate from any relationships with other EXTRANEOUS VARIABLEs. For example, if you want to compare the second language course achievement of two class groups, it may provide a fairer result if you remove statistically the language aptitude difference between the classes. Thus, when you want to compare a variable in two or more groups and suspect that the groups are not similar in terms of some important background variable (such as age, or aptitude) that is likely to effect the DV, you can specify this background variable as a covariate and then run an ANCOVA to test the group difference while controlling for this covariate. In this way, ANCOVA is like PARTIAL CORRELATION because it includes the variable whose effects you want to partial out in the analysis in order to separate them from the other effects. Thus, we get a purer picture of group differences than when just using ANOVA that does not allow the use of any covariates. ANCOVA is also the same as SEQUENTIAL MULTIPLE REGRESSION, with the covariate added at one stage and the IV added next. It tells us whether our IV adds significantly to the model when the covariate is already in the model.

ANCOVA carries with it all of the assumptions of any ANOVA test (e.g., NORMALITY, HOMOGENEITY OF VARIANCE). In addition, there are two additional assumptions that are important to meet when performing an ANCOVA: LINEARITY and HOMOGENEITY OF REGRESSION.

More specifically, ANCOVA requires the following pattern of correlations:

1) Covariates should be at least moderately correlated with the DV (e.g., $r > .30$). This makes it worthwhile to use up an extra degree of freedom for each covariate that is included. If the correlation between a covariate and a DV is too small, very little variance will be partialled out of the DV before examining group differences. At the same time, the degrees of freedom for the ERROR TERM are reduced, although the actual error term itself is not reduced substantially, leading to a slightly higher CRITICAL VALUE that is required to reach significance than would be the case without adding the covariate. Thus, the calculated F value has to jump a little higher when covariates are added. If the covariate is substantially correlated with the DV, the loss in a degree of freedom is more than compensated by the reduction in ERROR VARIANCE, making it easier to reach significance.

2) Covariates should be reliably measured. ANCOVA assumes that covariates are measured without error, which is a rather unrealistic assumption in much applied linguistics research. Some variables that you may wish to control, such as age, can be measured reasonably re-

liably; others which rely on a scale may not meet this assumption. Correlations between unreliable variables are less powerful than those with high reliability.
3) There should be low correlations among covariates if multiple CONTINUOUS VARIABLEs are added to an ANCOVA design. Variables that are highly correlated within a side (e.g., within IVs) lead to COLLINEARITY problems (e.g., instability and bias). ANCOVA assumes that the relationship between the DV and each of your covariates is linear (straight-line). If you are using more than one covariate, it also assumes a linear relationship between each of the pairs of your covariates. Violations of this assumption are likely to reduce the power (sensitivity) of your test. SCATTERPLOTs can be used to test for linearity, but these need to be checked separately for each of your groups (i.e. the different levels of your IV). Thus, it is always best to choose covariates that are relatively uncorrelated with each other.
4) Similarly, there should not be any appreciable correlation between covariates and grouping variables. In addition to collinearity problems, this could lead to a violation of an important assumption in ANCOVA, that of homogeneity of regressions. This impressive-sounding assumption requires that the relationship between the covariate and DV for each of your groups is the same. This is indicated by similar SLOPEs on the regression line for each group. Unequal slopes would indicate that there is an INTERACTION between the covariate and the TREATMENT. If there is an interaction, then the results of ANCOVA are misleading. In other words, a significant correlation between a covariate and the treatment can lead to violation of the assumption of homogeneity of regression, thereby invalidating the use of ANCOVA.

There are at least two occasions when ANCOVA can be used. Firstly, it is used in situations where a variable may be confounded with the IV and might affect the DV. Secondly, it is used when a *test-retest* design is used to allow for initial differences between groups that may mask differences in improvements. The scores on the pretest are treated as a covariate to control for pre-existing differences between the groups. However when, prior to introducing the experimental treatments, it is known that a strong correlation exists between the covariate and the DV, and that the groups are not equal with respect to the covariate, the following two options are available to a researcher: a) subjects can be randomly reassigned to groups, after which the researcher can check that the resulting groups are equivalent with respect to the covariate; or b) the covariate can be integrated into the study as a second IV.

Covariates can be entered into any of the ANOVA tests—ONE-WAY ANOVA, FACTORIAL ANOVA, and even REPEATED-MEASURES ANOVA. Analysis of covariance can be also used with multivariate designs (see MULTIVARIATE ANALYSIS OF COVARIANCE). There is no nonparametric alternative to an ANCOVA.

see also ONE-WAY ANCOVA, TWO-WAY ANCOVA, THREE-WAY ANCOVA, REPEATED-MEASURES ANCOVA

 Clark-Carter 2010; Dörnyei 2007; Harlow 2005; Larson-Hall 2010; Pallant 2010; Sheskin 2011; Tabachnick & Fidell 2007

analysis of dispersion
another term for MULTIVARIATE ANALYSIS OF VARIANCE

analysis of variance
also **ANOVA**
a term which describes a group of inferential statistical procedures which is used to analyze data from designs that involve *two* or *more* groups. Analysis of variance (for which the acronym ANOVA is often employed) is a *parametric* statistical procedure for comparing two or more group means to see if there are any statistically significant differences among them. ANOVA can be applied to a variety of research designs and takes specific names that reflect the design to which it has been applied. The computational details of the analysis become more complex with the design, but the essence of the test remains the same. The first distinction that is made is in the number of INDEPENDENT VARIABLEs (IVs) in the research design. If there is simply one IV, then the ANOVA is called a ONE-WAY ANOVA. If two IVs have been manipulated in the research, then a TWO-WAY ANOVA can be used to analyze the data; likewise if three IVs have been manipulated, a *three*-way ANOVA is appropriate. The logic of the test extends to any number of IVs. However, for ease of interpretation, researchers rarely go beyond a three-way ANOVA (ANOVAs involving more than one IV are known as FACTORIAL ANOVAs).

The second distinction that needs to be made is whether data in different conditions are *independent* or *related*. If data representing different levels (e.g., gender with two levels: female/male) of an IV are independent (i.e., collected from different groups or subjects), then an independent ANOVA can be used. If, for example, two IVs have been used and all levels of all variables contain data from different groups, then a *two*-way (independent) ANOVA could be employed, and so on. When data are related, for example, when the same groups or subjects have provided data for all levels of an IV or all levels of several IVs, a REPEATED MEASURES ANOVA can be employed. As with independent designs, it is possible to have *one*-way, *two*-way, *three*-way, *n*-way repeated measures ANOVAs.

A final type of ANOVA is used when a mixture of independent and related data have been collected. These *mixed* designs require at least two IVs, one of which has been manipulated using different groups or subjects (and so data are independent) and the other of which has been manipulated using the same groups or subjects (and so data are related). In these situations, a MIXED ANOVA (also called *between-within ANOVA*) is used. It is possible to combine different numbers of IVs measured using different groups or the same groups to come up with *three*-way, *four*-way, or *n*-way mixed ANOVAs.

All the ANOVAs above have some common features. All of them produce a statistic called the **F value** (commonly referred to as an **F ratio**), which is the ratio of the BETWEEN-GROUPS VARIANCE to the WITHIN-GROUPS VARIANCE. The *observed* value of F is compared with CRITICAL VALUEs of F from a special distribution known as the F DISTRIBUTION, which represents the values of F that can be expected at certain levels of probability. If the observed value exceeds the critical value for a small PROBABILITY (typically $p < .05$), you tend to infer that the model is a significant fit of the observed data or, in the case of experiments, that the experimental manipulation or treatment has had a significant effect on performance. The larger the between-groups variance relative to the within-groups variance, the larger the calculated value of F, and the more likely it is that the differences among the groups means reflect true effects of the IV rather than ERROR VARIANCE. If the F ratio is statistically significant ($p < .05$), a POST HOC COMPARISON test is, then, conducted to determine which means are significantly different from each other.

The main difference among ANOVAs is the effects that they produce. In an ANOVA with one IV, a single value of F is produced that tests the effect of that variable. In factorial ANOVAs, however, multiple Fs are produced: one for each effect and one for every combination of effects (see INTERACTION).

📖 Dörnyei 2007; Gray 2009; Larson-Hall 2010; Mackey & Gass 2005; Porte 2010; Salkind 2007

analytical statistics
another term for INFERENTIAL STATISTICS

analytic hierarchy
a process through which qualitative findings are built from the original raw data. It is described as a form of conceptual scaffolding within which the structure of the analysis is formed. The process is iterative (see ITERATION) and thus constant movement up and down the hierarchy is needed. The analytic process requires three forms of activity: data management in which the raw data are reviewed, labeled, sorted and synthesized; descriptive accounts in which the analyst makes use of the ordered

data to identifying key dimensions, map the range and diversity of each phenomenon and develop classifications and typologies; and explanatory accounts in which the analyst builds explanations about why the data take the forms that are found and presented.
 Ritchie & Lewis 2003

analytic induction
a process of developing constructs such as categories, statements of relationship, and generalizations as well as the theory resulting from integrating categories and generalizations by examining incidents, events, and other information relevant to a topic. Abstraction from the concrete to a more inclusive formulation is a key task in analytic induction. Analytic induction asks the following of any event, activity, situation, or attribute: 'What kind of event, activity, situation, or attribute is this particular one?' Classification is another central feature of analytic induction. From a close analysis of an initial case, constructs are generated and are refined through consideration of succeeding instances.
 Given 2008

analytic realism
a humanistic approach to qualitative methodology, particularly ETHNOGRAPHY, focusing on what they called the empirical world of lived experience (see EMPIRICISM). Like SUBTLE REALISM, analytic realism rejects the dichotomy of REALISM and RELATIVISM, although it is argued that analytic realism places the stronger emphasis on knowledge verification. Ontological assumptions (see ONTOLOGY) concern the social world, and this is conceptualized as interpreted rather than literal. Epistemologically (see EPISTEMOLOGY), interpretation is accepted as a valid way of knowing even though knowledge is considered relative to a perspective and it is accepted that different researchers, and research conducted at different points in time, may come to different conclusions. So, although analytic realism shares with NATURALISM a faith in immersive understanding, it includes a particular concern with the INTERPRETIVE VALIDITY of research accounts and is careful to specify criteria increasing the validity of reports. Criteria include clear delineation of the research context and method, reflexive reporting, and attention to the multivocality of members' perspectives. Such procedures do not ensure the objective truth of findings given that the report is considered to be truth only as the researcher has come to understand it, but they make the researchers claims better open to evaluation.
see also SCIENTIFIC REALISM, CRITICAL REALISM, NAIVE REALISM
 Given 2008

ANCOVA
an abbreviation for ANALYSIS OF COVARIANCE

ANOVA
an abbreviation for ANALYSIS OF VARIANCE

ANOVA F test
another term for OMNIBUS F TEST

Ansari-Bradley test
a NONPARAMETRIC TEST for testing the EQUALITY OF VARIANCEs of two POPULATIONs having the common MEDIAN. In some instances, it may be necessary to test for differences in spread while assuming that the centers of two populations are identical. One example is comparing two assay methods to see which is more precise. ASSUMPTIONS for this test are that within each sample the observations are independent and identically distributed. Further, the two samples must be independent of each other, with equal medians.
see also SIEGEL-TUKEY TEST; KLOTZ TEST, CONOVER TEST, MOSES TEST
 Sahai & Khurshid 2001

anti-foundationalism
see POSTSTRUCTURALISM

antimode
see MODE

APA style
guidelines set forth by the American Psychological Association for preparing research reports.
 American Psychological Association 2010

a-parameter
see ITEM CHARACTERISTIC CURVE

a posteriori test
another term for POST HOC TEST

appendix
a section of a RESEARCH REPORT which includes the material that cannot be logically included in the main body or textual body of the research report or the relevant materials too unwieldy to include in the main body. The appendix usually includes: tools of research, statistical tables and sometime raw-data. Even the material of minor importance e.g., forms,

letters, reminders, INTERVIEW sheets, blank QUESTIONNAIREs, charts, tables, lengthy questions, report of cases (if follow-up or case studies have been conducted). The important thing to remember is that appendices should be cross-referenced in the text. The readers should be made aware at what point during the report they need to turn to the appendix and make use of the information. Without such clear signposting, the appendices will just take on the form of some additional information that has been included at the end to pad out the report.

Like the main text, an appendix may include headings and subheadings as well as tables, figures, and displayed equations. All appendix tables and figures must be cited within the appendix and numbered in order of citation.

see also TITLE, ABSTRACT, INTRODUCTION, METHOD, RESULTS, DISCUSSION, REFERENCES

📖 American Psychological Association 2010; Henn et al. 2006

applied linguistics

an academic discipline which is concerned with the relation of knowledge about language to decision making in the real world. Generally, applied linguistics can be defined as the theoretical and empirical investigation of real-world problems in which language is a central issue. In this sense applied linguistics mediates between theory and practice. Applied linguistics can be described as a broad interdisciplinary field of study concerned with solutions to problems or the improvement of situations involving language and its users and uses. The emphasis on application distinguishes it from the study of language in the abstract—that is, general or theoretical linguistics.

But there is another tradition of applied linguistics, which belongs to linguistics; it is sometimes called **Linguistics-Applied** (L-A) but perhaps 'applications of linguistics' would be a more appropriate title for this tradition. This version has become more noticeable in the last 20 years as theoretical linguistics has moved back from its narrowly formalist concern to its former socially accountable role (e.g., in Bible translation, developing writing systems, dictionary making). The differences between these modes of intervention is that in the case of linguistics applied the assumption is that the problem can be reformulated by the direct and unilateral application of concepts and terms deriving from linguistic enquiry itself. That is to say, language problems are amenable to linguistics solutions. In the case of applied linguistics, intervention is crucially a matter of mediation. It has to relate and reconcile different representations of reality, including that of linguistics without excluding others.

📖 Cook 2003; Davies & Elder 2004; Simpson 2011

applied research

a type of RESEARCH which is designed to deal with human and societal problems in the hopes of finding solutions to real-world problems. Applied research focuses on the use of knowledge rather than the pursuit of knowledge for its own sake. A motivation behind applied research is to engage with people, organizations, or interests beyond the academic discipline and for knowledge to be useful outside the context in which it was generated. A great deal of research in the field of teaching is, of course, applied research. Second language educators, for example, have investigated why some students are reluctant to contribute to class discussions, what is the most effective type of feedback on student essays, and what is the most productive number of vocabulary items to introduce at one time.

Applied research is more limited in its questions and conclusions. It does not attempt to define a theory of language learning that accounts for all language learners; rather it sets forth findings that apply to a particular time, place, and context.

see also BASIC RESEARCH

📖 Mckay 2006; Sapsford & Jupp 2006

approximate replication

see REPLICATION

approximate test

see CONSERVATIVE TEST

a priori test

also **planned test, a priori comparison, planned contrasts, planned comparison**

a test (comparison or contrast) which is specified before the data are collected or analyzed. A priori tests are used when you wish to test specific preplanned hypotheses concerning the differences (usually base on theory, experience, or the results of previous studies) between a subset of your groups (e.g., 'Do Groups 1 and 3 differ significantly?'). These comparisons need to be specified, or planned, before you analyze your data, not after fishing around in your results to see what looks interesting! Here you are interested in certain specific contrasts a priori, where the number of such contrasts is usually small. Some caution needs to be exercised with this approach if you intend to specify a lot of different contrasts.

A priori tests are done without regard to the result of the OMNIBUS F TEST. In other words, the researcher is interested in certain specific contrasts, but not in the omnibus F test that examines all possible contrasts. In this situation the researcher could care less about the multitude of possible contrasts and need not even examine the *F* test; but rather the concern is only with a few contrasts of substantive interest. In addition, a priori comparisons do not control for the increased risks of TYPE I ERRORs. In other words there is an increased risk of thinking that you have found a significant result when in fact it could have occurred by chance. Fewer planned comparisons are usually conducted (due to their specificity) than POST HOC TESTs (due to their generality), so planned contrasts generally yield narrower CONFIDENCE INTERVALs, are more powerful, and have a higher likelihood of a Type I error than post hoc comparisons. If there are a large number of differences that you wish to explore, it may be safer to use post hoc tests, which are designed to protect against Type I errors.

📖 Lomax 2007; Pallant 2010

arbitrary scale

a RATING SCALE which is developed on ad hoc basis and is designed largely through the researcher's own subjective selection of items. The researcher first collects few statements or items which s/he believes are unambiguous and appropriate to a given topic. Some of these are selected for inclusion in the measuring instrument and then people are asked to check in a list the statements with which they agree. The chief merit of such scales is that they can be developed very easily, quickly and with relatively less expense. They can also be designed to be highly specific and adequate. Because of these benefits, such scales are widely used in practice. At the same time there are some limitations of these scales. The most important one is that we do not have objective evidence that such scales measure the concepts for which they have been developed. We have simply to rely on researcher's insight and competence.

see also LIKERT SCALE, SEMANTIC DIFFERENTIAL SCALE, DIFFERENTIAL SCALE, CUMULATIVE SCALE

📖 Kothari 2008

archival data

data that have already been collected, typically by the individual teacher, school, or district rather than by a researcher. Student absenteeism, graduation rates, suspensions, standardized state test scores, and teacher grade-book data are all examples of archival data that might be used in educational research or assessment. It is not uncommon for researchers to combine several different types of archival data in a single study.

Archival data is particularly suited for studying certain kinds of questions. First, it is uniquely suited for studying social and psychological phenomena that occurred in the historical past. We can get a glimpse of how people thought, felt, and behaved by analyzing records from earlier times. Second, archival research is useful for studying social and behavioral changes over time. Third, certain research topics require an archival approach because they inherently involve documents such as newspaper articles, magazine advertisements, or speeches. Finally, researchers sometimes use archival sources of data because they cannot conduct a study that will provide the kind of data they desire or because they realize a certain event needs to be studied after it has already occurred.

The major limitation of archival research is that the researcher must make do with whatever measures are already available. Sometimes, the existing data are sufficient to address the research question, but often important measures simply do not exist. Even when the data contain the kinds of measures that the researcher needs, the researcher often has questions about how the information was initially collected and, thus, concerns about the reliability and validity of the data.
 Leary 2011; Lodico et al. 2010

area sampling
also **block sampling**

a type of PROBABILITY SAMPLING which is quite close to CLUSTER SAMPLING and is often talked about when the total geographical area of interest happens to be big one. Area sampling is a form of sampling in which the clusters that are selected are drawn from maps rather than listings of individuals, groups, institutions or whatever. Sometimes a further subsample is taken in which case the phrase MULTISTAGE SAMPLING is used. If clusters happen to be some geographic subdivisions, in that case cluster sampling is better known as area sampling. In other words, cluster designs, where the primary SAMPLING UNIT represents a cluster of units based on geographic area, are distinguished as area sampling. Under area sampling we first divide the total area into a number of smaller non-overlapping areas, generally called geographical clusters, then a number of these smaller areas are randomly selected, and all units in these small areas are included in the sample.

Area sampling is specially helpful where there are no adequate population lists, which are replaced instead by maps. However, the boundaries on such maps must be clearly defined and recognizable, both at the stage of sampling and at the stage of data collection. This form of sampling is not appropriate where the aim of the research is to follow a COHORT of individuals over time because of the population changes within the areas that have been selected in the sample.

see also SIMPLE RANDOM SAMPLING, SYSTEMATIC SAMPLING, STRATIFIED SAMPLING, CLUSTER SAMPLING, MULTI-PHASE SAMPLING
 Kothari 2008; Sapsford & Jupp 2006

arithmetic mean
another term for MEAN

array

a simple arrangement of the individual scores or values of a data set arranged in order of magnitude, from the smallest to the largest value. For example, for the data set (2, 7, 5, 9, 3, 4, 6), an ordered array is (2, 3, 4, 5, 6, 7, 9).
    Sahai & Khurshid 2001

assignment matrix

another term for CLASSIFICATION MATRIX

association

another term for CORRELATION

assumption(s)

certain specific conditions that should be satisfied for the application of certain statistical procedures in order to produce valid statistical results. The principal assumptions are those which come up most frequently in applied linguistics studies: INDEPENDENCE ASSUMPTION, NORMALITY, HOMOGENEITY OF VARIANCE, LINEARITY, MULTICOLLINEARITY, and HOMOSCEDASTICITY. For example, ANALYSIS OF VARIANCE generally assumes normality, homogeneity of variance and independence of the observations. In some cases, these assumptions are not optional; they must be met for the statistical test to be meaningful. However, the assumptions will be of lesser or greater importance for different statistical tests. In addition, arguments have been proposed that certain statistics are ROBUST to violations of certain assumptions. Nonetheless, it is important for readers to verify that the researcher has thought about and checked the assumptions underlying any statistical tests which were used in a study and that those assumptions were met or are discussed in terms of the potential effects of violations on the results of the study.

Checking your data numerically and graphically can help you determine if data meet the assumptions of the test. If your data do not meet the assumptions of the test, then you will have less power to find the true results.
    Brown 1988, 1992

asymptotic

see NORMAL DISTRIBUTION

attenuation

also **correlation for attenuation**

a statistics which is used for correcting CORRELATION between two measures, when both measures are subject to MEASUREMENT ERROR. Many variables in applied linguistics are measured with some degree of

error or unreliability. For example, intelligence is not expected to vary substantially from day to day. Yet scores on an intelligence test may vary suggesting that the test is unreliable. If the measures of two variables are known to be unreliable and those two measures are correlated, the correlation between these two measures will be attenuated or weaker than the correlation between those two variables if they had been measured without any error. The greater the unreliability of the measures, the lower the real relationship will be between those two variables. The correlation between two measures may be corrected for their unreliability if we know the RELIABILITY of one or both measures.
 Cramer & Howitt 2004

attitudinal question
see QUESTIONNAIRE

attrition
another term for MORTALITY

audio computer-assisted self-interviewing
also **ACASI**
a methodology for collecting data that incorporates a recorded voice into a traditional COMPUTER-ASSISTED SELF-INTERVIEWING (CASI). Respondents participating in an audio computer-assisted self-interviewing (ACASI) SURVEY read questions on a computer screen and hear the text of the questions read to them through headphones. They then enter their answers directly into the computer either by using the keyboard or a touch screen, depending on the specific hardware used. While an interviewer is present during the interview, s/he does not know how the respondent answers the survey questions, or even which questions the respondent is being asked.
Typically the ACASI methodology is incorporated into a longer COMPUTER-ASSISTED PERSONAL INTERVIEW (CAPI). In these situations, an interviewer may begin the face-to-face interview by asking questions and recording the respondent's answers into the computer herself/himself. Then in preparation for the ACASI questions, the interviewer will show the respondent how to use the computer to enter his/her own answers. ACASI offers all the benefits of CASI, most notably:

a) the opportunity for a respondent to input her/his answers directly into a computer without having to speak them aloud to the interviewer (or risk having them overheard by someone else nearby);
b) the ability to present the questions in a standardized order across all respondents;

c) the ability to incorporate far more complex skip routing and question customization than is possible for a paper-based SELF-ADMINISTERED QUESTIONNAIRE; and
d) the opportunity to eliminate questions left blank, inconsistent responses, and out-of-range responses.

In addition, the audio component allows semi-literate or fully illiterate respondents to participate in the interview with all of the same privacy protections afforded to literate respondents. This is significant, because historically, in self-administered surveys it was not uncommon for individuals who could not read to either be excluded from participation in the study altogether or to be included but interviewed in a traditional interviewer-administered manner, resulting in the potential for significant mode effects.
 Lavrakas 2008

auditing
another term for PEER REVIEW

audit trail
an indicator which provide a mechanism by which others can determine how decisions were made and the uniqueness of the situation. It documents how the study was conducted, including what was done, when, and why. All research, regardless of paradigm, approach, or methods, should be auditable. It is expected that research be open and transparent. Readers should not be left in the dark in relation to any aspect of the research process. The audit trail contains the raw data gathered in INTERVIEWs and OBSERVATIONs, records of the inquirer's decisions about whom to interview or what to observe and why, files documenting how working hypotheses were developed from the raw data and subsequently refined and tested, the findings of the study, and so forth. The researcher must keep thorough notes and records of activities and should keep data well organized and in a retrievable form. S/he should provide information on the sample of people studied, the selection process, contextual descriptions, methods of data collection, detailed FIELDNOTES, tape recordings, videotapes, and other descriptive material that can be reviewed by other people. Using the audit trail as a guide, an independent third-party auditor can examine the inquirer's study in order to attest to the dependability of procedures employed and to examine whether findings are confirmable—that is, whether they are logically derived from and grounded in the data that were collected. A complete presentation of procedures and results enables the reader to make a judgment about the rep-

licability (see REPLICATION) of the research within the limits of the natural context.
📖 Ary et al. 2010; O'Leary 2004

authentic assessment
another term for PERFORMANCE ASSESSMENT

autocorrelation
a measure of the linear relationship between two separate instances of the same RANDOM VARIABLE often expressed as a function of the lag time between them. Often employed for TIME-SERIES DESIGN analysis, autocorrelation is the same as calculating the correlation between two different time series, except that the same time series is used twice—once in its original form and once lagged one or more time periods. When autocorrelation is used to quantify the linear relationship between values at points in space that are a fixed distance apart it is called **spatial autocorrelation**. Similarly, an autocorrelation between the two observations of a time series after controlling for the effects of intermediate observations is called **partial autocorrelation**. As with correlation the possible values lie between -1 and +1 inclusive, with unrelated instances having a theoretical autocorrelation of 0. An autocorrelation of +1 represents perfect positive correlation (i.e. an increase seen in one time series will lead to a proportionate increase in the other time series), while a value of -1 represents perfect negative correlation (i.e. an increase seen in one time series results in a proportionate decrease in the other time series).
Autocorrelation can be employed to evaluate either a CONTINUOUS or CATEGORICAL VARIABLE for randomness.
see also SERIAL CORRELATION
📖 Everitt & Skrondal 2010; Sahai & Khurshid 2001; Sheskin 2011; Upton & Cook 2008

autoethnography
a form of self-narrative that places the self within a social context. Autoethnography includes methods of research and writing that combine autobiography and ETHNOGRAPHY. The term has a dual sense and can refer either to the ethnographic study of one's own group(s) or to autobiographical reflections that include ethnographic observations and analysis. In autoethnography there is both self-reference and reference to culture. It is a method that combines features of life history and ethnography. The term autoethnography has been used both by qualitative researchers, who emphasize the connections between ethnography and autobiography, and by literary critics who are mainly concerned with the voices of ethnic autobiographers.
Autoethnography can be associated with forms of the following: first, native anthropology or self-ethnography in which those who previously

were the objects of anthropological inquiry come to undertake ETHNOGRAPHIC RESEARCH themselves on their own ethnic or cultural group; second, ethnic autobiography in which autobiographers emphasize their ethnic identity and ethnic origins in their life narrative; and third, autobiographical ethnography—a reflexive approach in which ethnographers analyze their own subjectivity and life experiences (usually within the context of fieldwork).

In literary theory, autoethnography is frequently viewed as a form of counter-narrative. Memoirs, life histories, and other forms of self-representation are analyzed as autoethnographies when they deal with topics such as transnationalism, biculturalism or other forms of border crossing, and local cultural practices. Ethnographers make use of such texts to explore these issues in the context of life experiences and cultural constructions of these. Ethnographers have also adopted the term autoethnography to label forms of self-reflexivity.

see also QUALITATIVE RESEARCH, LIFE HISTORY RESEARCH
📖 Sapsford & Jupp 2006

average

a number which represents the usual or typical value in a set of data. Average is virtually synonymous with measures of CENTRAL TENDENCY. Common averages in statistics are the MEAN, MEDIAN, and MODE. There is no single conception of average and every average contributes a different type of information. For example, the mode is the most common value in the data whereas the mean is the numerical average of the scores and may or may not be the commonest score. There are more averages in statistics than are immediately apparent. For example, the HARMONIC MEAN occurs in many statistical calculations such as the STANDARD ERROR of differences often without being explicitly mentioned as such.

In TESTS OF SIGNIFICANCE, it can be quite important to know what measure of central tendency (if any) is being assessed. Not all statistics compare the arithmetic means or averages. Some NONPARAMETRIC TESTS, for example, make comparisons between medians.

see also GEOMETRIC MEAN
📖 Cramer & Howitt 2004

average inter-item correlation

a measure of INTERNAL CONSISTENCY RELIABILITY which uses all of the items on your instrument that are designed to measure the same construct. You first compute the CORRELATION between each pair of items, as illustrated Figure A.1. For example, if you have six items, you will have 15 different item pairings (15 correlations). The average inter-item correlation is simply the average or MEAN of all these correlations. In the example, you find an average inter-item correlation of .90 with the individual correlations ranging from .84 to .95.

see also CRONBACH'S ALPHA, KUDER-RICHARDSON FORMULAS, SPLIT-HALF RELIABILITY, AVERAGE ITEM-TOTAL CORRELATION

📖 Trochim & Donnelly 2007

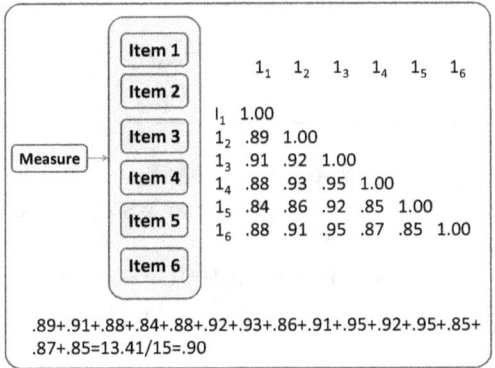

Figure A.1. The Average Inter-Item Correlation

average item-total correlation

a measure of INTERNAL CONSISTENCY RELIABILITY which uses the inter-item correlations (the CORRELATION of each item with the sum of all the other relevant items). In addition, you compute a total score for the six items and use that as a seventh variable in the analysis.

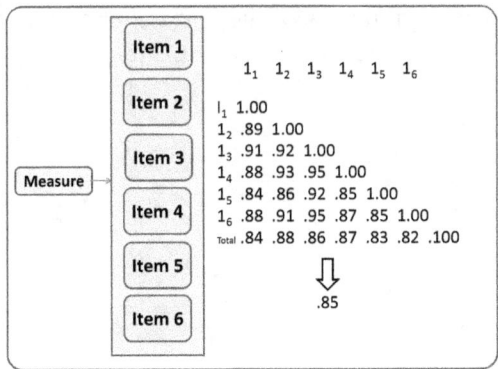

Figure A.2. Average Item-Total Correlation

Figure A.2 shows the six item-to-total correlations at the bottom of the CORRELATION MATRIX. They range from .82 to .88 in this sample analysis, with the average of these at .85.
see also CRONBACH'S ALPHA, KUDER-RICHARDSON FORMULAS, SPLIT-HALF RELIABILITY, AVERAGE INTER-ITEM CORRELATION
📖 Trochim & Donnelly 2007

axial coding
see CODING

axiology
the study of value. In QUALITATIVE RESEARCH, there is an assumption that all research is value-laden, and includes the value systems of the researcher, the theory, research methodology, and research paradigm, as well as the social and cultural norms of the researcher and participants.
see also EPISTEMOLOGY, ONTOLOGY, NATURALISM
📖 Heigham & Croker 2009

B

balanced data
see BALANCED DESIGN

balanced design
also **orthogonal design**
a term which is used to denote a FACTORIAL DESIGN with two or more FACTORs having an equal number of values or observations in each CELL or LEVEL of a factor, and where each TREATMENT occurs the same number of times at all the levels. Experimental data that are obtained by using an orthogonal design are called **balanced data** (also called **orthogonal data**). With a balanced design, each of the two INDEPENDENT VARIABLEs (IVS) and the INTERACTION are independent of each other. Each IV can be significant or non-significant, and the interaction can be significant or non-significant without any influence from one or the other effects. In contrast, when the groups or cells have unequal group values, the analysis is called the UNBALANCED DESIGN.
 Hatch & Lazaraton 1991; Porte 2010; Sahai & Khurshid 2001

bar chart
another term for BAR GRAPH

bar graph
also **bar chart, bar diagram, barplot**
a graph with a series of bars next to each other which illustrates the FREQUENCY DISTRIBUTION of nominal or ordinal values. In a bar graph, as shown in Figure B.1, scores are represented on the **horizontal axis** (also called **X axis, abscissa**), and frequencies of occurrence for each score are represented along the **vertical axis** (also called **Y axis, ordinate**). Here the X axis is labeled from left to right, which corresponds to low to high. Similarly, the height of each bar is the score's frequency. The larger the frequency of occurrence, the taller, or longer, the bar. The bars in a bar graph represent CATEGORICAL DATA, and do not imply a continuum. To indicate that each bar is independent of the other bars and represent discrete, or categorical data, such as frequencies or percentages of occurrence in different groups or categories, these bars should not touch (i.e., there are gaps between the bars).

Occasionally, we may want to compare data from two or more groups within each category, in addition to comparing the data across categories. To facilitate such comparison, we can use multiple joint bars within each category (see COMPOUND HISTOGRAM).
 Heiman 2011; Ravid 2011

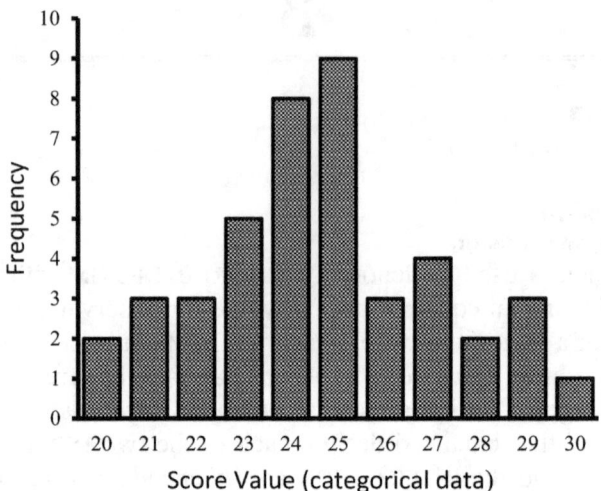

Figure B.1. An Example of Bar Graph

barplot
another term for BAR GRAPH

Bartlett's test
a test procedure for testing three or more INDEPENDENT SAMPLES for HOMOGENEITY OF VARIANCEs before using an ANALYSIS OF VARIANCE procedure. Bartlett's test is useful whenever the assumption of equal variances across samples is made. Bartlett's test is sensitive to departures from NORMALITY. That is, if your samples come from nonnormal distributions, then Bartlett's test may simply be testing for nonnormality. The LEVENE'S TEST is an alternative to the Bartlett's test that is less sensitive to departures from normality.
see also BOX'S M TEST, COCHRAN'S C TEST, HARTLEY'S TEST, LEVENE'S TEST, BROWN-FORSYTHE TEST, O'BRIEN TEST
📖 Cramer & Howitt 2004; Everitt & Skrondal 2010; Tabachnick & Fidell 2007; Upton & Cook 2008

baseline measurement
a measure to assess scores on a VARIABLE prior to some INTERVENTION or change. It is the starting point before a variable or treatment may have had its influence. The basic sequence of the research would be baseline measurement → treatment → post-treatment measure of same variable.
📖 Cramer & Howitt 2004

basement effect
another term for FLOOR EFFECT

base number
see POWER

basic research
also **fundamental research, pure research**
a type of research which is designed to acquire knowledge for the sake of knowledge. Basic research deals mainly with generating highly abstract constructs and theories that may have little apparent practical use. It is conducted to investigate issues relevant to the confirmation or disconfirmation of theoretical or empirical positions. The major goal of basic research is to acquire general information about a phenomenon, with little emphasis placed on applications to real-world examples of the phenomenon. For example, basic research studies are not, at first sight, very appealing to the classroom teacher who is looking for immediate ways to improve his/her students' learning. Nevertheless, these studies are important for looking at the underlying linguistic, psychological, or sociological mechanisms that might be eventually applied in the classroom. In fact, one might argue that this type of research reveals the theoretical foundations on which all other research rests. For example, unless we have demonstrated in basic research that the brain processes information in a certain way, it would be difficult to promote a teaching method that elicits this type of brain processing.

Often basic research is undertaken in disciplines like biology, physics, astronomy, and geology and is used by researchers who want to verify theories of their discipline. Cosmologists, for example, may be concerned about-testing theories about the origin of the universe. Physicists may be concerned about verifying the qualities of molecules. But basic research is also a tradition in applied linguistics. Research that seeks to verify such things as the order that learners acquire grammatical rules or the importance of input in language learning are examples of basic research in the field of second language acquisition (SLA).
see also APPLIED RESEARCH
📖 Bordens & Abbott 2011; Mckay 2006; Perry 2011

Bayesian *t*-value
see WALLER-DUNCAN *t*-TEST

Bayes' Theorem
another term for WALLER-DUNCAN *t*-TEST

before-after design
another term for ONE-GROUP PRETEST-POSTTEST DESIGN

behavioral question
see QUESTIONNAIRE

bell-shaped curve
another term for NORMAL DISTRIBUTION

bell-shaped distribution
another term for NORMAL DISTRIBUTION

beta (B)
an abbreviation for UNSTANDARDIZED PARTIAL REGRESSION COEFFICIENT

beta (β)
an abbreviation for STANDARDIZED PARTIAL REGRESSION COEFFICIENT

beta (β)
see TYPE I ERROR

beta (β) coefficient
another term for STANDARDIZED PARTIAL REGRESSION COEFFICIENT

beta (β) error
another term for TYPE II ERROR

beta (β) weight
another term for BETA (β) COEFFICIENT

between-groups design
another term for BETWEEN-SUBJECTS DESIGN

between-groups factor
also **between-groups independent variable, between-subjects factor, between-subjects independent variable**
a *categorical* INDEPENDENT VARIABLE (IV) which is studied using INDEPENDENT SAMPLES in all CONDITIONs. If it is a between-groups (subjects) factor, then each participant can be in only one of the levels of the IV. In contrast, a **within-groups factor** (also called **within-subjects factor, within-groups independent variable, within-subjects independent variable, repeated-measures factor, within-participants factor, nested variable**) is an IV which is studied using related samples in all conditions. If it is a within-groups variable, then each participant will be included in all of the levels of the variable. For example, if the subjects receive instruction in only one teaching method, this is a between-groups IV because their

scores are only found in one level of the Teaching Method variable. However, if they received instruction in the three different teaching methods and scores were recorded after each type of instruction, this would be a within-groups variable since the same subjects' scores were in all levels of the variable.

Studies which measure between-groups and within-groups factors are called BETWEEN-GROUPS and WITHIN-GROUPS DESIGNs respectively.
📖 Larson-Hall 2010; Perry 2011

between-groups factorial ANOVA
another term for FACTORIAL ANOVA

between-groups factorial design
another term for FACTORIAL DESIGN

between-groups independent variable
another term for BETWEEN-GROUPS FACTOR

between-groups sum of squares
another term for SUM OF SQUARES BETWEEN GROUPS

between-groups variability
another term for SYSTEMATIC VARIANCE

between-groups variance
another term for SYSTEMATIC VARIANCE

between-subjects design
also **between-groups design, independent samples design, randomized-groups design, independent measures design, unrelated design, uncorrelated design**
an EXPERIMENTAL DESIGN in which there is at least one BETWEEN-GROUPS FACTOR (e.g., gender, teaching method). This between-groups INDEPENDENT VARIABLE (IV) compares different groups of subjects. For example, a researcher who compares reading achievement scores for students taught by one method with scores for an equivalent group of students taught by a different method is using a between-subjects design. The basic idea behind this type of design is that participants can be part of the treatment group or the control group, but cannot be part of both. Every participant is only subjected to a single treatment condition or group. This lowers the chances of participants suffering boredom after a long series of tests or, alternatively, becoming more accomplished through practice and experience, skewing the results. In between-groups

designs, the differences among subjects are uncontrolled and are treated as error.

Between-subjects designs can theoretically contain any number of between-subjects IVs. They may be called **one-way, two-way, three-way between-subjects** (or groups) **design**s, or higher, depending on how many IVs are included. A between-subjects design with two or more IVs is called a FACTORIAL DESIGN. When using a factorial design, the IV is referred to as a *factor* and the different values of a factor are referred to as *levels*.

The most appropriate statistical analysis for a between-subjects design is ANOVA, which takes into account the fact that the measures are independent.

Between-subjects designs can be contrasted with WITHIN-SUBJECTS DESIGNs.

 Cramer & Howitt 2004; Sheskin 2011

between-subjects factor
another term for BETWEEN-GROUPS FACTOR

between-subjects factorial ANOVA
another term for FACTORIAL ANOVA

between-subjects factorial design
another term for FACTORIAL DESIGN

between-subjects independent variable
another term for BETWEEN-GROUPS FACTOR

between-subjects *t*-test
another term for INDEPENDENT SAMPLES *t*-TEST

between-subjects variability
another term for SYSTEMATIC VARIANCE

between-subjects variance
another term for SYSTEMATIC VARIANCE

between-within design
another term for MIXED DESIGN

bias
any error that may distort a statistical result of a research study in one direction. Bias may derive either from a conscious or unconscious tendency on the behalf of the researcher to collect, interpret or present data in

such a way as to produce erroneous conclusions that favor their own beliefs or commitments. Bias is usually considered to be a negative feature of research and something that should be avoided. It implies there has been some deviation from the truth either as a consequence of the limitations of the research method or from the data analysis. It is associated with research VALIDITY (i.e., the extent to which the inquiry is able to yield the correct answer).

Bias is also caused by SYSTEMATIC ERRORs that may either be motivated or unmotivated. If the bias is motivated, that motivation may either be conscious (**willful bias**) or unconscious (**negligent bias**). If the bias is unmotivated then the resulting bias will be negligent. The use of the term systematic in such a definition of bias implies that the error is not random (see MEASUREMENT ERROR), that is, a false result has not arisen by random chance. Unmotivated bias suggests that researchers may be unaware of their own tendencies to collect or interpret data in terms of their own particular commitment. Ignorance of this is little defense as errors which may represent a deviation from the truth should be recognized and acknowledged.

Closely related to bias are **holistic fallacy, elite bias**, and **going native**. The first has to do with seeing patterns and themes that are not really there. The second is concerned with giving too much weight to informants who are more articulate and better informed, making the data unrepresentative. The third, going native, occurs when the researcher adopts the perspective of their own participants and consequently may also adopt their participants' particular biases.

Bias is a concern of both QUANTITATIVE and QUALITATIVE RESEARCH. In particular quantitative researchers are concerned with measurement or SAMPLING BIAS, that is, where the results found from the research sample do not represent the general population. However qualitative research is by no means immune to bias, and indeed could be considered to be particularly prone to bias when the researcher is the main instrument of enquiry. It may occur while the researcher is engaged in RESEARCH DESIGN, SAMPLING, FIELD WORK, DATA ANALYSIS, or report writing.

📖 Sahai & Khurshid 2001; Bloor & Wood 2006

biased sample

a SAMPLE selected in such a manner that certain units of a sampled POPULATION are more likely to be included in the sample than others. Thus, the sample is not a representative one of the population as a whole. NON-PROBABILITY SAMPLING, especially CONVENIENCE or PURPOSIVE SAMPLING often produces a biased sample.

📖 Sahai & Khurshid 2001

Bibliography
see REFERENCES

bidirectional hypothesis
another term for NONDIRECTIONAL HYPOTHESIS

bimodal distribution
see MODE

binary logistic regression
see LOGISTIC REGRESSION

binary variable
another term for DICHOTOMOUS VARIABLE

B-index
see ITEM ANALYSIS

binomial distribution
a PROBABILITY DISTRIBUTION which describes the PROBABILITY of an event or outcome occurring on a number of independent occasions or trials when the event has the same probability of occurring on each occasion. For example, a coin flip is a binomial variable that can result in only one of two outcomes. The binomial distribution results when the following five conditions are met:

1) There is a series of N trials;
2) On each trial, there are only two possible outcomes;
3) On each trial, the two possible outcomes are mutually exclusive;
4) There is independence between the outcomes of each trial; and
5) The probability of each possible outcome on any trial stays the same from trial to trial.

When these requirements are met, the binomial distribution tells us each possible outcome of the N trials and the probability of getting each of these outcomes.
The binomial distribution is associated with the RANDOM VARIABLEs.
Cramer & Howitt 2004; Pagano 2009; Upton & Cook 2008

binomial test
a NONPARAMETRIC TEST procedure which compares the observed frequencies of the two categories of a DICHOTOMOUS VARIABLE to the frequencies that are expected under a BINOMIAL DISTRIBUTION with a specified probability parameter. For example, when you toss a coin, the

PROBABILITY of a head equals 1/2. Based on this HYPOTHESIS, a coin is tossed 40 times, and the outcomes are recorded (heads or tails). From the binomial test, you might find that 3/4 of the tosses were heads and that the observed significance level is small (.0027). These results indicate that it is not likely that the probability of a head equals 1/2; the coin is probably biased. The binomial test examines the proposition that the proportion of counts that you have fits a binomial distribution. It starts with the assumption that either of two choices is equally likely. The binomial test can be used both for a single sample and two DEPENDENT SAMPLES. For two dependent samples, it is required that each of subjects has two scores.

The binomial test is similar to the SIGN TEST in that (1) the data are nominal in nature, (2) only two response categories are set up by the researcher, and (3) the response categories must be mutually exclusive. The binomial test is also like the sign test in that it can be used with a single group of people who are measured just once, with a single group of people who are measured twice (e.g., in pretest and posttest situations), or with two groups of people who are matched or are related in some logical fashion. The binomial and sign tests are even further alike in that both procedures lead to a data-based *P*-VALUE that comes from tentatively considering the NULL HYPOTHESIS to be true.

The only difference between the sign test and the binomial test concerns the flexibility of the null hypothesis. With the sign test, there is no flexibility. This is because the sign test's always says that the objects in the population are divided evenly into the two response categories. With the binomial test, however, researchers have the flexibility to set up with any proportionate split they wish to test.
 📖 Huck 2012; Sheskin 2011; SPSS Inc. 2011

binomial variable
 another term for DICHOTOMOUS VARIABLE

biodata
 see FILL-IN ITEM

biographical study
 a form of NARRATIVE INQUIRY which depicts the life experiences of an individual. The method is defined as the study, use, and collection of life documents that describe significant points in an individual's life as reported by others. Biographical writings appear in various fields and disciplines and are designed to reflect the history of one's life.
 📖 Tailore 2005

biological reductionism
see REDUCTIONISM

biplot
a graphical representation of multivariate data (data containing information on two or more VARIABLEs) in which all the variables are represented by a point. In addition to showing the relationship between variables, the technique is useful in displaying any hidden structure or pattern among the individuals and for displaying results found by more conventional methods of analysis. Biplots can be considered as the multivariate analogue of SCATTERPLOTs.
Sahai & Khurshid 2001; Upton & Cook 2008

bipolar scale
another term for SEMANTIC DIFFERENTIAL SCALE

biserial coefficient of correlation
another term for BISERIAL CORRELATION COEFFICIENT

biserial correlation coefficient
also **biserial coefficient of correlation,** r_{bis}, r_b
a measure of association between a CONTINUOUS VARIABLE and an artificially dichotomized variable (i.e., having underlying continuity and normality) with two categories represented by the numbers 0 and 1. The biserial correlation coefficient is employed if both variables are based on an INTERVAL/RATIO SCALE, but the scores on one of the variables have been transformed into a dichotomous NOMINAL SCALE. An example of a situation where an interval/ratio variable would be expressed as a dichotomous variable is a test based on a normally distributed interval/ratio scale for which the only information available is whether a subject has passed or failed the test.
This method is rarely used, partly because it has certain problems entailed in its calculation and in its use when the distributions are not normal. As an alternative, in such a situation it would be permissible to use PHI CORRELATION COEFFICIENT.
Bachman 2004; Brown 1988, 1992; Richards & Schmidt 2010

bivariate analysis
a form of statistical analysis which involves the simultaneous analysis of two VARIABLEs where neither is an *experimental* INDEPENDENT VARIABLE and the desire is simply to study the relationship between the variables. Bivariate analysis involves the exploration of interrelationships between variables and, hence, possible influences of one variable on another. Calculation of statistics to assess the degree of relationship between

two variables would be an example of a bivariate statistical analysis. Any measure of association that assesses the degree of relationship between two variables is referred to as a *bivariate measure of association*. Bivariate graphs such as the SCATTERPLOTS display the relationship between two variables.
see also UNIVARIATE ANALYSIS, MULTIVARIATE ANALYSIS
📖 Cramer & Howitt 2004; Peers 1996; Sheskin 2011; Tabachnick & Fidell 2007

bivariate distribution
another term for SCATTERPLOT

bivariate normal distribution
a distribution which involves two variables. The assumption of *bivariate normality* (one of the assumptions for PEARSON PRODUCT-MOMENT CORRELATION COEFFICIENT) states that each of the variables and the linear combination of the two variables are normally distributed. Another characteristic of a bivariate normal distribution is that for any given value of the X variable, the scores on the Y variable will be normally distributed, and for any given value of the Y variable, the scores on the X variable will be normally distributed. In conjunction with the latter, the variances for the Y variable will be equal for each of the possible values of the X variable, and the variances for the X variable will be equal for each of the possible values of the Y variable.
Related to the bivariate normality assumption is the assumption of HOMOSCEDASTICITY. When the assumption of bivariate normality is met, the two variables will be homoscedastic.
A generalization of a bivariate normal distribution to three or more random variables is known as **multivariate normal distribution**
📖 Sheskin 2011

bivariate polygon
see FREQUENCY POLYGON

bivariate regression
another term for SIMPLE REGRESSION

block sampling
another term for AREA SAMPLING

bogus question
also **fictitious question**
a question that asks about something that does not exist. Bogus question is included in a QUESTIONNAIRE to help the researcher estimate the extent to which respondents are providing ostensibly substantive answers to

questions they cannot know anything about, because it does not exist. Bogus questions are a valuable way for researchers to gather information to help understand the nature and size of respondent-related MEASUREMENT ERROR.

The data from bogus questions, especially if several bogus questions are included in the questionnaire, can be used by researchers to (a) filter out respondents who appear to have answered wholly unreliably, and/or (b) create a scaled variable based on the answers given to the bogus questions and then use this variable as a COVARIATE in other analyses. When a new topic is being studied—that is, one that people are not likely to know much about—it is especially prudent to consider the use of bogus questions.

📖 Lavrakas 2008

Bonferroni adjustment
also **Bonferroni correction, Bonferroni test, Bonferroni t, Bonferroni-Dunn test, Dunn test, Dunn correction, Dunn multiple comparison test**

a procedure for guarding against an increase in the PROBABILITY of a TYPE I ERROR when performing multiple significance tests. Bonferroni adjustment is an adjustment made to the ALPHA (α) LEVEL whereby the alpha level is divided by the number of tests. This results in a new alpha level, and to be statistical a test must be below this level. Because researchers obviously do not want to conclude that the INDEPENDENT VARIABLE has an effect when it really does not, they take steps to control type I error when they conduct many statistical analyses. The conventional level for determining whether two groups differ is the .05 or 5% level. At this level the probability of two groups differing by chance when they do not differ is 1 out of 20 or 5 out of 100. The most straightforward way of preventing Type I error inflation when conducting many tests is to set a more stringent alpha level than the conventional .05 level. Researchers sometimes use the Bonferroni adjustment in which they divide their desired alpha level (such as .05) by the number of tests they plan to conduct. For example, if we wanted to conduct 10 t-TESTs to analyze all pairs of MEANs in a study, we could use an alpha level of .005 rather than .05 for each t-test we ran. (We would use an alpha level of .005 because we divide our desired alpha level of .05 by the number of tests we will conduct; .05/10 = .005.) If we did so, the likelihood of making a Type I error on any particular t-test would be very low (.005), and the overall likelihood of making a Type I error across all 10 t-tests would not exceed our desired alpha level of .05.

This test has generally been recommended as an A PRIORI TEST for planned comparisons even though it is a more conservative (i.e., less powerful) test than some POST HOC TESTs for unplanned comparisons. It can be used for equal and unequal group sizes where the VARIANCEs are equal. Where the variances are unequal, it is recommended that the GAMES-HOWELL MULTIPLE COMPARISON be used. This involves calculating a critical difference for every pair of means being compared which uses the STUDENTIZED RANGE TEST.

Although this adjustment protects us against inflated Type I error when we conduct many tests, it has a drawback: As we make alpha more stringent and lower the probability of a Type I error, the probability of making a Type II error (and missing real effects of the independent variable) increases. That is, we are more likely to be making a TYPE II ERROR in which we assume that there is no difference between two groups when there is a difference.

see also FALSE DETECTION RATE, DUNCAN'S NEW MULTIPLE RANGE TEST
📖 Cramer & Howitt 2004; Everitt & Skrondal 2010; Gamst et al. 2008; Larson-Hall 2010; Leary 2011; Sahai & Khurshid 2001

bootstrap
an approach to validating a multivariate model by drawing a large number of subsamples and estimating models for each subsample. The bootstrap is an application of RESAMPLING TECHNIQUE which takes the DISTRIBUTION of the obtained data in order to generate a SAMPLING DISTRIBUTION of the particular statistic in question. It is based on the general assumption that a RANDOM SAMPLE can be used to determine the characteristics of the underlying population from which the sample is derived. The term bootstrap is derived from the saying that a person lifts oneself up by one's bootstraps. Within the framework of the statistical procedure, bootstrapping indicates that a single sample is used as a basis for generating multiple additional samples; in other words, one makes the most out of what little resources one has. The crucial feature or essence of bootstrapping methods is that the obtained SAMPLE DATA are, conceptually speaking at least, reproduced an infinite number of times to give an infinitely large sample. Given this, it becomes possible to sample from the 'bootstrapped POPULATION' and obtain outcomes which differ from the original sample. So, for example, imagine the following sample of 10 scores obtained by a researcher:

5, 10, 6, 3, 9, 2, 5, 6, 7, 11

There is only one sample of 10 scores possible from this set of 10 scores—the original sample (i.e. the 10 scores above). However, if we endlessly repeated the string as we do in bootstrapping then we would get

5, 10, 6, 3, 9, 2, 5, 6, 7, 11, 5, 10, 6, 3, 9, 2, 5, 6, 7, 11, 5, 10, 6, 3, 9, 2, 5, 6, 7, 11, 5, 10, 6, 3, 9, 2, 5, 6, 7, 11, 5, 10, 6, 3, 9, 2, 5, 6, 7, 11, 5,

10, 6, 3, 9, 2, 5, 6, 7, 11, 5, 10, 6, 3, 9, 2, 5, 6, 7, 11, ..., 5, 10, 6, 3, 9, 2, 5, 6, 7, 11, etc.

With this bootstrapped population, it is possible to draw random samples of 10 scores but get a wide variety of samples many of which differ from the original sample. This is simply because there is a variety of scores from which to choose now. So long as the original sample is selected with care to be representative of the wider situation, it has been shown that bootstrapped populations are not bad population estimates despite the nature of their origins. The difficulty with bootstrapping statistics is the computation of the sampling distribution because of the sheer number of samples and calculations involved.

Bootstrap is used in circumstances where there is reasonable doubt regarding the characteristics of the underlying population distribution from which a sample is drawn. The most frequent justification for using the bootstrap is when there is reason to believe that data may not be derived from a normally distributed population. Another condition that might merit the use of the bootstrap is one involving a sample that contains one or more outliers.
📖 Cramer & Howitt 2004; Hair et al. 2010; Sheskin 2011

boundary effect

the effect which occurs when a test is too easy or too difficult for a particular group of test takers, resulting in their scores tending to be clustered toward the top of the distribution (CEILING EFFECT) or the bottom of the distribution (FLOOR EFFECT). When tests are very easy or difficult for a given group of participants, skewed distribution of scoring will result.
📖 Richards & Schmidt 2010

bounding

a technique used in PANEL DESIGNs to reduce the effect of TELESCOPING on behavioral frequency reports. Telescoping is a memory error in the temporal placement of events; that is, an event is remembered, but the remembered date of the event is inaccurate. This uncertainty about the dates of events leads respondents to report events mistakenly as occurring earlier or later than they actually occurred. Bounding reduces telescoping errors in two ways. First, bounding takes advantage of the information collected earlier to eliminate the possibility that respondents report events that occurred outside a given reference period. Second, bounding provides a temporal reference point in respondents' memory, which helps them correctly place an event in relation to that reference point.
📖 Lavrakas 2008

box-and-whisker plot
another term for BOXPLOT

boxplot
also **box-and-whisker plot, hinge plot**
a way of representing data graphically. This visual display (see Figure B.2) is extremely helpful for representing distributions, since it includes visual representation of two DESCRIPTIVE STATISTICS—the MEDIAN and SEMI-INTERQUARTILE RANGE of a score distribution. In a box-and-whisker plot, the score distribution is displayed in a way that provides information about both the midpoint of the distribution and the relative variability of the scores. Boxplots provide information about group centers, spread, and shape of a distribution. The first step in constructing a box-and-whisker plot is to first find the median, the lower QUARTILE, and the upper quartile of a given set of data. For example, take the following set of scores from fifteen subjects:

82 54 27 100 34 59 61 68 78 85 84 18 91 93 50

First we rewrite the data in order, from smallest length to largest:

18 27 34 50 54 59 61 *68* 78 82 84 85 91 93 100

Now we find the median of all the numbers. The median (i.e., *68*) is the value exactly in the middle of an ordered set of numbers. Next, we consider only the values to the left of the median: 18 27 34 *50* 54 59 61. We now find the median of this set of numbers. Thus *50* is the median of the scores less than the median of all scores, and therefore is the lower quartile. Now consider only the values to the right of the median: 78 82 84 *85* 91 93 100. We now find the median of this set of numbers. The median *85* is therefore called the upper quartile. Now we can construct the actual box and whisker graph, as shown below.

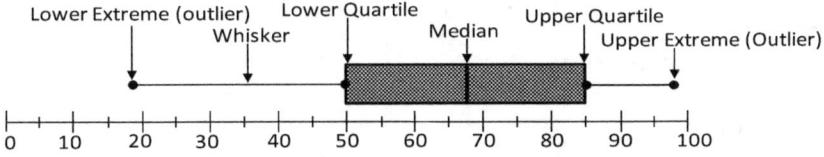

Figure B.2. An Example of Boxplot

The line drawn in the box marks the median, or midpoint of distribution, which is the point at which 50% of scores are above and 50% of scores are below. For a skewed distribution, the median is not in the middle of

its box—it is somewhat off-center—while for the normal distribution the line is directly in the center of the box. The range of scores within the shaded box is known as the INTERQUARTILE RANGE (IQR) and contains the scores that fall within the 25th to 75th PERCENTILE. If the distributions have EQUAL VARIANCE, the length of their boxes (or IQR) will be very similar. However, a skewed distribution has a much longer box than the normal distribution. The drawn lines from the left and right sides of the box are known as whiskers—hence the box plot is sometimes called the box-and-whisker plot. They indicate the points above and below which the highest and lowest ten percent of the cases occur. Points that lie outside the box are identified as lower and upper extreme scores (or OUTLIERs). Boxplot is a useful device for spotting outliers in a set of data.
 Bachman 2004; Clark-Carter 2010; Larson-Hall 2010

box's *M* test

a test which is used to determine whether the VARIANCE and COVARIANCE matrices of two or more DEPENDENT VARIABLEs in a MULTIVARIATE ANALYSIS OF VARIANCE or MULTIVARIATE ANALYSIS OF COVARIANCE are similar or homogeneous across the groups, which is one of the assumptions underlying this analysis. If the STATISTICAL SIGNIFICANCE does not exceed the critical level (i.e., nonsignificance), then the equality of the covariance matrices is supported. If the test shows statistical significance, then the groups are deemed different and the assumption is violated. If this test is significant, it may be possible to reduce the variances by transforming the scores by taking their SQUARE ROOT or natural logarithm.
see also COCHRAN'S *C* TEST, BARTLETT'S TEST, HARTLEY'S TEST, LEVENE'S TEST, BROWN-FORSYTHE TEST, O'BRIEN TEST
 Cramer & Howitt 2004; Hair et al. 2010; Tabachnick & Fidell 2007

b-parameter
see ITEM CHARACTERISTIC CURVE

bracketing
see PHENOMENOLOGY

branching
a QUESTIONNAIRE design technique used in SURVEY RESEARCH that utilizes skip patterns to ensure that respondents are asked only those questions that apply to them. This technique allows the questionnaire to be tailored to each individual respondent so that respondents with different characteristics, experiences, knowledge, and opinions are routed to applicable questions (e.g., questions about a treatment for reading difficulties

are only asked to respondents who have been diagnosed with dyslexia). Branching also is used to ask respondents to choose among a large number of response options without requiring them to keep all the response options in working memory.

Branching can be conditional, compound conditional, or unconditional. In conditional branching, a single condition is met where routing occurs based on the answer to a single question (i.e., if the answer to question 1 is *no*, then skip to question 3). In compound conditional branching, more than one condition must be met. The branching in this case is dependent on multiple answers, and routing occurs based on a combination of answers (i.e., if the answer to question 1 is *yes* or the answer to question 2 is *yes*, skip to question 5). Unconditional branching is a direct statement with no conditions, often used to bring the respondent back to a specific point in the main survey after following a branching sequence. The approaches to branching differ depending on survey administration.

see also CONTINGENCY QUESTION

📖 Lavrakas 2008

broad open question

see SHORT-ANSWER ITEM

Brown-Forsythe test

a test of HOMOGENEITY OF VARIANCEs for assessing whether a set of POPULATION VARIANCEs are equal. The Brown-Forsythe procedure has been shown to be quite ROBUST to nonnormality in numerous studies. The test is recommended for LEPTOKURTIC DISTRIBUTIONs (i.e., those with sharp peaks) (in terms of being robust to nonnormality, and providing adequate TYPE I ERROR protection and excellent power). Although the Brown-Forsythe procedure is recommended for leptokurtic distributions, the **O'Brien test** is recommended for other distributions (i.e., MESOKURTIC and PLATYKURTIC DISTRIBUTIONs). Like Brown-Forsythe procedure, O'Brien procedure is relatively robust to nonnormality.

see also BOX'S M TEST, COCHRAN'S C TEST, BARTLETT'S TEST, HARTLEY'S TEST, LEVENE'S TEST

📖 Everitt & Skrondal 2010; Lomax 2007

Bryant-Paulson simultaneous test

a POST HOC TEST which is used to determine which of three or more ADJUSTED MEANs differ from one another when the F RATIO (the ratio of the between-group variance to the within-group variance) in an ANALYSIS OF COVARIANCE is significant. The formula for this test varies according to the number of COVARIATEs and whether cases have been assigned to treatments at random or not.

📖 Cramer & Howitt 2004

C

CA
an abbreviation for CONVERSATION ANALYSIS

CALL
an abbreviation for COMPUTER-ASSISTED LANGUAGE LEARNING

canonical correlation
also **CC**
a multivariate statistical procedure that allows multiple INDEPENDENT VARIABLEs (IVs) and multiple DEPENDENT VARIABLEs (DVs). Canonical correlation (CC) is, in fact, a generalization of MULTIPLE REGRESSION (MR) that adds more than one DV or criterion to the prediction equation. It correlates two sets of variables with one another. The goal of CC is to identify pairs of linear combinations involving the two sets of variables that yield the highest CORRELATION with one another. For example, a researcher may want to compute the (simultaneous) relationship between three measures of scholastic ability with five measures of success in school.

CC involves the correlation between one set of X variables (which is comprised of two or more X variables and represents the IVs or predictors) and another set of Y variables (which is comprised of two or more Y variables and represents the criterion variables). However, these variables are not those as actually recorded in the data but abstract variables. There may be several LATENT VARIABLEs in any set of variables just as there may be several factors in FACTOR ANALYSIS. This is true for the X variables and the Y variables. Hence, in CC there may be a number of coefficients—one for each possible pair of a LATENT ROOT of the X variables and a latent root of the Y variables.

More specifically, in CC, there are several layers of analysis:

1) We would like to explore whether pairs of linear combinations (i.e., labeled as CANONICAL VARIATEs in CC) are significantly related.
2) We are interested in how the variables on the left (i.e., IVs) relate to their respective canonical variates, and how the variables on the right (i.e., DVs) relate to their respective canonical variates.
3) We would like to see how the variables on each side relate to the canonical variates on the other side.
4) We can conduct follow-up MRs, one for each DV, using the full set of IVs from CC as the IVs in each MR. This will provide insight about specific relationships among the IVs and each DV. To protect TYPE I ERROR rate, it may be preferred to use a conservative ALPHA

LEVEL, .01, or a BONFERRONI ADJUSTMENT that divides the desired alpha level (e.g., .05) by the number of follow-up analyses (e.g., $p = .05/2 = .025$). Researchers instead may choose the more traditional alpha level, .05.

CC is different from normal correlation, which involves the correlation between one variable and another. CC is similar to MR in that multiple IVs are allowed. CC differs from MR in that MR allows only a single DV, whereas CC allows two or more DVs. CC is similar to DISCRIMINANT FUNCTION ANALYSIS (DFA) and LOGISTIC REGRESSION (LR) in that multiple IVs are allowed with all three methods. CC is different from both DFA and LR in that the latter two methods usually have only a single *categorical* DV, whereas CC allows two or more usually *continuous* DVs. CC is similar to ANALYSIS OF COVARIANCE (ANCOVA) and MULTIVARIATE ANALYSIS OF VARIANCE (MANOVA) in requiring the GENERAL LINEAR MODEL ASSUMPTIONS (i.e., NORMALITY, LINEARITY, and HOMOSCEDASTICITY) when making inferences to the population. CC differs from ANCOVA and MANOVA in that CC is a correlational method that does not have to include any CATEGORICAL VARIABLEs and is not focused on mean differences between groups. Finally, CC is similar to MR, DFA, and LR in its focus on weighted functions of the variables, where the most interpretable weights are correlational (ranging from -1 to +1).

CC is most likely to be useful in situations where there is doubt that a single variable in and of itself can serve as a suitable criterion variable. Consequently, by determining if a set of criterion variables correlate with a set of predictor variables, a clearer picture may emerge regarding the relationship between the dimensions represented by the X and Y variables.

📖 Brown 1992; Cramer & Howitt 2004; Harlow 2005; Sheskin 2011

canonical variable
see MULTIVARIATE ANALYSIS OF VARIANCE

canonical variate
a term which is employed in CANONICAL CORRELATION (CC) to identify any linear combination comprised of X (or Y) variables that is correlated with a linear combination of Y (or X) variables. The procedure in CC searches for the set of canonical variates that yields the maximum CORRELATION COEFFICIENT. The next set of canonical variates (uncorrelated with the first) is then identified which yields the next highest correlation, and so on.

📖 Harlow 2005; Sheskin 2011

CAPI
an abbreviation for COMPUTER-ASSISTED PERSONAL INTERVIEWING

carryover effect
another term for ORDER EFFECT

case
see CASE STUDY

case study
one of the most common qualitative approaches to research (see QUALITATIVE RESEARCH) which aims to understand social phenomena within a single or small number of naturally occurring settings. Case study is the study of the particularity and complexity of a single **case**. Cases are primarily people, but researchers can also explore in depth a program, an institution, an organization, a school, a class, or a community. In fact, almost anything can serve as a case as long as it constitutes a single entity with clearly defined boundaries. To study the selected cases, case study researchers usually combine a variety of data collection methods such as INTERVIEWs, OBSERVATION, VERBAL PROTOCOLs, narrative accounts (see NARRATIVE INQUIRY), document archives (see ARCHIVAL DATA), and audio or video recording. Thus, the case study is not a specific technique but rather a method of collecting and organizing data so as to maximize understanding of the unitary character of the social being or object studied.
There are three types of case study:

a) the **intrinsic case study** in which interest lies purely in one particular case itself. The intrinsic case study is conducted to understand a particular case that may be unusual, unique, or different in some way. It does not necessarily represent other cases or a broader trait or problem for investigation. There is no attempt at all to generalize from the case being studied, compare it to other cases, or claim that it illustrates a problem common to other, similar cases. The emphasis is on gaining a deep understanding of the case itself. For example, if you were not interested in improving support and instruction for your second language students but rather simply wished to understand the lived experience of your two participants, you would be conducting an intrinsic case study;
b) the **instrumental case study** in which a case is studied with the goal of illuminating a particular issue, problem, or theory. It is intended to provide insights into a wider issue while the actual case is of secondary interest; it facilitates understanding of something else. While the

intrinsic case study requires a primarily descriptive approach, with an eye toward the particularity of the case at hand, the instrumental case study is more likely to require interpretation and evaluation, in addition to description. For example, a researcher might study how Mrs. Brown teaches phonics, for example, in order to learn something about phonics as a method or about the teaching of reading in general. The researcher's goal in such studies is more global and less focused on the particular individual, event, program, or school being studied. Researchers who conduct such studies are more interested in drawing conclusions that apply beyond a particular case than they are in conclusions that apply to just one specific case. Instrumental case studies may be used to develop conceptual categories or illustrate, support, or challenge theoretical assumptions. In other words, case studies—both intrinsic and instrumental—may lay the groundwork for future studies by providing basic information about the realms in which little research has been conducted; and

c) the **multiple** (or collective) **case study** where there is even less interest in one particular case, and a number of cases are studied jointly in order to investigate a phenomenon or general condition. Again, one issue, problem, or theory is focused upon, but the researcher chooses to study more than one case to shed light on a particular issue if doing so will lead to a better understanding, and perhaps better theorizing, about a still larger collection of cases. Your study is a multiple case study, as you study one issue and compares different students (i.e., undergraduate and graduate) to see how their experiences are similar or different, for the benefit of a broader group of cases—future undergraduate and graduate students in the intensive English program (IEP). You could also have compared students going into different departments or faculties, or students who come from different language backgrounds.

Case study approach has been productive and highly influential in applied linguistics. In the area of second language (L2) teaching and learning, case studies are frequently used to trace the language development of a particular group of learners. These studies are usually associated with a *longitudinal* approach, in which observations of the phenomena under investigation are made at periodic intervals for an extended period of time. A case study in L2 teaching might focus on a single teacher and perhaps a small group of students in order to explore how the relationship develops as the latter settle into a new language school. The institutional setting would need to be carefully delineated and we would need to know a lot about the background of the individuals involved, so a number of IN-DEPTH INTERVIEWs would be necessary and these might be linked to lesson observation and perhaps also to critical incidents. Documentary evidence might also be sought out where relevant and the researcher would aim to develop a rich picture of the experiences of those involved within this particular setting, perhaps including narrative accounts as well as descriptive vignettes. In discussing the case, attention will be drawn to features of particular interest, relating these to broader issues and developing explanations where appropriate.

As with all sound research, case study researchers must strive for VALIDITY and RELIABILITY in their investigation. In terms of EXTERNAL VALIDITY, one of the major criticisms of case study research is that a single case provides very little evidence for generalizing. Accepting the definition of validity used in experimental research is not warranted because case studies do not claim to be based on a representative sample in which statistical procedures can verify generalizations. Statistical generalizations are valid for EMPIRICAL RESEARCH, but case study research depends on analytical generalizations (see INDUCTIVE REASONING, ANALYTIC INDUCTION) in which the findings of a study can lend support to some broader theory.

In regard to reliability, case study researchers, like all researchers, must make certain that if another researcher were to conduct a comparable case study, they would come to similar findings. In order to accomplish this, case study researchers must carefully document all the procedures they follow in as much detail as possible.

Dörnyei 2007; Fraenkel & Wallen 2009; McKay 2006; Richards 2003

CASI
an abbreviation for COMPUTER ASSISTED SELF-INTERVIEWING

CAT
an abbreviation for COMPUTER ADAPTIVE TESTING

catalytic validity
a type of VALIDITY which embraces the paradigm of CRITICAL THEORY. Catalytic validity simply strives to ensure that research leads to action. However, the story does not end there, for discussions of catalytic validity are substantive; like critical theory, catalytic validity suggests an agenda. The agenda for catalytic validity is to help participants to understand their worlds in order to transform them. The agenda is explicitly political, for catalytic validity suggests the need to expose whose definitions of the situation are operating in the situation. It is suggested that the criterion of *fairness* should be applied to research, meaning that it should (a) augment and improve the participants' experience of the world, and (b) that it should improve the empowerment of the participants. In this respect the research might focus on what might be (the leading edge of

innovations and future trends) and what could be (the ideal, possible futures).
Catalytic validity requires solidarity in the participants, an ability of the research to promote emancipation, autonomy and freedom within a just, egalitarian and democratic society to reveal the distortions, ideological deformations and limitations that reside in research, communication and social structures Valid research, if it is to meet the demands of catalytic validity, must demonstrate its ability to empower the researched as well as the researchers. How defensible it is to suggest that researchers should have such ideological intents is, perhaps, a moot point, though not to address this area is to perpetuate inequality by omission and neglect. Catalytic validity reasserts the centrality of ethics in the research process, for it requires the researcher to interrogate his/her allegiances, responsibilities, and self-interestedness.
📖 Cohen et al. 2011

categorical data
see CATEGORICAL VARIABLE

categorical variable
also **nominal variable, grouped variable, classification variable, discontinuous variable, non-metric variable**
a VARIABLE which can take on specific values only within a defined range of values. An often cited example is that of gender because you can either be male or female. There is no middle ground when it comes to gender; you must be one, and you cannot be both. Race, marital status, and hair color are other common examples of categorical variables. It is often helpful to think of categorical variables as consisting of discrete, mutually exclusive categories, such as male/female, white/black, single/married/divorced. A categorical variable that can assume only a finite or, at most, a countable number of possible values is called a **discrete variable**. A categorical variable that is normally not expressed numerically because it differs in kind rather than degree among elementary units is called a **qualitative variable**. When a categorical variable has only two possible categories or values, it is called a **dichotomous variable** (also called **binary variable, binomial variable**) (e.g., pass/fail, yes/no, male/female). A categorical variable which has more than two classes are called a **multinomial variable** (also called **polychomous variable, polytomous variable)**; examples are educational level, proficiency level, religious affiliation, and place of birth. The values of a categorical variable are known as **categorical data** (also called **non-metric data**).
To conduct statistics using most computer software, the gender variable, for example, would need to be coded using numbers to represent each group. The number we assign are arbitrary since it makes no difference

what number we assign to what category. For example, men may be labeled '0' and women may be labeled '1.' In this case, a value of 1 does not indicate a higher score than a value of 0. Rather, 0 and 1 are simply names, or labels, that have been assigned to each group.

see also INDEPENDENT VARIABLE, DEPENDENT VARIABLE, MODERATOR VARIABLE, INTERVENING VARIABLE, CONTINUOUS VARIABLE, EXTRANEOUS VARIABLE, CONFOUNDING VARIABLE

📖 Bachman 2004; Marczyk et al. 2005; Sahai & Khurshid 2001

causal-comparative research
also criterion-group study

a type of EX POST FACTO RESEARCH in which the investigator sets out to discover possible causes for a phenomenon being studied, by comparing the subjects in which the variable is present with similar subjects in whom it is absent. The basic design in this kind of study may be represented thus:

	Independent variable	Dependent variable
Experimental Group	X	O_1
Control Group		O_2

Using this model, the investigator hypothesizes the INDEPENDENT VARIABLE (IV) and then compares two groups, an experimental group which has been exposed to the presumed IV (X), and a control group which has not. (The dashed line in the model shows that the comparison groups E and C are not equated by random assignment). Alternatively, the investigator may examine two groups that are different in some way or ways and then try to account for the difference or differences by investigating possible antecedents. If, for example, a researcher chose such a design to investigate factors contributing to teacher effectiveness, the criterion group (O_1), the effective teachers, and its counterpart (O_2), a group not showing the characteristics of the criterion group, are identified by measuring the differential effects of the groups on classes of students. The researcher may then examine X, some variable or event, such as the background, training, skills and personality of the groups, to discover what might cause only some teachers to be effective.

The basic design of causal-comparative investigations is similar to an experimentally designed study. The chief difference resides in the nature of the IV, X. In a truly experimental situation, this will be under the control of the investigator and may therefore be described as manipulable. In the causal-comparative model, however, the IV is beyond his/her control, having already occurred. It may therefore be described in this design as non-manipulable.

Criterion-group or causal-comparative studies may be seen as bridging the gap between DESCRIPTIVE RESEARCH methods on the one hand and TRUE EXPERIMENTAL (research) DESIGN on the other.
see also CAUSAL RESEARCH
📖 Cohen et al. 2011

causal hypothesis
a HYPOTHESIS which suggests that input X will affect outcome Y, as in, for example, an EXPERIMENTAL DESIGN. An **associative hypothesis**, on the other hand, describes how variables may relate to each other, not necessarily in a causal manner (e.g., in CORRELATIONAL RESEARCH).
📖 Cohen et al. 2011

causal model
see PATH ANALYSIS

causal relationship
a relationship in which one variable is hypothesized or has been shown to affect another variable. The DEPENDENT VARIABLE is assumed to depend on the INDEPENDENT VARIABLE (IV). The IV must occur before the DV. However, a variable which precedes another variable is not necessarily a cause of that other variable. Both variables may be the result of another variable.
To demonstrate that one variable causes or influences another variable, we have to be able to manipulate the independent or causal variable and to hold all other variables constant. If the DV varies as a function of the IV, we may be more confident that the IV affects the DV. For example, if we think that noise decreases performance, we will manipulate noise by varying its level or intensity and observe the effect this has on performance. If performance decreases as a function of noise, we may be more certain that noise influences performance.
In order to attribute a causal relationship between two events, A and B, three conditions are typical: (a) B must not precede A in time, (b) A and B must covary together to a recognizable degree, and (c) no alternative explanation accounts as well as or better for the covariation between A and B.
see also PATH ANALYSIS
📖 Cramer & Howitt 2004; Porte 2010

causal research
also **co-relational research**
a type of EX POST FACTO RESEARCH which is concerned with identifying the antecedents of a present condition. Causal research involves the collection of two sets of data, one of which will be retrospective, with a

view to determining the relationship between them. The basic design of such an experiment may be represented thus:

    Independent variable   Dependent variable
               X   O

Although one variable in an ex post facto study cannot be confidently said to depend upon the other as would be the case in a truly experimental investigation, it is nevertheless usual to designate one of the variables as independent (X) and the other as dependent (O). The left to right dimension indicates the temporal order, though having established this, we must not overlook the possibility of reverse causality. A researcher may, for example, attempt to show a relationship between the quality of a music teacher's undergraduate training (X) and his/her subsequent effectiveness as a teacher of his/her subject (O). Measures of the quality of a music teacher's college training can include grades in specific courses, overall grade average and self-ratings, etc. Teacher effectiveness can be assessed by indices of student performance, student knowledge, student attitudes, and judgment of experts, etc. Correlations between all measures were obtained to determine the relationship. Where a strong relationship is found between the independent and dependent variables, three possible interpretations are open to the researcher:

- that the variable X has caused O.
- that the variable O has caused X.
- that some third unidentified, and therefore unmeasured, variable has caused X and O.

It is often the case that a researcher cannot tell which of these is correct. The value of causal studies lies chiefly in their exploratory or suggestive character. While they are not always adequate in themselves for establishing CAUSAL RELATIONSHIPs among variables, they are a useful first step in this direction in that they do yield measures of association.
see also CAUSAL-COMPARATIVE RESEARCH
📖 Cohen et al. 2011

cause variable
    another term for INDEPENDENT VARIABLE

CC
    an abbreviation for CANONICAL CORRELATION

CEEB score
    a STANDARD SCORE which stands for College Entrance Examination

Board. This standard score is used for SAT (Scholastic Achievement Test), the GRE (Graduate Record Exam), TOEFL paper-and-pencil, and other tests. The subtests for these exams all have a MEAN of 500 and a STANDARD DEVIATION of 100. To convert z SCOREs to CEEB scores, multiply the z scores by 100 and add 500, as follows:

$$CEEB = 100z + 500$$

Clearly, CEEB scores are very similar to T SCOREs. In fact, they are exactly the same except that CEEB scores always have one extra zero. So to convert a T score to CEEB, just add a zero. In other words, if a student's T score is 30, his/her CEEB score will be 300.
 📖 Brown 2005; Lomax 2007

ceiling effect
 an effect which occurs when scores on a measuring instrument (e.g., a test) are approaching the maximum they can be. In other words, a ceiling effect occurs when many of the scores on a measure are at or near the maximum possible score. Tests with a ceiling effect are too easy for many of the examinees, and we do not know what their scores might have been if there had been a higher ceiling. For example, if we gave a 60-item test and most of the scores fell between 55 and 60, we would have a ceiling effect. Thus, there would be bunching of values close to the upper point. A graph of the FREQUENCY DISTRIBUTION of such scores would be negatively skewed (see SKEWED DISTRIBUTION). Failure to recognize the possibility that there is a ceiling effect may lead to the mistaken conclusion that the INDEPENDENT VARIABLE has no effect.
 see also FLOOR EFFECT
 📖 Ary et al. 2010; Cramer & Howitt 2004

cell
 a category of counts or values in a CONTINGENCY TABLE. A cell is a location in a contingency table, and the corresponding frequency is the **cell frequency** (also called **cell count**). The mean of all the data in a particular cell or level of a factor is called **cell mean**. A cell may refer to just single values of a CATEGORICAL VARIABLE. However, cells can also be formed by the intersection of two or more LEVELs or categories of the two (or more) independent categorical variables. Thus, a 2 × 3 (two-by-three) cross-tabulation or contingency table has six cells. Similarly, a 2 × 2 × 2 FACTORIAL ANOVA has a total of eight cells.
 According to the type of variable, the contents of the cells will be frequencies (e.g., for CHI-SQUARE TEST) or scores (e.g., for ANALYSIS OF VARIANCE).
 📖 Cramer & Howitt 2004

cell count
another term for CELL FREQUENCY

cell frequency
see CELL

cell mean
see CELL

censored data
data items in which the true value is replaced by some other value. Censored data frequently arise in many LONGITUDINAL STUDIes where the event of interest has not occurred to a number of subjects at the completion of the study. Moreover, the loss to follow-up often leads to censoring since the outcomes remain unknown. Consequently, one must employ approximate scores instead of exact scores to represent the observations that cannot be measured with precision. Two obvious options that can be employed to negate the potential impact of censored data are: (a) use of the MEDIAN in lieu of the MEAN as a MEASURE OF CENTRAL TENDENCY; and (b) employing an inferential statistical test that uses rank-orders instead of interval/ratio scores. A sample that has some of its values, usually the largest and/or smallest, censored is called **censored sample**.
 Sahai & Khurshid 2001; Sheskin 2011; Upton & Cook 2008

censored regression analysis
a form of REGRESSION where the values of the DEPENDENT VARIABLE are censored or truncated. The analysis of such a model is also called **tobit analysis**.
 Sahai & Khurshid 2001; Upton & Cook 2008

censored sample
see CENSORED DATA

central limit theorem
a probability theory which describes the SAMPLING DISTRIBUTION of the MEAN. It is an important tool in INFERENTIAL STATISTICS which enables certain conclusions to be drawn about the characteristics of SAMPLEs compared with the POPULATION. The theorem states that as the size of a sample increases, the shape of the sampling distribution approaches normal whatever the shape of the population. The significance of this important theory is that it allows us to use the normal PROBABILITY DISTRIBUTION even with sample means from populations which do not have a normal distribution. This fact enables us to make statistical inferences

using tests based on the approximate normality of the mean, even if the sample is drawn from a population that is not normally distributed.

Part of the practical significance of this is that samples drawn at random from a population tend to reflect the characteristics of that population. The larger the sample size, the more likely it is to reflect the characteristics of the population if it is drawn at random. With larger sample sizes, statistical techniques on the NORMAL DISTRIBUTION will fit the theoretical assumptions of the technique increasingly well. Even if the population is not normally distributed, the tendency of the sampling distribution of means towards normality means that PARAMETRIC STATISTICS may be appropriate despite limitations in the data. With means of small-sized samples, the distribution of the sample means tends to be flatter than that of the normal distribution so we typically employ the *t* DISTRIBUTION rather than the normal distribution.

📖 Boslaugh & Watters 2008; Cramer & Howitt 2004

central location
another term for CENTRAL TENDENCY

central tendency
also **grouping, central location**
any measure or index which describes the central value in a distribution of data. Central tendency is the central point in the distribution that describes the most typical behavior of a group. It can refer to a wide variety of measures. These measures provide a sense of the location of the distribution. A measure of central tendency is a number that is a summary that you can think of as indicating where on the variable most scores are located; or the score that everyone scored around; or the typical score; or the score that serves as the address for the distribution as a whole. The MEAN, MEDIAN, and MODE are the most commonly used **measures of central tendency** (also called **measures of location**). For NORMAL DISTRIBUTIONs, these measures are all the same. For SKEWED DISTRIBUTIONs, they can differ considerably. Less common measures of centrality are the WEIGHTED MEAN, the TRIMMED MEAN, and the GEOMETRIC MEAN.

see also DISPERSION

📖 Peers 1996; Porte 2010

centroid
see DISCRIMINANT FUNCTION ANALYSIS

cf
an abbreviation for CUMULATIVE FREQUENCY

CFA
an abbreviation for CONFIRMATORY FACTOR ANALYSIS

chain referral sampling
another term for SNOWBALL SAMPLING

chain sampling
another term for SNOWBALL SAMPLING

chance agreement
a measure of the proportion of times two or more observers would agree in their measurement or assessment of a phenomenon under investigation simply by chance.
see also COHEN'S KAPPA
 Sahai & Khurshid 2001

chance sampling
another term for SIMPLE RANDOM SAMPLING

chance variable
another term for RANDOM VARIABLE

chaos theory
a term coined to designate a scientific discipline which is concerned with investigating the apparently random and chaotic behavior of a system or phenomenon by use of DETERMINISTIC MODELs. Chaos theory assumes that small, localized perturbations in one part of a complex system can have widespread consequences throughout the system. The vivid example often used to describe this concept, known as the *butterfly effect*, is that the beating of a butterfly's wings can lead to a hurricane if the tiny turbulence it causes happens to generate a critical combination of air pressure changes. The key word here is 'if,' and much of chaos theory is concerned with attempts to model circumstances based on this conditional conjunction.
In general, chaos theory states that the world and universe in which we live are filled with turbulence, fractalness, and difference. Such dynamism is the very nature of our world/universe. Equilibrium, balance, simple harmony and conformity, norming, classification, and even equality and justice are human constructs.
see also COMPLEXITY THEORY
 Given 2008

characteristic root
another term for EIGENVALUE

CHAT
a coding unit for oral data. Whereas T-UNITs and SOC tend to focus primarily on linguistic accuracy, the CHAT system is aimed at discourse. CHAT was developed as a tool for the study of first and second language acquisition as part of the CHILDES database. It has become an increasingly common system for the coding of conversational interactions and employs detailed conventions for the marking of such conversational features as interruptions, errors, overlaps, and false starts. A standard but detailed coding scheme such as CHAT is particularly useful in QUALITATIVE RESEARCH. For example, in CONVERSATION ANALYSIS, researchers typically eschew a focus on quantifying data and concentrate instead on portraying a rich and detailed picture of the interaction, including its sequencing, turn taking, and repair strategies among participants in a conversation. Thus, whereas a researcher conducting a quantitative study might code a transcript for errors in past-tense formation, another researcher undertaking conversation analysis might mark the same transcript with a much more detailed coding system, marking units such as length of pauses and silences, stress, lengthening of vowels, overlaps, laughter, and indrawn breaths. It is important to realize that many researchers working in qualitative paradigms, including those working on conversation analysis, have argued that quantification of coding does not adequately represent their data.
 Mackey & Gass 2005

checklist
a set of questions that present a number of possible answers, and the respondents are asked to check those that apply. For example, 'What type of teaching aids do you use in your classes?' (check as many as apply):

- chalkboard □
- overhead projector □
- computer projector □
- videotapes □
- other □

see also OBSERVATIONAL SCHEDULE, DICHOTOMOUS QUESTION, MULTIPLE-CHOICE ITEM, RATIO DATA QUESTION, MATRIX QUESTIONS, CONSTANT SUM QUESTIONS, RANK ORDER QUESTION, CONTINGENCY QUESTION, NUMERIC ITEM
 Ary et al. 2010

CHILDES
a database which was designed to facilitate language acquisition research. It allows researchers to study conversational interactions among

child and adult first and second language learners and includes a variety of languages and situations/contexts of acquisition, including bilingual and disordered acquisition, as well as cross-linguistic samples of narratives. It consists of three main components: CHILDES (Child Language Data Exchange System), a database of transcribed data; CHAT, guidelines for transcription and methods of linguistic coding; and **CLAN**, software programs for analyzing the transcripts through, for example, searches and frequency counts. It is also possible in CHILDES to link transcripts to digital audio and video recordings.
📖 Mackey & Gass 2005

chi-square (χ^2)
an abbreviation for CHI-SQUARE TEST

chi-square distribution
a distribution which is considered as a sum of squares of k independent VARIABLEs, where each variable follows a NORMAL DISTRIBUTION with MEAN 0 and STANDARD DEVIATION 1. The parameter k is known as the number of DEGREEs OF FREEDOM. The distribution is frequently used in many applications of statistics, for example, in testing the *goodness of fit* of models (see GOODNESS-OF-FIT TEST) and in analyzing count data in frequency tables. The CHI-SQUARE TEST is based on chi-square distribution.
📖 Sahai & Khurshid 2001

chi-squared test
another term for CHI-SQUARE TEST

chi-square goodness-of-fit test
also **one-way chi-square test, one-way goodness-of-fit chi-square test, one-variable chi-square test**
a type of CHI-SQUARE TEST which explores the OBSERVED FREQUENCIES or proportion of cases that fall into the various LEVELs (two or more categories) of a single *categorical* INDEPENDENT VARIABLE, and compares these with hypothesized values. When chi-square is used as a measure of goodness-of-fit, the smaller chi-square is, the better the fit of the observed frequencies to the expected ones. A chi-square of *zero* indicates a perfect fit.
The one-way chi-square test is based on the following ASSUMPTIONS:

1) Participants are categorized along one variable having two or more categories, and we count the frequency in each category;
2) Each participant can be in only one category (that is, you cannot have repeated measures);

3) Category membership is independent: The fact that an individual is in a category does not influence the probability that another participant will be in any category;
4) We include the responses of all participants in the study; and
5) For theoretical reasons, the expected frequency of each cell is 5 or more.

see also CHI-SQUARE TEST FOR HOMOGENEITY, CHI-SQUARE TEST OF INDEPENDENCE

📖 Ary et al. 2010; Heiman 2011; Pallant 2010; Sheskin 2011

chi-square group-independence test
another term for CHI-SQUARE TEST OF INDEPENDENCE

chi-square test
also **chi-squared test**, **Pearson's chi-square**
a NONPARAMETRIC TEST and a test of *significance* (pronounced 'ky' similar to 'by' and symbolized by the lowercase Greek letter χ) which is used to compare actual or **observed frequencies** with **expected frequencies** in SAMPLE DATA to see whether they differ significantly. Observed frequencies, as the name implies, are the actual frequencies obtained by observation. Expected frequencies are theoretical frequencies that would be observed when the NULL HYPOTHESIS is true. The chi-square test is most often used with *nominal* data, where observations are grouped into several discrete, mutually exclusive categories, and where one counts the frequency of occurrence in each category. The test works by comparing the *categorically* coded data (observed frequencies) with the frequencies that you would expect to get in each cell of a table by chance alone (expected frequencies). In fact, this procedure is used to test the relationship between the variables (how well they go together) rather than how one variable affects another. It does not allow us to make cause-effect claims. For example, a researcher makes use of the chi-square test to see if males and females differ in their choice of foreign language to study in high school, where the school offers Japanese, Spanish, and French. The variable of gender (with two levels or two groups inside the variable) is *categorical*, as is choice of foreign language (with three levels).

The chi-square test is, generally, based on the following ASSUMPTIONS:

1) Observations must be independent—that is, the subjects in each sample must be randomly and independently selected.
2) The categories must be mutually exclusive: Each observation can appear in one and only one of the categories in the table.
3) The observations are measured as frequencies.

The table of values to be analyzed in a chi-square test of independence is known as a CONTINGENCY TABLE. That is because in this type of analysis, we are testing whether the number of cases in one category of one variable are contingent upon (i.e., dependent or independent of) the other variable. This test is used to detect an association between data in rows and data in columns, but it does not indicate the strength of any association.

The Chi-squared test is more accurate when large frequencies are used—all of the expected frequencies should be more than 1, and at least 80% of the expected frequencies should be at least 5. If these conditions are not met, the Chi-squared test is not valid and therefore cannot be used. If the Chi-squared test is not valid and a 2 × 2 (two-by-two) table is being used, FISHER'S EXACT-TEST can sometimes be utilized. If there are more than two rows and/or columns, it may be possible to regroup the data so as to create fewer columns. Doing this will increase the cell frequencies, which may then be large enough to meet the requirements. For example, if you have four age groups (0-7, 8-14, 15-21 and 22-28 years), it might be reasonable to combine these to produce two age groups (0-14 and 15-28 years).

There are three types of chi-square statistical tests. One is used when you have only one INDEPENDENT VARIABLE (IV), and want to examine whether the distribution of the data is what is expected. This is called the CHI-SQUARE GOODNESS-OF-FIT TEST. The other type of chi-square is used when you have two IVs, with two or more levels each. This is used when you want to examine whether there is a relationship between the variables. This is called the CHI-SQUARE TEST OF INDEPENDENCE. It tests the hypothesis that there is no relationship between the two CATEGORICAL VARIABLEs. This is probably the more common chi-square test in the field of applied linguistics research. The third type is CHI-SQUARE TEST FOR HOMOGENEITY which examine whether the relationship between TREATMENT and outcome is the same across gender, for example.

Unlike INFERENTIAL STATISTICS such as t-TESTs and ANOVA which are appropriate only when the DEPENDENT VARIABLEs being measured are *continuous* (measured on INTERVAL or RATIO SCALEs), the chi-square statistic investigates whether there is a relationship between two categorical variables. The chi-square is not a measure of the degree of relationship. It is merely used to estimate the likelihood that some factor other than chance accounts for the apparent relationship.

The chi-square test is a valuable tool for analyzing frequency data, but is restricted to studying no more than two categorical variables at a time. When there are three or more categorical variables, it is necessary to use more complex procedures such as LOG-LINEAR ANALYSIS.

Ary et al. 2010; Hatch & Lazaraton 1991; Larson-Hall 2010; Mackey & Gass 2005; Marczyk et al. 2005; Porte 2010; Sapsford & Jupp 2006; Stewart 2002; Urdan 2010

chi-square test for homogeneity
 a type of CHI-SQUARE TEST which is employed to compare the distribution of frequency counts across different populations. Put differently, the chi-square test for homogeneity evaluates if a single CATEGORICAL VARIABLE with two (or more) LEVELs has the same distribution in two (or more) samples. If sample data are displayed in a CONTINGENCY TABLE, the expected frequency count for each cell of the table is at least 5.
 see also CHI-SQUARE TEST OF INDEPENDENCE, CHI-SQUARE GOODNESS-OF-FIT TEST
 📖 Sheskin 2011

chi-square test of independence
 also **chi-square group-independence test, two-way group-independence chi-square test, two-way chi-square test, multidimensional chi-square test, two-variable chi-square test**
 a type of CHI-SQUARE TEST which is used when you count the frequency of category membership along two INDEPENDENT VARIABLEs (IVs). The purpose of the Chi-square test is to examine whether the frequency that participants fall into the LEVELs or categories of one variable depends on the frequency of falling into the categories on the other variable. It tests the relationship between two *categorical* IVS each with two or more levels and a DEPENDENT VARIABLE in the form of a frequency count. For example, we want to see if males and females differ in their choice of foreign language to study in high school, where the school offers Japanese, Spanish, and French. The variable of gender (with two levels or two groups inside the variable) is categorical, as is choice of foreign language (with three levels).
 The assumptions of the two-way chi-square are the same as for the ONE-WAY CHI-SQUARE TEST. The chi-square test of independence evaluates the general hypothesis that the two variables are independent of one another. Another way of stating that two variables are independent of one another is to say that there is a zero CORRELATION between them. A zero correlation indicates there is no way to predict at above chance in which category an observation will fall on one of the variables, if it is known which category the observation falls on the second variable. In other words, when variables are independent, there is no correlation, and using the categories from one variable is no help in predicting the frequencies for the other variable. Thus, a significant two-way chi-square indicates a significant correlation between the variables. To determine the size of this correlation, we compute either the PHI CORRELATION COEFFICIENT (ϕ) or the **contingency coefficient** (C), which is used to describe a significant two-way chi-square that is not a 2 × 2 (two-by-two) design (it is a 2 × 3, a 3 × 3, and so on). Squaring ϕ or C gives the proportion of variance accounted for, which indicates how much more accurately the fre-

quencies of category membership on one variable can be predicted by knowing category membership on the other variable.
see also CHI-SQUARE GOODNESS-OF-FIT TEST, CHI-SQUARE TEST FOR HOMOGENEITY
📖 Ary et al. 2010; Heiman 2011; Pallant 2010; Sheskin 2011

choice distribution
another term for DISTRACTOR EFFICIENCY

CI
an abbreviation for CONFIDENCE INTERVAL

circularity
another term for SPHERICITY

CLAN
see CHILDES

classical test theory
also **true score model, true score theory, classical true score, CTT**
a test theory that assumes that a test taker's **observed score** (X), a score that a person actually received on a test, is an additive composite of two components: **true score** (i.e., the true ability) of the respondent on that measure and ERROR SCORE (due to factors other than the ability being tested) (see Figure C.1).

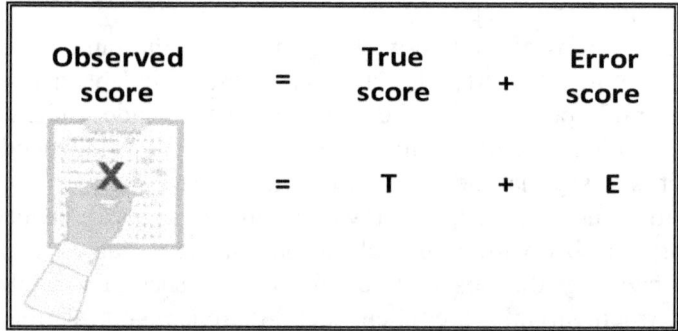

Figure C.1. The Basic Equation of True Score Theory

According to this theory, the true score remains constant and any non-systematic variation in the observed score is due to the error score. Note that you observe the X score; you never actually see the true or error scores. Because of error, the obtained score is sometimes higher than the true score and sometimes lower than the true score. For instance, a student may get a score of 85 on a test. That is the score you observe, an X

of 85. However the reality might be that the student is actually better at the test than that score indicates. Assume the student's true ability is 89 ($T = 89$). That means that the error for that student is = 4. While the student's true ability may be 89, s/he may have had a bad day, may not have had breakfast, may have had an argument with someone, or may have been distracted while taking the test. Factors like these can contribute to errors in measurement that make the students' observed abilities appear lower than their true or actual abilities.

The classical test theory only takes a unitary ERROR TERM into account, even though errors actually come from multiple sources. This means that RELIABILITY assessment must rest on multiple procedures and indicators (for example, TEST-RETEST RELIABILITY, SPLIT-HALF RELIABILITY, CRONBACH'S ALPHA), each one accounting for a different error source. Thus, a high test-retest reliability means that we can trust that measure independently of the occasion when it is measured, but it tells us nothing about whether we can trust that measure independently of the system (human being or instrument) which actually makes the measurement. Consequently, multiple reliabilities exist within classical test theory, for instance across occasions, across raters, across items, and so forth. This represents a major limit of the classical approach to reliability, as it cannot account for multiple error sources. Classical test theory treats all errors to be random, and thus CTT reliability estimates do not distinguish systematic error. Far more importantly, classical theory of reliability cannot account for the interaction among different sources of error. For instance, neither cronbach's alpha nor test-retest reliabilities are useful when consistency across items changes across occasions. GENERALIZABILITY THEORY, instead, represents a more general approach to the assessment of the reliability of a score.

📖 Bachman 1990; Leary 2011; Richards & Schmidt 2010; Trochim & Donnelly 2007

classical true score
another term for CLASSICAL TEST THEORY

classification matrix
also **confusion matrix, assignment matrix, prediction matrix**
a means of assessing the predictive ability of the DISCRIMINANT FUNCTION(s). Created by cross-tabulating actual group membership with predicted group membership, this matrix consists of numbers on the diagonal representing correct classifications and off-diagonal numbers representing incorrect classifications.

📖 Hair et al. 2010

classification question
another term for FACTUAL QUESTION

classification variable
another term for CATEGORICAL VARIABLE

closed-ended item
another term for CLOSED-FORM ITEM

closed-ended question
another term for CLOSED-FORM ITEM

closed-ended response
another term for CLOSED-FORM ITEM

closed-form item
also **fixed response item, fixed-ended response, closed-ended response, closed-form question, closed question, restricted question, closed-response question, closed-ended question, closed-ended item, closed-response item**
a type of item or question posed by researchers to participants in research projects that specifies the parameters within which participants can frame their answers. Closed-form items typically provide possible responses in the questions, request specific facts, or may even limit responses to *yes* or *no*. As such, they assume that people's experiences may be reduced to facts that can be coded with preestablished researcher-generated categories. Closed-form items are worded to eliminate possibilities for participants to introduce their own topics or provide answers that do not fit the researcher's coding schemes. Such questions are frequently used in a way that formulates the human subject as passive, responding to a neutral researcher working to elicit specific facts concerning research topics. Highly structured, closed-form items are useful in that they can generate frequencies of response amenable to statistical treatment and analysis. They also enable comparisons to be made across groups in the sample. They are quicker to code up and analyze than word-based data and, often, they are directly to the point and deliberately more focused than OPEN-FORM ITEMs. For example, a question might require a participant to choose either 'yes or no', 'agree or disagree'. A statement might be given requiring participants to indicate their level of agreement on a 5-point scale (see LIKERT SCALE). The main advantage of using the closed form is that the data elicited are easy to record and analyze with statistical procedures.
Such an item might look like the following (Table C.1).

The following is a list of communicative activities. Please circle how *effective* you believe each one is for second/foreign language learning.

Classroom activities	Not at all effective	Somewhat effective	Fairly effective	Very effective
Debate	1	2	3	4
Grammer drills	1	2	3	4
Group	1	2	3	4
Pair work	1	2	3	4

Table C.1. An Example of a Closed-Form Item

In general closed-form items (such as DICHOTOMOUS QUESTIONs, MULTIPLE-CHOICE ITEMs, RATIO DATA QUESTIONs, MATRIX QUESTIONS, CONSTANT SUM QUESTIONS, RANK ORDER QUESTIONS, CONTINGENCY QUESTIONs, CHECKLISTs, NUMERIC ITEMs) are quick to complete and straightforward to code (e.g., for computer analysis), and do not discriminate unduly on the basis of how articulate respondents are. On the other hand, they do not enable respondents to add any remarks, qualifications and explanations to the categories, and there is a risk that the categories might not be exhaustive and that there might be bias in them.
📖 Best & Kahn 2006; Dörnyei 2003; Given 2008; Perry 2011

closed-form question
another term for CLOSED-FORM ITEM

closed question
another term for CLOSED-FORM ITEM

closed-response item
another term for CLOSED-FORM ITEM

closed-response question
another term for CLOSED-FORM ITEM

cloze test
a reading passage (perhaps 150 to 300 words) in which roughly every *sixth* or *seven* word has been deleted; the test-taker is required to supply words that fit into those blanks. The cloze test results are good measures of overall proficiency. According to theoretical constructs underlying this claim, the ability to supply appropriate words in blanks requires a number of abilities that lie at the heart of competence in a language: knowledge of vocabulary, grammatical structure, discourse structure, reading skills and strategies, and an internalized *expectancy grammar* (enabling one to predict an item that will come next in a sequence). It was argued that successful completion of cloze items taps into all of those abilities, which were said to be the essence of global language proficiency.
📖 Brown 2010

cluster analysis

an advanced statistical technique in MULTIVARIATE ANALYSIS that determines a classification or taxonomy from multiple measures of an initially unclassified set of individual or objects. Put simply, cluster analysis a set of statistical multivariate techniques which are used to sort variables, individuals, respondents, objects, and the like, into groups on the basis of their similarity with respect to a set of attributes. These groupings are known as clusters (see Figure C.2). The objective is to identify certain homogenous subgroups or clusters of participants within a given SAMPLE who share similar combinations of characteristic. The sets of measurements pertaining to individuals being studied, known as *profiles*, are compared and individuals that are close or similar are classified as being in the same cluster or group.

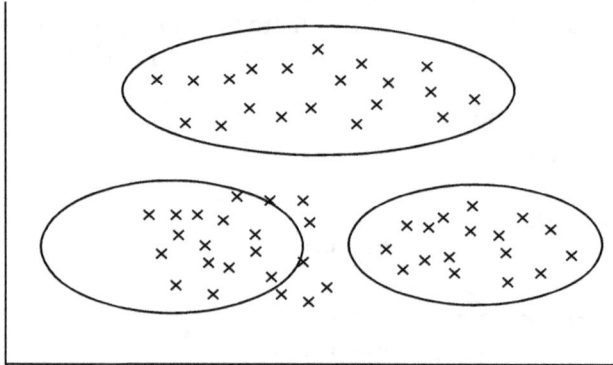

Figure C.2. Schematic Diagram for Clusters of Data

Cluster analysis appears to be less widely used than FACTOR ANALYSIS, which does a very similar task. One advantage of cluster analysis is that it is less tied to the CORRELATION COEFFICIENT than factor analysis is. In other words, factor analysis makes the groupings based on patterns of variation (correlation) in the data whereas cluster analysis makes groupings on the basis of distance (proximity). In addition, factor analysis is primarily concerned with grouping variables.

In many instances, the grouping in cluster analysis is actually a means to an end in terms of a conceptually defined goal. The more common roles cluster analysis can play in conceptual development include the following:

• *Data reduction*: A researcher may be faced with a large number of observations that are meaningless unless classified into manageable groups. Cluster analysis can perform this data reduction procedure objectively by reducing the information from an entire POPULATION or

sample to information about specific groups. For example, if we can understand the attitudes of a population by identifying the major groups within the population, then we have reduced the data for the entire population into profiles of a number of groups. In this fashion, the researcher provides a more concise, understandable description of the observations, with minimal loss of information.
- HYPOTHESIS *generation*: Cluster analysis is also useful when a researcher wishes to develop hypotheses concerning the nature of the data or to examine previously stated hypotheses.

There are two main types of cluster analysis, **hierarchal clustering** and **non-hierarchical clustering**. In hierarchical clustering, clusters of variables are formed in a series or hierarchy of stages. Initially there are as many clusters as variables. At the first stage, the two variables that are closest are grouped together to form one cluster. At the second stage, either a third variable is added or agglomerated to the first luster containing the two variables or two other variables are grouped together to form a new cluster, whichever is closest. At the third stage, two variables may be grouped together, a third variable may be added to an existing group of variables or two groups may be combined. So, at each stage only one new cluster is formed according to the variables, the variable and cluster or the clusters that are closest together. At the final stage all the variables are grouped into a single cluster.

Non-hierarchical clustering follows a different path. During the process, sample members are put into a predefined number of clusters. As a first step, the statistical program takes the first N members of the sample (N equals the number of clusters defined prior to the analysis) and defines these as the centers of N clusters. Following this, the whole data set is partitioned into N clusters by assigning sample members to the predefined cluster center that they are closest to. Finally, on the basis of the position of the cluster members, new centers are identified and sample members are regrouped according to these new centers. The procedure is repeated until the centers become stable, that is, until they show no change after further regrouping.

Both hierarchical and non-hierarchal clustering techniques have their advantages and disadvantages. On the one hand, hierarchical clustering is difficult to apply if the SAMPLE SIZE is too large. On the other hand, the results of non-hierarchical clustering are highly dependent on the initial cluster centers. To avoid these limitations, clustering is often done in two stages: first, hierarchical clustering is carried out on a smaller subsample. Based on this first step, the number of clusters and their positions (i.e., the initial cluster centers) are defined and subsequently non-hierarchical clustering is run on the whole sample by inputting the cluster centers defined previously, and the procedure of non-hierarchical clustering is iterated until stable cluster centers are received.

Cluster analysis can also be criticized for working too well in the sense that statistical results are produced even when a logical basis for clusters is not apparent. Thus, the researcher should have a strong conceptual basis to deal with issues such as why groups exist in the first place and what variables logically explain why objects end up in the groups that they do. Even if cluster analysis is being used in conceptual development as just mentioned, some conceptual rationale is essential. The following are the most common criticisms that must be addressed by conceptual rather than empirical support:

- *Cluster analysis is descriptive, atheoretical, and noninferential.* Cluster analysis has no statistical basis upon which to draw inferences from a sample to a population, and many contend that it is only an exploratory technique. Nothing guarantees unique solutions, because the cluster membership for any number of solutions is dependent upon many elements of the procedure, and many different solutions can be obtained by varying one or more elements.
- *Cluster analysis will always create clusters, regardless of the actual existence of any structure in the data.* When using cluster analysis, the researcher is making an assumption of some structure among the objects. The researcher should always remember that just because clusters can be found does not validate their existence. Only with strong conceptual support and then validation are the clusters potentially meaningful and relevant.
- *The cluster solution is not generalizable because it is totally dependent upon the variables used as the basis for the similarity measure.* This criticism can be made against any statistical technique, but cluster analysis is generally considered more dependent on the measures used to characterize the objects than other multivariate techniques. With the **cluster variate** (i.e., a set of variables or characteristics representing the objects to be clustered and used to calculate the similarity between objects) completely specified by the researcher, the addition of SPURIOUS VARIABLEs or the deletion of relevant variables can have a substantial impact on the resulting solution. As a result, the researcher must be especially cognizant of the variables used in the analysis, ensuring that they have strong conceptual support.

see also STRUCTURAL EQUATION MODELING

 Dörnyei 2007; Hair et al. 2010; Sahai & Khurshid 2001; Sapsford & Jupp 2006

clustered bar chart
see COMPOUND HISTOGRAM

cluster sampling
a type of PROBABILITY SAMPLING which is particularly appropriate when the POPULATION of interest is infinite, when a list of the members of the population does not exist, or when the geographic distribution of the individuals is widely dispersed. Cluster sampling involves grouping the population and then selecting the groups or the clusters rather than individual elements for inclusion in the SAMPLE (see Figure C.3). These clusters are often based on naturally occurring groupings, such as geographical areas or particular institutions.

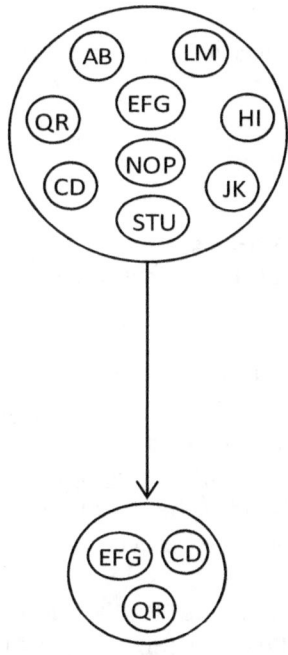

Figure C.3. Schematic Diagram for Cluster Sampling

In populations spread over a substantial geographical area, random sampling is enormously expensive since random sampling maximizes the amount of travel and consequent expense involved. Thus, it is fairly common to employ cluster samples in which the larger geographical area is subdivided into representative clusters or sub-areas. Suppose a researcher wants to survey students' proficiency levels in a particularly large community. It would be completely impractical to select students and spend an inordinate amount of time traveling about in order to test them. By cluster sampling, the researcher can select a specific number of schools and then examine all the students in those selected schools. Each school would be a cluster.

Cluster sampling is similar to SIMPLE RANDOM SAMPLING except that groups rather than individuals are randomly selected (that is, the SAMPLING UNIT is a group rather than an individual).

Cluster sampling is widely used in small-scale research. In a cluster sample the parameters of the wider population are often drawn very sharply. A researcher, therefore, would have to comment on the generalizability of the findings. The researcher may also need to stratify within this cluster sample if useful data, i.e., those which are focused and which demonstrate discriminability, are to be acquired.

see also SYSTEMATIC SAMPLING, STRATIFIED SAMPLING, AREA SAMPLING, MULTI-PHASE SAMPLING

📖 Clark-Carter 2010; Cohen et al. 2011; Fraenkel & Wallen 2009; Kothari 2008; Sapsford & Jupp 2006

cluster variate
see CLUSTER ANALYSIS

Cochran–Mantel–Haenszel test
another term for MANTEL-HAENSZEL TEST

Cochran's *C* test
a test procedure for testing three or more INDEPENDENT SAMPLES for HOMOGENEITY OF VARIANCEs before using an ANALYSIS OF VARIANCE procedure. Cochran's C test is based on the ratio of the largest SAMPLE VARIANCE to the sum of all the sample variances. Like BARTLETT'S TEST, however, it is found to be sensitive to any departures from NORMALITY. It has been found to be even less ROBUST to nonnormality than HARTLEY'S TEST.

see also BOX'S *M* TEST, LEVENE'S TEST, BROWN-FORSYTHE TEST, O'BRIEN TEST, MANTEL-HAENSZEL TEST, COCHRAN'S *Q* TEST

📖 Lomax 2007; Sahai & Khurshid 2001

Cochran's *Q* test
a NONPARAMETRIC TEST which is used to determine whether the frequencies of a dichotomous DEPENDENT VARIABLE differ significantly for more than two related samples or groups. If the measure taken is dichotomous, for example, *yes* or *no*, or can be converted into one or more dichotomies, then Cochran's Q can be used. An example would be if researchers wanted to compare students' choices of modules on applied linguistics, research methods, and historical issues to see whether some modules were more popular than others.

The Cochran's Q test is an extension of the MCNEMAR'S TEST to a design involving more than two DEPENDENT SAMPLES. In the case of two dependent samples the Cochran's *Q* test will yield a result that is equivalent to that obtained with the McNemar's test.

see also COCHRAN'S *C* TEST, MANTEL-HAENSZEL TEST

📖 Clark-Carter 2010; Cramer & Howitt 2004; Sheskin 2011

codebook
    also **data codebook**
a written or computerized list that provides a clear and comprehensive description of the VARIABLEs that will be included in the database. The codebook applies to any project that involves collecting and analyzing data. A detailed codebook is essential when the researcher begins to analyze the data. Moreover, it serves as a permanent database guide, so that the researcher, when attempting to reanalyze certain data, will not be stuck trying to remember what certain variable names mean or what data were used for a certain analysis. Ultimately, the lack of a well-defined data codebook may render a database uninterpretable and useless. Once the coding of the QUESTIONNAIRE items has been completed and a computer data file has been created, the questionnaires are usually put into storage and not looked at again (except for special occasions when something needs to be double-checked). Given the general shortage of storage facilities, it is inevitable that sooner or later the questionnaire piles find their way into the trashcan, which will leave the computer file as the only record of the survey data. In order to make these records meaningful for people who have not been involved in creating it, it is worth compiling a codebook. This is intended to provide a comprehensive and comprehensible description of the data set that is accessible to anyone who would like to use it. It usually contains:

- the name of each variable that has been entered in the data set (e.g., gender, languages spoken).
- a brief description of the variable and/or the citation of the actual item as it occurred in the questionnaire.
- the location of each variable in the computer record (e.g., specified in columns or sequence numbers).
- the CODING FRAME for each variable, including the range of valid codes (i.e. minimum and maximum values) and the code used for missing data.
- a note of any special instructions or actions taken in the course of coding/keying the data.

see also DATA CODING

📖 Dörnyei 2003; Marczyk et al. 2005

coding
a process of disassembling and reassembling the data in GROUNDED

THEORY. Data are disassembled when they are broken apart into lines, paragraphs, or sections. These fragments are then rearranged, through coding, to produce a new understanding that explores similarities, differences, across a number of different cases. The early part of coding should be confusing, with a mass of apparently unrelated material. However, as coding progresses and themes emerge, the analysis becomes more organized and structured. In grounded theory there are three types of coding: *open, axial* and *selective coding*, the intention of which is to deconstruct the data into manageable chunks in order to facilitate an understanding of the phenomenon in question. **Open coding** involves exploring the data and identifying units of analysis to code for meanings, feelings, actions, events and so on. The researcher codes up the data, creating new codes and categories and subcategories where necessary, and integrating codes where relevant until the coding is complete.

Axial coding seeks to make links between categories and codes, to integrate codes around the axes of central categories; the essence of axial coding is the interconnectedness of categories. Hence codes are explored, their interrelationships are examined, and codes and categories are compared to existing theory. Think of a wheel with a center and spokes extending. The spokes are all related to the central category. A visual model is developed, called an *axial coding paradigm*.

Selective coding is used to develop propositions or hypotheses based on the model, showing how the categories are related. The resulting theory can take the form of a narrative statement, a picture, or a series of hypotheses. That is, the researcher identifies a story line and writes a story that integrates the categories in the axial coding model. As coding proceeds the researcher develops concepts and makes connections between them.

see also CONSTANT COMPARISON METHOD

📖 Cohen et al. 2011; Strauss & Corbin 1998

coding frame

(in coding QUESTIONNAIRE data) a classification scheme that offers a numerical score for every possible answer to an item. Coding frame is used to categorize the answers to questionnaire items in order to facilitate analysis. The minimum number of categories is two, as with yes/no questions or gender data: *Yes* and male are usually coded 1, whereas *no* and female are coded 2. For some OPEN-ENDED QUESTIONs (e.g., what foreign languages have you learned in the past?) the coding frame can have many more categories—in fact, as many as the number of different answers in all the questionnaires. With such items the coding frame is continuously extended, with every new language mentioned by the respondents being assigned a new number.

The coding frame of every item will need to have a special category for cases when no answer has been given (e.g., because someone overlooked the item or intentionally avoided it)—such missing data are often coded 9 or 99 (rather than 0, which can be confused with several other meanings).

With CLOSED-ENDED ITEMs the coding frame is usually very straightforward: each pre-determined response option is assigned a number (e.g., strongly disagree = 1, disagree = 2, neutral = 3, agree = 4, strongly agree = 5). The coding of open-ended items, however, often goes beyond mechanical conversion and requires a certain amount of subjective interpretation and summary on the part of the coder. Here the task is to condense the detailed information contained in the responses into a limited number of categories; thus, the assigned codes can be seen as shorthand symbols standing for the longer replies. Ongoing decisions will need to be made about whether to label two similar but not completely identical responses as the same or whether to mark the difference somehow.

see also CODEBOOK

 Dörnyei 2003

coefficient

a *number* that represents the amount of an attribute

coefficient alpha

another term for CRONBACH'S ALPHA

coefficient of alienation

also *k*

a statistic that indicates the amount of variation that two VARIABLEs do not have in common. Coefficient of alienation is obtained as the ratio of the RESIDUAL SUM OF SQUARES to the TOTAL SUM OF SQUARES. It is interpreted as the amount of error in predicting values of the DEPENDENT VARIABLE that could not be eliminated by using values of the INDEPENDENT VARIABLES. If there is a perfect CORRELATION between two variables then the coefficient of alienation is zero. If there is no correlation between two variables then the coefficient of alienation is one. In a sense, then, it is the opposite of the COEFFICIENT OF DETERMINATION. The square of coefficient of alienation is called **coefficient of nondetermination (k^2)**, which represents that part of the dependent variable's total variation not accounted for by linear association with the independent variable.

 Cramer & Howitt 2004; Sahai & Khurshid 2001

coefficient of correlation

another term for CORRELATION COEFFICIENT

coefficient of determination
also *r* square, r^2

an index of the amount of variation that two variables have in common. Coefficient of determination is simply the square of PEARSON PRODUCT-MOMENT CORRELATION COEFFICIENT between the two variables:

$$\text{Coefficient of determination} = r^2$$

This provides a clearer indication of the meaning of the size of a correlation as it gives the proportion of the variance that is shared between two variables. Coefficient of determination tells you how much of the variance of *Y* is in common with the variance of *X*. To convert this to percentage of variance, just multiply by 100 (shift the decimal place two columns to the right). For example, two variables that correlate r = .2 share only .2 × .2 = .04 = 4 per cent of their variance. There is not much overlap between the two variables. A correlation of r = .5, however, means 25 per cent shared variance (.5 × .5 = .25). A correlation of +.80 or -.80 means that the two variables have $.80^2$ or 64 percent of their variance in common with each other. If correlation coefficient is zero, we account for none of the variance. If it equals - 1.00 or + 1.00, we can perfectly account for 100% of the variance. And if it is in between, the more variance we account for, the stronger the relationship.

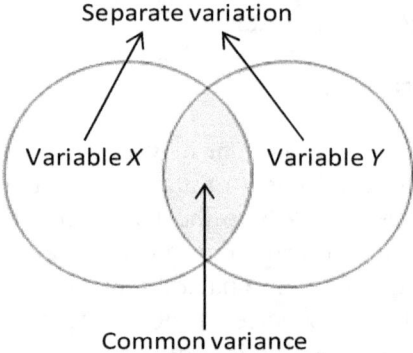

Figure C.4. Schematic Representation of Covariation or Common Variance

The notion of covariation or **common variance** is illustrated in Figure C.4, in which the total amount of variation in each variable is represented by a circle. The overlap of the circles represents the common or shared variance. The greater the common variance, between the two variables, the stronger the relationship. The coefficient of determination is a useful index for evaluating the meaning of size of a correlation. It also reminds one that positive and negative correlations of the same magnitude, for

example, $r = .5$ and $r = -.5$, are equally useful for prediction and other uses because both have the same coefficient of determination, $r^2 = .25$. The coefficient of determination ranges from 0 to +1. If it is 1 ($r = +1$), you can predict individuals' scores on one variable perfectly from their scores on the other variable.
 Ary et al. 2010; Cramer & Howitt 2004; Leary 2011; Pallant 2010

coefficient of multiple correlation
another term for MULTIPLE CORRELATION COEFFICIENT

coefficient of multiple determination
see MULTIPLE CORRELATION COEFFICIENT

coefficient of nondetermination
see COEFFICIENT OF ALIENATION

coefficient of stability
see TEST-RETEST RELIABILITY

coefficient of variation
also **CV**

the STANDARD DEVIATION (*SD*) of the SAMPLE divided by the ARITHMETIC MEAN (*M*) of a set of scores. Coefficient of variation (CV) is often presented as the given ratio multiplied by 100. It would seem intuitive to suggest that samples with big *M* scores of, say, 100 are likely to have larger variation around the *M* than samples with smaller *M*s. In order to indicate relative variability adjusting the variance of samples for their SAMPLE SIZE, we can calculate the CV. This allows comparison of variation between samples with large *M*s and small *M*s. Essentially, it scales down (or possibly up) all *SD*s as a ratio of a single unit on the MEASUREMENT SCALE. Thus, if a sample *M* is 39 and its *SD* is 5.3, we can calculate the CV as follows:

$$CV = \frac{SD}{M} = \frac{5.3}{39} = .14$$

CV is useful because the *SD* of data must always be understood in the context of the *M* of the data. Instead, the actual value of the CV is independent of the unit in which the measurement has been taken, so it is a dimensionless number (cannot be measured on a scale of physical units). For comparison between data sets with different units or widely different *M*s, one should use the CV instead of the *SD*. Unlike the *SD*, CV cannot be used directly to construct CONFIDENCE INTERVALs for the *M*.
 Cramer & Howitt 2004

Cohen's *d*
also *d*

an index of EFFECT SIZE that measures the difference between two *independent sample* means in terms of STANDARD DEVIATION units. This is a group difference index of effect size. Cohen's *d* can start from zero and range as high as it needs to. A value of .20 is generally considered a small effect size, .50 a medium effect size, and .80 or more a large effect size. Knowing the amount of effect a particular variable had will help the researcher (and the reader) in other contexts to decide on whether to apply this treatment in other less constrained situations. Information about effect size is also extremely useful to the field when other researchers are trying to establish the most powerful statistical test to use for their study. The researcher will want to have selected a test that is powerful enough to give him or her the assurance that a TYPE I ERROR or TYPE II ERROR will not be made in reporting results.
see also META-ANALYSIS
📖 Larson-Hall 2010; Pallant 2010; Porte 2010

Cohen's *f*
also *f*

an index of EFFECT SIZE that measures the MEAN differences of three or more groups. It is generally appropriate for MULTIPLE REGRESSION and ANALYSIS OF VARIANCE. This is a group index of effect size, but it is not used as frequently as COHEN'S *d*. It measures differences between groups in terms of the number of STANDARD DEVIATIONs they differ by. The following values as criteria for identifying the magnitude of an effect size have been proposed: (a) a small effect size is one that is greater than .10 but not more than .25; (b) A medium effect size is one that is greater than .25 but not more than .40; and (c) A large effect size is greater than .40.

Cohen's *f* can easily be converted from an ETA-SQUARED effect size.
📖 Larson-Hall 2010; Sheskin 2011

Cohen's kappa
also **kappa coefficient, kappa (κ)**

a measure of agreement which is used in calculating INTERRATER RELIABILITY representing the average rate of agreement for entire set of scores, accounting for the frequency of both agreements and disagreements by category. In a dichotomous coding scheme (e.g., coding forms as targetlike or nontargetlike), Cohen's kappa requires that the researcher determine how many forms both raters coded as targetlike, how many were coded as targetlike by the first rater and as nontargetlike by the second, how many were coded as nontargetlike by the first and as targetlike by the second, and so on. The final calculation of kappa involves more detail on agreement and disagreement than simple percentage systems, and it also accounts for chance.

see also PERCENTAGE AGREEMENT

📖 Mackey & Gass 2005

cohort

a group of individuals who experienced the same life event within the same time and share some common characteristic. Commonly used cohorts include all people born in the same year (called birth cohorts), all people hired at the same time, and all people who graduate in a given year.

📖 Ruspini 2002

cohort study

a type of LONGITUDINAL MIXED DESIGN which is somewhere in between PANEL and a TREND STUDY. In a cohort study, a specific POPULATION is tracked over a specific period of time but selective SAMPLING within that SAMPLE occurs. This means that some members of a COHORT may not be included each time. In cohort studies, rather than observing the exact same people in each wave (as the panel study does), a series of *repeated cross-sectional surveys* are administered to selective member each time. The study, in fact, focuses on a category of people who share a similar life experience in a specified time period. For example, a school system might follow the high school graduating class(es) of 2004 over time and ask them questions about higher education, work experiences, attitudes, and so on. From a list of all the graduates, a RANDOM SAMPLE is drawn at different points in time, and data are collected from that sample. Thus, the population remains the same during the study, but the individuals surveyed are different each time.

The underlying idea behind any cohort study is that long-term social change must be interpreted within the context of generational change. By following one generation throughout its entire life-course, the consequences of growth, maturity, and ageing are rendered visible. Furthermore, it also becomes possible to investigate the influence of a variety of events that take place over the course of time and, likewise, to understand whether a specific event has influenced an entire generation in the same way. Consequently, cohort studies are particularly suitable when studying populations that are subject to radical changes.

Cohort studies can be either prospective or retrospective. A **prospective cohort study** usually studies one or more cohorts, at successive intervals, over a period of time, while a **retrospective cohort study** gathers retrospective information about just one cohort at a time and may thus be made up of more than one study. Because of this, retrospective studies may evince, simultaneously, both cross-sectional features (samples are

only interviewed once) and prospective panel features (they offer information about the life histories of the interviewees).
see also ROTATING PANELS, SPLIT PANELS, LINKED PANELS, ACCELERATED LONGITUDINAL DESIGN, DIARY STUDY
📖 Ary et al. 2010; Dörnyei 2007; Neuman 2007; Ruspini 2002

collaborative research
another term for PARTICIPATORY ACTION RESEARCH

collapsing
in a TWO-WAY ANOVA, averaging together all scores from all levels of one FACTOR in order to calculate the MAIN EFFECT means for the other factor.
📖 Heiman 2011

collinearity
another term for MULTICOLLINEARITY

column sum of squares
another term for SUM OF SQUARES FOR COLUMNS

combination
see PERMUTATION

commonsense realism
another term for NAIVE REALISM

common variance
see COEFFICIENT OF DETERMINATION

comparative research
a broad term which refers to the evaluation of the similarities, differences, and associations between entities. Entities may be based on many lines such as statements from an INTERVIEW or individual, symbols, social groups, and cross-national comparisons. Comparative research is used within most qualitative approaches, such as comparisons by core emic categories in ethnographic studies (see ETHNOGRAPHY), within-case comparisons in PHENOMENOLOGY, CASE STUDY comparisons, and examination of contrasts in narrative and DISCOURSE ANALYSIS.
The underlying goal of comparative research is to search for similarity and variation between the entities that are the object of comparison. The examination of similarity often means the application of a more general theory and a search for universals or underlying general processes across different contexts or categories. The ONTOLOGY of patterns or categories

is assumed to be universal and independent of time and space. In other words, the comparison should be broad enough to allow researchers to compare at a *higher level* of abstraction. However, it remains difficult to determine these general patterns. For this reason, comparative research is often used to separate patterns that are more general and isolate regularities or discrepancies from the context-laden environment.
see also HISTORICAL RESEARCH
📖 Given 2008

comparison group
see CONTROL GROUP

comparisonwise error rate
also **per-comparison error rate**
the SIGNIFICANCE LEVEL at which each test or comparison is carried out in an experiment. In a multiple comparison procedure, one is concerned with individual comparisons as well as sets of such comparisons. In individual comparisons, the SIGNIFICANCE LEVEL is referred to as comparisonwise error rate.
see also EXPERIMENTWISE ERROR RATE
📖 Everitt & Skrondal 2010; Pagano 2009; Upton & Cook 2008

compensatory demoralization
another term for DEMORALIZATION

compensatory rivalry
another term for JOHN HENRY EFFECT

complete observer
also **non-participant observer**
a type of PARTICIPANT OBSERVATION in which the researcher does not participate at all and whose role is also kept away from the people who are being observed. The role of the complete observer is typified in the one-way mirror, the video-cassette, the audio-cassette and the photograph. The best illustration of the non-participant observer role is perhaps the case of the researcher sitting at the back of a classroom coding up every three seconds the verbal exchanges between teacher and students by means of a structured set of observational categories. The qualitative researcher simply observes and records events as they occur. No attempt is made to alter the situation in any way. These are considered naturalistic observations.
see also PARTICIPANT AS OBSERVER, OBSERVER AS PARTICIPANT, COMPLETE PARTICIPANT
📖 Ary et al. 2010; Given 2008

complete participant
also **covert participant**
a type of PARTICIPANT OBSERVATION which involves a researcher to take on an insider role in the group being studied, and maybe who does not even declare that s/he is a researcher. For example is a researcher who becomes a certified teacher and takes a position in a school for the purpose of conducting research without telling anyone. In the Internet world, a researcher may join a listserve or chat room or virtual world in order to examine the online world of a particular subgroup.
see also COMPLETE OBSERVER, PARTICIPANT AS OBSERVER, OBSERVER AS PARTICIPANT
📖 Ary et al. 2010; Given 2008

complex comparison
another term for NONPAIRWISE COMPARISON

complexity theory
a research paradigm which looks at the world in ways which break with simple cause-and-effect models, linear predictability, and a dissection approach to understanding phenomena, replacing them with organic, non-linear and holistic approaches in which relations within interconnected networks are the order of the day. Here key terms are feedback, recursion, emergence, connectedness, and self-organization. Out go the simplistic views of linear causality, the ability to predict, control, and manipulate, and in come uncertainty, networks and connection, self-organization, emergence over time through feedback and the relationships of the internal and external environments, and survival and development through adaptation and change.
Complexity theory suggests that phenomena must be looked at holistically; to atomize phenomena into a restricted number of variables and then to focus only on certain factors is to miss the necessary dynamic interaction of several parts. This theory offers considerable leverage into understanding societal, community, individual, and institutional change; it provides the nexus between macro- and micro-research in understanding and promoting change. Complexity theory seriously undermines the value of experiments and positivist research (see POSITIVISM).
see also CHAOS THEORY
📖 Cohen et al. 2011; Given 2008

component analysis
another term for PRINCIPLE COMPONENTS ANALYSIS

composite comparison
another term for NONPAIRWISE COMPARISON

compound histogram
also **compound bar chart**
a form of BAR GRAPH which allows the introduction of a second VARIABLE to the analysis. A compound bar chart, as shown in Figure C.5, might involve the use of a second variable gender. Each bar of the simple bar chart would be differentiated into a section indicating the proportion of males and another section indicating the proportion of females. In this way, it would be possible to see pictorially whether there is a gender difference in terms of the four types of university course chosen, for example.

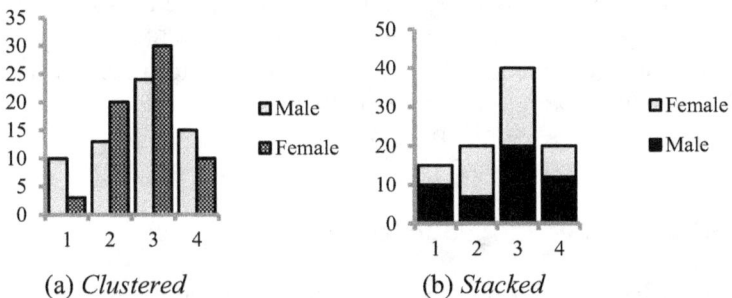

Figure C.5. Compound Histograms

In a **clustered bar chart** (Figure C.5a), the bars for the two genders are placed side by side rather than stacked (i.e., **stacked bar chart**, Figure C.5b) into a single column so that it is possible to see the proportions of females going to university, males going to university, females not going to university, and males not going to university more directly. Compound bar charts work well only when there are small numbers of values for each of the variables. With many values the charts become too complex and trends more difficult to discern.
 Cramer & Howitt 2004; Larson-Hall 2010

compound symmetry
a special case of SPHERICITY which exists when both of the following conditions have been met: a) HOMOGENEITY OF VARIANCE; and b) homogeneity of covariance (i.e., all of the population covariances are equal to one another.
 Sheskin 2011

comprehensive sampling
see PURPOSIVE SAMPLING

computer adaptive testing
also **CAT**

a type of testing which attempts to match the difficulty of test items to the knowledge and skill level of the student being assessed by tailoring the test so that a pre-selected sequence of items is administered based on whether or not the response to the previous item is correct. In computerized adaptive testing, a computer administers the items and gathers the examinee's responses, but its most distinctive feature is that the items finally administered depend on the examinee's ability. The test then adapts to the examinee's performance on the items. The advantages of CAT over traditional achievement tests include reduced testing time, the need for fewer items at a given level of MEASUREMENT ERROR, minimized frustration for students who perform poorly, and more precise estimates of achievement across the entire distribution.
see also ITEM RESPONSE THEORY
📖 Fernandez-Ballesteros 2003

computer-assisted language learning
also **CALL**

the search for and study of applications of the computer in the teaching or learning of a second or foreign language. Computer Assisted Language Learning (CALL) is often perceived, somewhat narrowly, as an approach to language teaching and learning in which the computer is used as an aid to the presentation, reinforcement, and assessment of material to be learned, usually including a substantial interactive element. CALL may take place in classrooms, homes, libraries, computer cafés, etc. It also happens at different times and in different economic, cultural, political, social, and linguistic realms that embody different understandings, goals, and standards. CALL research considers computer technologies that are not limited to desktop computers but include any form of electronic, chip-driven technology and the software that makes it run: These include personal digital assistants (PDAs); cell phones with text messaging and Web searching capabilities; laptops and peripherals, such as digital cameras, scanners, printers, and piano keyboards; and software from word processors to movie makers. These technologies provide language, culture, and other content, both explicit and implicit, through a variety of modes including visual, oral, textual, and graphical.

More specifically, CALL has been divided into seven general types of activity. One of the most important is *writing*. This includes word processing, text analysis, and desktop publishing, often combined with communication over a local area network (LAN). Though student use of spell checkers and grammar checkers is common in these types of activities, much more sophisticated and interactive approaches are also possible. Many second language (L2) teachers, for example, now request their students to use computers to write essays then to e-mail each other what they have written or to post their essays on a LAN. The students then discuss and correct each other's writing, engaging in meaningful discourse and creating knowledge through interaction.

A second type of CALL is *communicating*. This includes e-mail exchanges, student discussions with each other or with their teacher on LANs, MOOs (sites on the Internet where student do role-playing games and talk with each other), and real-time chat. These activities are particularly useful for foreign language teaching where students share the same first language because they create the need to use the foreign language for authentic communication.

Another CALL activity is use of *multimedia*. This includes courseware presented on CD-ROM or online for study of specific skills such as pronunciation or grammar, and integrated skills-based or communicative practice where hyperlinks allow students to access a range of supplementary material for learning support. Often teacher-created programs are course-specific and are designed to quiz students over material covered in class.

Other CALL activities involve the *Internet*, such as Web searches for information and student construction of home pages. Related to this is the field of *information literacy*, a concept similar to *computer literacy* and referring to the ability to obtain information from the Internet and process it selectively and critically. The tremendous amount of online resources means that teacher evaluation of Web sites and L2 learning materials has now become an important aspect of Internet-based activities.

An additional use of CALL is *concordancing* and *referencing*, or using a corpus to examine the range of usages for grammar and vocabulary items, and using online dictionaries for definitions and usage information.

Yet another significant use of CALL is *distance learning*. Some college professors teach some or all of their courses online. Research on distance learning and courses with online components suggests that online students make the same gains as those achieved by students receiving a regular 'brick-and-mortar' lecture. An additional aspect of distance learning is the teacher creation of Web pages to disseminate their lesson plans, course material, research papers, and other material. Many teachers routinely take attendance online and post course outlines, specific activities, tests, drills, and so on, on their home pages. Veteran teachers may recall when there was often a filing cabinet of time-tested activities, lessons, and tests in the teachers' office for instructors to browse through and copy. Now this 'filing cabinet' has moved online to hundreds of sites, including listening laboratories, Test of English as a Second Language (TOEFL) practice, reading and writing activities and exercises, tests, holiday-related and other types of cultural activities, Web page design, and so forth. Again, teachers are required to be able to evaluate sites and online materials.

Another important use of CALL is *test taking*. There is extensive research on computer-assisted language testing (CALT), suggesting that computer-based tests, particularly those that respond to learners' choices by presenting subsequent items at varying levels of difficulty, are effective in building language skills because they provide immediate feedback and multimedia support by access to dictionaries, grammatical explanations, and audio and video material for study of test items. Because the TOEFL is now administered by computer, students routinely use CD-ROM TOEFL practice tests and other self-tests. Furthermore, many teachers have developed their own tests, checked them for RELIABILITY and VALIDITY, and posted them on home pages for others to use, or have developed freeware for course-specific test creation.

With new learning programs arriving regularly, today, CALL is one of the more dynamic areas in applied linguistics.

📖 Egbert & Petrie 2005; Fotos & Browne 2004; Levy 1997

computer-assisted personal interviewing
also **CAPI**

a data collection technique which is used by an in-person interviewer (i.e., face-to-face interviewing) who uses a computer to administer the QUESTIONNAIRE to the respondent and captures the answers onto the computer.

📖 Lavrakas 2008

computer assisted self-interviewing
also **CASI**

a technique for data collection in which the respondent uses a computer to complete the QUESTIONNAIRE without an interviewer administering it to the respondent. This assumes the respondent can read well (enough) or that the respondent can hear the questions well in cases in which the questions are prerecorded and the audio is played back for the respondent one question at a time (see AUDIO COMPUTER ASSISTED SELF-INTERVIEWING). A primary rationale for CASI is that some questions are so sensitive that if researchers hope to obtain an accurate answer, respondents must use a highly confidential method of responding. For a successful CASI effort, the survey effort must consider three factors: (1) the design of the questions, (2) the limitations of the respondent, and (3) the appropriate computing platform.

📖 Lavrakas 2008

concept mapping

the graphical display of concepts and their interrelations. Concept mapping is a general method that can be used to help any individual or group to describe ideas about some topic in a pictorial form. Several methods currently go by names such as *concept mapping*, *mental mapping*, or *concept webbing*. All of them are similar in that they result in a picture of someone's ideas. Concept mapping is primarily a group process and so it is especially well suited for situations where teams or groups of researchers have to work together. The other methods work primarily with individuals. Second, it uses a structured facilitated approach. Specific steps are followed by a trained facilitator in helping a group articulate its ideas and understand them more clearly. Third, the core of concept mapping consists of several state-of-the-art *multivariate* statistical methods (involving three or more variables at the same time) that analyze the input from all of the individuals and yield an aggregate group product. Finally, the method requires the use of specialized computer programs that can handle the data from this type of process and accomplish the correct analysis and mapping procedures.

Essentially, concept mapping is a structured process, focused on a topic or construct of interest, involving input from one or more participants, that produces an interpretable pictorial view (concept map) of their ideas and concepts and how these are interrelated. Concept mapping helps people to think more effectively as a group without losing their individuality. It helps groups capture complex ideas without trivializing them or losing detail (see Figure C.6).

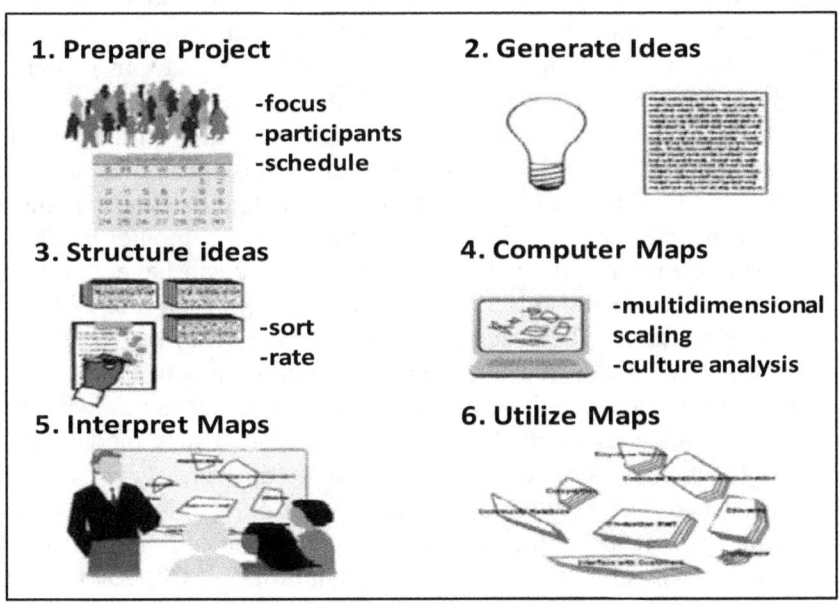

Figure C.6. The Steps in Concept-Mapping Process

A concept-mapping process involves six steps that can take place in a single day or can be spread out over weeks or months depending on the situation. The process can be accomplished with everyone sitting around a table in the same room or with the participants distributed across the world using the Internet. The steps are as follows:

- *Preparation.* Step one accomplishes three things. The facilitator of the mapping process works with the initiator(s) (those who requested the process initially) to identify who the participants will be. A mapping process can have hundreds or even thousands of STAKEHOLDERS participating, although there is usually a relatively small group of between 10 and 20 stakeholders involved. Second, the initiator works with the stakeholders to develop the focus for the project. For instance, the group might decide to focus on defining a program or treatment, or it might choose to map all of the expected outcomes. Finally, the group decides on an appropriate schedule for the mapping.
- *Generation.* The stakeholders develop a large set of statements that address the focus. For instance, they might generate statements describing all of the specific activities that will constitute a specific social program, or generate statements describing specific outcomes that could result from participating in a program. A variety of methods can be used to accomplish this including traditional brainstorming, brainwriting, NOMINAL GROUP TECHNIQUEs, FOCUS GROUPs, qualitative text analysis, and so on. The group can generate up to 200 statements in a concept-mapping project. This is a software limitation, in most situations, around 100 statements is the practical limit in terms of the number of statements they can reasonably handle.
- *Structuring.* The participants do two things during structuring. First, each participant sorts the statements into piles of similar statements. They often do this by sorting a deck of cards that has one statement on each card; but they can also do this directly on a computer by dragging the statements into piles that they create. They can have as few or as many piles as they want. Each participant names each pile with a short descriptive label. Then each participant rates each of the statements on some scale. Usually the statements are rated on a 1-to-5 scale for their relative importance, where a 1 means the statement is relatively unimportant compared to all the rest; a 3 means that it is moderately important, and a 5 means that it is extremely important.
- *Representation.* This is where the analysis is done; this is the process of taking the sort and rating input and representing it in map form. Two major statistical analyses are used. The first—MULTIDIMENSIONAL SCALING—takes the sort data across all participants and develops the basic map where each statement is a point on the map and statements

that were piled together by more people are closer to each other on the map. The second analysis—CLUSTER ANALYSIS—takes the output of the multidimensional scaling (the point map) and partitions the map into groups of statements or ideas, into clusters. If the statements describe program activities, the clusters show how to group them into logical groups of activities. If the statements are specific outcomes, the clusters might be viewed as outcome constructs or concepts.
- *Interpretation.* To interpret the conceptualization, we assemble certain materials and follow a specific sequence of steps—a process that has been developed on the basis of our experiences with many different projects. The materials consist of the original statements and clusters, a series of maps depicting these statements and clusters as well as related variable data, and rating comparison graphs known as pattern matches (graphs comparing average cluster ratings for a rating variable between demographic groups, points in time, or other variables) and go-zones (bivariate (X-Y) graphs that show the average ratings for two variables on each statement within a specific cluster).
- *Utilization.* At this point, the group discusses ways to use the final concept maps, pattern matches, and go-zones to enhance either planning or evaluation. The uses of these tools are limited only by the creativity and motivation of the group. For planning, these results might be used for structuring the subsequent planning effort or as the framework for an outline of a planning report. In evaluation, the concept map, pattern matching, and go-zones can act as an organizing device for operationalizing and implementing the program, as a guide for measurement development, or as a framework for examining patterns of outcomes.

 Kane & Trochim 2007; Trochim & Donnelly 2007

conceptual definition
see OPERATIONAL DEFINITION

conceptual replication
another term for CONSTRUCTIVE REPLICATION

conceptual research
a research type which is related to some abstract idea(s) or theory. It is generally used by philosophers and thinkers to develop new concepts or to reinterpret existing ones.
see also EMPIRICAL RESEARCH
 Kothari 2008

conclusion
see DISCUSSION

conclusion validity
another term for STATISTICAL VALIDITY

concomitant variable
another term for COVARIATE

concurrent validity
see CRITERION-RELATED VALIDITY

condition
another term for LEVEL

confidence bands
also **confidence belts**
(in REGRESSION ANALYSIS) dashed lines on each side of an estimated REGRESSION LINE or curve that have a specified PROBABILITY of including the line or curve in the POPULATION, as shown in Figure C.7.

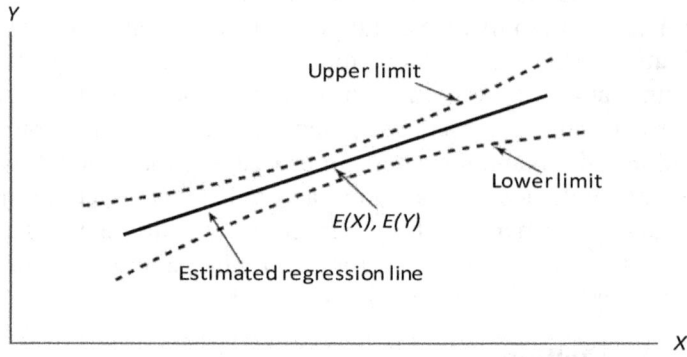

Figure C.7. An Example of Confidence Bands

The confidence bands can be constructed by determining CONFIDENCE INTERVALs for the regression line for the entire range of X values. One can then plot the upper and lower **confidence limits** (the lower and upper limits of a confidence interval) obtained for several specified values of X and sketch the two curves that connect these points.
📖 Sahai & Khurshid 2001

confidence belts
another term for CONFIDENCE BANDS

confidence interval
also **CI**
a range of values with a lower limit and an upper limit within which an

unknown POPULATION PARAMETER value is expected to lie with a certain degree of PROBABILITY, or **confidence level** (also called *level of confidence, confidence coefficient*). It is the probability that the interval contains the value of the parameter of interest. The SAMPLE MEAN which serves as the center of the interval is used to estimate the POPULATION MEAN. The STANDARD ERROR OF THE MEAN is also used in constructing confidence intervals (CIs). When we select multiple samples of the same size from two different populations, or when we repeat a certain intervention with multiple samples of the same size chosen from the same population, the differences between the two means are normally distributed. This distribution has its own mean and standard deviation. The CIs in these studies provide the lower and upper limits of the distribution of the differences between the means.

Traditionally, the two confidence levels that have been used in HYPOTHESIS TESTING are the .95 and .99 levels. The exact Z SCORE values associated with these two levels are 1.96 and 2.58 respectively. For example, a 95% confidence level indicates that we are 95% confident (or there is a 95% probability) that an unknown population parameter value will fall within that interval. A confidence level is reported as 1 - α (SIGNIFICANCE LEVEL), which is usually equal to (1 - .05) = .95, i.e., the level of likelihood that a score falls within a prespecified range of scores, and, like the significance level (α), is specified by the researcher.

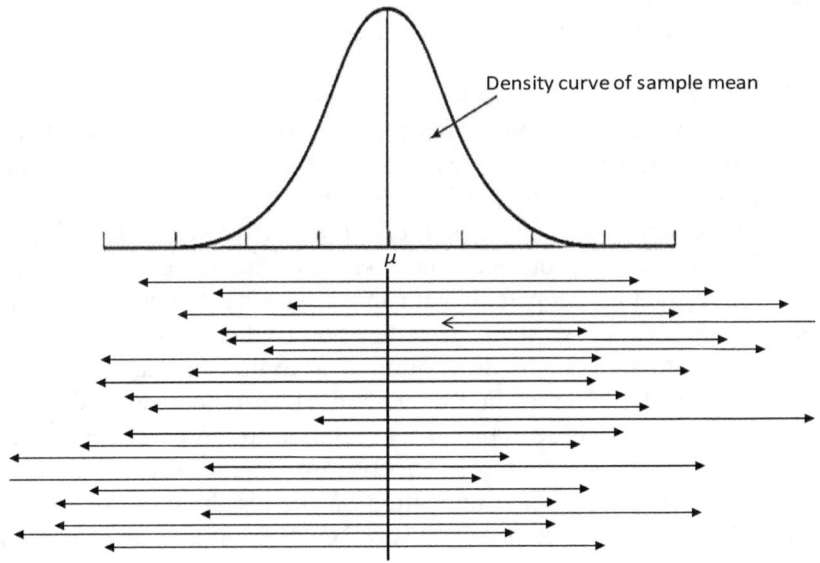

Figure C.8. A Schematic Diagram for Confidence Interval

The Figure C.8 shows one hundred 95% confidence intervals for the population mean. Each confidence interval is derived from a RANDOM SAMPLE from the same distribution. The intervals differ in width and location because of variations in the sample means and variances. On average, 95% of such confidence intervals will include the true value of the population mean (μ).

The concept of CIs can be applied to virtually any statistic. However, it is probably best understood initially in terms of the CI of the mean. CIs are often promoted as an alternative to POINT ESTIMATEs (conventional significance testing). They are both based on the same hypothesis testing approach. CIs are set values. Consequently they may not be as informative as the exact values available for point estimates using computers. CIs are also claimed to allow greater understanding of the true importance of trends in the data. This is basically because the CI is expressed in terms of a range on the original SCALE OF MEASUREMENT (i.e., the measurement scale on which the calculations were based).

see also TYPE I ERROR

 Bachman 2004; Cohen et al. 2011; Kirk 2008; Richards & Schmidt 2010; Sahai & Khurshid 2001; Upton & Cook 2008

confidence level
see CONFIDENCE INTERVAL

confidence limits
see CONFIDENCE BAND

confidentiality

a way of protecting a participant's right to privacy. This means that although researchers know who has provided the information or are able to identify participants from the information given, they will in no way make the connection known publicly; the boundaries surrounding the shared secret will be protected. The essence of the matter is the extent to which investigators keep faith with those who have helped them. It is generally at the access stage or at the point where researchers collect their data that they make their position clear to the hosts and/or subjects. They will thus be quite explicit in explaining to subjects what the meaning and limits of confidentiality are in relation to the particular research project. On the whole, the more sensitive, intimate or discrediting the information, the greater is the obligation on the researcher's part to make sure that guarantees of confidentiality are carried out in spirit and letter.

A number of techniques have been developed to allow public access to data and information without confidentiality being betrayed:

- *deletion of identifiers* (for example, deleting the names, addresses or other means of identification from the data released on individuals).
- *crude report categories* (for example, releasing the year of birth rather than the specific date, profession but not the speciality within that profession, general information rather than specific).
- *micro-aggregation* (that is, the construction of *average persons* from data on individuals and the release of these data, rather than data on individuals).
- *error inoculation* (deliberately introducing errors into individual records while leaving the aggregate data unchanged).

It is suggested that confidentiality can be protected by obtaining signed statements indicating non-disclosure of the research, restricting access to data which identify respondents, seeking the approval of the respondents before any disclosure about respondents takes place, non-disclosure of data (e.g. subsets that may be able to be combined to identify an individual).
 Cohen et al. 2011

confirmability

the extent to which the research is free of bias in the procedures and the interpretation of results. Because it may be impossible to achieve the levels of OBJECTIVITY that quantitative studies strive for, qualitative researchers are concerned with whether the data they collect and the conclusions they draw would be confirmed by others investigating the same situation. It involves making available full details of the data on which claims or interpretations are based so that other researchers can examine the data and confirm, modify or reject the first researcher's interpretation. It also refers to the neutrality of the findings, which is the qualitative counterpart of objectivity.

There are a number of strategies for enhancing confirmability. The AUDIT TRAIL is the main strategy for demonstrating confirmability. After the study, a researcher can conduct a data audit that examines the data collection and analysis procedures and makes judgments about the potential for bias or distortion. By providing a complete audit trail, the researcher enables another researcher to arrive or not arrive at the same conclusions given the same data and context. Another researcher can take a devil's advocate role with respect to the results, and this process can be documented. The researcher can actively search for and describe negative instances that contradict prior observations. Other strategies used to enhance confirmability include TRIANGULATION of methods, PEER REVIEW, and reflexivity (the use of self-reflection to recognize one's own biases and to actively seek them out).

see also TRANSFERABILITY, DEPENDABILITY, CREDIBILITY
 Ary et al. 2010; Dörnyei 2007; Mackey & Gass 2005; Trochim & Donnelly 2007

confirmatory factor analysis
also **CFA**
a type of FACTOR ANALYSIS which, like EXPLORATORY FACTOR ANALYSIS (EFA), is used to examine the relationships between a set of measured variables and a smaller set of *constructs* or *factors* that might account for them. With EFA, all measured variables are related to every factor by a FACTOR LOADING estimate. Simple structure results when each measured variable loads highly on only one factor and has smaller loadings on other factors. Confirmatory factor analysis (CFA), however, assumes relatively precise advance knowledge and allows a researcher to specify a priori what these relationships might look like and then to test the accuracy of these formal hypotheses. In fact, the researcher has preconceived thoughts on the actual structure of the data, based on theoretical support or prior research. The question in CFA is: 'Are the CORRELATIONs among variables consistent with a hypothesized factor structure?'
More specifically, with CFA, the researcher must specify both the number of factors that exist for a set of variables and which factor each variable will load on before results can be computed. Thus, the statistical technique does not assign variables to factors. Instead, the researcher makes this assignment based on the theory being tested before any results can be obtained. Moreover, a variable is assigned to only a single factor (construct), and cross-loadings (loading on more than a single factor) are not assigned. CFA is applied to test the extent to which a researcher's a priori, theoretical pattern of factor loadings on prespecified constructs (variables loading on specific constructs) represents the actual data. Thus, instead of allowing the statistical method to determine the number of factors and loadings as in EFA, CFA statistics tell us how well our theoretical specification of the factors matches reality (the actual data). In a sense, CFA is a tool that enables us to either confirm or reject our preconceived theory.
CFA is often performed through STRUCTURAL EQUATION MODELING.
 Hair et al. 2010; Ho 2006; Leary 2011; Pallant 2010; Tabachnick & Fidell 2007

confirmatory research
see DEDUCTIVE REASONING

confirming and disconfirming sampling
another term for NEGATIVE CASE SAMPLING

confounder
 another term for CONFOUNDING VARIABLE

confounding factor
 another term for CONFOUNDING VARIABLE

confounding variable
 also **spurious variable, confounding factor, confounder**
 a variable which may affect the DEPENDENT and INDEPENDENT VARIABLEs and confuse or confound the apparent nature of the relationship between them. Two variables are confounded if they vary together in such a way that it is impossible to work out which one is responsible for an observed effect. For example, imagine a study wherein two L2 teaching methodologies were compared. The first was given to a group of teenage students and the second to a group of adults. If a difference between TREATMENTs were revealed, it would be impossible to tell if one treatment were more effective than the other, or if teaching methodology treatments are more effective for one age group than the other. In such an example, age and treatment would have been confounded. In most studies, researchers aim to control for these confounding variables. In any study there is potentially an infinite variety of possible confounding variables. Researchers comment on the influence of confounding variables, after the study has been complete, because these variables may have operated to explain the relationship between the independent and dependent variable, but were not or could not be easily assessed.
 see also MODERATOR VARIABLE, INTERVENING VARIABLE, CATEGORICAL VARIABLE, CONTINUOUS VARIABLE, EXTRANEOUS VARIABLE, PARTIAL CORRELATION, SEMI-PARTIAL CORRELATION COEFFICIENT
 📖 Cramer & Howitt 2004

confound variance
 another term for ERROR VARIANCE

confusion matrix
 another term for CLASSIFICATION MATRIX

conover test
 a NONPARAMETRIC TEST procedure for testing the EQUALITY OF VARIANCEs of two POPULATIONs having different MEDIANs. The test has rather a low STATISTICAL POWER.
 see also MOSES TEST, KLOTZ TEST, ANSARI-BRADLEY TEST, SIEGEL-TUKEY TEST
 📖 Sahai & Khurshid 2001

consensus task
a measurement technique which generally involves pairs or groups of learners who must come to an agreement on a certain issue. For example, ten individuals are stranded on an island, but only five can fit into a boat to get to the mainland. Characteristics are provided for each individual, and the pair or group must come to an agreement about which five should get into the boat. This task allows for a less guided discussion than do other tasks, but it does not guarantee that there will be interaction. One individual might not participate, or, if the task is not engaging, participants might take only a few minutes to pick five individuals without giving elaborate justification. As with other methods, instructions are important to ensure that the participants understand the need to participate. For example, each participant can be assigned a role of an individual and argue for that person's suitability for the boat.
Another type of consensus task is a *dictogloss task*. In this type of task, learners work together to reconstruct a text that has been read to them. It is possible to choose a text based on content, vocabulary, or particular grammatical structures. In its normal mode of delivery (although this could be modified for the purposes of research), the text is read aloud twice at normal speed. Participants can take notes on the first reading, the second reading, both, or neither. This will depend on the researcher's goals. Because the text is read at normal speed (unlike a typical DICTATION), the participants cannot write down everything. Following the readings, participants can work in dyads or small groups to reconstruct the text while maintaining the meaning of the original.
see also JIGSAW TASK
📖 Mackey & Gass 2005

consequentialism
the belief that ends justify means; that is, that the results of actions determine their rightness or wrongness. Any particular action is neither intrinsically good nor bad; rather, it is good or bad because of its results in a particular context—its consequences.
📖 Heigham & Croker 2009

consequential validity
a type of VALIDITY which argues that the ways in which research data are used (the consequences of the research) are in keeping with the capability or intentions of the research, i.e., the consequences of the research do not exceed the capability of the research and the action-related consequences of the research are both legitimate and fulfilled. Clearly, once the research is in the public domain, the researcher has little or no control over the way in which it is used. However, and this is often a political matter, research should not be used in ways in which it was not intended

to be used, for example by exceeding the capability of the research data to make claims, by acting on the research in ways that the research does not support (e.g. by using the research for illegitimate epistemic support), by making illegitimate claims by using the research in unacceptable ways (e.g., by selection, distortion) and by not acting on the research in ways that were agreed, i.e., errors of omission and commission.

A clear example of consequential validity is *formative assessment*. This is concerned with the extent to which students improve as a result of feedback given, hence if there is insufficient feedback for students to improve or if students are unable to improve as a result of—a consequence of—the feedback, then the formative assessment has little consequential validity.

📖 Cohen et al. 2011

conservative test

a term which is used to describe a STATISTICAL TEST in which the probability of a TYPE I ERROR is smaller than ALPHA (α) (the nominal or stated level). When the CRITICAL VALUE is increased greatly, the test procedure is referred to as being conservative. Put differently, conservative procedures provide greater control over Type I error risk, but do so at the expense of lower POWER (i.e., higher risk of TYPE II ERROR). A statistical test when its level of significance is exactly equal to the nominal or stated level is called **exact test**. Often, it is not possible to obtain a test with a level of significance exactly equal to nominal or stated level, and then the test is referred to as an **approximate test**.

see also LIBERAL TEST

📖 Huck 2012; Sahai & Khurshid 2001

constant

see VARIABLE

constant comparison method

a process used in GROUNDED THEORY by which the properties and categories across the data are compared continuously until no more variation occurs, i.e., SATURATION is reached. In constant comparison the researcher compares the new data with existing data and categories so that the categories achieve a perfect fit with the data. If there is a poor fit between data and categories, or indeed between theory and data, then the categories and theories have to be modified until all the data are accounted for. New and emergent categories are developed in order to be able to incorporate and accommodate data in a good fit, with no discrepant cases. The purpose of the constant comparative method of joint coding and analysis is to generate theory by using explicit coding and analytic procedures. That theory is not intended to ascertain universality or the proof of suggested causes or other properties. Since no proof is involved, the constant comparison method requires only saturation of data—not consideration of all available data.

In constant comparison data are compared across a range of situations, times, groups of people, and through a range of methods. The process resonates with the methodological notion of TRIANGULATION. The constant comparison method involves four stages: comparing incidents and data that are applicable to each category; integrating these categories and their properties; bounding the theory; setting out the theory. The first stage here involves coding of incidents and comparing them with previous incidents in the same and different groups and with other data that are in the same category. The second stage involves **memoing** (i.e., a process by which the researcher writes down his/her ideas about the evolving theory throughout the coding process) and further coding. Here the constant comparative units change from comparison of incident with incident to comparison of incident with properties of the category that resulted from initial comparisons of incidents. The third stage—of delimitation—occurs at the levels of the theory and the categories and in which the major modifications reduce as underlying uniformities and properties are discovered and in which theoretical saturation takes place. The final stage—of writing theory—occurs when the researcher has gathered and generated coded data, memos, and a theory, and this is then written in full.

Constant comparison combines the elements of inductive category coding with simultaneously comparing these with the other events and social incidents that have been observed and coded over time and location. This enables social phenomena to be compared across categories, where necessary giving rise to new dimensions, codes, and categories. Constant comparison can proceed from the moment of starting to collect data, to seeking key issues and categories, to discovering recurrent events or activities in the data that become categories of focus, to expanding the range of categories. This process can continue during the writing-up process, which should be ongoing, so that a model or explanation of the phenomena can emerge that accounts for fundamental social processes and relationships.

see also CODING

📖 Cohen et al. 2011

constant sum questions

CLOSED-FORM ITEMs in which the respondents are asked to distribute a given number of marks (points) between a range of items. For example:

Please distribute a total of 10 points among the sentences that you think most closely describe your behavior. You may distribute these freely: they may be spread out, or awarded to only a few statements, or all allocated to a single sentence if you wish.

I can take advantage of new opportunities	[ ]
I can work effectively with all kinds of people	[ ]
Generating new ideas is one of my strengths	[ ]
I can usually tell what is likely to work in practice	[ ]
I am able to see tasks through to the very end	[ ]
I am prepared to be unpopular for the good of school	[ ]

This enables priorities to be identified, comparing highs and lows, and for equality of choices to be indicated, and, importantly, for this to be done in the respondents' own terms. It requires respondents to make comparative judgments and choices across a range of items. For example, we may wish to distribute 10 points for aspects of an individual's personality:

Talkative	[ ]
Cooperative	[ ]
Hard-working	[ ]
Lazy	[ ]
Motivated	[ ]
Attentive	[ ]

This means that the respondent has to consider the relative weight of each of the given aspects before coming to a decision about how to award the marks. To accomplish this means that the all-round nature of the person, in the terms provided, has to be considered, to see, on balance, which aspect is stronger when compared to another.

The difficulty with this approach is to decide how many marks can be distributed (a round number, for example 10, makes subsequent calculation easily comprehensible) and how many statements/items to include, e.g., whether to have the same number of statements as there are marks, or more or fewer statements than the total of marks. Having too few statements/items does not do justice to the complexity of the issue, and having too many statements/items may mean that it is difficult for respondents to decide how to distribute their marks. Having too few marks available may be unhelpful, but, by contrast, having too many marks and too many statements/items can lead to simple computational errors by respondents. Our advice is to keep the number of marks to ten and the number of statements to around six to eight.

Constant sum data are ordinal, and this means that nonparametric analysis can be performed on the data.

see also DICHOTOMOUS QUESTION, MULTIPLE CHOICE ITEMS, RATIO DATA QUESTION, MATRIX QUESTIONS, RANK ORDER QUESTION, CONTINGENCY QUESTION
 Cohen et al. 2011

constitutive definition
another term for CONCEPTUAL DEFINITION

construct
also **trait**
an abstract hypothetical concept (such as intelligence, creativity, anxiety, underachievement, motivation, self-concept, and reading readiness) that cannot be directly observed or measured but that is considered to exist on theoretical grounds. For example, people can observe that individuals differ in what they can learn and how quickly they can learn it. To account for this observation, scientists invented the construct called intelligence. They hypothesized that intelligence influences learning and that individuals differ in the extent to which they possess this trait. Although we hypothesize that intelligence exists, we cannot see it. We cannot surgically open up someone's brain and locate intelligence. However, based on theory, we know that that person has intelligence. Some of us have more intelligence, and some of us have less intelligence.
Defining constructs is a major concern for researchers. The further removed constructs are from the empirical facts or phenomena they are intended to represent, the greater the possibility for misunderstanding and the greater the need for precise definitions. Constructs may be defined in a way that gives their general meaning, or they may be defined in terms of the operations by which they will be measured or manipulated in a particular study. The former type of definition is called a CONCEPTUAL DEFINITION; the latter is known as an OPERATIONAL DEFINITION. To measure constructs, they must be operationally defined, that is, defined in terms of how they will be measured. The operational definition allows researchers to identify the variables that are being used to measure the construct. So, if we operationally define intelligence as a score on the *Stanford Intelligence Test*, other researchers understand that in our study, intelligence is conceptualized as the ability to successfully complete the items on the test. Of course, operational definitions are limited, and the construct of intelligence is much broader and more complex. Therefore, some researchers might also include a more conceptual definition of intelligence, such as intelligence is the ability to solve complex problems.
 Ary et al. 2010; Lodico et al. 2010; Porte 2010

constructed-response item
also **productive response item**
a type of test item or test task that requires test takers to respond to a series of OPEN-ENDED QUESTIONs by writing, speaking, or doing something rather than choose answers from a ready-made list. The most commonly used types of constructed-response items include FILL-IN ITEMs, SHORT-ANSWER ITEMs, and PERFORMANCE ASSESSMENT.
see also SELECTED-RESPONSE ITEM
 Brown 2005; Richards & Schmidt 2010

construct-irrelevant variance
the extent to which test scores are affected by variables that are extraneous (see EXTRANEOUS VARIABLE) to the CONSTRUCT. Low scores should not occur because the test contains something irrelevant that interferes with people's demonstration of their competence. Construct-irrelevant variance could lower scores on an achievement test for individuals with limited reading skills or limited English skills. Reading comprehension is thus a source of construct-irrelevant variance in an achievement test and would affect the validity of any interpretations made about the individuals' science achievement.
see also CONSTRUCT UNDERREPRESENTATION
 Ary et al. 2010; Messick 1995

constructive replication
see REPLICATION

constructivism
ontological (see ONTOLOGY) and epistemological (see EPISTEMOLOGY) views which disallow the existence of an external objective reality independent of an individual from which knowledge may be collected or gained. Instead, each individual constructs knowledge and his/her experience through social interaction. This research paradigm represents a change from the focus on explaining phenomena typical in the natural sciences to an emphasis on understanding, which is deemed more appropriate for investigating phenomena in the human sciences. In terms of methods, constructivist QUALITATIVE RESEARCH studies typically emphasize PARTICIPANT OBSERVATION and interviewing for data generation as the researcher aims to understand a phenomenon from the perspective of those experiencing it. The researcher's understanding is co-constructed with that of the participants through their mutual interaction within the research setting and dialogic interaction through researcher-initiated data generation efforts such as interviewing.

see also PSYCHOLOGICAL CONSTRUCTIVISM, OBJECTIVISM, SUBJECTIVISM
📖 Given 2008

construct underrepresentation
an assessment that is too narrow and fails to include important dimensions of the construct. The test may not adequately sample some kinds of content or some types of responses or psychological processes and thus fails to adequately represent the theoretical domain of the construct. Individuals' scores on an intelligence test may be misleading because the test did not measure some of the relevant skills that, if represented, would have allowed the individuals to display their competence. Or, a scale designed to measure general self-concept might measure only social self-concept and not academic and physical components of self-concept.
see also CONSTRUCT-IRRELEVANT VARIANCE
📖 Ary et al. 2010; Messick 1995

construct validity
a type of VALIDITY which deals with the degree to which the instruments used in a study measure the CONSTRUCT that is being examined. In this type of validity agreement is sought on the operationalized forms of a construct, clarifying what we mean when we use this construct (see OPERATIONAL DEFINITION). The researcher needs to describe the characteristics of the constructs in a way which would enable an outsider to identify these characteristics if they came across them. If the researcher fails to provide specific definitions, then we need to read between the lines. For example, if a study, investigates listening comprehension, and the DEPENDENT VARIABLE is a written cloze test, then the default definition of listening comprehension is the ability to complete a written cloze passage. If we were to find such a definition unacceptable, we would be questioning the construct validity of the study. Or, imagine a researcher wished to assess a child's intelligence (assuming, for the sake of this example, that it is a unitary quality). The researcher could say that s/he construed intelligence to be demonstrated in the ability to sharpen a pencil. How acceptable a construction of intelligence is this? Is not intelligence something else (e.g., that which is demonstrated by a high result in an intelligence test)?
To establish construct validity the researcher would need to be assured that his/her construction of a particular issue agreed with other constructions of the same underlying issue, e.g., intelligence, creativity, anxiety, motivation. This can be achieved through CORRELATIONs with other measures of the issue or by rooting the researcher's construction in a wide literature search which teases out the meaning of a particular construct (i.e., a theory of what that construct is) and its constituent ele-

ments. Demonstrating construct validity means not only confirming the construction with that given in relevant literature, but also looking for counter-examples which might falsify the researcher's construction. When the confirming and refuting evidence is balanced, the researcher is in a position to demonstrate construct validity, and can stipulate what s/he takes this construct to be. In the case of conflicting interpretations of a construct, the researcher might have to acknowledge that conflict and then stipulate the interpretation that will be used.

In QUALITATIVE RESEARCH construct validity must demonstrate that the categories that the researchers are using are meaningful to the participants themselves i.e., that they reflect the way in which the participants actually experience and construe the situations in the research, that they see the situation through the actors' eyes.

Construct validity is addressed by CONVERGENT VALIDITY and DISCRIMINANT VALIDITY or techniques.

Construct validity is one of the most complex types of validity, in part because it is a composite of multiple validity approaches that are occurring simultaneously. This might include aspects of CONTENT, CONCURRENT, and PREDICTIVE VALIDITY. Therefore, many researchers consider construct validity to be a superordinate or overarching type of validity. Fully establishing construct validity also involves a lengthy process of collecting evidence from many studies over time.

see also INTERNAL VALIDITY, EXTERNAL VALIDITY, FACE VALIDITY

📖 Trochim & Donnelly 2007; Cohen et al. 2011

contaminated normal distribution
another term for MIXED NORMAL DISTRIBUTION

content analysis
a procedure which is used to convert written or spoken information into data that can be analyzed and interpreted. Content analysis is a QUALITATIVE RESEARCH technique which is used to quantify aspects of written or spoken text or of some form of visual representation. It is used for analyzing and tabulating the frequency of occurrence of themes, emotions topics, ideas, opinions and other aspects of the content of written and spoken communication. Materials analyzed can be textbooks, newspapers, television programs, speeches, musical compositions, essays, advertisements, magazine articles, or any other types of DOCUMENTs. Content analysis, for example, could be used to determine the frequency of occurrence of references to males, females, adults, children, Caucasians, non-Caucasians, etc., in a set of language teaching materials, in order to discover if any particular attitudes or themes were unintentionally being communicated in the material.

Content analysis starts with a sample of texts (the units), defines the units of analysis (e.g., words, sentences) and the categories to be used for analysis, reviews the texts in order to code them and place them into categories, and then counts and logs the occurrences of words, codes and categories. From here statistical analysis and quantitative methods are applied, leading to an interpretation of the results. Put simply, content analysis involves coding, categorizing (creating meaningful categories into which the units of analysis—words, phrases, sentences etc.—can be placed), comparing (categories and making links between them), and concluding—drawing theoretical conclusions from the text.

A major advantage of content analysis is that it is unobtrusive. A researcher can observe without being observed, since the contents being analyzed are not influenced by the researcher's presence. Information that might be difficult, or even impossible, to obtain through direct OBSERVATION or other means can be gained unobtrusively through analysis of textbooks and other communications, without the author or publisher being aware that it is being examined. Another advantage of content analysis is that it is extremely useful as a means of analyzing INTERVIEW and observational data. A third advantage of content analysis is that the researcher can delve into records and documents to get some feel for the social life of an earlier time. S/he is not limited by time and space to the study of present events. A fourth advantage accrues from the fact that the logistics of content analysis are often relatively simple and economical—with regard to both time and resources—as compared to other research methods. This is particularly true if the information is readily accessible, as in newspapers, reports, books, periodicals, and the like. Lastly, because the data are readily available and almost always can be returned to if necessary or desired, content analysis permits replication of a study by other researchers. Even live television programs can be videotaped for repeated analysis at later times.

A major disadvantage of content analysis is that it is usually limited to recorded information, although the researcher may, of course, arrange the recordings, as in the use of open-ended QUESTIONNAIREs or PROJECTIVE TECHNIQUES. The other main disadvantage is in establishing VALIDITY. Assuming that different analysts can achieve acceptable agreement in categorizing, the question remains as to the true meaning of the categories themselves. As with any measurement, additional evidence of a criterion or construct nature is important. In the absence of such evidence, the argument for content validity rests on the persuasiveness of the logic connecting each category to its intended meaning. For example, our interpretation of the data on social studies research assumes that what was clear or unclear to us would also be clear or unclear to other researchers or readers. Similarly, it assumes that most, if not all, researchers would agree as to whether definitions and particular threats to internal validity were present in a given article. While we think these are reasonable assumptions, that does not make them so. With respect to the use of content analysis in HISTORICAL RESEARCH, the researcher normally has records only of what has survived or what someone thought was of sufficient importance to write down. Because each generation has a somewhat different perspective on its life and times, what was considered important at a particular time in the past may be viewed as trivial today. Conversely, what is considered important today might not even be available from the past.

see also SECONDARY RESEARCH

📖 Clark-Carter 2010; Cohen et al. 2011; Fraenkel & Wallen 2009; Richards & Schmidt 2010

content-referenced test
another term for CRITERION-REFERENCED TEST

content validity
the extent to which the instrument must show that it fairly and comprehensively covers the domain or items that it purports to cover. It is unlikely that each issue will be able to be addressed in its entirety simply because of the time available or respondents' motivation to complete, for example, a long QUESTIONNAIRE. If this is the case, then the researcher must ensure that the elements of the main issue to be covered in the research are both a fair representation of the wider issue under investigation (and its weighting) and that the elements chosen for the research sample are themselves addressed in depth and breadth. Careful sampling of items is required to ensure their representativeness. For example, if the researcher wished to see how well a group of students could spell 1,000 words in French but decided to have a sample of only 50 words for the spelling test, then that test would have to ensure that it represented the range of spellings in the 1,000 words—maybe by ensuring that the spelling rules had all been included or that possible spelling errors had been covered in the test in the proportions in which they occurred in the 1,000 words. Frequently a **table of specification**s is used to help estimate the content representativeness. The specifications include content items the test is supposed to measure and the measures of how well and how completely the items represent content areas.

see also CRITERION-RELATED VALIDITY, CONSTRUCT VALIDITY, INTERNAL VALIDITY, EXTERNAL VALIDITY, FACE VALIDITY

📖 Cohen et al. 2011

contingency coefficient
see CHI-SQUARE TEST OF INDEPENDENCE

contingency question
  a CLOSED-FORM ITEM which depends on responses to earlier question, for example: 'if your answer to question (1) was *yes* please go to question (4)'. The earlier question acts as a filter for the later question, and the later question is contingent on the earlier, and is a branch of the earlier question (see BRANCHING). Some QUESTIONNAIREs will write in words the number of the question to which to go (e.g., 'please go to question 6'); others will place an arrow to indicate the next question to be answered if your answer to the first question was such-and-such.
  For example, in a SURVEY designed to assess faculty interest in using computer-assisted testing, the following question might be used:

1. Are you interested in using computer-assisted testing in your classes?
1) NO (if NO, please go to question 6)
2) YES
3) UNDECIDED
2. If YES, would you use the computer-assisted testing for
1) QUIZZES
2) TESTS
3) BOTH

  Faculty members who indicated in question 1 that they were not interested in computer-assisted testing would not even have to read the next four questions but could proceed to question 6, the next relevant question.
  Filter questions can be complex. Sometimes, you have to have multiple filter questions to direct your respondents to the correct subsequent questions. Contingency and filter questions may be useful for the researcher, but they can be confusing for the respondent as it is not always clear how to proceed through the sequence of questions and where to go once a particular branch has been completed. It is found that respondents tend to ignore, misread and incorrectly follow branching instructions, such that item nonresponse occurs for follow-up questions that are applicable only to certain subsamples and respondents skip over, and therefore fail to follow-up on those questions that they should have completed. It is also found that the increased complexity of the questionnaire brought about by branching instructions negatively influenced its correct completion.
  see also DICHOTOMOUS QUESTION, MULTIPLE CHOICE ITEMS, RATIO DATA QUESTION, MATRIX QUESTIONS, CONSTANT SUM QUESTIONS, RANK ORDER QUESTION
  📖 Ary et al. 2010; Cohen et al. 2011; Trochim & Donnelly 2007

contingency table
  also **cross-classification table, cross-tabulation table, crossbreak table, r × c contingency table, r × c table**
  a table with two or more rows and two or more columns that shows the intersection of two or more CATEGORICAL VARIABLEs. This table pro-

duces the CELLs in which EXPECTED and OBSERVED FREQUENCIES can be compared. More specifically, contingency table refers to as an r × c table because the 'r' in r × c refers to row and the 'c' to column. Rows and columns are always named in this order, a convention also followed in describing matrices and in subscript notation. For example, a 2 × 2 table (see Table C.2) can be thought of as an r × c table where r and c both equal 2. The phrase 'r × c' is read as 'r by c' and the same convention applies to specific tables sizes, so '2 × 2' is read as '2 by 2.' A 2 × 2 table contingency table lists the frequency of the joint occurrence of two LEVELs (or possible outcomes), one level for each of the two categorical variables. The levels for one of the categorical variables correspond to the columns of the table, and the levels for the other categorical variable correspond to the rows of the table. A contingency table also contains the sums of the values of each row and column (i.e., row and column totals). These sums are also called the '**marginal**s' of the table. The sum of column or row marginals corresponds to the SAMPLE SIZE or grand total.

		Independent Variable 1		
Independent Variable 2		Level A	Level B	Total
	Level A	Cell A	Cell B	$A + B$
	Level B	Cell C	Cell D	$C + D$
	Total	$A + C$	$B + D$	

Table C.2. An Example of a 2 × 2 Contingency Table

The primary interest in constructing contingency tables is usually to determine whether there is any association (in terms of statistical dependence) between the two categorical variables, whose counts are displayed in the table. A table displaying two variables is called a **two-way table**, three variables three-way, and so on. It is so called because the categories of one variable are contingent on or tabulated across the categories of one or more other variables. This table may be also described according to the number of levels or categories in each variable. For example, a 2 × 2 table consists of two variables which each have two levels or categories. A 2 × 3 table has one variable with two levels and another variable with three levels. Similarly, a 3 × 3 × 3 table has three variables which each have three levels or categories. A measure of the global association between the two categorical variables is the CHI-SQUARE TEST. Such tables are commonly made when using a chi-square test. Three- and higher-dimensional tables (called **multidimensional contingency tables**) which summarize information from more than two categorical vari-

ables are analyzed by using log-linear models (see LOG-LINEAR ANALYSIS) and related procedures.
📖 Larson-Hall 2010; Upton & Cook 2008; Urdan 2010

continuous data
see CONTINUOUS VARIABLE

continuous variable
also **metric variable, ungrouped variable, dimensional variable**
a variable which is measured on INTERVAL or RATIO SCALEs of measurement. Continuous variables can theoretically take on any value along a continuum. With continuous variables the number of possible values is theoretically unlimited because the abilities or attributes that these variables represent are assumed to vary continuously. For example, age is a continuous variable because, theoretically at least, someone can be any age. Test scores, income, temperature, weight, and height are other examples of continuous variables. A continuous variable that is normally expressed numerically because it differs in degree rather than kind is called **quantitative variable** (also called **numerical variable**). Data that are obtained on measures of a continuous variable, i.e., using interval and ratio scales of measurement are called **continuous data** (also called **metric data**).

Obviously, the type of data produced from using continuous variables differs from the type of data produced from using CATEGORICAL VARIABLEs. In some circumstances, researchers may decide to convert some continuous variables into categorical variables. For example, rather than using age as a continuous variable, a researcher may decide to make it a categorical variable by creating discrete categories of age, such as under age 40 or age 40 or older. Income, which is often treated as a continuous variable, may instead be treated as a categorical variable by creating discrete categories of income, such as under $25,000 per year, $25,000-$50,000 per year, and over $50,000 per year.

The benefit of using continuous variables is that they can be measured with a higher degree of precision. For example, it is more informative to record someone's age as 47 years old (continuous) as opposed to age 40 or older (categorical). The use of continuous variables gives the researcher access to more specific data.

see also INDEPENDENT VARIABLE, DEPENDENT VARIABLE, MODERATOR VARIABLE, INTERVENING VARIABLE, EXTRANEOUS VARIABLE, CONFOUNDING VARIABLE
📖 Bachman 2004; Marczyk et al. 2005; Sahai & Khurshid 2001; Urdan 2010

control group
a group of participants who do not receive any TREATMENT. In EXPERI-

MENTAL DESIGNs, a control group is the untreated group with which an **experimental group** (also called **treatment group, intervention group**) who receive the treatment of interest is contrasted. It consists of units of study that did not receive the treatment whose effect is under investigation. For many QUASI-EXPERIMENTAL DESIGNs, treatments are not administered to participants, as in TRUE EXPERIMENTAL DESIGNs. Rather, treatments are broadly construed to be the presence of certain characteristics of participants, such as female gender, adolescence, and low language proficiency, or features of their settings, such as private schools or participation in a program of interest. Thus, the control group in quasi-experimental studies is defined to be those lacking these characteristics (e.g., males, respondents who are older or younger than adolescence, those of high and medium language proficiency) or absent from selected settings (e.g., those in public schools, nonparticipants in a program of interest). Control groups may alternatively be called *baseline groups*.

In a true experiment, control groups are formed through RANDOM ASSIGNMENT of respondents, as in BETWEEN-SUBJECTS DESIGNs, or from the respondents themselves, as in WITHIN-SUBJECTS DESIGNs. Random assignment supports the assumption that the control group and the experimental group are similar enough (i.e., equivalent) in relevant ways so as to be genuinely comparable. In true experimental studies and between-subject designs, respondents are first randomly selected from the SAMPLING FRAME; then they are randomly assigned into either a control group or an experimental group or groups. At the conclusion of the study, outcome measures (such as responses on one or more DEPENDENT VARIABLEs, or distributions on QUESTIONNAIRE items) are compared between those in the control group and those in the experimental group(s). The effect of a treatment (e.g., a different incentive level administered to each group) is assessed on the basis of the difference (or differences) observed between the control group and one or more experimental group.

Similarly, in within-subjects designs, respondents are randomly selected from the sampling frame. However, in such cases, they are not randomly assigned into control versus experimental groups. Instead, baseline data are gathered from the respondents themselves. These data are treated as control data to be compared with outcome measures that are hypothesized to be the result of a treatment after the respondents are exposed to the experimental treatment. Thus, the respondents act as their own control group in within-subject designs.

More common than comparing a treatment group to a group receiving no treatment (true control group) is the situation in which researchers compare groups receiving different treatments. These are called **comparison group**s. The majority of educational experiments study the difference in the results of two or more treatments rather than the difference in the results of one treatment versus no treatment at all. For example, it would be pointless to compare the spelling achievement of an experimental group taught by method A with a control group that had no spelling instruction at all. Instead, researchers compare groups receiving method A and method B treatments. Comparison of groups receiving different treatments provides the same control over alternative explanations, as does comparison of treated and untreated groups. Comparisons are essential in scientific investigation. Comparing a group receiving treatment with either an equivalent group receiving no treatment or an equivalent group or groups receiving alternative treatment makes it possible to draw well-founded conclusions from the results.

📖 Ary et al. 2010; Lavrakas 2008

control group rivalry
another term for JOHN HENRY EFFECT

control group time series design
also multiple time-series design
a variation of TIME-SERIES DESIGN and essentially the same as the NONEQUIVALENT GROUPS PRETEST-POSTTEST DESIGN, with the exception that the DEPENDENT VARIABLE is measured at multiple time points both before and after presentation of the INDEPENDENT VARIABLE or TREATMENT to the EXPERIMENTAL GROUP, as depicted here (where O_1, O_2, O_3, O_4 = pretest, O_5, O_6, O_7, O_8 = posttest, NR = nonrandom assignment, and X = treatment):

Experimental group (NR)	O_1 O_2 O_3 O_4	X	O_5 O_6 O_7 O_8
Control group (NR)	O_1 O_2 O_3 O_4		O_5 O_6 O_7 O_8

The CONTROL GROUP, again representing an intact group, would be measured at the same time as the experimental group but would not experience the treatment. The control group permits the necessary comparison. This design overcomes the weakness of SIMPLE INTERRUPTED TIME-SERIES DESIGN—that is, failure to control HISTORY as a source of extraneous variance. The control group permits the necessary comparison. If the experimental group shows a gain from O_4 to O_5 but the control group does not show a gain, then the effect must be caused by treatment rather than by any contemporaneous events, which would have affected both groups.

Although this design is not randomized, it can be quite strong in terms of its ability to rule out other explanations for the observed effect. This design enables us to examine trends in the data, at multiple time points, before, during, and after an intervention (allowing us to evaluate the plausibility of certain threats to INTERNAL VALIDITY). Unlike SIMPLE INTERRUPTED TIME-SERIES DESIGN, this design allows us to make both within-group and between-group comparisons, which may further reduce concerns of alternative explanations associated with history. Regrettably, this design does not involve RANDOM ASSIGNMENT and thus is unable to eliminate all threats to internal validity.

Other variations of the time-series design include adding more control groups, more observations, or more experimental treatments.

📖 Ary et al. 2010; Campbell & Stanley 1963; Marczyk et al. 2005

control variable
see EXTRANEOUS VARIABLE

convenience sampling
a type of NON-PROBABILITY SAMPLING which involves choosing the nearest individuals to serve as respondents and continuing that process until the required SAMPLE SIZE has been obtained. In practice, having access to all members of the entire POPULATION is often impossible due to time or financial constraints. Instead researchers access participants from a population that is readily available (see Figure C.9). Captive audiences such as students or student teachers often serve as respondents based on convenience sampling. The researcher simply chooses the SAMPLE from those to whom s/he has easy access. For example, if the target population is all learners of EFL who attend an English-medium university, but the researcher only has access to a sample from learners of EFL who attend the English-medium university where s/he teaches, s/he uses this group because it is convenient.

Convenience sampling differs from PURPOSIVE SAMPLING in that expert judgment is not used to select a representative sample of elements. Rather, the primary selection criterion relates to the ease of obtaining a sample. Ease of obtaining the sample relates to the cost of locating elements of the population, the geographic distribution of the sample, and obtaining the interview data from the selected elements. In convenience sampling the representativeness of the sample is generally less of a concern than in purposive sampling. Whether one can apply their findings from a convenience sample to a larger target population depends on how well one can show that the sample corresponds to the larger population on important characteristics. This is done by providing clear descriptions of how the sample shares these features. The study should also be replicated, that is, repeated, with a number of similar samples to decrease the likelihood that the results obtained were simply a one-time occurrence.

see also QUOTA SAMPLING, DIMENSIONAL SAMPLING, SNOWBALL SAMPLING, SEQUENTIAL SAMPLING, VOLUNTEER SAMPLING, OPPORTUNISTIC SAMPLING

110 convergent validity

📖 Cohen et al. 2011; Dörnyei 2007; Fraenkel & Wallen 2009; Gall et al. 2006; Lavrakas 2008; Perry 2011

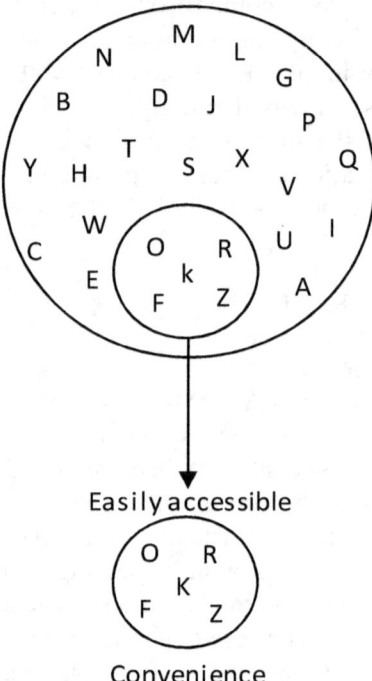

Figure C.9. A Schematic Diagram for Convenience Sampling

convergent validity
a type of CONSTRUCT VALIDITY which implies that different methods for researching the same construct should give a relatively high intercorrelation. This means that measures of constructs that theoretically should be related to each other are, in fact, observed to be related to each other (i.e., you should be able to show a correspondence or convergence between similar constructs. To establish convergent validity, you need to show that measures that should be related are in reality related.
In Figure C.10, you see four measures (each is an item on a scale) that all purport to reflect the construct of self-esteem. For instance, Item 1 might be the statement, 'I feel good about myself,' rated using a 1-to-5 scale. You theorize that all four items reflect the idea of self-esteem. On the bottom part of the figure (Observation), you see the intercorrelations of the four scale items. This might be based on giving your scale out to a sample of respondents. You should readily see that the item intercorrelations for all item pairings are extremely high. The correlations provide

support for your theory that all four items are related to the same construct.
see also DISCRIMINANT VALIDITY
📖 Cohen et al. 2011; Trochim & Donnelly 2007

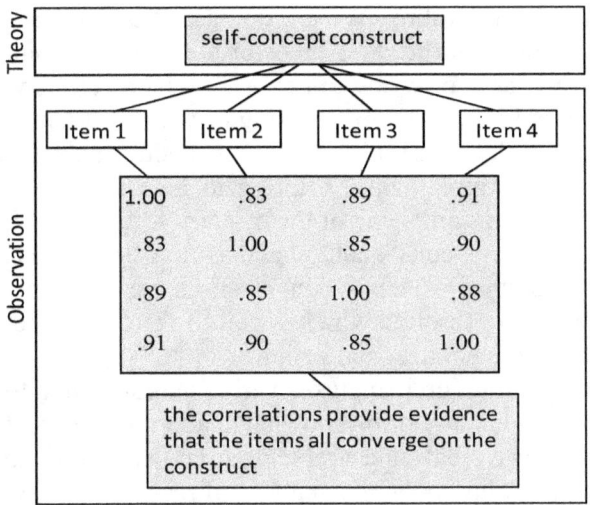

Figure C.10. Convergent Validity Correlations

conversation analysis
also CA

a QUALITATIVE RESEARCH approach which is founded on a sociological conceptualization of the basically social nature of language use in human interaction. However as the work in conversation analysis (CA) has developed, it has come to be a truly multi-disciplinary field. CA is a field of study concerned with the norms, practices, and competences underlying the organization of social interaction. Despite its name, it is concerned with all forms of spoken interaction including not only everyday conversations between friends and acquaintances, but also interactions in medical, educational, mass media and socio-legal contexts, relatively monologic interactions such as lecturing or speech-making and technologically complex interactions such as web-based multiparty communication. Regardless of the interaction being studied, CA starts from the perspective that the details of conduct in interaction are highly organized and orderly and, indeed, that the specificities of meaning and understanding in interaction would be impossible without this orderliness.

The central sociological insight of CA is that it is through conversation that we conduct the ordinary, and perhaps extraordinary, affairs of our lives. When people talk with one another, they are not merely communicating thoughts, information, or knowledge. Our relationships with one another, and our sense of who we are to one another, are generated, manifest, maintained and managed in and through our conversations, whether face-to-face or on the telephone. People construct, establish, reproduce, and negotiate their identities, roles, and relationships in conversational interaction. In our interactions with others, we do not just talk; conversation is not language idling. We are doing things, such as inviting someone over, asking them to do a favor or a service, blaming or criticizing them, greeting them or trying to get on first name terms with them, disagreeing or arguing with them, advising or warning them, apologizing for something one did or said, complaining about one's treatment, telling about troubles, sympathizing, offering to help and the like. These and other such activities are some of the primary forms of social action. They are as real, concrete, consequential and as fundamental as any other form of conduct. So when we study conversation, we are investigating the actions and activities through which social life is conducted. It is therefore primarily an approach to social action.

As a research technique it analyzes verbal output from a totally inductive perspective without any prior knowledge about the context of the participants. Resulting verbal data are seldom coded or transformed into numerical data. CA insists on the analysis of real, recorded data, segmented into turns of talk that are carefully transcribed. Generally speaking, the conversation analyst does not formulate research questions prior to analyzing the data. The goal is to build a convincing and comprehensive analysis of a single case, and then to search for other similar cases in order to build a collection of cases that represent some interactional phenomenon.

Two key analytical themes within CA are *sequential organization* and *categorization*. Sequential organization analysis examines how utterances can perform different actions depending on their sequential position within the conversation. *Turn-taking* is one fundamental aspect of sequential organization which is displayed through conversation. Thus it is suggested that conversation is organized in **adjacency pair**s such as question followed by answer; accusation followed by denial; compliment followed by acceptance. The sense of the second part of the adjacency pair is dependent on the first part. Breaches in such turn-taking (for example, when a question is followed by a further question in reply) are rare and suggest a breakdown in the order of the interaction. Breaches are useful to conversation analysts as it is usually when the rules have been subverted that the rules themselves become more explicit to the analysts.

Categorization is a further concern of conversation analysts and has its roots in the ethnomethodological tradition's ideas of membership category analysis (MCA). MCA rests on the principle that people are what they are as a result of their activities and thus it is by identifying activities that people may be defined as being one thing or another. For example the family may be a membership categorization device in which baby and mother are categories and from which category-bounding activities may include living together and caring.

Although the influence of CA is growing, it is methodologically very demanding and requires a ferocious attention to detail that not all researchers can muster. Some critics have also argued that its insistence on looking only at what can be discovered in the talk means that its contribution to our understanding, however valuable in itself, must necessarily remain very limited.

📖 Bloor & Wood 2006; Lazaraton 2003; Perry 2011; Richards 2003

Cook's distance

a diagnostic measure commonly used in REGRESSION ANALYSIS to detect the presence of an OUTLIER. Cook's distance measures the degree to which outliers affect the regression and it takes into account a person's score on the DEPENDENT as well as the INDEPENDENT VARIABLEs. The values of measure greater than 1 suggest the undue influence of the value on the corresponding REGRESSION COEFFICIENTs.

see also MAHALANOBIS DISTANCE D^2, LEVERAGE

📖 Larson-Hall 2010; Sahai & Khurshid 2001

cooperative suppression

another term for RECIPROCAL SUPPRESSION

corpus

a collection of naturally occurring samples of language which have been collected and collated for easy access by researchers and materials developers who want to know how words and other linguistic items are actually used. A corpus may vary from a few sentences to a set of written texts or recordings. In language analysis, corpuses usually consist of a relatively large, planned collection of texts or parts of texts, stored and accessed by computer. A corpus is designed to represent different types of language use, e.g., casual conversation, business letters, ESP (English for specific purposes) texts.

A number of different types of corpuses may be distinguished, for example:

1) *specialized corpus*: a corpus of texts of a particular type, such as academic articles, student writing, etc.
2) *general corpus or reference corpus*: a large collection of many different types of texts, often used to produce reference materials for language learning (e.g. dictionaries) or used as a base-line for comparison with specialized corpora.

3) *comparable corpora*: two or more corpora in different languages or language varieties containing the same kinds and amounts of texts, to enable differences or equivalences to be compared.
4) *learner corpus*: a collection of texts or language samples produced by language learners.
see also CORPUS LINGUISTICS
 Richards & Schmidt 2010

corpus linguistics
an approach to investigating language structure and use through the analysis of large databases of real language examples stored on computer. Issues amenable to corpus linguistics include the meanings of words across registers, the distribution and function of grammatical forms and categories, the investigation of lexico-grammatical associations (associations of specific words with particular grammatical constructions), the study of discourse characteristics, register variation, and (when learner corpora are available) issues in language acquisition and development.
 Richards & Schmidt 2010

correlated groups
another term for DEPENDENT SAMPLES

correlated measures design
another term for WITHIN-SUBJECTS DESIGN

correlated samples
another term for DEPENDENT SAMPLES

correlated samples design
another term for WITHIN-SUBJECTS DESIGN

correlated subjects design
another term for WITHIN-SUBJECTS DESIGN

correlated *t*-test
another term for PAIRED-SAMPLES *t*-TEST

correlation
also **association**
a measure of the strength of the *relationship* or *association* between two or more two VARIABLEs. By relationship, we mean that variations in one entity correspond to variations in the other. For example, we may know, on the basis of previous research, that learning a second or foreign language is correlated with motivation, so that under similar conditions of

language learning, individuals who are highly motivated tend to learn languages more quickly than those who are not highly motivated. In this case, the correlation is a relationship between two constructs—motivation and language ability. If we were to observe that individuals who received high scores on a test of grammar also received high scores on a test of vocabulary, the correlation is a relationship between two variables—two sets of test scores.

On way of thinking about correlation is as an indicator of how much two variables covary. When the scores on two different distributions vary together, they covary, so that they share some common variation. In the example above, with tests of grammar and vocabulary, we could say that these two sets of scores covary. The statistics that indicates the amount of covariation between two variables is called the **covariance** (i.e., a measure of how the two variables vary together). If the covariance is large and positive then this is because people who were low on one variable tended to be low on the other and people who were high on one tended to be high on the other, and suggests a positive relationship between the two variables. Similarly, a large negative covariance suggests a negative relationship. Covariance of zero shows no relationship between the two variables.

However, there is a problem with covariance being used as the measure of the relationship: it does not take the size of the variance of the variables into account. Hence, if in a study one or both of the variables had a large variance then the covariance would be larger than in another study where the two variances were small, even if the degree of relationship in the two studies were similar. Therefore, using covariance we would not be able to compare relationships to see whether one relationship was closer than another. For example, we might wish to see whether IQ and second language proficiency were as closely related in one country as they were in another. Accordingly, we need a measure that takes the variances into account. The CORRELATION COEFFICIENT is such a measure.

see also CORRELATION COEFFICIENT, PARTIAL CORRELATION, MULTIPLE CORRELATION COEFFICIENT

📖 Clark-Carter 2010; Larson-Hall 2010; Bachman 2004

correlational research

a type of NONEXPERIMENTAL RESEARCH in which the researcher investigates the relationship between two, or more, naturally occurring VARIABLES. The variables are examined to determine if they are related and, if so, the direction and magnitude of that relationship. In this type of research, the distinction between INDEPENDENT VARIABLEs (IVs) and DEPENDENT VARIABLEs (DVs) is usually arbitrary and many researchers prefer to call IVs *predictor variable*s and DVs *criterion variable*s.

Correlational research does not seek to show causality (that one variable is causing a change to occur in another). Rather, the main purpose of correlational research is to determine, through application of a quantitative statistical analysis, whether a relationship exists between the variables under investigation. One might make predictions based on these relationships, but not statements of causality. For example, if such a relationship does exist, the strength and the direction of the relationship are reported numerically in what is referred to as a CORRELATION COEFFICIENT. Scores from this analysis fall somewhere along the correlation coefficient's range of negative 1 to positive 1. Note that negative and positive do not have any moral value attached to them in this context. A highly negative relationship is not a relationship that is bad but one that results from scores on two variables moving in opposite directions: an increase in one variable is accompanied by a decrease in the other variable being studied.

The basic design for correlational research is straightforward. First, the researcher specifies the problem by asking a question about the relationship between the variables of interest. The variables selected for investigation are generally based on a theory, previous research, or the researcher's observations. The population of interest is also identified at this time. In simple correlational studies, the researcher focuses on gathering data on two (or more) measures from a single group of subjects. For example, you might correlate vocabulary and reading comprehension scores for a group of high school students.

see also EX POST FACTO RESEARCH

 Fraenkel & Wallen 2009; Harlow 2005; Lodico et al. 2010; Mackey & Gass 2005; Urdan 2010

correlation coefficient
also coefficient of correlation

a statistical index that reveals the strength and direction of the relationship or association between two VARIABLEs. Describing relationship in terms such as 'strong', 'moderate', 'weak', 'positive' and 'negative' is not very precise. Furthermore, such terms do not derive directly from the data themselves, but from the conceptualization of CORRELATION. Thus, in order to investigate correlations empirically, we need a numerical statistic that precisely summarizes these qualities, and that is based on observed data, or variable. This is exactly what a correlation coefficient provides. A graphical method for depicting the relationship among two variables is to plot the pair of scores on X and Y for each individual on a two-dimensional figure known as a SCATTERPLOT.

There are two fundamental characteristics of correlation coefficients researchers care about. The first of these is the direction of the correlation coefficient. The direction of the relationship has to do with whether the relationship is positive or negative. The sign (+ or -) of the correlation coefficient indicates the nature or direction of the linear relationship that exists between the two variables. A positive sign indicates a direct linear relationship, whereas a negative sign indicates an indirect (or inverse) linear relationship. A **positive correlation** occurs when as scores on variable X increase (from left to right), scores on variable Y also increase (from bottom to top). A direct linear relationship is one in which a change on one variable is associated with a change on the other variable in the same direction. That is, an increase on one variable is associated with an increase on the other variable, and a decrease on one variable is associated with a decrease on the other variable. When there is a direct relationship, subjects who have a high score on one variable will have a high score on the other variable, and subjects who have a low score on one variable will have a low score on the other variable. A **negative correlation**, sometimes called an **inverse correlation**, occurs when as scores on variable X increase (from left to right), scores on variable Y decrease (from top to bottom). A negative relationship indicates that change on one variable is associated with a change on the other variable in the opposite direction. That is, an increase on one variable is associated with a decrease on the other variable, and a decrease on one variable is associated with an increase on the other variable). When there is an indirect linear relationship, subjects who have a high score on one variable will have a low score on the other variable, and vice versa.

The second fundamental characteristic of correlation coefficients is the strength or magnitude of the relationship. Some correlation coefficients range in strength from -1 to +1 and some between 0 and 1. Thus, the value of coefficient can never be less than -1 (i.e., coefficient cannot equal -1.2, -50, etc.) or be greater than +1 (i.e., coefficient cannot equal 1.2, 50, etc.). The closer a positive value of coefficient is to +1, the stronger the direct relationship between the two variables; whereas the closer a positive value of a coefficient to 0, the weaker the direct relationship between the variables. A perfect positive correlation of +1 reveals that for every member of the sample or population, a higher score on one variable is related to a higher score on the other variable. The closer a negative value of coefficient is to -1, the stronger the indirect relationship between the two variables, whereas the closer a negative value of coefficient is to 0, the weaker the indirect relationship between the variables. A perfect negative correlation of -1 indicates that for every member of the sample or population, a higher score on one variable is related to a lower score on the other variable.

Once a correlation coefficient has been computed, there remains the problem of interpreting it. There are three cautions to be borne in mind when one is interpreting a correlation coefficient. First, a coefficient is a simple number and must not be interpreted as a percentage. A correlation of .50, for instance, does not mean 50 per cent relationship between the variables. Further, a correlation of .50 does not indicate twice as much relationship as that shown by a correlation of .25. A correlation of .50 actually indicates more than twice the relationship shown by a correlation of .25. In fact, as coefficients approach +1 or -1, a difference in the absolute values of the coefficients becomes more important than the same numerical difference between lower correlations would be. A way of determining the degree to which you can predict one variable from the other is to calculate an index called the COEFFICIENT OF DETERMINATION, which is the square of the correlation coefficient.

Second, a correlation does not necessarily imply a cause-and-effect relationship between two factors, as we have previously indicated. It should not therefore be interpreted as meaning that one factor is causing the scores on the other to be as they are. There are invariably other factors influencing both variables under consideration. Suspected cause-and-effect relationships would have to be confirmed by subsequent experimental study.

Third, a correlation coefficient is not to be interpreted in any absolute sense. A correlational value for a given sample of a population may not necessarily be the same as that found in another sample from the same population. Many factors influence the value of a given correlation coefficient and if researchers wish to extrapolate to the populations from which they drew their samples they will then have to test the significance of the correlation.

There are many different correlation coefficients or measures of association in applied linguistics literature, and the appropriateness of their use depends on the LEVELs OF MEASUREMENT (nominal, ordinal, interval, ratio) and distributions (normal, non-normal) of the two variables under investigation. These include the PEARSON PRODUCT-MOMENT CORRELATION COEFFICIENT, POINT-BISERIAL CORRELATION COEFFICIENT, BISERIAL CORRELATION COEFFICIENT, TETRACHORIC CORRELATION COEFFICIENT, PHI CORRELATION COEFFICIENT, CONTINGENCY COEFFICIENT, CRAMER'S V, GOODMAN-KRUSKAL'S LAMBDA, SPEARMAN RANK ORDER CORRELATION COEFFICIENT, KENDALL'S RANK-ORDER CORRELATION COEFFICIENT, GOODMAN-KRUSKAL'S GAMMA, GOODMAN-KRUSKAL'S TAU, SOMER'S d, and ETA (η), among others.

📖 Bachman 2004; Cohen et al. 2011; Cramer & Howitt 2004; Kirk 2008; Lomax 2007; Richards & Schmidt 2010; Sheskin 2011; Urdan 2010

correlation for attenuation
another term for ATTENUATION

correlation line
 another term for REGRESSION LINE

correlation matrix
 also **correlation table**
 a symmetrical table which shows the CORRELATIONs or intercorrelations between a set of variables. The variables are listed in the first row and first column of the table. The diagonal of the table shows the correlation of each variable with itself which is 1 (see Table C.3).

Variables	1. Spelling	2. Phonics	3. Vocabulary	4. Lang. mech	5. Total battery
1. Spelling	1	0.63	0.45	0.57	0.82
2. Phonics	0.63	1	0.39	0.68	0.78
3. Vocabulary	0.45	0.39	1	0.85	0.86
4. Lang. mech	0.57	0.68	0.85	1	0.91
5. Total battery	0.82	0.78	0.86	0.91	1

Table C.3. An Example of Correlation Matrix

Because the information in the diagonal is always the same, it may be omitted. The values of the correlations in the lower left-hand triangle of the matrix are the mirror image of those in the upper right-hand triangle. Because of this, the values in the upper right-hand triangle may be omitted. Thus, the table can be reorganized to present the results more efficiently. Table C.4 may look as if it lacks some information, but, in fact, it contains all the information needed.
 Cramer & Howitt 2004; Ravid 2011

Variables	1. Spelling	2. Phonics	3. Vocabulary	4. Lang. mech	5. Total battery
1. Spelling					
2. Phonics	0.63				
3. Vocabulary	0.45	0.39			
4. Lang. mech	0.57	0.68	0.85		
5. Total battery	0.82	0.78	0.86	0.91	

Table C.4. An Example of Correlation Matrix

correlation ratio
 another term for ETA

correlation table
 another term for CORRELATION MATRIX

counterbalanced design
 also **rotation experiment, cross-over design, switch-over design**
 a design in which several TREATMENT conditions or interventions are tested simultaneously and the number of groups in the study equals the number of interventions. All the groups in the study receive all interven-

tions, but in a different order. In effect, this design involves a series of replications; in each replication the groups are shifted so that at the end of the experiment each group has been exposed to each condition. This design should be used when random assignment is not possible and when it is expected that the different treatments will not interfere too much with each other. This design is particularly useful when the researcher uses INTACT GROUPs (i.e., preexisting classes).

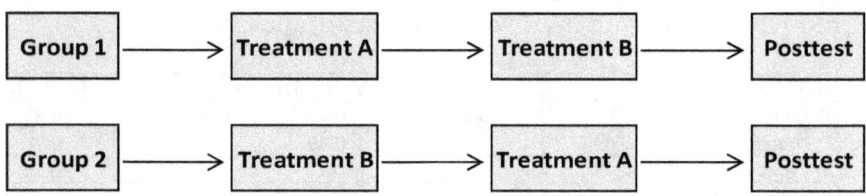

Figure C.11. Schematic Representation of a Counterbalanced Design with Two Conditions

The simplest type of counterbalanced design is used when there are two possible conditions, A and B (see Figure C.11). As with the standard RE-PEATED MEASURES DESIGN, the researchers want to test every subject for both conditions. They divide the subjects into two groups and one group is treated with condition A, followed by condition B, and the other is tested with condition B followed by condition A. For example, a classroom teacher could use a counterbalanced study to compare the effectiveness of two methods of instruction on learning second language grammar. The teacher could choose two intact classes and two units of subject matter comparable in the nature of the concepts, difficulty of concepts, and length. It is essential that the units be equivalent in the complexity and difficulty of the concepts involved. During the first replication of the design, class (group) 1 is taught unit 1 by method A and class (group) 2 is taught unit 1 by method B. An achievement test over unit 1 is administered to both groups. Then class 1 is taught unit 2 by method B and class 2 is taught unit 2 by method A; both are then tested over unit 2. After the study, the column means are computed to indicate the mean achievement for both groups (classes) when taught by method A or method B. A comparison of these column mean scores through an ANALYSIS OF VARIANCE indicates the effectiveness of the methods on achievement in science. If you have three conditions (see Figure C.12), the process is exactly the same, and you would divide the subjects into 6 groups, treated as orders ABC, ACB, BAC, BCA, CAB and CBA.

In complete counterbalancing, the order of presentation of conditions to participants is systematically varied so that: (1) each participant is exposed to all of the conditions of the experiment; (2) each condition is presented an equal number of times; (3) each condition is presented an equal number of times in each position; and (4) each condition precedes and follows each other condition an equal number of times. The problem with complete counterbalancing is that for complex experiments, with multiple conditions, the PERMUTATIONs quickly multiply and the research project becomes extremely unwieldy. For example, four possible conditions requires 24 orders of treatment (4 × 3 × 2 × 1), and the number of participants must be a multiple of 24, due to the fact that you need an equal number in each group.

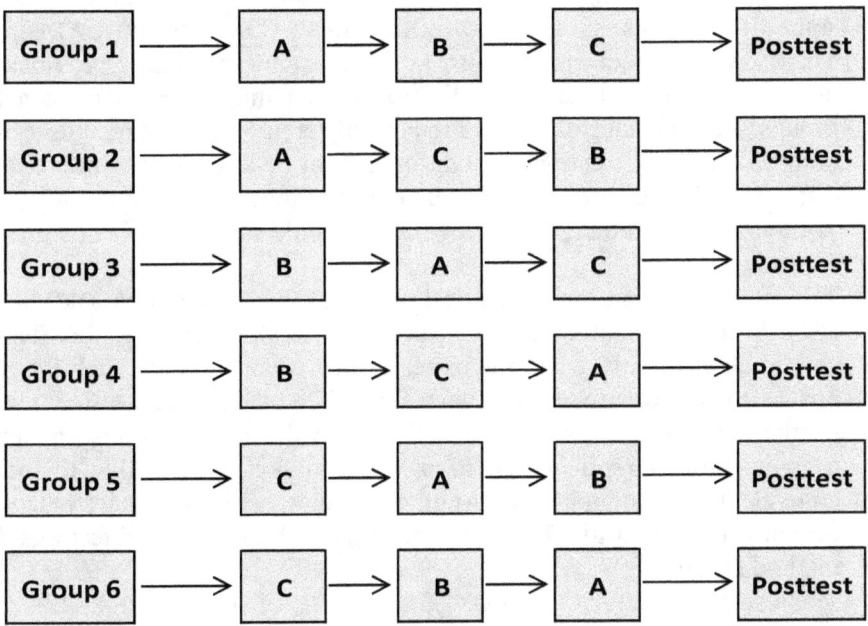

Figure C.12. Schematic Representation of a Counterbalanced Design with Three Conditions

As the number of experimental conditions increase, complete counterbalancing becomes more difficult to implement, since the number of subjects required increases substantially. When it is not possible to completely counterbalance the order of presentation of the conditions, alternative less complete counterbalancing procedures are available. One such incomplete counterbalanced measures design is the LATIN SQUARE DESIGN, which attempts to circumvent some of the complexities and keep the experiment to a reasonable size.

Another context in which it is worth considering counterbalancing is when samples of individuals are being measured twice on the same variable. For example, the researcher may be interested in changes of children's IQs over time. To give exactly the same IQ test twice would encourage the claim that PRACTICE EFFECTs are likely to lead to increases in IQ at the second time of measurement. By using two different versions (forms) of the test this criticism may be reduced. As the two different versions may vary slightly in difficulty, it would be wise to give version A to half of the sample first followed by version B at the second administration, and also give version B first to the other half of the sample followed by version A. Of course, this design will not totally negate the criticism of practice effects. There are more complex designs in which some participants do not receive the first version of the test which may be helpful in dealing with this issue. Counterbalanced design overcomes some of the weaknesses of NONEQUIVALENT CONTROL GROUP DESIGN. That is, when intact groups must be used, counterbalancing provides an opportunity to rotate out any differences that might exist between the groups. Because all treatments are administered to all groups, the results obtained for each treatment condition cannot be attributed to preexisting differences in the subjects. If one group should have more aptitude on the average than the other, each X treatment would benefit from this greater aptitude.

The main shortcoming of this design is that there may be an ORDER EFFECT from one treatment condition to the next. Therefore, this design should be used only when the experimental treatments are such that exposure to one treatment will have no effect on subsequent treatments. Furthermore, one must establish the equivalence of learning material used in various replications. It may not always be possible to locate equivalent units of material. Another weakness of the counterbalanced design is the possibility of boring students with the repeated testings this method requires.

see also NONEQUIVALENT CONTROL GROUP DESIGN, TIME-SERIES DESIGN, EQUIVALENT MATERIAL DESIGN, RECURRENT INSTITUTIONAL CYCLE DESIGN, SEPARATE-SAMPLE PRETEST-POSTTEST CONTROL GROUP DESIGN, SEPARATE SAMPLE-PRETEST-POSTTEST DESIGN

 Ary et al. 2010; Best & Kahn 2006; Brown 1988; Cramer & Howitt 2004; Mackey & Gass 2005; Sheskin 2011

covariance
see CORRELATION

covariance structure analysis
another term for STRUCTURAL EQUATION MODELING

covariate
also **covariate variable, concomitant variable**
an INDEPENDENT VARIABLE (IV) which is measured so that it can be controlled statistically and its effect is removed statistically from the

study during the analysis. More specifically, it denotes an IV which researcher includes not so much to examine its effect on the DEPENDENT VARIABLE (DV) but to subtract out its influence from the other IVs. The intention is to produce more precise estimates of the effect of the IV of main interest. For example, if a researcher was looking at the relationship between student age and second language (L2) examination success, the researcher might first want to remove any effects due to the amount of time spent studying the L2. Covariates are can be either *categorical* or *continuous*, although in the field of applied linguistics research they are by and large continuous. Covariate can be entered into all types of ANOVA model. After adjusting for the influence of covariates, a standard ANOVA or MANOVA is carried out. This adjustment process (known as ANCOVA or MANCOVA) usually allows for more sensitive tests of treatment effects.

Failing to consider covariates could hinder the interpretation of relationships between IVs and DVs, especially with NONRANDOM SAMPLEs. Covariates help to statistically isolate an effect, especially when RANDOM ASSIGNMENT and/or manipulation are not accomplished. When several well-selected covariates (i.e., CONFOUNDING, EXTRANEOUS VARIABLEs) are included in a study, and the relationship between the IVs and DVs still holds after controlling for the effects of one or more covariates, there is greater assurance that we have isolated the effect.

 Hair et al. 2010; Harlow 2005; Larson-Hall 2010; Porte 2010; Urdan 2010

covariate variable
another term for COVARIATE

coverage error
a SELECTION ERROR which arises when the POPULATION list from which the SAMPLE of cases is drawn is incomplete. This happens, e.g., when TELEPHONE INTERVIEWs are conducted; all those who do not have a telephone are excluded from the sample a priori, which results in error. In fact, coverage error results because of *undercoverage* and *overcoverage*. Undercoverage occurs when members of the target population are excluded. Overcoverage occurs when units are included erroneously. The net coverage error is the difference between the undercoverage and the overcoverage.
see also SAMPLING ERROR, NONRESPONSE ERROR
 Corbetta 2003; O'Leary 2004

cover letter
a type of QUESTIONNAIRE administration in POSTAL SURVEYs. In the absence of a live contact person, the cover letter has the difficult job to sell the survey, that is, to create rapport with the respondents and to convince

them about the importance of the survey and of their role in contributing to it. In addition to this public relations function, the cover letter also needs to provide certain specific information and directions. To write a letter that meets all these requirements is not easy, particularly in view of the fact that it needs to be short at the same time. If it is more than a page it is likely to be tossed aside and then find its way into the trashcan unread. So writing this letter is something we do not want to rush. The cover letter should assure the respondent that all information will be held in strict confidence or that the questionnaire is anonymous. The matter of sponsorship also might well be mentioned. Of course, a stamped, addressed return envelope should be included. To omit this virtually guarantees that many of the questionnaires will go into the wastebasket. Some researchers suggest that two copies of the questionnaire be sent, one to be returned when completed and the other to be placed in the respondent's own file.

Cover letters usually address the following points:

- Who the writer is.
- The organization that is sponsoring or conducting the study.
- What the survey is about and why this is important or socially useful.
- Why the recipient's opinion is important and how s/he was selected.
- Assurance that all responses will be kept confidential.
- How to return the completed questionnaire.
- The date by which the completed questionnaire should be returned.
- What to do if questions arise (e.g., a contact name and telephone number).
- Possible reward for participation.
- Thank you!
- Signature, preferably by a person of recognized stature.
- Attached stamped addressed envelope.

Ary et al. 2010; Best & Kahn 2006; Dörnyei 2003

covert participant
another term for COMPLETE PARTICIPANT

c-parameter
see ITEM CHARACTERISTIC CURVE

Cramer's V
also **Cramer's phi, Cramer's V coefficient, ϕ_c, V**

an EFFECT SIZE for a CHI-SQUARE analysis that provides information about the strength of the association between two CATEGORICAL VARIABLEs whose data are cross-classified in a 2 × 2 (two-by-two) or higher-

order CONTINGENCY TABLE. Cramer's V is the extension of PHI CORRELATION COEFFICIENT. For a 2 × 2 contingency table, Cramer's V gives exactly the same value as the phi coefficient.
  Larson-Hall 2010; Sahai & Khurshid 2001

Cramer's V coefficient
another term for CRAMER'S V

credibility
(in QUALITATIVE RESEARCH) a term which refers to the truthfulness of the inquiry's findings. Credibility or truth value involves how well the researcher has established confidence in the findings based on the research design, participants, and context. The researcher has an obligation to represent the realities of the research participants as accurately as possible and must provide assurances in the report that this obligation was met. The term credibility in qualitative research is analogous to INTERNAL VALIDITY in quantitative research.

Credibility is used by qualitative researchers to ensure that the picture provided by the researcher is as full and complete as possible. In qualitative research credibility can be addressed by prolonged engagement in the field, persistent OBSERVATION, TRIANGULATION of methods, sources, investigators and theories, PEER DEBRIEFING, NEGATIVE CASE SAMPLING, and MEMBER CHECKS.

see also TRANSFERABILITY, DEPENDABILITY, CONFIRMABILITY, OBJECTIVITY
  Ary et al. 2010; Cook & Campbell 1979; Lodico et al. 2010; Perry 2011

criterion-based sampling
another term for PURPOSIVE SAMPLING

criterion-referenced test
also **content-referenced test, domain-referenced test, objectives-referenced test, CRT**

a test which is constructed to allow users to interpret examinee test performance in relation to well-defined domains of content and/or behaviors. A criterion-referenced test does not use a norming group to establish guidelines for interpreting test results. Instead one or more criteria are used to decide how well the examinee has done. In other words, unlike NORM-REFERENCED TEST, each subject's score is meaningful without reference to the other subjects' scores. The criteria are predetermined before administering the test and are used to establish cut points. A **cut point** is a point on the test score scale used to classify people into different categories such as high, middle, or low ability. For instance, all respondents scoring over 80% correct might be considered high ability, those between

50% and 80% average ability, and those below 50% below average. Moreover, the distribution of scores on a CRT need not necessarily be normal. If all the subjects know 100 percent of the material on all the objectives, then all the subjects should receive the same score with no variation at all. For example, a driving test is usually criterion-referenced since to pass it requires the ability to meet certain test items regardless of how many others have or have not passed the driving test. If the subject meets the criteria, then s/he passes the examination.

A criterion-referenced test provides the researcher with information about exactly what a subject has learned, what s/he can do. The intention here is to indicate whether students have achieved a set of given criteria, regardless of how many others might or might not have achieved them, hence variability or range is less important here.

More recently an outgrowth of criterion-referenced testing has seen the rise of **domain-referenced test**s (DRT). Here considerable significance is accorded to the careful and detailed specification of the content or the domain which will be assessed. The domain is the particular field or area of the subject that is being tested. For DRTs, the items are sampled from a general, but well-defined, domain of behaviors (e.g., overall business English ability), rather than from individual course objectives (e.g., the course objectives of a specific intermediate level business English class), as is often the case in what might be called **objective-referenced tests** (ORTs). The domain is set out very clearly and very fully, such that the full depth and breadth of the content are established. Test items are then selected from this very full field, with careful attention to sampling procedures so that representativeness of the wider field is ensured in the test items. The student's achievements on that test are computed to yield a proportion of the maximum score possible, and this, in turn, is used as an index of the proportion of the overall domain that s/he has grasped. So, for example, if a domain has 1,000 items and the test has 50 items, and the student scores 30 marks from the possible 50, then it is inferred that s/he has grasped 60 per cent ($\{30 \div 50\} \times 100$) of the domain of 1,000 items. Here inferences are being made from a limited number of items to the student's achievements in the whole domain; this requires careful and representative sampling procedures for test items. The results on a DRT can therefore be used to describe a student's status with regard to the domain in a manner similar to the way in which ORT results are used to describe the student's status on small subsets for each course objectives. Thus, the term domain-referenced and objectives-referenced describe variant sampling techniques within the overall concept of criterion-referenced testing.

see also ITEM ANALYSIS, ITEM SPECIFICATIONS
📖 Brown 2005; Perry 2011

criterion-referenced validity
another term for CRITERION-RELATED VALIDITY

criterion-related validity
also **empirical validity, criterion-referenced validity, criterion validity**
a form of VALIDITY which endeavors to relate the results of one particular measuring instrument to another external criterion or standard which is relevant, reliable, and free from bias. A criterion is a second test or other assessment procedure presumed to measure the same variable. Within this type of validity there are two principal forms: **predictive validity** and **concurrent validity**. To obtain evidence of predictive validity, researchers allow a time interval to elapse between administration of the instrument and obtaining the criterion scores. Predictive validity is achieved if the data acquired at the first round of research correlate highly with data acquired at a future date. For example, if the results of examinations taken by 16-year-olds correlate highly with the examination results gained by the same students when aged 18, then we might wish to say that the first examination demonstrated strong predictive validity. Or, the Scholastic Assessment Test (SAT) that many U.S. high school students take measures scholastic aptitude—the ability of a student to perform in college. If the SAT has high predictive validity, then students who get high SAT scores will subsequently do well in college. If students with high scores perform the same as students with average or low scores, then the SAT has low predictive validity.

A variation on this theme is encountered in the notion of concurrent validity. To have concurrent validity, an instrument must be associated with a preexisting instrument that is judged to be valid and reliable so that the data gathered from using one instrument must correlate highly with data gathered from using another instrument at nearly the same time. For example, you create a new test to measure intelligence. For it to be concurrently valid, it should be highly correlated with existing IQ tests (assuming the same definition of intelligence is used). This means that most people who score high on the old measure should also score high on the new one, and vice versa. The two measures may not be perfectly associated, but if they measure the same or a similar construct, it is logical for them to yield similar results. Concurrent validity is very similar to its partner—predictive validity—in its core concept (i.e., agreement with a second measure); what differentiates concurrent and predictive validity is the absence of a time element in the former; concurrence can be demonstrated simultaneously with another instrument.

A key index in both forms of criterion-related validity is the CORRELATION COEFFICIENT. A correlation coefficient indicates the degree of relationship that exists between the scores individuals obtain on two instruments. A positive relationship is indicated when a high score on one of the instruments is accompanied by a high score on the other or when a low score on one is accompanied by a low score on the other. A negative relationship is indicated when a high score on one instrument is accompanied by a low score on the other, and vice versa. All correlation coefficients fall somewhere between +1 and +1. When a correlation coefficient is used to describe the relationship between a set of scores obtained by the same group of individuals on a particular instrument and their scores on some criterion measure, it is called a **validity coefficient**.

see also CONTENT VALIDITY, CONSTRUCT VALIDITY, INTERNAL VALIDITY, EXTERNAL VALIDITY, FACE VALIDITY

📖 Cohen et al. 2011; Cramer & Howitt 2004; Neuman 2007; Richards & Schmidt 2010

criterion sampling
see PURPOSIVE SAMPLING

criterion validity
another term for CRITERION-RELATED VALIDITY

criterion variable
another term for DEPENDENT VARIABLE

critical case sampling
see PURPOSIVE SAMPLING

critical applied linguistics
an interdisciplinary critical approach to English applied linguistics. One of the central concerns in this approach is exposing the political dimensions and power relations involved in mainstream applied linguistics, in areas like language teaching, language policy and planning, language testing, language rights, CRITICAL LITERACY, CRITICAL PEDAGOGY, CRITICAL DISCOURSE ANALYSIS, and so forth. In the case of critical applied linguistics, the interest is addressing social problems involving language. Its proponents consider it an indispensable part of the intellectual activity that is applied linguistics, especially because applied linguistics claims as its mission the study of language with implications for everyday life, or the real world. Critical applied linguists believe it is incumbent upon them to link language issues to general social issues (e.g., unemployment) and to be more than a student of language-related situations, namely to be an agent for social change. Generally, this is done within a broad political framework.

📖 Berns 2010

critical discourse analysis
  also **CDA**
  a type of discourse analytical research that primarily studies the way social power abuse, dominance, and inequality are enacted, reproduced, and resisted by text and talk in the social and political context. Critical discourse analysis (CDA), which is a domain of CRITICAL APPLIED LINGUISTICS, investigates how language use may be affirming and indeed reproducing the perspectives, values, and ways of talking of the powerful, which may not be in the interests of the less powerful. The relationship between language, power, and ideology is a crucial focal point. CDA consists of an interdisciplinary set of approaches which attempt to describe, interpret and explain this relationship.
  More specifically, in CDA, *critical* is usually taken to mean studying and taking issue with how dominance and inequality are reproduced through language use: Analysis, description and theory formation play a role especially in as far as they allow better understanding and critique of social inequality, based on gender, ethnicity, class, origin, religion, language, sexual orientation and other criteria that define differences between people. Their ultimate goal is not only scientific, but also social and political, namely change. In that case, social discourse analysis takes the form of a critical discourse analysis. CDA is critical of how unequal language use can do ideological work. Ideologies are representations of aspects of the world which contribute to establishing and maintaining relations of power, domination, and exploitation. When language use reflects inequality, CDA argues that sustained use of such unequal representations does ideological work because it tacitly affirms inequitable social processes. A key assumption in this argument is that there is a 'dialectical' or 'bi-directional' relationship between social processes and language use. With such a focus on the ideological effects of unequal language use, CDA is especially drawn to texts where the marginal and relatively powerless are (mis)represented by the powerful.
  Usually in CDA, the concept of *discourse* has two different but related senses. The first (discourse 1) is *language in use*. The discourse 1 of a conversation refers to the meanings made in interaction with those features of context which are deemed relevant, e.g., tone of voice of participants, facial movements, hand-gestures. If the conversation is recorded, its 'text' would be the transcription of the conversation. Discourse 1 refers to meanings made in reading too, that is, those meanings we derive from the text in line with the knowledge we possess, the amount of effort we invest, our values, how we have been educated and socialized, our gender, etc.
  A second meaning of discourse (discourse 2) in CDA refers to discourses as ways of talking about the world which are tightly connected to ways of

seeing and comprehending it. The discourses place limits on the possibilities of articulation (and by extension, what to do or not to do) with respect to the area of concern of a particular institution, political program, etc. For example, different religions promote their own discourses which frame explanation of natural behavior. Roman Catholicism now approves of 'the big bang' theory of the universe's birth (scientific discourse) but that its genesis was by divine means (religious discourse). So, it is the powerful who ultimately control discourse 2 and have the means to regenerate it (e.g. newspaper moguls).

In CDA, *analysis* consists of three stages: *description*, *interpretation* and *explanation*. In the first stage, description stage, the text should be described as rigorously and as comprehensively as possible relative to the analytical focus. A key descriptive tool used in CDA is SYSTEMIC FUNCTIONAL LINGUISTICS (SFL). Systematicity in the description stage is important since this helps ground interpretation of how the text might lead to different discourses 1 for different readers in different discourse practices or the situations of language use, e.g., a political speech, a chat between strangers at a bus stop, a debate on TV.

The focus in the interpretation stage is concerned with conjecturing the cognition of readers/listeners, how they might mentally interact with the text. This refers to as *processing analysis*. Critique in the interpretation stage means pointing to a misrepresentation or a cognitive problem. This might mean that some significant information is absent from a particular text, which leads to the reader either being misled or not being fully apprised of the most relevant facts. This stage also seeks to show how wider social and cultural contexts and power relations within them (the second meaning of discourse) might shape the interpretation (discourses 1) of a text.

In explanation stage, CDA critically explains connections between texts and discourse(s) circulating in the wider social and cultural context, the *sociocultural practice*. Critique here involves showing how the 'ideological function of the misrepresentation or unmet need' helps 'in sustaining existing social arrangements'.

Thus, CDA is both a theory and a method. Researchers who are interested in the relationship between language and society use CDA to help them describe, interpret, and explain such relationships. CDA is different from other discourse analysis methods because it includes not only a description and interpretation of discourse in context, but also offers an explanation of why and how discourses work. CDA is a domain of CRITICAL APPLIED LINGUISTICS.

The terms **critical linguistics** (CL) and CDA are often used interchangeably. In fact, more recently the term CDA seems to have been preferred and is being used to denote the theory formerly identified as CL. The

manifold roots of CDA lie in rhetoric, text linguistics, anthropology, philosophy, socio-psychology, cognitive science, literary studies and sociolinguistics, as well as in applied linguistics and pragmatics. Nowadays, however, some scholars prefer the term **critical discourse studies** (CDS).
📖 Hyland & Paltridge 2011; Rogers 2011; Simpson 2011

critical discourse studies
see CRITICAL DISCOURSE ANALYSIS

critical ethnography
see ETHNOGRAPHY

critical inquiry
also **critical research**

a meta-process of investigation which questions currently held values and assumptions and challenges conventional social structures. Critical inquiry invites both researchers and participants to discard what they term false consciousness in order to develop new ways of understanding as a guide to effective action. Critical inquiry perspective is not content to interpret the world but also to change it. The assumptions that lie beneath critical inquiry are that:

- Ideas are mediated by power relations in society.
- Certain groups in society are privileged over others and exert an oppressive force on subordinate groups.
- What are presented as facts cannot be disentangled from ideology and the self-interest of dominant groups.
- Mainstream research practices are implicated, even if unconsciously, in the reproduction of the systems of class, race and gender oppression.

Those adhering to the critical inquiry perspective accuse interpretivists of adopting an uncritical stance towards the culture they are exploring, whereas the task of researchers is to call the structures and values of society into question.
📖 Gray 2009

critical linguistics
see CRITICAL DISCOURSE ANALYSIS

critical literacy
an approach to developing literacy skills that contextualize the reader and the text within socio-historical frames and the cultural and political environments of reader and text. In its broadest sense, critical literacy is also an approach to life, to language, to agency, and to the search for truths

that are omitted from the text, as well as the reasons why those omissions occur. Critical literacy implies approaches to teaching literacy in the classroom, yet it also embodies empowerment, emancipation, and the ability of school people (teachers and students and others) to manifest change through language.

The aims of critical literacy include those of a more traditional vein, which is to facilitate the development of literacy skills in children. Critical literacy goes beyond a notion of literacy skills as performance skills (i.e., the learner's achievement in conventional reading/writing). Teachers who use critical literacy aspire to help children create a sense of self as a reader/writer in the world—a knowledge of what written text accomplishes, and for whom. Further, it acknowledges a child's agency; through critical literacy, both students and teachers can become agents for social change.

While some teachers may feel a reluctance to engage in what they deem *political* education, it warrants stating that educational acts are inherently political. Teachers who fear a critical approach to teaching may not understand that teaching methods aligned with status quo ideologies can also serve to perpetuate oppressive social forces. Although that may not be a purposeful choice on the part of such teachers, it is a result of traditional teaching methodologies. Teaching is thus inherently political. Critical literacy is a means by which educators can uncover buried political assumptions and their eventual outcomes in the lives of children.

Critical literacy researchers continue to study the relationships between language, power, and identity in the classroom. As research about critical literacy continues, it is increasingly incorporated in various iterations as an approach to literacy instruction in the classroom. Students in bilingual classrooms are often falsely considered to have a deficit in learning simply because they are not native speakers of English. Critical literacy approaches, on the other hand, value the diversity in perspective and interpretation that bilingual and bicultural students bring to the classroom. Bilingual students thrive on critical literacy approaches that facilitate biliteracy development, while contributing to the creation of critical citizens of our world who understand the power of language in creating social change.
📖 GonzÁlez 2008

critical multiplism
the philosophy that researchers should use many ways of obtaining evidence regarding a particular HYPOTHESIS rather than relying on a single approach.
📖 Leary 2011

critical pedagogy
a philosophy of education which is as an educational movement, guided by passion and principle, to help students develop consciousness of freedom, recognize authoritarian tendencies, and connect knowledge to power and the ability to take constructive action. Critical pedagogy includes relationships between teaching and learning. Its proponents claim that it is a continuous process of what they call unlearning, learning, and relearning, reflection, evaluation, and the impact that these actions have on the students, in particular students whom they believe have been historically and continue to be disenfranchised by what they call traditional schooling. Central to the development of critical pedagogy is the need to explore how pedagogy functions as a cultural practice to produce rather than merely transmit knowledge within the asymmetrical relations of power that structure teacher–student relations.

Also referred to as critical pedagogy, **participatory pedagogy** aims to create classroom environments that help learners first to understand more fully their local conditions and circumstances, and second, to take action toward changing their lives. One way this is done is by helping learners understand the myriad ways in which the contexts of their lives are publicly constructed and the means they have available for recreating their worlds in ways that are meaningful and appropriate for them.

According to critical pedagogy, goal of research is social change. Critical pedagogy is distinguished by being grounded in analysis of ideology, power, and inequality, and in addition it seeks the transformation of schools and other institutions, in order to undermine social hierarchies that are sustained by these institutions. This task is a formidable one, requiring not only carefully considered research methods, but also an analysis of educational innovation and change, an understanding of the local politics of language policy in schools, and a practical involvement in the daily work of teaching and learning. In this undertaking, the hierarchical separation of research and teaching, and of researchers and language teachers, must also be critically examined and transformed. Although some researchers fear that critical pedagogy has politicized scholarship, the crisis of language loss among indigenous people and pervasive economic, social, and political inequalities based on language will continue to motivate language planning scholars to participate in language maintenance and revitalization programs, as well as efforts to develop language policies that further social justice.
📖 Hinkel 2011; Hornberger 2008

critical realism
an ONTOLOGY that can conceptualize reality, support theorizing, and guide empirical work in the natural and human sciences. Critical realism views reality as complex and recognizes the role of both AGENCY and

structural factors in influencing human behavior. It can be used with QUALITATIVE and/or QUANTITATIVE RESEARCH methods. Critical realism is one of a range of postpositivist approaches positioned between POSITIVISM and CONSTRUCTIVISM. Critical realism simultaneously recognizes the existence of knowledge independent of humans but also the socially embedded and fallible nature of scientific inquiry. Among other criticisms, positivism is viewed as failing to acknowledge the inherent social nature of knowledge development, the influence of underlying unobservable factors/powers, and the meaning-centered nature of humans. However, constructivist philosophies are also criticized for overprivileging these human perspectives and attendant problematic variations of relativism that cannot adequately resolve competing claims to knowledge or account for knowledge development.

To resolve these epistemological issues the existence of three realms of reality is identified: the *actual*, the *real*, and the *empirical*. The actual domain refers to events and outcomes that occur in the world. The real domain refers to underlying relations, structures, and tendencies that have the power to cause changes in the actual realm. Most often these causal influences remain latent; however, under the right circumstances, factors in the real domain can act together to generate causal changes in the actual domain. These causal changes are neither uniform nor chaotic but are somewhat patterned. The empirical dimension refers to human perspectives on the world (i.e., of the actual and real domains). This could be perspectives of an individual or, in a wider sense, of scientific inquiry. The real and actual domains can be perceived only fallibly. Hence, this ontology advocates the existence of an objective reality formed of both events and underlying causes, and although these dimensions of reality have objective existence, they are not knowable with certainty.

Other tenets of critical realism tend to emerge from this ontological basis. A strong focus in theorizing and research informed by critical realism is placed on understanding causality and explaining events in the actual domain. This movement from events to their causes, known as ABDUCTION, is contrasted with other common goals of research to describe, predict, correlate, and intervene.

Critical realism attempts to respond to and understand reality as it exists in the actual and real domains. Hence, being led by the nature of that reality is of overriding importance and takes precedence over disciplinary, methodological, or ideological predisposition because each of these could distort perceptions of reality. This results in a postdisciplinary vent that seeks to be led by reality in all its complexity and to avoid simplification, narrowness, and distortion.

In the realm of the real, critical realism views behavior as being influenced by both agency and structural factors. Although humans have a degree of agency, this is always constrained by wider structural factors that are viewed as surrounding the individual. Although culture can be conceived as being dependent on and created only through the existence of humans, critical realism argues that culture exists independent of individuals. Likewise, social phenomena are made possible by the presence of humans but are deemed to be external to individuals and have existence and the power to constrain whether this is recognized by individuals or not.

see also SCIENTIFIC REALISM, SUBTLE REALISM, ANALYTIC REALISM, NAIVE REALISM, DISCOURSE ANALYSIS

📖 Given 2008

critical region
another term for REJECTION REGION

critical research
another term for CRITICAL INQUIRY

critical theory
a foundational perspective from which analysis of social action, politics, science, and other human endeavors can proceed. Research drawing from critical theory has critique (assessment of the current state and the requirements to reach a desired state) at its center. Critique entails examination of both action and motivation; that is, it includes both what is done and why it is done. In application, it is the use of dialectic, reason, and ethics as means to study the conditions under which people live.

The significance of critical theory for research is immense, for it suggests that much social research is comparatively trivial in that it accepts rather than questions given agendas for research. Critical theorists would argue that the positivist (see POSITIVISM) and INTERPRETIVE PARADIGMs are essentially technicist, seeking to understand and render more efficient an existing situation, rather than to question or transform it.

see also CATALYTIC VALIDITY

📖 Cohen et al. 2011; Given 2008

critical value
the theoretical value of a TEST STATISTIC (e.g., t STATISTIC, F STATISTIC) that leads to rejection of the NULL HYPOTHESIS at a given LEVEL OF SIGNIFICANCE. Put differently, critical value is the minimum value of a statistic at which the results would be considered statistically significant. The critical value is related to the level of significance chosen. It provides a cut off point for the REGION OF REJECTION and the REGION OF

ACCEPTANCE of the null hypothesis. It is used as a confidence measure to determine whether a null hypothesis can be retained or it can be rejected. Put simply, the critical value is the value that the researcher might expect to observe in the sample simply because of chance. If the observed statistics is smaller than the critical value, the null hypothesis is accepted. If the observed statistics is greater than the critical value for that statistic, then the null hypothesis is rejected. Having rejected the null hypothesis, one of the two alternatives is automatically accepted (see NULL HYPOTHESIS). For example, if you look at the statistical tables for the t DISTRIBUTION, the critical value of t (with 5 DEGREES OF FREEDOM using the .01 SIGNIFICANCE LEVEL is 4.03. This means that for the PROBABILITY VALUE to be less than or equal to .01, the value of the t statistic obtained from the calculation must be 4.03 or greater. The critical value for any hypothesis test depends on the significance level at which the test is carried out, and whether the test is one or two-tailed.
📖 Brown 1988; Mackey & Gass 2005; Porte 2010

Cronbach's alpha
also **alpha (α) reliability, Cronbach's alpha reliability, coefficient alpha, alpha coefficient of reliability, Cronbach's coefficient alpha**
an approach to estimating the INTERNAL CONSISTENCY RELIABILITY of a measuring instrument (e.g., a test) based on information about (a) the number of items on the test, (b) the variance of the scores of each item, and (c) the variance of the total test scores. The Cronbach's alpha provides a coefficient of **inter-item correlation**s, i.e., the CORRELATION of each item with the sum of all the other relevant items. This is a measure of the internal consistency among the items (not, for example, the people) and the most common way to assess the reliability of self-report items (e.g., QUESTIONNAIRE). It measures the degree to which the items in an instrument are related. The Cronbach's alpha has a maximum value of 1. Values closer to 1 reflect a stronger relationship between the test items. For an instrument with a high alpha, participants who score high on one item on the test would also score high on other items on the test. Similarly, participants who score low on one item of the test would also score low on the other items on the test. Tests with low alphas would indicate that there was little similarity of responses.
The Cronbach's alpha does the same thing as the KUDER-RICHARDSON FORMULAS except that it is used when the items are scored with more than two possibilities. When items are scored dichotomously, it yields the same result as the *KR*20, but it can also be used when items are not scored dichotomously (it can be used for either dichotomous or continuously scored items). One use of this method is on RATING SCALEs (e.g., LIKERT SCALE), where participants are asked to indicate on a multipoint scale the degree to which they agree or disagree. As with the *KR* formu-

las, the resulting RELIABILITY COEFFICIENT is an overall average of the correlations among all possible pairs of items. If the test items are heterogeneous—that is, they measure more than one trait or attribute—the reliability index as computed by either coefficient alpha or *KR20* will be lowered. Furthermore, these formulas are not appropriate for SPEED TESTS because item variances will be accurate only if each item has been attempted by every person.

see also SPLIT-HALF RELIABILITY, AVERAGE INTER-ITEM CORRELATION, AVERAGE ITEM-TOTAL CORRELATION

📖 Ary et al. 2010; Cohen et al. 2011; Richards & Schmidt 2010

Cronbach's alpha reliability
another term for CRONBACH'S ALPHA

Cronbach's coefficient alpha
another term for CRONBACH'S ALPHA

crossbreak table
another term for CONTINGENCY TABLE

cross-classification table
another term for CONTINGENCY TABLE

crossed factorial design
see NESTED DESIGN

cross-lagged panel correlation
the CORRELATION between two variables, X and Y, which is calculated at two different points in time. Then, correlations are calculated between measurements of the two variables across time. For example, we would correlate the scores on X taken at Time 1 with the scores on Y taken at Time 2. Likewise, we would calculate the scores on Y at Time 1 with those on X at Time 2. If X causes Y, we should find that the correlation between X at Time 1 and Y at Time 2 is larger than the correlation between Y at Time 1 and X at Time 2 (see Figure C.13). This is because the relationship between a cause (variable X) and its effect (variable Y) should be stronger if the causal variable is measured before rather than after its effect.

Cross-lagged panel correlation is consequently often employed in the analysis of PANEL DESIGNs.

📖 Leary 2011

cross-over design

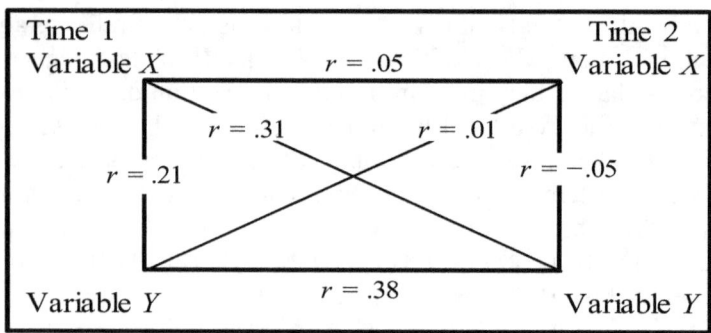

Figure C.13. A Schematic Diagram for a Cross-Lagged Panel Correlation

cross-over design
another term for COUNTER BALANCED DESIGN

cross product
the product of multiplying each individual's scores on two variables.
📖 Urdan 2010

cross-sectional design
another term for CROSS-SECTIONAL DESIGN

cross-sectional study
also **cross-sectional design, cross-sectional survey, cross-sectional research**
the study of a group of different individuals or subjects at a single point in time. A cross-sectional study is one that produces a snapshot of a population at a particular point in time. Details about an event or phenomenon are gathered once, and once only, for each subject or case studied. Consequently, cross-sectional studies offer an instant, but static, photograph of the process being studied. Their one-off nature makes such studies easier to organize and cheap as well as giving them the advantage of immediacy, offering instant results. The epitome of the cross-sectional study is a national census in which a representative SAMPLE of the population consisting of individuals of different ages, different occupations, different educational and income levels, and residing in different parts of the country, is interviewed on the same day.
In a LONGITUDINAL STUDY of vocabulary development, for example, a researcher would compare a measure of first-grade students' vocabulary skills in 2000 with one when they were fourth-grade students in 2003 and seventh-grade students in 2006. A cross-sectional study would compare the vocabulary skills of a sample of children from grades 1, 4, and 7 in 2006. In cross-sectional research designs time is not considered one of

the study VARIABLEs. Researchers collect data that cannot be directly observed, but instead are self-reported, such as opinions, attitudes, values, and beliefs. The purpose often is to examine the characteristics of a population. Cross-sectional data can be collected by SELF-ADMINISTERED QUESTIONNAIREs. Cross-sectional data can also be collected by INTERVIEWs. Cross-sectional data can be gathered from individuals, groups, organizations, or other units of analysis. Because cross-sectional data are collected at one point in time, researchers typically use the data to determine the frequency distribution of certain behaviors, opinions, attitudes, or beliefs.

Cross-sectional data can be highly efficient in testing the associations between two variables (see CORRELATIONAL RESEARCH). These data are also useful in examining a research model that has been proposed on a theoretical basis. The biggest limitation of cross-section data is that they generally do not allow the testing of causal relationships, except when an experiment is embedded within a cross-sectional survey. Cross-sectional data are not also appropriate for examining changes over a period of time.
see also SIMULTANEOUS CROSS-SECTIONAL STUDY, REPEATED CROSS-SECTIONAL STUDY
 Ary et al. 2010; Cohen et al. 2011; Dörnyei 2007; Lavrakas 2008; Ravid 2011

cross-sectional research
another name for CROSS-SECTIONAL STUDY

cross-sectional survey
another name for CROSS-SECTIONAL STUDY

cross-tabulation table
another term for CONTINGENCY TABLE

cross-validation
a procedure for applying the results of statistical analysis from one SAMPLE of subjects to a new sample of subjects in order to assess the RELIABILITY of the estimated parameters. It is frequently used in REGRESSION and other multivariate statistical procedures (see MULTIVARIATE ANALYSIS).
 Sahai & Khurshid 2001

CRT
an abbreviation for CRITERION-REFERENCED TEST

crude realism
another term for NAIVE REALISM

crude score
　another term for RAW SCORE

CTT
　an abbreviation for CLASSICAL TEST THEORY

cube
　a number that is multiplied by itself three times. For example, 2.7 cubed is written as 2.7^3 and means $2.7 \times 2.7 \times 2.7 = 19.683$. Another way of putting it is to say 2.7 to the power of 3. It is also 2.7 to the exponent of 3. It is occasionally met with in statistical calculations though not the common ones.
　📖 Cramer & Howitt 2004

cultural portrait
　see ETHNOGRAPHY

cultural validity
　a type of VALIDITY which is related to ECOLOGICAL VALIDITY. This is particularly an issue in cross-cultural, inter-cultural and comparative kinds of research, where the intention is to shape research so that it is appropriate to the culture of the researched, and where the researcher and the researched are members of different cultures. Cultural validity is defined as the degree to which a study is appropriate to the cultural setting where research is to be carried out. Cultural validity applies at all stages of the research, and affects its planning, implementation and dissemination. It involves a degree of sensitivity to the participants, cultures, and circumstances being studied.
　Cultural validity entails an appreciation of the cultural values of those being researched. This could include: understanding possibly different target culture attitudes to research; identifying and understanding salient terms as used in the target culture; reviewing appropriate target language literature; choosing research instruments that are acceptable to the target participants; checking interpretations and translations of data with native speakers; and being aware of one's own cultural filters as a researcher.
　📖 Cohen et al. 2011

cumulative frequency
　also *cf*
　a FREQUENCY which accumulates by incorporating earlier values in the range. In a cumulative frequency distribution, the cumulative frequency for a given score represents the frequency of a score plus the frequencies of all scores which are less than that score. A distribution showing the

cumulative frequency of all scores is called a **cumulative frequency distribution**. It can be presented in a table or graph.

X	Frequency (f)	Cumulative frequency	Cumulative proportion	Cumulative percentage
15	3	20	20/20 = 1	100%
14	2	17	17/20 = .85	85%
13	2	15	15/20 = .75	75%
12	0	13	13/20 = .65	65%
11	4	13	13/20 = .65	65%
10	2	9	9/20 = .45	45%
9	1	7	7/20 = .35	35%
8	0	6	6/20 = .30	30%
7	4	6	6/20 = .30	30%
6	2	2	2/20 = .10	10%
	N = 20			

Table C.5. A Cumulative Frequency Distribution

Table C.5 represents a cumulative frequency distribution for a distribution comprised of $N = 20$ scores. Each of the scores that occur in the distribution is listed in the first column (X). Scores are arranged ordinally, with the lowest score at the bottom of the distribution, and the highest score at the top of the distribution. The cumulative frequency for the lowest score will simply be the frequency for that score, since there are no scores below it. To get the cumulative frequency for the next higher score, 7 in this case, we add its frequency (4) to the frequency of the previous score (2), which gives us a cumulative frequency of (6) (4+2). Following this procedure, we get cumulative frequencies of (6) (6+0) for a score of 8 and (7) (6+1) for a score of 9, and so on, up to 20 for the top score, 15. The cumulative frequency for the highest score will always equal N, the total number of scores in the distribution. In some instances a cumulative frequency distribution may present cumulative proportions (which can also be expressed as probabilities) or cumulative percentages in lieu of and/or in addition to cumulative frequencies. A **cumulative proportion** for a score is obtained by dividing the cumulative frequency of the score by N. A cumulative proportion is converted into a **cumulative percentage** by moving the decimal point for the proportion two places to the right. A cumulative proportion or percentage for a given score represents the proportion or percentage of scores that are equal to or less than that score. When the term cumulative probability is employed, it means the likelihood of obtaining a given score or any score below it (which is numerically equivalent to the cumulative proportion

for that score). The cumulative frequency which is expressed as a proportion or percentage of the total number of values is known as **cumulative relative frequency**.
📖 Sahai & Khurshid 2001; Sheskin 2011

cumulative frequency distribution
see CUMULATIVE FREQUENCY

cumulative frequency polygon
see FREQUENCY POLYGON

cumulative percentage
see CUMULATIVE FREQUENCY

cumulative proportion
see CUMULATIVE FREQUENCY

cumulative relative frequency
see CUMULATIVE FREQUENCY

cumulative relative frequency polygon
see FREQUENCY POLYGON

cumulative scale
also **Guttman scaling**
a RATING SCALE consisting of a series of statements to which a respondent expresses his/her agreement or disagreement. The special feature of this type of scale is that statements form a cumulative series. This, in other words, means that the statements are related to one another in such a way that an individual, who replies favorably to say item No. 3, also replies favorably to items No. 2 and 1, and one who replies favorably to item No. 4 also replies favorably to items No. 3, 2 and 1, and so on. This being so an individual whose attitude is at a certain point in a cumulative scale will answer favorably all the items on one side of this point, and answer unfavorably all the items on the other side of this point. The individual's score is worked out by counting the number of points concerning the number of statements s/he answers favorably. If one knows this total score, one can estimate as to how a respondent has answered individual statements constituting cumulative scales. The major scale of this type of cumulative scales is the **Guttman's scalogram**. The technique is also known as **scalogram analysis**, or at times simply **scale analysis**. It refers to the procedure for determining whether a set of items forms a **unidimensional scale**. A scale is said to be unidimensional if the responses fall into a pattern in which endorsement of the item reflecting

the extreme position results also in endorsing all items which are less extreme. Under this technique, the respondents are asked to indicate in respect of each item whether they agree or disagree with it (see Table C.5).

Table C.5. A Response Pattern in Scalogram Analysis

Item number				Respondent score
4	3	2	1	
X	X	X	X	4
–	X	X	X	3
–	–	X	X	2
–	–	–	X	1
–	–	–	–	0

X = Agree
– = Disagree

A score of 4 means that the respondent is in agreement with all the statements which is indicative of the most favorable attitude. But a score of 3 would mean that the respondent is not agreeable to item 4, but s/he agrees with all others. In the same way one can interpret other values of the respondents' scores. This pattern reveals that the universe of content is scalable.
see also LIKERT SCALE, SEMANTIC DIFFERENTIAL SCALE, DIFFERENTIAL SCALE, ARBITRARY SCALE
📖 Kothari 2008

Curriculum Vitae
see RÉSUMÉ

curvilinearity
a term which denotes a *nonlinear* relationship. In a curvilinear relationship, as the values of X increase, the values of Y increase up to a point, at which further increases in X are associated with decreases in Y. Curvilinearity, unlike LINEARITY, might occur when the points plotted form a curve rather than a straight line (e.g., the CORRELATION begins highly positive but finishes highly negative)—the result is not a straight line of correlation (indicating linearity) but a curved line (indicating curvilinearity). A practical way of determining whether the relationship between two VARIABLES is linear or curvilinear is to examine a SCATTERPLOT of the data. (see Figure C.14). This non-linear form of relationship is described as **polynomial relationship**. Examples of curvilinear relationships might include:

- pressure from the teacher and student achievement
- degree of challenge and student achievement
- assertiveness and success
- age and muscular strength
- age and concentration
- age and cognitive abilities.
- room temperature and comfort

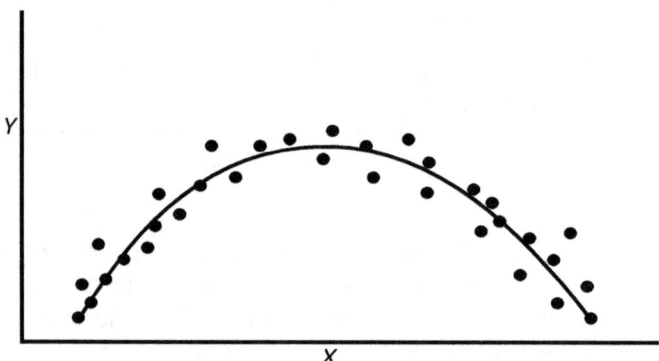

Figure C.14. *An Example of a Curvilinear Relationship*

It is suggested that the variable *age* frequently has a curvilinear relationship with other variables, and that poorly constructed tests can give the appearance of curvilinearity if the test is too easy (a CEILING EFFECT where most students score highly) or if it is too difficult, but that this curvilinearity is, in fact, spurious, as the test does not demonstrate sufficient item difficulty or discriminability.

The usually recommended CORRELATION COEFFICIENT for curvilinear data is ETA (η), which is related to ANOVA. The PEARSON CORRELATION COEFFICIENT is not suitable when the relationship is curvilinear. Under certain circumstances it is possible to transform one or both of the variables in a non-linear relationship so that the relationship becomes linear and then PEARSON *r* can be applied to the data.

In planning CORRELATIONAL RESEARCH, then, attention will need to be given to whether linearity or curvilinearity is to be assumed.

📖 Ary et al. 2010; Cohen et al. 2011; Heiman 2011; Howell 2010

cut point
see CRITERION-REFERENCED TEST

CV
an abbreviation for COEFFICIENT OF VARIATION

D

d
an abbreviation for COHEN'S *d*

data
information collected in a research study. Data may be oral and recorded onto audio and/or videotapes; they may be written, in the forms of essays, test scores, diaries, or check marks on OBSERVATION SCHEMEs; they may appear in electronic format, such as responses to a computer-assisted accent modification program; or they may be visual, in the form of eye movements made while reading text at a computer or gestures made by a teacher in a classroom. Different kinds of data require different approaches to statistical analysis.
see also MEASUREMENT SCALE, DATA CODING
📖 Porte 2010

data analysis
the process of reducing accumulated data collected in research to a manageable size, developing summaries, looking for patterns, and performing statistical analysis. Quantitative data are usually in the form of numbers that researchers analyze using various statistical procedures. Even verbal data, such as compositions written by high school students, would be converted through the scoring process to a numerical form. The analysis of the numerical data in QUANTITATIVE RESEARCH provides evidence that supports or fails to support the HYPOTHESIS of the study. Based on the number of variables under investigation, UNIVARIATE ANALYSIS, BIVARIATE ANALYSIS, and MULTIVARIATE ANALYSIS are used for analysis of quantitative data.

In contrast, qualitative data generally take the form of words (descriptions, observations, impressions, recordings, and the like). Examples include responses to open-ended questions on a survey, the transcript from an interview or focus group session, notes from a log or diary, or field notes. Data might come from many people, a few individuals, or a single case.

The researcher must organize and categorize or code the large mass of data so that they can be described and interpreted. Although the qualitative researcher does not deal with statistics, analyzing qualitative data is not easy. It is a time-consuming and painstaking process.
see also GROUNDED THEORY, CONVERSATION ANALYSIS, CODING
📖 Ary et al. 2010

data codebook
another term for CODEBOOK

data coding
a research technique and procedure in which data that have been collected are turned into classes or categories (i.e., codes) for the purpose of counting or tabulation. Once data are collected, it is necessary to organize them into a manageable, easily understandable, and analyzable base of information, and searching for and marking patterns in the data. When researchers code, they are trying to make sense of the data by systematically looking through it, clustering or grouping together similar ideas, phenomena, people, or events, and labeling them. Coding helps researchers find similar patterns and connections across the data. It helps researchers get to know the data better and to organize their thinking, and it also makes storage and retrieval of data easier. Some types of data can be considered ready for analysis immediately after collection; for example, language test scores such as those from the TOEFL. However, for other types of data, after they are collected they need to be prepared for coding.
There is a wide range of different types of data in applied linguistics research. One common type of data is oral. Oral data may come from a range of sources, including, for example, native speaker-learner interviews, learners in pairs carrying out communicative tasks in a laboratory setting, or learners in small groups and their teacher in a noisy second language classroom setting. Oral data usually need to be transcribed in some way for coding and analysis. Transcriptions of oral data can yield rich and extensive second language data, but in order to make sense of them they must be coded in a principled manner.
Data coding entails looking for and marking patterns in data regardless of modality. Therefore, the first step of data processing involves converting the respondents' answers to numbers by means of coding procedures. Because numbers are meaningless in themselves and are too easy to mix up, a major element of the coding phase is to define each variable and then to compile coding specifications for every possible value that the particular variable can take. It is important to note that there is a range of different types of MEASUREMENT SCALEs that a researcher might employ in applied linguistics research. Naturally, the way the data are coded depends in part on the scales used to measure the variables. NOMINAL DATA include cases in which entities may be the same or different but not more or less, as an example, the part of speech of a given word in a particular sentence, or interpretation of a sentence, is a nominal variable: a word either can be classified as an adjective or it cannot. In general, there are two ways nominal data can be coded, depending on whether the research

involves a DICHOTOMOUS VARIABLE (i.e., a variable with only two values, e.g., + /- native speaker) or a variable with several values. When dealing with dichotomous variables, researchers may choose to employ signs such as + or -. Alternatively, and particularly when working with a computer-based statistical program such as SPSS, researchers may wish to use numerical values (e.g., 1 and 2). If the data are not dichotomous and the researcher has to deal with a variable with several values, additional numbers can be used to represent membership in particular categories. For instance, to code the native languages of each of these fictional study participants, a numerical value could be assigned to each of the languages spoken (e.g., Arabic = 1, English= 2, German = 3, Spanish = 4, etc.).

ORDINAL DATA are usually coded in terms of a ranking. For example, with a data set consisting of test scores from a group of 100 students, one way to code these data would be to rank them in terms of highest to lowest scores. The student with the highest score would be ranked 1, whereas the student with the lowest would be ranked 100. In this scenario, when multiple students have identical scores, ranks are typically split. For example, if two learners each received the fourth highest score on the test, they would both be ranked as 3.5. Alternatively, instead of using a 100-item list, the scores could be divided into groups (e.g., the top 25%) and each group assigned a number. For example, a 1 would signify that the individual scored within the top 25%, whereas a 4 would show that the participant scored in the bottom 25%.

Dividing learners into ranked groups can be particularly useful when using a test where the researcher does not have full confidence in the fine details of the scoring. For instance, a researcher may not believe that a student who scores 88 is very much better than a student who scores only 80. In this case, an ordinal scale could be the appropriate way of indicating that the two students are close together, and better than the other groups, without making claims about differences between those students. ORDINAL SCALEs can also be used to roughly separate learners from each other; for example, in a study using a battery of second language working memory tests, the researcher might be interested in examining the data from learners with high and low working memory scores more closely, but might wish to discount the data from learners in the middle-range scores on the basis that they are not differentiated clearly enough. In this case, the middle 50 percent of learners could be assigned as middle scorers, and only data from students in the top and bottom 25% would be used. There could also be several other cut-off points besides the exact test scores used for the ranking, including points based on measures of CENTRAL TENDENCY.

INTERVAL SCALEs, like ordinal scales, also represent a rank ordering. However, in addition, they show the interval, or distance, between points in the ranking. Thus, instead of simply ordering the scores of the test, we could present the actual scores in a table. This would allow us to see not only which scores are higher or lower (as in the ordinal scale), but also the degree to which they differ. Other data that are typically coded in this way include age, number of years of schooling, and number of years of language study. It should be kept in mind, however, that the impact on learning may be different at different intervals. For example, the difference between scores 1 and 10 may have the same interval as those between 90 and 100 on a test, but the impact is quite different. Similarly, the difference between 2 and 3 years of instruction may be the same interval as the difference between 9 and 10 years. In each case, the difference is only 1 year, but that year might be very different in terms of the impact on language production for a learner who is at the advanced, near-native stage, as compared to a learner who is in the early stages of acquisition. These are issues that merit careful consideration in the coding stages of a research study.

A number of coding units or categories for oral and written data have been proposed over the years. Three of the most common of these are T-UNIT, SUPPLIANCE IN OBLIGATORY CONTEXTS, and CHAT. Regardless of the potential utility of standard coding systems in increasing the generalizability of findings, the goal is always to ascertain how best to investigate one's own research questions.
 Mackey & Gass 2005

data screening

an initial examination of a data set to check for any errors or discrepancies in the data. The technique is also useful for checking the quality of the data and identifying any possible OUTLIERs.
 Sahai & Khurshid 2001

data transformation

a mathematical procedure or adjustment which is applied to scores in an attempt to make the DISTRIBUTION of the scores fit requirements. Data transformations are used to correct for the violations of ASSUMPTIONS of a statistical procedure. Conclusions derived from the statistical analyses performed on the transformed data are generally applicable to the original data. Data transformation involves performing a mathematical operation on each of the scores in a set of data, and thereby converting the data into a new set of scores which are then employed to analyze the results of an experiment. Adding 5 to each score is a transformation or converting *number correct* into *percent correct* is a transformation.

Data transformation has some advantages: in addition to making scores easier to work with and more comparable, data transformation allows the researcher reduce the impact of OUTLIERs; it can be also employed to equate heterogeneous group variances, as well as to normalize a nonnormal distribution. In fact, a transformation which results in HOMOGENEITY OF VARIANCEs, at the same time often normalizes data.

More specifically, most statistical procedures assume that the variables being analyzed are normally distributed. Analyzing variables that are not normally distributed can lead to serious overestimation or underestimation (see TYPE I ERROR). Therefore, before analyzing their data, researchers should carefully examine variable distributions. Although this is often done by simply looking over the FREQUENCY DISTRIBUTIONs, there are many, more objective methods of determining whether variables are normally distributed. Typically, these involve examining each variable's skewness (see SKEWED DISTRIBUTION), and whether it looks the same to the left and right of the center point and its KURTOSIS. Many variables within particular sample populations are not normally distributed. Therefore, researchers often rely on one of several transformations to potentially improve the normality of certain variables. For example, if the data form a negatively skewed distribution then squaring each score could reduce the skew and then it would be permissible to employ a parametric test on the data. If you are using a statistical test that looks for differences between the means of different levels of an INDEPENDENT VARIABLE then you must use the same transformation on all the data. The most frequently used transformations are the SQUARE ROOT TRANSFORMATION, LOG TRANSFORMATION, and RECIPROCAL TRANSFORMATION.
📖 Clark-Carter 2010; Marczyk et al. 2005; Sheskin 2011

data triangulation
a type of TRIANGULATION in which the researcher investigates whether the data collected with one procedure or instrument confirm data collected using a different procedure or instrument. The researcher wants to find support for the observations and conclusions in more than one data source. Convergence of a major theme or pattern in the data from these various sources lends CREDIBILITY to the findings. Generally, data triangulation involves the application of time and space for data collection. **Space triangulation** attempts to overcome the parochialism of studies conducted in the same country or within the same subculture by making use of cross-cultural techniques. The vast majority of studies in our field are conducted at one point only in time, thereby ignoring the effects of social change and process. **Time triangulation** goes some way to rectifying these omissions by making use of CROSS-SECTIONAL and LONGITUDINAL RESEARCH methods. The use of PANEL STUDIes and TREND STUDIes may also be mentioned in this connection. The weaknesses of each of

these methods can be strengthened by using a combined approach to a given problem.
see also INVESTIGATOR TRIANGULATION, THEORETICAL TRIANGULATION, METHODOLOGICAL TRIANGULATION
 Cohen et al. 2011

debriefing

the procedure through which research participants are told about the nature of a study after it is completed. Debriefing of participants takes place at the conclusion of the study, and it involves revealing the purposes of the research. It should be done as soon as possible after completion of the study, preferably immediately after participation. It is important to provide a written debriefing so that participants leave the research experience with a tangible description of the activities they just performed. An oral debriefing is also recommended if the research participation was stressful or the research design was complicated.

A good debriefing accomplishes four goals. First, the debriefing clarifies the nature of the study for participants. Although the researcher may have withheld certain information at the beginning of the study, the participant should be more fully informed after it is over. This does not require that the researcher give a lecture regarding the area of research, only that the participant leave the study with a sense of what was being studied and how his/her participation contributed to knowledge in an area.

The second goal of debriefing is to remove any stress or other negative consequences that the study may have induced. For example, if participants were provided with false feedback about their performance on a test, the deception should be explained. In cases in which participants have been led to perform embarrassing or socially undesirable actions, researchers must be sure that participants leave with no bad feelings about what they have done.

A third goal of the debriefing is for the researcher to obtain participants' reactions to the study itself. Often, if carefully probed, participants will reveal that they did not understand part of the instructions, were suspicious about aspects of the procedure, were disturbed by the study, or had heard about the study from other people. Such revelations may require modifications in the procedure.

The fourth goal of a debriefing is more intangible. Participants should leave the study feeling good about their participation. Researchers should convey their genuine appreciation for participants' time and cooperation, and give participants the sense that their participation was important.

The debriefing can be done in person, upon completion of the study, or it can be done via correspondence (surface mail or email) after the researchers have completed some of their analyses. Waiting until this point

has the disadvantage of providing delayed rather than immediate feedback, but it has the advantage of providing the participants with interesting, first-hand knowledge of the study findings.
📖 Leary 2011; VanderStoep & Johnston 2009

deception
a research technique in which participants are misinformed about the true nature and purpose of a study. Deception is ethical if the researcher can demonstrate that important results cannot be obtained in any other way. It is often difficult to find naturalistic situations in which certain behaviors occur frequently. For example, a researcher may have to wait a long time for a teacher to reinforce students in a certain way. It may be much easier for the researcher to observe the effects of such reinforcement by employing the teacher as a confederate.
📖 Bordens & Abbott 2011; Fraenkel & Wallen 2009

decile
a distribution which is divided into 10 equal parts, each of which contains 10% of the total observations (see Table D.1). The percentile points at the 10th, 20th, 30th, ..., and 90th percentiles are called the first decile ($D1$), second decile ($D2$), third decile ($D3$), ... , and ninth decile ($D9$), respectively. Thus, a score that corresponds to the 10th percentile falls at the upper limit of the first decile of the distribution. A score that corresponds to the 20th percentile falls at the upper limit of the second decile of the distribution, and so on. The **interdecile range** is the difference between the scores at the 90th percentile (the upper limit of the ninth decile) and the 10th percentile.
see also PERCENTILE, QUARTILE QUINTILE
📖 Sahai & Khurshid 2001; Sheskin 2011

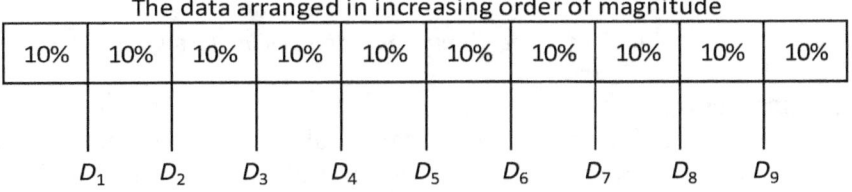

Table D.1. Schematic Representation of Deciles of a Data Set

decimals
a convenient way of writing fractions or fractions of numbers without using the fraction notation. Fractions are simply parts of whole numbers such as a half, a fifth, a tenth, a seventeenth, a hundredth and a thousandth—or two-fifths or three-fifths and so forth. The simplest way of

writing fractions is for example $\frac{2}{5}$ or $\frac{7}{12}$ though this is not used generally in statistics. For many purposes this sort of notation is fine. The difficulty with it is that one cannot directly add fractions together. Decimals are a notational system for expressing fractions of numbers as tenths, hundredths, thousands, etc., which greatly facilitates the addition of fractions. In the decimal system, there are whole numbers followed by a dot which is then followed by the fraction:

$$17.5$$

In the above number, 17 is the whole number, the dot indicates the beginning that a fraction will follow and the number after the dot indicates the size of the fraction. The first number after the dot is the number of tenths that there are. In the above example we therefore have five tenths which is $\frac{5}{10}$ which simplifies to $\frac{1}{2}$ or a half. The following number has three numbers after the decimal point:

$$14.623$$

The first number 6 is the number of tenths. The second number 2 is the number of hundredths, and the final 3 refers to the number of thousandths. Thus, in full $14.623 = 14$ and $\frac{6}{10}$ and $\frac{2}{100}$ and $\frac{3}{1000}$. This is actually the same as 14 and $\frac{623}{1000}$. The system goes on to the number of ten thousandths, the number of hundred thousandths, millionths and beyond. Table D.2 illustrates the components of the decimal number 423.7591.
📖 Cramer & Howitt 2004

4	2	3	.	7	5	9	1
Four hundred	Twenty	three	Decimal point	Seven tenth	five hundredth	Nine thousandth	One ten thousandth

Table D.2. The Components of a Decimal Number

deconstruction
a method of philosophical and literary analysis which questions the fundamental conceptual distinctions, or oppositions, in Western philosophy through a close examination of the language and logic of philosophical and literary texts. The commonsense notion of knowledge is that it consists of signs that systematically represent objective and subjective states of affairs. Accurate representation is then believed to ground the meaning of signs (e.g., words, symbols, languages). This ensures that repeated use of signs will mean the same thing to the extent that what they represent will be more or less stable. But deconstruction reverses this commonsense perspective, showing that it is the repetition of signs that gen-

erates belief in objectivity and subjectivity (as categories that transcend sign systems). Nothing is really outside of a text. And texts iterate, mutate, and shift without direction, intention, or purpose. Deconstruction is an artful strategy rather than a method per se, for if it were formulated explicitly enough to be called a method, it would be deconstructable itself. It has been used to deconstruct highly influential theories and philosophies that subtly privilege masculinity over femininity, science over art, mind over body, and other binaries that have supported/constituted power relations in modernity.
📖 Given 2008

DCT
an abbreviation for DISCOURSE COMPLETION TEST

deductive inference
another term for DEDUCTIVE REASONING

deductive reasoning
also **deductive inference**
a mode of reasoning that uses a top-down approach to knowing. Researchers use deductive reasoning by first making a general statement (HYPOTHESIS) based on a theory and then seeking specific evidence that would support or disconfirm that statement (see Figure D.1). They employ what is known as the **hypothetic-deductive method** or **hypothesis-testing method**, which begins by forming a hypothesis.

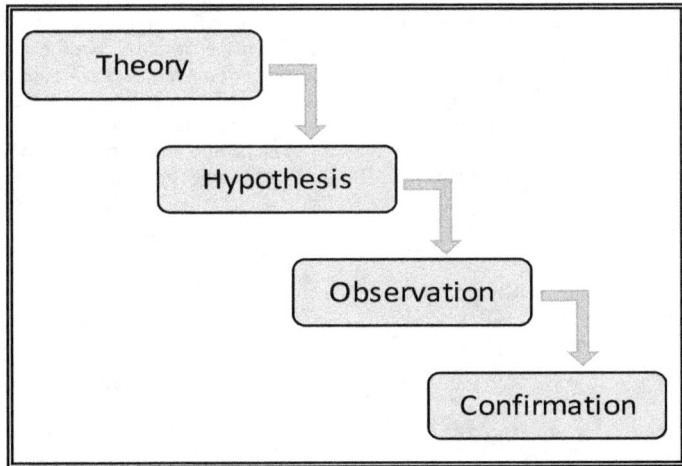

Figure D.1. Schematic Representation of Deductive Reasoning

For example, one might hypothesize that small classes would result in a greater amount of student learning than large classes. This hypothesis would be based on a theory or a knowledge base composed of the results of previous research studies. The next step in the hypothetic-deductive approach is to collect data to see if the hypothesis is true or should be rejected as false. And finally, the researcher makes a decision based on the data to either accept or reject the hypothesis or prediction. As such, deductive approach is sometimes called **confirmatory research**, which tries to find evidence to support (i.e., confirm) a hypothesis.

The hypothetic-deductive method is most closely associated with quantitative approaches, which summarize data using numbers. Hypotheses and methods of data collection in QUANTITATIVE RESEARCH are created before the research begins. Hypotheses or theories are then tested, and when supported, these hypotheses or theories are typically considered to be generalizable, i.e., applicable to a wide range of similar situations and populations (see GENERALIZABILITY, EXTERNAL VALIDITY).

see INDUCTIVE REASONING, HYPOTHESIS TESTING
Lodico et al. 2010

degrees of freedom
also *df*, v

the minimum amount of data needed to calculate a statistic. The number of degrees of freedom, abbreviated *df*, and also denoted by v (the lower-case Greek letter *nu*, pronounced *new*), in a DISTRIBUTION is the number of independent units of information in a SAMPLE that are free to vary in calculating a statistic when certain restrictions are imposed on the data set. Degrees of freedom measure the quantity of information available in sample data for estimating the POPULATION PARAMETERs. It is a characteristic of the statistic being employed and is equal to the number of values that can be freely chosen when calculating the statistic. To illustrate, suppose a teacher asks a student to name any five numbers that come into his/her mind. The student would be free to name any five numbers s/he chooses, so we would say that the student has 5 degrees of freedom. Now suppose the teacher tells the student to name five numbers but to make sure that the mean of these five numbers is 20. The student now is free to name any numbers for the first four, but for the last number s/he must name the number that will make the total for the five numbers 100 in order to arrive at a MEAN of 20. If the student names, as the first four numbers, 10, 16, 20, and 35, then the fifth number must be 19. The student has five numbers to name and one restriction, so his/her degrees of freedom are 5 - 1 = 4. We can show this as a formula:

$$df = N - 1$$
$$= 5 - 1$$
$$= 4$$

Now suppose the teacher asks the student to name seven numbers in such a way that the first three have a mean of 10 and all seven have a mean of 12. Here, we have seven numbers and two restrictions, so

$$df = N - 2$$
$$= 7 - 2$$
$$= 5$$

When the unknown population STANDARD DEVIATION is estimated from the sample standard deviation, one degree of freedom is lost. The one degree of freedom is lost because the sample statistic (s) is derived from the deviations about the sample mean that must always sum to 0. Thus, all but one of the deviations is free to vary, or $df = N - 1$.
The appropriate degree of freedom for each statistical procedure appears with the formula defining the test statistic. For example, in a 2 × 2 (two-by-two) CONTINGENCY TABLE with fixed MARGINALs, only one of the four cell frequencies is free to vary, and therefore the table has single degree of freedom associated with it. Often, the number of degrees of freedom on which a SAMPLE STATISTIC is based depends on the SAMPLE SIZE (N) and the number of sample statistics used in its calculation. Whenever the t DISTRIBUTION is used to make inferences about a POPULATION MEAN with unknown variance, the required t distribution has $N - 1$ degrees of freedom. Similarly, in order to consult tables of CRITICAL VALUEs, the researcher needs to know the degrees of freedom.
📖 Ary et al. 2010; Best & Kahn 2006; Larson-Hall 2010

deliberate sampling
another term for PURPOSIVE SAMPLING

delphi technique
the written partner to the NOMINAL GROUP TECHNIQUE. This technique has the advantage that it does not require participants to meet together as a whole group. This is particularly useful in institutions where time is precious and where it is difficult to arrange a whole group meeting. The process of data collection resembles that of the nominal group technique in many respects: it can be set out in a three-stage process:

1) The leader asks participants to respond to a series of questions and statements in writing. This may be done on an individual basis or on a small group basis—which enables it to be used flexibly, e.g., within a department, within an age phase.
2) The leader collects the written responses and collates them into clusters of issues and responses (maybe providing some numerical data

on frequency of response). This analysis is then passed back to the respondents for comment, further discussion and identification of issues, responses and priorities. At this stage the respondents are presented with a group response (which may reflect similarities or record differences) and the respondents are asked to react to this group response. By adopting this procedure the individual has the opportunity to agree with the group response (i.e., to move from a possibly small private individual disagreement to a general group agreement) or to indicate a more substantial disagreement with the group response.

3) This process is repeated as many times as it is necessary. In saying this, however, the leader will need to identify the most appropriate place to stop the recirculation of responses. This might be done at a group meeting which, it is envisaged, will be the plenary session for the participants, i.e., an endpoint of data collection will be in a whole group forum.

By presenting the group response back to the participants, there is a general progression in the technique towards a polarizing of responses, i.e., a clear identification of areas of consensus and dissensus. The Delphi technique brings advantages of clarity, privacy, voice, and collegiality. In doing so it engages the issues of confidentiality, anonymity, and disclosure of relevant information while protecting participants' rights to privacy. It is a very useful means of undertaking behind-the-scenes data collection which can then be brought to a whole group meeting; the price that this exacts is that the leader has much more work to do in collecting, synthesizing, collating, summarizing, prioritizing, and recirculating data than in the nominal group technique, which is immediate. As participatory techniques both the nominal group technique and Delphi techniques are valuable for data collection and analysis in ACTION RESEARCH.
 Cohen et al. 2011

demoralization
also **resentful demoralization, compensatory demoralization**
a potential threat to EXTERNAL VALIDITY when the TREATMENT under study is sufficiently attractive that being assigned to the CONTROL GROUP is aversive. In this case, the control participants, because they were not given the desirable treatment, might be resentful or demoralized and put forth less effort than the members of the other group and this demoralization might affect their performance on the OUTCOME VARIABLE so as to bias the results of the study. Researchers sometimes avoid this source of bias either by promising to give the same treatment to the control participants after the study is completed or by providing services to the control

group that are equally attractive but not directed to the same outcomes as the experimental treatment.
📖 Ary et al. 2010; Bickman & Rog 1998; Cook & Campbell 1979

denominator
see NUMERATOR

density curve
another term for PROBABILITY DENSITY CURVE

dependability
the degree to which the results reported in a study can be trusted or are reliable. Dependability, the qualitative counterpart of RELIABILITY, can be regarded as a fit between what researchers record as data and what actually occurs in the natural setting that is being researched, i.e., a degree of accuracy and comprehensiveness of coverage. This is not to strive for uniformity; two researchers who are studying a single setting may come up with very different findings but both sets of findings might be reliable. In qualitative methodologies dependability includes fidelity to real life, context- and situation-specificity, authenticity, comprehensiveness, detail, honesty, depth of response and meaningfulness to the respondents. In reporting qualitative studies, researchers need to provide a rich description of the subjects involved in the study, the context for the study, and, most importantly, all of the steps the researcher took to carry out the study. Researchers also have to be certain that in selecting examples to illustrate particular conclusions, they select representative examples from their data rather than unusual or surprising instances.
Some strategies to investigate dependability are using an AUDIT TRAIL, TRIANGULATION, replication logic, stepwise replication, code-recoding, and interrater comparisons. To enhance reliability, the researcher wants to demonstrate that the methods used are reproducible and consistent, that the approach and procedures used were appropriate for the context and can be documented, and that external evidence can be used to test conclusions.
Dependability can be demonstrated by showing consistent findings across multiple settings or multiple investigators. Replication logic, which involves conducting the study in multiple locations or with multiple groups, is suggested for determining dependability of a study. According to this logic, the more times a finding is found true with different sets of people or in different settings and time periods, the more confident the researcher can be in the conclusions. Stepwise replication is another technique suggested for enhancing dependability. In this strategy, two investigators divide the data, analyze it independently, and then

compare results. Consistency of results provides evidence of dependability.

Intrarater and interrater agreement are strategies for assessing dependability (reliability). An intrarater method is the code-recode strategy: A researcher codes the data, leaves the analysis for a period of time, and then comes back and recodes the data and compares the two sets of coded materials. Because much qualitative research involves observation by multiple observers, some researchers suggest interrater or interobserver agreement methods for assessing dependability. For example, a researcher might randomly select a transcript and ask a peer to code the transcript using the coding labels identified by the researcher. The second coder would be free to add other codes s/he might identify. After the peer completes coding of the transcripts, the results are compared to the original coded transcript to determine whether both coders labeled components of the transcript the same.

see also TRANSFERABILITY, CONFIRMABILITY, CREDIBILITY, OBJECTIVITY

📖 Ary et al. 2010; Cohen et al. 2011; McKay 2006

dependent groups
another term for DEPENDENT SAMPLES

dependent samples
also **paired samples, matched samples, correlated samples, dependent groups, paired groups, matched groups, correlated groups, related groups, related samples**

groups of one or more SAMPLEs in which the values in one sample are related to the values in the other sample. Two samples are dependent when the method of sample selection is such that those individuals selected for sample 1 do have a relationship to those individuals selected for sample 2. In other words, the selections of individuals to be included in the two samples are correlated. You might think of the samples as being selected simultaneously such that there are actually pairs of individuals. For example, we have two dependent samples if the same individuals are measured at two points in time, such as during a pretest and a posttest. The scores on Y at time 1 will be correlated with the scores on Y at time 2 because the same individuals are assessed at both time points. Similarly, if subjects are matched or paired on relevant VARIABLEs first and then randomly assigned to treatments then we have two dependent samples. These may be IQ, mental age, socioeconomic status, age, gender, reading, pretest score, or other variables known to be related to the dependent variable of the study. In both cases we have natural pairs of individuals or scores. The extent to which the samples are independent or dependent determines the appropriate inferential test.

see also INDEPENDENT SAMPLES
📖 Lomax 2007

dependent samples design
another term for WITHIN-SUBJECTS DESIGN

dependent samples *t*-test
another term for PAIRED-SAMPLES *t*-TEST

dependent variable
also **criterion variable, response variable, explained variable, outcome variable, *Y* variable, effect variable**
a VARIABLE which is observed to determine what effect the other types of variables may have on it. The dependent variables (DVs) are the conditions or characteristics that appear, disappear, or change as the experimenter introduces, removes, or changes the INDEPENDENT VARIABLEs (IVs). For example, if you wanted to study the construct 'communicative competence' of a group of students, then the dependent variable is the construct and it might be operationalized as your students' scores or ratings on some measure of communicative competence. We expect performance on the dependent variable will be influenced by other variables. That is, it is dependent in relation to other variables in the study. Thus, the DVs are the measured changes attributable to the influence of the IVs. The distinction between dependent and independent variables is typically made on theoretical grounds to test a particular model of cause-effect HYPOTHESIS. It is also possible to have more than two DVs in an experiment. Typically, experiments involving two or more DVs are evaluated with multivariate statistical procedures (see MULTIVARIATE ANALYSIS). In NONEXPERIMENTAL RESEARCH, it is often more common to label the DV as the *criterion* or *response* variable.
see also MODERATOR VARIABLE, INTERVENING VARIABLE, CATEGORICAL VARIABLE, CONTINUOUS VARIABLE, EXTRANEOUS VARIABLE, CONFOUNDING VARIABLE
📖 Best & Kahn 2006; Hatch & Lazaraton 1991; Larson-Hall 2010; Porte 2010; Sheskin 2011; Urdan 2010

derived score
see RAW SCORE

descriptive discriminative analysis
see DISCRIMINANT ANALYSIS

descriptive realism
another term for NAIVE REALISM

descriptive research
an investigation that provides a picture of a phenomenon as it naturally occurs, as opposed to studying the impacts of the phenomenon or intervention. Descriptive research attempts to looks at individuals, groups, institutions, methods and materials in order to describe, compare, contrast, classify, analyze, and interpret the entities and the events that constitute their various fields of inquiry. It is concerned with conditions or relationships that exist; practices that prevail; beliefs, points of views, or attitudes that are held; processes that are going on; effects that are being felt; or trends that are developing. At times, descriptive research is concerned with how what is or what exists is related to some preceding event that has influenced or affected a present condition or event.
Descriptive research deals with the relationships between variables, the testing of hypotheses, and the development of generalizations, principles, or theories that have universal validity. The expectation is that, if variable A is systematically associated with variable B, prediction of future phenomena may be possible, and the results may suggest additional or competing hypotheses to test.
Descriptive research is used to establish the existence of phenomena by explicitly describing them, for example, the research may attempt to establish the existence of a specific strategy used by learners in which HYPOTHESIS-TESTING is involved. Descriptive research may provide measures of frequency, for example, of the occurrence of a particular syntactic form in the speech of second language learners at some stage in development. It is important to emphasize that while this type of research may begin with a question or HYPOTHESIS, the phenomena it describes are not manipulated or artificially elicited in any way.
Descriptive research shares characteristics with both QUALITATIVE and QUANTITATIVE RESEARCH. It is similar to qualitative research because it deals with naturally occurring phenomena, using data which may either be collected first hand or taken from already existing data sources such as data from other studies, student records, and so on, without intervention of an experiment or an artificially contrived treatment. It differs from qualitative research in that it often begins with preconceived hypotheses and a narrower scope of investigation and uses the logical methods of inductive or deductive reasoning to arrive at the generalizations. In this respect, it shares some of the qualities of quantitative research. The essential difference between descriptive and quantitative research is that descriptive research can be either *synthetic* (i.e., a holistic approach which attempts to capture the whole phenomenon) or *analytic* (an approach which focuses on the role of the constituents parts that make up the total phenomenon) in its approach to language phenomena being studied, while quantitative research must be analytic. Both types of

research can be hypothesis-driven, in that researcher starts with a theory or a specific research question. An equally important distinction between them is that in descriptive research no manipulation of naturally occurring phenomena occurs, while in quantitative research, manipulation and control become important measures of both internal and external validity.

Descriptive research is sometimes divided into CORRELATIONAL RESEARCH and EX POST FACTO RESEARCH, and other descriptive research that is neither correlational nor designed to find causation but describes existing conditions, such as SURVEY RESEARCH and CASE STUDY.
📖 Best & Kahn 2006; Cohen et al. 2011; Seliger & Shohamy 1989

descriptive statistics

a set of statistical procedures that are used to describe, organize and summarize characteristics of SAMPLE DATA in a clear and understandable way, both numerically and graphically. Some of the descriptive statistics procedures include MEASURES OF CENTRAL TENDENCY (such as the MEAN, MODE, or MEDIAN), and VARIABILITY (typically the VARIANCE or STANDARD DEVIATION) and in graphical presentations FREQUENCY DISTRIBUTION, BAR GRAPH, HISTOGRAM, FREQUENCY POLYGON, PIE CHART, NORMAL DISTRIBUTION, and SKEWED DISTRIBUTION.
see also INFERENTIAL STATISTICS, EXPLORATORY DATA ANALYSIS
📖 Porte 2010

descriptive validity

(in QUALITATIVE RESEARCH) the factual accuracy of the researcher's account that it is not made up, selective or distorted. It is the primary aspect of VALIDITY because all the other validity categories are dependent on it. It refers to what researcher him/herself has experienced and also to secondary accounts of things that could in principle have been observed, but that were inferred from other data. One useful strategy for ensuring this validity is INVESTIGATOR TRIANGULATION, i.e., using multiple investigators to collect and interpret the data.
see also INTERPRETIVE VALIDITY, THEORETICAL VALIDITY, EVALUATIVE VALIDITY
📖 Cohen et al. 2011; Dörnyei 2007

design validity

the extent to which the design is capable of answering the research question and/or the extent to which it can eliminate alternative explanations of the stated relationship (see INTERNAL VALIDITY). If the intent of the study is to generalize, then EXTERNAL VALIDITY questions have to be answered to estimate the design validity of the study.
📖 Ridenour & Newman 2008

deterministic model
a model that proposes that behavior is determined for an individual, rather than by an individual. Proponents place much weight on the regulation of behavior by subconscious processes. A deterministic model does not involve any random or probabilistic term. It is based on a relationship between any two outcomes or variables, such that the value of one is uniquely determined whenever the value of the other is specified.
see also CHAOS THEORY
📖 Given 2008

deviation IQ
a variety of STANDARD SCORE used to report 'intelligence quotients' (IQs) with a MEAN set at 100 and a STANDARD DEVIATION set at 15.
see also NORMAL DISTRIBUTION, WECHSLER SCALES
📖 Ary et al. 2010; Coaley 2010

deviation score
see STANDARD DEVIATION

DFA
an abbreviation for DISCRIMINANT FUNCTION ANALYSIS

d family of effect size
another term for GROUP DIFFERENCE INDEX

diary study
a research technique which offers the opportunity to investigate social, psychological, and physiological processes within everyday situations and asking research participants to keep regular records of certain aspects of their daily lives allows the researcher to capture the particulars of experience in a way that is not possible using other methods. It is important to note that the term diary studies usually refers to data obtained from solicited diaries only, that is, from accounts produced specifically at the researchers request, by an informant or informants. Diaries are particularly appropriate in recording routine or everyday processes that are otherwise unnoticed if not documented.

Many *qualitative* studies use diary analysis to observe, improve, or enhance people's practices by tracking their patterns and cycles. Diaries can provide researchers with enlarged and detailed snapshots of what people have experienced. Although diary formats vary, usually they do not offer open-ended questions but rather supply participants with a specific set of fixed responses. These optional answers can be in a dichotomous (yes/no) scaled, or multiple-choice format. Likewise, diaries can be constituted in the form of logs, ledgers, or calendars. When analyzing diaries, researchers have a variety of options. Diary studies are inherently longitudinal (see LONGITUDINAL RESEARCH) as they contain data recorded over time. Diaries lend themselves to MIXED METHODS RESEARCH while also offering rich subjective data. If researchers include open-ended questions in diaries, participant responses are usually coded thematically with an eye toward emerging themes and subthemes.

For example, a diary study in second language learning, acquisition, or teaching is an account of a second language experience as recorded in a first-person journal. The diarist may be a language teacher or a language learner—but the central characteristic of the diary studies is that they are introspective: The diarist studies his/her own teaching or learning. Thus s/he can report on affective factors, language learning strategies, and his/her own perceptions—facets of the language learning experience which are normally hidden or largely inaccessible to an external observer. On the other hand, some language learning diary studies have involved a third person analyzing the diaries of language learners or teachers. These are called indirect or nonintrospective studies. These are useful when the researcher is interested in studying the learning process of a group that s/he does not belong to, such as young learners or learners of particular languages or cultural backgrounds.

Diary studies can be used as the sole form of data collection in a research project, or as just one form in a broader study, possibly to triangulate (see TRIANGULATION) the information collected using an array of data collection techniques (for example, INTERVIEWs, OBSERVATIONs, class recordings, and so on), or different sources (students, teachers, administrators) to provide a broader and richer perspective.

Diary studies have often been classified into three categories depending on when the diary entries are to be made: interval-, signal-, and event-contingent designs. The **interval-contingent design** requires participants to report on their experiences at regular, predetermined intervals (e.g., every afternoon at 4 P.M.). **Signal-contingent design**s rely on some signaling device such as a pager, or programmed wristwatch or a phone call to prompt participants to provide diary reports. This design is often used when studying momentary experiences of people such as psychological states (e.g., happiness or stress). **Event-contingent design**s require participants to provide a self-report each time a specific event (such as a meeting with a second language speaker) occurs.

see also ROTATING PANELS, SPLIT PANELS, LINKED PANELS, COHORT STUDY, ACCELERATED LONGITUDINAL DESIGN, JOURNAL
📖 Dörnyei 2007; Given 2008; McKay 2006; Scott & Morrison 2005

dichotomous question

a CLOSED-FORM ITEM which requires a 'yes'/'no' response. The layout of a dichotomous question can be thus:

Sex (please tick):   Male ☐   Female ☐

The dichotomous question is useful, for it compels respondents to come off the fence on an issue. It provides a clear, unequivocal response. Further, it is possible to code responses quickly, there being only two categories of response. A dichotomous question is also useful as a *funneling* or sorting device for subsequent questions, for example: 'If you answered *yes* to question X, please go to question Y; if you answered *no* to question X, please go to question Z'. On the other hand, the researcher must ask, for instance, whether a yes/no response actually provides any useful information. Requiring respondents to make a yes/no decision may be inappropriate; it might be more appropriate to have a range of responses, for example in a RATING SCALE. There may be comparatively few complex or subtle questions which can be answered with a simple *yes* or *no*. A *yes* or a *no* may be inappropriate for a situation whose complexity is better served by a series of questions which catch that complexity. Furthermore, a simple dichotomous question might build in respondent bias. Indeed people may be more reluctant to agree with a negative statement than to disagree with a positive question.

see also MULTIPLE CHOICE ITEMS, RATIO DATA QUESTION, MATRIX QUESTIONS, CONSTANT SUM QUESTIONS, RANK ORDER QUESTION, CONTINGENCY QUESTION

📖 Cohen et al. 2011

dichotomous variable
see CATEGORICAL VARIABLE

dictation
a familiar language-teaching technique that evolved into a measurement technique. Essentially, respondents listen to a passage of 100 to 150 words read aloud by the examiner (or audiotape) and write what they hear, using correct spelling. The listening portion usually has three stages: an oral reading without pauses; an oral reading with long pauses between every phrase (to give the respondents time to write down what is heard); and a third reading at normal speed to give test-takers a chance to check what they wrote. Supporters argue that dictation is an INTEGRATIVE TEST because it taps into grammatical and discourse competence required for other modes of performance in a language. Success on a dictation requires careful listening, reproduction in writing of what is heard, and efficient short-term memory. Further, dictation test results tend to be correlate strongly with other tests of proficiency. RELIABILITY of scoring criteria for dictation tests can be improved by designing multiple-choice or exact method cloze test scoring.

📖 Brown 2010

dictogloss task
see CONSENSUS TASK

DIF
an abbreviation for DIFFERENTIAL ITEM FUNCTIONING

differential attrition
another term for MORTALITY

differential item functioning
also **DIF, item bias**
a procedure which allows one to judge whether items (and ultimately the test they constitute) are functioning in the same manner in various groups of examinees. In broad terms, this is a matter of measurement invariance; that is, is the test performing in the same manner for each group of examinees? Given that a test is comprised of items, questions soon emerged about which specific items might be the source of such bias. Given this context, many of the early item bias methods focused on (a) comparisons of only two groups of examinees, (b) terminology such as *focal* and *reference* groups to denote minority and majority groups, respectively, and (c) binary (rather than polytomous) scored items.
Due to the highly politicized environment in which item bias was being examined, two inter-related changes occurred. First, the expression item bias was replaced by the more palatable term differential item functioning or DIF in many descriptions. DIF was the statistical term that was used to simply describe the situation in which persons from one group answered an item correctly more often than equally knowledgeable persons from another group. Second, the introduction of the term differential item functioning allowed one to distinguish **item impact** from item bias. Item impact described the situation in which DIF exists because there were true differences between the groups in the underlying ability of interest being measured by the item. Item bias described the situations in which there is DIF because of some characteristic of the test item or testing situation that is not relevant to the underlying ability of interest (and hence the test purpose).
Research has primarily focused on developing sophisticated statistical methods for detecting or flagging DIF items rather than on refining methods to distinguish item bias from item impact and providing explanations for why DIF was occurring.
 Fernandez-Ballesteros 2003

differential scale
also **Thurstone scale**
a RATING SCALE under which the selection of items is made by a panel of

judges who evaluate the items in terms of whether they are relevant to the topic area and unambiguous in implication. The detailed procedure is as follows:

a) The researcher gathers a large number of statements, usually twenty or more, that express various points of view toward a group, institution, idea, or practice (i.e., statements belonging to the topic area).
b) These statements are then submitted to a panel of judges, each of whom arranges them in eleven groups or piles ranging from one extreme to another in position. Each of the judges is requested to place generally in the first pile the statements which s/he thinks are most unfavorable to the issue, in the second pile to place those statements which s/he thinks are next most unfavorable and s/he goes on doing so in this manner till in the eleventh pile s/he puts the statements which s/he considers to be the most favorable.
c) This sorting by each judge yields a composite position for each of the items. In case of marked disagreement between the judges in assigning a position to an item, that item is discarded.
d) For items that are retained, each is given its median scale value between one and eleven as established by the panel. In other words, the scale value of any one statement is computed as the median position to which it is assigned by the group of judges.
e) A final selection of statements is then made. For this purpose a sample of statements, whose median scores are spread evenly from one extreme to the other is taken. The statements so selected, constitute the final scale to be administered to respondents. The position of each statement on the scale is the same as determined by the judges.

After developing the scale as stated above, the respondents are asked during the administration of the scale to check the statements with which they agree. The median value of the statements that they check is worked out and this establishes their score or quantifies their opinion. It may be noted that in the actual instrument the statements are arranged in random order of scale value. If the values are valid and if the opinionnaire deals with only one attitude dimension, the typical respondent will choose one or several contiguous items (in terms of scale values) to reflect his/her views. However, at times divergence may occur when a statement appears to tap a different attitude dimension.

The Thurstone method has been widely used for developing differential scales which are utilized to measure attitudes. Such scales are considered most appropriate and reliable when used for measuring a single attitude. But an important deterrent to their use is the cost and effort required to develop them. Another weakness of such scales is that the values as-

signed to various statements by the judges may reflect their own attitudes. The method is not completely objective; it involves ultimately subjective decision process. Critics of this method also opine that some other scale designs give more information about the respondents attitude in comparison to differential scales.
see also LIKERT SCALE, SEMANTIC DIFFERENTIAL SCALE, CUMULATIVE SCALE, ARBITRARY SCALE
📖 Kothari 2008

differential selection
also **selection bias**
a threat to INTERNAL VALIDITY which can occur whenever a researcher does not randomly select his/her SAMPLEs when forming different groups for comparison purposes. Any preexisting differences between groups could result in differences between groups not due to the VARIABLE being investigated. The classical situation where this might occur is when two intact classrooms are used: one for the TREATMENT GROUP and the other for the CONTROL GROUP. Chances are that there are preexisting differences between the classes. Accordingly, these prior differences, and not the treatments, could account for any difference in the DEPENDENT VARIABLE (DV) between groups. Or, in a learning experiment, if more capable students are in the experimental group than in the control group, the former would be expected to perform better on the DV measure even without the experimental treatment. Differential selection or selection bias is also a threat when volunteers are used. People who volunteer for a study may differ in some important respects from nonvolunteers. If the researcher then compares volunteers with nonvolunteers following the experimental treatment, the researcher does not know if the differences are caused by the treatment or by preexisting differences between the two groups.
The best way to control selection bias is to use RANDOM ASSIGNMENT of subjects to groups. With random assignment, you cannot determine in advance who will be in each group; randomly assigned groups differ only by chance. Another way to eliminate the threat of differential selection of participants or using already-formed groups that might be different, most researchers give participants a pretest whenever they are forced to use intact groups.
see also HISTORY, MATURATION, STATISTICAL REGRESSION, MORTALITY, TESTING EFFECT, INSTRUMENTATION
📖 Ary et al. 2010; Lodico et al. 2010; Perry 2011

dimensional sampling
a type of NON-PROBABILITY SAMPLING and a further refinement of QUOTA SAMPLING. One way of reducing the problem of SAMPLE SIZE in quo-

ta sampling is to opt for dimensional sampling. It involves identifying various factors of interest in a POPULATION and obtaining at least one respondent of every combination of those factors. Thus, in a study of race relations, for example, researchers may wish to distinguish first, second and third generation immigrants. Their SAMPLING PLAN might take the form of a multi-dimensional table with ethnic group across the top and generation down the side. A second example might be of a researcher who may be interested in studying disaffected students, girls and secondary aged students and who may find a single disaffected secondary female student, i.e., a respondent who is the bearer of all of the sought characteristics.

see also CONVENIENCE SAMPLING, QUOTA SAMPLING, PURPOSIVE SAMPLING, SNOWBALL SAMPLING, SEQUENTIAL SAMPLING, VOLUNTEER SAMPLING, OPPORTUNISTIC SAMPLING

Dörnyei 2007; Cohen et al. 2011

dimensional variable
another term for CONTINUOUS VARIABLE

directional hypothesis
also **one-tailed hypothesis, one-way hypothesis, unidirectional hypothesis, one-sided hypothesis**

an ALTERNATIVE HYPOTHESIS chosen when the researcher, usually based on previous research, wishes to predict a relationship or assess the PROBABILITY of differences in one direction or the other. A directional hypothesis, unlike a NONDIRECTIONAL HYPOTHESIS, is tested with a ONE-TAILED TEST and is stated in words that 'A is greater than B' or 'B is greater than A.' For a CORRELATIONAL RESEARCH in which the CORRELATION is believed to be positive, the hypothesis under investigation would take the following form:

'There is a positive relationship between the two variables.'

Conversely, if the correlation in a study is believed to be negative, the hypothesis would take this form:

'There is a negative relationship between the two variables.'

Note that the directional hypothesis indicates *more* or *less*, whereas the nondirectional hypothesis indicates only difference, and not where the difference may lie; the decision to use either a directional hypothesis or a nondirectional hypothesis should be made early in the study, before any statistical tests are performed; you do not wait to see what the data look

like and then select a one-tailed or two-tailed test
📖 Ary et al. 2010; Brown 1988; Clark-Carter 2010; Lavrakas 2008

directional test
another term for ONE-TAILED TEST

discontinuous variable
another term for CATEGORICAL VARIABLE

discourse analysis
an umbrella term for a variety of approaches to understanding authentic language use in particular social contexts. A piece of discourse is an instance of spoken or written language that has describable internal relationships of form and meaning (for example, words, structures, and cohesion—the ways in which pronouns and conjunctions connect parts of text) that relate coherently to an external communicative function or purpose and a given audience/interlocutor. Competence in the production and interpretation of discourse is crucial for language learners; by extension, language teachers must understand how discourse is structured and how it can be analyzed so that they are better equipped to teach effectively and also so that they can foster their own professional development by using discourse analysis to analyze the nature of language use for themselves.
Discourse analysis as a domain of study traces its roots to various disciplines—anthropology, linguistics, philosophy, psychology, and sociology, to name a few. As a result of its multidisciplinary nature, there is no one right way to do discourse analysis. The discourse analytical approaches that have grown out of these interdisciplinary developments are many, including CRITICAL DISCOURSE ANALYSIS, CONVERSATION ANALYSIS, NARRATIVE ANALYSIS, *register* and *genre analyses, discursive psychology, interactional sociolinguistics,* the *ethnography of communication, stylistics, mediated discourse analysis, metadiscourse, corpus-based analysis, multimodal discourse analysis, rhetorical-grammatical analysis, argumentation analysis,* and many others.
Discourse analysis can answer a myriad of interesting questions such as the following:

- How do my ESL/EFL students perform telephone openings and closings? How do they write e-mail openings and closings?
- What do my students know about compliments or complaints in English? If I ask them to role play a situation that requires one of these speech acts, will they perform in the same way that native speakers of English do?

- My ESL/EFL students are required to write a research paper for our composition class. What types of *cohesive markers* (e.g., however and finally) do they use so that their papers read coherently?
- Students in my ESL/EFL class have a lot of trouble knowing when to use *will* and *be going* to talk about future time. If I analyze a corpus of English, will I be able to determine the contexts in which native speakers prefer one form over the other, or when they use them interchangeably?
- How is meaning negotiated in peer writing feedback sessions in my advanced composition class?
- Using a critical perspective to look at talk in my ESL/EFL classroom, how do my ESL/EFL students display their gendered, racial, and cultural identities through their talk?

Each of these questions really can be answered using discourse analysis, which is often used in CASE STUDY, ETHNOGRAPHY, and ACTION RESEARCH.

Discourse analysis is based on the following principles: First, discourse analysis as it is practiced in applied linguistics examines authentic data—authentic in the sense that it is produced spontaneously rather than elicited experimentally. That is, we analyze the discourse of naturally occurring events, not language that is produced solely for the sake of research. Whatever approach to discourse analysis we choose, context—the setting in which the discourse occurs, the participants who produce the discourse, and the roles, identities, and relationships that are involved in these settings and with these participants—is of critical importance in the approach. This is because our goal is to provide a rich description of language use in a particular setting, not to make sweeping claims across every possible context.

Second, discourse analysts, for the most part, focus on interaction between and among speakers rather than on monologic talk. An important concept in this regard is co-construction, which is defined as the joint creation of a form, interpretation, stance, action, activity, identity, institution, skill, ideology, emotion, or other culturally meaningful reality. The importance of this idea for understanding classroom talk may be obvious, but for many years linguists, second language acquisition researchers, and language testers have analyzed and assessed learner language as if it were solely the cognitive product of a speaker, with no important influence from those with whom the speaker is interacting.

Third, for discourse analysis of speech, data must be collected for analysis and a conventionalized system employed for representing the data visually. These transcription notation systems take various forms, from simple orthography to finely detailed notations of pronunciation, breathing, loudness, pitch, and the like.

Furthermore, discourse analysis is grounded in the data (see GROUNDED THEORY). That is, the researcher may have ideas about how some feature of language works, from experience or theory, perhaps, but the notions that we bring to our data should really only guide us in our analysis. They should not dictate or restrict the way that we look at our data. Whatever we think we already know, we must try to remain open-minded about what we are seeing. Of course, it is impossible to come to any analytic task with no preconceived notions, but many discourse analysts attempt to let findings emerge from the data, rather than imposing an a priori framework on the data.

Finally, discourse data are presented in papers or reports in the form of data fragments or examples taken from spoken or written text. Although some researchers code, quantify, and count certain discourse features (for example, the number of turns or average pause length), most discourse analysts rely on relevant examples from the actual language data to shed light on the ways that communication is structured in certain settings or with certain speakers. That is, discourse data are not usually combined and reported in terms of means or percentages; rather, the researcher needs to present enough data examples that exhibit the relevant features under study to convince readers that her/his analysis is explanatory and comprehensive.

📖 Bhatia et al. 2008; Heigham & Croker 2009

discourse completion task
also DCT, production questionnaire

a means of gathering contextualized data. Generally, a situation is provided and then the respondent is asked what s/he would say in that particular situation. This is particularly useful if one wants to investigate speech acts such as apologies, invitations, refusals, and so forth. One can manipulate relatively easily such factors as age differences or status differences between interlocutors. DCTs are implemented most frequently in writing, with the participants being given a description of a situation in which the speech act occurs. After the description, there is usually blank space where the response is required. The following example illustrates a situation in which a status difference may be a factor when trying to provide embarrassing information to someone:

You are a corporate executive talking to your assistant. Your assistant, who will be greeting some important guests arriving soon, has some spinach in his/her teeth.

....
....

There are other instances when one needs to force a response. One way to do this is not only to provide space for the response, but to sandwich that space between the stimulus and the response to the response. For example, the following discourse is supplied to elicit refusals:

Worker: As you know, I've been here just a little over a year now, and I know you've been pleased with my work. I really enjoy working here, but to be quite honest, I really need an increase in pay.

....
....

Worker: Then I guess I'll have to look for another job.

The term *production questionnaires* is a relatively new name for discourse completion tasks that have been the most commonly used ELICITATION technique in the field of interlanguage pragmatics.
📖 Dörnyei 2003; Mackey & Gass 2005

discrete-point test
a test which is constructed to measure the small bits and pieces of a language as in a MULTIPLE-CHOICE ITEM made up of questions constructed to measure the respondents' knowledge of different structures. One question on such a test might be written to measure whether the respondents know how the distinction between *a* and *an* in English. A major assumption that underlies the use of test questions like this is that a collection of such discrete-point questions covering different structures (or other language learning points), if taken together as a single score, will produce a measure of some global aspect of language ability. For example, a teacher who believes in discrete-point tests would argue that scores based on the administration of fifty narrowly defined discrete-point multiple-choice questions covering a variety of English grammatical structures will reveal something about the students' overall proficiency in grammar. A corollary to this general view would be that the individual skills (reading, writing, listening, and speaking) can be tested separately, and that different aspects of these skills (like pronunciation, grammar, vocabulary, culture, and so forth) can also be assessed as isolated phenomena.
see also INTEGRATIVE TEST
📖 Brown 2005

discrete variable
see CATEGORICAL VARIABLE

discriminant analysis
another term for DISCRIMINANT FUNCTION ANALYSIS

discriminant function analysis
also **discriminant analysis, DFA**
a *multivariate* statistical procedure which is concerned with the prediction of membership in one of two (or more) levels or categories of a single *categorical* DEPENDENT VARIABLE (DV) or criterion from scores on two or more *continuous* INDEPENDENT VARIABLEs (IVs) or predictors. That is, you want to know which variables best predict group membership. Discriminant function analysis (DFA) has widespread application in situations in which the primary objective is to identify the group to which an object (e.g., a person, an institute) belongs. Potential applications include predicting the success or failure of a second language learner, deciding whether an undergraduate student should be admitted to graduate level, classifying students as to vocational interests, or predicting whether a teaching program will be successful. In each instance, the objects fall into groups, and the objective is to predict and explain the bases for each object's group membership through a set of independent variables selected by the researcher. In many cases, the DV consists of two groups or classifications, for example, male versus female or high proficiency versus low proficiency. In other instances, more than two groups are involved, such as low, medium, and high classifications. DFA is capable of handling either two groups or multiple (three or more) groups. When two classifications are involved, the technique is referred to as **two-group discriminant analysis**. When three or more classifications are identified, the technique is referred to as **multiple discriminant analysis** (MDA). In fact, the goal of DFA is to maximize the distance between two or more groups, which in turn maximizes discriminability through a set of one or more functions of a specific rank, i.e., the number of functions required to maximize the separation between groups. These functions are typically linear combinations of the input variables, and are called **linear discriminant function**s (LDFs).

The principal ASSUMPTIONS underlying DFA involve the formation of the **variate** (a linear combination of variables with empirically determined weights) or DISCRIMINANT FUNCTION (NORMALITY, LINEARITY, and MULTICOLLINEARITY) and the estimation of the discriminant function (EQUAL VARIANCE and HOMOGENEITY OF VARIANCE-COVARIANCE MATRICES).

DFA is used in two situations: (a) when a difference is presumed in a categorical variable and more than one predictor variable is used to identify the nature of that difference or (b) when a set of predictor variables is being explored to see whether participants can be classified into categories on the basis of differences on the predictor variables. The term **descriptive discriminative analysis** (DDA) is used to describe the former, an example of which would be where two cultures are asked to rate a number of descriptions of people on the dimension of intelligence. For an illustration, imagine that you were comparing Iranian and Japanese people on the way they rated the intelligence of five hypothetical people whose descriptions you provided. Each hypothetical person had to be rated on the dimension, which ranged from Intelligent to Unintelligent. Thus, the classificatory variable was culture and the predictor variables were the ratings supplied for each of the hypothetical people. DFA would allow you to see whether the profiles of ratings that the two cultures gave you differed significantly. If they did then you can explore further to find out what was contributing to the difference.

The second approach is described as **predictive discriminative analysis** (PDA). An example of its use would be if an institute wanted to distinguish those who would be successful in bilingual training from those who would be unsuccessful on the basis of their profiles on a proficiency test. If the analysis achieved its aim, successful trainees would have similar profiles and would differ from the unsuccessful trainees. The ways in which the profiles of the two groups differed could then be used to screen applicants for training to decide who is likely to be successful.

DFA is the appropriate statistical technique for testing the HYPOTHESIS that the group means of a set of independent variables for two or more groups are equal. By averaging the discriminant scores for all the individuals within a particular group, we arrive at the group mean. This group mean is referred to as a **centroid**. When the analysis involves two groups, there are two centroids; with three groups, there are three centroids; and so forth. The centroids indicate the most typical location of any member from a particular group, and a comparison of the group centroids shows how far apart the groups are in terms of that discriminant function.

The test for the statistical significance of the discriminant function is a generalized measure of the distance between the group centroids. It is computed by comparing the distributions of the discriminant scores for the groups. If the overlap in the distributions is small, the discriminant function separates the groups well. If the overlap is large, the function is a poor discriminator between the groups. Two distributions of discriminant scores, as shown in Figure D.2, further illustrate this concept. The diagram (a) represents the distributions of discriminant scores for a function that separates the groups well, showing minimal overlap (the shaded area) between the groups. The diagram (b) shows the distributions of discriminant scores on a discriminant function that is a relatively poor discriminator between groups A and B. The shaded areas of overlap represent the instances where misclassifying objects from group A into group B, and vice versa, can occur.

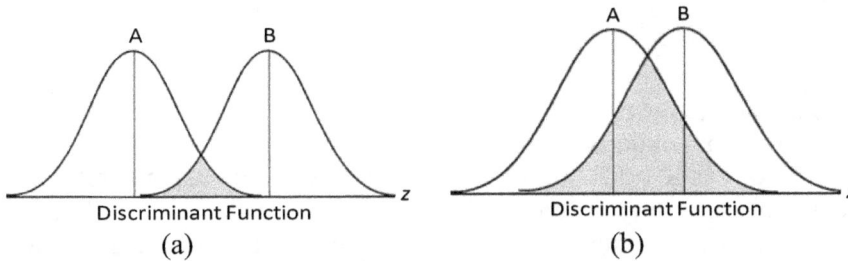

Figure D.2. Univariate Representation of Discriminant z Scores

DFA is mathematically equivalent to MULTIVARIATE ANALYSIS OF VARIANCE (MANOVA) in that there are one or more CATEGORICAL VARIABLEs on one side and two or more CONTINUOUS VARIABLEs on the other side. The main difference is that DFA uses the continuous (discriminating) variables as predictors of the categorical group membership DV. So, the focus in DFA is reversed between IVs and DVs compared with MANOVA. DFA can be classified as either a group-difference, or a prediction, statistical analysis. It is mainly used in examining what variables differentiate between groups most clearly. In this sense, the focus is on the groups. However, it is also analogous to a MULTIPLE REGRESSION (MR) analysis except that the dependent or outcome variable is categorical (with several levels or groups) with DFA, instead of continuous (as with MR). Similar to MR, DFA focuses on the weights, often the standardized ones (see STANDARDIZED PARTIAL REGRESSION COEFFICIENT), associated with each of the predictor variables. The variable(s) with the highest standardized discriminant weights are those that will also show the strongest group differences, so that these variables discriminate most clearly among the groups. DFA is also similar to LOGISTIC REGRESSION (LR) except that LR often uses categorical, as well as continuous IVs, and it does not require the traditional GENERAL LINEAR MODEL assumptions (i.e., NORMALITY, LINEARITY, and HOMOSCEDASTICITY) needed with DFA, MANOVA, MR, and other linear methods. DFA is also similar to CANONICAL CORRELATION, PRINCIPAL COMPONENTS ANALYSIS, and FACTOR ANALYSIS in that all four methods tend to focus on loadings that are correlations between variables and linear combinations or dimensions.

📖 Cramer & Howitt 2004; Hair et al. 2009; Harlow 2005; Seliger & Shohamy 1989

discriminant function

(in DISCRIMINANT FUNCTION ANALYSIS) a VARIATE of the INDEPENDENT VARIABLEs selected for their discriminatory power used in the prediction of group membership. The predicted value of the discriminant function is

the DISCRIMINANT Z SCORE, which is calculated for each object (e.g., person) in the analysis.
📖 Hair et al. 2010

discriminant validity
also **divergent validity**

a type of CONSTRUCT VALIDITY which suggests that using similar methods for researching different constructs should yield relatively low intercorrelations. In other words, measures of constructs that theoretically should not be related to each other are, in fact, observed not to be related to each other (i.e., you should be able to discriminate between dissimilar constructs). Such discriminant validity can also be yielded by FACTOR ANALYSIS, which clusters together similar issues and separates them from others.

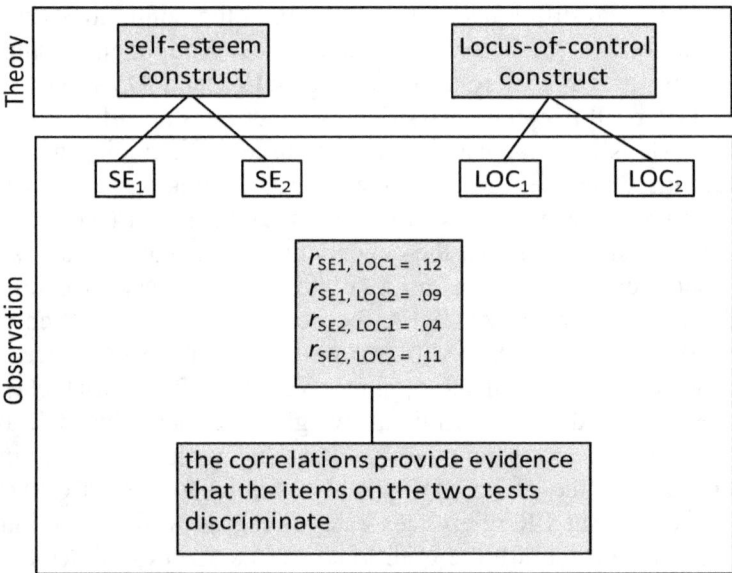

Figure D.3. Discriminant Validity Correlations

To establish discriminant validity, you need to show that measures that should not be related are in reality not related. In Figure D.3, you see four measures (each is an item on a scale). Here, however, two of the items are thought to reflect the construct of self-esteem; whereas the other two are thought to reflect locus of control. The top part of the figure shows the theoretically expected relationships among the four items. If you have discriminant validity, the relationship between measures from different constructs should be low. There are four correlations between measures that reflect different constructs, and these are shown on the bottom of the figure (Observation). You should see immediately that

these four cross-construct correlations are low (near zero) and certainly much lower than the convergent correlations (see CONVERGENT VALIDITY).
 Cohen et al. 2011; Trochim & Donnelly 2007

discriminant weight
also discriminant coefficient
(in DISCRIMINANT FUNCTION ANALYSIS) weight whose size relates to the discriminatory power of that INDEPENDENT VARIABLE across the groups of the DEPENDENT VARIABLE. Independent variables with large discriminatory power usually have large weights, and those with little discriminatory power usually have small weights. However, MULTICOLLINEARITY among the independent variables will cause exceptions to this rule.
 Hair et al. 2010

discriminant z score
a score which is defined by the DISCRIMINANT FUNCTION for each object in the analysis and usually stated in standardized terms. Also referred to as the Z SCORE, it is calculated for each object on each discriminant function and used in conjunction with the cutting score to determine predicted group membership. It is different from the z score terminology used for standardized variables.
 Hair et al. 2010

discussion
a section of a RESEARCH REPORT which follows the RESULTS section. After presenting the results, you are in a position to evaluate and interpret their implications, especially with respect to your original hypotheses (see HYPOTHESIS). Here you will examine, interpret, and qualify the results and draw inferences and conclusions from them. You should emphasize any theoretical or practical consequences of the results. You should open the discussion (sometimes headed *discussion*, sometimes *conclusion*, and sometimes both) section with a clear statement of the support or nonsupport for your original hypotheses, distinguished by primary and secondary hypotheses. If hypotheses were not supported, you should offer post hoc explanations. Similarities and differences between your results and the work of others should be used to contextualize, confirm, and clarify your conclusions. Do not simply reformulate and repeat points already made; each new statement should contribute to your interpretation and to the reader's understanding of the problem.

More specifically, your interpretation of the results should take into account (a) sources of potential BIAS and other threats to INTERNAL VALIDITY, (b) the imprecision of measures, (c) the overall number of tests or overlap among tests, (d) the EFFECT SIZEs observed, and (e) other limitations or weaknesses of the study. If an INTERVENTION is involved, you should discuss whether it was successful and the mechanism by which it was intended to work and/or alternative mechanisms. Also, you should discuss barriers to implementing the intervention or manipulation as well as the fidelity with which the intervention or manipulation was implemented in the study, that is, any differences between the manipulation as planned and as implemented.

You should acknowledge the limitations of your research, and address alternative explanations of the results. You should discuss the GENERALIZABILITY, or EXTERNAL VALIDITY, of the findings. This critical analysis should take into account differences between the target POPULATION and the accessed SAMPLE. For interventions, You should discuss characteristics that make them more or less applicable to circumstances not included in the study, how and what outcomes were measured (relative to other measures that might have been used), the length of time to measurement (between the end of the intervention and the measurement of outcomes), incentives, compliance rates, and specific settings involved in the study as well as other contextual issues.

The discussion section must be ended with a reasoned and justifiable commentary on the importance of your findings. This concluding section may be brief or extensive provided that it is tightly reasoned, self-contained, and not overstated. In this section, you might briefly return to a discussion of why the problem is important (as stated in the INTRODUCTION); what larger issues, those that transcend the particulars of the subfield, might hinge on the findings; and what propositions are confirmed or disconfirmed by the extrapolation of these findings to such overarching issues.

You may also consider the following issues:

- What is the theoretical, clinical, or practical significance of the outcomes, and what is the basis for these interpretations? If the findings are valid and replicable, what real-life psychological phenomena might be explained or modeled by the results? Are applications warranted on the basis of this research?
- What problems remain unresolved or arise anew because of these findings?

The responses to these questions are the core of the contribution of your study and justify why readers both inside and outside your own specialty should attend to the findings. Your readers should receive clear, unambiguous, and direct answers.

see also TITLE, ABSTRACT, METHOD, REFERENCES, APPENDIXES

📖 American Psychological Association 2010

dispersion
another term for VARIABILITY

disproportionate stratified sampling
see STRATIFIED SAMPLING

distractor efficiency
also choice distribution
the extent to which (a) the distractors lure a sufficient number of test takers, especially lower-ability ones, and (b) those responses are somewhat evenly distributed across all distractors. To illustrate, suppose a multiple-choice item with five choices, and responses across upper- and lower-ability students are distributed as follows:

Choices	A	B	C	D	E
High-ability students (10)	0	1	7	0	2
low-ability students (10)	3	5	2	0	0

Note: *C* is the correct response.

This item successfully attracts seven of ten high-ability students toward the correct response, while only two of the low-ability students get this one right. This item might be improved in two ways: (a) Distractors *D* does not fool anyone. No one picked it, and therefore it probably has no utility. A revision might provide a distractor that actually attracts a response or two. (b) Distractor *E* attracts more responses (2), from the high-ability group than the low-ability group (0). Perhaps it includes a subtle reference that entices the high group but is over the head of low group, and therefore the latter students do not even consider it. The other two distractors (*A* and *B*) seem to be fulfilling their function of attracting some attention from lower-ability students.
 Brown 2010; Farhady et al. 1995

distribution
the values of a characteristic or VARIABLE along with the FREQUENCY or PROBABILITY of their occurrence, often displayed in either tabular or graphic format. Hence, the distribution of scores in a sample is merely a tally or graph which shows the pattern of the various values of the score. The distribution of gender, for example, would be merely the number or proportion of males and females in the sample or population.
see also FREQUENCY DISTRIBUTION, NORMAL DISTRIBUTION, SKEWED DISTRIBUTION
 Sahai & Khurshid 2001

distribution-free tests
another term for NONPARAMETRIC TESTS

divergent validity
another term for DISCRIMINANT VALIDITY

document
a term which refers to a wide range of written, physical, and visual materials, including what other authors may term artifacts. Documents may be personal, such as autobiographies, diaries, and letters; official, such as files, reports, memoranda, or minutes; or documents of popular culture, such as books, films, and videos. Documents constitute the basis for most QUALITATIVE RESEARCH. **Document analysis** can be of written or text-based artifacts (textbooks, novels, journals, meeting minutes, logs, announcements, policy statements, newspapers, transcripts, birth certificates, marriage records, budgets, letters, e-mail messages, etc.) or of nonwritten records (photographs, audiotapes, videotapes, computer images, websites, musical performances, televised political speeches, virtual world settings, etc.). The analysis may be of existing artifacts or records, or in some cases the researcher may ask subjects to produce artifacts or documents, for example, asking participants to keep a journal about personal experiences, to write family stories, to draw pictures to express memories, or to explain thinking aloud as it is audiotaped.

Document may include primary data (collected by the researcher) or secondary data (collected and archived or published by others). Primary data documents include transcriptions of INTERVIEWs; PARTICIPANT OBSERVATION *fieldnotes*; photographs of field situations taken by the researcher as records of specific activities, rituals, and personas (with associated locational and descriptive data); and maps and diagrams drawn by the researcher or by field assistants or participants in a study (with accompanying explanations). These documents are filed systematically so that they can be readily recovered for classification, coding, and analysis. Most primary data documents archiving systems are computerized, although hard copies of materials also are kept.

Secondary data documents are materials that are important in describing the historical background and current situation in a community or country where the research is being conducted. They include maps, demographic data, measures of educational status (records of differences in types of graduation rates, etc.), and de-identified quantitative databases that include variables of interest to the researcher.

Examining records and documents is an unobtrusive approach to qualitative research and can be conducted as part of a study that includes other

forms of data collection or alone. The specific analytic approach is called CONTENT ANALYSIS.
📖 Ary et al. 2010; Given 2008

document analysis
see DOCUMENT

domain-referenced test
see NORM-REFERENCED TEST

double-barreled question
an item that include *two or more issues* in the one question. For example, 'Do you feel that the university should provide basic skills courses for students and give credit for those courses?' is a double-barreled question. When a respondent answers such a question, the researcher does not know whether the answer applies to both parts of the question or just to one. A *yes* answer to the preceding question may mean either that the respondent believes the university should offer basic skills courses and give credit for them or that it should offer the courses but not give credit for them. Double-barreled questions most frequently arise in attitudinal questions in which two attitude targets are asked as one construct. As a result, higher rates of item nonresponse (i.e., missing data) and unstable attitudes are likely to occur with double-barreled questions. This also leads to analytic problems and questions of CONSTRUCT VALIDITY, as the analyst does not know which barrel led to the respondent's answer.
📖 Ary et al. 2010; Lavrakas 2008

double-blind technique
see RESEARCHER EFFECT

double negative
a construction that employs *two* negatives, especially to express a single negation. A double (or more accurately, multiple) negative is considered unacceptable in Standard English when it is used to convey or reinforce a negative meaning, as in *He didn't say nothing* (meaning *he said nothing* or he *didn't say anything*). In QUESTIONNAIRE design, this is almost always a situation to be avoided. A double-negative usually creates an unnecessary amount of confusion in the mind of the respondent and makes it nearly impossible for the researcher to accurately determine what respondents were agreeing or disagreeing to. Such a question can increase item nonresponse (i.e., MISSING DATA) by increasing the percentage of respondents unable to understand the question. A more insidious problem is an increase in the number of responses from people who have misun-

derstood the question and responded based on that misunderstanding.
 Lavrakas 2008

doubly-multivariate design
see PROFILE ANALYSIS

dropout
another term for MORTALITY

DRT
an abbreviation for DOMAIN-REFERENCED TEST

dummy variable
a DICHOTOMOUS VARIABLE that can take on exactly two mutually exclusive values and that has been given numerical codes, usually 1 and 0. The 0 stands for whatever the 1 is not, and is thus said to be *dumb* or silent. Thus, when we use gender, for example, we are really coding it as 1 = female and 0 = not female (i.e., male). CATEGORICAL VARIABLEs with more than two categories are incorporated by a series of dummy variables. If the categorical variables have k categories then $k - 1$ dummy variables are required. For example, with four categories the three dummy variables (X_1, X_2, X_3) could be assigned values (1, 0, 0) for category 1, (0, 1, 0) for category 2, (0, 0, 1) for category 3, and (0, 0, 0) for category 4. Dummy variables enable the inclusion of categorical information in regression models.
 Lavrakas 2008; Leech et al. 2005; Upton & Cook 2008

Duncan's new multiple range test
see NEWMAN-KEULS TEST

Duncan's test
another term for DUNCAN'S NEW MULTIPLE RANGE TEST

Dunnett multiple comparison test
another term for DUNNETT'S TEST

Dunnett's test
also **Dunnett multiple comparison test**
a POST HOC TEST which is used to determine whether the MEAN of a CONTROL GROUP differs from that of two or more EXPERIMENTAL GROUPs following a significant F TEST in an ANALYSIS OF VARIANCE. Dunnett's test makes PAIRWISE COMPARISONs. However, Dunnett's test does not pair every mean with every other mean. Instead, the Dunnett's test compares the mean of a particular group in the study against each of

the remaining group means. Dunnett's test can be used for equal and unequal group sizes where the variances are equal. It is less conservative than BONFERRONI t because it does not assume that the contrasts are orthogonal (i.e., independent).
see also LIBERAL TEST, CONSERVATIVE TEST
 Everitt & Skrondal 2010; Huck 2012; Sahai & Khurshid 2001; Salkind 2007; Page et al. 2003

Dunn multiple comparison test
another term for BONFERRONI ADJUSTMENT

E

ecological correlation

a CORRELATION from combining data from multiple groups to calculate a CORRELATION COEFFICIENT. In many situations, we may be interested in investigating relationships among variables at the level of groups, rather than individual. However, because of possible ordering among groups themselves, combining data from groups to calculate a correlation coefficient can dramatically affect the value of the correlation coefficients. Suppose, for example, we were interested to see if there was a relationship between reading comprehension and mathematical reasoning in grade school students. We might administer tests of reading and mathematics to students at different grade levels, and find that within each grade, the correlation coefficient are quite small, say, .25 and .24. However, when we aggregate the data across grade levels, we might find that the ecological correlation is very high, .71. The relationship for combined groups thus is much stronger than for either of the two groups considered individually. In other situations, combining groups can have the opposite effect. Suppose, for example, we were to investigate the relationship between second language (L2) vocabulary knowledge and L2 reading comprehension at two different levels—beginning and advanced. We might find that within each of these groups the correlation coefficient is positive and quite high (e.g., .85 and .82). however, when we combine the two groups, we might find that the correlation coefficient is actually negative.
📖 Bachman 2004

ecological validity

(in QUALITATIVE RESEARCH) the extent to which behavior observed in one context can be generalized to another. In QUANTITATIVE RESEARCH, VARIABLEs are frequently isolated, controlled, and manipulated in contrived settings. For qualitative research a fundamental premise is that the researcher deliberately does not try to manipulate variables or conditions, that the situations in the research occur naturally. The intention here is to give accurate portrayals of the realities of social situations in their own terms, in their natural or conventional settings. For ecological validity to be demonstrated it is important to include and address in the research as many characteristics in, and factors of, a given situation as possible. The difficulty for this is that the more characteristics are included and described, the more difficult it is to abide by central ethical tenets of much research—non-traceability, anonymity and nonidentifiability.
see also VALIDITY
📖 Cohen et al. 2011

EDA
an abbreviation for EXPLORATORY DATA ANALYSIS

EFA
an abbreviation for EXPLORATORY FACTOR ANALYSIS

effect size
also **treatment magnitude, treatment effect, ES**
a value that indicates the proportion or percentage of variability on a DEPENDENT VARIABLE (DV) that can be attributed to variation on the INDEPENDENT VARIABLE (IV). Basically effect sizes tell you how important your statistical result is (whether it is *statistically significant* or not). It derived from the difference between the EXPERIMENTAL and CONTROL GROUPs as measured in some standard unit. The larger the effect size, the larger the differences between groups. When a researcher rejects the NULL HYPOTHESIS and concludes that an IV had an effect, an effect size is calculated to determine how strong the IVs effect (e.g., presence or absence of a bilingual program) was on the DV (e.g., academic performance). An effect size, in fact, gives the researcher insight into the magnitude of this strength. If the effect size is quite small, then it may make sense to simply discount the findings as unimportant, even if they are statistical. If the effect size is large, then the researcher has found something that it is important to understand.

As a proportion, effect size can range from 0, indicating no relationship between the IV and the DV, to 1, indicating that 100% of the variance in the DV is associated with the IV. For example, if we find that our effect size is .47, we know that 47% of the variability in the DV is due to the IV.

Whereas *P*-VALUEs and significance testing depend on the POWER OF A TEST and thus, to a large measure, on group sizes, effect sizes do not change no matter how many participants there are. It is not dependent on SAMPLE SIZE and therefore can allow comparisons across a range of different studies with different sample sizes (see META-ANALYSIS). This makes effect sizes a valuable of information, much more valuable than the question of whether a statistical test is *significant* or not.

Effect size is divided into two broad families—*group difference indexes* and *relationship indexes*—although it is important to note that in most cases there are algebraic calculations that can transform one kind into the other, and there are other kinds of effect sizes that do not fit into these categories, like ODDS RATIOs. Both the group difference and relationship effect sizes are ways to provide a standardized measure of the strength of the effect that is found. A **group difference index**, or mean difference measure is a type of effect size that measures the difference between two independent sample means, and expresses how large the difference is in

STANDARD DEVIATIONs. This type of effect size index is most commonly employed prior to conducting an experiment, in order to allow a researcher to determine the appropriate sample size to use to identify a hypothesized effect size. A standard measure of effect size is COHEN'S d. Other group difference index measures include COHEN'S f, **g index** (employed to compute the power of the BINOMIAL TEST for a single sample), **h index** (employed to compute the power of the Z TEST FOR TWO INDEPENDENT PROPORTIONS), **w index** (employed to compute the power of the CHI-SQUARE GOODNESS-OF-FIT TEST and the CHI-SQUARE TEST OF INDEPENDENCE), **q index** (represents the difference between two PEARSON PRODUCT-MOMENT CORRELATION COEFFICIENTs). Group difference indexes are also called the **d family of effect size**s. This family of effect sizes measures how much groups vary in terms of standard deviations of difference.

Relationship indexes (also called the **r family of effect size**s) measures how much an independent and DV vary together or, in other words, the amount of covariation in the two variables. This type of index expresses effect size in the form of a CORRELATION COEFFICIENT. It is computed at the conclusion of an experiment to indicate the proportion of variability on the DV that can be attributed to the IV. The more closely the two variables are related, the higher the effect size. So, for example, the relationship between height and weight among adults is quite closely related, and would have a high r value. Squared indices of r (i.e., R^2) and related quantities such as ETA-SQUARED (η^2), OMEGA-SQUARED (ω^2), PARTIAL ETA-SQUARED, and PARTIAL OMEGA-SQUARED are used for measures of strength of *association*, but because they are squared they lack directionality. These squared measures indicate the observed proportion of explained variance. Thus, they are called **percentage variance effect size**s (PV).

see also STATISTICAL POWER

Best & Kahn 2006; Cramer & Howitt 2004; Everitt & Howell 2005; Larson-Hall 2010; Leary 2011; Mackey & Gass 2005; Richards & Schmidt 2010; Sheskin 2011

effect variable
another term for DEPENDENT VARIABLE

EHA
an abbreviation for EVENT HISTORY ANALYSIS

eigenvalue
also **characteristic root, latent root**
the amount (not percentage) of VARIANCE accounted for by the VARIABLEs on a factor in a FACTOR ANALYSIS. Eigenvalue is the sum of the squared CORRELATIONs or loadings between each variable and that fac-

tor. The magnitude of a factor and its significance are assessed partly from the eigenvalue.
📖 Cramer & Howitt 2004

elicitation
also **elicitation technique, elicitation procedure**
any technique or procedure that is designed to get a person to actively produce speech or writing, for example asking someone to describe a picture, tell a story, or finish an incomplete sentence. In linguistics, these techniques are used to prompt native speakers to produce linguistic data for analysis. In teaching and second language research, the same and similar techniques are used to get a better picture of learner abilities or a fuller understanding of interlanguage than the study of naturally occurring speech or writing can provide.
📖 Richards & Schmidt 2010

elicitation technique
another term for ELICITATION

elicited imitation
an ELICITATION procedure in which a person has to repeat a sentence which s/he sees or hears. The basic assumption underlying elicited imitation is that if a given sentence is part of one's grammar, it will be relatively easy to repeat. When people are asked to repeat a sentence which uses linguistic rules which they themselves cannot or do not use, they often make changes in the sentence so that it is more like their own speech. Elicited imitation can be used to study a person's knowledge of a language. For example:

Stimulus sentence	Elicited imitation
Why *can't the man* climb over the fence?	Why *the man can't* climb over the fence?

📖 Mackey & Gass 2005; Richards & Schmidt 2010

elicitation procedure
another term for ELICITATION

elite bias
see BIAS

email survey
a SURVEY that sends the survey instrument (e.g., QUESTIONNAIRE) to a respondent via email and most often samples respondents via email. Similar to a WEB SURVEY, a survey conducted via email most typically uses electronic mail to contact members of the SAMPLE. With Web surveys,

the user is directed in the contact email to a Web site containing the questionnaire. With email surveys, the contact email contains the survey questionnaire and no survey Website is referenced. Generally, the email survey approach takes one of three forms: (1) a software file attached to the email, (2) an electronic document attached to the email, or (3) questionnaire text embedded in the email itself.
📖 Lavrakas 2008

embedded design

a MIXED METHODS RESEARCH design which is used when a researcher needs to answer a SECONDARY RESEARCH question that requires the use of different types of data within a traditional QUANTITATIVE or QUALITATIVE RESEARCH design. To accomplish this, one type of data collection and analysis is embedded or nested within the design associated with another type of data. For example, a researcher may need to embed qualitative data within a quantitative EXPERIMENTAL DESIGN and will conduct qualitative INTERVIEWs during the research study to understand the reasons for certain participants' behaviors. Less frequently, a researcher may embed quantitative SURVEY data within a traditionally qualitative CASE STUDY to help describe the broader context in which a case is situated. Unlike the TRIANGULATION DESIGN, the embedded design has a predominant method (quantitative or qualitative) that guides the research study.

The *weight* in this design is given to the predominant method, quantitative or qualitative, that guides the project and within which another method is embedded. The *mixing* of the quantitative and qualitative data occurs either at the data analysis stage if the data is collected concurrently (like in the triangulation design), or at the interpretation stage if the two types of data are collected sequentially (like in the EXPLANATORY and the EXPLORATORY DESIGNs). The quantitative and qualitative data analysis in this design is conducted separately because they seek to answer different research questions. Depending on the *timing* of the data collection, the structure of the report could follow either a *sequential* or *concurrent* design model.

The main advantage of the embedded design is that a researcher builds the study on a design that is well known (e.g., a case study). Another advantage is that a researcher can collect the two types of data at the same time. However, it might sometimes be challenging to integrate the quantitative and qualitative results because the two methods are used to answer different research questions. Nevertheless, due to the nature of the questions, researchers can present the two sets of results separately.
📖 Heigham & Croker 2009

emic perspective
see QUALITATIVE RESEARCH

empirical research
an evidence-based research type that relies on direct OBSERVATION and experimentation in the acquisition of new knowledge. Empirical research focuses on the collection, analysis, and interpretation of data that can be sensed or experienced in some way, either to answer research questions, to test hypotheses derived from theories, and/or to develop hypotheses or theories. The SCIENTIFIC METHOD is firmly based on the empirical research. In the empirical research, scientific decisions are made based on the data derived from direct observation and experimentation. For example, we have all made decisions based on feelings, hunches, or gut instinct. Additionally, we may often reach conclusions or make decisions that are not necessarily based on data, but rather on opinions, speculation, and a hope for the best.
The empirical research, with its emphasis on direct, systematic, and careful observation, is best thought of as the guiding principle behind all research conducted in accordance with the scientific method. It is data-based research, coming up with conclusions which are capable of being verified by observation or experiment. It is called as experimental type of research. In such research it is necessary to get at facts firsthand, at their source, and actively to go about doing certain things to stimulate the production of desired information. In such research, you must first provide yourself with a working HYPOTHESIS or guess as to the probable results. You then work to get enough facts (data) to prove or disprove your hypothesis. You then set up EXPERIMENTAL DESIGNs which you think will manipulate the persons or the materials concerned so as to bring forth the desired information. Such research is thus characterized by your control over the variables under study and your deliberate manipulation of one of them to study its effects. Empirical research is appropriate when proof is sought that certain variables affect other variables in some way.
see also CONCEPTUAL RESEARCH
Flood et al. 2005; Kothari 2008; Marczyk et al. 2005

empirical validity
another term for CRITERION-RELATED VALIDITY

empiricism
a philosophical doctrine that experience is the foundation of knowledge and that the project of gaining access to a reality other than experience is problematic. This can be contrasted with **rationalism**, which holds that knowledge comes from basic concepts known intuitively through reason such as innate ideas. According to empiricism, there are no innate struc-

tures in the mind; we experience particular things, not universal truths; we have no access to reality (unless we take experience to be the only reality) and cannot know things with certainty; theoretical statements are ultimately a form of shorthand, translatable into accounts of what has been, or might be, observed; and observation can hope to adjudicate between competing theories and determine which of them is more likely to be true. POSITIVISM has its origins in the classical theory of empiricism, and indeed borrowed from empiricism the idea that knowledge has its foundation in sense data. The principal problem that it encountered relates to the impossibility of accessing data through the senses without some prior theory to make sense of it. In short, observations are concept-dependent. This has to be distinguished from concept-determination, because this implies that theories developed about reality are observation-neutral. There would be no need to make observations if theory development was always prior to the making of observations.

It is presumably true to say that the majority of social scientists are empiricists in the weakest sense of the term, which involves the claim that experience, in the form of observation, is the ultimate source of knowledge without any specific implications about what forms that observation should take or about the nature of the relation between observation and theory. But this is only to say that most social scientists are committed to empirical inquiry and that very few of them believe that significant conclusions can be drawn on the basis of pure speculation, theology, philosophy, or unsupported intuition. In a similar way, the existence (or not) of innate ideas plays virtually no part in methodological thinking (although many cognitive scientists believe that the mind has innate, or innately channeled, processing systems).

📖 Given 2008; Scott & Morrison 2005

endogenous variable
see PATH ANALYSIS

epistemology
the term which is made up of the Greek-derived terms *episteme*, knowledge or science, and *logos*, knowledge, information, theory or account. Epistemology is the theory of knowledge, or as it is sometimes taken to mean, an analysis of the conditions, possibilities, and limits of our knowledge-gaining processes. A good deal of contemporary epistemology is concerned with the analysis of *propositional* knowledge (knowing that) and has not, by and large, focused on *procedural* knowledge (knowing how) and *acquaintance* knowledge (knowing who). Epistemology is often concerned with the nature, sources and justification of the major kinds of knowledge, for example how we may come to

know things through the senses in the form of empirical knowledge, or a priori knowledge that we may have from other sources or via logic.
 Given 2008

epoche
see PHENOMENOLOGY

EPSEM
an abbreviation which stands for the *equal probability of selection method* for selecting SAMPLEs. Every element or case in the POPULATION must have an equal PROBABILITY of selection for the sample.
see also PROBABILITY SAMPLING, RANDOM SELECTION, RANDOM ASSIGNMENT

EQS
(pronounced like the letter X) the name of one of the computer programs for carrying out STRUCTURAL EQUATION MODELING. The name seems to be an abbreviation for *equation systems*.
 Cramer & Howitt 2004

equal-interval scale
another term for INTERVAL SCALE

equality of variance
another term for HOMOGENEITY OF VARIANCE

equal variance
another term for HOMOGENEITY OF VARIANCE

equivalent-form reliability
another term for PARALLEL-FORM RELIABILITY

equivalent material design
a QUASI-EXPERIMENTAL DESIGN which uses the same group for both EXPERIMENTAL and CONTROL GROUPs in two or more cycles. The group may be used as a control group in the first cycle and as an experimental group in the second. The order of exposure to experimental and control can be revered, i.e., experimental first and control following. Essential to this design is the selection of learning materials different but as nearly equal as possible to the students and in difficulty of comprehension. The schematic representation of this design would be as follows, where O_1 = pretest, O_2 = posttest, X_A and X_B = equivalent materials:

$$O_1 \quad X_A \quad O_2 \quad O_1 \quad X_B \quad O_2$$

The simplicity and logic of this design are somewhat misleading and when examined in the light of the threats of INTERNAL VALIDITY, the design's weaknesses become apparent. Some of the limitations of the equivalent-material design can be partially minimized by a series of replications in which the order of exposure to experimental and control treatments is reversed. However, it is apparent that this design is not likely to equate materials, subjects, or experimental conditions.

see also NONEQUIVALENT CONTROL GROUP DESIGN, TIME-SERIES DESIGN, COUNTERBALANCED DESIGN, RECURRENT INSTITUTIONAL CYCLE DESIGN, SEPARATE-SAMPLE PRETEST-POSTTEST CONTROL GROUP DESIGN, SEPARATE-SAMPLE PRETEST-POSTTEST DESIGN

📖 Best & Kahn 2006; Campbell & Stanley 1963; Cook & Campbell 1966

equivalent time-samples design
also **reversal time-series design**

a variation of TIME-SERIES DESIGN and a multi-subject variation of the SINGLE-SUBJECT REVERSAL DESIGN which establishes causality by presenting and withdrawing an INTERVENTION, or INDEPENDENT VARIABLE, one to several times while concurrently measuring change in the DEPENDENT VARIABLE. Equivalent time-samples design uses one group as the EXPERIMENTAL and CONTROL GROUP. In this design the TREATMENT is present between some observations (i.e., measurements) and between others. As in the SIMPLE INTERRUPTED TIME-SERIES DESIGN, this design begins with a series of pretests to observe normal fluctuations in baseline. It measures behavior during at least three phases: before the treatment is introduced (A), after introducing the treatment (B), and again after withdrawing the treatment (A). This design may be represented as follows (where O = pretest and posttest, X = treatment, $-X$ = no treatment):

O   O   O   X   O   O   O   -X   O   O   O

In this case the design is called **ABA design**. Additional baselines and/or treatment phases may be added, further complicating the design; the most common of these designs are **ABAB** and **ABABA**, which is analogous to the single-subject reversal design.

Designs of this type have a number of limitations. Although they may minimize the effect of HISTORY, it is possible that they may increase the influence of MATURATION, INSTRUMENTATION, TESTING EFFECT, and MORTALITY.

📖 Best & Kahn 2006; Campbell & Stanley 1963; Cook & Campbell 1966; Marczyk et al. 2005

error
the variation in scores which the researcher has failed to control or

measure in a particular study. Once it is measured as an identifiable variable it ceases to be error. So variations in the scores on a measure which are the consequence of time of day, for example, are error if the researcher does not appreciate that they are due to variations in time of day and includes time of day as a variable in the study. Error may be due to poor RESEARCH DESIGN or METHODOLOGY, but it is not a mistake in the conventional sense. The objective of the researcher needs to be to keep error to a minimum as far as possible. Error makes the interpretation of trends in the data difficult since the greater the error, the greater the likely variation due to chance or unknown factors. Many factors lead to increased error—poor measurement techniques such as unclear or ambiguous questions and variations in the instructions given to participants, for instance.
see also MEASUREMENT ERROR, ERROR VARIANCE
📖 Cramer & Howitt 2004

error mean square

the term used in ANALYSIS OF VARIANCE for dividing the effect MEAN SQUARE to obtain the F RATIO. It is the error sum of squares divided by the error DEGREES OF FREEDOM. The smaller this term is in relation to the effect mean square, the bigger the F ratio will be and the more likely that the means of two or more of the groups will be statistically significant.
📖 Cramer & Howitt 2004

error of central tendency

see GENEROSITY ERROR

error of measurement

another term for MEASUREMENT ERROR

error of severity

see HALO EFFECT

error score

another term for MEASUREMENT ERROR

error sum of squares

also **residual sum of squares (SS_{res}), sum of squared residuals, sum of squared errors**

the sum of squared deviations of all individual data from the SAMPLE MEANs of their respective TREATMENT GROUPs which remains after the SUM OF SQUARES for the other effects has been removed. It is used to denote the VARIANCE in the DEPENDENT VARIABLE not yet accounted for

by the model. It is the NUMERATOR of the equation that represents *residual variability* (i.e., error variability that is beyond the researcher's control). If no independent variables are used for prediction, it becomes the squared errors using the mean as the predicted value and thus equals the TOTAL SUM OF SQUARES.
 Cramer & Howitt 2004; Sheskin 2011

error term
also **residual error**
a term used in a statistical model which represents the contribution from various OTHER VARIABLEs, known or unknown, which are omitted from the model. Each test of significance within an ANOVA depends on having a denominator (i.e., error term) of the F RATIO whose expected value includes all of the terms in the expectation of the NUMERATOR except the one term whose existence is denied by the NULL HYPOTHESIS.
 Hancock & Mueller 2010; Sahai & Khurshid 2001

error variability
another term for ERROR VARIANCE

error variance
also **unsystematic variance, within-groups variability, within-subjects variability, within-groups variance, within-subjects variance, confound variance, secondary variance, error variability**
the variability in the value of the DEPENDENT VARIABLE that is related to EXTRANEOUS VARIABLEs and not to the variability in the INDEPENDENT VARIABLE (IV) or TREATMENT. Error variance is that portion of the **total variance** (see Figure E.1) in a set of SAMPLE DATA that remains unaccounted for and is, in fact, beyond the control of a researcher.

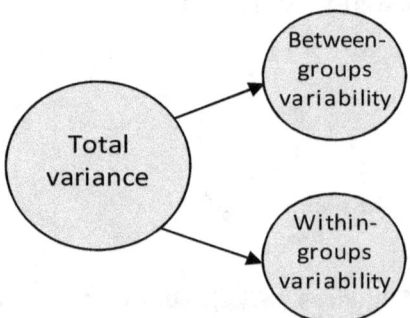

Figure E.1. Schematic Representation of the Total Variance

Error variance is the static in an experiment. It results from all of the unsystematic, uncontrolled, and unidentified variables that affect participants' behavior (i.e., extraneous variable). It is the variability among scores that cannot be attributed to the effects of the IV. Error variance may also be the result of within-individual variation when measures are obtained from the same individuals at different times, and it is influenced by variables such as attentiveness, practice, and fatigue. The total variance in a set of data also contains **systematic variance** (also called **between-groups variance, treatment variability, between-groups variability, between-subjects variance, between-subjects variability, primary variance, treatment variance**), which is related in an orderly, predictable fashion to the variables the researcher is investigating. It is essentially a measure of the variance of the means of the samples.

Not all of the total variability in participants' behavior is systematic variance. Factors that the researcher is not investigating may also be related to participants' behavior. Error variance is unrelated to the variables under investigation in a study. Even after a researcher has determined how much of the total variance is related to the variables of interest in the study (that is, how much of the total variance is systematic), some variance remains unaccounted for. This error variance can mask or obscure the effects of the variables in which researchers are primarily interested. The more error variance in a set of data, the more difficult it is to determine whether the variables of interest are related to variability in behavior.

The reason that error variance can obscure the systematic effects of other variables is analogous to the way in which noise or static can cover up a song that you want to hear on the radio. In fact, if the static is too loud (because you are sitting beside an electrical device, for example), you might wonder whether a song is playing at all. Similarly, you can think of error variance as noise or static—unwanted, annoying variation that, when too strong, can mask the real signal produced by the variables in which the researcher is interested.

The most common source of error variance is preexisting individual differences among participants. When participants enter an experiment, they already differ in a variety of ways—cognitively, physiologically, emotionally, and behaviorally. As a result of their preexisting differences, even participants who are in the same experimental condition respond differently to the IV, creating error variance.

Participants also differ in terms of transient states. Participants' moods, attitudes, and physical conditions can affect their behavior in ways that have nothing to do with the experiment. At the time of the experiment, some are healthy whereas others are ill. Some are tired; others are well rested. Some are happy; others are sad. Some are enthusiastic about participating in the study; others resent having to participate.

Error variance is also affected by differences in the environment in which the study is conducted. For example, external noise may distract some participants. Collecting data at different times during the day may create extraneous variability in participants' responses. To reduce error variance, researchers try to hold the environment as constant as possible as they test different participants.

Ideally, researchers should treat each and every participant within each condition exactly the same in all respects (i.e., avoid differential treatments). However, experimenters find it difficult to treat all participants in precisely the same way during the study.

MEASUREMENT ERROR or any uncontrolled or unexplained variation also contribute to error variance because it causes participants' scores to vary in unsystematic ways. It is also referred to as the error variance of the ERROR TERM.
 Leary 2011; Sahai & Khurshid 2001

ES

an abbreviation for EFFECT SIZE

estimate

a particular numerical value yielded by an ESTIMATOR for a given SAMPLE DATA. An estimate can be a mean, proportion, correlation coefficient or any other parameter value derived from a sample. An estimate is used to make inference about a target population whose true parameter value is unknown.
 Sahai & Khurshid 2001

estimated standard deviation

another term for SAMPLE STANDARD DEVIATION

estimated variance

another term for SAMPLE VARIANCE

estimator

the SAMPLE STATISTIC which is used to make inferences about an unknown PARAMETER. For example, one might use SAMPLE MEAN to estimate the value of the POPULATION MEAN.
see also SAMPLE, SAMPLE SIZE
 Sahai & Khurshid 2001

eta (η)

also **correlation ratio**

a CORRELATION COEFFICIENT for curvilinear data for which linear correlation coefficients such as PEARSON PRODUCT MOMENT CORRELATION

COEFFICIENT are not appropriate. This is a little misleading as eta gives exactly the same numerical value as Pearson correlation coefficient when applied to perfectly linear data. However, if the data are not ideally fitted by a straight line then there will be a disparity. In this case, the value of eta will be bigger (never less) than the corresponding value of Pearson correlation applied to the same data. Eta is interpreted in much the same way as the Pearson r, except that it ranges from 0 to 1, rather than from +1 to -1. The greater the disparity between the linear correlation coefficient and the curvilinear correlation coefficient, the less linear is the underlying relationship.

Eta requires data that can be presented as a ONE-WAY ANOVA. This means that there is a DEPENDENT VARIABLE which takes the form of numerical scores. The INDEPENDENT VARIABLE (IV) takes one of a number of different categories. These categories may be ordered (i.e., they can take a numerical value and, as such, represent scores on the IV). Alternatively, the categories of the IV may simply be nominal categories which have no underlying order.

📖 Cramer & Howitt 2004; Fraenkel & Wallen 2009; Porte 2010

eta² (η^2)
also eta squared

a measure of association that can be employed to determine the magnitude of EFFECT SIZE. Eta squared, symbolized by η^2 (the lowercase Greek letter eta), is interpreted as the proportion of the total variability of the DEPENDENT VARIABLE which is explained by the variation in the INDEPENDENT VARIABLE (IV). It can be used after a t-TEST which goes beyond the fact that there is a significant difference and gives us an indication of how much of the variability is due to our IV. Take an example of a t-test in the study of two different types of vocabulary instruction. Suppose that the t-test indicates that the learners from Group 1 score significantly better on their end of semester exam than do the learners from Group 2. You know that there is a difference between these groups, but you do not know how much of that difference can be explained by the IV (instruction type). You calculate η^2 and determine that $\eta^2 = .46$. That means that 46% of the variability in their scores can be accounted for by the instruction type. Or, 54% of the variability cannot be accounted for by the independent variable. η^2 is a relatively biased estimate of this proportion of the total variability in the population, and the biased estimate is usually larger than the true size of the effect.

📖 Larson-Hall 2010; Mackey & Gass 2005; Pagano 2009; Porte 2010

eta squared
another term for ETA² (η^2)

ethics

guidelines or sets of principles for good professional practice, which serve to advise and steer researchers as they conduct their work. The word ethics is derived from the Greek word *ethos* meaning a person's character, nature or disposition. Ethics is a branch of philosophy which is concerned with thinking about morality, integrity and the distinction between right and wrong.

see also INFORMED CONSENT

 Bloor & Wood 2006

ethnographic interview

an INTERVIEW which is similar to UNSTRUCTURED INTERVIEWs but within the context of the target research area, and extending beyond the restrictions of an unstructured interview by allowing interviewees to develop their responses in their own way, using their own frame of reference. The researcher here acts more as a facilitator, suggesting directions for discussion rather than controlling them and, at all times, maintaining a sense of freedom and informality for the informant. However, this appearance of informality does not necessarily result in incomparable, anecdotal data which can only be reported in case-study style. If the interviewer is sufficiently competent, ethnographic interviews can be steered through a broad range of subject matter and recorded data (note-taking is not advised with this approach) can be analyzed via CONTENT or DISCOURSE ANALYSIS following transcription.

see also NON-DIRECTIVE INTERVIEW, UNSTRUCTURED INTERVIEW; SEMI-STRUCTURED INTERVIEW, STRUCTURED INTERVIEW, INTERVIEW GUIDE, INFORMAL INTERVIEW, TELEPHONE INTERVIEW, FOCUS GROUP

 Brewerton & Millward 2001

ethnographic research

see ETHNOGRAPHY

ethnography

an approach to QUALITATIVE RESEARCH which comes largely from the field of anthropology. Literally the word ethnography means the description (graphy) of cultures (ethno). Ethnography is the in-depth study of naturally occurring behavior within a culture or entire social group. It seeks to understand the relationship between culture and behavior, with culture referring to the shared beliefs, values, concepts, practices, and attitudes of a specific group of people. It examines what people do and interprets why they do it. Ethnographers typically describe, analyze, and interpret culture over time using OBSERVATIONs and FIELD WORK as the primary data collecting strategies. The final product is a **cultural portrait** that incorporates the views of participants (EMIC PERSPECTIVE) as well as views of researcher (ETIC PERSPECTIVE). Ethnographic studies consider where people are situated and how they go about daily activities as well as cultural beliefs.

As a research methodology, **ethnographic research** requires avoidance of theoretical preconceptions and HYPOTHESIS TESTING in favor of prolonged direct observation, especially PARTICIPANT OBSERVATION, attempting to see social action and the activities of daily life from the participants' point of view, resulting in a long detailed description of what has been observed. Ethnography is an excellent way of crossing cultures and gaining insight into the life of organizations, institutions, and communities. It is ideal for generating initial hypotheses about something totally unknown. An ethnographic researcher provides a thick description of the target culture, that is, a narrative that describes richly and in great detail the daily life of the community as well as the cultural meanings and beliefs the participants attach to their activities, events, and behaviors. For this purpose ethnography uses an *eclectic* range of data collection techniques, including *participant* and *nonparticipant observation*, interviewing, and the ethnographer's own diary with FIELDNOTES and journal entries. These data sources are further supplemented by film or audio recordings as well as authentic documents and physical artifacts, and ethnographers may even use structured QUESTIONNAIREs that have been developed during the course of the field work. For example, in studying a particular group of second language learners, a researcher might observe the students in the classroom, with their peers outside the classroom, and at home with their families. They might also conduct IN-DEPTH INTERVIEWs with them as well as with their teachers, parents, and peers. All of this would be done in order to have multiple sources on which to build an interpretation of what is being studied. Note that it is not the data collection techniques that determine whether a study is an ethnography but rather the *sociocultural interpretation* that sets it apart from other forms of qualitative inquiry. Ethnography is not defined by how data are collected, but rather by the lens through which the data are interpreted. Ethnography can help educators and policymakers understand social and cultural issues that need to be addressed and provide insights into strategies that might be appropriate in a given culture or with particular marginalized groups.

There two main approaches to ethnography. **Realist ethnography** is the more traditional approach. In realist ethnography, the researcher tries to provide an objective account of the situation, typically from a third-person point of view. Standard categories are used, and factual information and closely edited quotes are presented as data. The researcher's interpretation occurs at the end. In **critical ethnography**, the researcher takes an advocacy perspective and has a value-laden orientation. The researcher is advocating for a marginalized group, challenging the status quo, or attempting to empower the group by giving it voice.

Applied linguistics as a field has an inherent interest in intercultural communication and, thus, ethnographic research has been embraced by scholars who look at language leaning as a profoundly social practice and see second language learning, second culture learning, and language socialization as inextricably bound. In addition, because of the increasingly situated nature of much recent SLA research, ethnography has also been utilized for the contextualized analysis of classroom discourse and school learning. In studies of language learning and use, the term ethnographic research is sometimes used to refer to the observation and description of naturally occurring language (e.g., between mother and child or between teacher and students), particularly when there is a strong cultural element to the research or the analysis. However, much of this research is quasi-ethnographic at best, since the requirements of prolonged observation and thick description are frequently not met.

A typical ethnography might be a study of a group of teachers in their institutional setting over a term or year, focusing particularly on their relationships with students as these are exemplified in staffroom and classroom behavior. The researcher might join the staff as a temporary teacher, taking fieldnotes, observing lessons, interviewing teachers (and perhaps students), even taping some staff meetings, focusing particularly on the ways in which teachers deal with new students in their classes and how these students are represented in staffroom talk.

The main drawback of the approach is concerned is that the need for prolonged engagement with the participants in their natural setting requires an extensive time investment that few academic researchers can afford. A further limitation of ethnographic studies is how to strike a balance between the insider and outsider perspective. If teachers, for example, are too familiar with a teaching context, they have biases, which may distort their interpretations. On the other hand, if teachers are unfamiliar with a teaching context they may not be able to get an insider's view of the dynamics in the classroom. Striking a balance between these two extremes is challenging because classroom teachers researching their own culture must simultaneously maintain membership for the sake of their identity and detach themselves from the culture sufficiently to describe it.

📖 Ary et al. 2010; Dörnyei 2007; McKay 2006; Richards 2003

ethnomethodology
a branch of sociology that studies how people organize and understand the activities of ordinary life. Ethnomethodology is concerned with how people make sense of their everyday world. More especially, it is directed at the mechanisms by which participants achieve and sustain interaction in a social encounter—the assumptions they make, the conven-

tions they utilize and the practices they adopt. Ethnomethodology, thus, seeks to understand social accomplishments in their own terms; it is concerned to understand them from within. The central aim for ethnomethodologists is to describe and analyze the practical procedures that members use to make sense of the social world. The intention is to focus upon identifying and understanding the methods which people employ to decide whether or not something is real.

Ethnomethodology also has similarities with SYMBOLIC INTERACTIONISM, which is concerned with the ways in which people define and share meanings of the social world through interaction. Like symbolic interactionism, ethnomethodology is also concerned with interactions, but ethnomethodology focuses on the methods by which people make sense of social worlds.

Ethnomethodologists examine the ways in which people go about their daily lives (at work, at home, at leisure etc.). Ethnomethodologists argue that in order to organize action, people need to make frequent decisions as to what is unquestionably true for them. Popular examples are that if people switch their computer on it is unquestionably true that poisonous gas will not emit from the hard disc, or if they make a cup of coffee it is unquestionably true that they will find it bitter without sugar. These decisions (to switch the computer on, to put sugar in one's coffee and so on), and taken-for-granted assumptions, pervade everyday activities.

A key feature of ethnomethodology is that it is concerned with people's practical actions in situated contexts. Using one of the previous examples of coffee making, the situated context may change if the coffee bean is a different brand to one's usual coffee or the coffee is made in a different kitchen. Therefore the practical situatedness of actions still provides for the possibility of improvisation in even the most routine activities. Ethnomethodologists are then able to study how people work out a course of action while they are engaged in the activity.

There are two types of ethnomethodologists: linguistic and situational. The **linguistic ethnomethodologist**s focus upon the use of language and the ways in which conversations in everyday life are structured. Their analyses make much use of the unstated taken-for-granted meanings, the use of indexical expressions, and the way in which conversations convey much more than is actually said. The **situational ethnomethodologist**s cast their view over a wider range of social activity and seek to understand the ways in which people negotiate the social contexts in which they find themselves. They are concerned to understand how people make sense of and order their environment. As part of their empirical method, ethnomethodologists may consciously and deliberately disrupt or question the ordered taken-for-granted elements in everyday situations in order to reveal the underlying processes at work, i.e., to see how people react.

One of the key criticisms of ethnomethodology is that in focusing on face-to-face interactions it ignores, and arguably denies, the existence and importance of wider complex social systems such as class structure and social norms. Therefore, it is argued, rather than being a comprehensive sociology, ethnomethodology can only aspire to be a sociological specialism which focuses on the details of face-to-face interactions. Ethnomethodologists have responded to this charge by arguing that their neglect of the wider social context is the result of their decision to treat as important that which their subjects are orientated to (everyday action). And it is undeniable that the constitutive practices of everyday life were under-researched before the development of ethnomethodological studies.

see also PHENOMENOLOGY
📖 Bloor & Wood 2006; Cohen et al. 2011

etic perspective
see QUALITATIVE RESEARCH

evaluation research
also **program evaluation**
the systematic gathering of information for purposes of decision making. Evaluation may use quantitative methods (e.g., tests), qualitative methods (e.g., observations, ratings), and value judgments. In language planning, evaluation frequently involves gathering information on patterns of language use, language ability, and attitudes towards language. In language program evaluation, evaluation is related to decisions about the quality of the program itself and decisions about individuals in the programs. It is the determination of how successful an educational program or curriculum is in achieving its goals. The evaluation of programs may involve the study of curriculum, objectives, materials, and tests or grading systems. The evaluation of individuals involves decisions about entrance to programs, placement, progress, and achievement. In evaluating both programs and individuals, tests and other measures are frequently used.

There are many different types of evaluations depending on the object being evaluated and the purpose of the evaluation. Perhaps the most important basic distinction in evaluation types is that between FORMATIVE EVALUATION and SUMMATIVE EVALUATION. Program evaluators tend to use both formative and summative information in identifying areas in need of improvement and in determining a program's success or failure.

Often, evaluation is construed as part of a larger managerial or administrative process. Sometimes this is referred to as the **planning-evaluation**

cycle. Usually, the first stage of such a cycle—the planning phase—is designed to elaborate a set of potential actions, programs, or technologies, and select the best for implementation. Depending on the organization and the problem being addressed, a planning process could involve any or all of these stages: the formulation of the problem, issue, or concern; the broad conceptualization of the major alternatives that might be considered; the detailing of these alternatives and their potential implications; the evaluation of the alternatives and the selection of the best one; and the implementation of the selected alternative. Although these stages are traditionally considered planning, a lot of evaluation work is involved. Evaluators are trained in needs assessment; they use methodologies—such as the CONCEPT MAPPING—that help in conceptualization and detailing, and they have the skills to help assess alternatives and make choice of the best one.

The evaluation phase also involves a sequence of stages that typically include the formulation of the major objectives, goals, and hypotheses of the program or technology; the conceptualization and operationalization of the major components of the evaluation (the program, participants, setting, and measures); the design of the evaluation, the details of how these components will be coordinated; the analysis of the information, both qualitative and quantitative; and the utilization of the evaluation results.

📖 Lodico et al. 2010; O'Leary 2004; Richards & Schmidt 2010; Trochim & Donnelly 2007

evaluative validity

(in QUALITATIVE RESEARCH) a type of VALIDITY which refers to the assessment of how the researcher evaluates the phenomenon studied (e.g., in terms of *usefulness, practicability, desirability*), that is how accurately the research account assigns value judgments to the phenomenon. Thus, this validity aspect concerns the implicit or explicit use of an evaluation framework (e.g., ethical or moral judgments) in a qualitative account, examining how the evaluative claims fit the observed phenomenon. Evaluative validity is gaining importance nowadays with various critical theories becoming increasingly prominent in the social science and also in applied linguistics.

see also DESCRIPTIVE VALIDITY, INTERPRETIVE VALIDITY, THEORETICAL VALIDITY

📖 Dörnyei 2007

event-contingent design

see DIARY STUDY

event history analysis
also **EHA**

a technique that allows researchers to assess the implicit risk of an event occurring. That is, we consider not only whether an event occurs, but when. Event history analysis (EHA) provides an understanding of the timing and history leading up to one single event or to events that may be repeated over time from which we can draw inferences about the process. More precisely, EHA is the name given to a wide variety of statistical techniques for the analysis of longitudinal data and for studying the movement over time (transitions) of subjects through successive states or conditions, including the length of the time intervals between entry to and exit from specific states. EHA is usually used in situations when the DEPENDENT VARIABLE is *categorical*. However, even changes noted in *continuous* dependent variables (measured on INTERVAL or RATIO SCALEs) can be dealt with.

Two types of event history models are parametric and semiparametric models. Parametric models assume that the time until an event occurs follows a specific distribution, such as the exponential, and the distribution of when the events happen can be thought of as time dependency in the data. Parametric distributions are most often used in engineering when the analyst has a strong understanding of the distribution of the risk of failing with respect to time. The primary advantage of parametric event history models is the ability to forecast.

Conversely, semiparametric models do not specify a distributional shape for the timing of events; rather semiparametric models are parameterized by the EXPLANATORY VARIABLEs. A semiparametric model is more appropriate when the primary objective is to understand the impact of covariates on the risk of an event. In this situation, duration dependence is considered a nuisance. Time-dependency can be thought of as the *left over* effects of time after the hazard rate has been conditioned by the covariates. If the model had been perfectly specified, there would be no time-dependency because the hazard rate would be fully characterized by the covariates.

 Menard 2008

exact replication
another term for LITERAL REPLICATION

exact test
see CONSERVATIVE TEST

exogenous variable
see PATH ANALYSIS

expected frequencies
　　see CHI-SQUARE TEST

experiential realism
　　a worldview or EPISTEMOLOGY which underlies the work of some QUANTITATIVE RESEARCHers. Experiential realism claims, as do antipositivist positions, that we cannot observe the world in a purely objective way, because our perception itself influences what we see and measure. In contrast to subjectivist positions, however, experiential realists believe that there is a limit to subjectivity. Humans are limited in their subjectivity by the fact that we use a limited number of schemas to formulate our views of the world. This is because our perception is embodied. We do not observe passively, but actively interact with the world through our bodies. Experiential realists see the use of metaphor as crucial to the way we make sense of the world around us. We use metaphors to understand our world. One of the main metaphors we use to do this is the subject/object schema, which divides the world up into objects (things) and subjects (people). This metaphor has its origins in the fact that in our dealings with the world we find that there is a distinction between an external world consisting of edges, surfaces, and textures that are not us, and those things that are us, the actor. As we move around our world, the objects remain invariant. Science, according to this view, is an activity that is based on this subject/object schema.
　　📖 Muijs 2004

experimental contamination
　　a situation that occurs when participants in one experimental condition are indirectly affected by the INDEPENDENT VARIABLE in another experimental condition because they interacted with participants in the other condition.
　　📖 Leary 2011

experimental design
　　see EXPERIMENTAL RESEARCH

experimental group
　　see CONTROL GROUP

experimental manipulation
　　another term for TREATMENT

experimental mortality
　　another term for MORTALITY

experimental research
  also **experimental study**
a type of QUANTITATIVE RESEARCH in which the experimenters manipulate certain stimuli, TREATMENTs, or environmental conditions and observe how the condition or behavior of the subject is affected or changed. Their manipulation is deliberate and systematic. They must be aware of other factors (EXTRANEOUS VARIABLEs) that could influence the outcome and remove or control them so that they can establish a logical association between manipulated factors and observed effects. Experimentation provides method of HYPOTHESIS TESTING. After experimenters define a problem, they propose a tentative answer or HYPOTHESIS. They test the hypothesis and confirm or refute it in the light of the controlled variable relationship that they have observed. It is important to note that the confirmability or rejection of the hypothesis is stated in terms of PROBABILITY rather than certainty.

Experimental design is the blueprint of the procedures that enable the researcher to test hypotheses by reaching valid conclusion about relationship between INDEPENDENT and DEPENDENT VARIABLEs. Selection of a particular design is based on the purpose of the experiment, the type of variables to be manipulated, the conditions or limiting factors under which it is conducted, and some other factors. Experimental designs can be classified according to the number of independent variables (IVs): *single-variable designs* and FACTORIAL DESIGNs. A single-variable design has one manipulated IV; factorial designs have two or more IVs, at least one of which is manipulated.

Experimental designs may also be classified according to how well they provide control of the threats to INTERNAL and EXTERNAL VALIDITY. They can be divided into those which do and those which do not show RANDOM SELECTION and RANDOM ASSIGNMENT (i.e., PRE-EXPERIMENTAL DESIGN, TRUE EXPERIMENTAL DESIGN, and QUASI-EXPERIMENTAL DESIGN). For example, true experimental designs require random selection and, where treatments are compared, random assignment to groups. Sometimes, especially in classroom research, neither random selection nor random assignment is possible. The researcher must work with an established class of students, (i.e., an INTACT GROUP).

The experimental designs that use at least two groups of subjects, one of which is exposed to the treatment (IV) and the other that does not receive the treatment or is exposed to another level of the treatment are called BETWEEN-SUBJECTS DESIGNs. However, it is possible to use experimental designs in which the same participants are exposed to different levels of the IV at different times. This type of design in which a researcher observes each individual in all of the different treatments is called a WITHIN-SUBJECTS DESIGN. It is also called a *repeated-measures*

design because the research repeats measurements of the same individuals under different treatment conditions. There are still other experimental designs, SINGLE-SUBJECT EXPERIMENTAL DESIGNs, which are limited to one or a few participant(s) who serves as both the TREATMENT and the CONTROL GROUPs.
see also NONEXPERIMENTAL RESEARCH
 Ary et al. 2010; Best & Kahn 2006; Hatch & Lazaraton 1991; Lavrakas 2008; Ravid 2011; Seliger & Shohamy 1989

experimental study
another term for EXPERIMENTAL RESEARCH

experimental treatment
another term for TREATMENT

experimental variable
another name for INDEPENDENT VARIABLE

experimenter bias
see RESEARCHER EFFECT

experimenter effect
another term for RESEARCHER EFFECT

experimentwise error rate
also **per-experiment error rate**
the PROBABILITY that at least one (i.e., one or more) of the inferences to be drawn from the same set of data will be wrong. Experimentwise error rate is equivalent to the probability of incorrectly rejecting at least one of the null hypotheses in an experiment involving one or more tests or comparisons. In other words, it is the probability of making a TYPE I ERROR anywhere among the comparisons in an experiment. In a multiple comparison procedure, it is the SIGNIFICANCE LEVEL associated with the entire set of comparisons of interest to the investigator.
see also COMPARISONWISE ERROR RATE
 Everitt & Skrondal 2010; Heiman 2011; Sahai & Khurshid 2001

expert review
another term for PEER REVIEW

explained variable
another term for DEPENDENT VARIABLE

explanatory design

a MIXED METHODS RESEARCH design which is used extensively in applied linguistics research. The word explanatory in the design name suggests explanation: qualitative findings are used to help explain, refine, clarify, or extend quantitative results. Quantitative and qualitative data are collected and analyzed in sequence: first quantitative data is collected and analyzed, and then qualitative data. A typical example would include conducting follow-up qualitative interviews of representative or extreme cases to more deeply explore quantitative results. An example of this is the exploration of Japanese ESL students' perceptions of the classroom activities and classroom-related behaviors of their English teachers in the United States and in Japan. The researchers first surveyed a large sample of Japanese ESL learners in both countries using a 49-item QUESTIONNAIRE, and then they conducted follow-up interviews with three students to help interpret and elaborate the results obtained from the SURVEY. Figure E.2 presents the visual diagram of the explanatory design procedures in this study.

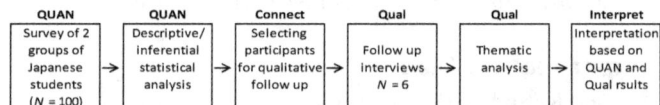

Figure E.2. Schematic Representation of Explanatory Design

The weight in this design is typically placed on quantitative data because the quantitative data collection represents the major aspect of this mixed methods data collection process; it also comes first in the sequence. The mixing of the two methods occurs at two stages in the research process: first, while developing the qualitative interview protocol and choosing the participants for in-depth exploration of the quantitative results; and second, while integrating the results from both quantitative and qualitative phases at the interpretation and discussion stage of the study. The data analysis typically involves several options. A researcher might choose to follow up on extreme or representative cases from the quantitative analysis, or seek to explain the quantitative results in more depth.

The structure of an explanatory design report typically follows the sequential character of the design: the quantitative data collection and analysis is described first, followed by the description of the qualitative data collection and analysis. A separate section in the report might discuss how the two phases were connected in the research process. During the discussion of the study results, a researcher explains how the qualitative findings helped elaborate or extend the quantitative results.

An advantage of the explanatory design is that its two separate phases make it straightforward and reasonably easy to implement for novice researchers. This sequential nature also makes it simple to describe and report on. However, compared to a straightforward quantitative study, an explanatory design study may take longer to complete.

see also QUANTITATIVE RESEARCH, QUALITATIVE RESEARCH, TRIANGULATION DESIGN, EMBEDDED DESIGN, EXPLORATORY DESIGN

📖 Heigham & Croker 2009

explanatory variable
another term for INDEPENDENT VARIABLE

exploratory data analysis
also **EDA**

a philosophy and strategy of research which puts the primary focus of the researcher on using the data as the starting point for understanding the matter under research. This is distinct from the use of data as a resource for checking the adequacy of theory. Classical or conventional approaches to data analysis are driven by a desire to examine fairly limited hypotheses empirically but, as a consequence, may ignore equally important features of the data which require understanding and explanation. In conventional approaches, the focus is on using techniques such as the t-TEST, ANOVA, and so forth, in order to establish the credibility of the model developed by the researcher largely prior to data collection. In exploratory data analysis, the emphasis is on maximizing the gain from the data by making more manifest the process of describing and analyzing the obtained data in their complexity without using a statistical model or having formulated a HYPOTHESIS. In exploratory data analysis, anomalous data such as the existence of OUTLIERs are not regarded as a nuisance but something to be explained as part of the model. Deviations from LINEARITY are seen as crucial aspects to be explained rather than a nuisance.

The major functions of exploratory data analysis are as follows:

1) To ensure maximum understanding of the data by revealing their basic structure.
2) To identify the nature of the important variables in the structure of the data.
3) To develop simple but insightful models to account for the data.

Many of the techniques used in exploratory data analysis would be regarded as very basic statistical *plots*, *graphs*, and *tables*. The STEM-AND-LEAF PLOT, BOX-AND-WHISKER PLOT, and PARETO CHART are graphical examples of exploratory data analysis. Also exploratory statistics such as

FACTOR ANALYSIS, PRINCIPLE COMPONENT ANALYSIS, MULTIDIMENTIAL SCALING, CLUSTER ANALYSIS, DISCRIMINANT FUNCTION ANALYSIS, GUTTMAN SCALING, PATH ANALYSIS, and LOGLINEAR ANALYSIS are used to explore relationships between variables by helping to identify (a) underlying variables, (b) similar subject performance, (c) group membership, (d) the existence of a scale, or (e) causal relationships.
see also DESCRIPTIVE STATISTICS, INFERENTIAL STATISTICS
📖 Brown 1992; Cramer & Howitt 2004; Harlow 2005

exploratory design
a MIXED METHODS RESEARCH design which is used when a researcher needs first to explore a topic using qualitative data before measuring or testing it quantitatively. This design is particularly appropriate when studying a topic which has been little explored, so there is little information about the relevant constructs and how to measure important variables. In this design, the qualitative data is collected and analyzed first, followed by the collection and analysis of the quantitative data. The researchers first explore a topic by collecting qualitative data to help identify principal themes and possibly generate a theory. Then, they collect quantitative data to examine the initial qualitative results, such as to test a theory or to develop a measurement instrument such as a questionnaire or survey.

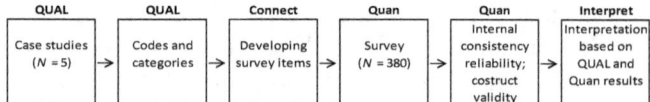

Figure E.3. Schematic Representation of Exploratory Design

For example, the exploratory design was used to investigate teachers' attitudes toward COMPUTER-ASSISTED LANGUAGE LEARNING (CALL). In the first phase, five case studies were conducted in four schools and a university to explore teachers' attitudes toward CALL. Next the qualitative findings from these studies were used to develop a 56-item questionnaire to measure those attitudes, which was then tested for reliability and validity with a larger sample of school and university teachers. Figure E.3 presents the visual diagram of the exploratory design procedures in this study.

The *weight* in the exploratory design is typically given to the qualitative data, because it provides the foundation for the quantitative exploration of the topic. The *mixing* of the two methods occurs while developing the quantitative survey items based on the qualitative data analysis and also while comparing the quantitative results with initial qualitative findings.

The most popular approach for data analysis is to use the qualitative themes and categories to develop the quantitative measurement instrument. In writing up the research, a researcher first reports the qualitative data collection and analysis and then explains the development of the instrument. Next, the quantitative data collection and analysis are discussed, and finally the overall results of the study are presented.

Like the EXPLANATORY DESIGN, the two-phase nature of the exploratory design makes it straightforward for a researcher to design, implement, and report on. However, like in the explanatory design, implementing the two separate phases of the study can be time consuming. In addition, developing a measurement instrument is not easy. A researcher must use careful procedures to ensure that it is grounded in the qualitative results—that it is not constructed from common sense or theory, but based upon the qualitative data collected—and that it is tested for RELIABILITY and VALIDITY.

see also QUALITATIVE RESEARCH, QUANTITATIVE RESEARCH, TRIANGULATION DESIGN, EMBEDDED DESIGN

📖 Heigham & Croker 2009

exploratory factor analysis
also EFA

a type of FACTOR ANALYSIS (FA) in which the researcher seeks to describe and summarize data by grouping together a large number of variables that are linearly correlated. The variables themselves may or may not have been chosen with potential underlying processes in mind. Exploratory factor analysis (EFA) explores the data and provides the researcher with information about how many constructs or factors are needed to best represent the data. EFA is usually performed in the early stages of research, when it provides a tool for consolidating variables and for generating hypotheses about underlying processes. The question in EFA is: 'What are the underlying processes that could have produced CORRELATIONs among these variables?'

For an illustration, imagine that a researcher wants to identify the major dimensions underlying a number of personality tests. S/he begins by administering the personality tests to a large sample of people ($N = 1000$), with each test supposedly measuring a specific facet of a person's personality (e.g., ethnocentrism, authoritarianism, and locus of control). Assume that there are 30 such tests, each consisting of ten test items. What the researcher will end up with is a mass of numbers that will say very little about the dimensions underlying these personality tests. On average, some of the scores will be high, some will be low, and some intermediate, but interpretation of these scores will be extremely difficult if not impossible. This is where FA comes in. It allows the researcher to reduce this mass of numbers to a few representative factors, which can then be used for subsequent analysis. FA is based on the assumption that all variables are correlated to some degree. Therefore, those variables that share similar underlying dimensions should be highly correlated, and those variables that measure dissimilar dimensions should yield low correlations. Using the earlier example, if the researcher intercorrelates the scores obtained from the 30 personality tests, then those tests that measure the same underlying personality dimension should yield high CORRELATION COEFFICIENTs, whereas those tests that measure different personality dimensions should yield low correlation coefficients. These high/low correlation coefficients will become apparent in the CORRELATION MATRIX because they form clusters indicating which variables hang together.

Suppose that you obtained participants' scores on five variables: A, B, C, D, and E. When you calculated the correlations among these five variables, you obtained the following correlation matrix:

Variables	A	B	C	D	E
A	1.00	.78	.85	.01	-.07
B	—	1.00	.70	.09	.00
C	—	—	.100	-.02	.04
D	—	—	—	1.00	.86
E	—	—	—	—	1.00

Table E.1. A Correlation Matrix

As shown in Table E.1, variables A, B, and C correlate highly with each other, but each correlates weakly with variables D and E. Variables D and E, on the other hand, are highly correlated. This pattern suggests that these five variables may be measuring only two different constructs: A, B, and C seem to measure aspects of one construct, whereas D and E measure something else. In the language of FA, two factors underlie these data and account for the observed pattern of correlations among the variables.

FA attempts to identify the minimum number of factors or dimensions that will do a reasonably good job of accounting for the observed relationships among the variables. At one extreme, if all of the variables are highly correlated with one another, the analysis will identify a single factor; in essence, all of the observed variables are measuring aspects of the same thing. At the other extreme, if the variables are totally uncorrelated, the analysis will identify as many factors as there are variables. If the variables are not at all related, there are no underlying factors that account for their interrelationships. Each variable is measuring something different, and there are as many factors as variables.

The solution to a FA is presented in a **factor matrix**. Table E.2 shows the factor matrix for the variables examined in the preceding correlation matrix.

Variables	Factor 1	Factor 2
A	.97	-.04
B	.80	.04
C	.87	.00
D	.03	.93
E	-.01	.92

Table E.2. A Factor Matrix

Down the left column of the factor matrix are the original variables—A, B, C, D, and E. Across the top are the factors that have been identified from the analysis. The numerical entries in the table are **factor loadings**, which are the correlation between the original variables and the factors, and the key to understanding the nature of a particular factor. Squared factor loadings indicate what percentage of the variance in an original variable is explained by a factor. A variable that correlates with a factor is said to load on that factor. The higher its loading, the more a variable contributes to and defines a particular factor. A factor loading is interpreted like a correlation coefficient: The larger it is (either positive or negative), the stronger the relationship of the variable to the factor. Researchers use these factor loadings to interpret and label the factors. By seeing which variables load on a factor, researchers can usually identify the nature of a factor. In interpreting the factor structure, researchers typically consider variables that load at least $\pm.30$ with each factor. That is, they look at the variables that correlate at least $\pm.30$ with a factor and try to discern what those variables have in common. By examining the variables that load on a factor, they can usually determine the nature of the underlying construct. For example, as you can see in Table E.2, variables A, B, and C each load greater than .30 on Factor 1, whereas the Factor loadings of variables D and E with Factor 1 are quite small. Factor 2, on the other hand, is defined primarily by variables D and E. This pattern indicates that variables A, B, and C reflect aspects of a single factor, whereas D and E reflect aspects of a different factor. In a real FA, we would know what the original variables were measuring, and we would use that knowledge to identify and label the factors we obtained. For example, we might know that variables A, B, and C were all related to language and verbal ability, whereas variables D and E were measures of conceptual ability and reasoning. Thus, Factor 1 would be a verbal ability factor and Factor 2 would be a conceptual ability factor.

To conclude, the distinctive feature of EFA is that the factors are derived from statistical results, not from theory. This means that the researcher runs the software and lets the underlying pattern of the data determine the factor structure. Thus, EFA is conducted without knowing how many factors really exist (if any) or which variables belong with which constructs. When EFA is applied, the researcher uses established guidelines to determine which variables load on a particular factor and how many factors are appropriate. The factors that emerge can only be named after the FA is performed. In this respect, EFA is different from the other type of FA, i.e., CONFIRMATORY FACTOR ANALYSIS.

📖 Best & Kahn 2006; Cohen et al. 2011; Fulcher 2003; Hair et al. 2010; Hatch & Farhady 1982; Ho 2006; Leary 2011; Mackey & Gass 2005; Pallant 2010; Tabachnick & Fidell 2007

exploratory research
another term for HYPOTHESIS-GENERATING RESEARCH

exponent
a symbol or number written above and to the right of another symbol or number to indicate the number of times that a quantity should be multiplied by itself. For example, the exponent 3 in the expression 2^3 indicates that the quantity 2 should be multiplied by itself three times, $2 \times 2 \times 2$. The exponent 2 in the expression R^2 indicates that the quantity R is multiplied by itself twice.

see also POWER
📖 Cramer & Howitt 2004

expository text
see NARRATIVE TEXT

ex post facto research
also **natural experiment**

a research design in which the researcher has no control over the selection and manipulation of the INDEPENDENT VARIABLE (IV) and examines the data *retrospectively* to establish possible causes, relationships or associations, and their meanings. When translated literally, ex post facto means *after the fact* or retrospectively. In the context of social, educational and applied linguistics research the ex post facto research refers to those studies which investigate the possible cause-and-effect relationships by observing an existing condition or state of affairs and searching back in time for plausible causal factors. The important thing is that the researcher is not interested in seeing the effect of a TREATMENT as such, but rather in studying the hypothesized effect of an IV after that effect has occurred (such as whether gender has any effect on motivation in second-language learning). The research is not attempting to show that performance has improved as a result of some instruction or other, nor is cause and effect being studied, no group assignment is organized or needed, and no variables are being manipulated to bring about a change.

Ex post facto research, then, is a method of finding out possible antecedents of events that have happened and cannot, therefore, be engineered or manipulated by the investigator. The following example will illustrate the basic idea. Imagine a situation in which there has been a dramatic increase in the number of fatal road accidents in a particular locality. An expert is called in to investigate. Naturally, there is no way in which s/he can study the actual accidents because they have happened; nor can s/he turn to technology for a video replay of the incidents. What s/he can do, however, is attempt a reconstruction by studying the statistics, examining the accident spots, and taking note of the statements given by victims and witnesses. In this way the expert will be in a position to identify possible determinants of the accidents. These may include excessive speed, poor road conditions, careless driving, frustration, inefficient vehicles, the effects of drugs or alcohol and soon. On the basis of his/her examination, s/he can formulate hypotheses as to the likely causes and submit them to the appropriate authority in the form of recommendations. These may include improving road conditions, or lowering the speed limit, or increasing police surveillance, for instance. The point of interest to us is that in identifying the causes retrospectively, the expert adopts an ex post facto perspective.

In ex post facto research the IV or variables have already occurred and in which the researcher starts with the observation of a DEPENDENT VARIABLE or variables. S/he then studies the IV or variables in retrospect for their possible relationship to, and effects on, the dependent variable or variables. The researcher is thus examining retrospectively the effects of a naturally occurring event on a subsequent outcome with a view to establishing a causal link between them. Interestingly, some instances of ex post facto designs correspond to EXPERIMENTAL RESEARCH in reverse. the researcher must consider the possibility of **reverse causality**—that the reverse of the suggested HYPOTHESIS could also account for the finding. Instead of saying that X causes Y, perhaps it is the case that Y causes X. Ex post facto research, unlike experimental research, does not provide the safeguards that are necessary for making strong inferences about causal relationships. Mistakenly attributing causation based on a relationship between two variables is called the **post hoc fallacy**. An investigator who finds a relationship between the variables in an ex post facto study has secured evidence only of some concomitant variation. Because the investigator has not controlled X or other possible variables that may have determined Y, there is less basis for inferring a causal relationship between X and Y.

Ex post facto designs are appropriate in circumstances where the more powerful experimental method is not possible. These would arise when, for example, it is not possible to select, control and manipulate the factors necessary to study cause-and-effect relationships directly; or when the control of all variables except a single IV may be unrealistic and artificial, preventing the normal interaction with other influential variables; or when laboratory controls for many research purposes would be impractical, costly or ethically undesirable. Ex post facto research is particularly suitable in contexts where the IV or variables lie outside the researchers' control. Ex post facto designs can also be used for text analysis too. The research tells us what is going on, not the effect of some treatment. We can examine text features (e.g., use of modals) and see how they vary across genres (e.g., narrative vs. procedural text). The analysis will describe what is already there, not a change brought about by some instructional treatment.

Two kinds of design may be identified in ex post facto research: CAUSAL RESEARCH and CAUSAL-COMPARATIVE RESEARCH.

see also CORRELATIONAL RESEARCH

📖 Ary et al. 2010; Cohen et al. 2011; Hatch & Lazaraton 1991

external criticism
see SYNTHESIS

external generalizability
see GENERALIZABILITY

external validity
the extent to which the research findings based on a SAMPLE of individuals or objects can be generalized to the same POPULATION that the sample is taken from or to other similar populations in terms of contexts, individuals, times, and settings. External validity is a very important concept in all types of research designs. In QUANTITATIVE RESEARCH, GENERALIZABILITY is often achieved by using a RANDOM SAMPLE of a representative group of the target population. For example, if a researcher wants to make generalizations about Iranian junior university students' attitudes toward communicative language teaching, the researcher would try to get a large representative sample of Iranian junior university students in order to make certain that the findings of the SURVEY can be generalized to all Iranian junior university students.

Some extraneous factors that can threaten the external validity of a study are: MULTIPLE-TREATMENT INTERACTION, SPECIFICITY OF VARIABLES,

TREATMENT DIFFUSION, RESEARCHER EFFECT, HALO EFFECT, HAWTHORNE EFFECT, NOVELTY EFFECT, JOHN HENRY EFFECT, ORDER EFFECT, DEMORALIZATION, SELECTION-TREATMENT INTERACTION, and PRETEST-TREATMENT INTERACTION.

The two main ways to improve external validity are *replication* and the careful *selection* of participants. Replication is the term used to describe repeating a piece of research. Replications can be conducted under as many of the original conditions as possible. While such studies will help to see whether the original findings were unique and merely a result of chance happenings, they do little to improve external validity. This can be helped by replications that vary an aspect of the original study, for example, by including participants of a different age or using a new setting. If similar results are obtained then this can increase their generalizability. There are a number of ways of selecting participants (see SAMPLING).

QUALITATIVE RESEARCHers use the term TRANSFERABILITY to mean the same thing as external validity.

see also CRITERION-RELATED VALIDITY, CONSTRUCT VALIDITY, INTERNAL VALIDITY, FACE VALIDITY, CONTENT VALIDITY

 Clark-Carter 2010; Lodico et al. 2010; McKay 2006

extraneous variable
also nuisance variable

an INDEPENDENT VARIABLE (IV) that the investigator has chosen to keep constant, neutralize, or otherwise eliminate so that it will not have an effect on the study. Because applied linguistics research may involve many variables interacting at the same time, variables other than the independent, DEPENDENT, and MODERATOR VARIABLEs must sometimes be accounted for without actually including them in the research. Such variables may be treated as **control variable**s, that is, variables that the researcher wants to inhibit from interfering with the interpretation of the results. The researcher must attempt to control, or neutralize, all independent extraneous or irrelevant variables that are not related to the purpose of the study. These extraneous variables will result in ERROR VARIANCE, variability among scores that cannot be attributed to the effects of the IV.

For example, consider a study of the effect of teaching Method X on English language proficiency. The researcher would be primarily interested in the relationship between the IV (method) and dependent variable (English proficiency). However, there are a number of variables which might have an impact on such a study: gender, years of language study, whether the students had lived with a native speaker, number of languages spoken at home, language aptitude, motivation, and so forth. The list of potential control variables could become quite long. The researcher might choose to control one variable by:

a) *Removing it from the study.* (e.g., living with a native speaker could be removed from the study as a variable by using only subjects who have never lived with a native speaker).
b) *Holding it constant.* (e.g., years of language study could be held constant by using only those students who had studied 6 years of English; or, if a researcher includes only boys as the subjects of a study, s/he is controlling the variable of gender. We would say that the gender of the subjects does not vary; it is a constant in this study).
c) *Making it a* COVARIATE. For instance, the researcher might choose to treat language aptitude as a covariate. Using scores on a language aptitude test, this variable could be controlled by including it as a covariate and statistically removing its effects.
d) *Using random selection.* If individuals are randomly selected (see RANDOM SAMPLING) when the researcher is forming the groups in a study and the number of people in each group is sufficiently large, the groups can be considered equivalent on all variables other than those purposely manipulated as independent, dependent, and moderator variables. This attribute of random selection explains why it is sometimes so prominently discussed in statistical studies.

see also INTERVENING VARIABLE, CATEGORICAL VARIABLE, CONTINUOUS VARIABLE, EXTRANEOUS VARIABLE, CONFOUNDING VARIABLE

 Brown 1988, 1992; Fraenkel & Wallen 2009; Hatch & Farhady 1982; Porte 2010

extreme case sampling
see PURPOSIVE SAMPLING

F

f
    an abbreviation for FREQUENCY. Also an abbreviation for COHEN'S *f*

F_{max}
    an abbreviation for HARTLEY'S TEST

face appearance
    another term for FACE VALIDITY

face-to-face interview
    also **in-person interview, personal interview**
    a data collection method where the researcher is in the same location as the participant and asks questions to which the participant responds. It is called face-to-face interview because the researcher and participant are facing each other during the interview conversation. Face-to-face interviews are generally the best choice when interviewing individuals who are geographically accessible. As with all types of interviews, researchers using face-to-face interviews learn about participants' views in their own words. In addition, by conducting interviews in person, researchers are better able to develop rapport with participants, thereby increasing the likelihood of learning details about their views. Interviewers can also make observations during interviews when they are physically present. Observations may include important nonverbal cues used by interviewees, including hand motions and head nodding. If the face-to-face interviews take place in the participants settings (e.g., their homes or places of work), then interviewers are able to observe individuals context as well.
    📖 Given 2008

face validity
    also **face appearance**
    a facet of VALIDITY that indicates the degree to which a measurement procedure appears to measure what it is supposed to measure. Face validity involves the judgment of the researcher or of research participants that the indicator really measures the CONSTRUCT. A measure has face validity if people think it does. It is a consensus method. For example, few people would accept a measure of college student math ability using a question that asked students: 2 + 2 =? This is not a valid measure of college-level math ability on the face of it. Or, if a test of reading comprehension contains many dialect words that might be unknown to the

test takers, the test may be said to lack face validity. The closer it looks like it is gathering the correct data, the more valid it looks.

In general, a researcher is more likely to have faith in an instrument whose content obviously taps into the construct s/he wants to measure than in an instrument that is not face valid. Examinees who do not feel that the procedure is measuring what they think it should measure might not be motivated to do their best. This, in turn, will affect the results of the study. People outside a study might also not see the relevance of a particular measurement technique and, therefore, not consider the results from such measurement useful for answering the researcher question (i.e., the consumer). Although this facet of validity is of lesser theoretical importance from a research perspective, it is the one that many practitioners in applied linguistics give most attention to. This has led some people to make incorrect conclusions about the validity of data that result from some measurement procedures.

see also CRITERION-RELATED VALIDITY, CONSTRUCT VALIDITY, INTERNAL VALIDITY, EXTERNAL VALIDITY, CONTENT VALIDITY

Perry 2011; Clark-Carter 2010

factor

see INDEPENDENT VARIABLE

factor analysis
also **FA**

a multivariate technique whose primary purpose is to define the underlying structure among the variables in the analysis. Factor analysis (FA) is a data reduction statistical procedure which allows you to condense a large set of variables (e.g., test scores, test items, QUESTIONNAIRE responses) down to a smaller, more manageable and representative number of constructs or variables that are highly interrelated, known as factors. In fact, it is used to determine which LATENT VARIABLEs or factors account for the CORRELATIONs among different OBSERVED VARIABLEs. FA is a method of grouping together variables which have something in common. It is a process which enables the researcher to take a set of variables and reduce them to a smaller number of underlying factors which account for as many variables as possible. It detects structures and commonalities in the relationships between variables. Thus, FA enables researchers to identify where different variables, in fact, are addressing the same underlying concept.

Factor analytic techniques can achieve their purposes from either an exploratory or confirmatory perspective (see EXPLORATORY FACTOR ANALYSIS and CONFIRMATORY FACTOR ANALYSIS).

The term FA encompasses a variety of different, although related techniques. One of the main distinctions is between what is termed PRINCI-

PAL COMPONENTS ANALYSIS (PCA) and FA. These two sets of techniques are similar in many ways and are often used interchangeably by researchers. Both attempt to produce a smaller number of linear combinations of the original variables in a way that captures (or accounts for) most of the variability in the pattern of correlations. They do differ in a number of ways, however. In principal components analysis, the original variables are transformed into a smaller set of linear combinations, with all of the variance in the variables being used. In FA, however, factors are estimated using a mathematical model, whereby only the shared variance is analyzed. Thus, if you are interested in a theoretical solution uncontaminated by unique and error variability FA is your choice. If on the other hand you simply want an empirical summary of the data set, PCA is the better choice.

see also CLUSTER ANALYSIS

📖 Best & Kahn 2006; Cohen et al. 2011; Fulcher 2003; Hair et al. 2010; Hatch & Farhady 1982; Ho 2006; Leary 2011; Mackey & Gass 2005; Pallant 2010; Tabachnick & Fidell 2007

factorial ANOVA
also **between-subjects factorial ANOVA, between-groups factorial ANOVA, multifactor ANOVA, multi-way ANOVA**

a PARAMETRIC TEST and an extension of the *t*-TEST and ONE-WAY ANOVA which involves the analysis of *two* or *more* FACTORs or independent variables (IVs). Factorial ANOVA is used in EXPERIMENTAL RESEARCH designs in which every LEVEL of every factor is paired with every level of every other factor. It allows the researcher to assess the effects of each IV separately, as well as the joint effect or INTERACTION of variables. It is used is designs where you have one *continuous* DEPENDENT VARIABLE and two or more *categorical* IVs each with two or more levels. If there are two IVs, we conduct a TWO-WAY ANOVA. The same logic can be extended to **three-way** and **four-way ANOVA**s, and so on (due to the complexity in interpreting higher-order interactions, most factorial designs are limited to three or four IVs or factors).

For factorial ANOVA the following ASSUMPTIONS must be met:

- The populations from which the samples were taken are normally distributed (see NORMALITY).
- HOMOGENEITY OF VARIANCE.
- The observations are all independent of one another, i.e., each participant's score is not related systematically to any other participant(s)'s score (see INDEPENDENCE ASSUMPTION).

One advantage of a factorial ANOVA over an INDEPENDENT SAMPLES *t*-TEST or ONE-WAY ANOVA is that the interaction between factors can be explored. The result of factorial ANOVA is F associated with each MAIN EFFECT (the effect of a single IV, by itself, on the dependent variable), and Fs associated with each interaction effect (the combined effect of two or more IVs). Main effects are usually followed up either with PLANNED COMPARISONs, which compare specific sets of means, or with POST HOC TESTs, which compare all combinations of pairs of means. In factorial ANOVAs, the interactions are typically more interesting than the main effects. Interactions are usually broken down using SIMPLE EFFECTs analysis or specific contrasts designed by the researcher.

There is no nonparametric alternative to a factorial ANOVA, but one could test the influence of each IV separately using the nonparametric KRUSKALL-WALLIS TEST.

see also REPEATED-MEASURES ANOVA

 Ho 2006; Larson-Hall 2010; Ravid 2011; Urdan 2010

factorial design
also **multifactor design, between-groups factorial design, between-subjects factorial design, multi-way design**
a design which is used to simultaneously evaluate the effect of two or more factors on a DEPENDENT VARIABLE (DV). When using a factorial design, the INDEPENDENT VARIABLE (IV) is referred to as a FACTOR and the different values of a factor are referred to as LEVELs (i.e., subdivisions of a factor). When a researcher wants to study the effects of two or more factors simultaneously, it makes more sense to manipulate these variables in one experiment than to run a single experiment for each one. In this type of design, we are concerned with the use of FACTORIAL ANOVA to investigate the relationship between one *continuous* DV (measured on INTERVAL or RATIO SCALEs) and two or more *categorical* IVs each of which may have several levels. A factorial design also permits a researcher to evaluate whether or not there is an INTERACTION between two or more IVs. By using factorial designs researchers can determine, e.g., if the TREATMENT interacts significantly with gender or age, i.e., the experimenter can determine if one treatment is more effective with boys and another with girls, or if older girls do better on the treatment than younger girls, whereas older and younger boys do equally well on the treatment.

Factorial designs are labeled either by the number of factors involved or in terms of the number of levels of each factor. They are identified with a shorthand notation such as 2×3 or 3×5. The general term is $r \times c$ (rows $\times$ columns). The first number tells the number of levels of one factor; the second number tells you the number of levels of the other factor. The simplest case of a factorial design would be to have two IVs with two levels or conditions of each, known as TWO-WAY FACTORIAL DESIGN or a 2 × 2 factorial design, which is read as '2 by 2.' For example, suppose we wanted to study the influence of gender (a factor with two levels: female/male) and first language background (a factor with two levels: e.g., Italian/Iranian) on second language reading. You have two IVs each with two levels. As represented graphically in Figure F.1, such a design is called a 2 × 2 factorial design.

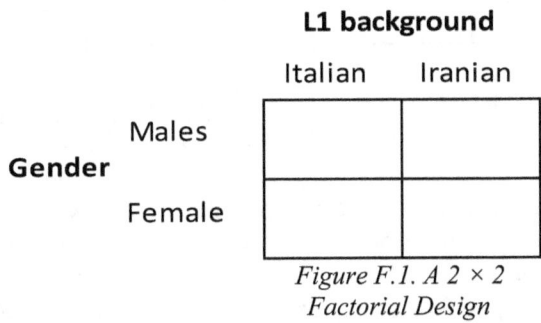

Figure F.1. A 2 × 2 Factorial Design

In a 2 × 3 design (as diagramed in Figure F.2), there are two IVs; one of which has two levels and the other one has three levels. Because there are six possible combinations of variables A and B, the design has six conditions.

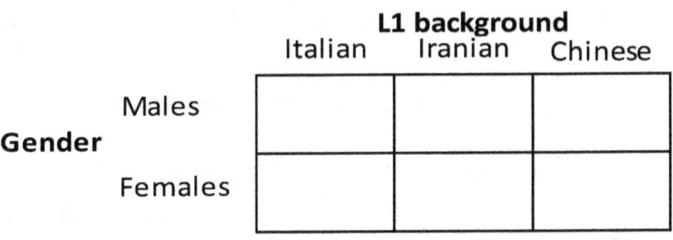

Figure F.2. A 2 × 3 Factorial Design

In a 3 × 3 design (as shown in Figure F.3), there are two IVs, each of which has three levels. Because there are nine possible combinations of variables A and B, the design has nine conditions.

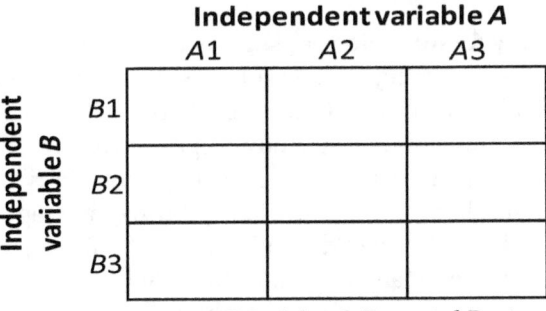

Figure F.3. A 3 × 3 Factorial Design

In a 4 × 2 design, IV A has four levels, and IV B has two levels, resulting in eight experimental conditions. The order of the numbers makes no difference and you could term this a 2 × 4 factorial design (see Figure F.4).

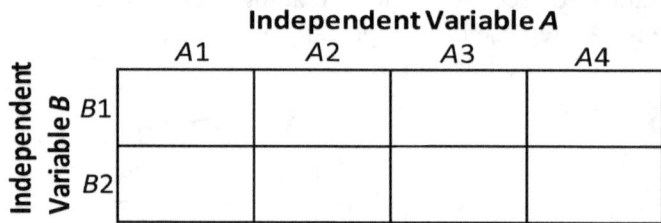

Figure F.4. A 4 × 2 Factorial Design

Of course, factorial designs can have more than two factors and more than two levels or conditions of each variable. For example, a **three-way factorial design**, such as a 2 × 2 × 2 design, has three IVs; each of the variables has two levels. In Figure F.5, for example, we see a design that has three IVs (labeled A, B, and C). Each of these variables has two levels, resulting in eight conditions that reflect the possible combinations of the three IVs. A 2 × 2 × 4 factorial design also has three IVs, but two of the IVs have two levels each and the other variable has four levels. Such a design is shown in Figure F.6. As you can see, this design involves 16 conditions that represent all combinations of the levels of variables A, B, and C.

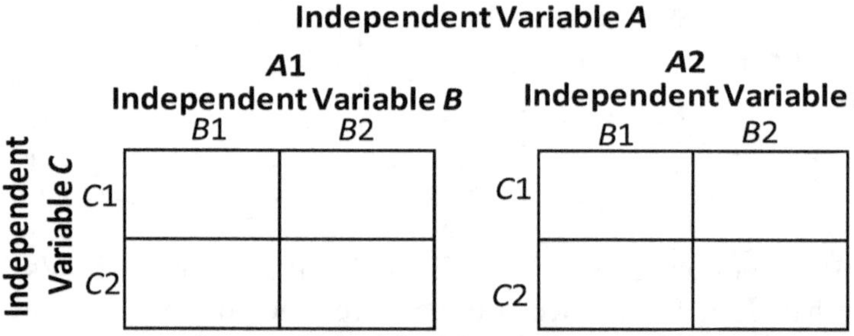

Figure F.5. A 2 × 2 × 2 Factorial Design

A **four-way factorial design**, such as a 2 × 2 × 3 × 3 design, would have four IVs—two would have two levels, and two would have three levels. As we add more IVs and more levels of our IVs, the number of conditions increases rapidly. A study might have three treatment conditions (e.g., three methods of reading instruction), the two genders, three age groups, and three intelligence levels (gifted, average, and mildly retarded) as the IVs. This would be a 3 × 2 × 3 × 3 factorial design.

We can tell how many experimental conditions (groups or CELLs) a factorial design has simply by multiplying the numbers in a design specification. For example, a 2 × 2 design has four different cells or conditions—that is four possible combinations of the two IVs (2 × 2 = 4). A 3 × 4 × 2 design has 24 different experimental conditions (3 × 4 × 2 = 24), and so on. A 3 × 2 × 3 × 3 factorial design would have a total of 54 subgroups or cells.

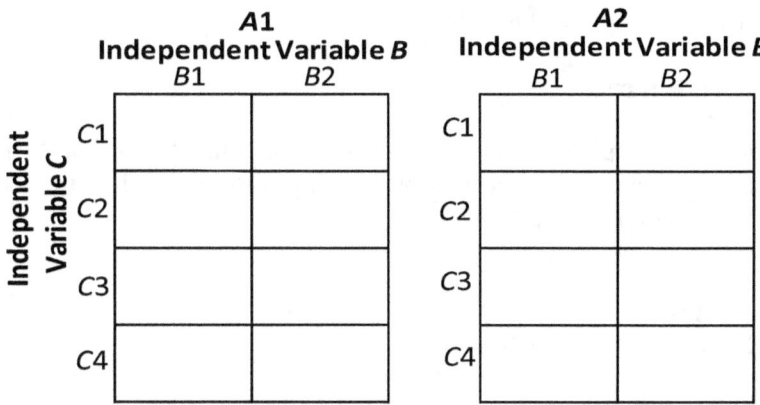

Figure F.6. A 2 × 2 × 4 Factorial Design

The factorial design has two important strengths. The primary advantage of factorial designs is that they enable us to empirically examine the effects of more than one IV, both individually and in combination, on the DV. The design, as its name implies, allows us to examine all possible combinations of factors in the study. A second and related strength is the efficiency of the factorial design. Because it allows us to test several hypotheses in a single research study, it can be more economical to use a factorial design than to conduct several individual studies, in terms of both number of participants and researcher effort.

 Best & Kahn 2006; Cohen et al. 2011; Leary 2011; Kothari 2008; Marczyk et al. 2005

factorial MANCOVA
see MULTIVARIATE ANALYSIS OF COVARIANCE

factorial MANOVA
see MULTIVARIATE ANALYSIS OF VARIANCE

factor loading
see EXPLORATORY FACTOR ANALYSIS

factor matrix
see FACTOR ANALYSIS

factual question
see QUESTIONNAIRE

fail-safe *N*
see FILE-DRAWER PROBLEM

false alarm
another term for TYPE I ERROR

false detection rate
also **FDR**

a correction applied to *P*-VALUEs to control the FAMILY-WISE ERROR RATE, which has much more power to find differences than the too conservative BONFERRONI TEST.
📖 Larson-Hall 2010

false negative
another term for TYPE II ERROR

false positive
another term for TYPE I ERROR

familywise error rate
also **FWE**

the PROBABILITY of making any error (especially a TYPE I ERROR) in a given family of inferences. If you run a large number of statistical tests all concerning the same research question then you need to think about controlling the familywise error rate by using some type of correction. When determining whether a finding is statistically significant, the significance level is usually set at .05 or less. If more than one finding is tested on a set of data, the probability of those findings being statistically significant increases the more findings or tests of significance that are made. There are various ways of controlling for the familywise error rate. Some of the tests for doing so are listed under MULTIPLE COMPARISON TESTs. One of the simplest is the BONFERRONI TEST.
see also COMPARISONWISE ERROR RATE, EXPERIMENTWISE ERROR RATE
📖 Everitt & Skrondal 2010; Larson-Hall 2010

F distribution
the distribution of the ratio of two estimates of variance and is used to compute PROBABILITY VALUEs in the ANALYSIS OF VARIANCE. Like the *t* DISTRIBUTION, the *F* distribution varies with DEGREES OF FREEDOM. However, the *F* distribution has two values for degrees of freedom, one for the NUMERATOR and one for the DENOMINATOR.
📖 Pagano 2009; Porte 2010

FDR
    an abbreviation for FALSE DETECTION RATE

FEW
    an abbreviation for FAMILYWISE ERROR RATE

fictitious question
    another term for BOGUS QUESTION

field diary
    a personal statement of the researcher's feelings, opinions, and perceptions about others with whom s/he comes in contact during the course of his/her work. Field diary provides a place where researchers can let their hair down, so to speak—an outlet for writing down things that the researcher does not want to become part of the public record. FIELD WORK is often an intense, emotionally draining experience, and a diary can serve as a way for the researcher to let out his/her feelings, yet still keep them private.
    see also FIELDNOTES
    📖 Fraenkel & Wallen 2009

field jottings
    quick notes about something the researcher wants to write more about later. Field jottings provide the stimulus to help researchers recall a lot of details they do not have time to write down during an observation or an interview.
    📖 Fraenkel & Wallen 2009

field log
    a sort of running account of how researchers plan to spend their time compared to how they actually spend it. A field log is, in effect, the researcher's plan for collecting his/her data systematically. A field log consists of books of blank, lined paper. Each day in the field is represented by two pages of the log. On the left page, the researcher lists what s/he plans to do that day—where to go, who to interview, what to observe, and so on. On the right side, the researcher lists what s/he actually did that day. As the study progresses, and things come to mind that the researcher wants to know, the log provides a place for them to be scheduled. The value of maintaining a log is that it forces the researcher to think hard about the questions s/he truly wants answered, the procedures to be followed, and the data really needed.
    see also FILEDNOTES
    📖 Fraenkel & Wallen 2009

fieldnotes
the most common method of recording the data collected during OBSERVATION. The researcher may make brief notes during the observation but then later expands his/her account of the observation as fieldnotes. Notes may supplement information from other sources, including documents and INTERVIEWs, or they may comprise the main research data. Fieldnotes contain what the researcher has seen and heard.
They have two components:

1) *The descriptive part*, which includes a complete description of the setting, the people and their reactions and interpersonal relationships, and accounts of events (who, when, and what was done); and
2) *The reflective part*, which includes the observer's personal feelings or impressions about the events, comments on the research method, decisions and problems, records of ethical issues, and speculations about data analysis. Fieldnotes may include photographs and audio and video recordings.

The researcher's reflections are identified as *observer comments* (OCs) to distinguish them from the descriptive information. Some researchers organize fieldnotes so as to have the descriptive information in one column and the observer comments in another column next to the descriptive notes. The researcher's fieldnotes present the data that will later be analyzed to provide an understanding of the research setting and the behavior of people within that setting. It can be said that the successful outcome of the study relies on detailed, accurate, and extensive fieldnotes. Observation sessions typically should last not more than 1 or 2 hours at a time; otherwise, so many data accumulate that it is difficult to record them all. Researchers may use audio and video recordings to facilitate data collection. New computer technologies may allow a researcher to digitally record a chat room session or a virtual world interaction. A disadvantage of some recording methods is that participants may be conscious of the camera or other recording device and behave differently or may try to avoid being filmed or photographed.
see also FIELD JOTTINGS, FIELD DIARY, FIELD LOG
 Ritchie & Lewis 2003

field research
 also **field study, field work**
a broad approach to QUALITATIVE RESEARCH or a method of gathering qualitative data by OBSERVATION or recording in as natural a setting as possible. Different procedures are used to obtain data. For example: (a) the recording of speakers to obtain speech samples for analysis of sounds, sentence structures, lexical use, etc. The people recorded may be

native speakers of a particular language or speakers using a second language; (b) INTERVIEWS, e.g., in bilingual or multilingual communities, to obtain information on language choice and/or attitudes to language, and (c) observation and/or video recording of verbal or non-verbal behavior in a particular situation.

see also FIELD JOTTINGS, FIELD DIARY, FIELD LOG, FIELDNOTES
📖 Richards & Schmidt 2010

field study
another term for FIELD RESEARCH

field work
another term for FIELD RESEARCH

file-drawer problem
a *bias* on the part of both authors and journals towards reporting statistically significant results. This means that other research may have been conducted that did not yield significance and has not been published. This is termed the file-drawer problem on the understanding that researchers' filing cabinets will contain their unpublished studies. This would mean that your meta-analysis is failing to take into account non-significant findings and in so doing gives a false impression of significance.

One method of assessing whether there is a file-drawer problem is to compute the number of non-significant studies that would have to be added to the meta-analysis to render it non-significant. This is known as the **fail-safe *N***. The fail-safe N is the number of unpublished, non-significant studies that would have to exist filed away in researchers' drawers in order to render the probability we have found for the meta-analysis non-significant.

📖 Clark-Carter 2010

fill-in item
an OPEN-FORM ITEM that requires the respondents to provide relatively brief bits of information. For instance, **biodata** items (or demographic items) are usually fill-in. Consider the following biodata items and notice how all of these fill-in items are relatively restricted in what they require the respondents to produce:

Name......................   Personality...............
Institution..................   Address....................
Sex..........................   Age........................

Biodata items can be used to collect information about respondents' learning history (how many years they have been studying the target language, certificates obtained, standardized test results like IELTS or TOEFL scores), professional history (highest professional qualification, number of years teaching, publications), teaching situation (types and number of classes taught, number of students in each class), or students' learning context (types and numbers of language classes offered, classes streamed into levels or not).

Another type of fill-in item is **sentence completion item**; this is an unfinished sentence (or PROMPT) that the respondent needs to complete. This has the advantage of helping the respondent focus on a clearly defined issue, so these questions can be answered relatively quickly; data analysis for this type of question is also fairly easy. Here is an example of a sentence completion item:

Three communicative activities that you often do in your classroom are:
....,
....,
and ....

The difference between fill-in and SHORT-ANSWER ITEMs is primarily in the length of what the respondents are required to produce. Fill-in items might call for responses of word or phrase length, while short-answer items usually call for responses involving a few phrases, sentences, or paragraphs.

📖 Best & Kahn 2006; Dörnyei 2003; Given 2008; Perry 2011

first-order partial correlation
see PARTIAL CORRELATION

Fisher's exact test
also Fisher's exact probability test
an alternative procedure to use of the CHI-SQUARE TEST for assessing the independence of two DICHOTOMOUS VARIABLEs forming a two-by-two CONTINGENCY TABLE particularly when the expected frequencies are small. Fisher's exact test is a test of *significance* (or *association*) for analyzing data in a 2 × 2 contingency table in which there are two LEVELs (i.e., categories) of a dichotomous INDEPENDENT VARIABLE (IV) in rows and two levels of other dichotomous IV in the columns. As such, it can be used in circumstances in which the assumptions of chi-square test such as minimal numbers of EXPECTED FREQUENCIES are not met. Fisher's exact test has the further advantage that exact probabilities are calculated even in the hand calculation, though this advantage is eroded by the use of powerful statistical packages which provide exact probabilities for

all statistics. The major disadvantage of the Fisher test is that it involves the use of *factorials* which can rapidly become unwieldy with substantial SAMPLE SIZEs.
📖 Cramer & Howitt 2004; Everitt & Skrondal 2010; Sahai & Khurshid 2001

Fisher's least significant difference
also **least significant difference test, Fisher's LSD test, LSD, protected *t*-test**
a POST HOC TEST which provides the most powerful (i.e., liberal) test with respect to identifying differences between pairs of MEANs, since it does not adjust the value of FAMILYWISE ERROR RATE. Fisher's least significant difference (LSD) should only be used after an OVERALL F TEST has established a significant difference. Otherwise, the risk of TYPE I ERRORs greatly increases, given the number of comparisons being made. Fisher's LSD test requires the smallest difference between two means in order to conclude that a difference is significant. However, since Fisher's LSD test does not reduce the value of familywise type I error rate, it has the highest likelihood of committing one or more Type I errors in a set/family of comparisons.
see also LIBERAL TEST, CONSERVATIVE TEST
📖 Sheskin 2011

Fisher's LSD test
another term for FISHER'S LEAST SIGNIFICANT DIFFERENCE

fixed effects
those effects whose parameters are fixed and are the only ones you want to consider. Fixed effects have informative labels for FACTOR levels, and the factor levels exhaust the possibilities. For fixed effects, you are interested in the LEVELs that are in your study and you do not want to generalize further. That is, you can only generalize your findings to these same levels in the population. Examples of fixed effects are TREATMENT type, gender, status as NS, child versus adult, first language, and second language.
see also RANDOM EFFECTS
📖 Hatch & Lazaraton 1991; Larson-Hall 2010

fixed-ended response
another term for CLOSED-FORM ITEM

fixed response item
another term for CLOSED-FORM ITEM

fixed variable
see RANDOM VARIABLE

flat distribution
see MODE

floor effect
also basement effect
an effect which occurs when a measuring instrument (e.g., a test) is too difficult and many scores are near the minimum possible score. For example, a vocabulary test administered as a pretest before students had a vocabulary class would likely show a floor effect. A graph of the frequency distribution of scores would be positively skewed. A test with a floor effect would not detect true differences in examinees' achievement either. Standardized tests typically cover a wide range of student performance, so it is not likely that many students would get all or almost all questions correct (CEILING EFFECT) or almost all questions wrong (floor effect).
see also BOUNDARY EFFECT
📖 Cramer & Howitt 2004

focused interview
another term for FOCUS GROUP

focus group
also focus group interview, focused interview
a form of GROUP INTERVIEW, though not in the sense of a backwards and forwards between interviewer and group. Rather, the reliance is on the interaction within the group who discuss a topic supplied by the researcher, yielding a collective rather than an individual view. The assumption is that individual attitudes, beliefs, and choices of action do not form in a vacuum. The focus group format is based on the collective experience of group brainstorming, that is, participants thinking together, inspiring and challenging each other, and reacting to the emerging issues and points. Hence the participants interact with each other rather than with the interviewer, such that the views of the participants can emerge—the participants rather than the researcher's agenda can predominate. It is from the interaction of the group that the data emerge.

In focus group interviews the interviewer is usually referred to as the *moderator*, and this special name reflects the fact that the researchers role differs from that in one-to-one interviews. Although they still need to ask questions, during the session they need to function more as facilitators of the discussion than as interviewers in the traditional sense. Because the dynamic of the focus group is one the unique features of this method, the researcher's role inevitably involves some group leadership functions, including making sure that nobody dominates the floor and that even the shyer participants have a chance to express their views. In addition, moderators need to prevent any dominating and inhibiting group opinion—or groupthink—from emerging by actively encouraging group members to think critically.

Focus groups typically consist of 6 to 12 people. The group should be small enough that everyone can take part in the discussion but large enough to provide diversity in perspective. Focus group discussions usually need to last at least 1 hour and possibly 2 hours. Groups should be homogeneous in terms of prestige and status to ensure comfort in expressing opinions.

When designing a focus group study, the two key technical questions to decide are (a) whether to have homogeneous or heterogeneous people in a group; and (b) how many groups to have. Although heterogeneous samples consisting of dissimilar people could in theory be useful in providing varied and rich data that covers all angles, it has been found that the dynamics of the focus group works better with homogeneous samples. Therefore, in order to obtain a wide range of information, the usual strategy is to have several groups which, as a whole, are different from each but each of which is made up of similar people; this is usually referred to as segmentation and it involves *within-group homogeneity* and *intergroup heterogeneity* in the sample.

With regard to the number of groups, the standard practice is to run several focus groups in any research project. Thus, in order to achieve adequate breadth and depth of information, it is usually recommended that a project involve 4-5 groups as a minimum, with a few more if possible. Focus groups might be useful to triangulate with more traditional forms of interviewing, QUESTIONNAIRE, and OBSERVATION.

see also ETHNOGRAPHIC INTERVIEW, NON-DIRECTIVE INTERVIEW, UNSTRUCTURED INTERVIEW, SEMI-STRUCTURED INTERVIEW, STRUCTURED INTERVIEW, INTERVIEW GUIDE, INFORMAL INTERVIEW, TELEPHONE INTERVIEW

📖 Cohen et al. 2011; Dörnyei 2007; Mckay 2006

focus group interview
    another term for FOCUS GROUP

follow up study
    another term for PANEL STUDY

follow-up test
    another term for POST HOC TEST

footnotes
    reference or comment at the bottom of a page or end of a chapter. Footnotes are used to provide additional content or to acknowledge copyright

permission status. *Content footnotes* supplement or amplify substantive information in the text; they should not include complicated, irrelevant, or nonessential information. Because they can be distracting to readers, such footnotes should be included only if they strengthen the discussion. A content footnote should convey just one idea; if you find yourself creating paragraphs or displaying equations as you are writing a footnote, then the main text or an APPENDIX probably would be a more suitable place to present your information. Another alternative is to indicate in a short footnote that the material is available online as supplemental material. In most cases, an author integrates a RESEARCH REPORT best by presenting important information in the text, not in a footnote.
Copyright permission footnotes acknowledge the source of lengthy quotations, scale and test items, and figures and tables that have been reprinted or adapted. Authors must obtain permission to reproduce or adapt material from a copyrighted source.
 American Psychological Association 2010

formative evaluation
also process evaluation
a type of EVALUATION RESEARCH which is an ongoing continuous process. The goal of formative evaluation is to provide information that will aid the development of particular change intervention programs. It investigates program delivery and asks how, and how well, a program is being implemented. It can assess strengths, weaknesses, opportunities, and threats, and often work to assess barriers and lubricants to implementation. Results are expected to inform decision-making related to program improvement, modification, and management. Formative data are collected and provided to program developers as the program is occurring, with the hope that such evidence will support the needed changes. For example, if one is evaluating a new reading program and the instruction is not being delivered according to the programs specific goals, the evaluator would provide this information to the program director so that the instruction could be improved. Formative evaluation includes several evaluation types:

- *Needs assessment* determines who needs the program, how great the need is, and what might work to meet the need.
- *Evaluability assessment* determines whether an evaluation is feasible and how STAKEHOLDERS can help shape its usefulness.
- *Structured conceptualization* (e.g., CONCEPT MAPPING) helps stakeholders define the program or technology, the target population, and the possible outcomes.

- *Implementation evaluation* monitors the fidelity of the program or technology delivery.
- *Process evaluation* investigates the process of delivering the program or technology, including alternative delivery procedures.

see also SUMMATIVE EVALUATION

📖 Lodico et al. 2010; O'Leary 2004; Richards & Schmidt 2010; Trochim & Donnelly 2007

four-way ANOVA
see FACTORIAL ANOVA

four-way factorial design
see FACTORIAL DESIGN

fractile
another term for QUANTILE

***F* ratio**
another term for *F* VALUE

free response item
another term for OPEN-FORM ITEM

frequency
also *f*

the number of times a particular event or outcome occurs, symbolized by the lowercase *f*. For example, the number of times a score occurs is the score's frequency. If we count the frequency of every score in the data, we create a FREQUENCY DISTRIBUTION. An alternative term, most common in statistical packages, is **frequency count**. This highlights the fact that the frequency is merely a count of the number of cases in a particular category. The symbol for the total number of scores in a set of data is the uppercase N. An N of 10 means we have 10 scores, or $N = 43$ means we have 43 scores. Note that N is not the number of different scores, so even if all 43 scores in a sample are the same score, N still equals 43. Counts of frequency data can be displayed visually in a HISTOGRAMs, STEM-AND-LEAF PLOTs, or BAR GRAPHs.

📖 Heiman 2011; Larson-Hall 2010

frequency count
see FREQUENCY

frequency curve
another term for FREQUENCY POLYGON

frequency distribution

a table or graph which gives the frequencies of values of any given variable. For QUALITATIVE VARIABLEs this is the number of times each of the categories occurs whereas for QUANTITATIVE VARIABLEs this is the number of times each different score (or range of scores) occurs. An example of a frequency distribution would be if the scores 0, 5, 5, 8, 9, 9, 12 were arranged in a tabular format. Specifically, each score in the range 0 to 12 would be recorded in one column, and an adjacent column would list the frequency of occurrence for each score.

The importance of a frequency distribution is simply that it allows the researcher to see the general characteristics of a particular variable for the cases or participants in the research. The frequency distribution may reveal important characteristics such as *asymmetry* and *skewedness* (see SKEWED DISTRIBUTION), NORMALITY, DISPERSION, *extreme scores* (see OUTLIER), and so on, in the case of score data. For qualitative data, it may help reveal categories which are very frequent or so infrequent that it becomes meaningless to analyze them further. Frequency distributions may be presented in a number of different forms such as SIMPLE FREQUENCY DISTRIBUTION, GROUPED FREQUENCY DISTRIBUTION, RELATIVE FREQUENCY, and CUMULATIVE FREQUENCY. While frequency distributions reflect the distribution of a single variable, there are variants on the theme which impose a second or third variable such as COMPOUND BAR CHARTs.

see also KURTOSIS, SKEWED DISTRIBUTION, NORMAL DISTRIBUTION, U-SHAPED DISTRIBUTION

Sheskin 2011; Cramer & Howitt 2004

frequency histogram

another term for HISTOGRAM

frequency polygon
also **frequency curve**

a graphical representation of a FREQUENCY DISTRIBUTION, applied to a large range of interval/ratio (i.e., continuous) scores, in which the horizontal axis (X axis) represents score values and the vertical axis (Y axis) represents frequency of occurrence. As shown in Figure F.7, a dot is placed over each score value at the height representing its frequency of occurrence. These dots are then joined by straight lines to form a polygon. Cumulative frequencies of interval/ratio data can also be displayed in the form of a polygon, known as the **cumulative frequency polygon** (sometimes referred to as the **ogive curve**).

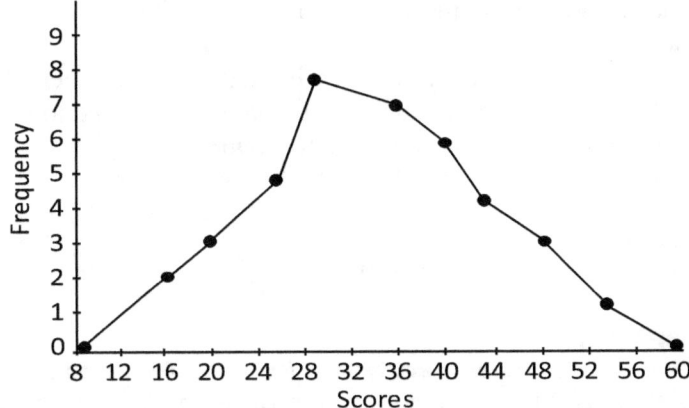

Figure F.7. A Frequency Polygon of the Frequency Distribution

As shown in Figure F.8, the differences between the frequency polygon and the cumulative frequency polygon are that the cumulative frequency polygon (a) involves plotting cumulative frequencies along the Y axis, (b) the points are plotted at the upper real limit of each interval, and (c) the polygon cannot be closed on the right-hand side. The cumulative frequency polygon cannot connect back to the X axis on the right-hand side because that would involve bringing the curve back to zero, which cannot happen as the cumulative frequencies can never decrease. For example, the cumulative frequency for the 32 interval is 10, indicating that there are 10 scores in that interval and below.

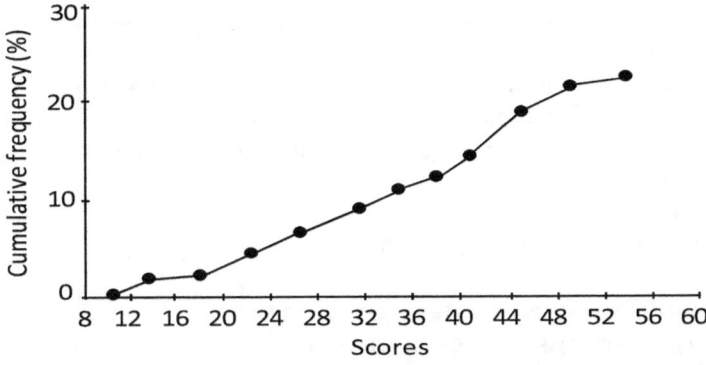

Figure F.8. An Example of Cumulative Frequency Polygon

One could also plot cumulative relative frequencies on the Y axis to reflect the percentage of students in the sample whose scores fell into a particular interval and below. This is known as the **cumulative relative frequency polygon**. All we have to change is the scale of the Y axis to cumulative relative frequency. The position of the polygon would remain the same.

The most famous frequency curve in statistics is the bell-shaped, NORMAL CURVE. A generalization of polygon which is used to represent a bivariate frequency distribution is called **bivariate polygon**.
📖 Cramer & Howitt 2004; Lomax 2007; Sahai & Khurshid 2001

Friedman's rank test
another term for FRIEDMAN'S TEST

Friedman's test
also Friedman's two-way analysis of variance, Friedman's rank test
a classic rank-based method for comparing multiple dependent or CORRELATED GROUPS. Friedman's test is a *nonparametric* alternative to ONE-WAY REPEATED MEASURES ANOVA which is used for three or more related or matched samples that cannot be compared by means of an *F* TEST either because the scores are *ordinal* in nature or because the NORMALITY or HOMOGENEITY OF VARIANCE assumptions cannot be satisfied. Whereas the WILCOXON MATCHED-PAIRS SIGNED-RANKS TEST is used to analyze two sets of scores obtained from the same individuals, the Friedman's test is used when there are three or more related sets of scores. It is used when you have one *categorical* INDEPENDENT VARIABLE with three or more levels (the same participants are measured three or more times, e.g., Time 1, Time 2, Time 3, or under three or more different conditions) and one ordinal dependent variable. Thus, each participant produces three scores, one in each of the three conditions. This makes it possible to make a direct comparison between each participant's three scores in all the conditions.

Like the MANN-WHITNEY *U* TEST and KRUSKAL-WALLIS TEST, the calculation of the Friedman's test is based on ranks within each case. The scores for each variable are ranked, and the mean ranks for the variables are compared.

see also NONPARAMETRIC TESTS
📖 Cohen et al. 2011; Larson-Hall 2010

Friedman's two-way analysis of variance
another term for FRIEDMAN'S TEST

F statistic
see *F* TEST

F test
a statistical test which is based on an ***F* statistic** (i.e., any statistic that has an *F* DISTRIBUTION). Two commonly used *F* tests are ***F* test for analysis**

of variance and *F* test for two population variances. *F* test for analysis of variance is a statistical test for comparing the MEANs of several POPULATIONs used in the ANALYSIS OF VARIANCE. Under the NULL HYPOTHESIS of no difference between the POPULATION MEANs, the two mean squares (between and within) are approximately equivalent and their ratio (*F* statistic) is nearly equal to 1. In comparison of the means of two INDEPENDENT GROUPS, the *F* test is equivalent to the TWO-SAMPLE *t*-TEST. In REGRESSION ANALYSIS, the *F* statistic is used to test the joint significance of all the variables in the model.

F test for two population variances is used to compare the variances of two POPULATIONs. It makes its comparisons directly in the form of a ratio, with the larger SAMPLE VARIANCE serving as the NUMERATOR and the smaller serving as the DENOMINATOR. This is the simplest use of the *F* statistic for testing the difference between the variances of two independent normal populations. The *F* test for two population variances may be used to compare two distributions for HOMOGENEITY OF VARIANCEs before proceeding to perform *t*-test.

The *F* test, unlike the *t*-test, is not ROBUST with respect to violation of the NORMALITY assumption. Hence, unless the normality assumption is fulfilled, the probability of making a TYPE I ERROR will not equal the preselected value of ALPHA (α). Unfortunately, the lack of robustness of the *F* test does not improve in large samples. In summary, the *F* test should not be used unless you have good reason for believing that the population distributions of the two variables are normal

📖 Kirk 2008; Sahai & Khurshid 2001

F test for analysis of variance
see *F* TEST

F test for two population variances
see *F* TEST

F value
see ANALYSIS OF VARIANCE

fundamental research
another term for BASIC RESEARCH

G

Games-Howell multiple comparison
a POST HOC TEST which is used to determine which of three or more MEANs differ from one another when the *F* RATIO in an ANALYSIS OF VARIANCE is significant. It was developed to deal with groups with unequal variances (see HOMOSCEDASTICITY). It can be used with groups of equal or unequal size. It is based on the STUDENTIZED RANGE TEST.
📖 Cramer & Howitt 2004

gamma (γ)
an abbreviation for GOODMAN-KRUSKAL'S GAMMA

Gaussian curve
another term for NORMAL DISTRIBUTION

Gaussian distribution
another term for NORMAL DISTRIBUTION

generalizability
the extent to which the results of a study can be extended to a greater POPULATION. Underlying the idea of VALIDITY and RELIABILITY in both QUANTITATIVE and QUALITATIVE RESEARCH is the concept of generalizability. In quantitative research, the degree to which a study can be generalized to other contexts can be determined through statistical procedures, which verify that the results obtained were not due to chance (see EXTERNAL VALIDITY). Because in qualitative research, the population is generally quite limited and the amount of control exerted by the researcher is minimal, statistical measures cannot be used to achieve generalizability. Often the goal of a qualitative research is to understand what happens in one particular classroom or what the experiences are of specific language learners and teachers. A useful strategy to examine generalizability is to include in the qualitative account the participants' own judgments about the generalizability of the targeted issue/phenomenon.

There are two main areas where the generalizability of the research could be in question. Firstly, there may be a question over the degree to which the particular conditions pertaining in the study can allow the results of the study to be generalized to other conditions—the tasks required of the participants, the setting in which the study took place or the time when the study was conducted. Secondly, we can question whether aspects of the participants can allow the results of a study to be generalized to other

people—whether they are representative of the group from which they come, and whether they are representative of a wider range of people.
Generalizability is divided into **internal generalizability** and **external generalizability**. Both aspects of generalizability refer to the extension of the account to persons, times or settings other than those directly studied, but internal generalizability concerns generalizing within the community or institution observed, whereas external generalizability refers to generalizing to other communities or institutions.
see also CREDIBILITY, DEPENDABILITY, CONFIRMABILITY, PROXIMAL SIMILARITY MODEL
📖 Cohen et al. 2011; Dörnyei 2007; Lodico et al. 2010; Mckay 2006

generalizability study
see GENERALIZABILITY THEORY

generalizability theory
also **G-theory**
a measurement model which enables us to investigate the relative effects of multiple sources of variance in test scores. Generalizability theory which was developed as an alternative approach to CLASSICAL TEST THEORY defines a score as a sample from the universe of all the admissible observations, characterized by one or more conditions of measurement. Here, the true score (i.e., the true ability) is defined as the **universe score**, that is the average of all the observations in the universe of admissible observations, and errors are defined by the conditions of measurement. Items, raters, occasions, tests, and so forth, are examples of the conditions of measurement, and each one accounts for part of the variability of the observed scores. Generalizability theory is designed to estimate the multiple components of the obtained score variability, and to use them to explore the effects of different sources of MEASUREMENT ERROR. Consequently, it allows the investigation of several sources of variation simultaneously, and the estimation of the error in generalizing an observed result to the universe defined by each of them.
Generalizability theory is founded upon the statistical model of the ANALYSIS OF VARIANCE (ANOVA). In ANOVA, the total variance is partitioned according to the INDEPENDENT VARIABLEs in the design. Similarly, generalizability theory uses the ANOVA model to estimate the variance components associated with the sources of variation that affect the score under investigation. In other words, the sources of variation define a model of the score, and specify which error source (by itself or combined with others) affects the measure and how much it does. In generalizability theory, sources of variation other than the object of measurement are defined as *facets*, while groupings within a facet are defined as *conditions* (FACTORs and LEVELs represent their analogues in FACTORIAL

ANOVA). Facets may be considered as either *random* or *fixed*, likewise factors in ANOVA. Conditions within a random facet are considered as randomly sampled from the universe of conditions that define that facet. Specifying a facet as random allows the researcher to generalize to all the conditions within that facet, including those not explicitly included in the design. For instance, items of a test may be regarded as conditions within a random facet, since researchers are not usually interested to those particular items, but consider them as a sample drawn from the population of items that measure the same theoretical construct. Specifying a facet as fixed, instead, implies that all the conditions within that facet have been included in the model, or that the researcher is willing to generalize only to the conditions included in the design. Individuals enter as a source of variation in all the generalizability theory models, usually as the object of measurement. This means that the variance associated with the individuals represents actual differences among persons, whereas the variance associated with the facets reflects error.

Furthermore, G-theory extends CLASSICAL TEST THEORY in several ways:

1) G-theory allows us to estimate the relative effects of multiple sources of error, including interactions among the different sources, in one analysis;
2) G-theory focuses on variance components that indicate the magnitude of each source of measurement error;
3) G-theory provides a mechanism for optimizing the RELIABILITY of measurement by adjusting the numbers of conditions of the different facets of measurement; and
4) G-theory allows us to distinguish between relative and absolute errors, thus providing reliability estimates that are appropriate for both NORM- and CRITERION-REFERENCED TESTs.

In the context of generalizability theory, research conducted to explore the impact of different facets of the universe on a test score is referred to as **generalizability study** (also called **G-study**).
 Bachman 2004; Fernandez-Ballesteros 2003

general linear model
also GLM
a general model that will bring together the main types of statistical analysis. The term *general* simply means that the model applies equally to REGRESSION ANALYSIS and to the analysis of variables in ANALYSIS OF VARIANCE. Turning to the term *linear*, the basic notion is that this refers to the nature of the lines. The assumption of LINEARITY is that the lines are straight lines. In both regression and analysis of variance the as-

sumption is that relationships between variables are defined by the SLOPEs of straight lines.
 Greene & Oliveira 2005; Sahai & Khurshid 2001

generalized linear model
a class of linear models that allows the theory and methodology to be applicable to a much more general class of linear models, of which the normal theory is a special case. Such models allow the use of sample data that follow a nonnormal PROBABILITY DISTRIBUTION. Estimates of parameters in such models are generally determined by the method of MAXIMUM LIKELIHOOD ESTIMATE.
 Sahai & Khurshid 2001

generosity error
see RATING ERROR

geometric mean
also **GM**
the nth root of the multiplication of N scores. So the geometrical mean of 2, 9, and 12 is

$$\sqrt[3]{2 \times 9 \times 12} = \sqrt[3]{216} = 6$$

The geometric mean of 3 and 6 is

$$\sqrt[2]{3 \times 6} = \sqrt[2]{18} = 4.24$$

The geometric mean has no obvious role in basic everyday statistical analysis. It is important, though, since it emphasizes that there are more meanings of the concept of mean than the ARITHMETIC MEAN or average.
 Cramer & Howitt 2004

G-G
an abbreviation for GREENHOUSE-GEISSER CORRECTION

***g* index**
see EFFECT SIZE

GLM
an abbreviation for GENERAL LINEAR MODEL

GM
an abbreviation for GEOMETRIC MEAN

going native
see BIAS

Goodman-Kruskal's gamma
also **gamma (γ)**

a bivariate measure of *association* which is employed with ORDINAL VARIABLEs (rank-order data) which is summarized within the format of an ordered CONTINGENCY TABLE. The measure ranges from -1 to +1 and takes into account only the number of untied pairs. Computation of gamma is recommended when there are many ties in a set of data, and thus it becomes more efficient to summarize the data within the format of an ordered r × c contingency table. An ordered r × c contingency table consists of r × c cells, and is comprised of r rows and c columns. In the model employed for Goodman-Kruskal's gamma, each of the rows in the contingency table represents one of the r levels of the *X* variable, and each of the columns represents one of the c levels of the *Y* variable (or vice versa). Since the contingency table that is employed to summarize the data is ordered, the categories for both the row and the column variables are arranged sequentially with respect to magnitude/ordinal position. To illustrate, if a subject is categorized on the lowest level of the row variable and the highest level of the column variable, that subject is concordant with respect to ordering when compared with any other subject who is assigned to a lower category on the row variable than s/he is on the column variable. On the other hand, that subject is discordant with respect to ordering when compared with another subject who is assigned to a higher category on the row variable than s/he is on the column variable.
 Sahai & Khurshid 2001; Sheskin 2011

Goodman-Kruskal's lambda
also **lambda (λ)**

a measure of *association* between the two variables forming a CONTINGENCY TABLE. Goodman-Kruskal's lambda is a measure of the proportional increase in accurately predicting the outcome for one CATEGORICAL VARIABLE when we have information about a second categorical variable, assuming that the same prediction is made for all cases in a particular category. For example, we could use this test to determine how much our ability to predict whether students pass or fail a test is affected by knowing their sex. We can illustrate this test with the data in Table G.1 which show the number of females and males passing or failing a test.

If we had to predict whether a particular student had passed the test disregarding whether they were female or male, our best bet would be to say they had passed as most of the students passed (164 out of 200). If we did this we would be wrong on 36 occasions. How would our ability to predict whether a student had passed be increased by knowing whether they were male or female? If we predicted that the student had passed and we also knew that they were female we would be wrong on 12 occasions, whereas if they were male we would be wrong on 24 occasions. If we knew whether a student was female or male we would be wrong on 36 occasions. This is the same number of errors as we would make without knowing the sex of the student, so the proportional increase knowing the sex of the student is zero. The value of lambda varies from 0 to 1. Zero means that there is no increase in predictiveness whereas one indicates that there is perfect prediction without any errors.

	Pass	Fail	Total
Female	108	12	120
Males	56	24	80
Total	164	36	200

Table G.1. Number of Females and Males Passing or Failing a Test

This test is asymmetric in that the proportional increase will depend on which of the two variables we are trying to predict. For this case, lambda is about 0.15 if we reverse the prediction in an attempt to predict the sex of the student on the basis of whether they have passed or failed the test. The test assumes that the same prediction is made for all cases in a particular row or column of the table. For example, we may assume that all females have passed or that all males have failed.
 Cramer & Howitt 2004; Sahai & Khurshid 2001

Goodman-Kruskal's tau
a measure of the proportional increase in accurately predicting the outcome of one CATEGORICAL VARIABLE when we have information about a second categorical variable where it is assumed that the predictions are based on the their overall proportions. We can illustrate this test with the data in Table G.1 (under the entry for GOODMAN-KRUSKAL'S LAMBDA) where we may be interested in finding out how much our ability to predict whether a person has passed or failed a test is increased by our knowledge of whether they are female or male. If we predicted whether a person had passed on the basis of the proportion of people who had passed disregarding whether they were female or male, we would be correct for .82 (164/200 = .82) of the 164 people who had passed, which is for 134.48 of them (.82 × 164 = 134.48). If we did this for the people who had failed, we would be correct for .18 (36/200 = .18) of the 36

people who had failed, which is for 6.48 of them (.18 × 36 = 6.48). In other words, we would have guessed incorrectly that 59.04 of the people had passed (200 - 134.48 - 6.48 = 59.04) which is a probability of error of .295 (59.04/200 = .295).

If we now took into account the sex of the person, we would correctly predict that the person had passed the test:

For .90 (108/120 = .90) of the 108 females who had passed, which is for 97.20 of them (.90 × 108 = 97.20),
for .70 (56/80 = .70) of the 56 males who had passed, which is for 39.20 of them (.70 × 56 = 39.20),
for .10 (12/120 = .10) of the 12 females who had failed, which is for 1.20 of them (.10 × 12 = 1.20), and
for .30 (24/80 = .30) of the 24 males who had failed, which is for 7.20 of them (.30 × 24 = 7.20).
📖 Cramer & Howitt 2004

goodness-of-fit test
a statistical procedure performed to test whether to accept or reject a hypothesized PROBABILITY DISTRIBUTION describing the characteristics of a population. Put simply, goodness-of-fit tests are employed to determine whether the distribution of scores in a SAMPLE conforms to the distribution of scores in a specific theoretical or empirical POPULATION distribution. Goodness-of-fit tests are somewhat unique when contrasted with other types of inferential statistical tests, in that when conducting a goodness-of-fit test a researcher generally wants or expects to retain the NULL HYPOTHESIS. In other words, the researcher wants to demonstrate that a sample is derived from a distribution of a specific type (e.g., a NORMAL DISTRIBUTION). On the other hand, in employing most other inferential tests, a researcher wants or expects to reject the null hypothesis—i.e., the researcher wants or expects to demonstrate that one or more samples do not come from a specific population or from the same population. It should be noted that the ALTERNATIVE HYPOTHESIS for a goodness-of-fit test generally does not stipulate an alternative distribution that would become the most likely distribution for the data if the null hypothesis is rejected.

The two most commonly employed goodness-of-fit tests are the CHI-SQUARE GOODNESS-OF-FIT TEST and the KOLMOGOROV-SMIRNOV GOODNESS-OF-FIT TEST for a single sample.
📖 Sheskin 2011

grand mean
the statistical average for all of the cases in all of the groups on the DEPENDENT VARIABLE.

graphic rating scale
see RATING SCALE

Greenhouse-Geisser correction
also **G-G**
a correction that is used when data in an REPEATED-MEASURES ANOVA does not satisfy the assumption of SPHERICITY. It is recommended always using a correction even if statistical tests indicate that your data do satisfy the assumption of sphericity. The Greenhouse-Geisser correction is more conservative than the HUYNH-FELDT CORRECTION. In other words, it is more likely to avoid a TYPE I ERROR but increase the likelihood of a TYPE II ERROR.
see also MAUCHLY'S TEST
📖 Clark-Carter 2010; Larson-Hall 2010

grounded theory
a general methodology of analysis in QUALITATIVE RESEARCH which seeks to build systematic theoretical statements inductively from CODING and analyzing observational data, by developing and refining conceptual categories which are then tested and retested in further data collection. The emphasis in this methodology is on the generation of theory which is grounded in the data. Grounded theory, indeed, holds that concepts and hypotheses (see HYPOTHESIS) should not precede the gathering of information, in that theory is rooted in the reality observed and it is the researcher's task to discover it. According to the advocates of this point of view, theory should be generated by empirical observation (they use the term *generate* as opposed to *verify*)—that is, the concepts and hypotheses should be extracted from reality, rather than imposing preconceived theoretical schemes on reality. The researcher does not begin with a particular theory in mind but adopts an inductive approach that allows theory to develop from the data. This is different from other types of research which might seek to test a hypothesis that has been formulated by the researcher. They argue that this approach yields theories that fit the data better and work better, in that the categories are discovered by examining the data themselves; moreover, such theories are easier for the ordinary person to understand, as they are deduced from his/her own way of thinking. Thus, grounded theory can help to forestall the opportunistic use of theories that have dubious fit and working capacity, and which are often adopted by researchers out of intellectual laziness and acquiescence to the dominant fashion.
In grounded theory studies, the number of people to be studied is not specified at the beginning of the research. This is because the researcher, at the outset, is unsure of where the research will take her/him. Instead, s/he continues with the data collection until SATURATION point is

reached. Grounded theory is therefore flexible and enables new issues to emerge that the researcher may not have thought about previously.

Data collection in grounded theory is similar to that of ETHNOGRAPHY, although OBSERVATION and INTERVIEWs are not necessarily privileged and if necessary the researcher can draw on a wide range of sources (for example photographs, documents) along with a comprehensive literature review which takes place throughout the data collection process. This literature review helps to explain emerging results.

A typical grounded theory project might involve a study of the experience of the first few weeks at a new language school from the learners' point of view. Learners might be asked OPEN-ENDED QUESTIONs about their views of language learning, the experience of arriving at a new institution and the approaches to language learning that they encountered; they might be asked to keep learner diaries; the researcher might observe lessons and interview teachers, collect a variety of documents (administrative and academic) and read accounts of other initial language-learning experiences. What might emerge is a theory about the ways in which a dominant view of what language learning involves comes to be shared by the students.

Because grounded theory does not demand the extended exposure necessary for a full ethnography but still offers a means of developing an understanding of educational contexts, it is a tradition that is likely to have strong practical appeal to TESOL practitioners. Perhaps the greatest attraction of grounded theory is that it offers a systematic way of analyzing and interpreting the data, normally a messy and frustrating process that is traditionally seen as something of a mystery, causing even the best researchers to feel at sea. Establishing categories from qualitative data, laments one group of ethnographic researchers, seems rather like a simultaneous left-brain right-brain exercise, so the practical guidelines offered in this tradition are reassuring. However, the process of analysis is still very time-consuming and the need to produce a theory can put considerable pressure on the researcher. Critics have reacted negatively to the strong focus on method, the place of the researcher and the status of the theories produced, but the growing popularity of this tradition cannot be ignored.

📖 Cohen et al. 2011; Dawson 2007; Glaser & Strauss 1967; Richards 2003; Ridenour & Newman 2008

group administration

a type of QUESTIONNAIRE administration which is the most common method of having questionnaires completed. One reason for this is that the typical targets of the SURVEYs are language learners studying within institutional contexts, and it is often possible to arrange to administer the instrument to them while they are assembled together, for example, as part of a lesson or slotted between certain other organized activities. The other reason for the popularity of this administration format is that it can overcome some of the problems just mentioned with regard to POSTAL SURVEYs or ONE-TO-ONE ADMINISTRATION. Groups of students are typically captive groups in the sense that a response rate of nearly 100% can be achieved with them, and because a few questionnaire administrators can collect a very large number of questionnaires, it is easier to make sure that all of them are adequately trained for the job. There are, however, some important points to consider:

- Because respondents have to work individually this format may not be appropriate for children under about age 10.
- With larger groups, or with groups of less mature kids, more than one field worker at a time is needed to help to answer questions and to distribute/collect the questionnaires.
- In group administration contamination through copying, talking, or asking questions is a constant danger.
- The negative influence of deviant kids may create an inappropriate climate for sincere and thoughtful work.

see also SELF-ADMINISTERED QUESTIONNAIRE
 Dörnyei 2003

group difference index
see EFFECT SIZE

grouped data
data values that have been sorted and grouped into class intervals, in order to reduce the number of scoring categories to a manageable level when the data range very widely. Data available in class intervals are then summarized by a FREQUENCY DISTRIBUTION. Individual values of the original data are not retained. Thus, with grouped data, one may not know the exact values of the observations falling within the class intervals.
 Sahai & Khurshid 2001

grouped frequency distribution
a FREQUENCY DISTRIBUTION that lists frequencies for class intervals rather than individual scores. The data are grouped in intervals of equal range and each frequency represents the number of data values in one of the intervals. When we have too many scores to produce a manageable ungrouped distribution, we create a grouped distribution, and then we report the total FREQUENCY (f), RELATIVE FREQUENCY ($rel.f$), CUMULATIVE FREQUENCY (cf), or PERCENTILE of all scores in each group.

Score	f	rel.f	cf	Percentile
40-44	2	.08	25	100
35-39	2	.08	23	92
30-34	0	.00	21	84
25-29	3	.12	21	84
20-24	2	.08	18	72
15-19	4	.16	16	64
10-14	1	.04	12	48
5-9	4	.16	11	44
0-4	7	.28	7	28

Table G.2. Grouped Distribution Showing f, rel.f, cf, and Percentile

For example, look at the grouped distribution shown in Table G.2. In the score column, '0-4' contains the scores 0, 1, 2, 3, 4, and '5-9' contains scores 5 through 9, and so on. The f for each group is the sum of the frequencies for the scores in that group. Thus, the scores between 0 and 4 have a total f of 7, while, for the highest scores between 40 and 44, the total f is 2. Likewise, the combined relative frequency of scores between 0 and 4 is .28, while for scores between 40 and 44 it is .08. Each cumulative frequency is the number of scores that are at 44 or below the highest score in the group. Thus, 7 scores are at 4 or below while 25 scores are at 44 or below. (Because 44 is the highest score, we know that is 25.) Finally, each percentile indicates the percent of scores that are below the highest score in the group, so the score of 4 is at the 28th percentile, and the score of 44 is at the 100th percentile.
📖 Heiman 2011

grouped variable
   another term for CATEGORICAL VARIABLE

grouping
   another term for CENTRAL TENDENCY

group interview
   a means of collecting data in research. Group interviews are useful where a group of people have been working together for some time or common purpose, or where it is seen as important that everyone concerned is aware of what others in the group are. Group interviews can generate a wider range of responses than in individual interviews. They might be useful for gaining an insight into what might be pursued in subsequent individual interviews. Group interviews are often quicker than individual interviews and hence are timesaving. They can also bring to-

gether people with varied opinions, or as representatives of different collectivities. They are also very useful when interviewing children.

Group interviews require skillful chairing and attention to the physical layout of the room so that everyone can see everyone else. Group size is also an issue; too few and it can put pressure on individuals, too large and the group fragments and loses focus. A group of around six or seven is an optimum size, though it can be smaller for younger children. The duration of an interview may not be for longer than, at most, fifteen minutes, and it might be useful to ensure that distractions are kept to a minimum. Simple language to the point and without ambiguity (e.g., avoiding metaphors) is important.

see also FOCUS GROUP

📖 Cohen et al. 2011

G-study
another term for GENERALIZABILITY STUDY

Guttman scaling
another term for CUMULATIVE SCALE

Guttman's scalogram
see CUMULATIVE SCALE

Guttman split-half method
see SPLIT-HALF RELIABILITY

H

***H*₀**
an abbreviation for NULL HYPOTHESIS

***H*₁**
an abbreviation for ALTERNATIVE HYPOTHESIS

***H*ₐ**
an abbreviation for ALTERNATIVE HYPOTHESIS

halo effect
a threat to QUESTIONNAIRE and EXTERNAL VALIDITY which refers to the rater's belief in the goodness of participants (the participants have haloes around their heads!), such that the more negative aspects of their behavior or personality are neglected or overlooked. For example, a researcher might rate a student who does good academic work as also being superior in intelligence, popularity, honesty, perseverance, and all other aspects of personality. The halo effect concerns the human tendency to overgeneralize. If our overall impression of a person or a topic is positive, we may be disinclined to say anything less than positive about them even if it comes to specific details. For many students, for example, a teacher they love is perfect in everything s/he does—which is obviously not true. Halo effect is contrasted with the **horns effect**, which refers to the rater's belief in the badness of the participants (the participants have devils' horns on their heads!), such that the more positive aspects of their behavior or personality are neglected or overlooked. For example, if we have a generally unfavorable impression of a person, we are likely to rate the person low on all aspects.
see also HAWTHORNE EFFECT, NOVELTY EFFECT, PRETEST-TREATMENT INTERACTION, MULTIPLE-TREATMENT INTERACTION, SPECIFICITY OF VARIABLES, TREATMENT DIFFUSION, RESEARCHER EFFECT
📖 Ary et al. 2010; Dörnyei 2003; Cohen et al. 2011

haphazard sampling
another term for OPPORTUNISTIC SAMPLING

harmonic mean
the number of scores divided by the sum of $1/X$ for each score. The harmonic mean of 3 and 6 is:

$$\frac{2}{\frac{1}{3}+\frac{1}{6}} = \frac{2}{.333+.167} = \frac{2}{.5} = 4$$

The harmonic mean of 3, 6 and 7 is

$$\frac{3}{\frac{1}{3}+\frac{1}{6}+\frac{1}{7}} = \frac{3}{.333+.167+.143} = \frac{3}{.643} = 4.67$$

The harmonic mean is rarely directly calculated as such in statistics. It is part of the calculation of the UNRELATED t-TEST, for example.
see also GEOMETRIC MEAN, ARITHMETIC MEAN
📖 Cramer & Howitt 2004

Hartley's test
also **maximum *F*-ratio test, F_{max}**
a test procedure for testing three or more INDEPENDENT SAMPLES for HOMOGENEITY OF VARIANCEs before using an ANALYSIS OF VARIANCE procedure. Hartley's test is based on the ratio between the largest and smallest SAMPLE VARIANCEs. Like Bartlett's test, however, it is found to be sensitive (i.e., not very ROBUST) to any departures from NORMALITY. It assumes normal population distributions and requires equal sample sizes.
see also BOX'S M TEST, COCHRAN'S C TEST, BARTLETT'S TEST, LEVENE'S TEST, BROWN-FORSYTHE TEST, O'BRIEN TEST
📖 Everitt 2001; Everitt & Skrondal 2010; Lomax 2007; Sahai & Khurshid 2001; Tabachnick & Fidell 2007; Upton & Cook 2008

Hawthorne effect
a threat to EXTERNAL VALIDITY which refers to the tendency of subjects to improve their performance under observation, simply because they are aware that they are being studied or are involved in an experiment so that the results of the study are more closely related to this pleasure than anything that actually occurs in the research. Procedures to control this problem are: using **unobtrusive measure**s (data-collection procedures that involve no intrusion into the naturally occurring course of events and in which subjects are unaware they are being studied), telling control subjects they are also in an experiment even if they are to receive no manipulation, and allowing an adaptation period during which no observations are made.
see also NOVELTY EFFECT, PRETEST-TREATMENT INTERACTION, MULTIPLE-TREATMENT INTERACTION, SPECIFICITY OF VARIABLES, TREATMENT DIFFUSION, RESEARCHER EFFECT, HALO EFFECT
📖 Brown 1988

hermeneutical phenomenology
   another term for INTERPRETIVE PHENOMENOLOGY

hermeneutics
   the study of the theory and the practice of understanding and interpretation. Hermeneutics is built on the assumption that interpretation is not a straightforward activity even though people do it all the time when they interact with others and the world. It is characterized as an approach to the analysis of textual material, such as interview transcripts, diaries, auto/biographies, that emphasizes the importance of understanding the meaning of the material from the perspective of the individual who produced it. It is associated largely with nineteenth century German philosophy, but also has connections with PHENOMENOLOGY and the psychoanalysis of Freud. Hermeneutics challenges both the aim of social science and its reliance on a narrow conception of understanding encouraged by scientific methods. According to a hermeneutic perspective, social reality is seen as socially constructed, rather than being rooted in objective fact. Hence, hermeneutics argues that interpretation should be given more standing than explanation and description. Social reality is too complex to be understood through the process of observation. The scientist must interpret in order to achieve deeper levels of knowledge and also self-understanding. Inquiry, therefore, is no longer framed as a separate event from that which is being inquired into; both must be acknowledged in the final analysis.
   Although not having an explicit method, hermeneutics has influenced the theory and practice of QUALITATIVE RESEARCH in several ways. First, because language (and other symbolic meaning systems) mediates people's experiences of the world, qualitative inquirers are paying closer attention to the language used by research participants while also acknowledging the symbolic systems they too inhabit and that give shape to their study. Second, theorists' contributions have informed how qualitative researchers talk about data collection, analysis, and representation, as each is seen as part of a dialogic, dynamic, holistic, and self-reflective process where interpretation and understandings are developed continuously along the way rather than as separate stages of a study. Finally, the hermeneutic potential that the space of difference between self and other opens up has caused theorists to call on social inquirers to reenvision their role not as elicitors of information that benefit social science, but as promoters of cross-cultural dialogue where understanding of self and other occur concurrent to inquiring into the world people share.
   📖 Given 2008; Gray 2009

heterogeneity of variance
   see HOMOGENEITY OF VARIANCE

heterogeneous sampling
another term for MAXIMUM VARIATION SAMPLING

heteroscedasticity
see HOMOSCEDASTICITY

heuristic research
a process that begins with a question or a problem which the researcher tries to illuminate or find an answer to. The question itself is usually focused on an issue that has posed a personal problem and to which answers are required. It seeks, through open-ended inquiry, self-directed search and immersion in active experience, to get inside the question by becoming one with it. One of the primary processes of heuristic research is self-dialogue in which the researcher enters into a conversation with the phenomenon and is questioned by it. It is hoped that the process will lead to self-discoveries, awareness, and enhanced understanding. Through this, the researcher is able to develop the skills and ability to understand the problem itself and, in turn, to develop the understanding of others.

Philosophically, heuristic inquiry does not start from the premise that there is an external objective truth to be discovered. In contrast, it starts phenomenologically from the belief that understanding grows out of direct human experience and can only be discovered initially through self-inquiry. Heuristic research, then, is autobiographical, providing for a deep, personal analysis. It is richly descriptive, but also strongly subjective, and weak in terms of GENERALIZABILITY.

Heuristic research, then, involves the researcher in:

- A deep personal questioning of what it is they wish to research.
- Living, sleeping and merging with the research question.
- Allowing inner workings of intuition to extend understanding of the question.
- Reviewing all the data from personal experiences to identify tacit meanings.
- Forming a creative synthesis, including ideas for and against a proposition.

see also QUALITATIVE RESEARCH
  Gray 2009

hierarchal clustering
see CLUSTER ANALYSIS

hierarchical design
another term for NESTED DESIGN

hierarchical multiple regression
another term for SEQUENTIAL MULTIPLE REGRESSION

higher order mixed design
see MIXED DESIGN

h index
see EFFECT SIZE

hinge plot
another term for BOXPLOT

hired hands
see INVESTIGATOR TRIANGULATION

histogram
also **frequency histogram**
a diagram consisting of rectangular bars to illustrate the FREQUENCY of a particular score or range of scores. By convention, in a histogram, scores are represented on the horizontal axis (X axis), and frequencies of occurrence for each score are represented along the vertical axis (Y axis). The lower values of both vertical and horizontal axes are recorded at the intersection of the axes (at the bottom left side).

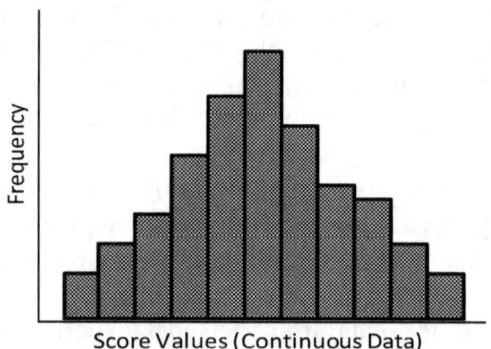

Figure H.1. An Example of Histogram

As you can see in Figure H.1, the values on both axes increase as they get farther away from the intersection.
A histogram is similar to a BAR GRAPH except that in a histogram adjacent bars touch. A bar graph is for more discrete CATEGORICAL VARIABLEs such as gender, while a histogram is for more CONTINUOUS VARIABLEs such as age. A histogram can also help detect any unusual observations (OUTLIERs), or any gaps in the data. Histograms can give information about whether distributions are symmetrically distributed or

skewed (see NORMAL DISTRIBUTION, SKEWED DISTRIBUTION), and whether they have one mode (peak) or several, and a histogram with an overlaid normal curve can be evaluated to see whether the data should be considered normally distributed.
📖 Clark-Carter 2010; Porte 2010

historical research
a type of research which goes beyond data gathering to analyze and develop theoretical and holistic conclusions about historical events and periods. In this type of research, some aspect of the past is studied, either by perusing documents of the period or by interviewing individuals who lived during the time. The researcher then attempts to reconstruct as accurately as possible what happened during that time and to explain why it did. Historical research includes a critical examination of sources, interpretation of data, and analysis that focuses on the narrative, interpretation, and use of valid and reliable evidence that supports the study conclusions. A researcher might want to investigate, for example, the trends in bilingual education in a particular city or district from its beginnings to the present. Also, one might investigate the methods used to teach reading in the past or study school practices and policies such as grade retention. Some of the data collected in historical research might be quantitative, such as when an investigator compares a school district's reading achievement scores when one teaching method was used with the scores obtained when another method was in vogue.
Perhaps more so than in any other form of research, the historical researcher must adopt a critical attitude toward any and all sources s/he reviews. A researcher can never be sure about the genuineness and accuracy of historical sources. A memo may have been written by someone other than the person who signed it. A letter may refer to events that did not occur or that occurred at a different time or in a different place. A document may have been forged or information deliberately falsified. Key questions for any historical researcher are: Was this document really written by the supposed author (i.e., is it genuine)? Is the information contained in this document true (i.e., is it accurate)? The first question refers to what is known as external criticism, the second to what is known as internal criticism. The process of blending external criticism and internal criticism is called SYNTHESIS.
The principal advantage of historical research is that it permits investigation of topics and questions that can be studied in no other way. It is the only research method that can study evidence from the past. In addition, historical research can make use of a wider range of evidence than most other methods (with the possible exceptions of ETHNOGRAPHIC RESEARCH and CASE STUDY). It thus provides an alternative and perhaps richer source of information on certain topics that can also be studied

with other methodologies. A researcher might, for example, wish to investigate the HYPOTHESIS that 'curriculum changes that did not involve extensive planning and participation by the teachers involved usually fail(ed)' by collecting interview or observational data on groups of second language teachers who (1) have and (2) have not participated in developing curricular changes (a CAUSAL-COMPARATIVE RESEARCH), or by arranging for variations in teacher participation (an EXPERIMENTAL RESEARCH). The question might also be studied, however, by examining documents prepared over the past 50 years by disseminators of new curricula (their reports), by teachers (their diaries), and so forth.

A disadvantage of historical research is that the measures used in other methods to control for threats to INTERNAL VALIDITY are simply not possible in a historical study. Limitations imposed by the nature of the sample of documents and the instrumentation process (CONTENT ANALYSIS) are likely to be severe. Researchers cannot ensure representativeness of the sample, nor can they (usually) check the RELIABILITY and VALIDITY of the inferences made from the data available. The possibility of bias due to researcher characteristics (in data collection and analysis) is also always present.

see also COMPARATIVE RESEARCH

📖 Ary et al. 2010; Fraenkel & Wallen 2009; Given 2008

history

a threat to INTERNAL VALIDITY which refers to events or incidents that take place during the course of the study that might have an unintended and uncontrolled-for impact on the study's final outcome (or the DEPENDENT VARIABLE). EMPIRICAL RESEARCH does not take place in a vacuum and therefore we might be subject to the effects of unanticipated events while the study is in progress. These events tend to be global enough that they affect all or most of the participants in a study. They can occur inside or outside the study and typically occur between the pre- and post-measurement phases of the dependent variable. The impact of history as a threat to internal validity is usually seen during the post-measurement phase of the study and is particularly prevalent if the study is longitudinal. Accordingly, the longer the period of time between the pre- and post-measure, the greater the possibility that a history effect could have confounded the results of the study.

For example, suppose a researcher is running a study on improving the second language of young children using some new teaching methodology over a period of several months. During that time, a new bilingual TV program is put on national TV. If the researcher found any difference between the treatment and control groups, could s/he be certain that the results were only due to the new methodology? Could the new methodology have interacted with the new TV program in such a way as to produce

the results? Had the program not appeared when it did, the new methodology might not have produced the same results. Consequently, the researcher could not be sure what caused the changes in language behavior, if any were observed. The best way to minimize the history effect is to document the impact of the events so that later we may neutralize it by using some kind of statistical control.
see MATURATION, STATISTICAL REGRESSION, MORTALITY, TESTING EFFECT, INSTRUMENTATION, DIFFERENTIAL SELECTION
📖 Dörnyei 2007; Perry 2011

HIT
an abbreviation for HOLTZMAN INKBLOT TEST

hit ratio
the percentage of subjects correctly classified by the LOGISTIC REGRESSION model. Hit ratio is calculated as the number of subjects in the diagonal of the CLASSIFICATION MATRIX divided by the total number of subjects.
📖 Hair et al. 2010

Hochberg's sequential method
a POST HOC TEST which uses a specific sequential method called a *step-up* approach as a more powerful alternative to the BONFERRONI ADJUSTMENT. Sequential methods use a series of steps in the correction, depending on the result of each prior step. Contrasts are initially conducted and then ordered according to P-VALUEs (from smallest to largest in the step-up approach). Each step corrects for the previous number of tests rather than all the tests in the set. This test is a good, high power alternative to the other modified Bonferroni approaches as long as CONFIDENCE INTERVALs are not needed.
📖 Everitt & Howell 2005

holistic fallacy
see BIAS

Holtzman Inkblot test
also **HIT**
a PROJECTIVE TECHNIQUE and a modification of the RORSCHACH TEST which consists of 45 inkblot cards (and not 10 inkblots as we find in case of Rorschach test) which are based on color, movement, shading and other factors involved in inkblot perception. Only one response per card is obtained from the subject (or the respondent) and the responses of a subject are interpreted at three levels of form appropriateness. Form responses are interpreted for knowing the accuracy or inaccuracy of re-

spondent's percepts; shading and color for ascertaining his/her affectional and emotional needs; and movement responses for assessing the dynamic aspects of his/her life. Holtzman Inkblot test or HIT has several special features or advantages. For example, it elicits relatively constant number of responses per respondent. Secondly, it facilitates studying the responses of a respondent to different cards in the light of norms of each card instead of lumping them together. Thirdly, it elicits much more information from the respondent then is possible with merely 10 cards in Rorschach test; the 45 cards used in this test provide a variety of stimuli to the respondent and as such the range of responses elicited by the test is comparatively wider.

There are some limitations of this test as well. One difficulty that remains in using this test is that most of the respondents do not know the determinants of their perceptions, but for the researcher, who has to interpret the protocols of a subject and understand his/her personality (or attitude) through them, knowing the determinant of each of his/her response is a must. This fact emphasizes that the test must be administered individually and a post-test inquiry must as well be conducted for knowing the nature and sources of responses and this limits the scope of HIT as a group test of personality. The usefulness of HIT for purposes of personal selection, vocational guidance, etc. is also to be established.

see also SOCIOMETRY, THEMATIC APPERCEPTION TEST, ROSENZWEIG TEST, RORSCHACH TEST, TOMKINS-HORN PICTURE ARRANGEMENT TEST
📖 Kothari 2008

homogeneity of regression

the extent to which the REGRESSION COEFFICIENTs being similar or homogeneous in an ANALYSIS OF COVARIANCE or MULTIVARIATE ANALYSIS OF COVARIANCE for the different categories or groups of an INDEPENDENT VARIABLE. In other words, the relationship between the COVARIATE and the DEPENDENT VARIABLE is constant across different TREATMENT levels. Homogeneity of regression assumes that the SLOPE of the REGRESSION LINE is the same for each group. When the slopes of the regression models for the individual groups are significantly different, that is, when the slope for one group differs significantly from the slope of at least one other group, then the assumption of homogeneity of regression has been violated. The results of such analyses are difficult to interpret if the regression coefficients are not homogeneous because this means that the relationship between the covariate and the dependent variable is not the same across the different groups.
📖 Cramer & Howitt 2004; Gamst et al. 2008; Larson-Hall 2010

homogeneity of variance
also equal variance, equality of variance

the degree to which the VARIANCEs of two or more SAMPLEs are similar or homogeneous. In an ANALYSIS OF VARIANCE, when samples are assumed to have been drawn from POPULATIONs with equal variances, they are said to exhibit homogeneity of variances. Many of the PARAMETRIC TESTS of significance require that the variances of the underlying populations, from which the samples are drawn, should be homogeneous. In REGRESSION ANALYSIS, homogeneity of variances is the condition in which the variance of the DEPENDENT VARIABLE is the same for all the values of the INDEPENDENT VARIABLE. By contrast, when samples differ markedly in terms of magnitude of their variances, they are said to exhibit **heterogeneity of variance**s. This property of data sets is known as HETEROSCEDASTICITY.

The violation of homogeneity of variances apparently has little effect on the results if the SAMPLE SIZEs are equal. If the sample sizes are seriously different (in a ratio of 3 or more to 1), this assumption should be tested empirically by the researcher before continuing with the analysis. Just as with the assumption of NORMALITY, there are different ways of examining the homogeneity of variances in one's own data. First and most simple is just to look at the numerical output for the STANDARD DEVIATIONs because the variances are simply the standard deviations squared. If there are big differences in these squared values, there are probably violations of this assumption. Another way of checking variances is to look at side-by-side BOXPLOTs of groups. Although the box in the boxplot is not the standard deviation (it is the area from the 25th to 75th QUANTILE), it is showing the amount of VARIABILITY in the central part of the distribution and thus can be examined for a rough sense of variance. There are also several statistical tests of homogeneity of variance such as BOX'S M TEST, COCHRAN'S C TEST, BARTLETT'S TEST, HARTLEY'S TEST, and LEVENE'S TEST. They are very strict because they assess normality as well. (exceptions are LEVENE'S TEST, BROWN-FORSYTHE TEST, and O'BRIEN TEST which are not typically sensitive to departures from normality).

Violations of homogeneity usually can be corrected by transformation of the dependent variable scores. Interpretation, however, is then limited to the transformed scores. Another option is to use untransformed variables with a more stringent a LEVEL OF SIGNIFICANCE (for nominal $\alpha = .05$, use .025 with moderate violation, and .01 with severe violation).

The multivariate analog of homogeneity of variance is **homogeneity of variance-covariance matrices**. As for univariate homogeneity of variance, inflated TYPE I ERROR rate occurs when the greatest dispersion is associated with the smallest sample size. The formal test Box's M is, too strict with the large sample sizes, usually necessary for multivariate applications of ANOVA.

see also INDEPENDENCE ASSUMPTION, LINEARITY, MULTICOLLINEARITY, HOMOSCEDASTICITY
 Brown 1992; Cramer & Howitt 2004; Everitt 2001; Everitt & Skrondal 2010; Larso-Hall 2010; Sahai & Khurshid 2001; Tabachnick & Fidell 2007

Homogeneity of variance-covariance matrices
see HOMOGENEITY OF VARIANCE

homogeneous sampling
see PURPOSIVE SAMPLING

homogeneous selection
a method that can make groups reasonably comparable on an EXTRANEOUS VARIABLE by selecting SAMPLEs that are as homogeneous as possible on that variable. If the experimenter suspects that age is a variable that might affect the DEPENDENT VARIABLE, s/he would select only children of a particular age. By selecting only 6-year-old children, the experimenter would control for the effects of age as an extraneous INDEPENDENT VARIABLE. Similarly, if intelligence is likely to be a variable affecting the dependent variable of the study, then subjects would be selected from children whose IQ scores are within a RESTRICTED RANGE—for example, 100 to 110. This procedure has thus controlled the effects of IQ. From this resulting homogeneous population, the experimenter randomly assigns individuals to groups and can assume that they are comparable on IQ. Beginning with a group that is homogeneous on the relevant variable eliminates the difficulty of trying to match subjects on that variable. Although homogeneous selection is an effective way of controlling extraneous variables, it has the disadvantage of decreasing the extent to which the findings.
see also RANDOM ASSIGNMENT, RANDOMIZED MATCHING
 Ary et al. 2010

homoscedasticity
also **homoskedasticity**
a term which consists of *homo* (meaning same) and *scedastic* (meaning scatter). Homoscedasticity exists in a set of data if the relationship between two CONTINUOUS VARIABLEs is of equal strength across the whole range of both. For *ungrouped* data, the assumption of homoscedasticity is that the variability in scores for one continuous variable (X) is roughly the same at all values of another continuous variable (Y). In other words, when data are homoscedastic the accuracy of a prediction based on the REGRESSION LINE will be consistent across the full range of both variables. To illustrate, if data are homoscedastic and a strong positive CORRELATION is computed between X and Y, the strong positive correlation

will exist across all values of both variables. However, if for high values of X the correlation between X and Y is a strong positive one, but the strength of this relationship decreases as the value of X decreases, the data show **heteroscedasticity**. Heteroscedasticity, the failure of homoscedasticity, is caused either by *nonnormality* of one of the variables or by the fact that one variable is related to some transformation of the other. As a general rule, if the distribution of one or both of the variables employed in a correlation is saliently skewed (see SKEWED DISTRIBUTION), the data are likely to be heteroscedastic. When, however, the data for both variables are distributed normally (see NORMALITY), the data will be homoscedastic.

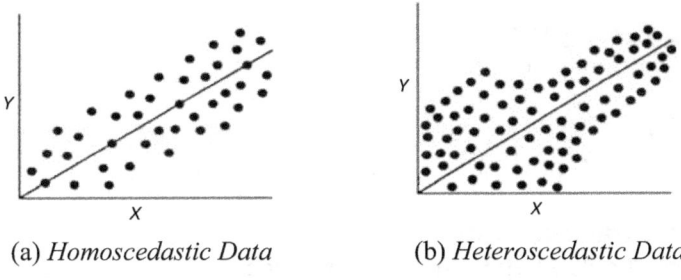

(a) *Homoscedastic Data*   (b) *Heteroscedastic Data*

Figure H.2. *Homoscedastic versus Heteroscedastic Data*

One way to check this assumption is to examine a SCATTERPLOT of the two variables and determine whether or not the points that deviate away from the straight line are about the same distance from the line all the way along it. Figure H.2 presents two regression lines. In Figure H.2a, which represents homoscedastic data, the distance of the data points or values (i.e., dots on the graph) from the regression line is about the same along the entire length of the line. Figure H.2b, on the other hand, represents heteroscedastic data, since the data are not dispersed evenly along the regression line. Specifically, in Figure H.2b the data points are close to the line for high values of X, yet as the value of X decreases, the data points become further removed from the line. Thus, the strength of the positive correlation is much greater for high values of X than it is for low values. This translates into the fact that a subject's Y score can be predicted with a greater degree of accuracy if the subject has a high score on the X variable as opposed to a low score.

For GROUPED DATA, homoscedasticity is the same as the assumption of HOMOGENEITY OF VARIANCE when one of the variables is *categorical*, the other is *continuous*. That is, the variability in the DEPENDENT VARIABLE is expected to be about the same at all levels of the INDEPENDENT VARIABLE. Homoscedasticity is a general assumption for all PARAMETRIC TESTS.

see also INDEPENDENCE ASSUMPTION, NORMALITY, LINEARITY, MULTI-COLLINEARITY, CATEGORICAL VARIABLE, CONTINUOUS VARIABLE
📖 Brown 1992; Larson-Hall 2010; Sheskin 2011

homoskedasticity
another term for HOMOSCEDASTICITY

horizontal axis
see BAR GRAPH

horns effect
see HALO EFFECT

Hotelling-Lawley trace
another term for HOTELLING'S TRACE CRITERION

Hotelling's T^2
another term for HOTELLING'S TRACE CRITERION

Hotelling's trace criterion
also **Hotelling's T^2, Hotelling-Lawley trace**
a *multivariate* test criterion and an extension of the INDEPENDENT SAMPLES t-TEST which can be employed to analyze the data for an experiment that involves a single INDEPENDENT VARIABLE (IV) comprised of two LEVELs (i.e., groups) and multiple DEPENDENT VARIABLEs (DVs). For example, there might be two DVs, such as score on an academic achievement test and attention span in the classroom, and two levels of type of therapy, emphasis on perceptual training versus emphasis on academic training. It is not legitimate to use separate t-tests for each DV to look for differences between groups because that inflates TYPE I ERROR due to unnecessary multiple significance tests with (likely) correlated DVs. Instead, Hotelling's trace criterion is used to see if groups differ on the two DVs combined. Hotelling's trace criterion is a special case of MULTIVARIATE ANALYSIS OF VARIANCE, just as the t-TEST is a special case of univariate ANALYSIS OF VARIANCE, when the IV has only two groups.
see also WILKS' LAMBDA, HOTELLING'S TRACE CRITERION, PILLAI'S CRITERION, ROY'S GCR CRITERION
📖 Clark-Carter 2010; Cramer & Howitt 2004; Everitt & Skrondal 2010; Sheskin 2011; Tabachnick & Fidell 2007

H-range
another term for INTERQUARTILE RANGE

HSD test
another term for TUKEY'S TEST

H test
another term for KRUSKAL-WALLIS TEST

Huynh-Feldt correction
a correction that is used when data in an REPEATED-MEASURES ANOVA do not satisfy the assumption of SPHERICITY. It is recommended always using a correction even if statistical tests indicate that your data do satisfy the assumption of sphericity. The Huynh-Feldt correction is more liberal (and thus gives more power) than the GREENHOUSE-GEISSER CORRECTION.
see also MAUCHLY'S TEST
📖 Larson-Hall 2010

hypothesis
an educated and testable guess or hunch, generally based on prior research and/or theory, to be subjected to the process of verification or disconfirmation. A hypothesis is a tentative statement of the relationship between two or more VARIABLEs and its validity remains to be tested and becomes the basis for further investigation. It is a proposition about the factual and conceptual elements; it is a brilliant guess about the solution of a problem. A key feature of all hypotheses is that each must make a prediction. Hypotheses are the researcher's attempt to explain the phenomenon being studied, and that explanation should involve a prediction about the variables being studied. These predictions are then tested by gathering and analyzing data, and the hypotheses can either be supported or refuted on the basis of the data. In their simplest forms, hypotheses are typically phrased as *if-then statements*. Hypotheses are made and evaluated in both QUANTITATIVE RESEARCH and QUALITATIVE RESEARCH. A quantitative researcher usually states an a priori expectation about the results of the study in one or more research hypotheses before conducting the study, because the design of the research study and the planned research design often is determined by the stated hypotheses. Thus, one of the advantages of stating a research hypothesis is that it requires the researcher to fully think through what the RESEARCH QUESTION implies, what measurements and variables are involved, and what statistical methods should be used to analyze the data. In other words, every step of the research process is guided by the stated research questions and hypotheses, including the sample of participants, research design, data collection methods, measuring instruments, data analysis methods, possible results, and possible conclusions. The research hypotheses are usually derived from the stated research questions and the problems being inves-

tigated. After the research hypotheses are stated, inferential statistical methods are used to test these hypotheses to answer the research questions and make conclusions regarding the research problems. Generally, in quantitative research designs, hypothesis testing and the use of inferential statistical methods begin with the development of specific research hypotheses that are derived from the study research questions. Research hypotheses differ from research questions in that hypotheses are specific statements in terms of the anticipated differences and relationships, which are based on theory or other logical reasoning and which can be tested using statistical tests developed for testing the specific hypotheses. In qualitative research, however, hypotheses emerge gradually in the course of the research itself.

see also NULL HYPOTHESIS, DIRECTIONAL HYPOTHESIS, NONDIRECTIONAL HYPOTHESIS, CAUSAL HYPOTHESIS, GROUNDED THEORY, HYPOTHESIS TESTING

Lavrakas 2008; Marczyk et al. 2005; Richards & Schmidt 2010

hypothesis-generating research
see INDUCTIVE REASONING

hypothesis testing
also **test of hypothesis**

a procedure for testing hypotheses about a POPULATION PARAMETER of interest. Hypothesis testing is a scientific approach to assessing beliefs about a reality or phenomenon under investigation. It is a decision-making process where two possible decisions are weighed in a statistical fashion. In a way this is much like any other decision involving two possibilities, such as whether to carry an umbrella with you today or not. In statistical decision making, the two possible decisions are known as hypotheses. SAMPLE DATA are then used to help us select one of these decisions. The two types of hypotheses competing against one another are known as the NULL HYPOTHESIS and the ALTERNATIVE HYPOTHESIS. A null hypothesis is usually tested and either rejected in favor of an alternative hypothesis or not rejected, in which case the alternative hypothesis cannot be sustained.

The following are general steps in hypothesis testing:

1) State a null hypothesis based on the specific question or phenomenon to be investigated.
2) State an alternative hypothesis. This may be a DIRECTIONAL HYPOTHESIS or a NONDIRECTIONAL HYPOTHESIS, depending on the problem being investigated as defined in the null hypothesis.

3) Specify the LEVEL OF SIGNIFICANCE. This is commonly taken as .05 and represents the maximum acceptable PROBABILITY of incorrectly rejecting the null hypothesis.
4) Determine an appropriate SAMPLING DISTRIBUTION of the SAMPLE STATISTIC of interest. Select a ONE-TAILED TEST or a TWO-TAILED TEST, depending on the alternative hypothesis.
5) Evaluate the STANDARD ERROR or, more generally, an estimate of the standard error of the sample statistic; the formula for the standard error depends on the sample statistic in question.
6) Compute the true value of the TEST STATISTIC and locate its value on the sampling distribution.
7) Reject or do not reject the null hypothesis, depending on whether or not the sample statistic is located on the sampling distribution at or beyond the value of the test statistic at a given level of significance.

It is now a standard convention to report a P-VALUE as justification for rejecting null hypothesis, which is the probability of obtaining a result equal to or more extreme than the observed value of the test statistic if the null hypothesis were true.

Because we are dealing with sample statistics in our decision-making process, and trying to make an inference back to the population parameter(s), there is always some risk of making an incorrect decision. In other words, the sample data might lead us to make a decision that is not consistent with the population. We might decide to take an umbrella and it does not rain, or we might decide to leave the umbrella at home and it rains. Thus, as in any decision, the possibility always exists that an incorrect decision may be made. This uncertainty is due to SAMPLING ERROR, which we will see can be described by a probability statement. That is, because the decision is made based on sample data, the sample may not be very representative of the population and therefore leads us to an incorrect decision. If we had population data, we would always make the correct decision about a population parameter. Because we usually do not, we use inferential statistics to help make decisions from sample data and infer those results back to the population. The types of decision errors that might be made in the decision-making process are called TYPE I ERROR and TYPE II ERROR.
 Lomax 2007; Sahai & Khurshid 2001

hypothesis-testing method
another term for HYPOTHETIC-DEDUCTIVE METHOD

hypothetic-deductive method
see INDUCTIVE REASONING

I

ICC
an abbreviation for ITEM CHARACTERISTIC CURVE

IF
an abbreviation for ITEM FACILITY

ID
an abbreviation for ITEM DISCRIMINATION

ideation
see PHENOMENOLOGY

imitation of the treatment
another term for TREATMENT DIFFUSION

independence assumption
an ASSUMPTION which denotes the *independence* of groups and observations. The independence of groups implies that there must be no association between the groups in a study. Put another way, knowing the data in one group should give no information about the data in another group. The most obvious violations of this assumption occur when the same people appear in more than one group. Likewise, the independence of observations means that the performance of any given individual is independent of the performance of other individuals. In other words, there is no association between the observations within a group. For instance, if students within a group were copying answers from one another on a test, this assumption would be violated because the scores on the tests would no longer be independent of each other.

Some statistical tests (e.g., INDEPENDENT SAMPLES *t*-TEST) assume independence assumption, whereas others (e.g., DEPENDENT SAMPLES *t*-TEST) allow for repeated measures of the same people. When assumed for a particular statistic, the assumption can be checked by answering one question: 'Is there any reason to believe that there is association between the observations made on the groups in this study?' If the independence assumption for some statistical tests such as independent samples *t*-test is not met, then probability statements about the TYPE I and TYPE II ERRORs will not be accurate; in other words, the probability of a Type I or Type II error may be increased as a result of the assumption not being met. In general, the assumption can be met by keeping the individuals separate from one another through experimental control so that the scores on the

DEPENDENT VARIABLE *Y* for sample *A* do not influence the scores for sample *B*.
see also NORMALITY, HOMOGENEITY OF VARIANCE, LINEARITY, MULTI-COLLINEARITY, HOMOSCEDASTICITY
📖 Brown 1988, 1992; Lomax 2007

independence of groups
see ASSUMPTIONS

independence of observations
see ASSUMPTIONS

independent groups
another term for INDEPENDENT SAMPLES

independent groups *t*-test
INDEPENDENT SAMPLES *t*-TEST

independent measures design
another term for BETWEEN-SUBJECTS DESIGN

independent samples
also **independent groups, unrelated samples**
SAMPLEs that are selected from two (or more) POPULATIONs such that all the observations of one sample are chosen independently of the observations of the other sample(s). Two samples are independent when the method of sample selection is such that those individuals selected for sample 1 do not have any relationship to those individuals selected for sample 2. In other words, the selections of individuals to be included in the two samples are unrelated or uncorrelated such that they have absolutely nothing to do with one another. Because the individuals in the two samples are independent of one another, their scores on the dependent variable *Y* will also be independent of one another. Independence is often achieved in experiments by assigning the subjects to the TREATMENT groups by RANDOM ASSIGNMENT. The extent to which the samples are independent or dependent determines the appropriate inferential test.
see also DEPENDENT SAMPLES
📖 Lomax 2007; Sahai & Khurshid 2001

independent samples design
another term for BETWEEN-SUBJECTS DESIGN

independent samples *t*-test
also **independent groups *t*-test, unrelated *t*-test, independent *t*-test, uncorrelated *t*-test, between-subjects *t*-test, two-sample *t*-test**

a type of *t*-TEST used when we want to compare the MEANs of two INDEPENDENT SAMPLES (e.g., males/females, or *experimental/control groups*), on a *continuous* DEPENDENT VARIABLE (DV). In this case, we collect information on only one occasion, but from two different groups of participants to see whether there is a statistically significant difference in the mean scores for the two groups. If we have more than two groups, we will need to use ANALYSIS OF VARIANCE instead. For example, if you wanted to compare the average vocabulary knowledge of 50 randomly selected men to that of 50 randomly selected women, you would conduct an independent samples *t*-test. Note that the sample of men is not related to the sample of women, and there is no overlap between these two samples (i.e., one cannot be a member of both groups). Therefore, these groups are independent, and an independent samples *t*-test is appropriate. To conduct an independent samples *t*-test, you need one *independent* CATEGORICAL VARIABLE and one *dependent* CONTINUOUS VARIABLE. The INDEPENDENT VARIABLE (IV) in a *t*-test is simply a variable with only two LEVELs or categories (e.g., men and women). In this type of *t*-test, we want to know whether the mean scores on the DV differ according to which group one belongs to (i.e., the level of the IV). Using the earlier example, we may want to know if the average vocabulary knowledge of people (the dependent continuous variable) depends on whether the person is a man or a woman (gender of the person is the independent categorical variable).

There are several assumptions underlying this test:

- INDEPENDENCE ASSUMPTION, i.e., the groups are independent of each other;
- NORMALITY, i.e., the DV is normally distributed within each group; and
- HOMOGENEITY OF VARIANCE, i.e., the two groups come from two POPULATIONs whose variances are approximately the same.

The *t*-test is considered a ROBUST statistic. Therefore, even if the assumption of the homogeneity of variance or normality is not fully met, the researcher can probably still use the test to analyze the data. As a general rule, it is desirable to have similar group sizes, especially when the groups are small. As in several other statistical tests, researchers usually try to have a group size of at least 30. Larger samples are more stable and require a smaller *t*-VALUE (compared with smaller samples) to reject the NULL HYPOTHESIS)

When the homogeneity of variance assumption is not met and there are unequal numbers of observations in the samples, the usual method to use as an alternative to the independent *t*-test is the WELCH'S TEST. When the

data are *ordinal*, none of these procedures as such are recommended, as they have been specifically designed for continuous DVs. The nonparametric alternative to an independent-samples *t*-test is the MANN-WHITNEY *U* TEST.
 Dörnyei 2007; Larson-Hall 2010; Lomax 2007; Mackey & Gass 2005; Pallant 2010; Peers 1996; Ravid 2011

independent scientific review
another term for PEER REVIEW

independent *t*-test
another term for INDEPENDENT SAMPLES *t*-TEST

independent variable
also **experimental variable, treatment variable, cause variable, predictor variable, explanatory variable, *X* variable**
a VARIABLE which is selected, systematically manipulated, and measured by the researcher. Implicitly, independent variable (IV) is the variable that we think causes a change in the other variable (i.e., DEPENDENT VARIABLE). IVs are antecedent to dependent variables (DVs) and are known or are hypothesized to influence the DV. For example, if the researcher wants to investigate the effect of his/her instruction on reading scores of his/her students, then instruction is the IV because that is what the researcher wants to investigate. The IV can be conceptualized as input factors, TREATMENT conditions, or treatment effects. It is possible to have more than one IV in an experiment. Experimental designs that involve more than one IV are referred to as FACTORIAL DESIGNs. In such experiments, the number of IVs will correspond to the number of factors. In fact, IVs that allocate respondents to different groups are called **factor**s which will be comprised of two or more LEVELs.
In NONEXPERIMENTAL RESEARCH, it is often more common to label the IV as the *predictor* or *explanatory* variable, which is used to predict or explain parts of the variance of the dependent or *criterion* variable. For example, you might measure language learning aptitude, motivation, and level of anxiety to explain students' scores on a language proficiency test, such as the TOEFL. The measurements for aptitude, motivation, and anxiety will be your predictor or explanatory variables. You will try to predict or explain differences in TOEFL scores through the differences in scores on aptitude, motivation, and anxiety.
see also MODERATOR VARIABLE, INTERVENING VARIABLE, CATEGORICAL VARIABLE, CONTINUOUS VARIABLE, EXTRANEOUS VARIABLE, CONFOUNDING VARIABLE
 Brown 1988; Hatch & Farhady 1982; Heiman 2011; Larson-Hall 2010; Lavrakas 2008; Sheskin 2011

in-depth interview
a detailed and extended INTERVIEW covering a wide range of topics in order to obtain as much information as possible and to explore unknown variables that are introduced during the interview. Depth interview is a technique designed to elicit a vivid picture of the participant's perspective on the research topic through a semi-structured exchange with the individual. It is designed to discover underlying motives and desires. Such interviews are held to explore needs, desires, and feelings of respondents. In other words, they aim to elicit unconscious as also other types of material relating especially to personality dynamics and motivations. Researchers engage with participants by posing questions in a neutral manner, listening attentively to participants' responses, and asking follow-up questions and PROBES based on those responses. They do not lead participants according to any preconceived notions, nor do they encourage participants to provide particular answers by expressing approval or disapproval of what they say. As such, depth interviews require great skill on the part of the interviewer and at the same time involve considerable time. Unless the researcher has specialized training, depth interviewing should not be attempted.
📖 Kothari 2008; Mack et al. 2005; Richards & Schmidt 2010

indicator variable
another term for MANIFEST VARIABLE

inductive inference
another term for INDUCTIVE REASONING

inductive reasoning
also **inductive inference**
a mode of reasoning moving from specific facts and observations to broader generalizations and theory; a process that is part of the scientific way of knowing whereby observations or other bits of information (data) are collected, without preconceived notions of their relationships (see HYPOTHESIS), with the assumption that relationships will become apparent, that conclusions will emerge from the data. As shown in Figure I.1, rather than beginning with a theory, an explanation, or an interpretation and then seeking evidence to confirm, disconfirm, (as in DEDUCTIVE REASONING), in inductive reasoning, you begin with specific observations and measures, begin detecting patterns and regularities, formulate some tentative hypotheses that you can explore, and finally end up developing some theories, explanations, and interpretations to reflect or represent those particulars.

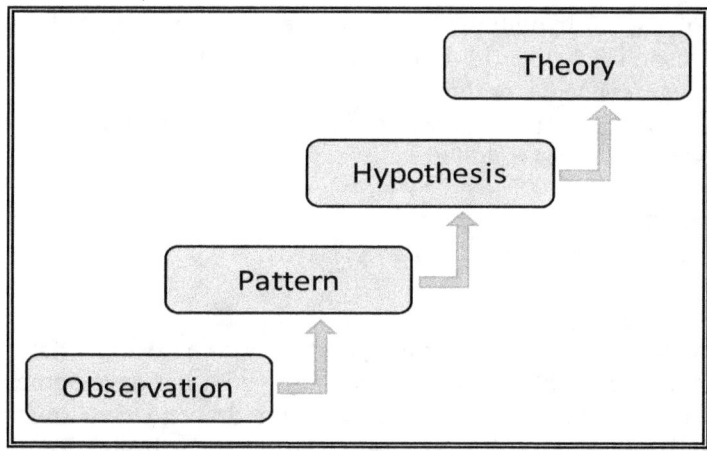

Figure I.1. Schematic Representation of Inductive Reasoning

Inductive reasoning often referred to as *a bottom-up approach* to knowing in which the researcher uses particular observations to build an abstraction or to describe a picture of the phenomenon that is being studied. Inductive reasoning usually leads to inductive methods of data collection where the researcher (1) systematically observes the phenomena under investigation, (2) searches for patterns or themes in the observations, and (3) develops a generalization from the analysis of those themes. So the researcher proceeds from specific observations to general statements—a type of discovery approach to knowing. Since there is no established theory on which to draw and the research is trying to develop theory, inductive approach is sometimes called **exploratory research** or **hypothesis-generating research**, which explores some phenomena prior to the development of any hypothesis and seeks to answer research questions without testing any hypothesis.

The inductive hypothesis-generating method represents one of the two general routes to knowledge used in applied linguistics research (the other route is DEDUCTIVE REASONING). Inductive reasoning is most closely associated with qualitative approaches to research, which collect and summarize data using VERBAL PROTOCOLs, OBSERVATIONs, INTERVIEWs, and CONTENT ANALYSIS. Qualitative researchers are often said to take inductive heuristic approaches to data collection because they formulate hypotheses only after they begin to make observations, interview people, and analyze documents. These hypotheses are examined and modified by further data collection rather than being accepted or rejected outright. Qualitative researchers believe that full understanding of phenomena is dependent on the context, and so they use theories primarily after data collection to help them interpret the patterns observed. However, ultimately qualitative researchers do attempt to make claims about the

truth of a set of hypotheses. Quantitative researchers may also use inductive reasoning as they look for similar experiences and results and form new ideas, concepts, or theories.
see also QUALITATIVE RESEARCH, QUANTITATIVE RESEARCH
📖 Given 2008; Lodico et al. 2010

inductive statistics
another term for INFERENTIAL STATISTICS

inferential statistics
also **inductive statistics, sampling statistics, analytical statistics**
a branch of STATISTICS that is concerned with the development and applications of methods and techniques for drawing generalizations (see GENERALIZABILITY) about a POPULATION on the basis of data obtained from a RANDOM SAMPLE, usually with a certain degree of uncertainty associated with it. Inferential statistics helps us to make inferences, estimates, or predictions about the characteristics of other groups of individuals on the basis of scores obtained from a single group. The rationale behind inferential statistics is that since the SAMPLE represents the population, what holds true for the sample probably also holds true for the population from which the sample was drawn. There are two broad categories of inferential statistics known as PARAMETRIC and NONPARAMETRIC TESTS. They deal with the parameters of the population from which researchers have drawn samples.
see also DESCRIPTIVE STATISTICS
📖 Marczyk et al. 2005; Perry 2011; Sahai & Khurshid 2001

informal interview
an interview in which (a) different questions are asked for each person being interviewed; (b) the same person is interviewed on several occasions; and (c) the length of the interview is completely open ended. Conversation is not being used here in the general sense of informal interactions that have no particular agenda because these conversations do have a purpose; however, in comparison to other types of interviews these interviews are very unstructured. The strength of an informal interview is that the interviewer can be very responsive to individual respondents and deal with topics as they arise in the conversation. The disadvantage is that a good deal of time is required to collect systematic information. Also because different questions will generate different answers, it is more difficult to find patterns in the data gathered. One context where this type of interview is valuable is when researchers want to conduct an intensive CASE STUDY of one or more teachers or students. For example, if researchers want to find out why particular students are having a great deal of difficulty in class, they might undertake a series of interviews with

these students over the course of the semester to find out what linguistic factors and nonlinguistic factors are contributing to the learners difficulty in acquiring English.
see also ETHNOGRAPHIC INTERVIEW, NON-DIRECTIVE INTERVIEW, UNSTRUCTURED INTERVIEW, SEMI-STRUCTURED INTERVIEW, STRUCTURED INTERVIEW, INTERVIEW GUIDE, TELEPHONE INTERVIEW, FOCUS GROUP
📖 Mckay 2006

informant

an individual from whom a researcher is able to obtain information relating to the customs, values, attitudes, and behaviors of the individual or wider group. The informant is a special category of research participant because of a particular expertise or knowledge that is brought to QUALITATIVE RESEARCH. Informants know and understand the kind of information that is of interest to researchers. They offer an insider's perspective and in-depth information that can represent the views of a group or even a community. It is the capacity to represent the knowledge of a larger group that distinguishes informants from other types of participants such as respondents to a QUESTIONNAIRE and people who are the subject of OBSERVATION. Qualitative researchers use informants in many research contexts, particularly ethnographies (see ETHNOGRAPHY), needs assessments, FOCUS GROUPs, policy evaluations, and ACTION RESEARCH. An informant's contribution to research may be a single INTERVIEW or continual involvement. An informant will usually provide data through IN-DEPTH INTERVIEWs, often face to face or by telephone. Sometimes an informant will assist during all stages of the research cycle, from identification of research questions to reviewing drafts of research findings.

There are advantages and disadvantages to using informants. Informants are advantageous because they can assist researchers in gaining trust and credibility within a community, they allow the collection of in-depth information and continuing clarification of data, they may represent a diversity of people's views (including those of silent minorities), they may save researchers time and resources, and they are important gatekeepers for gaining access to additional participants. Disadvantages include the possibility that informants will pass on their own biases and political agendas, thereby influencing the RELIABILITY and VALIDITY of information obtained. The informant technique can easily be combined with other methods, and TRIANGULATION of informant data by using other techniques of data collection is recommended. Good informants are more than just experts in the area of inquiry; they also reflect on it. This means that they can express a range of informed thoughts, feelings, insights, opinions, and facts about a topic. Researchers will often choose informants by asking members of a community to identify individuals who are both knowledgeable and respected for their expertise in the subject of inquiry. For example, to gain an understanding of popular culture in a high school, informants might include leaders from the student in-groups as well as teachers who are respected by students. These informants may suggest additional informants. An informant is unique by virtue of particular status, experience, or knowledge. An informant is in the know for whatever a researcher is investigating. During the initial stages of research, an informant may give new information to a researcher. During the later stages, the information should serve to clarify and validate what the researcher has learned.

📖 Brewerton & Millward 2001; Given 2008

informed consent
the procedures in which individuals choose whether to participate in an investigation after being informed of facts that would be likely to influence their decisions. This definition involves four elements: *competence*, *voluntarism*, *full information* and *comprehension*. Competence implies that responsible, mature individuals will make correct decisions if they are given the relevant information. It is incumbent on researchers to ensure they do not engage individuals incapable of making such decisions because of immaturity or some form of psychological impairment. Voluntarism entails applying the principle of informed consent and thus ensuring that participants freely choose to take part (or not) in the research and guarantees that exposure to risks is undertaken knowingly and voluntarily. This element can be problematical, especially in the field of medical research where unknowing patients are used as guinea-pigs. Full information implies that consent is fully informed, though in practice it is often impossible for researchers to inform subjects on everything, e.g., on the statistical treatment of data; and on those occasions when the researchers themselves do not know everything about the investigation. In such circumstances, the strategy of reasonably informed consent has to be applied. Comprehension refers to the fact that participants fully understand the nature of the research project, even when procedures are complicated and entail risks. Suggestions have been made to ensure that subjects fully comprehend the situation they are putting themselves into, e.g., by using highly educated subjects, by engaging a consultant to explain difficulties, or by building into the research scheme a time lag between the request for participation and decision time. If these four elements are present, researchers can be assured that subjects' rights will have been given appropriate consideration.

Informed consent requires an explanation and description of several factors, including, for example:

- the purposes, contents, and procedures of the research
- any foreseeable risks and negative outcomes, discomfort or consequences and how they will be handled
- benefits that might derive from the research
- incentives to participate and rewards from participating
- right to voluntary non-participation, withdrawal, and rejoining the project
- rights and obligations to CONFIDENTIALITY and non-disclosure of the research, participants, and outcomes
- disclosure of any alternative procedures that may be advantageous
- opportunities for participants to ask questions about any aspect of the research
- signed contracts for participation

There are many more issues, and researchers will need to decide what to include in informed consent. Not least among these is the issue of volunteering. Participants may feel coerced to volunteer (e.g., by a school principal), or may not wish to offend a researcher by refusing to participate, or may succumb to peer pressure to volunteer (or not to volunteer), or may wish to volunteer for reasons other than the researcher's (e.g., to malign a school principal or senior colleagues, to gain resources for his/her department, or to gain approval from colleagues). Researchers have to ensure that volunteers have real freedom of choice if informed consent is to be fulfilled.
see also ETHICS
📖 Cohen et al. 2011

in-person interview
another term for FACE-TO-FACE INTERVIEW

instrument
any device which is used to collect the data. Instruments can be presented in written, audio, or visual format. Responses can be gathered via paper-and-pencil tests, computer administered tests, video camera, or audiotape recorder. Other studies may not involve any data-gathering instruments, but may involve personal OBSERVATIONs of subjects or objects. These studies typically use video or audio recording to keep a record of the data in case there is need for validation, but the actual data collection is done by an observer or a group of observers. In some studies, confusion between the instruments and the materials used in the treatment can occur if the reader is not careful. One might think of the material as the stimulus that elicits the behavior that is measured or observed by the instrument. For example, one examined the cognitive processing that sub-

jects went through while taking a CLOZE TEST. The cloze test was not the instrument of the study, however, but rather the material used to elicit the subjects' think-aloud responses that were audiotaped. Whether the subjects got the items on the test correct was a secondary issue to the study. The data of interest were the participants' verbal responses.
📖 Perry 2011

instrumental case study
see CASE STUDY

instrument decay
changes in INSTRUMENTATION over time that may affect the INTERNAL VALIDITY of a study. Instrumentation can create problems if the nature of the instrument (including the scoring procedure) is changed in some way or another. This is often the case when the instrument permits different interpretations of results (as in essay tests) or is especially long or difficult to score, thereby resulting in fatigue of the scorer. Fatigue often happens when a researcher scores a number of tests one after the other; s/he becomes tired and scores the tests differently (for example, more rigorously at first, more generously later). The principal way to control instrument decay is to schedule data collection and/or scoring so as to minimize.
📖 Fraenkel & Wallen 2009

instrumentation
a threat to INTERNAL VALIDITY which refers to the level of RELIABILITY and VALIDITY of the measuring instrument (e.g., a test) or measurement procedures being used to assess the effectiveness of the INTERVENTION. If your assessments do not accurately measure the variables, the result is an inaccurate assessment of performance. Therefore, even if at the end of your study you demonstrate a difference between groups, it might not be due to the manipulation of the IV but simply a function of poor assessments or a result of a change in the instruments used during the study. The change in the way the dependent variable was measured from the first time to the second time, rather than the treatment, may bring about the observed outcome. Changes may involve the type of measuring instrument, the difficulty level, the scorers, the way the tests are administered, using different observers for pre- and postmeasures, INSTRUMENT DECAY, and so on. For example, if one test of English proficiency were used (e.g., a multiple-choice test) as a pretest and another test of English proficiency (e.g., an essay test) were used as a posttest, you would not know whether any change in test score was due to increase in ability or difference in the difficulty level between the two tests. Unless the two tests are parallel in all possible ways, the results between the two tests

cannot be compared. Instrumentation is a problem in LONGITUDINAL RESEARCH because the way measures are made may change over a period of time.

see also DIFFERENTIAL SELECTION, HISTORY, MATURATION, STATISTICAL REGRESSION, MORTALITY, TESTING EFFECT

 Ary et al. 2010; Lodico et al. 2010; Marczyk et al. 2005; Perry 2011; Ravid 2011

intact group

a group that is made up of all individuals in a given class, school, university, institution, etc. There are situations when RANDOM SELECTION of individuals may not be feasible. For example, in second language research we often need to use intact classes for our studies, and in these cases the participants cannot be randomly assigned to one of the EXPERIMENTAL or CONTROL GROUPs.

Intact classes are commonly and often by necessity used in research for the sake of convenience.

 Mackey & Gass 2005

intact group design

another term for STATIC-GROUP COMPARISON DESIGN

integer

see SYSTEMATIC SAMPLING

integrative meta-analysis

see META-ANALYSIS

integrative test

a test that requires a test taker to use several language skills at the same time such as a DICTATION TEST, which requires the learner to use knowledge of grammar, vocabulary, and listening comprehension. Integrative tests attempt to measure the actual aspects of activities that one must normally perform in using language. The rationale for integrative tests is that since language is for the purpose of communication, language tests should concentrate on the communicative use of language in tasks that are similar to those in real-life situations. The integrative tests, unlike DISCRETE-POINT TESTs, treat language as a dynamic system whose various subskills are assessed all at the same time. Proponents of integrative test method centered their arguments on what became known as the **unitary trait hypothesis**, which suggested an indivisible view of language proficiency: that vocabulary, grammar, phonology, the four skills, and other discrete points of language could not be disentangled from each other in language performance. This hypothesis contended that there is a general factor of language proficiency such that all the discrete points do

not add up to that whole. However, unitary trait position is seriously questioned by some specialists in the field of language testing.
Another type of integrative test method is CLOZE TEST.
📖 Brown 2005, 2010; Farhady et al. 1995

intensity sampling
see PURPOSIVE SAMPLING

interaction
also **interaction effect**
the simultaneous effect of two or more INDEPENDENT VARIABLEs (IVs) on at least one DEPENDENT VARIABLE (DV) in which their joint effect is significantly greater (or significantly less) than the sum of the parts. Put differently, interaction effect is the result of two or more IVs combining to produce a result different from those produced by either IV alone. An interaction effect occurs when one IV differs across the levels of at least one other IV. When there is more than one IV in an ANOVA we may find that the effect of the IVs is different depending on how the IVs are combined. For example, looking at the IVs of age and first language (L1) on reading ability in Persian second language (L2), if we find that being older when you start learning an L2 is difficult no matter whether you have L1 English or L1 Japanese, the IVs are parallel. However, if we find that being older is only more difficult if your L1 is English but not Japanese, then there is an interaction between the two variables. Thus, a two-way FACTORIAL DESIGN provides information about two **main effect**s (the effect of a single IV, by itself, on the DV without considering the effect of the other variables). That is, in a factorial design with two IVs, A and B, we can ask whether there is (1) a main effect of A (an effect of variable A, ignoring B), (2) a main effect of B (ignoring A), and (3) an interaction of A and B. A main effect reflects the effect of a particular IV while ignoring the effects of the other IVs. When we examine the main effect of a particular IV, we pretend for the moment that the other IVs do not exist and test the overall effect of that IV by itself. A factorial design will have as many main effects as there are IVs. For example, because a 2×3 design has two IVs, we can examine two main effects.

A three-way design, such as a $2 \times 2 \times 2$, or a $3 \times 2 \times 4$ design, provides even more information. First, we can examine the effects of each of the three IVs separately—that is, the main effect of A, the main effect of B, and the main effect of C. In each case, we can look at the individual effects of each IV while ignoring the other two. Second, a three-way design allows us to look at three two-way interactions—interactions of each pair of IVs while ignoring the third IV. Thus, we can examine the interaction of A by B (while ignoring C), the interaction of A by C (while ignoring B), and the interaction of B by C (while ignoring A). Each two-way interaction tells us whether the effect of one IV is different at different levels of another IV. For example, testing the B by C interaction tells us whether variable B has a different effect on behavior in Condition C1 than in Condition C2. Third, a three-way factorial design gives us information about the combined effects of all three IVs—the three-way interaction of A by B by C. If statistical tests show that this three-way interaction is significant, it indicates that the effect of one variable differs depending on which combination of the other two variables we examine. For example, perhaps the effect of IV A is different in Condition B1C1 than in Condition B1C2, or that variable B has a different effect in Condition A2C1 than in Condition A2C2.

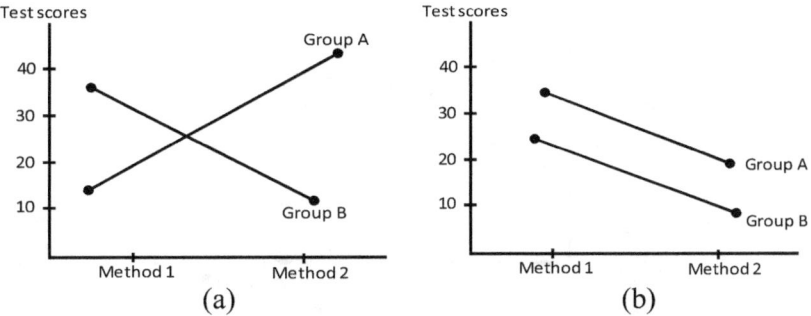

Figure I.2. A Graph Showing a Statistically Significant Interaction (a), and a Graph Showing an Interaction that is not Statistically Significant (b)

Often the best way of interpreting and understanding an interaction is by a graph. A nonsignificant interaction is represented by parallel lines, and a significant interaction is represented by nonparallel lines. Suppose, for example, that we want to conduct a study to investigate two methods designed to increase the reading ability of second- and third-grade second language students using two behavior modification methods. In this study, students' grade level is one IV; the second IV is the behavior modification method (Method 1 and Method 2). Half of the students in grade two (group A) and half of the students in grade three (group B) are taught using Method 1. The other half in each class is taught using Method 2. The DV is the students' reading ability scores. Figure I.2 shows two possible outcomes of the study: the interaction is significant and the lines intersect (a); and the interaction is not significant and the lines are parallel (b). Figure I.2a shows that there was an interaction effect between the behavior modification method and student grade level. We can conclude that Method 1 was more effective with Group B, and Method 2 was more effective with Group A regarding their reading ability. Figure I.2b shows no interaction effect. Method 1 was more effective for both Group A and

B, and Method 2 was less effective for both Groups. In addition, Group B who were taught using Method 1 and Group B who were taught using Method 2 scored lower than Group A who were taught using either Method 1 or Method 2.

There are two types of significant interactions: (a) disordinal, where the lines intersect (Figure I.2a); and (b) ordinal, where the lines do not intersect (Figure I.3). Therefore, an interaction may be significant even if the two lines do not intersect, as long as they are not parallel. Although the two lines representing the two groups do not cross, they are on a *collision course*, which is typical of a significant interaction effect.

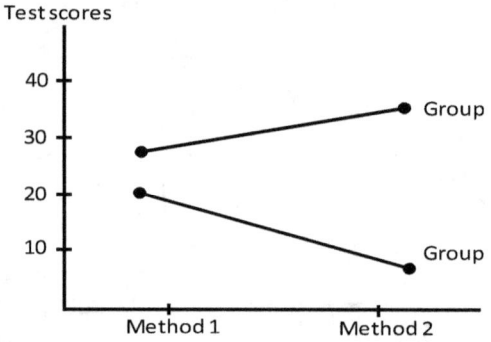

Figure I.3. A Graph Showing a Significant Interaction

Logically, factorial designs can have any number of IVs and thus any number of conditions. For practical reasons, however, researchers seldom design studies with more than three or four IVs. A two-way interaction is usually easy to interpret, but four- and five-way interactions are quite complex. Interactions can be found only in those factorial designs that include two or more IVs. If we find an interaction effect, then very rarely will the main effect still be of interest. This is because the main effects can only be interpreted in light of how they interact together.

 Larson-Hall 2010; Leary 2011; Marczyk et al. 2005; Ravid 2011; Trochim & Donnelly 2007

interaction analysis
also **interaction process analysis**
any of several procedures for measuring and describing the behavior of students and teachers in classrooms, (a) in order to describe what happens during a lesson (b) to evaluate teaching (c) to study the relationship between teaching and learning (d) to help teacher-trainees learn about the process of teaching. In interaction analysis, classroom behavior is ob-

served and the different types of student and teacher activity are classified, using a classification scheme.
📖 Richards & Schmidt 2010

interaction-based research
a type of research whose goal is usually to manipulate the kinds of interactions in which learners are involved, the kind of feedback they receive during interaction, and the kind of output they produce in order to determine the relationship between the various components of interaction and second language learning. The most common way of gathering data is to involve learners in a range of carefully planned tasks. There are a variety of ways of categorizing task types. For example, a common distinction is to classify *tasks* as *one-way* and *two-way*. In a one-way task, the information flows from one person to the other, as when a learner describes a picture to his/her partner. In other words, the information that is being conveyed is held by one person. In a two-way task, there is an information exchange whereby both parties (or however many participants there are in a task) hold information that is vital to the resolution of the task. For example, in a story completion task, a learner may hold a portion of the information and must convey it to another person before the task can be successfully completed.
Another way to classify tasks is to consider the resolution of the task. Is there one correct outcome, as in a closed task (e.g., when two learners need to identify exactly five differences between two pictures), or do the participants need to agree on a common outcome or conclusion, as in an open task such as a discussion activity?
Considering these dimensions, researchers need to be creative in eliciting interactive data. Frequently, one is interested in eliciting certain grammatical structures, with the idea that interactive feedback on nontargetlike forms might be associated with learning, possibly reflected through changes in the learners' output on the particular structures about which they have received feedback. Thus, it is always important to pilot whatever instrument is selected to make sure that opportunities for the production of appropriate forms and feedback are being provided.
Some general ways of eliciting interactive data include picture description tasks, spot the difference tasks, JIGSAW TASKs, CONSENSUS TASKs, and consciousness-raising tasks.
📖 Mackey & Gass 2005

interaction effect
another term for INTERACTION

interaction process analysis
another term for INTERACTION ANALYSIS

interactive focus group

a variation on traditional FOCUS GROUP which is characterized by a resistance to one facilitator or leader, collaboration in forming research questions, multiple voices, flexibility of conversation and direction, and collaborative writing and analysis. Interactive focus groups let researchers analyze, reflect, and share in vivo, using their group discourse itself as a method of inquiry as well as data to be analyzed. Interactive focus groups allow researchers to equalize the hegemonic power relationship between traditional research participants and researchers through a dialogic process that views all of those involved in the research process as co-participants. The focus of the interactive focus group is threefold: to discuss the topic at hand, to jointly reflect on the discussion in the group, and to analyze the discourse used in the discussion as a way of understanding how meaning is constructed in the group.

Unlike traditional focus groups, which are highly constrained and organized, in interactive focus groups the discussion is as unstructured as possible, allowing for multiple perspectives. Although interactive focus groups have ringleaders, all participants are co-researchers, yielding a group process somewhere between that of a leaderless group and a group with all leaders. At different times, different participants may take the lead.

Unlike traditional focus groups in which participants are strangers to each other, and thus their interactions have few consequences past the group session, interactive focus groups typically consist of participants already in an existing bona fide group or relationship, and the purpose is to observe how their prior group culture plays itself out in the focus group environment and to watch a system in action and interaction. This process entails multiple focus group sessions to build on previous sessions and encourage reflection, empathy, and trust between sessions. In analysis of interactive focus group sessions, the conversation itself can be investigated as a speech event to understand the joint construction of meaning taking place during the sessions through conversation and interaction.

Interactive focus groups are a moral and ethical methodological choice that let participants have a say in how the research is conducted given that they are able to exert control over the conversation. This approach provides an opportunity to tilt the balance of power in the research relationship from one single researcher to the group as co-participants.
📖 Dawson 2007; Given 2008

interaction sum of squares

another term for SUM OF SQUARES FOR INTERACTION

interactive interview
an interpretive practice for getting an in-depth and intimate understanding of people's experiences. Emphasizing the communicative and joint sensemaking that occurs in interviewing, this approach involves the sharing of personal and social experiences of both respondents and researchers, who tell (and sometimes write) their stories in the context of a developing relationship.

Interactive interviewing is a collaborative communication process occurring between researchers and respondents in small group settings. The goal of an interactive interview is for all of those participating, usually two to four people (including the primary researcher), to act both as researchers and as research participants. Each person has the opportunity to share his/her story in the context of the developing relationships among all participants. Interactive interviewing works especially well when all participants also are trained as researchers. If that is not the case, however, participants can be given an important role in determining the research process and its contents as well as in interpreting the meaning of the interviews.

Likewise, the feelings, insights, and stories that the primary researcher brings to the interactive session are as important as those brought by other participants; the understandings that emerge among all parties during interaction—what they learn together—are as compelling as the stories each person brings to the session. Ideally, all participants should have some history together or be willing to work to develop a strong affiliation. It is helpful for the researcher as well as the co-participants to have personal experience with the topic under investigation; if that is not the case, the researcher should be willing to take on the roles and lived experiences of other participants in this regard. This strategy is particularly useful when the researcher is examining personal topics that require reciprocity and the building of trust.

Interactive interviewing requires considerable time, multiple interview sessions, and attention to communication and emotions. It also may involve participating in shared activities outside the formal interview situation. This approach does not have rigid rules for proceeding; rather, it is flexible and continually guided by the ongoing interaction within the interview context. Participants engaged in this kind of research must be open to vulnerability and emotional investment while working through the intricacies of sensitive issues. In some cases, research roles may overlap with friendship, caretaking, and therapeutic roles, and the primary researcher must have plans in place for coping with that possibility.

Interactive interviewing reflects the way in which relationships develop in real life as conversations where one person's disclosures and self-probing invite another's disclosures and self-probing, where an increas-

ingly intimate and trusting context makes it possible for a person to reveal more of himself or herself and to probe deeper into another's feelings and thoughts, where listening to and asking questions about another person's plight lead to greater understanding of one's own plight, and where the examination and comparison of experiences offer new insight into both lives.
📖 Given 2008

intercept
a place on a SCATTERPLOT where a plotted line strikes the vertical axis (*Y* axis). In REGRESSION ANALYSIS, intercept is the predicted value of the DEPENDENT VARIABLE when the value of the INDEPENDENT VARIABLE is equal to zero. The point where the regression line for *X* predicted on the basis of *Y* crosses the *X* axis is called the ***X* intercept**. The point where the regression line for *Y* predicted on the basis of *X* crosses the *Y* axis is called ***Y* intercept**. These points mark the location of the regression line.

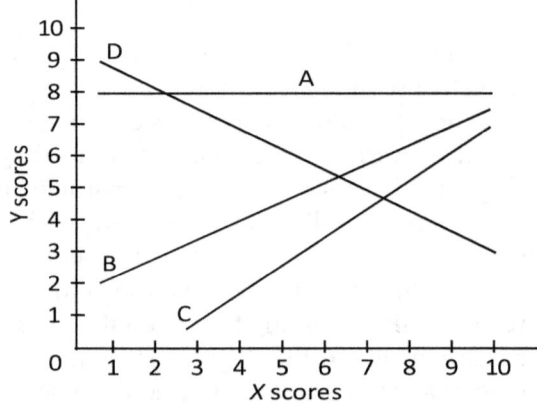

Figure I.4. An Example of Intercept

In Figure I.4, line B intercepts the *Y* axis at +2, so the *Y* intercept is +2. If we extended line C, it would intercept the *X* axis at a point below the *Y* axis, so its *Y* intercept is a negative *Y* score. Because line D reflects a negative relationship, its *Y* intercept is the relatively high *Y* score of 9. Finally, line A exhibits no relationship, and its *Y* intercept equals +8.
see also SLOPE
📖 Heiman 2011; Sahai & Khurshid 2001

intercoder reliability
another term for INTERRATER RELIABILITY

interdecile range
see DECILE

interfractile range
another term for INTERQUARTILE RANGE

interim summary
a short report prepared about one-third of the way through data collection in QUALITATIVE RESEARCH in order to review the quantity and quality of the data, confidence in its RELIABILITY, the presence and nature of any gaps or puzzles that have been revealed, and to judge what still needs to be collected in the time available.
📖 Walliman 2006

inter-item consistency
another term for INTERNAL CONSISTENCY RELIABILITY

inter-item correlation
see CRONBACH'S ALPHA

interjudge reliability
another term for INTERRATER RELIABILITY

internal consistency reliability
also **inter-item consistency**
a measure of the degree to which the items or parts of a test are homogeneous, equivalent, or consistent with each other. It is based on a single test administration and obviates the need for parallel forms of a test (see PARALLEL-FORMS RELIABILITY), which are often expensive and difficult to develop. Internal consistency reliability is often estimated by the following approaches: CRONBACH'S ALPHA, KUDER-RICHARDSON FORMULAS, SPLIT-HALF RELIABILITY, AVERAGE INTER-ITEM CORRELATION, and AVERAGE ITEM-TOTAL CORRELATION.
📖 Richards & Schmidt 2010

internal criticism
see SYNTHESIS

internal generalizability
see GENERALIZABILITY

internal validity
a degree to which a design successfully demonstrates that changes in a DEPENDENT VARIABLE are caused by changes in an INDEPENDENT VARI-

ABLE. The extent to which EXTRANEOUS VARIABLEs affect the change in the dependent variable is the extent to which the internal validity is influenced. Unlike EXTERNAL VALIDITY, internal validity is concerned with the degree to which the results of the study are due to the independent variable(s) under consideration that are measured, controlled, or manipulated and not due to anything else. Researchers favoring more qualitative approaches use the term CREDIBILITY to mean the same thing as internal validity.

There are a number of extraneous factors that can affect the results of a study that will lower the internal validity of a study: HISTORY, MATURATION, STATISTICAL REGRESSION, MORTALITY, TESTING EFFECT, INSTRUMENTATION, DIFFERENTIAL SELECTION, and SELECTION-MATURATION INTERACTION. Of course, some of the problems described as external validity problems, such as HAWTHORNE EFFECT, JOHN HENRY EFFECT, DEMORALIZATION, and EXPERIMENTER EFFECT, can also be internal validity problems.

see also CRITERION-RELATED VALIDITY, CONSTRUCT VALIDITY, CONTENT VALIDITY, FACE VALIDITY

📖 Ary et al. 2010; Cook & Campbell 1979; Lodico et al. 2010; Perry 2011

Internet survey
also Web survey, WWW survey

a SURVEY that sample respondents via the Internet, gather data from respondents via the Internet, or both. Using the Internet to conduct survey research provides a great many opportunities and a great many challenges to researchers. The Internet survey can be viewed as a considerably enhanced replacement of the EMAIL SURVEY, where text QUESTIONNAIREs are emailed to respondents, who are then asked to return the completed questionnaire by email. However, the Internet survey overcomes many of the inherent limitations of email surveys. The possibilities of visual and audio stimulation, the online interactive capabilities, and the potential of enhanced skip patterns available in the design of an Internet survey make it an extremely powerful survey data collection tool, far superior to the email survey. On the other hand the Internet survey may often suffer from serious problems of coverage, representativeness, and nonresponse bias.

📖 Lavrakas 2008

interobserver reliability
another term for INTERRATER RELIABILITY

interpenetrated survey design
a SURVEY that randomly assigns respondent cases to interviewers. This is done to lower the possibility that interviewer-related MEASUREMENT ER-

ROR is of a nature and size that would bias the survey's findings. This type of design addresses survey errors associated with the survey instrument and the recording of responses by the interviewer. One way to reduce subjective interviewer error is to develop a survey using an interpenetrated design—that is, by ensuring a random assignment of respondents to interviewers. Surveys employing an interpenetrated design, when such is warranted, will tend to reduce the severity of interpretation errors resulting from the conflation of INTERVIEWER BIAS with some other statistically relevant variable that might serve as a basis for assigning respondents. It will also typically reduce the overall standard error of response variance, especially for types of questions that inherently require some judgment or interpretation in recording by the interviewer.
📖 Lavrakas 2008

interpretive meta-analysis
see META-ANALYSIS

interpretive paradigm
see NORMATIVE PARADIGM

interpretive phenomenology
also **hermeneutical phenomenology**

a school which is based on the assumption that humans are interpretation through and through. Humans dwell in the world with no capacity to be completely free of the world. Interpretive phenomenology holds that there is no access to brute data (i.e., data containing no presuppositions or preunderstandings). Human science mirrors humans in that humans are the kind of beings who allow other beings to be revealed and known.

Interpretive phenomenology focuses on understanding practical worlds, skilled know-how, situated understanding, and embodied lived experiences. The embodied knower is irrevocably connected to the world and is socially constituted. Rigor involves staying true to the text, engaging in consensual validation, and allowing the readers to participate in the validation process by presenting texts associated with the interpretations made by the researcher. Phenomena to be interpreted may be found in practical worlds, cultural encounters, experiences of coping, skilled know-how, habits, practices, and common meanings. The interpreter uses PARTICIPANT OBSERVATION, OBSERVATION, first-person experience/near accounts of real events, videotapes, interviews, and all sources of text.

Interpretive phenomenology can be contrasted with **transcendental phenomenology** that seeks to reduce things down to their essence—their least interpreted essence of a thought or mental process. Transcendental phenomenology seeks to bracket presuppositions and try to approach

something as though one had no prior experiences, ideas, suppositions, or expectations.
📖 Given 2008

interpretive validity

(in QUALITATIVE RESEARCH) the ability of the research to accurately portraying the meaning attached by participants to what is being studied by the researcher and the degree to which the participants' viewpoints, thoughts, feelings, intentions, and experiences are accurately understood and portrayed. It is argued that good qualitative research focuses on what the various tangible events, behaviors, or objects mean to the participants. Interpretive validity, then, focuses on the quality of the portrayal of this participant perspective. Two primary strategies are used to enhance this validity: **member check**s (also called **respondent validation, participant feedback**) and **low-inference descriptor**s. Member checks involve discussing the findings with the participants. Member checks ask the question, 'Do the people who were studied agree with what you have said about them?' At the end of the data collection period, the researcher may ask participants to review and critique FIELDNOTES or tape recordings for accuracy and meaning. Or, the researcher's sharing his/her interpretations of the data with the participants can help clear up miscommunication, identify inaccuracies, and help obtain additional useful data. In member checks, the researcher solicits feedback from the participants about the study's findings. 'Has the researcher accurately described and interpreted their experience?' Feedback from the participants may help the researcher gain further insight and/or call attention to something that s/he missed. Furthermore, through member checking, the researcher demonstrates courtesy to the participants by letting them read what has been written about them.

Using many low-inference descriptors such as verbatim or direct quotations helps the reader experience the participants' world. Using tape recorders or video cameras enables the researcher to use these descriptors. Rich, THICK DESCRIPTION also helps the research convey an understanding of the study's context. These descriptions are very detailed, helping the reader see the setting, or if reporting themes from interviews, using the actual words of the respondents.

see also DESCRIPTIVE VALIDITY, THEORETICAL VALIDITY, EVALUATIVE VALIDITY
📖 Ary et al. 2010; Cohen et al. 2011; Dörnyei 2007; Johnson & Christensen 2000

interquartile range
also **IQR, interfractile range, H-range**

a common measure of DISPERSION which is the difference between the third and first QUARTILEs. Unlike the RANGE, the interquartile range

(IQR) is the difference between the score that marks the 75th PERCENTILE (the third quartile, denoted by Q_3) and the score that marks the 25th percentile (the first quartile, denoted by Q_1). To put it another way, this is a measure of variability that is based on the range of the middle 50 per cent of the test scores while discarding the upper 25% and the lower 25% of the distribution (see Figure I.5). The formula for the IQR is:

$$IQR = Q_3 - Q_1$$

Interquartile range is useful with ordinal scores and with highly SKEWED DISTRIBUTIONs. To determine the interquartile range, we begin by locating the first and third quartiles, similar to the way we located the MEDIAN. If, for example the 25th percentile was 5 and the 75th percentile is 8. Therefore the interquartile range would be 8 - 5 = 3.

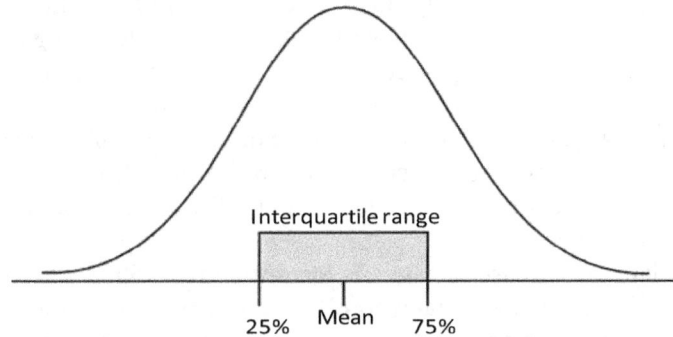

Figure I.5. An Example of Interquartile Range

When interquartile range is divided by 2 the result is the **semi-interquartile range** (SIQR) (also called **quartile deviation**), i.e., 3/2 = 1.5. When quoting a median the appropriate measure of spread is the semi-interquartile range. The formula for the SIQR is:

$$SIQR = \frac{Q_3 - Q_1}{2}$$

Interquartile range is the appropriate indicator of variability for ordinal scaled test scores, and is thus a natural companion to the median. In addition, because interquartile range is a ROBUST measure that is no strongly affected by extreme scores (i.e., OUTLIERs), it is particularly useful for describing the variability in distributions with one or more extreme scores, even when those scores are intervally scaled. In NORM-REFERENCED TESTs with large numbers of test scores and symmetric distributions (see NORMAL DISTRIBUTION), we will typically find that about

50 per cent of the scores occur within one interquartile range of the median.

However, the interquartile range suffers from problems that are just the opposite of those found with the range. Specifically, the interquartile range discards too much of the data. If we want to know whether one set of photographs is judged more variable than another, it may not make much sense to toss out those scores that are most extreme and thus vary the most from the MEAN.

see also BOXPLOT

📖 Bachman 2004; Clark-Carter 2010; Howell 2010; Larson-Hall 2010

interrater reliability
also **interobserver reliability, interjudge reliability, intercoder reliability**
a type of RELIABILITY that refers to the degree to which different observers/raters agree in their observations/ratings of the behavior of participants. Researchers typically determine the reliability of the raters by either computing a CORRELATION COEFFICIENT or calculating a percentage of agreement. For example, two researchers might score the same group of student essays using a six-point holistic scoring rubric. The degree to which the two raters agreed would indicate the level of interrater reliability. If a study reports an interrater reliability of .90, this would indicate that the two raters agreed on their rating 90% of the time and disagreed 10% of the time.

Also related to the use of raters is **intrarater reliability**. The type of consistency this addresses relates to observers/raters giving the same results if they were given the opportunity to observe/rate participants on more than one occasion. We would expect high agreement within the same person doing the rating over time if the attribute being observed is stable and the observer/rater understood the task. However, if the rater is not clear about what s/he is supposed to observe/rate, there will be different results, and CORRELATIONs or percentages of agreement will be low.

Two common measures of calculating interrater reliability are COHEN'S KAPPA and AGREEMENT COEFFICIENT.

📖 McKay 2006; Perry 2011; Richards & Schmidt 2010; VanderStoep & Johnston 2009

interrupted time-series design
another term for TIME-SERIES DESIGN

interval-contingent design
see DIARY STUDIES

interval data
see INTERVAL SCALE

interval estimate

the process of estimation of a PARAMETER in terms of an interval that contains the actual value of the parameter with a given PROBABILITY. The method for calculating an interval estimate from the SAMPLE DATA is known as an **interval estimator**.

see also CONFIDENCE INTERVAL, POINT ESTIMATE

📖 Sahai & Khurshid 2001

interval estimator

see INTERVAL ESTIMATE

interval scale
also **equal-interval scale**

a type of MEASUREMENT SCALE which categorize and rank order the data, thereby including the characteristics of NOMINAL and ORDINAL VARIABLES. However, an additional type of information is that of how large the difference is between one number and another. In other words, in addition to information about distinctiveness and ordering, interval scales provide information about the intervals, or distances between the data in the measurement scale. Interval scales thus answer three questions: 'are they different?', 'which is larger?', and 'how much larger?' Examples of interval scales include virtually all language test scores as well as other scales used to measure things like attitude, aptitude, IQ, and learning styles. Interval scales also assume that the distance between the scores is equal. They measure CONTINUOUS VARIABLEs in which the distance between any two positions is of known size. One unit on the scale represents the same magnitude on the trait or characteristic being measured across the whole range of that scale. For example, if language proficiency is measured on an interval scale, a difference between a score of 50 and 51 would be considered to be the same difference as that between 23 and 24. A continuous variable which is measured using an interval scale is called **interval variable**. Similarly, data which are measured on an interval scale are called **interval data**.

Interval scales can have an arbitrary zero, but it is not possible to determine for them what may be called an absolute zero or the unique origin. The primary limitation of the interval scale is the lack of a true zero; it does not have the capacity to measure the complete absence of a trait or characteristic.

📖 Bachman 2004; Brown 1992; Dörnyei 2007; Marczyk et al. 2005; Porte 2010; Sahai & Khurshid 2001

interval variable

see INTERVAL SCALE

intervening variable
also mediating variable, mediator variable
an abstract theoretical label which is applied to the relationship or process that links the INDEPENDENT VARIABLE (IV) and DEPENDENT VARIABLE (DV) but is not directly observable. An intervening variable is an in-the-head variable; it cannot be seen, heard, or felt; it is inferred from behavior. An intervening variable can be conceptualized as intermediate and thus intervenes between or changes the nature of the relationship between IV and DV. In some situations, the intervening variable label may be used to describe a variable that was unexpected in the study, yet surfaced because it might explain the relationship between the IV and DV. For instance, it might turn out that any difference discovered in the average TOEFL scores of the Method X and control groups was caused by an unanticipated intervening variable rather than by the different methods. The teacher of the Method X class might have been more lively and interesting than the teacher of the control group. Thus, any differences in student performance in English proficiency might have been due to differences in teaching style (an intervening variable), which were not anticipated in the study, yet could explain any relationship that was found. An intervening variable is the same thing as a MODERATING VARIABLE. The only difference is that the intervening variable has not been or cannot be identified in a precise way for inclusion in the research. Researchers generally prefer to avoid such surprises by anticipating and controlling potential intervening variables.

see also MODERATOR VARIABLE, CATEGORICAL VARIABLE, CONTINUOUS VARIABLE, EXTRANEOUS VARIABLE, CONFOUNDING VARIABLE

📖 Brown 1988, 1992; Harlow 2005; Hatch & Farhady 1982; Hatch & Lazaraton 1991; Porte 2010

intervention
another term for TREATMENT

intervention group
another term EXPERIMENTAL GROUP

interview
a data collection method in which a researcher and participant engage in a conversation focused on questions related to a research study. These questions usually ask participants for their thoughts, opinions, perspectives, or descriptions of specific experiences. Interview is a face to face verbal interchange in which one person, the interviewer, attempts to elicit information or expressions of opinions or belief from another person or persons. It provides a way of generating data by asking people to talk about their everyday lives. Its main function is to provide a framework in

which respondents can express their own thoughts in their own words. It generally takes the form of a conversation between two people (although they can involve larger groups (see FOCUS GROUP). Since everyone has experience of talking to people, there is a tendency to assume that conducting interviews is easy to do and requires little skill. This leads to the notion that anyone can do an interview. Nothing could be further from the truth. Interviews are not just conversations. They are conversations with a purpose to collect information about a certain topic or research question. These conversations do not just happen by chance; rather they are deliberately set up and follow certain rules and procedures. The interviewer initiates contact and the interviewee consents. Both parties know the general areas the interview will cover. The interviewer establishes the right to ask questions and the interviewee agrees to answer these questions. The interviewee also should be aware that the conversation will be recorded in some way and is therefore on record.

Establishing trust and familiarity, demonstrating genuine interest in what the respondent says and appearing non-judgmental are all necessary skills for conducting effective interviews. The interviewer has to develop an effective balance between talking and listening. This involves remembering what the respondent has said and knowing when and when not to interrupt. The interviewer also has to decide whether to use a tape-recorder to record the data and/or to take notes. In other words, interviews are rarely straightforward. They involve the interviewer considering different options and often making difficult choices. The interview itself requires the interviewer to possess, or learn, a number of skills and to be able to apply these skills effectively during the interaction with respondents. Interviews can yield rich and valid data but they are by no means an easy option.

Interviews are used both in QUANTITATIVE and QUALITATIVE RESEARCH. However, there are key differences between the two approaches. Quantitative interviews typically involve the use of a structured SURVEY instrument that asks all respondents the same questions in the same order and the responses are amenable to statistical analysis. Qualitative interviews are more flexible and open-ended. They are often used to develop ideas and research hypotheses rather than to gather facts and statistics. While the qualitative researcher may want to count or enumerate certain aspects of the data, there is less focus on quantification. Qualitative researchers are more concerned with trying to understand how ordinary people think and feel about the topics of concern to the research. Moreover, whereas quantitative research methods gather a narrow amount of information from a large number of respondents, qualitative interviews gather broader, more in-depth information from fewer respondents. In this sense, qualitative interviews are concerned with micro-analysis. Interviews are more or less taken at face value for what they have to tell the researcher about the particular issue being discussed. They can be used as a stand-alone data collection method to provide rich information in the respondents' own words. They allow respondents to say what they think and to do so with greater richness and spontaneity.

There are six basic types of questions that can be asked of participants during the interview. The six types are *background (or demographic) questions, knowledge questions, experience (or behavior) questions, opinion (or values) questions, feelings questions, and sensory questions.*

Background (or demographic) questions are routine sorts of questions about the background characteristics of the respondents. They include questions about education, previous occupations, age, income, and the like.

Knowledge questions pertain to the factual information (as contrasted with opinions, beliefs, and attitudes) respondents possess. Knowledge questions about a school, for example, might concern the kinds of courses available to students, graduation requirements, the sorts of extracurricular activities provided, school or university rules, enrollment policies, and the like. From a qualitative perspective, what the researcher wants to find out is what the respondents consider to be factual information (as opposed to beliefs or attitudes).

Experience (or behavior) questions focus on what a respondent is currently doing or has done in the past. Their intent is to elicit descriptions of experience, behaviors, or activities that could have been observed but (for reasons such as the researcher not being present) were not. Examples might include, 'If I had been in your class during the past semester, what kinds of things would I have been doing?' or, 'If I were to follow you through a typical day here at your school, what experiences would I be likely to see you having?'

Opinion (or values) questions are aimed at finding out what people think about some topic or issue. Answers to such questions call attention to the respondent's goals, beliefs, attitudes, or values. Examples might include such questions as, 'What do you think about the principal's new policy concerning absenteeism?' or, 'What would you like to see changed in the way things are done in your grammar class?'

Feelings questions concern how respondents feel about things. They are directed toward people's emotional responses to their experiences. Examples might include such questions as, 'How do you feel about the way students behave in this school?' or, 'To what extent are you anxious about going to grammar class?'

Sensory questions focus on what a respondent has seen, heard, tasted, smelled, or touched. Examples might include questions such as, 'When you enter your classroom, what do you see? or, 'How would you describe what your class sounds like?' Although this type of question could be considered as a form of experience or behavior question, it is often overlooked by researchers during an interview. Further, such questions are sufficiently distinct to warrant a category of their own.

Often interviews are combined or triangulated with other methods (see TRIANGULATION). Sometimes they are used to ensure that the questions that will appear in a widely circulated QUESTIONNAIRE are valid and understandable. Alternatively they may be used as follow-up to a questionnaire. This allows the researcher to explore in more depth interesting issues that may have emerged from the standard questionnaire. Interviews can thus lead to the development of new ideas and hypotheses and throw up new dimensions to be studied. In this way, interviews may complement questionnaire data.

see also ETHNOGRAPHIC INTERVIEW, NON-DIRECTIVE INTERVIEW, UN-STRUCTURED INTERVIEW, SEMI-STRUCTURED INTERVIEW, STRUCTURED INTERVIEW, INFORMAL INTERVIEW, TELEPHONE INTERVIEW, FOCUS GROUP

deMarrais & Lapan 2004; Dörnyei 2007; Fraenkel & Wallen 2009; Mckay 2006; Patton 1990

interviewer bias
see POSTAL SURVEY

interview guide
also **interview schedule, interview protocol, topic guide**
a plan for interviewer. A complete interview process involves a series of carefully designed steps, with the preparation starting well before the first interview session. Interview guides summarize the content that researchers cover during. At one extreme, they may provide very minimal directions, leading to less structured interviews that are designed primarily to explore the participant's own perspective on the research topic. At the other extreme, interview guides may contain elaborate specifications to ensure that the researcher's topics of interest are thoroughly covered.

After the initial sampling plan has been finalized and ethical issues such as INFORMED CONSENT have been considered, the researcher needs to prepare a detailed interview guide, which will serve as the main research instrument. The main function of the interview guide is to help the interviewer in a number of areas by:

a) ensuring that the domain is properly covered and nothing important is left out by accident;
b) suggesting appropriate question wordings;
c) offering a list of useful probe questions to be used if needed;

d) offering a template for the opening statement; and
e) listing some comments to bear in mind.
📖 Dörnyei 2007; Given 2008

interview protocol
another term for INTERVIEW GUIDE

interview schedule
another term for INTERVIEW GUIDE

intrarater reliability
see INTERRATER RELIABILITY

intrinsic case study
see CASE STUDY

introduction
a RESEARCH REPORT section which serves the overall purpose of putting the study in perspective. Generally, the introduction section tells you which area of the field is involved and then narrows to the specific specialization and topic that was investigated. This goal is normally accomplished through a review of the relevant literature (see LITERATURE REVIEW) and a statement of the purpose of the study (see STATEMENT OF PURPOSE).
see also ABSTRACT, INTRODUCTION, METHOD, RESULTS, DISCUSSION, REFERENCES, APPENDIXES
📖 Brown 1988

introspective method
a qualitative data collection method which is used for observing and reflecting on one's thoughts, feelings, motives, reasoning processes, and mental states with a view to determining the ways in which these processes and states determine our behavior. The various ways of eliciting self-reflections from respondents is usually referred to under the umbrella term introspective method. It subsumed several different approaches that all aim at helping the respondents to vocalize what is/was going through their minds when making a judgment, solving a problem or performing a task. Two of the most commonly introspective methods used in QUALITATIVE RESEARCH are VERBAL REPORT and DIARY STUDY. Verbal report is often used with ACTION RESEARCH and DISCOURSE ANALYSIS; diary study can be more broadly used in NARRATIVE INQUIRY, CASE STUDY, ETHNOGRAPHY, action research, and even MIXED METHODS RESEARCH.
📖 Dörnyei 2007; Heigham & Croker 2009; Mckay 2006; Nunan 1992

inverse correlation
    another term for NEGATIVE CORRELATION

inverse transformation
    another term for RECIPROCAL TRANSFORMATION

investigator triangulation
    a type of TRIANGULATION in which researchers attempt to increase the VALIDITY and trustworthiness of their findings by deploying more than one investigator in the collection and analysis of data. Investigator triangulation allows for additional insights in the process of making sense of the data as it brings different perspectives and different epistemological assumptions that may inform the research results. However, the researchers should be cautious caution against the use of untrained students and unmotivated research assistants (sometimes called the **hired hand**s) who may end up damaging the trustworthiness of any research findings through lack of engagement and accountability. It is generally recommended that co-investigators be full research partners through all stages of the research project, not only to guard against the hired-hand syndrome, but also to allow for the full play of competing theories and to provide an ongoing opportunity to deal with researcher biases and conflicts.
    Respondent or member validation is a related cross-checking strategy that does not usually extend as far as making people co-investigators, but does invite research participants and other STAKEHOLDERS in the research project to comment on research findings. Respondents may corroborate or refute the conclusions reached by the investigators by providing alternative perspectives.
    see also DATA TRIANGULATION, THEORETICAL TRIANGULATION, METHODOLOGICAL TRIANGULATION
    📖 Cohen et al. 2011; Given 2008

IQR
    an abbreviation for INTERQUARTILE RANGE

IRT
    an abbreviation for ITEM RESPONSE THEORY

item analysis
    a testing procedure which is used to determine flaws in test items, to evaluate the effectiveness of distractors (if the items are in a multiple-choice format), and to determine item statistics for use in subsequent test development work. Item analysis can take numerous forms, but when testing for norm-referenced purposes (see NORM-REFERENCED TEST),

there are three types of analyses that are typically applied: **item format analysis** (an analysis to ensure that the testees answer the items correctly only if they know the concept or ability being tested, not because of a poorly designed item), ITEM FACILITY and ITEM DISCRIMINATION. In developing CRITERION-REFERENCED TESTs, three other concerns become paramount: **item quality analysis** (analysis to determine the degree to which test items are valid for the overall purposes and content of the course program involved), the **item difference index** (an item statistic that indicates the degree to which an item is distinguishing between the testees who know the material or have the skill being taught, and those who do not.), and the **B-index** (an item statistic that compares the item facilities of those testees who passed a test with the item facilities of those who failed it) for each item.
see also ITEM SPECIFICATIONS
 Brown 2005; Fernandez-Ballesteros 2003

item bias
another term for DIFFERENTIAL ITEM FUNCTIONING

item characteristic curve
also **ICC**
a graphical representation between an individual's probability of obtaining a correct response on a given item and his/her level of ability. In other words, an item characteristic curve (ICC) can be drawn to express the relationship between the test taker's ability and his/her performance on a given item. ICC is a key concept in ITEM RESPONSE THEORY. It looks like a non-linear REGRESSION LINE (item performance regressed on ability) and provides an estimate of the probability of success on a test item for examinees at different ability levels.
Ability is usually represented by the Greek letter **theta** (θ), while item difficulty is expressed as a number from 0 to 1. The ICC is drawn as a smooth curve on a graph in which the vertical axis represents the probability of answering an item and the horizontal axis represents examinee ability on a scale in which θ has a mean of 0 and a STANDARD DEVIATION of 1. Figure I.6 shows the ICC for the three-parameter logistic model which can be applied to test items scored 0 or 1 (e.g., correct/incorrect or true/false). Each item in the model is described by three parameters: the **c-parameter** (the *guessing parameter*) is the probability of low-performing examinees answering an item correctly by guessing (.20 is a typical value), the **b-parameter** is the point on the ability continuum where an examinee has a probability of $(1 + c)/2$ of giving a correct answer (this parameter corresponds to ITEM DIFFICULTY in the CLASSICAL TEST MODEL), and the **a-parameter** is proportional to the

SLOPE of the curve at the point *b* on the ability continuum (this parameter corresponds to ITEM DISCRIMINATION in the classical test model).

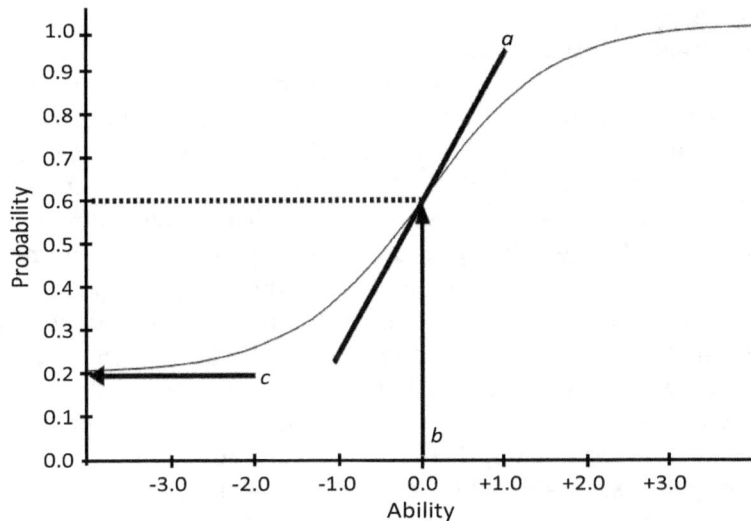

Figure I.6. Item Characteristic Curve for a Three-Parameter Model

The ICC is a monotonically increasing function, so that examinees with higher ability (higher value of θ) will always be predicted to have a higher probability of answering a given item correctly. For harder items the ICCs are shifted to the higher end of the ability scale. Thus, examinees always have lower probabilities of success on harder items than easier items (as it should be). For easier items the ICCs are shifted to the lower end of the ability scale. The special property of ICCs is that they are defined over the ability scale on which items and scores are reported, and are independent of the examinee samples to which they are applied. The discriminating power of a test item influences the slope of the ICC. More discriminating items have steeper slopes, less discriminating items have lower slopes. The slope of the ICC has a substantial influence on the usefulness of a test item for estimating ability.
see also ITEM INFORMATION FUNCTION
📖 Bachman 1990, 2004; Boslaugh & Watters 2008; Fernandez-Ballesteros 2003

item difference index
see ITEM ANALYSIS

item differentiation
another term for ITEM DISCRIMINATION

item difficulty
another term for ITEM FACILITY

item discrimination
also ID, item differentiation
the extent to which an item differentiates between high- and low-ability test takers. An item on which high-ability respondents (who did well in the test) and low-ability ones (who did not) score equally well would have poor item discrimination (ID) because it did not discriminate between the two groups. Conversely, an item that garners correct response from most of the high-ability group and incorrect responses from most of the low-ability group has good discrimination power. Suppose your class of 30 students has taken a test. Once you have calculated final scores for all 30 students, divide them roughly into thirds—that is, create three rank-ordered ability groups including the top 10 scores, the middle 10, and the lowest 10. To find out which of your 50 or so test item were most powerful in discriminating between high and low ability, eliminate the middle group (see Table I.1), leaving two groups with results that might look something like the following on a particular item:

Item 23	Correct	Incorrect
High-ability students (top 10)	7	3
Low-ability (bottom 10)	2	8

Table I.1. The Number of Correct versus Incorrect Answers by Low- and High-Ability Students

Using the ID formula (7 - 2 = 5/10 = .50), you would find that this item has an ID of .50, or a moderate level. The formula for calculating ID is:

$$ID = \frac{CH - CL}{1/2\ N}$$

where
CH refers to the number of correct responses to that particular item given by the examinees in the high group
CL refers to the number of correct responses to that particular item given by the examinees in the low group
½ N refers to the total number of responses divided by 2

High discriminating power would approach a perfect 1, which means that all the subjects in the high group answered an item correctly and all the subjects in the low group answered the item wrongly. That is the item has the highest discriminating power. In most case, you would want to dis-

card an item that scored near zero. As with ITEM FACILITY, no absolute rule governs the establishment of acceptable and unacceptable ID indices. Logically, the closer the value of ID to unity, the more discriminating the item.
📖 Brown 2010; Farhady et al. 1995

item easiness
another term for ITEM FACILITY

item facility
also **IF, item easiness, item difficulty**
the extent to which an item is easy or difficult for the proposed group of test takers. An item that is too easy (say, 99 percent of respondents get it right) or too difficult (99 percent get it wrong) really does nothing to separate high-ability and low-ability test-takers. It is not really performing much work for you on a test. IF simply reflects the percentage of the examinees answering a given item correctly. The formula for IF is:

$$IF = \frac{\Sigma C}{N}$$

where
ΣC = sum of the correct responses
N = total number of responses

For example, if you have an item on which 13 out of 20 test takers respond correctly, your IF index is 13 divided by 20 or .65 (65%). There is no absolute IF value that must be met to determine if an item should be included in the test as is, modified, or thrown out, but appropriate test items will generally have IFs that range between .37 and .63. That is, the items with facility indexes beyond .63 are too easy, and items with facility indexes below .37 are too difficult. Two good reasons for occasionally including a very easy item (.85 or higher) are to build in some affective feelings of success among lower-ability respondents and to serve as a warm-up items. And very difficult items can provide a challenge to the highest-ability respondents.

By determining item facility, you can easily find out *item difficulty*, which is the proportion of wrong responses.
see also ITEM DISCRIMINATION
📖 Brown 2010; Farhady et al. 1995

item format
a reference to the form, plan, structure, arrangement, or layout of individual test items, including whether the items require test takers to select a

response from existing alternative responses (SELECTED-RESPONSE ITEM) or to construct a response (CONSTRUCTED-RESPONSE ITEM).
see also ITEM ANALYSIS
 Cohen & Swerdlik 2010

item format analysis
see ITEM ANALYSIS

item information function
a feature of ITEM RESPONSE THEORY (IRT) models which refers to the amount of information a given item provides for estimating an individual's level of ability, and is a function of both the SLOPE of the ITEM CHARACTERISTIC CURVE (ICC) and the amount of variation at each ability level. In general, the steeper the slope of the ICC and the smaller the variation, the greater the information function. Thus, a given item will have differing information functions at different levels of ability. That is, a difficult item will provide very little information at low levels of ability, since virtually all individuals at these levels will get the item wrong. Similarly, an easy item that high ability individuals uniformly answer correctly will not provide much information at this ability level. Thus the information function of a given item will be at its maximum for individuals whose ability is at or near the value of the difficulty parameter.
 Bachman 1990, 2004

itemized rating scale
see RATING SCALE

item quality analysis
see ITEM ANALYSIS

item response theory
also **IRT, latent trait theory**
a modern measurement theory, as opposed to CLASSICAL TEST THEORY, which covers a range of models based on the probability of a test taker with a certain underlying ability getting a particular item right or wrong. Most of these models assume that a test is *unidimensional* (i.e., a single trait or ability underlies performance on a given item). Further, they assume that an OBSERVED SCORE is indicative of a person's ability on an underlying construct, which is often referred to as a *latent trait*. The trait is assumed to be a continuous, unobservable variable. These assumptions are explicitly stated in the ITEM CHARACTERISTIC CURVE, which is the cornerstone of item response theory (IRT) models. Using IRT, test designers can create a scale, usually scaled from around -4 to +4, upon which all items or tasks can be placed, and the value on the scale is the

ITEM DIFFICULTY. Test takers who take the items can be placed on to the same scale, and their scores are interpreted as person ability. As such, there is a direct connection between ability and difficulty. All models assume that when student ability = item difficulty, the probability of a test taker getting the item correct will be .5. On a scale, therefore, some items would have lower values (be easier), and the probability of more able students passing would be very high. As the difficulty value of the item rises, a test taker must be more able to have a chance of getting the item correct.

There are several different models commonly used in IRT which vary in terms of the number of parameters they include: a *one-parameter* IRT model, often referred to as the RASCH MODEL, includes only a difficulty parameter (the b-parameter); a *two-parameter* IRT model includes a difficulty parameter and a discrimination parameter (the a-parameter); while a *three-parameter* IRT model includes, in addition to parameter for difficulty and discrimination, a pseudo-chance, or guessing parameter (the c-parameter), which is an estimate of the probability that low-ability test takers will respond to the item correctly. IRT uses item scores, typically 0 or 1, of test takers to estimate these item parameters.

IRT models, in relation to classical test theory models, have the following advantages:

1) IRT models are falsifiable, i.e., the fit of an IRT model can be evaluated and a determination made as to whether a particular model is appropriate for a particular set of data.
2) Estimates of examinee ability are not test-dependent; they are made in a common metric that allows comparison of examinees that took different tests.
3) Estimates of item difficulty are not examinee-dependent; item difficulty is expressed in a common metric that allows comparison of items administered to different groups.
4) IRT provides individual estimates of STANDARD ERRORs for examinees, rather than assuming (as in classical test theory) that all examinees have the same STANDARD ERROR OF MEASUREMENT.
5) IRT takes item difficulty into account when estimating examinee ability, so two people with the same number of items correct on a test could have different estimates of ability if one answered more difficult questions correctly than did the other.

One consequence of points 2 and 3 is that in IRT, estimates of examinee ability and item difficulty are invariant. This means that, apart from MEASUREMENT ERROR, any two examinees with the same ability have the same probability of answering a given item correctly, and any two items of comparable difficulty have the same probability of being answered correctly by any examinee.

IRT models can also be applied in contexts where there is no right or wrong answer. For instance, in a QUESTIONNAIRE measuring attitudes, the meaning of item difficulty could be described as the probability of endorsing an item and theta (θ) as the degree or amount of the quality being measured.

see also ITEM CHARACTERISTIC CURVE, ITEM INFORMATION CURVE, ITEM INFORMATION CURVE

📖 Bachman 2004; Boslaugh & Watters 2008; Fulcher & Davidson 2007

item specifications

the clear item description for the purpose of test writing. Item descriptions include the following elements:

1) *General description*: A brief general description of the knowledge or skills being measured by the item.
2) *Sample item*: An example item that demonstrates the desirable item characteristics (further delimited by the stimulus and response attributes below).
3) *Stimulus attributes*: A clear description of the stimulus material, that is, the material that will be encountered by the respondents, or the material to which they will be expected to react through the response attributes below.
4) *Response attributes*: A clear description of the types of (a) options from which respondents will be expected to select their receptive language choices (responses), or (b) standards by which their productive language responses will be judged.
5) *Specification supplement*: for some items, supplemental material will be necessary for clarifying the four previous elements; for example, the specification supplement might include a list of vocabulary items from which the item writer should draw, or a list of grammatical forms, or list of functions of the language.

see also ITEM ANALYSIS
📖 Brown 2005

iteration

a process of moving back and forth between data collection and analysis. Researchers are in agreement that the participant selection process should remain open in a QUALITATIVE RESEARCH as long as possible so that after initial accounts are gathered and analyzed, additional participants can be added who can fill gaps in the initial description or can expand or even challenge it. Although iteration is a key process in qualita-

tive SAMPLING, it cannot go on for ever. Scholars agree that ideally the iterative process should go on until the researchers reach SATURATION.
📖 Dörnyei 2007

ITS design
another term for TIME-SERIES DESIGN

J

jackknife
a *nonparametric* technique for estimating STANDARD ERROR of a STATISTIC. The procedure consists of taking repeated subsamples of the original SAMPLE of n independent observations by omitting a single observation at a time. Thus, each subsample consists of $n - 1$ observations formed by deleting a different observation from the sample. The jackknife estimate and its standard error are then calculated from these truncated subsamples.
see also BOOTSTRAP
📖 Upton & Cook 2008

jigsaw task
a two-way task in which individuals have different pieces of information. In order to solve the task, they must orally interact to put the pieces together. One example of a jigsaw task is a map task in which participants are given a map of a section of a city. Each participant is provided with different information about street closings, and they must explain to each other about which streets are closed and when. Once this portion is completed, they have to work together to determine a route from Point A to Point B by car, keeping in mind that certain streets are closed.
Alternatively, each person can be given a map with pre-blocked-off streets. In this instance, participants would receive a separate blank map in order to draw the route, with instructions not to show the original map to each other. Another example of a jigsaw task is a story completion, or a story sequencing task, in which different individuals are given parts of a story (written or pictorial) with instructions to make a complete story. Important point about jigsaw tasks is that, because they involve an information exchange, they require participants to interact while completing the task.
see also CONSENSUS TASK
📖 Mackey & Gass 2005

John Henry effect
also **control group rivalry, compensatory rivalry**
a threat to EXTERNAL VALIDITY which occurs when the difference between the CONTROL GROUP and the TREATMENT GROUP is due to competition rather than the TREATMENT. John Henry effect can arise when control group members are aware of the treatment given to the experimental group and respond with increased competition in an effort to do just as well as the experimental group in spite of not receiving the experimental treatment (just as the mythical John Henry increased his efforts in a

competition against technological innovation). Researchers can attempt to avoid this threat by trying to curtail both awareness of and expectations about the presumed benefits of the experimental treatment.

see also MULTIPLE-TREATMENT INTERACTION, SPECIFICITY OF VARIABLES, TREATMENT DIFFUSION, RESEARCHER EFFECT, HALO EFFECT, HAWTHORNE EFFECT, NOVELTY EFFECT, ORDER EFFECT, DEMORALIZATION, SELECTION-TREATMENT INTERACTION, PRETEST-TREATMENT INTERACTION

📖 Perry 2011

journal
one of the most effective research tools to mine the rich personal experiences and emotions of participants' inner lives. When sensitive topics are studied, journals often allow participants to feel comfortable with their degrees of self-disclosure. Likewise, introverts or those who have been marginalized may feel particularly comfortable when voicing their ideas in private writing. Journal use is also particularly valuable when little attention has been devoted to a topic and the study seeks to elicit fresh data from first-person experiences. When analyzing journal entries, a system of thematic or CONTENT ANALYSIS is usually applied. This form of coding allows for categories and themes to emerge from the journal entries. Qualitative researchers read the journals looking for causal connections, patterns, recurring issues, and reactions; sub- or by-themes may also be noted and categorized. Although journal entries are often completely unstructured, researchers may also ask guided questions to encourage participants to write more specifically about a discrete experience or event.

📖 Given 2008

judgmental sampling
another term for PURPOSIVE SAMPLING

K

k
the number of LEVELs or groups in an EXPERIMENTAL DESIGN or individual study. Also an abbreviation for COEFFICIENT OF ALIENATION.

k^2
an abbreviation for COEFFICIENT OF NONDETERMINATION

kappa (κ)
an abbreviation for COHEN'S KAPPA

Kendall's coefficient of concordance
also **Kendall's *W*, *W***
a statistic which is a measure of how much a set of raters or judges agree when asked to put a set of objects in rank order. Kendall's coefficient of concordance is appropriately used to determine the tendency of agreement among three or more sets of ordinal data. If, for example, a study were to be made of the way four teachers agree in ranking students' ability to speak Farsi, Kendall's *W* could be used. This coefficient cannot have negative values. It ranges between 0 which would be no agreement between the judges to +1 which would denote perfect agreement between them. It also allows for a judge to give two objects the same rank.
 Brown 1988, 1992

Kendall's *W*
another term for KENDALL'S COEFFICIENT OF CONCORDANCE

Kendall's partial rank correlation coefficient
a measure of partial *association* for ordinal variables in which one or more other ordinal variables may be partialled out or controlled. Its calculation is similar to that of PARTIAL CORRELATION except that KENDALL'S RANK CORRELATION TAU *b* is used instead of PEARSON CORRELATION COEFFICIENT in the formula.
 Cramer & Howitt 2004

Kendall's rank correlation tau *a*
see KENDALL'S RANK-ORDER CORRELATION COEFFICIENT

Kendall's rank correlation tau *b*
see KENDALL'S RANK-ORDER CORRELATION COEFFICIENT

Kendall's rank correlation tau *c*
see KENDALL'S RANK-ORDER CORRELATION COEFFICIENT

Kendall's rank-order correlation coefficient
also **Kendall's tau (τ), tau(τ)**

a test of RANK CORRELATION which is used between two ORDINAL VARIABLES (i.e., ranked data). The Kendall tau (τ), unlike SPEARMAN RHO (ρ), is more suitable when there are many ties in the rankings. A negative value means that lower ranks on one variable are associated with higher ranks on the other variable. A positive value means that higher ranks on one variable go together with higher ranks on the other variable. A zero or close to zero value means that there is no linear association between the two variables. There are three forms of this measure called **Kendall's rank correlation tau *a*, Kendall's rank correlation tau *b*** and **Kendall's rank correlation tau *c***. *Kendall's Tau a* should be used when there are no ties or tied ranks. It can vary from -1 to 1. It can be calculated with the following formula:

$$Tau\ a = \frac{\text{number of concordant pairs} - \text{number of discordant pairs}}{\text{total number of pairs}}$$

A concordant pair is one in which the first case is ranked higher than the second case, while a discordant pair is the reverse in which the first case is ranked lower than the second case.
Kendall's Tau b should be used when there are ties or tied ranks. It can vary from -1 to 1 if the table of ranks is square and if none of the row and column totals are zero. It can be calculated with the following formula: where T_1 and T_2 are the numbers of tied ranks for the two variables.

$$Tau\ b = \frac{\text{number of concordant pairs} - \text{number of discordant pairs}}{\sqrt{\text{total number of pairs} - T_1 \times (\text{total number of pairs} - T_2)}}$$

Kendall's Tau c (also called **Kendall-Stuart Tau-c**) should be used when the table of ranks is rectangular rather than square as the value of tau *c* can come closer to -1 or 1. It can be worked out with the following formula: where S is the number of columns or rows whichever is the smaller.

$$Tau\ c = \frac{(\text{number of concordant pairs} - \text{number of discordant pairs}) \times 2 \times S}{\text{number of cases}^2 \times (S - 1)}$$

📖 Cramer & Howitt 2004; Larson-Hall 2010

Kendall's tau
another term for KENDALL'S RANK-ORDER CORRELATION COEFFICIENT

Kendall-Stuart Tau-*c*
another term for KENDALL'S RANK CORRELATION TAU *c*

Klotz test
a NONPARAMETRIC TEST for testing the EQUALITY OF VARIANCE of two POPULATIONs having the same MEDIAN. More efficient than the ANSARI-BRADLEY TEST.
📖 Everitt & Skrondal 2010

Kolmogorov-Smirnov goodness-of-fit test
another term for KOLMOGOROV-SMIRNOV TEST FOR ONE SAMPLE

Kolmogorov-Smirnov test for one sample
also **Kolmogorov-Smirnov goodness-of-fit test, one-sample Kolmogorov-Smirnov test**
a NONPARAMETRIC TEST which uses ranked data for determining whether the distribution of scores on an ORDINAL VARIABLE differs significantly from some theoretical distribution for that variable. For example, we could compare the distribution of the outcome of throwing a die 60 times with the theoretical expectation that it will land with 1 up 10 times, with 2 up 10 times, and so forth, if it is an unbiased die. The largest absolute difference between the CUMULATIVE FREQUENCY of the observed and the expected frequency of a value is used to determine whether the observed and expected distributions differ significantly.
📖 Cramer & Howitt 2004; Larson-Hall 2010

Kolmogorov-Smirnov test for two independent samples
also **Kolmogorov-Smirnov two-sample test, two-sample Kolmogorov-Smirnov test**
a NONPARAMETRIC TEST which determines whether the distributions of scores on an ORDINAL (ranked) VARIABLE differ significantly for two UNRELATED SAMPLES. As is the case with the Kolmogorov-Smirnov goodness-of-fit test, computation of the test statistic for the Kolmogorov-Smirnov test for two INDEPENDENT SAMPLES involves the comparison of two CUMULATIVE FREQUENCY distributions. Whereas the Kolmogorov-Smirnov goodness-of-fit test compares the cumulative frequency distribution of a single sample with a hypothesized theoretical or empirical cumulative frequency distribution, the Kolmogorov-Smirnov test for two independent samples compares the cumulative frequency distributions of two independent samples. If, in fact, the two samples are derived from the same population, the two cumulative frequency distributions would be expected to be identical or reasonably close to one another. The test protocol for the Kolmogorov-Smirnov test for two independent samples is based on the principle that if there is a significant

difference at any point along the two cumulative frequency distributions, the researcher can conclude there is a high likelihood the samples are derived from different populations.
📖 Sheskin 2011

Kolmogorov-Smirnov two-sample test
another term for KOLMOGOROV-SMIRNOV TEST FOR TWO INDEPENDENT SAMPLES

KR20
an abbreviation for KUDER-RICHARDSON FORMULA 20

KR21
an abbreviation for KUDER-RICHARDSON FORMULA 21

Kruskal-Wallis test
also **Kruskal-Wallis *H* test, *H* test**
a NONPARAMETRIC TEST alternative to ONE-WAY ANOVA which is employed with ordinal (rank-order) data in a HYPOTHESIS TESTING situation involving a design with three or more INDEPENDENT GROUPS of participants. Kruskal-Wallis test is used to determine whether the mean ranked scores for three or more unrelated or INDEPENDENT SAMPLES differ significantly and is calculated based on the sums of the ranks of the combined groups. Hence, the Kruskal-Wallis procedure can be thought of as an extension of the MANN-WHITNEY U TEST in the same way that a one-way ANOVA is typically considered to be an extension of an INDEPENDENT SAMPLES t-TEST—the Kruskal-Wallis and Mann-Whitney tests are mathematically equivalent when used to compare two groups.
Kruskal-Wallis test produces a value (denoted by H), whose probability of occurrence is checked by the researcher in the appropriate statistical table. This procedure does not assume population NORMALITY nor HOMOGENEITY OF VARIANCE, as does parametric ANOVA, and requires only ordinal scaling of the DEPENDENT VARIABLE. It is used when violations of population normality and/or homogeneity of variance are extreme or when interval or ratio scaling are required and not met by the data. In addition, there must be at least five scores in each sample to use the probabilities given in the table of chi-square.
The logic involves first testing the null hypothesis of no difference among the various means. If the null hypothesis is rejected, then multiple comparisons can be made between various pairs of means. For example, Kruskal-Wallis test enable you to see, whether there are differences between three or more groups (e.g., classes, schools, groups of teachers) on a RATING SCALE. The scores for all the samples are ranked together. If there is little difference between the sets of scores, their mean ranks

should be similar. The statistic for this test is CHI-SQUARE TEST which can be corrected for the number of ties or TIED SCORES.
see also NONPARAMETRIC TESTS, FRIEDMAN'S TEST
📖 Brown 1988; Cohen et al. 2011; Cramer & Howitt 2004; Ho 2006; Huck 2012; Pagano 2009; Perry 2011

Kuder-Richardson formulas
also *KR* formulas
measures which are used to estimate the INTERNAL CONSISTENCY RELIABILITY of a test with items that are dichotomously scored (such as yes/no, correct/incorrect or true/false items). There are two types of the Kuder-Richardson formulas: **Kuder-Richardson formula 20** (*KR20*) and **Kuder-Richardson formula 21** (*KR21*). *KR20* is based on information about (a) the number of items on the test, (b) the difficulty of the individual items, and (c) the VARIANCE of the total test scores. The formula for *KR20* is:

$$KR20 = \frac{k}{k-1}\left\{\frac{s^2 - \Sigma pq}{s^2}\right\}$$

where
k = number of items on the test
s^2 = the estimate of the variance of test scores, and
Σpq = the sum of the variances of all items.

A formula that is easier to use (not requiring calculation of ITEM FACILITY) but less accurate than *KR20* is *KR21*, which is based on information about (a) the number of items on the test, (b) the MEAN of the test, and (c) the variance of the total test scores, all of which are readily available, but requires an assumption that all items are equal in item difficulty. The formula for *KR21* is:

$$KR21 = \frac{k}{k-1}\left\{\frac{\bar{X}(k-)\bar{X}}{ks^2}\right\}$$

where
k = number of items on the test
$\bar{X}$ = mean of the test scores, an
s^2 = the estimate of the variance of test scores.

This method is by far the least time-consuming of all the reliability estimation procedures. It involves only one administration of a test and employs only easily available information. Because the Kuder-Richardson procedures stress the equivalence of all the items in a test, they are especially appropriate when the intention of the test is to measure a single

trait. For a test with homogeneous content, the reliability estimate will be similar to that provided by the SPLIT-HALF RELIABILITY. For a test designed to measure several traits, the Kuder-Richardson reliability estimate is usually lower than reliability estimates based on a correlational procedure.
see also CRONBACH'S ALPHA, PARALLEL-FORM RELIABILITY, AVERAGE INTER-ITEM CORRELATION, AVERAGE ITEM-TOTAL CORRELATION
📖 Fulcher & Davidson 2007; Richards & Schmidt 2010

Kuder-Richardson formula 20
see KUDER-RICHARDSON FORMULAS

Kuder-Richardson formula 21
see KUDER-RICHARDSON FORMULAS

kurtosis
the degree of peakedness in a DISTRIBUTION. Kurtosis describes how thin or broad the distribution is. Kurtosis provides information regarding the height of a distribution relative to the value of its STANDARD DEVIATION. The most common reason for measuring kurtosis is to determine whether data are derived from a normally distributed population. Kurtosis is often described within the framework of the following three general categories, all of which are depicted by representative frequency distributions in Figure K.1—**mesokurtic distribution, leptokurtic distribution,** and **platykurtic distribution**. Each of the distributions in Figure K.1 is symmetrical, since the distribution of scores above (to the right of) the central score is a mirror image of the distribution below (to the left of) the central score. These three distributions differ, however, in their degree of peakedness, or what statisticians refer to as kurtosis. As shown in Figure K.1b, if the distribution is pointy (i.e., relatively tall and thin) with a small range of values (there is too much data in the center of it), it is called leptokurtic. The scores in a leptokurtic distribution tend to be clustered much more closely around the MEAN than they are in either a mesokurtic or platykurtic distribution. Because of the latter, the value of the standard deviation for a leptokurtic distribution will be smaller than the standard deviation for the latter two distributions (if we assume the range of scores in all three distributions is approximately the same). The tails of a leptokurtic distribution are heavier/thicker than the tails of a mesokurtic distribution.

If the distribution is flat with a wide range of values (it is too flat at the peak of the normal curve), Figure K.1c, it is called platykurtic. The scores in a platykurtic distribution tend to be spread out more from the mean than they are in either a mesokurtic or leptokurtic distribution. Because of the latter, the value of the standard deviation for a platykurtic distribution will be larger than the standard deviation for the latter two distributions (if we assume the range of scores in all three distributions is approximately the same). The tails of a platykurtic distribution are lighter/thinner than the tails of a mesokurtic distribution.

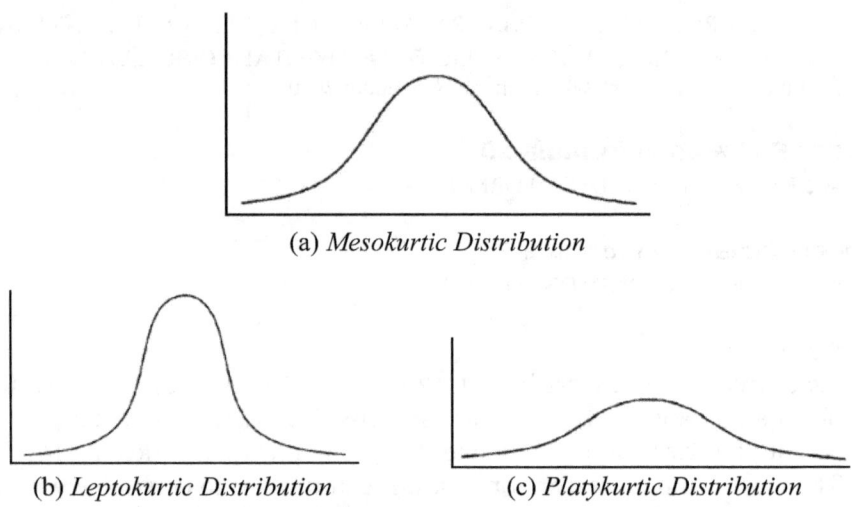

(a) *Mesokurtic Distribution*

(b) *Leptokurtic Distribution*   (c) *Platykurtic Distribution*

Figure K.1. *Representative Types of Kurtosis*

The distribution represented in Figure K.1a is somewhere in the middle (known as mesokurtic, i.e., like the NORMAL DISTRIBUTION, it is neither markedly tall and thin nor flat and wide), as is typical of the score distributions obtained with many NORM-REFERENCED TESTs.

📖 Clark-Carter 2010; Cramer & Howitt 2004; Larson-Hall 2010; Sheskin 2011

L

lag value
see AUTOCORRELATION

lambda (λ)
an abbreviation for GOODMAN-KRUSKAL'S LAMBDA. Also an abbreviation for WILKS' LAMBDA

language aptitude test
a test which is designed to measures capacity or general ability of a person to learn a foreign language and ultimate success in that undertaking. Two well-known standardized language aptitude tests are: the Modern Language Aptitude Test (MLAT) and the Pimsleur Language Aptitude Battery (PLAB). Both are English language tests and require students to perform a number of language-related tasks. The MLAT, for example, consists of five different tasks:

1) *Number learning*: Examinees must learn a set of numbers through aural input and then discriminate different combinations of those numbers.
2) *Phonetic script*: Examinees must learn a set of correspondences between speech sound and phonetic symbols.
3) *Spelling clues*: Examinees must read words that are spelled somewhat phonetically, and then select from a list the one word whose meaning is closest to the disguised word.
4) *Words in sentences*: Examinees are given a key word in a sentence and are then asked to select a word in a second sentence that performs the same grammatical function as the key word.
5) *Paired associates*: Examinees must quickly learn a set of vocabulary words from another language and memorize their English meanings.

Standardized aptitude tests are seldom used today. Instead, attempts to measure language aptitude more often provide learners with information about their styles and their potential strength and weaknesses, with follow-up strategies for capitalizing on the strength and overcoming the weaknesses. A test that claims to predict success in learning a language is undoubtedly flawed because we now know that with appropriate self-knowledge, active strategic involvement in learning, and/or strategies-based instruction, virtually everyone can succeed eventually. To pigeonhole learners a priori, before they have even attempted to learn a language, is to presuppose failure or success without substantial cause.
📖 Brown 2010

latent root
another term for eigenvalue

latent trait theory
another term for ITEM RESPONSE THEORY

latent variable
see MANIFEST VARIABLE

Latin square design
a term which is derived from an ancient word puzzle game that focused on placing Latin letters in a matrix such that each letter appeared only once in each row and column. In practice, Latin squares have two fundamental uses. The first use is to employ a Latin square as a research method or experimental design technique to ensure that a NUISANCE VARIABLE (i.e., an uncontrolled or incidental factor) such as time of day or type of experimenter is not confounded with the treatment(s) under study. The second use controls for the possible confounding influence of these nuisance variable(s) by incorporating this information into the statistical analysis through an adjustment of the subsequent ERROR TERM.

In a WITHIN-SUBJECTS DESIGN one method of controlling for the potential influence of practice or fatigue (both of which represent examples of ORDER EFFECTs) is by employing a Latin square design. This type of design which provides incomplete counterbalancing (see COUNTERBALANCED DESIGN) attempts to circumvent some of the complexities and keep the experiment to a reasonable size. It is more likely to be considered as a reasonable option for controlling for order effects when the INDEPENDENT VARIABLE is comprised of many LEVELs and consequently it becomes prohibitive to employ complete counterbalancing. If we conceptualize a within-subjects design as being comprised of n rows (corresponding to each of the n subjects) and n columns (corresponding to each of the n treatments/conditions), we can define a Latin square design as one in which each condition appears only one time in each row and only one time in each column. For example, in Figure L.1, there are $n = 4$ subjects and $n = 4$ treatments. Thus, the configuration of the design is a 4 × 4 Latin square. The four treatments are identified by the letters A, B, C, and D. Subject 1 receives the treatments in the order A, B, C, D, Subject 2 receives the treatments in the order C, A, D, B, and so on. As noted above, this design does not employ complete counterbalancing since, with 4 conditions, there are 24 possible presentation orders for the conditions. Thus, a minimum of 24 subjects will be required in order to have complete counterbalancing.

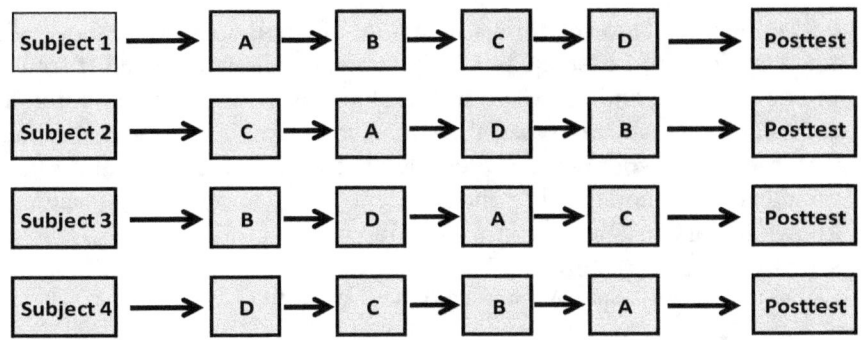

Figure L.1. Schematic Representation of a 4 × 4 Latin Square Design

The purpose of the Latin square arrangement is to equally distribute any order effects that are present over the *n* treatments. A Latin square design, however, will only provide effective control for order effects if there is no INTERACTION between order of presentation and the treatments. However, within this context, an interaction between order of presentation and treatment will be present if the performance of subjects on a given treatment is not only a function of the treatment itself, but also depends on which treatments precede it. In point of fact, the absence of an interaction between order of presentation and treatments is critical in any within-subjects design, since if an interaction is present it will not be possible to obtain a pure measure for any treatment effects that may be present.
📖 Sheskin 2011

LDFs
an abbreviation for LINEAR DISCRIMINANT FUNCTIONS

least significant difference test
another term for FISHER'S LEAST SIGNIFICANT DIFFERENCE

least squares estimation
another term for LEAST SQUARES METHOD OF ANALYSIS

least squares means
another term for ADJUSTED MEANS

least squares method of analysis
also **method of least squares analysis, least squares estimation**
the most commonly employed method of REGRESSION ANALYSIS which is a linear regression procedure that derives the straight line which provides the LINE OF BEST FIT for a set of data. Least squares is a common way to measure errors in statistical analysis. The least squares formula is

best known for favoring things with a lot of small errors over those with a few large errors. Least squares keeps track of all errors, even if some are in one direction and some are in the other direction. It is also referred to as **ordinary least squares** (OLS) to distinguish it from the method of **weighted least squares**, a preferable alternative when estimating the parameters of a model using independent observations whose values are known to vary in accuracy in a specified way.
see also ADJUSTED MEANS
📖 Larson-Hall 2010; Sahai & Khurshid 2001; Sheskin 2011

leniency error
another term for GENEROSITY ERROR

Leptokurtic
see KURTOSIS

level
also condition
a term which is used to describe the conditions or categories of a FACTOR in a given study. Put simply, a level is a subdivision of an INDEPENDENT VARIABLE. A CATEGORICAL VARIABLE, by definition, can include a number of categories. These categories are called levels. For instance, for a variable like gender, there are two levels, female and male. For a variable like foreign language proficiency, there might be three levels— elementary, intermediate, and advanced. Or, if the study concerned geographic area, a student might be subclassified as South American, European, Middle Eastern, or Asian so that comparisons among these levels of second language student could be made. The variable would consist of four levels. This definition of levels will prove important in thinking about statistical studies because of the concept of independence. If the levels of a variable are made up of two or more different groups of people, they are viewed as independent. For instance, in a study comparing the means of an EXPERIMENTAL GROUP and a CONTROL GROUP, the groups can be independent only if they were created using different groups of people. Many statistics can only be applied if the groups being compared are independent (e.g., ONE-WAY ANOVA, FACTORIAL ANOVA, INDEPENDENT-SAMPLES t-TEST).

However, there are studies in which it might be necessary or desirable to make repeated observations on the same group of people. For instance, a researcher might want to compare the means of a single group of students before and after some type of language instruction in what is called a pretest-posttest study. Such investigations are called repeated measures studies (see WITHIN-SUBJECTS DESIGN), and the groups can be said to lack independence because they are the same people. When independ-

ence cannot be assumed, different choices of statistics must be made (e.g., REPEATED MEASURES ANOVA, PAIRED-SAMPLES *t*-TEST). Thus it is important to understand the difference between independent levels of a variable (which were created by using different groups of people) and repeated levels of a variable (which were created through repeated measures or observations of the same people).
📖 Brown 1988, 1992; Hatch & Farhady 1982; Hatch & Lazaraton 1991; Porte 2010

level of measurement
another term for MEASUREMENT SCALE

level of significance
another term for SIGNIFICANCE LEVEL

Levene's median test
another term for LEVENE'S TEST

Levene's test
also **Levene's median test**
a test procedure which is used to assess the EQUALITY OF VARIANCEs in different SAMPLEs. Some common statistical procedures (e.g., ANALYSIS OF VARIANCE and *t*-TEST) assume that variances of the POPULATIONs from which different samples are drawn are equal. Levene's test assesses this assumption. For example, Levene's test is employed to test whether the variance (variation) of scores for the two or more groups (e.g., males and females) is the same. It tests the NULL HYPOTHESIS that the POPULATION VARIANCEs are equal. If the resulting P-VALUE of Levene's test is less than some CRITICAL VALUE (typically .05), the obtained differences in SAMPLE VARIANCEs are unlikely to have occurred based on RANDOM SAMPLING. Thus, the null hypothesis of equal variances is rejected and it is concluded that there is a difference between the variances in the population (i.e., variances are heterogeneous).

One advantage of Levene's test is that it does not require NORMALITY of the underlying data. Levene's test is often used before a comparison of means. When Levene's test is significant, modified procedures are used that do not assume equality of variance. However, it suffers from too much sensitivity when data sets are large and not enough sensitivity (power) when data sets are small.

see also BOX'S M TEST, COCHRAN'S C TEST, BARTLETT'S TEST, HARTLEY'S TEST, BROWN-FORSYTHE TEST, O'BRIEN TEST
📖 Larson-Hall 2010; Pallant 2010; Tabachnick & Fidell 2007

leverage
    also **hat element**
    a measure of whether an individual person's data contain OUTLIERs. It assesses whether a person's set of scores across the INDEPENDENT VARIABLEs (IVs) is a multivariate outlier. Thus, a person might not be an outlier on any single IV but the pattern of his/her scores across the IVs may be an outlier.
    see also COOK'S DISTANCE, MAHALANOBIS DISTANCE D^2
    📖 Clark-Carter 2010

liberal test
    a STATISTICAL TEST with the LEVEL OF SIGNIFICANCE greater than or equal to the nominal value. If it is known that the actual level of significance of a liberal test is not much greater than alpha (α) (the nominal value), the liberal test can be recommended. Liberal procedures provide less control over TYPE I ERROR, but this disadvantage is offset by increased POWER (i.e., more control over TYPE II ERROR).
    see also CONSERVATIVE TEST
    📖 Huck 2012; Sahai & Khurshid 2001

library research
    another term for SECONDARY RESEARCH

life history research
    a genre of NARRATIVE INQUIRY that distinguishes itself from other genres by the extent to which it takes into account the social, historical, and cultural contexts within which the story is situated. While life history research may focus on a particular period or aspect of a person's life, these are usually considered within the context of the person's whole life. A distinction should perhaps be drawn between a biography (see BIOGRAPHICAL STUDY), where the focus is on the individual life as an unfolding story, and life history, where the context plays an important part. In fact, the two approaches are very close and could be included under the broader umbrella of CASE STUDY.
Life history research can help us to understand learners' beliefs and assumptions about learning. As language educators working with learners from other cultures, we all know how important it is to be aware of cultural differences and their expression in the learning environment. One way of gaining a better understanding of learners from other cultures is to explore their stories for underlying assumptions. This, thus, makes narrative research, and more specifically life history research, a valuable approach for language educators. In addition to providing insight into learners' assumptions and beliefs about how they learn, life history research also enables researchers to access the identity of the participants.

Insights into learners' identities can be instrumental in understanding a number of language learning issues, including motivation, affect, learning styles, and choice of learning strategies. In a classroom setting, language learning histories can provide valuable information about who the learners are and how they learn. Whether in the classroom or the larger community one of the benefits of life history research is that it allows individual voices to be heard, especially those of the disenfranchised—people who have historically been marginalized in the research process, such as disabled people, gays and lesbians, and racial and ethnic minorities. These voices from the margins have the potential to change theory by prompting us to take a critical look at the existing canon or standard.

A possible example might be a life history of the teacher in our encounter, using this as a way of deepening our understanding of the encounter between teacher and new students that we are taking as our theme. Over a period of time and through a number of in-depth interviews, supported perhaps by lesson observation (to prompt questions and deepen the researcher's understanding) and documentary evidence (photographs, reports, influential texts, etc.), the researcher would develop an account of the individual, their beliefs and experiences. This can then be used, as with any good case study, to deepen our understanding of teachers and the world that they inhabit.

At the heart of any life history research is the prolonged INTERVIEW, which usually consists of a series of interviews. The length of such interviews can vary from between a couple of hours to totals well into double figures.

 Heigham & Croker 2009; Richards 2003

likelihood ratio chi-square

a version of CHI-SQUARE TEST which utilizes natural logarithms. It is different in some respects from the more familiar form which should be known as chi-square. It is useful where the components of an analysis are to be separated out since this form of chi-square allows accurate addition and subtraction of components. Because of its reliance on natural logarithms, likelihood ratio chi-square is a little more difficult to compute. Apart from its role in LOG-LINEAR ANALYSIS, there is nothing to be gained by using likelihood ratio chi-square in general. With calculations based on large frequencies, numerically the two differ very little anyway.

 Cramer & Howitt 2004

Likert scale
also **summated scale**

a type of RATING SCALE which includes a number of statements which express either a favorable or unfavorable attitude towards the given object to which the respondent is asked to react. The respondent indicates his/her agreement or disagreement with each statement in the instrument. Each response is given a numerical score, indicating its favorableness or unfavorableness, and the scores are totaled to measure the respondent's attitude. In other words, the overall score represents the respondent's position on the continuum of favorable-unfavorableness towards an issue. Likert scales are called summated because they are method of combining several VARIABLEs that measure the same concept into a single variable in an attempt to increase the RELIABILITY of the measurement. In most instances, the separate variables are summed and then their total or average score is used in the analysis.

In a Likert scale, the respondent is asked to respond to each of the statements in terms of several degrees, usually five degrees (but at times 3 or 7 may also be used) of agreement or disagreement. For example: For example, when asked to express opinion whether one 'reads English without looking up every new word', the respondent may respond in any one of the following ways: (1) strongly agree, (2) agree, (3) undecided, (4) disagree, (5) strongly disagree.

Such a scale could be set out like the following thus:

Instructions: Following are a number of statements with which some people agree and others disagree. We would like you to indicate your opinion after each statement by putting an 'X' in the bracket that best indicates the extent to which you agree or disagree with the statement. Thank you very much for your help.

I. I write down my feelings in a language learning diary.
1 = strongly agree   [ ]
2 = agree   [ ]
3 = undecided   [ ]
4 = disagree   [ ]
5 = strongly disagree   [ ]

II. I use English words in a sentence so that I can remember them.
1 = strongly agree   [ ]
2 = agree   [ ]
3 = undecided   [ ]
4 = disagree   [ ]
5 = strongly disagree   [ ]

We find that these five points constitute the scale. At one extreme of the scale there is strong disagreement with the given statement and at the other, strong agreement, and between them lie intermediate points. Each point on the scale carries a score. Response indicating the least favorable is given the least score (say 1) and the most favorable is given the highest score (say 5). The Likert scaling technique, thus, assigns a scale value to each of the five responses. The same thing is done in respect of each and every statement in the instrument. This way the instrument yields a total score for each respondent, which would then measure the respondent's favorableness toward the given point of view. If the instrument consists of, say 30 statements, the following score values would be revealing.

30 × 5 = 150 Most favorable response possible
30 × 3 = 90 A neutral attitude
30 × 1 = 30 Most unfavorable attitude

The scores for any individual would fall between 30 and 150. If the score happens to be above 90, it shows favorable opinion to the given point of view, a score of below 90 would mean unfavorable opinion and a score of exactly 90 would be suggestive of a neutral attitude. These two examples both indicate an important feature of an attitude scaling instrument, namely the assumption of unidimensionality in the scale, i.e., the scale should be measuring only one thing at a time.

The statements on Likert scales should be characteristic, that is, expressing either a positive/favorable or a negative/unfavorable attitude toward the object of interest. Neutral items (e.g., 'I think Iranian are all right') do not work well on a Likert scale because they do not evoke salient evaluative reactions; extreme items (e.g., 'Iranians are absolutely brilliant!') are also to be avoided.

The procedure for developing a Likert-type scale is as follows:

1) As a first step, the researcher collects a large number of statements which are relevant to the attitude being studied and each of the statements expresses definite favorableness or unfavorableness to a particular point of view or the attitude and that the number of favorable and unfavorable statements is approximately equal.
2) After the statements have been gathered, a trial test should be administered to a number of subjects. In other words, a small group of people, from those who are going to be studied finally, are asked to indicate their response to each statement by checking one of the categories of agreement or disagreement using a five point scale as stated above.
3) The response to various statements are scored in such a way that a response indicative of the most favorable attitude is given the highest score of 5 and that with the most unfavorable attitude is given the lowest score, say, of 1.
4) Then the total score of each respondent is obtained by adding his/her scores that s/he received for separate statements.
5) The next step is to array these total scores and find out those statements which have a high discriminatory power. For this purpose, the researcher may select some part of the highest and the lowest total

scores, say, the top 25 per cent and the bottom 25 per cent. These two extreme groups are interpreted to represent the most favorable and the least favorable attitudes and are used as criterion groups by which to evaluate individual statements. This way we determine which statements consistently correlate with low favorability and which with high favorability.
6) Only those statements that correlate with the total test should be retained in the final instrument and all others must be discarded from it.

The Likert-type scale has several advantages. Mention may be made of the important ones:

1) It is relatively easy to construct the Likert-type scale in comparison to THURSTONE SCALE because Likert-type scale can be performed without a panel of judges.
2) Likert-type scale is considered more reliable because under it respondents answer each statement included in the instrument. As such it also provides more information and data than does the Thurstone scale.
3) Each statement, included in the Likert-type scale, is given an empirical test for discriminating ability and as such, unlike Thurstone scale, the Likert-type scale permits the use of statements that are not manifestly related (to have a direct relationship) to the attitude being studied.
4) Likert-type scale can easily be used in respondent-centered and stimulus-centered studies i.e., through it we can study how responses differ between people and how responses differ between stimuli.
5) Likert-type scale takes much less time to construct; moreover, it has been reported in various research studies that there is high degree of CORRELATION between Likert-type scale and Thurstone scale.

However, there are several limitations of the Likert-type scale as well. One important limitation is that, with this scale, we can simply examine whether respondents are more or less favorable to a topic, but we cannot tell how much more or less they are. There is no basis for belief that the five positions indicated on the scale are equally spaced. The interval between strongly agree and agree, may not be equal to the interval between agree and undecided. This means that Likert scale does not rise to a stature more than that of an ORDINAL SCALE, whereas the designers of Thurstone scale claim it to be an INTERVAL SCALE. One further disadvantage is that often the total score of an individual respondent has little clear meaning since a given total score can be secured by a variety of answer patterns. It is unlikely that the respondent can validly react to a short statement on a printed form in the absence of real-life qualifying situations. Moreover, there remains a possibility that people may answer according to what they think they should feel rather than how they do feel. This particular weakness of the Likert-type scale is met by using a CUMULATIVE SCALE.

In spite of all the limitations, the Likert-type summated scales are regarded as the most useful in a situation wherein it is possible to compare the respondent's score with a distribution of scores from some well defined group. They are equally useful when we are concerned with a program of change or improvement in which case we can use the scales to measure attitudes before and after the program of change or improvement in order to assess whether our efforts have had the desired effects. We can as well correlate scores on the scale to other measures without any concern for the absolute value of what is favorable and what is unfavorable. All this accounts for the popularity of Likert-type scales in applied linguistics relating to measuring of attitudes.

see also SEMANTIC DIFFERENTIAL SCALE, DIFFERENTIAL SCALE, CUMULATIVE SCALE, ARBITRARY SCALE, MATRIX QUESTIONS

 Cohen et al. 2011; Dörnyei 2003; Dörnyei & Taguchi 2010; Kothari 2008

linear discriminant functions
see DISCRIMINANT ANALYSIS

linearity
an ASSUMPTION that often applies in the correlational and prediction family of statistics. Linearity means that there is a straight-line relationship between the two VARIABLEs involved. This assumption can be checked by examining a SCATTERPLOT of the two variables. When two variables are perfectly linearly related, the points of a scatterplot fall on a straight line (called a REGRESSION LINE). The more the points tend to fall along a straight line, the stronger the linear relationship. However, linearity cannot always be assumed (see CURVILINEARITY).

see also CORRELATION

 Brown 1992; Clark-Carter 2010; Cohen et al. 2011; Larson-Hall 2010; Porte 2010

line graph
a graph which allows you to inspect the mean scores of a CONTINUOUS VARIABLE across a number of different values of a CATEGORICAL VARIABLE (e.g., time 1, time 2, time 3), depicted on the two axes. The horizontal axis (X) indicates values that are on a continuum. The vertical axis (Y) can be used for various types of data. A line connects the data points or values (i.e., dots on the graph) on the graphs. Line graphs are also useful for graphically exploring the results of a ONE- or TWO-WAY ANOVA.

Figure L.2 shows mean test scores of second-grade students in one school over the last four years.

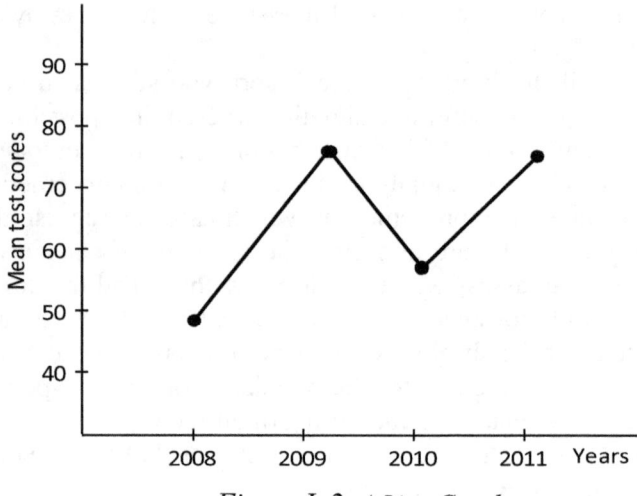

Figure L.2. A Line Graph

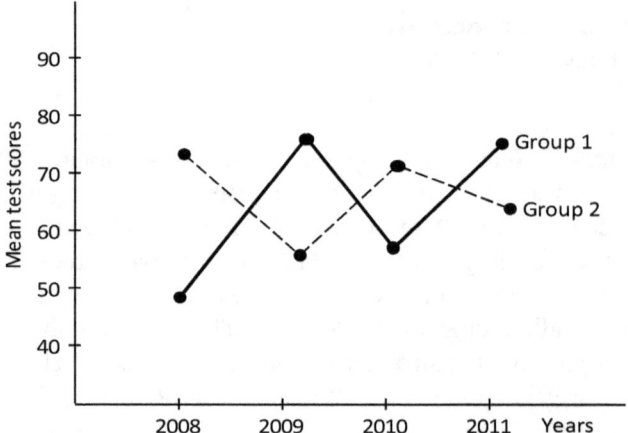

Figure L.3. A Line Graph Showing Mean Test Scores of Two Groups over a Four-Year period

A big advantage of the line graph is that more than one group can be shown on the same graph simultaneously. Each group can be presented by a different kind of line (e.g., broken or solid). Figure L.3 shows mean test scores of two groups of students over a four-year period.

📖 Pallant 2010; Ravid 2011

line of best fit
another term for REGRESSION LINE

linguistic ethnomethodology
see ETHNOMETHODOLOGY

Linguistics-Applied
see APPLIED LINGUISTICS

linked panels
also administrative panels
a type of LONGITUDINAL MIXED DESIGN which are created arbitrarily from existing data which has not been originally collected for longitudinal purposes but which contain codes (usually names accompanied by dates and places of birth) that allow the participants to be matched with other data obtained from them (e.g., census data).
see also ROTATING PANELS, SPLIT PANELS, COHORT STUDY, ACCELERATED LONGITUDINAL DESIGN, DIARY STUDY
📖 Dörnyei 2007

LISREL
an abbreviation for Linear Structural Relationships. It is one of several computer programs for carrying out STRUCTURAL EQUATION MODELING.

literal replication
see REPLICATION

literature review
also review of the literature
the systematic identification, location, and analysis of documents containing information related to a research problem. The phrase 'review of literature' consists of two words: *review* and *literature*. In RESEARCH METHODOLOGY the term literature refers to the knowledge of a particular area of investigation of any discipline which includes theoretical, practical and its research studies. The term review means to organize the knowledge of the specific area of research to evolve an edifice of knowledge to show that you study would be an addition to this field. The task of review of literature is highly creative and tedious because you have to synthesize the available knowledge of the field in a unique way to provide the rationale for your study. In other words, you avoid the problem of reinventing the wheel by examining issues that have already been investigated. You can contribute to knowledge in a field by exploring something that has not been adequately examined.
The review of literature is essential due to the following reasons:

1) One of the early steps in planning a research work is to review research done previously in the particular area of interest and relevant area quantitative and qualitative analysis of this research usually gives you an indication of the direction.
2) It is very essential for you as an investigator to be up-to-date in your information about the literature, related to your own problem already done by others. It is considered the most important pre-requisite to actual planning and conducting the study.
3) It avoids the replication of the study of findings to take an advantage from similar or related literature as regards, to methodology, techniques of data collection, procedure adopted and conclusions drawn. You can justify your own endeavor in the field.
4) It provides theories, ideas, explanations, or HYPOTHESIS which may prove useful in the formulation of a new problem. You formulate your hypothesis on the basis of review of literature. It also provides the rationale for the study.
 Brown 1988; Mckay 2006; Singh 2006

logarithmic transformation
also **log transformation**
a type of DATA TRANSFORMATION. There is a wide variety of log transformations. In general, however, a logarithm is the POWER to which a BASE NUMBER has to be raised to get the original number. As with SQUARE ROOT TRANSFORMATION, if a VARIABLE contains values less than 1, a CONSTANT must be added to move the minimum value of the distribution.
see also RECIPROCAL TRANSFORMATION
 Marczyk et al. 2005

logical positivism
see POSITIVISM

logistic coefficient
a coefficient in the logistic regression model that acts as the weighting factor for the INDEPENDENT VARIABLEs in relation to their discriminatory power. Logistic coefficient is similar to a REGRESSION WEIGHT or DISCRIMINANT COEFFICIENT.
 Hair et al. 2010

logistic regression
also **LR**
a *multivariate* prediction method and a development of MULTIPLE REGRESSION (MR) that has the added advantage of holding certain variables constant in order to assess the independent influence of key variables of

interest. Logistic regression (LR) is suitable for assessing the influence of two or more *continuous* (metric) or *categorical* (non-metric) INDEPENDENT VARIABLEs or predictors on one categorical DEPENDENT VARIABLE or criterion (e.g., win/lose, fail/pass, yes/no). The subjects fall into one of two groups, and the objective is to predict and explain the bases for each subject's group membership through a set of predictor variables selected by the researcher. LR is useful because it does not rely on some of the ASSUMPTIONS (e.g., HOMOSCEDASTICITY, NORMALITY, and LINEARITY) on which MR is based. MR is not suitable when you have categorical criterion variables. For multiple regression, your criterion variable (the thing that you are trying to explain or predict) needs to be a CONTINUOUS VARIABLE, with scores reasonably normally distributed. In contrast, LR allows you to test models to predict CATEGORICAL VARIABLEs with two or more LEVELs or categories. Your predictor variables can be either categorical or continuous, or a mix of both in the one model. LR enables you to assess how well your set of predictor variables predicts or explains your categorical criterion variable. It gives you an indication of the adequacy of your model (set of predictor variables) by assessing goodness of fit. It provides an indication of the relative importance of each predictor variable or the INTERACTION among your predictor variables. It also provides a summary of the accuracy of the classification of cases based on the MODE, allowing the calculation of the sensitivity and specificity of the model and the positive and negative predictive values.

Like correlation, LR provides information about the strength and direction of the association between the variables. In addition, LR coefficients can be used to estimate ODDS RATIO for each of the predictor variables in the model. These odds ratios can tell us how likely a dichotomous outcome is to occur given a particular set of predictor variables. The model could also be used to estimate the odds ratios for each variable.

LR can be seen as a more versatile version of **logit analysis** (the equivalent of multiple regression but with categorical data) in which the restrictions on the LEVELs OF MEASUREMENT are not as severe. It can also be used in a similar way to DISCRIMINANT ANALYSIS in that it can attempt to classify participants into their original categories to see how accurate it is at predicting group membership. However, in LR the predictor variables can be categorical, continuous, or a combination of both. In addition, LR is more flexible than discriminant analysis, since unlike the latter its reliability does not depend on certain restrictive normality assumptions regarding the underlying population distributions for the predictor variables.

LR can be divided into **binary logistic regression**, which is similar to linear regression except that it is used when the criterion variable is dichotomous, and **multinomial logistic regression**, which is used when the criterion variable has more than two categories, but that is complex and less common. In cases for which three or more groups form the dependent variable, DISCRIMINANT ANALYSIS is better suited.

📖 Cramer & Howitt 2004; Hair et al. 2010; Harlow 2005; Leech et al. 2005; Marczyk et al. 2005; Pallant 2010; Sheskin 2011; Tabachnick & Fidell 2007; Walliman 2006

logit analysis
see LOGISTIC REGRESSION

log-linear analysis
also **log-linear path analysis**

a complex analysis which may be regarded as an extension of the CHI-SQUARE TEST to CONTINGENCY TABLEs involving three or more VARIABLEs. Log-linear analysis is analogous to chi-square in that you use observed and expected frequencies to evaluate the STATISTICAL SIGNIFICANCE of your data. An important difference between chi-square and log-linear analysis is that log-linear analysis can be easily applied to experimental research designs that include more than two INDEPENDENT VARIABLEs whereas chi-square is normally limited to the two-variable case. Like chi-square, log-linear analysis involves nominal or CATEGORICAL DATA. However, it can be used for score data if the scores are subdivided into a small number of divisions (e.g., 1-5, 6-10, 11-15, etc.). A three-variable cross-tabulation table cannot be analyzed properly using chi-square because the table has too many dimensions, though researchers in the past commonly would carry out numerous smaller two-variable chi-squares derived from this sort of table. Such an approach cannot fully analyze the data no matter how thoroughly applied. There is no simple way of calculating the expected frequencies for three or more variables. In log-linear analysis, the objective is to find the model which best fits the empirical data. The fit of the model to the empirical data is assessed by using chi-square (usually LIKELIHOOD RATIO CHI-SQUARE). This version of the chi-square formula has the major advantage that the values of chi-square it provides may be added or subtracted directly without introducing error. Significant values of chi-square mean that the data depart from the expectations of the model. This indicates that the model has a poor fit to the data. A non-significant value of chi-square means that the model and the data fit very well. In log-linear analysis, what this means is that the cross-tabulated frequencies are compared with the expected frequencies based on the selected model (selected combination of MAIN EFFECTs and INTERACTION EFFECTs). The closer the actual frequencies are to the expected (modeled) frequencies, the better the model is.

The models created in log-linear analysis are based on the following components:

1) *The overall mean frequency.* This would be the equal-frequencies model. Obviously if all of the individual cell means are the same as the overall mean, then we would need to go no further in the analysis since the equal-frequencies model applies.
2) *The main effects.* A gender main effect would simply mean that there are different numbers of males and females in the analysis. As such, in much research main effects are of little interest, though in other contexts the main effects are important. For example, if it were found that there was a main effect of gender in a study, this might be a finding of interest as it would imply either more men in the group or more women in the group.
3) *Two-way interactions*—combinations of two variables (by collapsing the categories or cells for all other variables) which show larger or smaller frequencies which can be explained by the influence of the main effects operating separately.
4) *Higher order interactions* (what they are depends on the number of variables under consideration).
5) *The saturated model*—this is simply the sum of all the above possible components. It is always a perfect fit to the data by definition since it contains all of the components of the table. In log-linear analysis, the strategy is often to start with the saturated model and then remove the lower levels (the interactions and then the main effects) in turn to see whether removing the component actually makes a difference to the fit of the model. For example, if taking away all of the highest order interactions makes no difference to the data's fit to the model, then the interactions can be safely dropped from the model as they are adding nothing to the fit. Generally the strategy is to drop a whole level at a time to see if it makes a difference. So three-way interactions would be eliminated as a whole before going on to see which ones made the difference if a difference was found.

Log-linear analysis involves heuristic methods of calculations which are only possible using computers in practice since they involve numerous approximations towards the answer until the approximation improves only minutely. The difficulty is that the interactions cannot be calculated directly. One aspect of the calculation which can be understood without too much mathematical knowledge is the expected frequencies for different components of a log-linear model. These are displayed in computer printouts of log-linear analysis.

Interaction in log-linear analysis is often compared with interactions in ANOVA. The key difference that needs to be considered, though, is that the frequencies in the various cells are being predicted by the model (or pattern of independent variables) whereas in ANOVA it is the means

within the cells on the dependent variable which are being predicted by the model.
📖 Bordens & Abbott 2011; Cramer & Howitt 2004

log-linear path analysis
another term for LOG-LINEAR ANALYSIS

longitudinal design
another term for LONGITUDINAL RESEARCH

longitudinal method
another term for LONGITUDINAL RESEARCH

longitudinal mixed design
a LONGITUDINAL DESIGN type which combines aspects of *cross-sectional* and *panel* studies, thus involving an extensive and an intensive research component. This extensive element is typically *quantitative* and the intensive component lends itself to QUALITATIVE RESEARCH. The qualitative and quantitative traditions of longitudinal research are complementary. While this is true in theory, currently there is a marked imbalance in the social science between the relative weight given to these two paradigms, with quantitative studies being dominant. However, because longitudinal studies are inherently concerned with the micro- and macro-levels of development and change (e.g., individual growth and community change), the mixing of approaches is theoretically warranted. In addition, the sheer complexity of various dynamic patterns also suggests that a combination of qualitative and quantitative methods might be appropriate to do a longitudinal analysis full justice. For these reasons, longitudinal research is encouraged to capitalize on the strength of MIXED METHODS RESEARCH designs. In order to increase the strengths and reduce the weaknesses of certain longitudinal inquiry types, various creative longitudinal designs such as ROTATING PANELS, SPLIT PANELS, LINKED PANELS, COHORT STUDY, ACCELERATED LONGITUDINAL DESIGN and DIARY STUDY have been introduced.
see also CROSS-SECTIONAL STUDY, PANEL STUDY
📖 Dörnyei 2007

longitudinal research
also **longitudinal design, longitudinal study, longitudinal method, longitudinal survey**
a research type in which a single group of participants is studied over time. Longitudinal research is used to describe a variety of studies that are conducted over a period of time. Often, the word *developmental* is employed in connection with longitudinal studies that deal specifically

with aspects of human growth. Longitudinal designs are used most frequently to study age-related changes in how people think, feel, and behave. For example, we might use a longitudinal design to study how the strategies that children use to remember things change as they get older. To do so, we could follow a single group of children over a period of several years, testing their memory strategies when they were 4, 8, and 12 years old.

Longitudinal research gathers data over an extended period of time; a short-term investigation may take several weeks or months; a long-term study can extend over many years. It is also defined in terms of both the data and the design that are used in the research. A longitudinal investigation is research in which (a) data are collected for two or more distinct time periods; (b) the subjects or cases analyzed are the same or are comparable (i.e., drawn from the same POPULATION) from one period to the next; and (c) the analysis involves some comparison of data between periods.

Longitudinal research serves two primary purposes: to *describe* patterns of change, and to *explain* casual relationships. Although these two aims are interrelated, they do not always coincide because the researcher may obtain precise information about the temporal order of events without detecting any casual connection between these events.

Longitudinal studies suffer several disadvantages: First, they are time-consuming and expensive, because the researcher is obliged to wait for growth data to accumulate. Second, there is the difficulty of sample MORTALITY. Inevitably during the course of a long-term study, subjects drop out, are lost or refuse further cooperation. Such attrition makes it unlikely that those who remain in the study are as representative of the population as the sample that was originally drawn. Sometimes attempts are made to lessen the effects of sample mortality by introducing aspects of CROSS-SECTIONAL STUDY design, that is, topping up the original cohort SAMPLE SIZE at each time of retesting with the same number of respondents drawn from the same population. The problem here is that differences arising in the data from one SURVEY to the next may then be accounted for by differences in the persons surveyed rather than by genuine changes or trends. A third difficulty has been termed TESTING EFFECT. Often, repeated interviewing results in an undesired and confusing effect on the actions or attitudes under study, influencing the behavior of subjects, sensitizing them to matters that have hitherto passed unnoticed, or stimulating them to communication with others on unwanted topics. Fourth, longitudinal studies can suffer from the interaction of biological, environmental and intervention influences.

Finally, they pose considerable problems of organization due to the continuous changes that occur in students, staff, teaching methods and the like. Such changes make it highly unlikely that a study will be completed in the way that it was originally planned.

Longitudinal research has traditionally been associated with the QUANTITATIVE RESEARCH, aiming at providing statistical pictures of wider social trends. In such studies societies are studied from the social structure *downwards* rather than from the individual or personal network *upwards*. Recently, however, there has been a move in the social science to make longitudinal QUALITATIVE RESEARCH more prominent. The distinctiveness of such studies is given by interplay of the temporal and cultural dimensions of social life, offering a bottom-up understanding of how people move through time and craft the transition processes. Thus, the qualitative move offers us a *close-up* of the fabric of real lives as opposed to the quantitative *long shot*. The focus is on the plot and detailed story lines of the key actors rather than the grand vistas of the epic picture.

Longitudinal designs are closely related to TIME-SERIES DESIGNs but in the case of longitudinal designs, the independent variable is time itself. That is, nothing has occurred between one observation and the next other than the passage of time.

PANEL STUDY, TREND STUDY, RETROSPECTIVE LONGITUDINAL STUDY and SIMULTANEOUS CROSS-SECTIONAL STUDY are four main design types of longitudinal approaches.

see also CROSS-SECTIONAL STUDY, LONGITUDINAL MIXED DESIGN

Cohen et al. 2011; Dörnyei 2007; Leary 2011; Perry 2011

longitudinal study
another term for LONGITUDINAL RESEARCH

longitudinal survey
another term for LONGITUDINAL RESEARCH

low-inference descriptors
see INTERPRETIVE VALIDITY

LR
an abbreviation for LOGISTIC REGRESSION

LSD
an abbreviation for FISHER'S LEAST SIGNIFICANT DIFFERENCE

M

magnitude estimation

a well-established research tool used as a ranking procedure. Magnitude estimation is useful when one wants not only to rank items in relation to one another, but also to know how much better X is than Y. It has been used when eliciting grammatical knowledge not as an absolute (yes or no), but as a matter of gradation (i.e., which sentence is more acceptable than another?).
 Mackey & Gass 2005

Mahalanobis distance D^2

a measure of *distance* involving multivariate data useful in discriminating between two POPULATIONs. Mahalanobis D^2 is the two-sample version of HOTELLING'S T^2. It is based on CORRELATIONs between variables by which different patterns can be identified and analyzed. It gauges similarity of an unknown sample set to a known one. In other words, it is a multivariate EFFECT SIZE. It has found extensive applications in many fields including CLUSTER ANALYSIS, PROFILE ANALYSIS, and DISCRIMINANT FUNCTION ANALYSIS.

see also COOK'S DISTANCE, LEVERAGE, MULTIVARIATE ANALYSIS
 Larson-Hall 2010; Sahai & Khurshid 2001

mail survey

another term for POSTAL SURVEY

main effect

see INTERACTION

MANCOVA

another term for MULTIVARIATE ANALYSIS OF COVARIANCE

manifest variable

also **indicator variable, observed variable**

a term used to describe a variable where the measure of that variable represents that variable. For example, an IQ test score may be used as a direct measure of the theoretical CONSTRUCT of intelligence. However, a measure, like an IQ score, is often not a perfect representation of the theoretical construct as it may not be totally reliable and may assess other variables as well. For example, an IQ score may also measure knowledge in particular areas. Consequently, a manifest variable is distinguished from a **latent variable** (also known as **unobserved variable**), which is a hypothesized or unobserved construct and as such, cannot be measured

directly. It can only be approximated by observable or measured variables.
📖 Cramer & Howitt 2004; Sahai & Khurshid 2001

Mann-Whitney *U* test
also **Wilcoxon test, Wilcoxon-Mann-Whitney test, Mann-Whitney-Wilcoxon test, Wilcoxon rank-sums test, rank sums test, WMW test, *U* test, *U***

a *nonparametric* rank-based test which is alternative to a *parametric* INDEPENDENT SAMPLES *t*-TEST for comparing two INDEPENDENT GROUPS on the basis of their ranks above and below the MEDIAN. Mann-Whitney *U* test is used with one *categorical* INDEPENDENT VARIABLE with two LEVELs (e.g., gender: female/male) and one *ordinal* DEPENDENT VARIABLE. It is often used in place of the *t*-test for independent groups when there is an extreme violation of the NORMALITY or HOMOGENEITY OF VARIANCE assumptions or when the data are scaled at a level that is not appropriate for the *t*-test (i.e., the data are ordinal in nature). Mann-Whitney *U* test enables us to see, for example, whether there are differences between two INDEPENDENT SAMPLES (e.g., males and females) on a RATING SCALE. It is used to determine whether scores from two unrelated or independent samples differ significantly from one another. It tests whether the number of times scores from one sample are ranked higher than scores from the other sample when the scores for both samples have been ranked in a single sample. If the two sets of scores are similar, the number of times this happens should be similar for the two groups. If the samples are 20 or less, the STATISTICAL SIGNIFICANCE of the smaller *U* value is used. If the samples are greater than 20, the *U* value is converted into a Z VALUE. The value of *z* has to be 1.96 or more to be statistically significant at the .05 two-tailed level or 1.65 or more at the .05 one-tailed level.

Sometimes the Wilcoxon-Mann-Whitney test is described as a method for comparing MEDIANs. However, it is relatively unsatisfactory for this purpose because it is not based on a direct estimate of the population medians. For example, there are situations where power decreases as the difference between the population medians increases, and CONFIDENCE INTERVALs for the difference cannot be computed.

see also KRUSKAL-WALLIS TEST, WILCOXON SIGNED-RANKS TEST
📖 Pagano 2009; Sahai & Khurshid 2001; Urdan 2010; Wilcox 2003

Mann-Whitney-Wilcoxon test
another term for MANN-WHITNEY *U* TEST

MANOVA
an abbreviation for MULTIVARIATE ANALYSIS OF VARIANCE

Mantel-Haenszel chi-square test
another term for MANTEL-HAENSZEL TEST

Mantel-Haenszel test
also **Mantel-Haenszel chi-square test, Cochran–Mantel–Haenszel test**
a test that allows for testing the NULL HYPOTHESIS of independence between two DICHOTOMOUS VARIABLEs (e.g., success and failure). Mantel-Haenszel test is used when the effect of the EXPLANATORY VARIABLE on the RESPONSE VARIABLE is influenced by COVARIATEs that can be controlled. The test assumes that any association between the dichotomous variables is unaffected by the third variable. It is often used in studies where RANDOM ASSIGNMENT of subjects to different TREATMENTs cannot be controlled, but influencing covariates can. In the this test, the data are arranged in a series of associated 2×2 (two-by-two) CONTINGENCY TABLEs, the null hypothesis is that the observed response is independent of the treatment used in any 2×2 contingency table. The test's use of associated 2×2 contingency tables increases the ability of the test to detect associations (the POWER of the test is increased).
see also CHI-SQUARE TEST, COCHRAN'S C TEST, COCHRAN'S Q TEST
📖 Upton & Cook 2008

marginal
see CONTINGENCY TABLE

margin of error
the range of MEANs (or any other statistic) which are reasonably likely possibilities for the POPULATION value. Put simple, the margin of error is a common summary of SAMPLING ERROR, referred to regularly in the research, which quantifies uncertainty about a SURVEY result. This is normally expressed as the CONFIDENCE INTERVAL. An important factor in determining the margin of error is the size of the sample (see SAMPLE SIZE). Larger samples are more likely to yield results close to the target POPULATION quantity and thus have smaller margins of error than more modest-sized samples.
📖 Cramer & Howitt 2004

masking variable
another term for SUPPRESSOR VARIABLE

matched groups
another term for DEPENDENT SAMPLES

matched pairs design
another term for MATCHED SUBJECTS DESIGN

matched-pairs *t*-test
another term for PAIRED-SAMPLES *t*-TEST

matched samples
another term for DEPENDENT SAMPLES

matched samples design
another term for MATCHED SUBJECTS DESIGN

matched-samples *t*-test
another term for PAIRED-SAMPLES *t*-TEST

matched subjects design
also **matched pairs design, matched samples design, randomized matched subjects posttest-only control group design**
a TRUE EXPERIMENTAL DESIGN in which participants are allocated to CONTROL and EXPERIMENTAL GROUPs randomly but, unlike POSTTEST-ONLY CONTROL GROUP DESIGN, the basis of the allocation is that one member of the CONTROL GROUP is matched (see RANDOMIZED MATCHING) to a member of the EXPERIMENTAL GROUP on the several INDEPENDENT VARIABLES (IVs) considered important for the study (e.g., those IVs that are considered to have an influence on the DEPENDENT VARIABLE (DV), such as sex, age, ability). So, first, pairs of participants are selected who are matched in terms of the IV under consideration (e.g., whose scores on a particular measure are the same or similar), and then each of the pair is randomly assigned to the control or experimental group. RANDOM ASSIGNMENT takes place at the pair rather than the group level. The flip of a coin can be used to assign one member of each pair to the treatment group and the other to the control group.
This design can be diagramed as follows (where M = matched subjects, X = treatment, and O = posttests:

$$\begin{array}{lcc} \text{Experimental Group } (M) & X & O \\ \text{Control Group } (M) & & O \end{array}$$

The matched-subjects design serves to reduce the extent to which experimental differences can be accounted for by initial differences between the groups; that is, it controls preexisting intersubject differences on variables highly related to the DV that the experiment is designed to affect. The random procedure used to assign the matched pairs to groups adds to the strength of this design. Although this ensures effective matching of control and experimental groups, in practice it may not be easy to find sufficiently close matching, particularly in a field experiment, although finding such a close match in a field experiment may increase the control of the experiment considerably. Matched pairs designs are useful if the researcher cannot be certain that individual differences will not obscure treatment effects, as it enables these individual differences to be controlled. The researcher should pay attention to the need to specify the degree of variance of the match. For example, if the subjects were to be matched on, for example, linguistic ability as measured in a standardized test, it is important to define the limits of variability that will be used to define the matching (e.g. ± 3 points). As before, the greater the degree of precision in the matching here, the closer will be the match, but the greater the degree of precision the harder it will be to find an exactly matched sample.

One way of addressing this issue is to place all the subjects in rank order on the basis of the scores or measures of the DV. Then the first two subjects become one matched pair (which one is allocated to the control group and which to the experimental group is done randomly, e.g., by tossing a coin), the next two subjects become the next matched pair, then the next two subjects become the next matched pair, and so on until the sample is drawn. Here the loss of precision is counterbalanced by the avoidance of the loss of subjects (see COUNTERBALANCED DESIGN).
see also WITHIN-SUBJECTS DESIGN
📖 Ary et al. 2010; Cohen et al. 2011

matched-subjects factorial design
an experimental design involving two or more INDEPENDENT VARIABLEs in which participants are first matched into homogenous blocks and then, within each block, are randomly assigned to the experimental conditions
see also WITHIN-SUBJECTS DESIGN, BETWEEN-SUBJECTS DESIGN
📖 Leary 2011

matched *t*-test
another term for PAIRED-SAMPLES *t*-TEST

matching
another term for RANDOMIZED MATCHING

matching item
a type of test item or test task that requires test takers to indicate which entries (e.g. words or phrases) on one list are the correct matches for entries on another list. More specifically, matching items consist of two groups listed in columns—the left-hand column containing the questions or items to be thought about and the right-hand column containing the possible responses to the questions. The respondent pairs the choice from the right-hand column with the corresponding question or item in the left-hand column. The information given in the left-hand column will be

called the *matching item premise* and that shown in the right-hand column will be labeled *options*. In constructing matching items, more options should be supplied than premises so that the respondents cannot narrow down the choices as they progress through the test simply by keeping track of the options that they have already used. In addition, the options should be usually shorter than the premises because most respondents will read a premise then search through the options for the correct match.
see also SELECTED-RESPONSE ITEM
📖 Brown 2005; Richards & Schmidt 2010

materials

a subsection in the METHOD section of a RESEARCH REPORT which gives you the opportunity to describe any materials that were used in the study. The materials are also sometimes included in APPENDIXes. Teaching materials, QUESTIONNAIREs, RATING SCALEs, TESTs, and so forth should be described in detail unless they are well known. Any other pertinent information, such as the range of possible scores, scoring methods used, types of questions, and types of scales, should be included. The RELIABILITY and VALIDITY of any tests or scales should appear in this section as well.
see also PARTICIPANTS, PROCEDURES, ANALYSES
📖 Brown 1988

matrix questions

CLOSED-FORM ITEMs which are not types of questions but concern the layout of questions. Matrix questions enable the same kind of response to be given to several questions, for example 'strongly disagree' to 'strongly agree'. The matrix layout helps to save space. The following is an example:

Instructions: Please complete the following by placing a tick in one space only, as follows: 1 = not at all; 2 = very little; 3 = a little; 4 = quite a lot; 5 = a very great deal.

How much do you use the following for assessment purposes?

	1	2	3	4	5
1. commercially published tests	[ ]	[ ]	[ ]	[ ]	[ ]
2. your own made-up tests	[ ]	[ ]	[ ]	[ ]	[ ]
3. students' projects	[ ]	[ ]	[ ]	[ ]	[ ]
4. essays	[ ]	[ ]	[ ]	[ ]	[ ]
5. samples of students' work	[ ]	[ ]	[ ]	[ ]	[ ]

As you see, here five questions have been asked in only five lines, excluding, of course, the instructions and explanations of the anchor statements. Such a layout is economical of space. A second example (see the Table M.1) indicates how a matrix design can save a considerable amount of space in a QUESTIONNAIRE. Here the size of potential problems in conducting a piece of research is asked for, and data on how much these problems were soluble are requested. For the first issue (the size of the problem), 1 = no problem, 2 = a small problem, 3 = a moderate problem, 4 = a large problem, 5 = a very large problem. For the second issue (how much the problem was solved), 1 = not solved at all, 2 = solved only a very little, 3 = solved a moderate amount, 4 = solved a lot, 5 = completely solved.

Potential problems in conducting research	Size of the problem (1-5)	How much the problem was solved (1-5)
1. Gaining access to schools and teachers	[ ] [ ] [ ] [ ] [ ]	[ ] [ ] [ ] [ ] [ ]
2. Local political factors that impinge on the school	[ ] [ ] [ ] [ ] [ ]	[ ] [ ] [ ] [ ] [ ]
3. Resentment by principals	[ ] [ ] [ ] [ ] [ ]	[ ] [ ] [ ] [ ] [ ]
4. People vetting what could be used	[ ] [ ] [ ] [ ] [ ]	[ ] [ ] [ ] [ ] [ ]
5. Finding enough willing participants for your sample	[ ] [ ] [ ] [ ] [ ]	[ ] [ ] [ ] [ ] [ ]
6. Schools' or institutions' fear of criticism or loss of face	[ ] [ ] [ ] [ ] [ ]	[ ] [ ] [ ] [ ] [ ]
7. The sensitivity of the research: the issues being investigated	[ ] [ ] [ ] [ ] [ ]	[ ] [ ] [ ] [ ] [ ]

Table M.1. An Example of Matrix Questions

As shown in Table M.1, here 14 questions (7 × 2) have been able to be covered in just a short amount of space. Laying out the questionnaire like this enables the respondent to fill in the questionnaire rapidly. On the other hand, it risks creating a mind set in the respondent (a response set) in that the respondent may simply go down the questionnaire columns and write the same number each time (e.g., all number 3) or, in a rating scale, tick all number 3. Such response sets can be detected by looking at patterns of replies and eliminating response sets from subsequent analysis. The conventional way of minimizing response sets has been by reversing the meaning of some of the questions so that the respondents will need to read them carefully. However, it is argued that using positively and negatively worded items within a scale is not measuring the same underlying traits. They report that some respondents will tend to disagree with a negatively worded item, that the reliability levels of negatively worded items are lower than for positively worded items, and that negatively worded items receive greater nonresponse than positively worded items. Indeed some researchers argue against mixed-item formats, and supplement this by reporting that inappropriately worded items can induce an artificially extreme response which, in turn, compromises the reliability of the data. Mixing negatively and positively worded items in the same scale compromises both validity and reliability. Indeed it is suggested that respondents may not read negatively worded items as carefully as positively worded items.

see also DICHOTOMOUS QUESTION, MULTIPLE CHOICE ITEM, RATIO DATA QUESTION, CONSTANT SUM QUESTIONS, RANK ORDER QUESTION, CONTINGENCY QUESTION
📖 Cohen et al. 2011

matrix sampling
a procedure which is sometimes used when the SURVEY is long and the accessible POPULATION is large. This technique involves randomly selecting respondents, each of whom is administered a subset of questions, randomly selected from the total set of items. The practical advantage of using matrix sampling is the decrease in the time required for each individual to respond. This is an important advantage because one obstacle to obtaining a high response rate is the unwillingness of some individuals to take the time to answer a long QUESTIONNAIRE.
📖 Ary et al. 2010

maturation
a threat to INTERNAL VALIDITY in which the characteristics of groups may diverge, particularly in studies that are conducted over a long period of time. In other words, maturation deals with the natural and intrinsic changes that take place over time in the participants other than what is under study. Such areas as physical coordination and strength, emotional states, and cognitive structures change as people grow older. Studies that take place over longer periods of time are potentially subject to this interference.

see also STATISTICAL REGRESSION, MORTALITY, TESTING EFFECT, INSTRUMENTATION, DIFFERENTIAL SELECTION, HISTORY
📖 Perry 2011

Mauchly sphericity test
another term for MAUCHLY'S TEST

Mauchly's test
also **Mauchly sphericity test, Mauchly's test of sphericity**
a test of SPHERICITY in a REPEATED-MEASURES ANOVAs. A significant Mauchly's test indicates that the assumption of sphericity is not met. Violating this assumption inflates TYPE I ERROR rate. Like many tests, the ANALYSIS OF VARIANCE makes certain ASSUMPTIONS about the data used. Violations of these assumptions tend to affect the value of the test adversely. One assumption is that the variances of each of the CELLs should be more or less equal (see HOMOGENEITY OF VARIANCE). In repeated-measures ANOVAs, it is also necessary that the COVARIANCEs of the differences between each condition are equal. That is, subtract condition A from condition B, condition A from condition C etc., and calcu-

late the covariance of these difference scores until all possibilities are exhausted. The covariances of all of the differences between conditions should be equal. If not, then adjustments need to be made to the analysis such as finding a test which does not rely on these assumptions (e.g., a MULTIVARIATE ANALYSIS OF VARIANCE is not based on these assumptions and there are nonparametric versions of the related ANOVA).
  Cramer & Howitt 2004; Salkind 2007

Mauchly's test of sphericity
another term for MAUCHLY'S TEST

maximum F-ratio test
another term for HARTLEY'S TEST

maximum likelihood estimate
also **MLE**

a criterion for estimating a PARAMETER of a POPULATION of values such as the MEAN value. Maximum likelihood estimate is the value that is the most likely given the data from a SAMPLE and certain assumptions about the distribution of those values. This method is widely used in STRUCTURAL EQUATION MODELING. To give a very simple example of this principle, suppose that we wanted to find out what the PROBABILITY or likelihood was of a coin turning up heads. We had two hypotheses. The first was that the coin was unbiased and so would turn up heads .50 of the time. The second was that the coin was biased towards heads and would turn up heads .60 of the time. Suppose that we tossed a coin three times and it landed heads, tails, and heads in that order. As the tosses are independent, the joint probability of these three events is the product of their individual probabilities. So the joint probability of these three events for the first HYPOTHESIS of the coin being biased is .125 ($.5 \times .5 \times .5 = .125$). The joint probability of these three events for the second hypothesis of the coin being biased towards heads is .144 ($.6 \times .6 \times .4 = .144$). As the probability of the outcome for the biased coin is greater than that for the unbiased coin, the maximum likelihood estimate is .60. If we had no hypotheses about the probability of the coin turning up heads, then the maximum likelihood estimate would be the observed probability which is .67 ($2/3 = .67$).
  Cramer & Howitt 2004

maximum variation sampling
see PURPOSIVE SAMPLING

McNemar's change test
another term for MCNEMAR'S TEST

McNemar's chi-square test
another term for MCNEMAR'S TEST

McNemar's test
also **McNemar's chi-square test, McNemar's change test**
a NONPARAMETRIC TEST which is alternative to a *parametric* DEPENDENT SAMPLES *t*-TEST and can be used when all variables are *dichotomous*. McNemar's test is employed in a HYPOTHESIS TESTING situation which involves a design with two RELATED SAMPLES. It is a simple means of analyzing simple related nominal designs in which participants are classified into one of two categories on two successive occasions. Typically, McNemar's test is used to assess whether there has been change over time. It is a special case of the MANTEL-HAENSZEL CHI-SQUARE TEST which allows us to analyze nominal data when they can be formed into a single 2 × 2 (two-by-two) CONTINGENCY TABLE. For example, if we studied people's attitudes to applied linguistics as a science before and after a talk on the subject and asked them on each occasion whether or not they thought applied linguistics was a science, McNemar's test would be used. This test is only interested in those people who have changed opinion. As such, one measure can be described as the *before* measure and the second measure is the *after* measure.
see also COCHRAN'S *Q* TEST

Clark-Carter 2010; Cramer & Howitt 2004; Larson-Hall 2010; Sahai & Khurshid 2001; Sheskin 2011

MD
an abbreviation for MEAN DEVIATION

Mdn
an abbreviation for MEDIAN

MDS
an abbreviation for MULTIDIMENSIONAL SCALING

mean
also **arithmetic mean, *M*, $\bar{X}$**
the most commonly used MEASURE OF CENTRAL TENDENCY which is the sum of scores divided by the total number of scores, often represented by the following formula:

$$\bar{X} = \frac{\Sigma X}{N}$$

where
$\bar{X}$ (read as *X*-bar) is the symbol for the mean,

Σ is a summation sign (the uppercase Greek letter sigma),
N represents the total number of scores, and
ΣX is pronounced 'sum of X' and literally means to find the sum of the scores.

As an example, consider the scores 3, 4, 6, and 7. Adding the scores together produces ΣX = 20, and N is 4. Thus $\bar{X}$ = 20/4 = 5. Saying that the $\bar{X}$ of these scores is 5 indicates that the mathematical center of this distribution is located at the score of 5. (As here, the $\bar{X}$ may be a score that does not actually occur in the data). The mathematical center of the distribution must also be the point where most of the scores are located. This will be the case when we have a NORMAL and UNIMODAL DISTRIBUTION. For example, say that a test produced the scores of 5, 6, 2, 1, 3, 4, 5, 4, 3, 7, and 4, which are shown in Figure M.1. Here ΣX = 44, and N = 11, so the $\bar{X}$ score is 4. Computing the $\bar{X}$ is appropriate here because it is the point around which most of the scores are located: Most often the scores are at or near 4. Notice that Figure M.1 shows an approximately normal distribution. The $\bar{X}$ is the mathematical center of any distribution, and in a normal distribution, most of the scores are located around this central point.

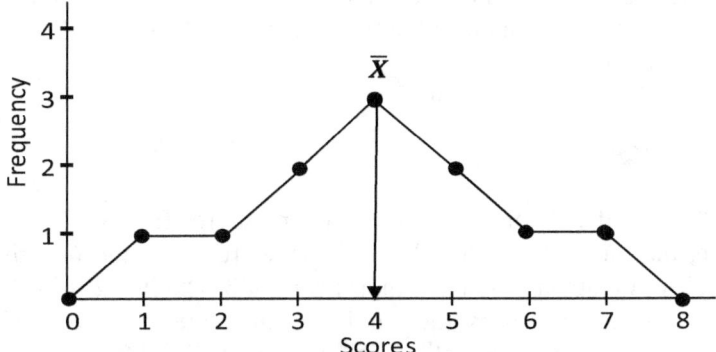

Figure M.1. Location of the Mean on a Symmetrical Distribution
The Vertical Line Indicates the Location of the Mean Score

The $\bar{X}$ is considered to be a comprehensive measure because it takes into account each and every score obtained in the group. No information is lost, and so any scores which somehow do not seem to fit in with the rest of the group's performance are also included in the calculation. The $\bar{X}$ is the center of a distribution because it is an equal distance from the scores above and below it. Therefore, the half of the distribution that is below the $\bar{X}$ balances with the half of the distribution that is above the $\bar{X}$. The sum of the deviations around the $\bar{X}$ always equals zero, regardless of the shape of the distribution. For example, in the skewed sample of 4, 5, 7 and 20, the $\bar{X}$ is 9, which produces deviations of -5, -4, -2 and + 11, respectively. Their sum is zero. The $\bar{X}$ is also amenable to algebraic treatment and is used in further statistical calculations. Thus, it is a relatively stable measure of central tendency.

However, the $\bar{X}$ suffers from some limitations. It is unduly affected by extreme items (see OUTLIERs). A couple of very high- or very low-scoring subjects in a relatively small group could displace this average measure to the left or the right of the middle ground because it must balance the entire distribution. You can see this starting with the symmetrical distribution containing the scores 1, 2, 2, 2, and 3. The $\bar{X}$ is 2, and this accurately describes most scores. However, adding the score of 20 skews the sample. Now the $\bar{X}$ is pulled up to 5. But most of these scores are not at or near 5. As this illustrates, although the $\bar{X}$ is always at the mathematical center, in a SKEWED DISTRIBUTION, that center is not where most of the scores are located. Thus, when the distribution is abnormal, it is unlikely that the $\bar{X}$ would be a safe measure of group tendency; it may not coincide with the actual value of an item in a series, and it may lead to wrong impressions, particularly when the item values are not given with the average. The solution is to use the MEDIAN to summarize a skewed distribution.

The mean is sometimes called the *arithmetic mean* to distinguish it from other forms of mean such as the HARMONIC MEAN or GEOMETRIC MEAN. see also MODE

📖 Heiman 2011; Perry 2011; Porte 2010

mean deviation
also *MD*

the MEAN of the absolute deviations of the scores from the mean. For example, the mean deviation (*MD*) of the scores of 2 and 6 is the sum of their absolute deviations from their mean of 3 which is 2 [(4 - 3 = 1) + (2 - 3 = -1) = 2] divided by the number of absolute deviations which is 2. The *MD* of these two deviations is 1 (2/2 = 1). The *MD* is not very widely used in statistics simply because the related concept of standard deviation is far more useful in practice.

📖 Cramer & Howitt 2004

mean score

ARITHMETIC MEAN of a set of scores.

mean square
also *MS*

a measure of the estimated POPULATION VARIANCE in ANALYSIS OF VARIANCE. Mean square (*MS*) is used to form the *F* RATIO which determines whether two VARIANCE ESTIMATEs differ significantly. In other words, it is used to determine if there exist significant differences in POPULATION MEANS. *MS* is the SUM OF SQUARES (or squared deviations) divided by the DEGREES OF FREEDOM.

The ratio of two *MS*s is known as **mean square ratio**.
📖 Cramer & Howitt 2004; Sahai & Khurshid 2001

mean square between-groups
(in a ONE-WAY ANOVA), the measure of variation between group MEANS (the mean of all the scores in a particular group) obtained by dividing the SUM OF SQUARES BETWEEN GROUPS by its DEGREES OF FREEDOM.
📖 Leary 2011; Sahai & Khurshid 2001

mean square ratio
see MEAN SQUARE

mean square within-groups
the average variance within experimental conditions. It is the sum of squares within-groups divided by the DEGREES OF FREEDOM within-groups.
📖 Leary 2011

measurement
the process of quantifying the characteristics of an object of interest according to explicit rules and procedures. The definition includes three distinguishing features: *quantification, characteristics*, and *explicit rules and procedures*. Quantification involves the assigning numbers, and this distinguishes measures from qualitative descriptions such as verbal accounts or nonverbal, visual representations. Non-numerical categories or rankings such as letter grades (A, B, C…), or labels (e.g., excellent, good, average…) may have the characteristics of measurement (see SCALE).

We can assign numbers to both physical and mental characteristics of persons. Physical attributes such as height and weight can be observed directly. In our research, however, we are almost always interested in quantifying mental attributes and abilities (sometimes called CONSTRUCT) which can only be observed indirectly. These mental attributes include characteristics such as aptitude, intelligence, motivation, field dependence/independence, attitude, native language, fluency in speaking, and achievement in reading comprehension.

The third distinguishing characteristic of measurement is that quantification must be done according to explicit rules and procedures. That is, the blind or haphazard assignment of numbers to characteristics of individuals cannot be regarded as measurement. In order to be considered a

measure, an observation of an attribute must be replicable, for other observers, in other contexts and with other individuals.
📖 Bachman 1990

measurement effect
another term for TESTING EFFECT

measurement error
also **error of measurement, error score**
an estimate of the discrepancy between the subjects' true scores (i.e., the true ability) and their OBSERVED SCOREs. Measurement error or error score is the variance in scores on a measurement instrument (e.g., a test) that is not directly related to the purpose of that measure. It is described as the variability in measurements of the same quantity on the same item. CLASSICAL TEST THEORY is a good simple model for measurement, but it may not always be an accurate reflection of reality. In particular, it assumes that any observation is composed of the true value plus some random error value. However, it is possible that some errors are systematic, that they hold across most or all of the members of a group. One way to deal with this notion is to revise the simple true score model by dividing the error component into two subcomponents, **random error** (also called **unsystematic error, random variation, chance variable**) and **systematic error** (also called **nonrandom error**). This can be represented by the following equation:

Observed score = true score + random error + systematic error

Random error represents deviation of an observed value from a true value that is due to pure chance rather than to one of the other factors being studied. It may inflate or depress any subject's score in an unpredictable manner. It is caused by any factors that randomly affect measurement of the variable across the sample. It takes no particular pattern and is assumed to cancel itself out over repeated measurements. For instance, people's moods can inflate or deflate their performance on any occasion. In a particular testing, some children may be in a good mood and others may be depressed. If mood affects the children's performance on the measure, it might artificially inflate the observed scores for some children and artificially deflate them for others. The important thing about random error is that it does not have any consistent effects across the entire sample. Instead, it pushes observed scores up or down randomly. You cannot see the random errors because all you see is the observed score (X). The important property of random error is that it adds variability to the data but does not affect average performance for the group. Because of this, random error is sometimes considered **noise**.

In contrast, systematic error is caused by any factors that systematically affect measurement of the variable across the sample. It inflates or depresses scores of identifiable groups in a predictable way. It has an observable pattern, is not due to chance, and often has a cause or causes that can be identified and remedied. For instance, if there is loud traffic going by just outside of a classroom where students are taking a test, this noise is liable to affect all of the children's scores—in this case, systematically lowering them. Unlike random error, systematic errors tend to be either positive or negative consistently; because of this, systematic error is sometimes considered to be BIAS in measurement.

Chance or random error that leads to inconsistency in scores can come from three sources:

1) *The individual being measured may be a source of error.* Fluctuations in individuals' motivation, interest, level of fatigue, physical health, anxiety, and other mental and emotional factors affect test results. As these factors change randomly from one measurement to the next, they result in a change or inconsistency in one's scores. Individuals may make more lucky guesses at one time than another. A student's breaking a pencil point on a SPEED TEST would increase the error component in the test results.

2) *The administration of the measuring instrument may introduce error.* An inexperienced person may depart from standardized procedures in administering or scoring a test. Testing conditions such as light, heat, ventilation, time of day, and the presence of distractions may affect performance. Instructions for taking the test may be ambiguous. The scoring procedure may be a source of error. Objectivity and precise scoring procedures enhance consistency, whereas subjectivity and vague scoring instructions depress it.

3) *The instrument may be a source of error.* Brevity of a test is a major source of unreliability. A small sample of behavior results in an unstable score. If a test is too easy and everyone knows most of the answers, students' relative scores again depend on only a few questions and luck is a major factor. If questions are ambiguous, lucky examinees respond in the way the examiner intended, whereas unlucky subjects respond in another equally correct manner, but their answers are scored as incorrect.

Whatever its source, measurement error undermines the RELIABILITY of the measures researchers use. In fact, the reliability of a measure is an inverse function of measurement error, i.e., the more measurement error present in a measuring instrument, the less reliable the measure is. Anything that increases measurement error decreases the consistency and reliability of the measure. A measure that has no error score (is all true score) is perfectly reliable; a measure that has no true score (is all error) has zero reliability.

The statistical models and methods for analyzing data measured with error are called *measurement error models*.

see also STANDARD ERROR OF MEASUREMENT

📖 Ary et al. 2010; Richards & Schmidt 2010; Sahai & Khurshid 2001; Salkind 2007; Trochim & Donnelly 2007

measurement scale
also **scale, level of measurement, scale of measurement, level of data**

the level or type of quantification produced by a MEASUREMENT. Scales are used to represent different ways of observing, organizing, quantifying and assigning numbers to language data. In addition, different types of scales can be said to measure with varying degrees of precision. The four types of scales are the NOMINAL, ORDINAL, INTERVAL, and RATIO SCALEs and can be arranged from least precise to most precise. Because these different scales provide increasing amount of information, from nominal scales up to ratio scales, they are sometimes called levels of measurement. At lower levels of measurement, assumptions tend to be less restrictive and data analyses tend to be less sensitive. At each level up the hierarchy, the current level includes all of the qualities of the one below it and adds something new.

Scales can be converted into other scales. It is possible to convert a scale that is higher on the hierarchy to one that is lower. The direction of scale conversion is only one-way (i.e. a ratio scale → an interval scale → an ordinal scale → a nominal scale), not the other way round. For example, if we had measured the amount of time spent studying a language in terms of hours, and found that we had an extremely wide range of values, we might categorize, or group, these values into ranges, such as 0 to 20, 21 to 40, 41 to 60, and so on, thus giving us an interval scale. Or, we can classify students into groups, such as high, intermediate and low, on the basis of scores on a test, thus reducing the interval scale of the test scores to an ordinal scale. While we may find it convenient in certain situations to convert numbers from a higher level to a lower level of measurement, we lose additional information provided in the original higher level. For this reason, we need to be sure that the information lost is compensated. Because we cannot generate additional information from nothing, it is obvious that we cannot convert numbers from lower levels of measurement to higher levels.

📖 Bachman 2004; Brown 1995, 2005; Richards & Schmidt 2010; Trochim & Donnelly 2007

measure of central tendency
see CENTRAL TENDENCY

measure of dispersion
another term for MEASURE OF VARIABILITY

measure of location
another term for MEASURES OF CENTRAL TENDENCY

measure of sampling adequacy
also MSA
measure calculated both for the entire correlation matrix and each individual variable evaluating the appropriateness of applying FACTOR ANALYSIS. Values above .50 for either the entire matrix or an individual variable indicate appropriateness.
📖 Hair et al. 2010

measure of variability
see DISPERSION

median
also *Mdn*
a MEASURE OF CENTRAL TENDENCY which is the middle value or score of a DISTRIBUTION. Median is simply another name for the score at the 50th PERCENTILE. If we rank-order the scores, the median is the score that falls in the middle. Median divides the distribution into two halves; in one half all items are less than median, whereas in the other half all items have values higher than median. To compute the median, we arrange the scores from lowest to highest. With an odd number of scores, the score in the middle position is the approximate median. For example, for the nine scores 1, 2, 3, 3, 4, 7, 9, 10, and 11, the score in the middle position is the fifth score, so the median is the score of 4. It is, in fact, the score at which 50% of the distribution falls below and 50% fall above. If there is an even number of test takers, however, you may find that the middle point occurs between two different scores in the distribution, depending on whether you begin with the lowest score and count up or with the highest score and count down. In such cases, the median is midway between these two scores. For example, for the ten scores 3, 8, 11, 11, 12, 13, 24, 35, 46, and 48, the middle scores are at position 5 (the score of 12) and position 6 (the score of 13). The average of 12 and 13 is 12.5, so the median is approximately 12.5. Thus, when there is an even number of test takers, the median may be a score that does not actually occur in the distribution.

A term that is closely related to the median is the **median location**. The median location of N numbers is defined as follows:

$$\text{Median location} = \frac{N+1}{2}$$

Thus, for five numbers the median location = $(5 + 1)/2 = 3$, which simply means that the median is the third number in an ordered series. For 12 numbers, the median location = $(12 + 1)/2 = 6.5$; the median falls between, and is the average of, the sixth and seventh numbers.

The median is the appropriate indicator of grouping for scores that are ordinally scaled. The most common examples of ordinally scaled scores in language measurement are those that are derived from ratings of samples of language, such as compositions or oral interviews. ORDINAL SCALEs provide information about how the scores are ordered, and the median, being the middle score in the distribution, tells us what point in the distribution the scores tend to group. The median is, thus, useful if our primary interest is in describing the relative ordering of students with respect to each other. In addition, the median is less sensitive to extreme scores (OUTLIERs) than the MEAN and this makes it a better measure than the mean for highly SKEWED DISTRIBUTIONs, whether these are of ordinal or interval scaled scores. Computing the median still ignores some information in the data because it reflects only the frequency of scores in the lower 50% of the distribution, without considering their mathematical values or considering the scores in the upper 50%.

see also MODE

Bachman 2004; Heiman 2011; Howell 2010; Kothari 2008; Porte 2010; Urdan 2010

median absolute deviation
also MAD

a MEASURE OF DISPERSION which plays an important role when trying to detect OUTLIERs. To compute it, first compute the sample MEDIAN, subtract it from every observed value, and then take absolute values.
Consider the 9 values:

12, 45, 23, 79, 19, 92, 30, 58, 132

the median is = 45, so $X_1 - M = 12 - 45 = 33$ and $X_2 - M = 0$. Continuing in this manner for all nine values yields:

33, 0, 22, 34, 26, 47, 15, 13, 87

The MAD is the median of the nine values just computed: 26.

Wilcox 2003

median location
see MEDIAN

median test
also **Mood's test, Mood's median test**
a NONPARAMETRIC TEST which is performed to test the HYPOTHESIS that two POPULATIONs have the same MEDIAN. The median test makes use of ranks and the BINOMIAL DISTRIBUTION to test hypotheses, i.e., where there are only two possible outcomes. It is used to determine whether the number of scores which fall either side of their common median differs for two UNRELATED SAMPLES. If the data of the two groups have the same or similar medians, we would expect that half of the subjects (or observations) in each of the groups would fall above and below the median of the combined groups. That is, we expect that if we find the median for all the subjects or all the observations, there would be as many from group 1 as from group 2 above the median and as many from each group below the median.
Cramer & Howitt 2004; Everitt & Skrondal 2010; Hatch & Lazaraton 1991; Sahai & Khurshid 2001

mediating variable
another term for INTERVENING VARIABLE

mediator variable
another term for INTERVENING VARIABLE

member checks
see INTERPRETIVE VALIDITY

memoing
see CONSTANT COMPARISON METHOD

mesokurtic
see KURTOSIS

meta-analysis
a term which refers to the statistical analysis of a large collection of analysis results from individual studies for the purpose of integrating the findings. Meta-analysis is a procedure that allows a researcher to systematically and statistically summarize the findings of several previous studies. In fact, meta-analysis refers to the analysis of the analyses. The term was introduced to describe a systematic approach to reviewing and synthesizing a large number of published research studies on a topic. The purpose of meta-analysis is to allow a research community to come to

some conclusion with respect to the validity of a HYPOTHESIS that is not based on one or two studies, but rather is based on a multitude of studies which have addressed the same general hypothesis. It connotes a rigorous alternative to the casual, narrative discussions of research studies which typify our attempts to make sense of the rapidly expanding research literature. It aims at determining a summery estimate of EFFECT SIZEs reported in the various studies, thus producing a combined superordinate result that synthesizes the individual studies. In most meta-analyses, researchers not only determine the degree to which certain variables are related, but also explore the factors that affect their relationship. For example, in looking across many studies, they may find that the relationship was generally stronger for male than for female participants, that it was stronger when certain kinds of measures were used, or that it was weaker when particular experimental conditions were present. Thus, not only is meta-analysis used to document relationships across studies, but it also can be used to explore factors that affect those relationships.

Generally, a meta-analyst, once having identified a set of research questions to investigate in a research domain (e.g., effectiveness of Spanish-English bilingual programs on Spanish first language children's academic performance in second language English), (a) searches for relevant studies, whether published or unpublished; (b) decides which studies to include in a meta-analysis, using a set of selection criteria; (c) codes each study for study characteristics; (d) calculates and then averages effect sizes from the studies; and (e) investigates relationships between study characteristics and effect sizes statistically.

Meta-analyses can be separated into two categories: integrative and interpretive. **Integrative meta-analysis** focuses on summarizing the data and is usually quantitative in nature (see QUANTITATIVE RESEARCH). **Interpretive meta-analysis** focuses on developing concepts and operationalizing concepts a priori. Interpretive analysis can be carried out using quantitative and qualitative approaches (see QUALITATIVE RESEARCH), does not have a priori concepts to test, and leads to the development of new interpretations from the analysis of multiple field studies. The goal is not to aggregate the data (e.g., determining and overall effect size) but to reinterpret. Quantitative meta-analysis reviews statistically a collection of analyses from related individual studies in order to provide a summarization or integration of the results. The core of this review is the calculation of an effect size. The effect size can be based on the difference between two groups divided by their pooled STANDARD DEVIATION or a CORRELATION between two variables. Qualitative meta-analysis also involves the synthesis of evidence from primary studies, but there are numerous forms of synthesis with different goals, though most are interpretive techniques.

Meta-analysis has three major advantages over a narrative review. Firstly, it allows the reviewer to quantify the trends that are contained in the literature by combining the effect sizes and combining the probabilities that have been found in a number of studies. Secondly, by combining the results of a number of studies the power of the statistical test (see STATISTICAL POWER) is increased. In this case, a number of non-significant findings that all show the same trend, may, when combined, prove to be significant. Thirdly, the process of preparing the results of previous research for a meta-analysis forces the reviewer to read the studies more thoroughly than would be the case for a narrative review.

📖 Best & Kahn 2006; Clark-Carter 2010; Dörnyei 2007; Given 2008; Richards & Schmidt 2010

meta-narrative

a term that can be understood in two ways: (1) as a narrative about narrative or (2) as a narrative above narrative. A narrative is a story that describes a particular sequence of events in the context of particular characters. The content and structure of narratives are deliberately (although sometimes unconsciously) selected to support a particular point of view and to encourage a particular interpretation or understanding. The analysis of narrative—that is, the narratives constructed in the course of thinking about narrative—creates meta-narratives. Similarly, researchers who use NARRATIVE ANALYSIS to study may construct meta-narratives in the course of their analyses.

Meta-narratives provide an organizing framework for knowledge and, through this mechanism, distinguish between knowledge that is legitimate and knowledge that is unjustified. People may also organize their experiences according to a meta-narrative. For example, the meta-narrative of psychoanalysis structures an individual's childhood memories differently from the meta-narrative of SYMBOLIC INTERACTIONISM. see also META-SYNTHESIS

📖 Given 2008

meta-synthesis

a term that refers to research approaches that integrate the collective products of extant bodies of QUALITATIVE RESEARCH findings using systematic, formal processes for the purpose of generating overarching inductively derived claims about phenomena of interest. Where sizeable bodies of published qualitative work exist within a field of study, meta-synthesis serves as an inquiry approach with the potential of generating comprehensive and substantial claims beyond those that can be warranted on the basis of individual qualitative studies. Meta-synthesis has become particularly popular in academic fields in which public policy is driven by reliance upon evidence because it offers the appeal of render-

ing the kinds of insights that qualitative research typically yields into more conclusive forms of knowledge within that evidentiary context.
see also META-NARRATIVE
📖 Given 2008

method
a section of a RESEARCH REPORT which describes what happened in the study. Method section should answer most of the Wh-questions. More specifically, this section should tell you (1) who participated in the study, including when and where (PARTICIPANTS), (2) what type of materials were used (MATERIALS), (3) what the participants were asked to do (PROCEDURES), and (4) how the analyses were performed (ANALYSES).
see also TITLE, ABSTRACT, INTRODUCTION, RESULTS, DISCUSSION, REFERENCES, APPENDIXES
📖 Brown 1988

method of least squares analysis
another term for LEAST SQUARES METHOD OF ANALYSIS

methodological triangulation
also **method triangulation**
a type of TRIANGULATION which uses the same method on different occasions or different methods on the same object of study. There are two categories of methodological triangulation: **within methods triangulation** and **between methods triangulation**. Triangulation within methods concerns the replication of a study as a check on RELIABILITY and theory confirmation. This form of triangulation is much less frequently used because it is limited to the use of just one method. Triangulation between methods involves the use of more than one method in the pursuit of a given objective. The between-methods type is a vehicle for cross validation when two or more distinct methods are found to be congruent and yield comparable data. This would involve the use of multiple methods to examine the same dimension of a research problem. For example, the effectiveness of a second language teacher may be studied by interviewing the teacher, observing his/her behavior, and evaluating performance records. Or, when interviews, related documents, and recollections of other participants produce the same description of an event or when a participant responds similarly to a question asked on three different occasions, one has evidence of CREDIBILITY.
Between-methods triangulation is the most conventional form and is used to test the data for the degree of EXTERNAL VALIDITY. Its frequent use is based on this fundamental assumption: The effectiveness of triangulation rests on the premise that the weaknesses in each single method will be compensated for by the counter-balancing strengths of another.

And, for all practical purposes, this type can be assumed to be the standard usage of triangulation.
see also DATA TRIANGULATION, INVESTIGATOR TRIANGULATION, THEORETICAL TRIANGULATION
📖 Ary et al. 2010; Cohen et al. 2011; Ridenour & Newman 2008

method triangulation
another term for METHODOLOGICAL TRIANGULATION

metric approach
see MULTIDIMENSIONAL SCALING

metric data
another term for CONTINUOUS DATA

metric variable
another term for CONTINUOUS VARIABLE

midsummary scores
those scores which are midway between values that cut off different fractions of the data in the upper and lower tails of the DISTRIBUTION. For example, one midsummary score might be midway between values cutting off the upper and lower eighths of the distribution; another might be midway between values cutting off the upper and lower fourths. If all of these midsummary scores equal the MEDIAN, it indicates that the distribution is symmetrical (see NORMAL DISTRIBUTION). If they are not all the same, the way they vary provides us with information about how the distribution departs from symmetry (see SKEWED DISTRIBUTION).
📖 Myers & Well 2003

minimal terminable unit
another term for T-UNIT

missing data
information that is not available for a subject (or case) about whom other information is available. Missing data are a nuisance to researchers and primarily result from errors in data collection or data entry or from the omission of answers by respondents. For example, missing data often occur when a respondent fails to answer one or more questions in a QUESTIONNAIRE. The researcher's challenge is to address the issues raised by missing data that affect the GENERALIZABILITY of the results. To do so, the researcher's primary concern is to identify the patterns and relationships underlying the missing data in order to maintain as close as possible the original distribution of values when any remedy is applied The extent

of missing data is a secondary issue in most instances, affecting the type of remedy applied. These patterns and relationships are a result of a *missing data process*, which is any systematic event external to the respondent (such as data entry errors or data collection problems) or any action on the part of the respondent (such as refusal to answer) that leads to missing values.
📖 Hair et al. 2010

mixed analysis of variance
also **mixed ANOVA, between-within ANOVA, split-plot ANOVA, mixed factorial ANOVA, mixed between-within ANOVA**
an analysis that contains both a BETWEEN-SUBJECTS and a WITHIN-SUBJECTS INDEPENDENT VARIABLE (IV). What is meant by a mixed ANOVA design is that it is a mixture between the same subjects and different subjects. To conduct a simple mixed between-within ANOVA, we need one between-subjects *categorical* IV (e.g., gender), one within-subjects categorical IV (e.g., time), and one *continuous* DEPENDENT VARIABLE (e.g., test scores). The ASSUMPTIONs for mixed ANOVA are similar to those for the REPEATED MEASURES ANOVA, except that the assumption of SPHERICITY must hold for levels of the within subjects variable at each level of between subjects variables. Thus, the F VALUE for the MAIN EFFECT of the between-subjects factor is unaffected by a lack of sphericity in the populations connected to the study. In contrast, the F values for the main effect of the within-subjects factor and for the INTERACTION are positively biased (i.e., turn out larger than they ought to) to the extent that the sphericity assumption is violated.

Imagine that experimenters want to compare the way that males and females rate their parents' IQs. In this design the IV gender which has two levels—male and female—is a between-subjects variable. The IV parent which has two levels—mother and father—is a within-subjects variable because each participant supplies data for each level of that variable.

It is possible to combine different numbers of IVs measured using different groups or the same groups to come up with **three-way, four-way,** or **n-way mixed ANOVAs**.

There is no *nonparametric* alternative to mixed ANOVA
📖 Clark-Carter 2010; Huck 2012; Pallant 2010

mixed ANOVA
another term for MIXED ANALYSIS OF VARIANCE

mixed between-within design
another term for MIXED DESIGN

mixed design
also **between-within design, split-plot design, mixed between-within design, mixed factorial design**

a design which involves two or more INDEPENDENT VARIABLEs (IVs) in which at least one of IVs is measured between-subjects (i.e., different subjects serve under each of the LEVELs of that IV) and at least one of the IVs is measured within-subjects (i.e., the same subjects or matched sets of subjects serve under all of the levels of that IV). In a **simple mixed design** (i.e., **two-way mixed design**), there are only two IVs, one a BETWEEN-SUBJECTS FACTOR and the other a WITHIN-SUBJECTS FACTOR; these variables are combined factorially. For example, you may want to investigate the impact of an INTERVENTION on students anxiety levels (using pretest and posttest), but you would also like to know whether the impact is different for males and females. In this case, you have two IVs: one is a between-subjects variable (gender: males/females); the other is a within-subjects variable (time of measurement: Time A/Time B). In this case, you would expose a group of both males and females to the intervention and measure their anxiety levels at Time A (pre-intervention) and again at Time B (after the intervention); this is a 2 × 2 (two-by-two) mixed factorial design with repeated measures on the second factor. The number of levels of each IV is not constrained by the design. Thus, we could have a 2 × 2, a 4 × 3, or even a 3 × 7 factorial design. Because there are two IVs, there are three effects of interest: the MAIN EFFECT of the between-subjects variable (A), the main effect of the within-subjects variable (B), and the two-way INTERACTION (A × B). Note that this is analogous to two-way BETWEEN-SUBJECTS and two-way WITHIN-SUBJECTS DESIGNs. Furthermore, the conceptual understanding of main effects and interactions in those designs carries forward to the simple mixed design. Main effects focus on the mean differences of the levels of each IV (e.g., A1 vs. A2) and interactions focus on whether or not the patterns of differences are parallel (e.g., A1 vs. A2 under B1 compared to A1 vs. A2 under B2). The primary difference between a simple mixed design and the between-subjects and within-subjects designs is in the way that the total variance of the DEPENDENT VARIABLE is partitioned. As is true for within-subjects designs, the total variance in a mixed design is divided into BETWEEN-SUBJECTS and WITHIN-SUBJECTS VARIANCE. The three effects of interest break out as follows:

- *The main effect of A:* The between-subjects variable A is subsumed in the between-subjects portion of the variance. It has its own between-subjects ERROR TERM that is used in computing the F RATIO associated with A.

- *The main effect of B*: The within-subjects variable B is subsumed in the within-subjects portion of the variance. It has its own within-subjects error term that is used in computing the F ratio associated with B. This error term is associated with the B factor and thus it is also used as an error term when computing the F ratio for the interaction effect.
- *The A × B interaction*: The interaction effect is subsumed in the within-subjects portion of the variance. It shares its within-subjects error term with the main effect of B.

Simple mixed designs have only two IVs and so, by definition, must have one of each type of variable. Complex mixed designs contain at least three IVs. For example, a **three-way mixed design** has two of one type and one of the other type of factor (e.g., two between-subjects factors and one within-subjects factor, or one between-subjects factor and two within-subjects factors). These designs are often called **higher order mixed design**s. Higher order mixed designs are specified by the number of between- and within-subjects factors they have. Generally, higher order mixed designs would follow the conventions of adding extra between-subjects or within-subjects factors.

📖 Gamst et al. 2008; Heiman 2011; Page et al. 2003; Pallant 2010; Sheskin 2011

mixed factorial design
another term for MIXED DESIGN

mixed methods research
also **multitrait-multimethod research, multi-methodological research, mixed model study**
a research approach for collecting, analyzing, and mixing *quantitative* and *qualitative* data at some stage of the research process within a single study in order to understand a research problem more completely. In mixed methods research, a researcher collects both numeric information (for example, through CLOSED-RESPONSE ITEMs on QUESTIONNAIREs) and text (from FACE-TO-FACE INTERVIEWs, picture descriptions, and so on) to better answer a study's research questions. The term mixing implies that the data or the findings are integrated and/or connected at one or several points within the study. The goal of mixed methods research is not to replace qualitative or quantitative approaches but, rather, to combine both approaches in creative ways that utilize the strengths of each within a single study. By mixing methods in ways that minimize weaknesses or ensure that the weaknesses of one approach do not overlap significantly with the weaknesses of another, the study is strengthened.

The most widely accepted notation system used in mixed methods designs, uses a plus sign (+) to indicate that the data collection and analysis of methods occur at the same time. An arrow (→) indicates that data collection and analysis occur in sequence. The *weight* or importance of the methods within the study should be denoted by using uppercase letters for prominence and lowercase letters to indicate less dominant methods. There are no specific rules that determine appropriate proportions of qualitative and quantitative research in a mixed methods study. Some researchers use parentheses to indicate methods that are embedded within other methods. The notation system rules are shown below:

Weighting priority
QUAL + QUAN (both are equally important)
QUAN + qual (quantitative approach is dominant)
QUAL + quan (qualitative approach is dominant)

Timing
QUAN → Qual (quantitative collection or analysis occurs first followed by qualitative collection/analysis)
QUAL → Quan (qualitative collection or analysis occurs first followed by quantitative collection/analysis)

Mixing
QUAL (quan)
QUAN (qual)

Mixed methods research has defined procedures for collecting, analyzing, and mixing quantitative and qualitative data in a study, based upon three main characteristics: (a) *timing*, (b) *weighting*, and (c) *mixing*. Timing refers to the sequence or order of the implementation of the quantitative and qualitative data collection and analysis procedures in the study when one phase builds on another. The two possible timing options include:

1) sequentially—collecting and analyzing the data one after the other (quantitative → qualitative, or qualitative → quantitative); or
2) concurrently—collecting and analyzing both quantitative and qualitative data at the same time (quantitative + qualitative).

Weighting refers to the relative importance or priority given to each type of data. The two possible weighting options include giving equal weight to the quantitative (QUAN) and qualitative (QUAL) data, or giving one type greater emphasis—to quantitative data (QUAN + qual) or qualitative data (QUAL + quan). When making the weighting decision, there are a number of things to consider: What is more strongly emphasized in the purpose statement, exploration (qualitative), or prediction (quantitative)? Which data collection process, quantitative or qualitative, is most central to the study? Which data analysis procedures, quantitative or qualitative, are more sophisticated, complex, and discussed more extensively when the study is presented?

Mixing refers to how the two methods, quantitative or qualitative, are integrated within the study. It is an essential component of mixed methods research. Mixing quantitative and qualitative data can occur at different stages in the study: during the data collection, the data analysis, or the interpretation of results. Deciding on how to mix depends on the purpose of the study, its design, and the strategies used for data collection and analysis. If the purpose of the study is to explain quantitative results that were obtained first, qualitative data can be collected after quantitative data by interviewing (or administering an open-response questionnaire) to a small number of participants, based on these quantitative results. Mixing here occurs at two points: when selecting participants for interview and creating interview questions grounded in the statistical results (connecting the quantitative and qualitative phases), and at the interpretation stage of the study, when discussing the results from the two phases. If the purpose of the study is to develop a closed-response questionnaire or SURVEY grounded in the views of the participants, first qualitative data is collected through interviews and then the questionnaire is developed; then quantitative data is collected using this questionnaire. Mixing here occurs while analyzing the qualitative data for codes and themes and transforming them into questionnaire items and scales. If the purpose of the study is to compare the quantitative and qualitative results, both quantitative and qualitative data are collected and analyzed separately. Mixing here occurs at the data interpretation stage, when the results from two data sets are compared.

Several arguments have been put forward about the value of mixing methods. The most important ones are:

1) *Increasing the strengths while eliminating the weaknesses.* The main attraction of mixed method research has been the fact that by using both qualitative and quantitative approaches researchers can bring out the best of paradigms, thereby combining qualitative and quantitative research strength. This is further augmented by the potential that the strengths of one method can be utilized to overcome the weaknesses of another method used in the study.
2) *Multi-level analysis of complex issues.* It has been suggested that the researchers can gain a better understanding of a complex phenomenon by converging numeric trends from quantitative data and specific details from qualitative data. Words can be used to add meaning to numbers and numbers can be used to add precision to words. It is

easy to think of situations in applied linguistics when the researchers are interested at the same time in both the exact nature (i.e., qualitative) and the distribution (i.e., quantitative) of a phenomenon (e.g., why do some teenage boys consider modern language learning girlish and how extensive is this perception. Mixed methods research is particularly appropriate for such multi-level analyses because it allows investigators to obtain data about both the individual and the broader societal context.

3) *Improved validity.* Mixed methods research has a unique potential to produce evidence for the validity of research outcomes through the convergence and correlation of the findings. Indeed improving the validity of research has been at the heart of the notion of triangulation. Corresponding evidence obtained through multiple methods can also increase the GENERALIZABILITY of the results.

4) *Reaching multiple audiences.* A welcome benefit of combining qualitative and quantitative methods is that the final results are usually acceptable for a larger audience than those of a monomethod study would be. A well-executed mixed method study has multiple selling points and can offer something to everybody, regardless of the paradigmatic orientation of the person.

However, there are also a number of weaknesses. It is difficult for a single researcher to carry out both quantitative and qualitative research. It is difficult to have equal skill sets in both methods, and especially if data are collected simultaneously, there is a great time commitment. The researcher must be able to understand the complexities of both approaches so as to make wise decisions about how they can appropriately be mixed. Conducting a mixed methods study is likely to be more expensive than using a single approach. Quantitizing and qualitizing data can have its own problems. Also, interpreting conflicting results may be difficult.

Although many models and designs have been discussed in the mixed methods literature, the four mixed methods designs most frequently used are EXPLANATORY DESIGN, EXPLORATORY DESIGN, TRIANGULATION DESIGN, and EMBEDDED DESIGN.

📖 Ary et al. 2010; Dörnyei 2007; Heigham & Croker 2009; Ridenour & Newman 2008

mixed model study
another term for MIXED METHODS RESEARCH

mixed multivariate analysis of variance
also **mixed MANOVA, doubly-multivariate design**
an analysis with both multiple DEPENDENT VARIABLEs (DVs) and WITHIN-SUBJECTS FACTORs. Mixed multivariate analysis of variance (mixed MANOVA) is mixed because there is a BETWEEN-GROUPS INDEPENDENT

VARIABLE (e.g., gender) and a within-groups independent variable (e.g., time). It is MANOVA because these are two (or more) DVs. Mixed MANOVAs are one way to analyze experimental studies that have more than one DV.
📖 Leech et al. 2005; Page et al. 2003

mixed normal distribution
also contaminated normal distribution

a classic way of illustrating some of the more important effects of nonnormality. Consider a situation where we have two subpopulations of individuals or things. Assume each subpopulation has a NORMAL DISTRIBUTION but that they differ in terms of their MEANs or VARIANCEs or both. When we mix the two populations together we get what is called a mixed, or contaminated, normal. Generally, mixed normals fall outside the class of normal distributions.

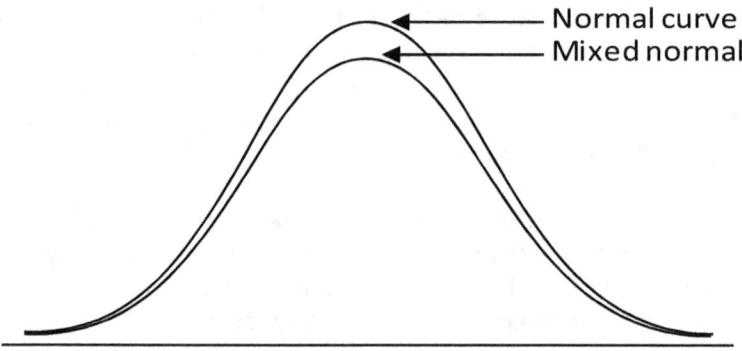

Figure M.2. An Example of Mixed Normal Distribution

As shown in Figure M.2, when the two normals mixed together have a common mean but unequal variances, the resulting probability curve is again symmetric about the mean, but even then the mixed normal is not a normal curve. Very small departures from normality can greatly influence the value of the population variance. The contaminated normal illustrates that two distributions can have substantially different variances even though their probability curves are very similar.
📖 Wilcox 2003

MLE
an abbreviation for MAXIMUM LIKELIHOOD ESTIMATE

Mo
an abbreviation for MODE

mode
 also **Mo**

a MEASURE OF CENTRAL TENDENCY which is the most frequently occurring score in a DISTRIBUTION of scores. Mode simply indicates which score in the distribution occurs most often, or has the highest frequency. In the following distribution of scores the mode is 5, since it occurs two times, whereas all other scores occur only once: 0, 1, 2, 5, 5, 8, 10. When a polygon has one hump, such as on the NORMAL CURVE, the distribution is called **unimodal**, indicating that one score qualifies as the mode. A distribution with more than one mode is referred to as a **multimodal distribution**. If it happens that two scores both occur with the highest frequency, the distribution would be described as a **bimodal distribution** (see Figure M.3), which represents one type of multimodal distribution. For example, consider the scores 2, 3, 4, 5, 5, 5, 6, 7, 8, 9, 9, 9, 10, 11, and 12. Here two scores, 5 and 9, are tied for the most frequently occurring score. This distribution is plotted in Figure M.3. Such a distribution was called bimodal because it has two modes.

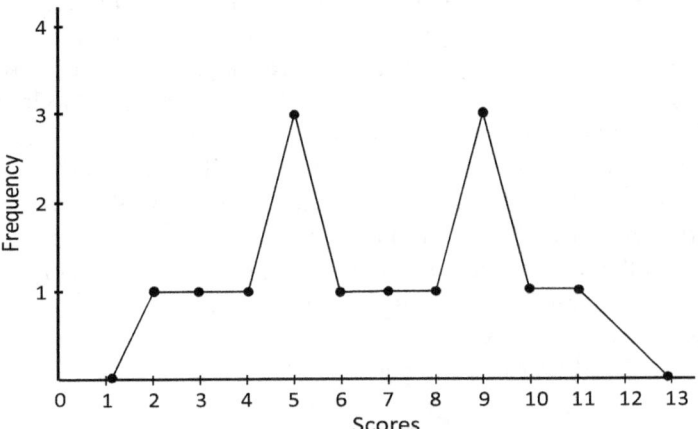

Figure M.3. A Bimodal Distribution

The mode(s) of a distribution can be pictured graphically as the peaks in the distribution. A NORMAL DISTRIBUTION has only one peak. A bimodal distribution has two distinct peaks, each reflecting relatively high-frequency scores. When the frequencies of all scores are the same the distribution is called **rectangular** or **flat**, as shown in Figure M.4. Sometimes the term **antimode** is used to denote the opposite of a mode in the sense that it corresponds to a (local) minimum frequency.

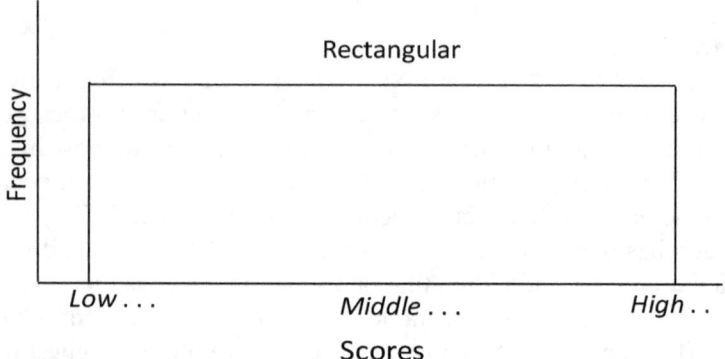

Figure M.4. A Rectangular Distribution

The mode is the appropriate indicator of grouping if the numbers we are describing constitute a NOMINAL SCALE. While it is relatively rare for test scores to be nominal, we sometimes use numbers to represent other variables that may be of interest to us, such as sex, native language, or group, as in particular class or section in multisection course. For variable such as these, the appropriate indicator of grouping is the mode, which is sometimes reported as a **percentage of the total frequency**. There are, however, two potential limitations with the mode. First, the distribution may contain many scores that are all tied at the same highest frequency. With more than two modes, we fail to summarize the data. In the most extreme case, we might obtain a **rectangular distribution**. A second problem is that the mode does not take into account any scores other than the most frequent score(s), so it may not accurately summarize where most scores in the distribution are located.

see also MEAN, MEDIAN

📖 Bachman 2004; Heiman 2011; Porte 2010; Sheskin 2011

model

a construct or formulation that provides a description of the assumed structure of a set of data. A model involves a set of assumptions about relationships used to describe the data structure in a manner that may aid in understanding the process assumed to have generated the data.

📖 Sahai & Khurshid 2001

moderating variable

another term for MODERATOR VARIABLE

moderator variable

also **moderating variable**

a special type of INDEPENDENT VARIABLE (IV) that the researcher has chosen to determine how, if at all, the relationship between the independent and DEPENDENT VARIABLEs (DVs) is affected, or moderated, by the moderator variable. Thus, if an experimenter thinks that the relationship between variables X and Y might be altered in some way by a third variable Z, then Z could be included in the study as a moderator variable. For example you may decide to study the degree to which the relationship between one year of Spanish study (the IV) and proficiency in Spanish (the DV) differed for males and females (the moderator variable). The essential difference between IV and moderator variables lies in how the researcher views each in the study. For IVs, the concern is with their direct relationship to the DV, whereas for moderator variables, the concern is with their effect on that relationship.

see also INTERVENING VARIABLE, CATEGORICAL VARIABLE, CONTINUOUS VARIABLE, EXTRANEOUS VARIABLE, CONFOUNDING VARIABLE

Brown 1988; Fraenkel & Wallen 2009

modernism

the rejection of tradition and authority in favor of reason, science, and objectivity, closely associated with Western thought and the scientific method. From the point of view of POSTMODERNISM, modernism is not contemporary, but out of date.

see also POSITIVISM

Richards & Schmidt 2010

molar behavior

see OBSERVATION

molecular behavior

see OBSERVATION

monotonic regression

a type of REGRESSION ANALYSIS that falls within the general category of *nonparametric* regression analysis. The latter type of analysis is based on the fact that if two variables (which are represented by interval/ratio data) are monotonically related to one another, the rankings on the variables will be linearly related to one another.

see SPEARMAN RANK ORDER CORRELATION COEFFICIENT

Sheskin 2011

monotonic relationship

see SPEARMAN RANK ORDER CORRELATION COEFFICIENT

Monte Carlo method
also **Monte Carlo simulation**
a term that has most commonly been used in the solution of any mathematical and statistical problem by performing sampling experiments involving generation of random numbers from a given PROBABILITY DISTRIBUTION. It provides an empirical method of finding solutions to many mathematical and statistical problems for which no simple analytical solutions are available. Thus, any statistical test which is based on calculating the probability of a variety of outcomes consequent of randomly allocating a set of scores is a Monte Carlo method.
see also BOOTSTRAP
📖 Cramer & Howitt 2004; Everitt & Skrondal 2010; Sahai & Khurshid 2001

Monte Carlo simulation
another term for MONTE CARLO METHOD

Mood's median test
another term for MEDIAN TEST

Mood's test
another term for MEDIAN TEST

mortality
also **participant mortality, attrition, subject attrition, dropout, experimental mortality, differential attrition**
a threat to INTERNAL VALIDITY which refers to students who self-select themselves out of a group by dropping out of the study for any number of reasons, including transfer to another institution, serious illness or dropping out of school or universities. In essence, participants drop out of the study in a systematic and nonrandom way that can affect the original composition of groups formed for the purposes of the study. The potential net result of attrition is that the effects of the INDEPENDENT VARIABLE might be due to the loss of participants and not to the manipulation of the independent variable. People who drop out of a study often differ from those who remain in ways that distort research findings. For example, a researcher might lose some beginning-level second language learners from his/her sample because they lose interest and drop out. This might leave the study not only with proportionally more participants of higher ability levels, but with participants who have higher motivation.

Sometimes researchers drop participants from groups to produce equal numbers in each group (see CELL). The reason they do this is that many statistical procedures are easier to interpret when there are equal cell sizes. However, you want to check whether participants are dropped randomly. If this is done, there is less chance that a BIAS may occur. Another caveat is that, when dealing with smaller numbers of participants, the loss of even one participant can have a significant impact on the results. The conclusion is that when you read a research article, give attention to any irregularities in the sample. There should be clear documentation to show that the results of the study were not contaminated by any participant attrition.

see also TESTING EFFECT, INSTRUMENTATION, DIFFERENTIAL SELECTION, HISTORY, MATURATION, STATISTICAL REGRESSION
📖 Perry 2011

Moses test

a NONPARAMETRIC TEST for equal variability which can be employed in a HYPOTHESIS TESTING situation involving two INDEPENDENT SAMPLES. The Moses test is based on the following assumptions:

a) each sample has been randomly selected from the population it represents;
b) the two samples are independent of one another;
c) the original scores obtained for each of the subjects are in the format of interval/ratio data, and the DEPENDENT VARIABLE is a CONTINUOUS VARIABLE; and
d) the underlying populations from which the samples are derived are similar in shape.

The major difference between the Moses test and the SIEGEL-TUKEY TEST is that the Moses test does not assume that the two populations from which the samples are derived have equal medians (which is an assumption underlying the Siegel-Tukey test). Moses test is categorized as a test of ordinal data, by virtue of the fact that a ranking procedure constitutes a critical part of the test protocol.

see also KLOTZ TEST, ANSARI-BRADLEY TEST, CONOVER TEST
📖 Sheskin 2011

MR

an abbreviation for MULTIPLE REGRESSION

MRT

an abbreviation for DUNCAN'S NEW MULTIPLE RANGE TEST

MS

an abbreviation for MEAN SQUARE

MSA
an abbreviation for MEASURE OF SAMPLING ADEQUACY

mu (μ)
an abbreviation for POPULATION MEAN

multicollinearity
also collinearity
the presence of overlap or CORRELATION among the INDEPENDENT VARIABLES (IVs) or predictors. Multicollinearity creates common (shared) variance between IVs, thus decreasing the ability to predict the DEPENDENT VARIABLE or criterion as well as ascertain the relative roles of each IV. As multicollinearity increases, the total variance explained decreases. Moreover, the amount of unique (separate) variance for the IVs is reduced to levels that make estimation of their individual effects quite problematic. The assumption of multicollinearity is a problem if the variables in a study are too highly interrelated. If there is multicollinearity it means that the variables are too closely related and thus they should not be entered into the study because they explain the same part of the variance. This assumption, often applied in statistical procedures which are based on correlation and prediction (e.g., MULTIPLE REGRESSION), can easily be checked by examining a CORRELATION MATRIX for each pair of variables in a study.

Identifying multicollinearity can be a problem as, even if no two variables correlate highly multicollinearity can still be present because a combination of predictor variables might account for the variance in one of the predictor variables. In order to detect multicollinearity, a number of statistics are available. Two common ones, which are directly related, are **tolerance** and **variance inflation factor** (VIF). Tolerance is the proportion of variance in a predictor variable that is not predicted by the other predictor variables. It can be used to protect against multicollinearity. To find tolerance a multiple regression is conducted with the predictor variable of interest treated as the dependent variable or criterion which is then regressed on the other predictor variables. The R SQUARE (R^2) from that regression is put into the following equation:

$$\text{Tolerance} = 1 - R^2$$

A tolerance of 0 means that the IV under consideration is a perfect linear combination of IVs already in the model. A tolerance of 1 means that an IV is totally independent of other variables already in the model.

A second measure of multicollinearity is VIF, which is calculated simply as the inverse of the tolerance value. A large VIF suggests multicollinearity among the IVs. It is computed from the following equation:

Variance inflation factor = 1/tolerance

Thus, instances of higher degrees of multicollinearity are reflected in lower tolerance values and higher VIF values. There are a number of ways in which multicollinearity can be dealt with. The simplest is to remove one or more of the offending variables and re-run the analysis. It is also possible to create composite predictor variables by combining the problematic predictor variables either by adding them or by using PRINCIPAL COMPONENTS ANALYSIS.

see also SINGULARITY

📖 Clark-Carter 2010; Hair et al. 2010; Kirk 2008; Larson-Hall 2010

multidimensional chi-square test
another term for CHI-SQUARE TEST OF INDEPENDENCE

multidimensional contingency table
see CONTINGENCY TABLE

multidimensional scaling
also **MDS**

a class of *multivariate* techniques involving a graphical representation of statistical similarities or differences with a view to trace a map of how individuals' attitudes or characteristics cluster. The procedure consists of plotting pairs of values with highest CORRELATIONs closest together and those with the lowest correlations farther apart. Multidimensional scaling (MDS) provides useful methodology for portraying subjective judgments of diverse kinds. It is used when all the variables in a study are to be analyzed simultaneously and all such variables happen to be independent. The underlying assumption in MDS is that respondents perceive a set of objects as being more or less similar to one another on a number of dimensions (usually uncorrelated with one another) instead of only one. Through MDS techniques one can represent geometrically the locations and interrelationships among a set of points. In fact, these techniques attempt to locate the points, given the information about a set of interpoint distances, in space of one or more dimensions such as to best summarize the information contained in the interpoint distances. The distances in the solution space then optimally reflect the distances contained in the input data. For instance, if objects, say X and Y, are thought of by the respondent as being most similar as compared to all other possible pairs of objects, MDS techniques will position objects X and Y in such a way that the distance between them in multidimensional space is shorter than that between any two other objects.

MDS can be considered to be an alternative to FACTOR ANALYSIS. In general, the goal of the analysis is to detect meaningful underlying dimensions that allow the researcher to explain observed similarities or dissimilarities (distances) between the investigated objects. In factor analysis, the similarities between objects (e.g., variables) are expressed in the CORRELATION MATRIX. With MDS, you can analyze any kind of similarity or dissimilarity matrix, in addition to correlation matrices.

Two approaches, the metric and the non-metric approach, are usually talked about in the context of MDS. The **metric approach** to MDS treats the input data as INTERVAL SCALE data and solves applying statistical methods for the additive constant which minimizes the dimensionality of the solution space. This approach utilizes all the information in the data in obtaining a solution. The data (i.e., the metric similarities of the objects) are often obtained on a bipolar similarity scale on which pairs of objects are rated one at a time. If the data reflect exact distances between real objects, their solution will reproduce the set of interpoint distances. But as the true and real data are rarely available, we require random and systematic procedures for obtaining a solution. Generally, the judged similarities among a set of objects are statistically transformed into distances by placing those objects in a multidimensional space of some dimensionality.

The **non-metric approach** first gathers the non-metric similarities by asking respondents to rank order all possible pairs that can be obtained from a set of objects. Such non-metric data is then transformed into some arbitrary metric space and then the solution is obtained by reducing the dimensionality. In other words, this non-metric approach seeks a representation of points in a space of minimum dimensionality such that the rank order of the interpoint distances in the solution space maximally corresponds to that of the data. This is achieved by requiring only that the distances in the solution be monotone with the input data. The non-metric approach has come into prominence during the sixties with the coming into existence of high speed computers to generate metric solutions for ordinal input data.

The significance of MDS lies in the fact that it enables the researcher to study the perceptual structure of a set of stimuli and the cognitive processes underlying the development of this structure. Psychologists, for example, employ MDS techniques in an effort to scale psychophysical stimuli and to determine appropriate labels for the dimensions along which these stimuli vary. The MDS techniques, in fact, do away with the need in the data collection process to specify the attribute(s) along which the several brands, say of a particular product, may be compared as ultimately the MDS analysis itself reveals such attribute(s) that presumably underlie the expressed relative similarities among objects. Thus, MDS is an important tool in attitude measurement and the techniques falling under MDS promise a great advance from a series of unidimensional meas-

urements (e.g., a distribution of intensities of feeling towards single attribute), to a perceptual mapping in multidimensional space of objects. In spite of all the merits stated above, the MDS is not widely used because of the computation complications involved under it. Many of its methods are quite laborious in terms of both the collection of data and the subsequent analyses.
also PRINCIPLE COMPONENTS ANALYSIS
📖 Hatch & Lazaraton 1991; Kothari 2008

multifactor ANOVA
another term for FACTORIAL ANOVA

multifactor design
another term for FACTORIAL DESIGN

multilevel modeling
see NESTED DESIGN

multi-methodological research
another term for MIXED METHODS RESEARCH

multimodal distribution
see MODE

multinomial logistic regression
see LOGISTIC REGRESSION

multinomial variable
see CATEGORICAL VARIABLE

multi-phase sampling
a type of PROBABILITY SAMPLING in which there is a single unifying purpose throughout the sampling. In a multi-phase sample, the purposes change at each phase, for example, at phase one the selection of the sample might be based on the criterion of geography (e.g., students living in a particular region); phase two might be based on an economic criterion (e.g., schools whose budgets are administered in markedly different ways); phase three might be based on a political criterion (e.g., schools whose students are drawn from areas with a tradition of support for a particular political party), and so on. What is evident here is that the sample population will change at each phase of the research
📖 Cohen et al. 2011

multiple analysis of covariance
another term for MULTIVARIATE ANALYSIS OF COVARIANCE

multiple-baseline across-behaviors design
see SINGLE-SUBJECT MULTIPLE-BASELINE DESIGN

multiple-baseline across-participants design
see SINGLE-SUBJECT MULTIPLE-BASELINE DESIGN

multiple-baseline across-settings design
see SINGLE-SUBJECT MULTIPLE-BASELINE DESIGN

multiple baseline design
another term for SINGLE-SUBJECT MULTIPLE-BASELINE DESIGN

multiple case study
see CASE STUDY

multiple-choice item
a CLOSED-FORM ITEM which is made up of an *item stem*, or the main part of the item at the top, a *correct answer*, which is obviously the choice (usually, a, b, c, or d) that will be counted correct, and the *distractors*, which are those choices that will be counted as incorrect. These incorrect choices are called distractors because they should distract, or divert respondents' attention away from the correct answer if they really do not know which is correct. The term *options* refers collectively to all the alternative choices presented to the respondents including the correct answer and the distractors. The following is an example:

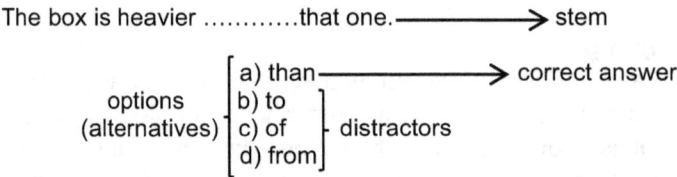

The appropriate selection and arrangement of suitable multiple-choice items on a test can be best accomplished by measuring items against three indices: ITEM FACILITY, ITEM DISCRIMINATION, and DISTRACTOR ANALYSIS.

see also DICHOTOMOUS QUESTION, RATIO DATA QUESTION, MATRIX QUESTIONS, CONSTANT SUM QUESTIONS, RANK ORDER QUESTION, CONTINGENCY QUESTION

📖 Brown 2005, 2010; Farhady et al. 1995

multiple coefficient of determination
another term for COEFFICIENT OF MULTIPLE DETERMINATION

multiple comparison test
another term for POST HOC TEST

multiple correlation
another term for MULTIPLE CORRELATION COEFFICIENT

multiple correlation coefficient
also **coefficient of multiple correlation, multiple correlation, multiple R, R**
a measure of the degree of linear association between multiple INDEPENDENT VARIABLEs or predictors, as a group, and the DEPENDENT VARIABLE or criterion simultaneously. Multiple correlation is used in MULTIPLE REGRESSION. In multiple regression a criterion variable is predicted using a multiplicity of predictor variables. For example, in order to predict IQ, the predictor variables might be social class, educational achievement and gender. For every individual, using these predictors, it is possible to make a prediction of the most likely value of their IQ based on these predictors. Quite simply, the multiple correlation is the correlation between the actual IQ scores of the individuals in the sample and the scores predicted for them by applying the multiple regression equation with these three predictors.
The computed multiple correlation coefficient is represented by the notation R. A computed value of R must fall within the range 0 to +1. Unlike PEARSON r value which is computed for two variables, the multiple correlation coefficient cannot be a negative number. The closer the value of R is to 1, the stronger the linear relationship between the criterion variable and the predictor variables, whereas the closer it is to 0, the weaker the linear relationship. Just as a PEARSON CORRELATION COEFFICIENT can be squared to indicate the percentage of variance in one variable that is accounted for by another (COEFFICIENT OF DETERMINATION), a multiple correlation coefficient can be squared to show the percentage of variance in the criterion variable that can be accounted for by the set of predictor variables. This **R^2**, (read as '**R square**') which is the square of the multiple correlation coefficient, is referred to as the **coefficient of multiple determination** (also called **multiple coefficient of determination, squared multiple correlation**). This proportion can be reexpressed as a percentage by multiplying the proportion by 100. It is commonly used in multiple regression to represent the proportion of variance in a criterion variable that is shared with or explained by two or more predictor variables.

see also CORRELATION, CORRELATION COEFFICIENT, PARTIAL CORRELATION, CANONICAL CORRELATION, *F* RATIO
 Cramer & Howitt 2004; Leary 2011

multiple discriminant analysis
see DISCRIMINANT FUNCTION ANALYSIS

multiple-I design
a variation of SINGLE-SUBJECT EXPERIMENTAL DESIGN in which several LEVELs of the INDEPENDENT VARIABLE (IV) are administered in succession, often with a baseline period between each administration. In such a design, the researcher obtains a baseline (A), then introduces one level of the IV (i.e., TREATMENT) (B) for a certain period of time. Then, this level is removed and another level of the IV is introduced (C). Of course, we could continue this procedure to create an **ABCDEFG design**. Often, researchers insert a baseline period between each successive introduction of a level of the IV, resulting in an **ABACA design**. After obtaining a baseline (A), the researcher introduces one level of the IV (B), then withdraws it as in an ABA design. Then a second level of the IV is introduced (C), then withdrawn (A). We could continue to manipulate the IV by introducing new levels of it, returning to baseline each time. Sometimes combinations of treatments are administered at each phase of the study.
 Ary et al. 2010; Leary 2011

multiple-occasions reliability
another term for TEST-RETEST RELIABILITY

multiple *R*
another term for MULTIPLE CORRELATION COEFFICIENT

multiple regression
also **MR**
a family of statistical techniques and an extension of SIMPLE REGRESSION which is employed to explore the relationship between one *continuous* DEPENDENT VARIABLE or criterion and a number of INDEPENDENT VARIABLES or predictors (usually *continuous*). Multiple regression (MR) is used for estimating or predicting a value for one criterion variable from two or more predictors. The researcher, thus, is concerned with multiple CORRELATION among a set of variables. The strength of the association between multiple predictor variables is determined by MULTIPLE CORRELATION COEFFICIENT.
MR analysis allows you to see:

a) how much the predictor variables, as a group, are related to the criterion variable,
b) the strength of the relationship between each predictor variable and the criterion variable while controlling for the other predictor variables in the model,
c) the relative strength of each predictor variable, and
d) whether there are INTERACTION EFFECTs between the predictor variables.

However, you have to be cautious: Variables may interact with each other and may be intercorrelated (see MULTICOLLINEARITY). The Figure M.5 shows graphically how, for example, the TOEFL score in English might be explained by 'hours of study', 'Modern Language Aptitude Test (MLAT) score', and 'personality.' What we see is that there are overlapping areas of variance among the predictor variables as well as with the criterion variable (the TOEFL score). For example, the score on the MLAT may correlate in part with how many hours an individual studies per week as well as with some part of the personality measure.

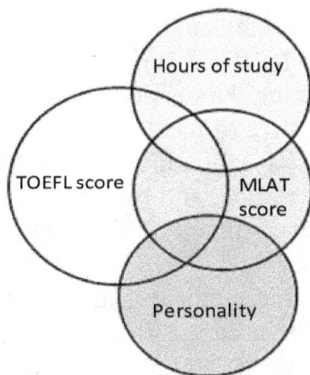

Figure M.5. Schematic Representation of Multiple Regression

MR makes a number of ASSUMPTIONS about the data: It does not like MULTICOLLINEARITY or SINGULARITY, and these certainly do not contribute to a good regression model; it is very sensitive to OUTLIERs (very high or very low scores); checking for extreme scores should be part of the initial DATA SCREENing process; others include NORMALITY, LINEARITY, and HOMOSCEDASTICITY.

There are two main general uses to this test. One use is to determine the strength and the direction of the linear association between criterion and a predictor controlling for the association of the predictors with each other and the criterion. The strength of the association is expressed in terms of the size of either the STANDARDIZED PARTIAL REGRESSION COEFFICIENT or the *unstandardized partial regression coefficient* which is symbolized by the small Greek letter β and its capital equivalent B respectively. Another use of MR is to determine how much of the VARIANCE in the criterion is accounted for by particular predictors. A multiple correlation coefficient (R) can be squared (i.e., R^2) to show the percentage of variance in the criterion variable that can be accounted for by the set of predictor variables.

Although MR analysis may result in a mechanism for reasonably accurate predictions, it does not provide sufficient control over the variables under study to allow a researcher to draw conclusions with regard to cause and effect. As is the case with *bivariate* correlation (correlation between two variables), multivariate correlation is not immune to the potential impact of EXTRANEOUS VARIABLEs that may be critical in understanding the causal relationship between the variables under study. It should be noted that there is a procedure called PATH ANALYSIS that employs correlational information to evaluate causal relationships between variables. Therefore, it is recommended that the resulting regression model be cross-validated. Minimally, this means replicating the results of the analysis on two subsamples, each representing a different half of the original SAMPLE. An even more desirable strategy is replicating the results on one or more INDEPENDENT SAMPLES that are representative of the POPULATION to which one wishes to apply the model. By cross-validating a model, one can demonstrate that it generates consistent results, and will thus be of practical value in making predictions among members of the reference population upon which the model is based.

MR can be classified as an intermediate method, somewhere between the bivariate methods of correlation and simple regression and multivariate methods such as CANONICAL CORRELATION. It differs from correlation and simple regression in that MR has more than one IV. It differs from canonical correlation in that MR is limited to just a single outcome or DV. MR differs from other predictive methods of DISCRIMINANT FUNCTION ANALYSIS (DFA) and LOGISTIC REGRESSION (LR) because both DFA and LR are used with a *categorical* dependent variable.

There are a number of different types of MR analyses that can be used, depending on the orders in which data on the independent variables can be entered into the analysis. The three main types of MR analyses are: STANDARD MULTIPLE REGRESSION, SEQUENTIAL MULTIPLE REGRESSION, and STATISTICAL MULTIPLE REGRESSION.

📖 Cohen et al. 2011; Cramer & Howitt 2004; Harlow 2005; Ho 2006; Pallant 2010; Sheskin 2011; Tabachnick & Fidell 2007; Urdan 2010

multiple time-series design
another term for CONTROL GROUP TIME SERIES DESIGN

multiple-treatment interaction
a threat to EXTERNAL VALIDITY. Some studies expose participants to multiple TREATMENTs that are part of some overarching treatment or simply expose them to more than one treatment. When this occurs, it might be difficult to determine which treatment resulted in any difference that might be found. For example, a researcher conducts a study that hopes to determine the effect that attending a private school has on achievement. In reality, a private school might include many different treatment components, all of which could affect achievement. For example, a private school might have much smaller class sizes and school uniforms. At the end of the study, the private school students seem to be outperforming their counterparts in public school classes. Could the results be generalizable to all private schools or just private schools with the same treatment components as the one under investigation? Multiple treatment interactions can be controlled by limiting the number of treatments delivered or delivering different treatments at different times. If one treatment has many components, seek out comparison groups receiving different components. For example, one might compare private schools that have smaller class sizes with those that have school uniforms.
see also SPECIFICITY OF VARIABLES, TREATMENT DIFFUSION, RESEARCHER EFFECT, HALO EFFECT, HAWTHORNE EFFECT, NOVELTY EFFECT, PRETEST-TREATMENT INTERACTION
📖 Lodico et al. 2010

multiple treatment interference
another term for ORDER EFFECT

multiple *t*-test
a test which is used to compare two or more pairs of MEANs. One option a researcher has available after computing an OMNIBUS F TEST is to run multiple t-tests (specifically INDEPENDENT SAMPLES t-TEST), in order to determine whether there is a significant difference between any of the pairs of means that can be contrasted. Multiple t-tests should only be employed for PLANNED COMPARISONs. Since multiple t-tests are only employed for planned comparisons, they can be conducted regardless of whether or not the omnibus F value is significant. Since multiple t-tests and FISHER'S LSD test are computationally equivalent, the term multiple t-tests/Fisher's LSD test will refer to a computational procedure which

can be employed for both planned and UNPLANNED COMPARISONs that does not adjust the value of FAMILYWISE ERROR RATE.
📖 Sheskin 2011

multistage random sampling
see MULTISTAGE SAMPLING

multistage sampling
a type of PROBABILITY SAMPLING and a further development of CLUSTER SAMPLING in which an attempt is made to reduce the geographical area covered. In multistage sampling, the researchers sequentially sample clusters from within clusters before choosing the final sample of participants. That is, the researchers begin by sampling large clusters, then sample smaller clusters from within the large clusters, then sample even smaller clusters, and finally obtain their sample of participants. Multistage sampling, in fact, involves selecting the sample in stages, i.e., taking samples from samples. This technique is applied in big inquiries extending to a considerably large geographical area like an entire country.

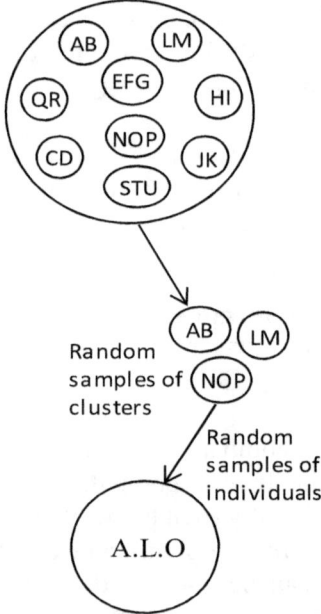

Figure M.6. Schematic Representation of a Two-Stage Sampling

Under multistage sampling the first stage may be to select large primary SAMPLING UNITs such as states, then cities, and then districts. In the next stage, we choose several particular schools from the selected districts.

We then select particular classrooms from the selected schools, and finally randomly sample students from each classroom. For example, in a two-stage random sampling, rather than randomly selecting 100 students from a population of 3,000 high school students located in 100 classes, the researcher might decide to select 25 classes randomly from the population of 100 classes and then randomly select 4 students from each class. This is much less time-consuming than visiting most of the 100 classes (see Figure M.6). If the technique of random-sampling is applied at all stages, the sampling procedure is described as **multistage random sampling**.

There are two advantages of this sampling design: (a) It is easier to administer than most single stage designs mainly because of the fact that SAMPLING FRAME under multistage sampling is developed in partial units; (b) a large number of units can be sampled for a given cost under multistage sampling because of sequential clustering, whereas this is not possible in most of the simple designs.

Cohen et al. 2011; Kothari 2008; Leary 2011

multitrait-multimethod research
another term for MIXED METHODS RESEARCH

multivariable analysis
see MULTIVARIATE ANALYSIS

multivariate analysis
a class of statistical methods and techniques which involve multiple INDEPENDENT VARIABLEs (IVs) or DEPENDENT VARIABLEs (DVs) in a single relationship or set of relationships. Multivariate analyses are complex group of statistical approaches and an extension of BIVARIATE ANALYSIS that are increasingly used for analyzing complicated data sets. They provide analysis when there are many IVs and/or many DVs, all correlated with one another to varying degrees. For example, if we were measuring a student's language proficiency and tests were given for reading, writing, and grammar, the resulting information would be multivariate data because it is based on three separate scores (three variables). Sometimes, the term **multivariable analysis** is used in contradistinction to multivariate analysis. When there are several IVs, but only a single DV, the term *multiple* or *multivariable* is preferable to multivariate.

With multiple DVs, a problem of inflated error rate (see TYPE I ERROR) arises if each DV is tested separately. Further, at least some of the DVs are likely to be correlated with each other, so separate tests of each DV reanalyze some of the same variance. Thus, multivariate tests are used.

A MULTIVARIATE ANALYSIS OF VARIANCE may be an appropriate way to analyze multivariate data. Other forms of multivariate analysis which are

useful if a researcher is interested in the wider perspective of how observations on several variables may be related include MULTIPLE REGRESSION, LOGISTIC REGRESSION, PRINCIPAL COMPONENT ANALYSIS, CANONICAL CORRELATION, FACTOR ANALYSIS, DISCRIMINANT FUNCTION ANALYSIS, and CLUSTER ANALYSIS. In addition, a number of multivariate test *criteria* or statistics are available for testing significance of MAIN EFFECTs and INTERACTIONs across groups such as WILKS' LAMBDA, HOTELLING'S TRACE CRITERION, PILLAI'S CRITERION, and ROY'S GCR CRITERION.
see also UNIVARIATE ANALYSIS
📖 Brown 1988; Clark-Carter 2010; Cramer & Howitt 2004; Everitt & Skrondal 2010; Hair et al. 2010; Harlow 2005; Peers 1996; Sheskin 2011; Tabachnick & Fidell 2007

multivariate analysis of covariance
also **multivariate ANCOVA, multiple analysis of covariance, MANCOVA**
a MANOVA with one or more COVARIATEs. Multivariate analysis of covariance (MANCOVA) is also the multivariate extension of ANCOVA. It is the same as ANCOVA except it has more than one DEPENDENT VARIABLE (DV). It is carried out on multiple DVs (two or more DVs) at the same time and where the DVs are related to each other. For example, imagine we wish to compare the reading ability and the mathematical ability of children in three schools: all-girls, all-boys and co-educational. Thus, you have one INDEPENDENT VARIABLE (IV): school type, with three levels, and you have two DVs: reading ability and mathematical ability, while controlling, for example, for age. In this example, age is a covariate, meaning that its effect is subtracted or controlled for. When only one IV is included, the analysis is referred to as a **one-way MANCOVA**, and when two or more IVs are included, the analysis is referred to as a **factorial MANCOVA** or *n*-way MANOVA (e.g., *two*-way, *three*-way, or *higher* MANCOVA).
Like MANOVA one advantage of this method is that the DVs analyzed together may be significant whereas the DVs analyzed separately may not be significant. When the combined or multivariate effect of the DVs is significant, it is useful to know which of the single or univariate effects of the DVs are significant. MANCOVA is also useful in the same ways as ANCOVA. First, in experimental work, it serves as a noise-reducing device where variance associated with the covariate(s) is removed from error variance; smaller error variance provides a more powerful test of mean differences among groups. Second, in nonexperimental work, MANCOVA provides statistical matching of groups when random assignment to groups is not possible. Prior differences among groups are accounted for by adjusting DVs as if all subjects scored the same on the covariate(s).
📖 Clark-Carter 2010; Cramer & Howitt 2004; Perry 2011; Tabachnick & Fidell 2007

multivariate analysis of variance
also **multivariate ANOVA, MANOVA, analysis of dispersion**
a generalization of ANALYSIS OF VARIANCE (ANOVA) to a situation in which there are several *continuous* DEPENDENT VARIABLEs (DVs). In MULTIVARIATE ANALYSIS OF VARIANCE (MANOVA), we ask whether there are significant group differences on the best linear combinations of our continuous DVs. As with ANOVA and ANALYSIS OF COVARIANCE (ANCOVA), MANOVA is a useful procedure whenever we have limited resources and want to identify which groups may need specific TREATMENTs or interventions. MANOVA can be used to identify which and how groups differ as well as on which DVs. In ANOVA, we allow one or more *categorical* INDEPENDENT VARIABLEs (IVs), each with two or more levels (groups), and one continuous DV. With MANOVA, we allow the same structure of IVs and two or more DVs. Thus, MANOVA allows for a much more realistic appraisal of group differences than does ANOVA. MANOVA also can be extended to incorporate one or more COVARIATEs, essentially becoming an ANCOVA that allows for two or more (continuous) DVs (i.e., MANCOVA). MANOVA is somewhat similar to DISCRIMINANT FUNCTION ANALYSIS (DFA) and LOGISTIC REGRESSION (LR), in that all three methods include at least one major CATEGORICAL VARIABLE. In MANOVA, the major categorical variable is on the independent side, whereas with DFA and LR, the DV is categorical. MANOVA differs from purely correlational methods such as MULTIPLE REGRESSION and other correlational methods (i.e., CANONICAL CORRELATION, PRINCIPAL COMPONENTS ANALYSIS, and FACTOR ANALYSIS) in that with MANOVA we are very interested in assessing the differing means between groups, whereas with the other methods the focus is not on the means but on correlations or weights between variables.

MANOVA is conducted on two or more continuous DVs simultaneously and where the DVs are interrelated in some way, or there should be some conceptual reason for considering them together. In cases where a study has one or more IV (with two or more LEVELs) and more than one DV, the researcher can perform a separate univariate ANOVA on each DV *or* analyze everything all at once using MANOVA. For example, if we wanted to look at whether people from different cultural backgrounds (IV1) varied on reading (DV1) and writing (DV2) ability, we could do two separate ANOVAs for each DV *or* we could do one MANOVA that does both at once. The rationale behind this is that the two DVs in this case are often highly correlated, in that they are both reflective of verbal ability. The MANOVA model, thus, can be used to test the MAIN EFFECTs of the IVs, INTERACTIONs between the IVs, and the degree of relationship between the DVs.

The ASSUMPTIONS of MANOVA include: INDEPENDENCE OF OBSERVATIONS (each person's scores are independent of every other person's scores), MULTIVARIATE NORMALITY, and HOMOGENEITY OF VARIANCE/covariance matrices (variances for each IV are approximately equal in all groups and covariances between pairs of DVs are approximately equal for all groups). MANOVA is ROBUST to violations of multivariate normality and to violations of homogeneity of variance/covariance matrices if groups are of nearly equal size.

Figure M.7 shows a set of hypothetical relationships between a single IV and four DVs. DV1 is highly related to the IV and shares some variance with DV2 and DV3. DV2 is related to both DV1 and DV3 and shares very little **unique variance** (the proportion of VARIANCE in the DV explained by an IV when controlling for all other IVs in the model) with the IV, although by itself in a univariate ANOVA might be related to the IV. DV3 is somewhat related to the IV, but also to all of the other DVs. DV4 is highly related to the IV and shares only a little bit of variance with DV3. Thus, DV2 is completely redundant with the other DVs, and DV3 adds only a bit of unique variance to the set. However, DV2 would be useful as a COVARIATE if that use made sense conceptually. DV2 reduces the total variance in DV1 and DV2, and most of the variance reduced is not related to the IV. Therefore, DV2 reduces the error variance in DV1 and DV3 (the variance that is not overlapping with the IV).

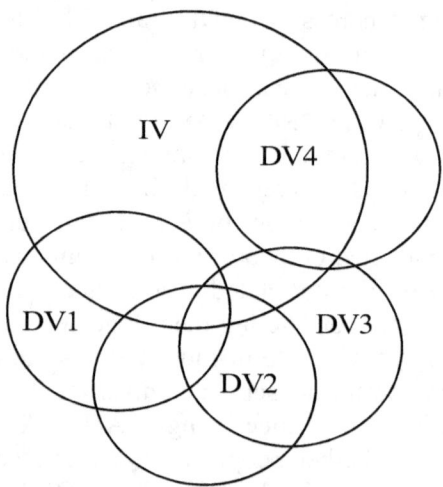

Figure M.7. Hypothetical Relationships among a Single IV and Four DVs

In the univariate analysis of variance, F TESTs are used to assess the hypotheses of interest. In the multivariate case, no single test statistic can be constructed that is optimal in all situations. Several multivariate statistics are available to test significance of main effects and interactions: WILKS' LAMBDA, HOTELLING'S TRACE CRITERION, PILLAI'S CRITERION, as well as ROY'S GCR CRITERION. Each of these four main indices has an associated F test for assessing whether group differences are significantly different from chance. If an overall finding is statistically significant, it would suggest that somewhere in the analysis there is a significant difference. Probably the most common follow-up to a significant MANOVA is to conduct a separate ANOVA for each DV. Researchers would hope to find a significant F test for each DV, indicating that these variables each show significant differences across two or more groups. However, if the MANOVA is not significant, examining the individual DVs using ANOVAs would run the risk of increasing type I errors.

Another follow-up, sometimes conducted in lieu of a set of ANOVAs, is to perform a separate ANCOVA for each DV, using the remaining DVs as covariates in each analysis. If these analyses revealed significant F tests, it would suggest that there were significant group differences on a DV after partialling out any overlapping variance among the remaining continuous DVs used in the MANOVA. Thus, we could examine group differences for the unique portion of each DV that is purged of any relationship with other DVs.

Still another possible follow-up procedure after a significant F test with MANOVA, is to conduct a single DFA with the same variables that were used in the MANOVA except that the roles (independent or dependent) are reversed. Thus, a DFA would use each of the continuous (dependent) variables from a MANOVA as the continuous IVs. The categorical (independent) grouping variable from MANOVA would now become the categorical DV in DFA. The goal would be to assess how each of the continuous variables discriminated among the groups of the DFA outcome variable.

MANOVA is used in two general cases: when the IVs all measure aspects of the same general construct (and, thus, lend themselves to analysis as a set), and when the researcher is concerned that performing separate analyses on several DVs will increase the possibility of making a TYPE I ERROR. In either case, MANOVA creates a new composite DV— a **canonical variable**—from the original DVs, then determines whether participants' scores on this canonical variable differ across conditions.

Mathematically speaking, there are no limits to the number of IVs or DVs that can be included in the analysis, and the IVs can be composed of two or more groups. When only one IV is included, the analysis is referred to as a **one-way MANOVA**, and when two or more IVs are included, the analysis is referred to as a **factorial MANOVA** or n-way MANOVA (e.g., *two*-way, *three*-way, or *higher* MANOVA). In the special case of one IV with two levels, the analysis is often referred to as a HOTELLING'S T.

Regardless of the study design, the goal of the MANOVA is to determine if the IV groups differ in their means on at least one linear combination of the DVs.

There is no *nonparametric* alternative to MANOVA.

see also PROFILE ANALYSIS

📖 Bachman 2004; Cramer & Howitt 2004; Everitt & Skrondal 2010; Harlow 2005; Leary 2011; Perry 2011; Porte 2010; Salkind 2007; Tabachnick & Fidell 2007; Upton & Cook 2008

multivariate ANCOVA
another term for MULTIVARIATE ANALYSIS OF COVARIANCE

multivariate ANOVA
another term for MULTIVARIATE ANALYSIS OF VARIANCE

multivariate *F*
another term for WILKS' LAMBDA

multivariate normality
the ASSUMPTION that each VARIABLE and all linear combinations of the variables in an analysis are normally distributed (see NORMALITY). As there are potentially a very large number of linear combinations, this assumption is not easy to test. When the data are *grouped* as in MULTIVARIATE ANALYSIS OF VARIANCE, the SAMPLING DISTRIBUTION of the MEANs of the DEPENDENT VARIABLEs in each of the CELLs has to be normally distributed as well as the variables' linear combinations. With relatively large SAMPLE SIZEs, the CENTRAL LIMIT THEOREM states that the sampling distribution of means will be normally distributed. If there is multivariate normality, the sampling distribution of means will be normally distributed. When the data are *ungrouped* as in DISCRIMINANT FUNCTION ANALYSIS and STRUCTURAL EQUATION MODELING, if there is multivariate normality each variable will be normally distributed and the relationship of pairs of variables will be linear and homoscedastic (see HOMOSCEDASTICITY).

📖 Cramer & Howitt 2004

multi-way ANOVA
another term for FACTORIAL ANOVA

multi-way design
another term for FACTORIAL DESIGN

N

n
an abbreviation for *number of cases* (generally in a subsample)

N
an abbreviation for *total number of cases*

naive realism
also **commonsense realism, descriptive realism, crude realism**
a viewpoint which asserts the ONTOLOGY that, under normal conditions, things are just as we perceive them to be and asserts the EPISTEMOLOGY that true knowledge can be identified through its correspondence with reality. Arguably, it is the commonsense philosophy adopted tacitly in daily life. Naive realism is an unsuitable position for inquiry into things that are not directly perceptible, but in itself it is compatible with both quantitative and qualitative methods and is drawn on within both positivist (see POSITIVISM) and postpositivist (see POSTPOSITIVISM) theories of science. see also REALISM, SCIENTIFIC REALISM, SUBTLE REALISM, ANALYTIC REALISM, CRITICAL REALISM
 Given 2008

narrative analysis
a family of analytic methods for interpreting texts that have in common a storied form. As in all families, there is conflict and disagreement among those holding different perspectives. Analysis of data is only one component of the broader field of NARRATIVE INQUIRY. Methods are case centered, and the cases that form the basis for analysis can be individuals, identity groups, communities, organizations, or even nations. Methods can be used to interpret different kinds of texts—oral, written, and visual. The term narrative is illusive, carrying many meanings and used in a variety of ways by different scholars, often used synonymously with story. In the familiar everyday form, a speaker connects events to a sequence that is consequential for later action and for the meanings listeners are supposed to take away from the story. Events are perceived as important, selected, organized, connected, and evaluated as meaningful for a particular listener. The definition emphasizes the contextual nature of oral stories; they are told (indeed performed) with the active participation of an audience and are designed to accomplish particular aims. Oral stories are strategic, functional, and purposeful. Other forms of oral communication include chronicles, reports, arguments, and question and answer exchanges.

Among scholars working in the human sciences with personal (first-person) accounts for research purposes, the narrative unit can differ, and its form is often linked to a discipline. In anthropology and social history, narrative can refer to a life story that the researcher weaves from threads of INTERVIEWs, OBSERVATIONs, and documents. At the other end of the continuum lies the very restrictive definition of social linguistics. Here, narrative refers to a discrete unit of discourse, an extended answer by a research participant to a single question, topically centered and temporally organized. Resting in the middle on a continuum of working definitions is research in psychology and sociology. Here, personal narrative encompasses long sections of talk—extended accounts of lives in context that develop over the course of single or multiple interviews or therapeutic conversations. The diversity of working definitions underscores the absence of a single meaning or unit of analysis. The term is employed in our field to refer to texts at several levels that overlap: stories told by research participants (stories, which are themselves interpretive), the interpretive account an investigator develops based on interviews and fieldwork observation (i.e., a story about stories), and even the interpretive narrative a reader constructs after engaging with the participant's and investigator's narratives.
📖 Given 2008

narrative inquiry
also narrative research

a QUALITATIVE RESEARCH approach for narratively inquiring into people and thus allowing for the intimate study of individuals' experiences over time and in context. Beginning with a narrative view of experience, researchers attend to place, temporality, and sociality, from within a methodological three-dimensional narrative inquiry space that allows for inquiry into both researchers' and participants' storied life experiences. Within this space, each story told and lived is situated and understood within larger cultural, social, and institutional narratives. Narrative inquiry is marked by its emphasis on relational engagement between researcher and research participants.

Narrative inquiry involves working with people's consciously told stories, recognizing that these rest on deeper stories of which people are often unaware. Participants construct stories that support their interpretation of themselves, excluding experiences and events that undermine the identities they currently claim. Whether or not they believe the stories they tell is relatively unimportant because the inquiry goes beyond the specific stories to explore the assumptions inherent in the shaping of those stories. No matter how fictionalized, all stories rest on and illustrate the story structures a person holds. As such, they provide a window into people's beliefs and experiences. Narratives allow researchers to present experience holistically in all its complexity and richness. They are therefore powerful constructions, which can function as instruments of social control as well as valuable teaching tools.

In its fullest sense, narrative inquiry requires going beyond the use of narrative as rhetorical structure, that is, simply telling stories, to an analytic examination of the underlying insights and assumptions that the story illustrates. Narrative inquiry is therefore rarely found in the form of a narrative. Hallmarks of the analysis are the recognition that people make sense of their lives according to the narratives available to them, that stories are constantly being restructured in the light of new events, and that stories do not exist in a vacuum but are shaped by lifelong personal and community narratives.

Narrative inquiry, across various disciplines and multiple professional fields, aims at understanding and making meaning of experience through conversations, dialogue, and participation in the ongoing lives of research participants. Each discipline and field of study brings slightly different ways of understanding and different contexts to the narrative study of experience that deepen the methodology of narrative inquiry. In the field of applied linguistics, researchers have made use of a variety of genres, including CASE STUDY, LIFE HISTORY RESEARCH, DIARY STUDY, BIOGRAPHICAL STUDY, autobiography, biography, and memoir.

Any research method, of course, has its limitations, and narrative is not suitable for all inquiries. The time commitment required makes it unsuitable for work with a large number of participants. It also requires close collaboration with participants and a recognition that the constructed narrative and subsequent analysis illuminates the researcher as much as the participant. Ethical issues are some of the most serious ones to be addressed. Exchanging stories is often understood within a larger story of friendship, so researchers may find disengagement difficult at the end of the research project. More seriously, when researchers take people's stories and place them into a larger narrative, they are imposing meaning on participants' lived experience. Although good practice demands that researchers share their ongoing narrative constructions, participants can never be quite free of the researcher's interpretation of their lives. The effects of this imposed restoring can be powerful.

see also META-NARRATIVE

📖 Bell 2002; Given 2008

narrative interview

an interview that is organized to facilitate the development of a text that can be interpreted through NARRATIVE ANALYSIS. Narrative analysis is guided by a theory of narrative, and these theories of narrative vary in the influence of the reader, the text, and the intent of the author on interpretation. For this reason, the content and structure of a narrative interview will depend both on the theory of narrative being used in the analysis and on the research question. That being said, there are some commonalities among all narratives that will facilitate interviews for use in narrative analysis. Informants often relate experiences in narrative format; that is, they select and order events in ways that both reflect their own meanings and convey those meanings to others. The content and structure of the narrative contains implied meanings that are as important to understanding the narrative as the overt meanings. Narrative interviews provide informants with many opportunities to select and order events themselves rather than to put events into a preordained structure. For this reason, narrative interviews are often organized temporally, in the manner of a life story or as in LIFE HISTORY RESEARCH. Questions such as, 'When did you first notice?', or 'How did you begin?' allow respondents to set the perimeters of the temporal context they find relevant. Decisions about relevant and irrelevant content are made during the course of the interview, both by the informant and in collaboration with the researcher, but no information is a priori ruled out, for any event or interpretation can contribute to the meaning of a story.

Narrative interviews can use semi-structured or unstructured formats depending upon the research question and the goal of the analysis. Questions should be sufficiently open-ended to encourage participants to explain themselves fully, but it is not necessary that every question elicit a story. Often narratives are constructed by the researcher from component parts offered by the informant across the interview or interviews. Questions that are closed (i.e., require a *yes* or *no* answer) or that offer a set of fixed choices (e.g., always, sometimes, never) do not facilitate the development of narratives. However, questions that begin, for example, 'Tell me a story about...' may intimidate informants who do not normally think in those terms. Narrative interviews, thus, require artful design, with questions carefully ordered to build on previous questions. Narrative interviews are also facilitated by the use of neutral PROBES that elicit information about actions and explanations. Questions such as, 'How did it happen that...?', or 'What did you do then?' elicit the thinking that underlies the connection of the events or experiences selected for the informants' story. Revealing those connections is the primary goal of the narrative interview.

see also ETHNOGRAPHIC INTERVIEW, NON-DIRECTIVE INTERVIEW, UNSTRUCTURED INTERVIEW, SEMI-STRUCTURED INTERVIEW, STRUCTURED INTERVIEW, INFORMAL INTERVIEW, TELEPHONE INTERVIEW, FOCUS GROUP, INTERACTIVE INTERVIEW, CLOSED-FORM ITEM, OPEN-FORM ITEM
📖 Given 2008

narrative research
another term for NARRATIVE INQUIRY

narrative text
a form of discourse that has been fixed by writing. Some postmodern scholars have defined text to include anything that can be interpreted, from a photograph to a film score. Scholars of rhetoric divide texts into different types depending on the author's intent. Narratives are characterized by temporal organization: beginning to middle to end. Events unfolding over time constitute the plot. Other central features of narratives include characters, a setting for the plot, and a theme or message that is conveyed both by the words of the story and by the selection and ordering of events that are included within it. Narratives, as compared to **expository text**s, use voice to convey a particular point of view—all narratives take a point of view, although the point of view may be that of an omniscient observer. Point of view is used to support the narratives theme by supporting the credibility or worthiness of the narrator. The purpose of a narrative text is to tell a story, usually the story of a resolution to a problem.

In contrast, the purpose of expository texts is to explain, inform, or teach. The voice of expository texts is therefore neutral and objective. Recipes and textbooks are examples of expository texts. Research reports are often structured as expository texts, using language that minimizes the author's voice and obscures the role of selection and exclusion of events or information in the development of a theme or message. Many QUALITATIVE RESEARCHers have decried this approach and developed alternative forms of research representation, some of which include narrative elements such as the story of the research or the researcher.

Both narrative and expository texts can be used as qualitative data. For example, interviewers may request expositions from informants, perhaps as journal entries or logs, or may elicit expositions in interviews and then fix those expositions as texts via transcription. Interviewers may also elicit narratives from informants, either in writing or as discourse. The boundary between expository and narrative texts is itself controversial. Some scholars contend that all texts are narrative because of the meanings they convey and because of the deliberate selection or omission of events or information. This liminality is nowhere more apparent than in qualitative research reports in which the exposition of findings, the voice of the author, the context of the study, and the narratives of informants come together.
📖 Given 2008

naturalism
an orientation which is concerned with the study of social life in real, naturally occurring settings; the experiencing, observing, describing, understanding and analyzing of the features of social life in concrete situations as they occur independently of scientific manipulation. It is the fo-

cus on natural situations that leads to the sobriquet naturalism, and it is signified by attention to what human beings feel, perceive, think, and do in natural situations that are not experimentally contrived or controlled. These naturally occurring situations are also sometimes called face-to-face situations, mundane interaction, micro-interaction or everyday life. Stress is laid on experiencing and observing what is happening naturally rather than hypothesizing about it beforehand, mostly by achieving first-hand contact with it, although researchers minimize their effect on the setting as much as possible. Stress is also laid on the analysis of people's meanings from their own standpoint, the feelings, perceptions, emotions, thoughts, moods, ideas, beliefs, and interpretative processes of members of society as they themselves understand and articulate them. Naturalism presents this as being true to the natural phenomena and from this is it easy to see why naturalism as a methodological position is partnered in research practice by a commitment to ETHNOGRAPHY and other QUALITATIVE RESEARCH methods.

There are ontological (see ONTOLOGY) and epistemological (see EPISTEMOLOGY) assumptions within this stance, which further highlight its contrast with POSITIVISM as a methodological position. Central to naturalism is the argument that human beings and social behavior are different from the behavior of physical and inanimate objects. People are meaning-endowing, in that they have the capacity to interpret and construct their social world and setting rather than respond in a simplistic and automatic way to any particular stimuli. Moreover, people are discursive, in that they have the capacity for language and the linguistic formulation of their ideas, and possess sufficient knowledge about discourse in order to articulate their meanings. Society, thus, is seen as either wholly or partially constructed and reconstructed on the basis of these interpretative processes, and people are seen as having the ability to tell others what they mean by some behavior, idea, or remark and to offer their own explanation of it or motive for it. Society is not presented as a fixed and unchanging entity, out there somewhere and external to the person, but is a shifting, changing entity that is constructed or reconstructed by people themselves. People live in material and bounded structures and locations, and these contexts shape their interpretative processes, so that we are not free to define the social world as if we existed as islands each one inhabited by ourselves alone. All social life is partially interdependent on the concrete situations and structures in which it exists, so society is not a complete invention (or reinvention) every time. But knowledge of the social world, in this methodological position, is inadequate if we do not also document, observe, describe, and analyze the meanings of the people who live in it. The theory of knowledge within naturalism thus sees it as essential for understanding the freely constructed character of human actions and institutions in the natural settings and contexts that influence and shape people's meanings. Thus, knowledge must be inductive not deductive (see DEDUCTIVE REASONING, INDUCTIVE REASONING). Naturalism is thus also closely associated with grounded theory as an analytical approach in the social sciences.

The three essential tenets of naturalism are therefore clear. The social world is not reducible to that which can be externally observed, but is something created or recreated, perceived and interpreted by people themselves. Knowledge of the social world must give access to actors' own accounts of it, among other things, at least as a starting point, and sometimes as the sole point. People live in a bounded social context, and are best studied in, and their meanings are best revealed in, the natural settings of the real world in which they live.

What is relevant here is the impact of these theoretical ideas on research practice. Four imperatives or requirements for social research follow from this methodological position. Social researchers in the humanistic model of social research need to meet one or more of these:

1) to ask people for their views, meanings and constructions;
2) to ask people in such a way that they can tell them in their own words;
3) to ask them in depth because these meanings are often complex, taken-for-granted and problematic; and
4) to address the social context which gives meaning and substance to their views and constructions.

These research imperatives go toward defining the attitude and approach of naturalist social researchers, predisposing them to focus on topics that can be approached through the exploration of people's meaning and giving them a preference for data collection techniques that can access these meanings.

 Miller & Brewer 2003

naturalistic inquiry

an approach to QUALITATIVE RESEARCH which is based on the underlying assumptions that knowledge about reality is mind dependent not value free, that hypotheses are always working hypotheses, and that reality is not a single construct but multiple constructs. Naturalistic inquiry endeavors on how people behave in natural settings while engaging in life experiences. It is based on the notion that context is essential for understanding human behavior, and acquiring knowledge of human experience outside of its natural context is not possible. This type of inquiry stems from the naturalistic paradigm (see NATURALISM) that situates itself opposite the positivist paradigm (see POSITIVISM).

The goal of naturalistic inquiry is to describe and understand human behavior as it occurs in its natural contexts. The naturalistic paradigm that influences inquiry makes several claims about how researchers make sense of human interactions. Naturalistic researchers understand reality as multiple and socially constructed and therefore subjective. Context interacts with human experience to create and shape human reality. Separating knowledge from its natural context is impossible. In order to understand human phenomena, researchers must enter the environments of the people or phenomena they seek to understand. Working in the scene or field links the researcher with the researched; they are inseparable and influence researchers' understanding of what they observe and how those observations are interpreted. Value-free inquiry is not possible because the researchers cannot separate their experiences from what they observe in the field. No researcher is neutral. These tenets of naturalistic inquiry influence how research is conducted and dictate the types of claims a researcher may make about human phenomena.

Several qualitative methodologies fall under the naturalistic umbrella. These methodologies rely primarily on some form of PARTICIPANT OBSERVATION, making the human researcher the instrument of data collection. Researchers need to purposively select the participants and scene necessary to respond to their interest in a topic or issue. Once in the field, researchers take fieldnotes documenting their observations. In addition to collecting data in the field, researchers may also conduct IN-DEPTH INTERVIEWs with informants to substantiate or supplement observations. Research is collected until theoretical SATURATION is reached.

Although situated in observations, study designs in naturalistic inquiry are emergent because human phenomena are unpredictable. In addition, this approach allows researchers the flexibility necessary to make adjustments to the focus of observations. Analysis of data uses GROUNDED THEORY, allowing researchers to situate findings and interpretation of those findings in the data. Findings are reported in a format that is conducive for describing human behavior in rich terms. Interpretations of findings should represent the experience of participants. Therefore, reports of a study's findings should resonate with participants. Resonance should not, however, compromise ethics in a naturalistic study. The spirit of naturalistic inquiry requires researchers to pay special attention to their human subjects to gain understanding of human interactions and behavior while maintaining ethical mandates like confidentiality and privacy.

The main kinds of naturalistic inquiry are: CASE STUDY, COMPARATIVE RESEARCH, RETROSPECTIVE INTERVIEW, LONGITUDINAL STUDY, ETHNOGRAPHY, GROUNDED THEORY, PHENOMENOLOGY, and BIOGRAPHICAL STUDY. The main methods for data collection in naturalistic inquiry are

participant observation, INTERVIEW and conversations, DOCUMENTs and FIELDNOTES, accounts, and notes and memos.
📖 Cohen et al. 2011; Given 2008; Gray 2009; Ridenour & Newman 2008

naturalistic observation
an OBSERVATION which involves observing organisms in their natural settings, the researcher does not attempt to manipulate that setting in any way, and no constraints (e.g., predetermined categories) are placed on the outcome of the investigation. Naturalistic observation seeks to provide authentic, rich descriptions of the behavior of interest as it naturally exists and unfolds in its real context. It emphasizes understanding and describing social activities from the point of view of the participants themselves. For example, a researcher who wants to examine the socialization skills of children may observe them while they are at a school playground, and then record all instances of effective or ineffective social behavior.

Data collection typically involves unstructured observation and informal interviewing, with note taking, audiorecording, and occasionally videorecording use to record data. Particular attention is paid to what participants say as a way to understand the meanings they attach to events and activities. Naturalistic observation is also characterized by emergent research design, PURPOSEFUL SAMPLING, and inductive data analysis. Believing that data must come from real life, researchers work to get as close to their data as possible. At the same time, investigators strive to be as unobtrusive as possible so as not to disrupt the natural setting being studied.

The primary advantage of the naturalistic observation approach is that it takes place in a natural setting, where the participants do not realize that they are being observed. Consequently, the behaviors that it measures and describes are likely to reflect the participants' true behaviors. The first and most fundamental principle is that of noninterference. Researchers who engage in naturalistic observation must not disrupt the natural course of events that they are observing. By adhering to this principle, researchers can observe events the way they truly happen. Second, naturalistic observation involves the observation and detection of invariants, or behavior patterns or other phenomena that exist in the real world. For example, individuals may be found to engage in similar ways, on certain times or days, in certain contexts, or when in the company of certain people or groups. Third, the naturalistic observation approach is particularly useful for exploratory purposes, when we know little or nothing about a certain subject. In this vein, naturalistic observation can provide a useful but global description of the participant and a series of events as opposed to isolated ones. Finally, the naturalistic observation method is basically descriptive. Although it can provide a somewhat detailed description of a phenomenon, it cannot tell us why the phenomenon occurred. Determining causation is left to experimental designs.

The major weakness of naturalistic observation is its potential for generating reactivity or OBSERVER EFFECT. This weakness may be addressed through the use of multiple observers and tests of INTERCODER RELIABILITY, although this strategy could result in even more reactivity in some settings, such as those involving only a few participants in a relatively small space. Member checking, while intrusive, is also helpful. Some researchers employ covert observation to reduce reactivity, although this approach is not always seen as acceptable in that it violates the principle of informed consent. Closely related to the problem of observer effect is the problem of OBSERVER BIAS, the idea that data will be limited by the characteristics of the individual collecting those data. Naturalistic observation typically yields large amounts of textual data that require a lot of time to manage and analyze. Finally, naturalistic observation is not effective for studying infrequently occurring or unpredictable behaviors, as this would require inordinate amounts of time in the field.

📖 Cohen et al. 2011; Given 2008; Marczyk et al. 2005

naturally occurring group design
another term for QUASI-EXPERIMENTAL DESIGN

negative case sampling
see PURPOSIVE SAMPLING

negative correlation
see CORRELATION COEFFICIENT

negatively skewed distribution
see SKEWED DISTRIBUTION

negative suppression
see SUPPRESSOR VARIABLE

NEGD
an abbreviation for NONEQUIVALENT-GROUPS DESIGN

negligent bias
see BIAS

nested variable
another term for within-subjects factor

nested design
also hierarchical design

a design in which LEVELs of one or more FACTORs are nested within one or more other factors. More specifically, given two factors A and B, the levels of B are said to be nested within the levels of A if each level of B appears with only a single level of A in the observations. That is, the levels of one factor do not occur at all levels of another factor. The FACTORIAL DESIGNs include all possible combinations of the levels of the independent variables (IVs). These designs are known as crossed or completely **crossed factorial design**s and allow researchers to examine the INTERACTION among the IVs or factors. Occasionally, however, researchers are unable or do not wish to employ a full factorial design. One instance of a design that is not a full factorial is the nested or hierarchical design. In BETWEEN-SUBJECTS DESIGNs, subjects are said to be nested within levels of the IV. That is, each subject is confined to only one level of each IV or combination of IVs. Nesting also occurs with IVs when levels of one IV are confined to only one level of another IV, rather than factorially crossing over the levels of the other IV.

Teaching techniques		
T1	T2	T3
Classroom 1	Classroom 2	Classroom 3
Classroom 4	Classroom 5	Classroom 6
Classroom 7	Classroom 8	Classroom 9

Table N.1. An Example of Nested Design

Nested designs are commonly found where subjects form small groups or blocks (e.g., classrooms) and the particular treatment is given to all members of the block. In such a case, the classroom is said to be nested in the particular treatment being studied. Take the example where the IV is various levels of teaching methods. Children within the same classroom cannot be randomly assigned to different methods but whole classrooms can be so assigned. The design is ONE-WAY BETWEEN-SUBJECTs where teaching methods is the IV and classrooms serve as subjects. For each classroom, the mean score for all children on the test is obtained, and the means serve as DEPENDENT VARIABLEs in ONE-WAY ANOVA. If the effect of classroom is also assessed, the design is nested or hierarchical, as shown in Table N.1. Classrooms are randomly assigned to and nested in teaching methods, and children are nested in classrooms. The ERROR TERM for the test of classroom is subjects within classrooms and teaching method, and the error term for the test of teaching method is classrooms within teaching technique. Nested models also are analyzed through **multilevel modeling**. It is a somewhat complicated but increasingly popular strategy for analyzing data in these situations.

Two important considerations concerning nested designs should be kept in mind: First, in a nested design it is not possible to investigate the A × B interaction effect because not all of the levels of factor B occur under all of the levels of factor A. Second, nested factors are typically random factors and therefore require a different error term in computing the F RATIO than fixed factors.

📖 Gamst et al. 2008; Tabachnick & Fidell 2007

net suppression
another term for NEGATIVE SUPPRESSION

network sampling
another term for SNOWBALL SAMPLING

Newman-Keuls test
also **NK test, Student-Newman-Keuls test, SNK test**
a POST HOC TEST which is used to determine whether three or more MEANs differ significantly in an ANALYSIS OF VARIANCE (ANOVA). Newman-Keuls (NK) test may be used regardless of whether the ANOVA is significant. It is based on the STUDENTIZED RANGE TEST. It assumes EQUAL VARIANCE and is approximate for unequal group sizes. The NK is quite similar to TUKEY'S TEST with several notable exceptions. The NK procedure is a contrast-based method. The NK procedure is more liberal than the Tukey's test as it has a higher family-wise error rate, a lower TYPE II ERROR rate, and therefore more power. The NK and Tukey's test are post hoc procedures used for testing pairwise contrasts (a comparison involving only two means) with equal observations per group. The NK is a stepwise or sequential test which is similar to **duncan's new multiple range test** (also called **Duncan's test, MRT**)—a modified form of the Newman-Keuls test—in that the means are first ordered in size. However, it differs in the SIGNIFICANCE LEVEL used. For the NK test the significance level is the same no matter how many comparisons there are. Consequently, differences are less likely to be significant for this test. Duncan's test is more liberal than the NK in terms of the Type I error rate, but has a lower Type II error rate and thus is more powerful.

📖 Cramer & Howitt 2004; Lomax 2007; Page et al. 2003

NH
an abbreviation for NULL HYPOTHESIS

noise
see MEASUREMENT ERROR

nominal data
see NOMINAL SCALE

nominal definition
another term for CONCEPTUAL DEFINITION

nominal group technique
a small group discussion that is structured to maximize each group member's participation. Each group member is first asked to silently write down their thoughts about a question or topic and then group members go around one by one sharing their thoughts. This structure helps avoid the dominance of any group member and minimizes conflict among members, which are some of the drawbacks of more traditional small group discussions (e.g., FOCUS GROUPs). This technique is very useful in gathering data from individuals and putting them into some order which is shared by the group, e.g., of priority, of similarity and difference, of generality and specificity. It also enables individual disagreements to be registered and to be built into the group responses and identification of significant issues to emerge. Further, it gives equal status to all respondents in the situation, for example, the voice of the new entrant to the teaching profession is given equal consideration to the voice of the headteacher of several years' experience. The attraction of this process is that it balances writing with discussion, a divergent phase with a convergent phase, space for individual comments and contributions to group interaction. It is a useful device for developing collegiality. All participants have a voice and are heard.
see also DELPHI TECHNIQUE
 Cohen et al. 2011; Kalof et al. 2008

nominal level of measurement
another term for NOMINAL SCALE

nominal scale
also **nominal level of measurement**
a type of MEASUREMENT SCALE which measure VARIABLEs that are *categorical*. In other words, nominal scales are appropriate when data are categorized into groups. These groupings might be natural or artificial. Naturally occurring nominal scales in language research would include gender (female/male), native language (Persian/German, etc.), academic status (under-graduate/graduate), and so forth. Artificial nominal scales might include groupings like assignment by a researcher to an EXPERI-

MENTAL or CONTROL GROUP, groups of elementary-, intermediate-, or advanced-level students, and so forth. Data obtained by using nominal scales of measurement are called **nominal data**.

Nominal scales are the least sophisticated type of measurement and are used only to qualitatively classify or categorize. They have no absolute zero point and cannot be ordered in a quantitative sequence, and there is no equal unit of measurement between categories. In other words, the numbers assigned to the variables are arbitrary and they have no mathematical meaning beyond describing the characteristic or attribute under consideration—they do not imply amounts of an attribute or characteristic. This makes it impossible to conduct standard mathematical operations such as addition, subtraction, division, and multiplication. Nominal scales provide information only about the distinctiveness of individuals on the attribute, and it is this property of numbers that enables us to differentiate among values for a given attribute. A numerical example of a nominal scale is the set of numbers assigned to football players. Frequently, these numbers have no meaning other than that they are convenient labels to distinguish the players from one another. To put it another way, nominal data answer the question: 'Are they different?'

see also ORDINAL SCALE, INTERVAL SCALE, RATIO SCALE, CATEGORICAL VARIABLE, CONTINUOUS VARIABLE

Bachman 1990, 2004; Howell 2010; Marczyk et al. 2005; Urdan 2010

nominal variable
another name for CATEGORICAL VARIABLE

nondirectional hypothesis
also **two-tailed hypothesis, two-way hypothesis, bi-directional hypothesis, two-sided hypothesis**

an ALTERNATIVE HYPOTHESIS that does not indicate the direction of the possible differences from the value specified by the NULL HYPOTHESIS. In other words, a nondirectional hypothesis, unlike a DIRECTIONAL HYPOTHESIS, is chosen when if there is no reason to hypothesize that an existing relationship will be in one direction or the other, positive or negative. A nondirectional hypothesis is tested with a TWO-TAILED TEST and is stated in words that 'A differs from B'. In Fact, the researcher may take the more conservative path of formulating a nondirectional hypothesis which leaves open the possibility of the relationship being in either direction. It would be formulated like this:

> 'There is a difference in levels of educational attainment between male and female students.'

What is not included in this hypothesis is any sense of whether it is believed that female attainment is likely to be higher than male attainment or vice versa; only that they will be different. In this sense there is no indication as to what the direction of the difference is. This nondirectional hypothesis essentially says the same thing as the following two directional hypotheses, but much more efficiently:

'There is a positive relationship between the two variables.'
'There is a negative relationship between the two variables.'

Thus, if a SAMPLE MEAN is observed that is either sufficiently greater or sufficiently less than the hypothesized value, the null hypothesis would be rejected. The direction of the difference is not important. However, if only one alternative to the null hypothesis is of interest, a directional hypothesis is used.
📖 Brown 1988; Clark-Carter 2010; Sahai & Khurshid 2001

nondirectional test
another term for TWO-TAILED TEST

non-directive interview
a research technique which derives from the therapeutic or psychiatric interview. The principal features of it are the minimal direction or control exhibited by the interviewer and the freedom the respondent has to express his/her subjective feelings as fully and as spontaneously as s/he chooses or is able. The respondent is encouraged to talk about the subject under investigation (usually himself) and to be free to guide the interview. There are no set questions, and usually no predetermined framework for recorded answers. The interviewer should prompt and probe, pressing for clarity and elucidation, rephrasing and summarizing where necessary and checking for confirmation of this, particularly if the issues are complex or vague.
It is an approach especially to be recommended when complex attitudes are involved and when one's knowledge of them is still in a vague and unstructured form.
see also ETHNOGRAPHIC INTERVIEW, UNSTRUCTURED INTERVIEW, SEMI-STRUCTURED INTERVIEW, STRUCTURED INTERVIEW, INTERVIEW GUIDE, INFORMAL INTERVIEW, TELEPHONE INTERVIEW, FOCUS GROUP
📖 Cohen et al. 2011; Corbetta 2003

non-directive question
another term for OPEN-FORM ITEM

nonequivalent comparison-group design
another term for NONEQUIVALENT CONTROL GROUP DESIGN

nonequivalent control group design
also **nonequivalent comparison-group design, nonequivalent-groups design (NEGD), non-randomized control group design, nonequivalent groups pretest-posttest design, non-randomized control group pretest-posttest design**
the most commonly used QUASI-EXPERIMENTAL DESIGN which is structurally quite similar to the TRUE EXPERIMENTAL DESIGN, but it does not employ RANDOM ASSIGNMENT. In nonequivalent control group design, the DEPENDENT VARIABLE (DV) is measured both before and after the TREATMENT, as shown below (where NR = nonrandom assignment, O = pretest and posttest, and X = treatment):

Experimental Group (NR)	O	X	O
Control Group (NR)	O		O

In this design, you most often use INTACT GROUPs that you think are similar as the EXPERIMENTAL and CONTROL GROUPs; you might pick two comparable classrooms or schools; you try to select groups that are as similar as possible, so you can fairly compare the treated one with the comparison one; but you can never be sure the groups are comparable. Put another way, it is unlikely that the two groups would be as similar as they would if you assigned them through a random lottery.
Perhaps the class designated the experimental group would have done better on the posttest without the experimental treatment. Thus, there is an initial SELECTION BIAS that can seriously threaten the INTERNAL VALIDITY of this design. Any prior differences between the groups may affect the outcome of the study. Under the worst circumstances, this can lead you to conclude that your study did not make a difference when in fact it did, or that it did make a difference when in fact it did not. The pretest, the design's most important feature, provides a way to deal with this threat. The pretest enables you to check on the equivalence of the groups on the DV before the experiment begins. In other words, the use of a pretest allows you to measure between-group differences before exposure to the intervention. This could substantially reduce the threat of selection bias by revealing whether the groups differed on the DV prior to the treatment. If there are no significant differences on the pretest, you can discount selection bias as a serious threat to internal validity and proceed with the study. If there are some differences, you can use ANCOVA to statistically adjust the posttest scores for the pretest differences.
Because both experimental and control groups take the same pretest and posttest, and the study occupies the same period of time, other threats to

internal validity, such as MATURATION, INSTRUMENTATION, HISTORY, and STATISTICAL REGRESSION should not be serious threats to internal validity. There are some possible internal validity threats, however, that this design does not control, namely threats resulting from an interaction of selection and some of the other common threats (e.g., interaction of selection and maturation, interaction of selection and statistical regression, and interaction of selection and instrumentation.

In summary, nonequivalent control group design is a good choice when random assignment of subjects to groups is not possible. The more similar the experimental and the control groups are at the beginning of the experiment, and the more this similarity is confirmed by similar group means on the pretest, the more credible the results of the nonequivalent control group design become. If the pretest scores are similar and selection-maturation and selection-regression interactions can be shown to be unlikely explanations of posttest differences, the results of this quasi-experimental design are quite credible.

see also TIME-SERIES DESIGN, EQUIVALENT MATERIAL DESIGN, COUNTERBALANCED DESIGN, RECURRENT INSTITUTIONAL CYCLE DESIGN, SEPARATE-SAMPLE PRETEST-POSTTEST CONTROL GROUP DESIGN, SEPARATE-SAMPLE PRETEST-POSTTEST DESIGN
📖 Ary et al. 2010; Marczyk et al. 2005

nonequivalent-groups design
another term for NONEQUIVALENT CONTROL GROUP DESIGN

nonequivalent groups pretest-posttest design
another term for NONEQUIVALENT CONTROL GROUP DESIGN

nonexperimental research
a type of QUANTITATIVE RESEARCH in which the researcher identifies VARIABLEs and may look for relationships among them but does not manipulate the variables. Major forms of nonexperimental research are relationship studies including EX POST FACTO RESEARCH, CORRELATIONAL RESEARCH, and SURVEY RESEARCH.
📖 Ary et al. 2010

non-hierarchical clustering
see CLUSTER ANALYSIS

non-metric approach
see MULTIDIMENSIONAL SCALING

non-metric data
another term for CATEGORICAL DATA

non-metric variable
another term for CATEGORICAL VARIABLE

nonorthogonal design
another term for UNBALANCED DESIGN

nonpairwise comparison
also **composite comparison, complex comparison**
a comparison which involves more than two MEANs. A nonpairwise comparison involves three or more groups, with these comparison groups divided into two subsets. The mean score for the data in each subset is then computed and compared. For example, suppose there are four comparison groups in a study: A, B, C, and D. The researcher might be interested in comparing the average of groups A and B against the average of groups C and D. This would be a nonpairwise comparison, as would a comparison between the first group and the average of the final two groups (with the second group omitted from the comparison). In contrast, a statistical comparison between two means is referred to as a **pairwise comparison** (also called **simple comparison**). The term pairwise simply means that groups are being compared two at a time. For example, pairwise comparisons among three groups labeled A, B, and C would involve comparisons of A versus B, A versus C, and B versus C. With four groups in the study, a total of six pairwise comparisons would be possible.
see also POST HOC TEST
📖 Huck 2012; Larson-Hall 2010

nonparametric procedure(s)
another term for NONPARAMETRIC TEST(s)

nonparametric test(s)
also **nonparametric statistic(s), distribution-free test(s), ranking test(s), nonparametric procedure(s)**
any of a large number of *inferential* techniques in statistics which do not involve assessing the characteristics of the POPULATION from characteristics of the SAMPLE. Nonparametric tests work with frequencies and rank-ordered scales, or may involve re-randomization and other procedures. Nonparametric tests are also well suited to small SAMPLE SIZEs, and rank tests are particularly helpful when OUTLIERs are present in a data set since ranks of raw scores are not affected by extreme values. Nonparametric tests are also called *distribution-free statistics* because they do not require that the data be normally distributed. They do not assume a regular BELL-SHAPED CURVE of distribution in the wider population; indeed the wider population is perhaps irrelevant as these tests are de-

signed for a given specific population, for example, a class in school. Because they make no ASSUMPTIONs about the wider population, the researcher must work with nonparametric statistics appropriate to *nominal* and *ordinal* LEVELs OF MEASUREMENT. In other words, they are generally used with NOMINAL and ORDINAL DATA or when the assumptions necessary for PARAMETRIC TESTS cannot be met.

The argument for using nonparametric tests is largely in terms of the inapplicability of parametric statistics to much data. Parametric statistics assume a NORMAL DISTRIBUTION. Data that do not meet this criterion may not be effectively analyzed by some statistics. For example, the distribution may be markedly asymmetrical (skewed) which violates the assumptions made when developing the parametric tests. The parametric tests may then be inappropriate. The other traditional argument for using nonparametric tests is that they use ordinal (rankable) data and do not require interval or ratio levels of measurement. This is an area of debate as some statisticians argue that it is the properties of the numbers which are important and not some abstract scale of measurement which is deemed to underlie the numbers. The general impression is that modern researchers err towards using parametric analyses as often as possible, resorting to nonparametric tests only when the distribution of scores is exceptionally skewed. This allows them to use some of the most powerful statistical techniques. Once nonparametric tests had ease of calculation on their side. This no longer applies with the ready availability of statistical computer packages.

The nonparametric methods include the BINOMIAL TEST, RUNS TEST, KOLMOGOROV-SMIRNOV TWO-SAMPLE TEST, KOLMOGOROV-SMIRNOV TEST FOR ONE SAMPLE, MANN-WHITNEY *U* TEST, MOSES TEST, WILCOXON SIGNED-RANK TEST, SIGN TEST, MCNEMAR'S TEST, KRUSKAL-WALLIS TEST, MEDIAN TEST, CHI-SQUARE TEST, FRIEDMAN'S TEST, MOOD'S TEST, and SPEARMAN RANK ORDER CORRELATION COEFFICIENT, among others.

 📖 Cohen et al. 2011; Cramer & Howitt 2004; Dörnyei 2007; Everitt & Skrondal 2010; Hatch & Lazaraton 1991; Mackey & Gass 2005; Sahai & Khurshid 2001

nonparametric statistic(s)
another term for NONPARAMETRIC TEST(S)

non-participant observer
another term for COMPLETE OBSERVER

nonprobability sample
another term for NONPROBABILITY SAMPLING

nonprobability sampling
also **nonrandom sampling**

any sampling procedure in which the PROBABILITY of an element being included in the SAMPLE is not known. A sample selected in such a manner is called a **nonprobability sample** (also called **nonrandom sample**). In nonprobability sampling, unlike PROBABILITY SAMPLING, researchers use preestablished criteria to select a sample. The selectivity which is built into a nonprobability sample derives from the researcher targeting a particular group, in the full knowledge that it does not represent the wider POPULATION; it simply represents itself. This is frequently the case in small scale research, for example, as with one or two schools, two or three groups of students, or a particular group of teachers, where no attempt to generalize is desired; this is frequently the case for some ETHNOGRAPHIC RESEARCH, ACTION RESEARCH, or CASE STUDY research. Small scale research often uses non-probability samples because, despite the disadvantages that arise from their non-representativeness, they are far less complicated to set up, are considerably less expensive, and can prove perfectly adequate where researchers do not intend to generalize their findings beyond the sample in question, or where they are simply piloting a QUESTIONNAIRE as a prelude to the main study.

Just as there are several types of probability sampling, so there are several types of non-probability sampling: CONVENIENCE SAMPLING, QUOTA SAMPLING, DIMENSIONAL SAMPLING, PURPOSIVE SAMPLING, SEQUENTIAL SAMPLING, VOLUNTEER SAMPLING, and SNOWBALL SAMPLING. Each type of sample seeks only to represent itself or instances of itself in a similar population, rather than attempting to represent the whole, undifferentiated population.

📖 Cohen et al. 2011; Sahai & Khurshid 2001

nonproportional quota sampling
see QUOTA SAMPLING

non-randomized control group design
another term for NONEQUIVALENT CONTROL GROUP DESIGN

non-randomized control group pretest-posttest design
another term for NONEQUIVALENT CONTROL GROUP DESIGN

nonrandom error
another term for SYSTEMATIC ERROR

nonrandom sample
see NONPROBABILITY SAMPLING

nonrandom sampling
another term for NONPROBABILITY SAMPLING

nonrecursive model
see PATH ANALYSIS

nonresponse bias
another term for NONRESPONSE ERROR

nonresponse error
also **nonresponse bias**
a SELECTION ERROR which is due to the fact that some subjects included in the SAMPLE either cannot be traced by the interviewer or refuse to respond. Individuals who have randomly selected for inclusion in a sample have the right to decline. This is not necessarily problematic if the characteristics of those who accept and those who decline are basically the same. But that is often not the case. For example, when it comes to SURVEYs, you often find that those who are most interested in a topic will be the ones willing to participate. Or, you may offer an inducement that appeals to those with a particular need for, or interest in, what is being offered. In both cases your eventuating sample will not be representative of your population.
see also COVERAGE ERROR, SAMPLING ERROR
 Corbetta 2003; O'Leary 2004

nonresponse rate
see RESPONSE RATE

normal curve
another term for NORMAL DISTRIBUTION

normal distribution
also **normal curve, bell-shaped curve, bell-shaped distribution, Gaussian curve Gaussian distribution**
a DISTRIBUTION of data where the probability curve rises smoothly from a small number of results at both extremes (the tails) to a large number of cases in the middle. One useful feature of the normal distribution is that a certain percentage of scores always falls between the MEAN and certain distances above and below the mean. These distances are described as how many STANDARD DEVIATIONs (SDs) above or below the mean a score falls. Approximately 34 per cent (precisely, 34.13 per cent) of the scores fall between the mean and one SD above it. Similarly, approximately 34 per cent (precisely, 34.13 per cent) of the scores fall between the mean and one SD below it. So about two thirds (precisely, 68.26 per

cent) of the scores will be in the area between one *SD* above and one *SD* below the mean. Another 13.5 per cent (precisely, 13.59 per cent) of the scores will fall in the area that is more than one *SD* above the mean but less than two *SD*s above the mean. Similarly, 13.5 per cent (precisely, 13.59 per cent) of the scores will fall in the area that is more than one *SD* below the mean but less than two *SD*s below the mean. Finally, another 2.15 per cent (precisely, 2.15 per cent) of the scores are higher than two *SD*s above the mean. Similarly, 2.15 of the scores will fall below two *SD*s below the mean. Less than .26 per cent (precisely, .13 + .13) of the scores fall further than 3 *SD*s below or above the mean. Thus, about 95 per cent (95.44 per cent) of measures lie between -2 and +2 *SD*s below and above the mean. About 99 per cent (99.74 per cent) of measures lie between -3 and +3 *SD*s below and above the mean. Figure N.1 illustrates the percentage of scores in each part of the normal curve.

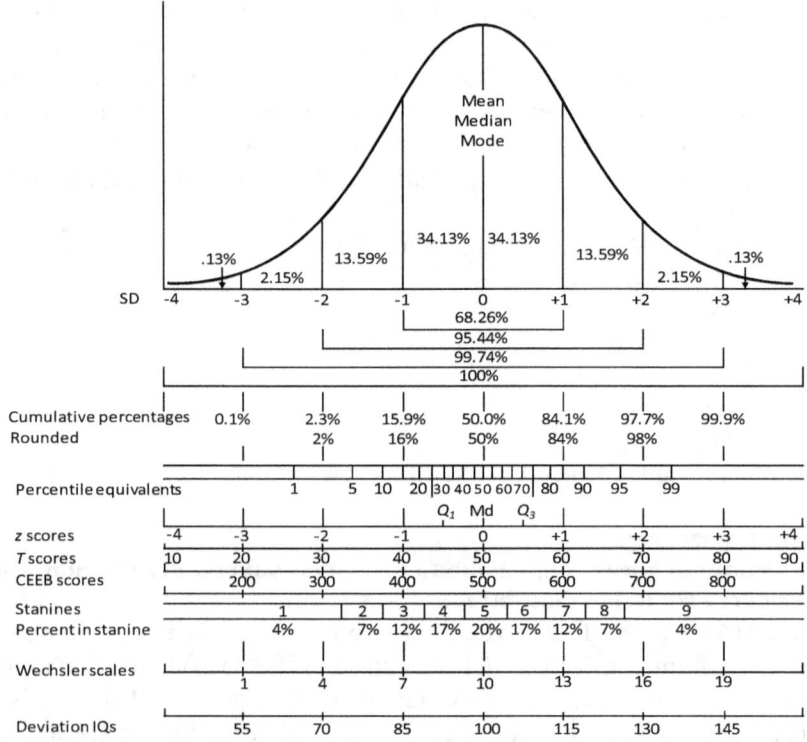

Figure N.1. *Relationships among Different Types of Test Scores in a Normal Distribution*

The first line under the curve shows standard deviations from -4 to +4. These are equivalent to Z SCOREs from -4 to +4 The CUMULATIVE PERCENTAGE line tells you that 15.9 percent of scores fall below -1 and 97.7

percent falls below +2, and so on. The line following cumulative percentage shows these cumulative percentage scores rounded to the nearest whole percentage. Multiplying each of these numbers by 100 gives you PERCENTILE RANK.

Percentile equivalents or scores are shown on the next line, which also shows the first QUARTILE (Q1 sets off the lowest 25% of scores), the MEDIAN, and the third quartile (Q3 sets off the lower 75% or upper 25% of scores). Note how slowly the percentile equivalents change below Q1 and above Q3 and how rapidly they change between these two points. The next line after percentile equivalents shows z scores, which are identical to the scores on the standard deviation line. Following the z score line are various STANDARD SCOREs transformed from z scores, including T SCORES, CEEB SCOREs, STANINEs, percent in stanine, WECHSLER SCALES, and Wechsler DEVIATION IQs. Note that 95 percent of the normal curve falls between plus and minus $z = 1.96$ and 99 percent falls between plus and minus $z = 2.58$. These boundaries become important when we discuss the use of the normal curve in INFERENTIAL STATISTICS.

There are many different normal distributions. Figure N.2 shows four normal distributions. Note that the two groups in Figure N.2a (Groups A and B) share the same mean, but Group A has a larger spread (i.e., Group A is more heterogeneous than Group B). Group B seems to be more homogeneous, and this group's scores tend to cluster closer to the mean. Next, examine Figure N.2b. Notice that Group C and Group D have the same spread, or VARIABILITY, but Group D has a higher mean than Group C. A normal distribution with a mean of zero and a standard deviation of one is called the **standard normal distribution**.

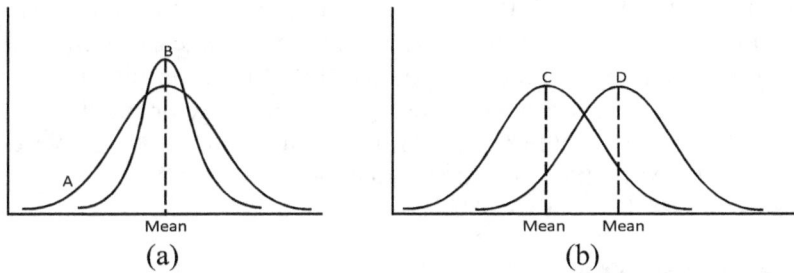

Figure N.2. Four Normal Distributions

Normal distribution has three fundamental characteristics. First, it is a **symmetrical distribution**, meaning that the upper half and the lower half of the distribution are mirror images of each other. If you fold the normal curve in half, the right side would fit perfectly with the left side; that is, it is not skewed. Second, the mean, MEDIAN, and MODE are all in the same place, in the center of the distribution (i.e., the top of the bell curve). Because of this second feature, the normal distribution is highest in the middle, it is unimodal, and it curves downward toward the top and bottom of the distribution. The curve is neither too peaked nor too flat and its tails are neither too short nor too long; it has no KURTOSIS. Finally, the normal distribution is **asymptotic**, meaning that the upper and lower tails of the distribution never actually touch the baseline, also known as the X axis.

see also BIVARIATE NORMAL DISTRIBUTION

Ary et al. 2010; Farhady 1995; Heiman 2011; Larson-Hall 2010; Leary 2011; Lodico et al. 2010; Porte 2010; Ravid 2011; Urdan 2010; Wilcox 2003

normality

an ASSUMPTION denoting that the data or scores on each VARIABLE should be normally distributed. Many of the PARAMETRIC TESTS of significance require that the distribution of the POPULATION(s) involved be normal or nearly normal in shape (see NORMAL DISTRIBUTION). The simplest methods for detecting violation of the normality assumption are graphical methods, such as STEM-AND-LEAF PLOTs, BOXPLOTs, or HISTOGRAMs, or statistical procedures such as the **Shapiro-Wilk test**. Another way to state this assumption is that neither of the two distributions should be skewed (see SKEWED DISTRIBUTION). Violations of this assumption are less troublesome if the SAMPLE SIZEs are large, which is to say that it is more important to worry about violations of this assumption if sample sizes are small. Nonetheless, the researcher (and the reader) can check for serious violations of this assumption by careful examination of the DESCRIPTIVE STATISTICS for all groupings in a study. If the descriptive statistics for all LEVELs of all variables indicate that the distributions are normal, there is no need to worry about violations of this assumption. Essentially, the distribution can be taken as normal if there is room for two or three STANDARD DEVIATIONs on either side of the MEAN and if there are no OUTLIERs (extremely large or small values).

see also INDEPENDENCE ASSUMPTION, HOMOGENEITY OF VARIANCE, LINEARITY, MULTICOLLINEARITY, HOMOSCEDASTICITY

Brown 1988, 1992; Lomax 2007

normative paradigm

a framework which contains two major orienting ideas: First, that human behavior is essentially rule governed; and second, that it should be investigated by the methods of natural science. The **interpretive paradigm**, in contrast to its normative counterpart, is characterized by a concern for the individual. Whereas normative studies are positivist (see POSITIVISM), all theories constructed within the context of the interpretive paradigm tend to be anti-positivist. The central endeavor in the context of the interpretive paradigm is to understand the subjective world of human experience. To retain the integrity of the phenomena being investigated, efforts are made to get inside the person and to understand from within. The imposition of external form and structure is resisted, since this reflects the viewpoint of the observer as opposed to that of the actor directly involved. Two further differences between the two paradigms may be identified at this stage: the first concerns the concepts of behavior and action; the second, the different conceptions of theory. A key concept within the normative paradigm, behavior refers to responses either to external environmental stimuli (another person, or the demands of society, for instance) or to internal stimuli (the need to achieve, for example). In either case, the cause of the behavior lies in the past. Interpretive approaches, on the other hand, focus on action. This may be thought of as behavior-with-meaning; it is intentional behavior and as such, future oriented. Actions are only meaningful to us in so far as we are able to ascertain the intentions of actors to share their experiences. A large number of our everyday interactions with one another rely on such shared experiences.

As regards theory, normative researchers try to devise general theories of human behavior and to validate them through the use of increasingly complex research methodologies which, some believe, push them further and further from the experience and understanding of the everyday world and into a world of abstraction. For them, the basic reality is the collectivity; it is external to the actor and manifest in society, its institutions and its organizations. The role of theory is to say how reality hangs together in these forms or how it might be changed so as to be more effective. The researcher's ultimate aim is to establish a comprehensive rational edifice, a universal theory, to account for human and social behavior.

But interpretive researchers begin with individuals and set out to understand their interpretations of the world around them. Theory is emergent and must arise from particular situations; it should be grounded on data generated by the research act. Theory should not precede research but follow it. Investigators work directly with experience and understanding to build their theory on them. The data thus yielded will include the meanings and purposes of those people who are their source. Further, the theory so generated must make sense to those to whom it applies. The aim of scientific investigation for the interpretive researcher is to understand how this glossing of reality goes on at one time and in one place and compare it with what goes on in different times and places. Thus theory becomes sets of meanings which yield insight and understanding of people's behavior. These theories are likely to be as diverse as the sets of human meanings and understandings that they are to explain. From an

interpretive perspective the hope of a universal theory which characterizes the normative outlook gives way to multifaceted images of human behavior as varied as the situations and contexts supporting them.
📖 Cohen et al. 2011

norm-referenced test
also **NRT**
a test that is designed to measure the subjects' global abilities (e.g., overall English proficiency, academic listening ability, reading comprehension). Each subject's score on such a test is interpreted relative to the scores of all other subjects who took the test. Such comparisons are usually done with reference to the concept of NORMAL DISTRIBUTION. The purpose of norm-referenced test (NRT) is to spread students out along a continuum of scores so that those with low abilities in a general area such as reading comprehension are at one end of the normal distribution, while those with high abilities are at the other end (with the bulk of the subjects falling between the extremes). In addition, while students may know the general format of the questions on an NRT (e.g., multiple-choice, true-false, dictation, or essay), they will typically not know before the test what specific content or skills will be covered by those questions.
Unlike a CRITERION-REFERENCED TEST, a norm-referenced test can only provide the researcher with information on how well one subject has achieved in comparison with another, enabling rank orderings of performance and achievement to be constructed. Hence a major feature of the norm-referenced test is its ability to discriminate between subjects and their achievements.
see also ITEM ANALYSIS, ITEM SPECIFICATIONS
📖 Brown 2005; Cohen et al. 2011; Perry 2011

novelty effect
a threat to EXTERNAL VALIDITY. Often a new TREATMENT is more effective than an older approach simply because it is new and different. After a while, the novelty wears off, and the new treatment is no better than the older treatment. For example, say that a high school teacher decided to put on a hat each time s/he was introducing a new concept in class. S/he uses this treatment in two of his/her classes (the TREATMENT GROUP) for two weeks but not in two other classes randomly assigned to be her/his CONTROL GROUP. S/he finds that the treatment group shows better understanding of the concepts than the control group. However, the effect may simply show that students pay attention when something new is happening in class. If s/he continues the hat routine for two months, s/he may find that it is no longer effective. The novelty effect means that a treatment is effective only when it is new or novel and that the treatment's effectiveness will not generalize beyond this initial period of time. In a re-

search study, reactive effects due to novelty are controlled for by extending the period of the study long enough so that any novelty effect will have worn off.
see also PRETEST-TREATMENT INTERACTION, MULTIPLE-TREATMENT INTERACTION, SPECIFICITY OF VARIABLES, TREATMENT DIFFUSION, RESEARCHER EFFECT, HALO EFFECT, HAWTHORNE EFFECT
📖 Lodico et al. 2010

NRT
an abbreviation for NORM-REFERENCED TEST

ns
an abbreviation for *not statistically significant*

nu (v)
an abbreviation for DEGREES OF FREEDOM

nuisance variable
another term for EXTRANEOUS VARIABLE

null hypothesis
also **zero hypothesis,** H_0**, NH**
a HYPOTHESIS which assumes that *no* or *zero* difference exists between two VARIABLEs. The null hypothesis (symbolized by H_0) is typically stated in words that 'A equals B' or 'there is no CORRELATION between variable A and B'. In general, the null hypothesis can be considered the hypothesis of 'no difference' or, more correctly, the hypothesis that the observed difference is entirely due to SAMPLING ERROR, i.e., that it occurred purely by chance. In a TEST OF SIGNIFICANCE, the rejection or acceptance of a null hypothesis is based on some LEVEL OF SIGNIFICANCE as a criterion. Whenever the PROBABILITY VALUE obtained under the null hypothesis is less than or equal to the predetermined level of significance, the null hypothesis is rejected. That is, when the difference between A and B is not significant, the null hypothesis is not rejected; when the difference is significant, the null hypothesis is rejected. Note that the null hypothesis is never proven right or wrong, or true or false, but is only rejected or not rejected at the arbitrarily chosen level of significance, i.e., .05, .01, .1, etc.

In addition to the null hypothesis, there is a hypothesis, termed **alternative hypothesis** (often represented by H_1, H_a, or **AH**), that states another potential outcome. When the null hypothesis is rejected, there is evidence in support of the alternative hypothesis. It is an opposite statement that the MEAN for group A is higher/lower than that for group B or there is a positive/negative correlation between variables A and B. If we ac-

cept H_0, then we are rejecting H_1 and if we reject H_0, then we are accepting H_1. Alternative hypotheses can be nondirectional or directional (see DIRECTIONAL HYPOTHESIS, NONDIRECTIONAL HYPOTHESIS).
The null hypothesis is the stronger hypothesis, requiring rigorous evidence not to support it. The alternative hypothesis is, perhaps, a fall-back position, taken up when the first—null—hypothesis is not confirmed. The latter is the logical opposite of the former. One should commence with the former and cast the research in the form of a null hypothesis, turning to the latter only in the case of finding the null hypothesis not to be supported.
see also TYPE I ERROR
📖 Brown 1988; Brown & Rodgers 2002; Hatch & Farhady 1982; Howell 2010; Porte 2010; Richards & Schmidt 2010; Sahai & Khurshid 2001

numerator
the number at the top of a fraction such a $\frac{4}{7}$. The numerator in this case is 4. The *denominator* is the bottom half of the fraction and so equals 7.

numerical scale
another term for ITEMIZED RATING SCALE

numerical variable
another term for QUANTITATIVE VARIABLE

numeric item
a CLOSED-FORM ITEM which is seemingly open-ended but is, in effect, closed-ended. These items ask for a specific numeric value, such as the respondent's age in years, or the number of foreign languages spoken by a person. What makes these items similar to closed questions is that we can anticipate the range of the possible answers and the respondent's task is to specify a particular value within the anticipated range. We could, in fact, list, for example for the age item, all the possible numbers (e.g., between 5 and 100) for the respondent to choose from (in a MULTIPLE-CHOICE ITEM fashion) but this would not be space-economical. However, computerized, on-line QUESTIONNAIREs often do provide these options in a pull-down menu for the respondent to click on the selected answer.
see also DICHOTOMOUS QUESTION, RATIO DATA QUESTION, MATRIX QUESTIONS, CONSTANT SUM QUESTIONS, RANK ORDER QUESTION, CONTINGENCY QUESTION, CHECKLIST
📖 Dörnyei 2003

O

objectives-referenced test
another term for CRITERION-REFERENCED TEST

objectivism
a notion that an objective reality exists and can be increasingly known through the accumulation of more complete information. Objectivism is thus an ONTOLOGY (the world exists, is real), and an EPISTEMOLOGY (knowledge can increasingly approximate the real nature, or quality, of its object—i.e., knowledge can become increasingly objective). Objectivist epistemology presupposes an objectivist ontology—to objectively know the world, there must be a real objective, definite world. (The inverse relation is not necessary—it is theoretically possible that a real world exists but cannot be known objectively because human perception is biased, for example.)
Positivists (see POSITIVISM) and many qualitative methodologists alike misconstrue objectivism as antithetical to QUALITATIVE RESEARCH methodology. Positivists take this opposition as repudiating any value to qualitative methodology. Many qualitative methodologists applaud the opposition between qualitative methodology and objectivism because they regard objectivism as an impersonal, reified, distorting concept that discounts the subjectivity of subjects and researchers. In this view, validating people's subjectivity requires eschewing objectivism.
see also SUBJECTIVISM, CONSTRUCTIVISM
📖 Given 2008

objectivity
a term that is commonly associated with QUANTITATIVE RESEARCH, broadly described as the extent to which research projects are undistorted by the *biases* of researchers. The VALIDITY, RELIABILITY, and GENERALIZABILITY of most EMPIRICAL RESEARCH projects are described as being dependent upon their objectivity. Consequently, quantitative researchers actively seek to ensure objectivity through a variety of means, including the standardization of testing procedures and the minimization of flexible data analysis and interpretation. Research projects from this perspective should be untainted by researcher characteristics and therefore repeatable. It is argued that only with such measures can the findings of studies be accurate and dependable. This view of objectivity as a necessary characteristic of research projects is usually associated with work that is rooted in the positivist (see POSITIVISM) or postpositivist (see POSTPOSITIVISM) tradition. This paradigm suggests that there is a single, identifiable truth that can be learned (or at least approached) through rigorous

scientific research. To this end, biases and personal viewpoints should be controlled for and as a result, irrelevant to the findings.

QUALITATIVE RESEARCHers use the term CONFIRMABILITY to mean the same thing as objectivity.

see also TRANSFERABILITY, DEPENDABILITY, CONFIRMABILITY, CREDIBILITY

📖 Dörnyei 2007; Mackey & Gass 2005; Trochim & Donnelly 2007

O'Brien test
see BROWN-FORSYTHE TEST

observation

a data collection method of generating data which involve the researcher immersing him/herself in a research setting, and systematically observing dimensions of that setting, interactions, relationships, actions, events, etc., within it. When collecting data using observational techniques, researchers aim to provide careful description of subjects' activities without unduly influencing the events in which the subjects are engaged. The distinctive feature of observation as a research process is that it offers an investigator the opportunity to gather live data from naturally occurring social situations. In applied linguistics, this can include a classroom or teachers' room, or any environment where language use is being studied, such as a bilingual family home or a work environment that is bilingual or has nonnative speakers. In this way, the researcher can look directly at what is taking place in situ rather than relying on second-hand accounts. The use of immediate awareness, or direct cognition, as a principal mode of research thus has the potential to yield more valid or authentic data than would otherwise be the case with mediated or inferential methods.

Observation can be of facts, such as the number of books in a classroom, the number of students in a class, the number of students who visit the school library in a given period. It can also focus on events as they happen in a classroom, for example, the amount of teacher and student talk, the amount of off-task conversation and the amount of group collaborative work. Further, it can focus on behaviors or qualities, such as the friendliness of the teacher, the degree of aggressive behavior or the extent of unsociable behavior among students.

Observations enable the researcher to gather data on:

- *the physical setting* (e.g., the physical environment and its organization);
- *the human setting* (e.g., the organization of people, the characteristics and makeup of the groups or individuals being observed, for instance, gender, class);

- *the interactional setting* (e.g., the interactions that are taking place, formal, informal, planned, unplanned, verbal, non-verbal, etc.); and
- *the program setting* (e.g., the resources and their organization, pedagogic styles, curricula and their organization).

However, the lack of control in observing in natural settings may render observation less useful, coupled with difficulties in measurement, problems of small samples, difficulties of gaining access and negotiating entry, and difficulties in maintaining anonymity.

Traditionally observation has been characterized as non-interventionist, where researchers do not seek to manipulate the situation or subjects, they do not pose questions for the subjects, nor do they deliberately create new provocations. QUANTITATIVE RESEARCH tends to have a small field of focus, fragmenting the observed into minute chunks that can subsequently be aggregated into a variable. QUALITATIVE RESEARCH, on the other hand, draws the researcher into the phenomenological complexity of participants' worlds; here situations unfold, and connections, causes, and CORRELATIONs can be observed as they occur over time. The qualitative researcher aims to catch the dynamic nature of events, to see intentionality, to seek trends and patterns over time.

There are numerous ways in which observations can be classified. One kind of observation available to the researcher lies on a continuum from *unstructured* (informal or casual) to *structured* (formal or systematic). A highly **structured observation** will know in advance what it is looking for (i.e. pre-ordinate observation) and will have its observation categories worked out in advance. A **semi-structured observation** will have an agenda of issues but will gather data to illuminate these issues in a far less predetermined or systematic manner. An **unstructured observation** will be far less clear on what it is looking for and will therefore have to go into a situation and observe what is taking place before deciding on its significance for the research. A semi-structured and, more particularly, an unstructured observation, will be hypothesis-generating rather than HYPOTHESIS-TESTING. The semi-structured and unstructured observations will review observational data before suggesting an explanation for the phenomena being observed. The structured observation, takes much time to prepare but the data analysis is fairly rapid, the categories having already been established, whilst the less structured approach, is quicker to prepare but the data take much longer to analyze. A structured observation is very systematic and enables the researcher to generate numerical data from the observations. Numerical data, in turn, facilitate the making of comparisons between settings and situations, and frequencies, patterns and trends to be noted or calculated. The observer adopts a passive, non-intrusive role, merely noting down the incidence of the factors being studied. Observations are entered on an OBSERVATIONAL SCHEDULE. In a nutshell, a structured observation will already have its hypotheses decided and will use the observational data to confirm or refute these hypotheses.

Another type of classification is based on the degree to which the observer is part of the behavior being observed (see PARTICIPANT OBSERVATION). Another way in which types of observation are classified relates to the level at which the behavior is being observed and recorded. **Molar behavior** refers to larger-scale behavior such as greeting a person who enters the room; this level of observation can involve interpretation by the observer as to the nature of the behavior. On the other hand, **molecular behavior** refers to the components that make up molar behavior, and is less likely to involve interpretation. For example, a molecular description of the behavior described earlier as greeting a person who enters the room might be described thus: 'extends hand to newcomer; grips newcomer's hand and shakes it; turns corners of mouth up and makes eye-contact, briefly; let's go of newcomer's hand'.

A final way to view types of observation is according to the theoretical perspectives of the researchers. Structured observation may use more interpretation and observe more molar behavior. ETHNOGRAPHY may entail more casual observation and interpretation, as well as introspection (see INTROSPECTIVE METHOD) on the part of the observer. Those employing ecological observation will be interested in the context and setting in which the behavior occurred and will be interested in inferring the meanings and intentions of the participants.

None of these ways of classifying observation are mutually exclusive. Different ways are complementary and may be used by the same researchers, in a form of TRIANGULATION. Alternatively, different approaches may form different stages in a single piece of research.

📖 Clark-Carter 2010; Cohen et al. 2011

observation checklist
another term for OBSERVATION SCHEDULE

observation schedule
also **observation scheme, observation checklist**
a form which is prepared prior to data collection that delineates the behavior and situational features to be observed and recorded during OBSERVATION. Observation schedules vary on a quantitative-qualitative continuum. More quantitative observation schedules sometimes referred to as *observation checklists*, use carefully and explicitly predefined categories of variables that can be counted and analyzed statistically. More qualitative observation schedules act as flexible guidelines for data collection, listing topics of interest and providing space to record notes

about new themes that emerge during observation. Heavily structured observation schedules are best suited to contexts where more is known about the topic of interest; more flexible, less structured observation schedules are more effective in situations where less is known about the research questions.

Observation schedules allow factual information to be recorded immediately. Factual data collected typically include some or all of relevant demographic information (e.g., age, gender), the role of participants in the research setting (e.g., job title), counts of the number of individuals present, and elements of the physical setting. Investigators also document what participants do (acts and activities) either by checking predetermined categories or by making notes about what is observed. What people say (words and the meanings ascribed to them) and relationships among participants are usually also of interest. In developing observation schedules, researchers attend to ease of use. More quantitative observation schedules will include explicitly defined categories that are exhaustive and mutually exclusive and that, wherever possible, avoid subjective measures requiring judgment or inference. More qualitative observation schedules seek to list as many emerging themes of interest to the project as is possible. Observation schedules are well suited to tracking time and if designed to do so, can capture the frequency, sequence and duration of events observed. Most researchers recommend leaving space on observation schedules, including the most explicitly quantitative forms, for recording data that do not fit into preselected categories and impressions and other more subjective data that may inform the study.
  Given 2008

observation scheme
   another term for OBSERVATION SCHEDULE

observed frequencies
   see CHI-SQUARE TEST

observed score
   see CLASSICAL TEST THEORY

observed significance level
   another term for PROBABILITY VALUE

observed variable
   another term for MANIFEST VARIABLE

observer as participant
   a type of PARTICIPANT OBSERVATION which involves the researchers to

reveal the fact that they were observing but not participate directly in the action being observed and maybe have less extensive contact with the group. Researchers are more participant than observer and may interact with subjects enough to establish rapport but do not really become involved in the behaviors and activities of the group. Their status as observer/researcher is known to those under study. Their role is more peripheral rather than the active role played by the participant observer. For example, a researcher could focus on observing a vocational training class for welfare recipients.

see also COMPLETE OBSERVER, PARTICIPANT AS OBSERVER, COMPLETE PARTICIPANT

📖 Ary et al. 2010; Given 2008

observer bias
see PARTICIPANT OBSERVATION

observer effect
see PARTICIPANT OBSERVATION

odds
the PROBABILITY that an event will occur divided by the probability that it will not occur. Odds can also be expressed as the ratio of the frequency of an event occurring to the frequency of other events occurring. Suppose, for example, that six out of nine students pass an exam. The probability of a student passing the exam is about .67 (6/9 = .667). The probability of a student failing the exam is about .33 (3/9 = .33 or 1 - .67 = .33). Consequently, the odds of a student passing the exam are about 2 (.667/.333 = 2). This is the same as the number of students passing the exam divided by the number of students failing it (6/3 = 2).

📖 Cramer & Howitt 2004

odds ratio
also *OR*
the ratio of the ODDS for a BINARY VARIABLE in two groups of subjects, for example, males and females. Put differently, the odds ratio represents the ratio of the odds favoring the occurrence of an event to that of another event. If the two possible states of the variable are labeled *success* and *failure* then the odds ratio is a measure of the odds of a success in one group relative to that in the other. In fact, it is a measure of association between two variables and can range from 0 upwards. An odds ratio of 1 indicates that there is no relationship between the variables. An odds ratio less than 1 indicates an inverse or negative relation and an odds ratio greater than 1 indicates a direct or positive relation. In a 2 × 2 (two-by-two) CONTINGENCY TABLE it is calculated by the formula (ad)/(bc),

where *a*, *b*, *c*, and *d* are the appropriate cell counts. Although the odds ratio can be extended beyond 2 × 2 tables, it becomes more difficult to interpret with larger contingency tables.
The odds ratio is a feature of LOGISTIC REGRESSION.
see also EFFECT SIZE
📖 Everitt & Skrondal 2010; Larson-Hall 2010; Sahai & Khurshid 2001; Sheskin 2011

off-line outlier
see OUTLIER

ogive curve
another term for CUMULATIVE FREQUENCY POLYGON

OLS
an abbreviation for ORDINARY LEAST SQUARES

omega² (ω^2)
also omega squared
the most commonly employed measure of TREATMENT EFFECT. Omega squared, symbolized by the notation ω^2 (the lowercase Greek letter omega), represents the proportion of VARIABILITY on the DEPENDENT VARIABLE that is associated with the INDEPENDENT VARIABLE in the underlying POPULATION. ω^2 is a relatively unbiased estimate of this proportion in the population.
see also ETA²
📖 Pagano 2009

omega squared
another term for OMEGA² (ω^2)

omnibus *F* test
also overall *F* test, ANOVA *F* test
a test which is used to determine whether three or more MEANs differ significantly from one another without being able to specify in advance of collecting the data which of those means differ significantly. It is the *F* RATIO in an ANALYSIS OF VARIANCE which determines whether the BETWEEN-GROUPS VARIANCE is significantly greater than the WITHIN-GROUPS VARIANCE. If there are good grounds for predicting which means differ from each other, an A PRIORI TEST should be carried out to see whether these differences are found. If differences are not expected, POST HOC TESTs should be conducted to find out which means or combination of means differ from each other.
📖 Cramer & Howitt 2004; Larson-Hall 2010

one-factor ANOVA
another term for ONE-WAY ANOVA

one-factor between-subjects ANOVA
another term for ONE-WAY ANOVA

one-factor within-subjects ANOVA
another term for ONE-WAY REPEATED MEASURES ANOVA

one-group posttest-only design
another term for ONE-SHOT DESIGN

one-group pretest-posttest design
also **before-after design**
a PRE-EXPERIMENTAL DESIGN type which is similar to ONE-SHOT DESIGN. The difference is that a pretest is given before the TREATMENT. Therefore, there are two tests: the pretest and the posttest (denoted by O). X is also used to symbolize the treatment in the following diagram of the design:

Experimental Group O X O

In one-group pretest-posttest design, the researcher gives a pretest (e.g., English vocabulary) to a group of students, provides some sort of treatment to the group (e.g., classroom instruction in English vocabulary), then gives them a posttest. The pretest and posttest means are then compared to determine whether learning took place.
The pretest and posttest do not have to be TESTS. They can be OBSERVATIONS. For example, you might observe the behavior of students using some OBSERVATION CHECKLIST before and after some special instruction. Test is just a cover term for all kinds of observations.
This design is sometimes referred to a REPEATED MEASURES DESIGN because the subjects are observed or measured twice on the independent variable. This design is an improvement over the one-shot design because the researcher has measured the gains that the subjects have made rather than just looking at how well everyone did at the end. However, without a CONTROL GROUP, the researcher still cannot make justified claims about the effect of the treatment. There is no way of determining whether any observed gain in means was due to the treatment itself, to normal teaching, or perhaps even to the effect of having taken the test twice (see testing effect). Two obvious extraneous variables not controlled in this design are HISTORY and MATURATION. Things happen between pretest and posttest, other than the experimental treatment, that

could affect learning. Between pretest and posttest, the subject grow mentally and physically, and they may learn experiences that could affect their achievement. History and maturation become more threatening to INTERNAL VALIDITY as the time between pre- and posttest increases. INSTRUMENTATION and STATISTICAL REGRESSION also present uncontrolled threats to internal validity of this design. Another weakness is that this design affords no way to assess the effect of the pretest. We know there is a PRACTICE EFFECT when subjects take a test a second time or even take an alternate form of the test—or they may learn something just from taking the test and will do better the second time. Without a control group to make a comparison possible, the results obtained in a one-group design are basically uninterpretable.

Ary et al. 2010; Brown 1988; Campbell & Stanley 1963; Cohen et al. 2011; Hatch & Farhady 1982; Hatch & Lazaraton 1991; Seliger & Shohamy 1989; Sheskin 2011

one-group time-series design
another term for SIMPLE INTERRUPTED TIME-SERIES DESIGN

one-parameter model
another term for RASCH MODEL

one-sample Kolmogorov-Smirnov test
another term for kolmogorov-smirnov test for one sample

one-sample *t*-test
also **single-sample *t*-test**

the least common type of *t*-TEST which is used to compare a single group (a SAMPLE) to a larger group (a POPULATION). In order to carry out this kind of a study the researcher must know prior to the start of the study the mean value of the population. One-sample t-test is used in situations in which the STANDARD DEVIATION (σ) of the population is unknown. For example, we may use the Graduate Record Examination (GRE) scores of second language graduate students (the sample) to test whether they are significantly different from the overall mean GRE in the university (the population). The purpose is to discover whether the sample can be regarded as being randomly selected from the specified population, or whether it is likely to have come from another population with a different mean.

Larson-Hall 2010; Miller 1984; Pagano 2009; Ravid 2011

one-sample *z* test
also **single-sample *z* test**

a PARAMETRIC TEST used in a one-sample experiment if (a) the population contains *interval* or *ratio* scores and (b) the STANDARD DEVIATION (σ) of the population is known. In the event the value of σ is unknown,

the data should be evaluated with the ONE-SAMPLE *t*-TEST. Of course, if the sample size is very small, the one-sample *t*-test provides a more accurate estimate of the underlying sampling distribution for the data. The single-sample *z* test is based on the following ASSUMPTIONS: a) the sample has been randomly selected from the population it represents (see PROBABILITY SAMPLING); and b) the distribution of data in the underlying population the sample represents is normal (see NORMALITY). If either of the aforementioned assumptions is saliently violated, the RELIABILITY of the *z* test statistic may be compromised.
 Sheskin 2011

one-shot case design
another term for ONE-SHOT DESIGN

one-shot design
also **one-shot case design, one-group posttest-only design**
a PRE-EXPERIMENTAL DESIGN type has only one group, a TREATMENT, and a posttest. Because there is only one group, there is no RANDOM ASSIGNMENT, no measurement before the treatment and no CONTROL GROUP. Students are given some experimental instruction or treatment (labeled *X*) for a given period of time. At the end of the specific period of time, the students receive some sort of test (labeled *O*), on the treatment. For example, in many teaching programs, teachers (and administrators) want to know whether students meet the objectives set for the course. At the end of the course, students take a test. The schematic representation for this design is:

Experimental Group   X   O

Although it has some features of an experiment (an intervention and a posttest), the lack of a pretest, of a control group, of random allocation, and of controls, renders this a flawed methodology. The main problem with this design is that there is no way of knowing the characteristics of the group or individual before the treatment or experience. It is open to almost all sorts of questions of INTERNAL and EXTERNAL VALIDITY. The results of such a study are neither valid nor generalizable. However, the design is useful as a means of pinpointing what to avoid in experimental research. It can also be used for preliminary testing of instruments.
 Campbell & Stanley 1963; Cohen et al. 2011; Hatch & Farhady 1982; Hatch & Lazaraton 1991; Seliger & Shohamy 1989

one-sided hypothesis
another term for DIRECTIONAL HYPOTHESIS

one-sided test
another term for ONE-TAILED TEST

one-tailed hypothesis
another term for DIRECTIONAL HYPOTHESIS

one-tailed test
also **one-sided test, directional test**
a SIGNIFICANCE TEST for which the ALTERNATIVE HYPOTHESIS is directional. Put differently, a one-tailed test is a test of hypothesis in which the rejection of the NULL HYPOTHESIS occurs in only one tail of the SAMPLING DISTRIBUTION of the TEST STATISTIC. The CRITICAL REGION of a one-tailed test is located completely at one end of the distribution of the test statistic. A one-tailed test takes into account deviations in only one direction from the value stated under the null hypothesis, either those that are greater than it or those that are less than it. With a one-tailed test the critical or rejection region is in one tail of the distribution and so we are willing to accept a result as statistically significant as long as its probability is .05 or less, on the predicted side of the distribution. In other words, 5% of possible occurrences are within the rejection region. For a .05 LEVEL OF SIGNIFICANCE, this region in a NORMAL CURVE is the point equal to $z = 1.645$. A z score of $+1.645$ leaves an area of .05 beyond it under the tail to the right of the distribution. A -1.645 z score leaves an area of .05 beyond it under the tail to the left of the distribution. These are the values needed for testing a one-tailed DIRECTIONAL HYPOTHESIS.

For a one-tailed test, we do not, as we would in TWO-TAILED TESTs, divide the 5 percent between the two sides of the curve. Rather, we place the whole 5 percent of chance error on one side of the curve. This means that the null hypothesis will be retained unless the observed difference is in the hypothesized direction. It is obvious that for rejecting a null hypothesis at a given level, a one-tailed test requires a smaller Z VALUE than a two-tailed test (compare $z = 1.645$ with $z = 1.96$, the z value required for a two-tailed test). Therefore, a one-tailed test makes it easier to reject the null hypothesis and thus increases the probability that the null hypothesis will be rejected if the difference is in the hypothesized direction.

In a positive directional hypothesis (see Figure O.1) we expect our group to perform better than normal for the POPULATION. For a positive directional (one-tailed) hypothesis we can reject the null hypothesis at the .05 level if the scores fall in the shaded area.

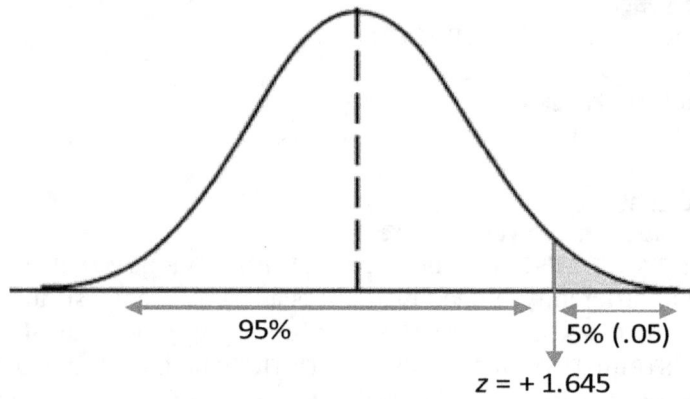

Figure O.1. A One-Tailed Test for a Positive Directional Hypothesis

Conversely, with a negative directional (one-tailed) hypothesis (see Figure O.2), we expect our group to perform worse than the population. For a negative directional hypothesis we can reject the null hypothesis at the .05 level of significance if the scores fall in the shaded area.

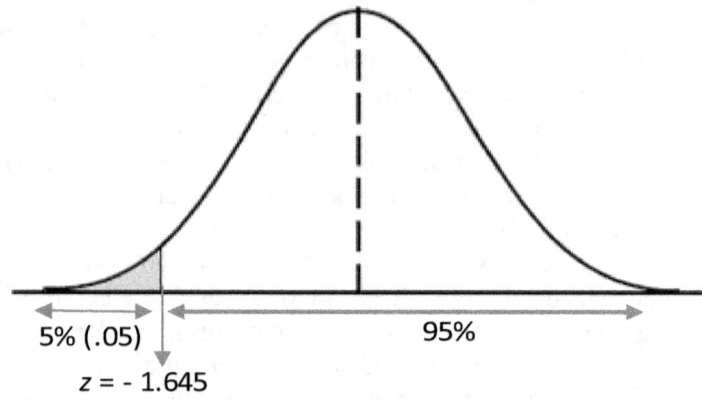

Figure O.2. A One-Tailed Test for a Negative Directional Hypothesis

The one-tailed test is a stronger test than the two-tailed test as it makes assumptions about the population and the direction of the outcome (i.e., that one group will score more highly than another), and hence, if supported, is more powerful than a two-tailed test.

📖 Ary et al. 2010; Brown 1988; Clark-Carter 2010; Everitt & Skrondal 2010; Hatch & Lazaraton 1991; Lavrakas 2008; Sahai & Khurshid 2001

one-to-one administration

a type of QUESTIONNAIRE administration which refers to a situation when someone delivers the questionnaire by hand to the designated person and arranges the completed form to be picked up later (e.g., handing out questionnaires to colleagues at work). This is a much more personal form of administration than MAIL SURVEYs and therefore the chances for the questionnaires to be returned are significantly better. The personal contact also allows the questionnaire administrator to create rapport with the respondent, to explain the purpose of the enquiry, and to encourage cooperation. Furthermore, with young children (i.e., less than ten years old) the administrator can be present while they complete the questionnaire to be available if help is needed.

see also GROUP ADMINISTRATION, SELF-ADMINISTERED QUESTIONNAIRE
 Dörnyei 2003

one-variable chi-square test

another term for CHI-SQUARE GOODNESS-OF-FIT TEST

one-way ANCOVA

an ANCOVA which involves one *categorical* INDEPENDENT VARIABLE (with two or more LEVELs or conditions), one *continuous* DEPENDENT VARIABLE (DV) (measured on INTERVAL or RATIO SCALEs), and one or more continuous COVARIATEs. One-way analysis of covariance is often used when evaluating the impact of an INTERVENTION or experimental manipulation, while controlling for pretest scores. All normal ONE-WAY ANOVA assumptions apply. These should be checked first. Additional ANCOVA assumptions are as follows:

1) the covariate is measured prior to the intervention or experimental manipulation;
2) the covariate is measured without error (or as reliably as possible);
3) the covariates are not strongly correlated with one another;
4) there is a linear relationship between the DV and the covariate for all groups (see LINEARITY); and
5) the relationship between the covariate and DV is the same for each of the groups.
 Pallant 2010

one-way ANOVA

also **single-factor ANOVA, single-factor between-subjects ANOVA, one-way between-subjects ANOVA, one-factor between-subjects ANOVA, one-factor ANOVA, one-way independent ANOVA, simple ANOVA**

a PARAMETRIC TEST which is used to compare the MEANs of two or more groups to see if the group means are significantly different from each other. A one-way ANOVA examines whether the differences between mean scores of two or more INDEPENDENT GROUPS are so great that we could not just ascribe the differences to chance fluctuations in scores. It involves one *continuous* dependent variable (DV) and one *categorical* INDEPENDENT VARIABLE (IV) (referred to as a FACTOR), which has a number of different LEVELs. These levels correspond to the different groups or conditions. For example, if a researcher is interested in investigating whether four ethnic groups (i.e., one categorical IV with four levels: Japanese, Chinese, Indian, Iranian) differ in their IQ scores (i.e., one continuous DV), the one-way ANOVA can be used. It is called one-way because you are looking at the impact of only one IV on your DV. One-way ANOVA is premised on the ASSUMPTIONS such as INDEPENDENCE OF GROUPS and OBSERVATIONS, NORMALITY, and HOMOGENEITY OF VARIANCE.

Usually, one-way ANOVA is used to test whether differences exist between three or more means; however, it can be applied to situations in which there are only two means to be compared. In fact, if you want to compare the means of two independent groups on a single variable, you can use either an INDEPENDENT SAMPLES t-TEST or a one-way ANOVA. The results will be identical, except instead of producing a t-VALUE, the ANOVA will produce an **F value**, which is the ratio of the BETWEEN-GROUPS VARIANCE (explained by the IV) to the WITHIN-GROUPS VARIANCE (referred to as the ERROR TERM) in an ANOVA. Because the t-test and the one-way ANOVA produce identical results when there are only two groups being compared, most researchers use the one-way ANOVA only when they are comparing three or more groups. The problem with running separate t-tests is that each time we run a t-test, we must make a decision about whether the difference between the two means is meaningful, or statistically significant. This decision is based on PROBABILITY, and every time we make such a decision, there is a slight chance we might be wrong. The more times we make decisions about the significance of t-tests, the greater the chances are that we will be wrong. In other words, the more t-tests we run, the greater the chances become of deciding that a t-test is significant (i.e., that the means being compared are really different) when it really is not. In still other words, running multiple t-tests increases the likelihood of making a TYPE I ERROR (i.e., rejecting the NULL HYPOTHESIS when, in fact, it is true). A one-way ANOVA fixes this problem by adjusting for the number of groups being compared.

One-way ANOVA produces multiple comparisons in two steps. First an F value is computed and checked for significance. A large F ratio indicates that there is more variability between the groups than there is within each group. If the F value is significant, it means that there is at least one significant difference amongst the group means. It does not, however, tell us which of the groups differ. In other words, because with more than two groups we have more than one contrast (i.e., with three groups—A, B, and C—we have three contrasts: A and B, B and C, or C and A), we need a second step to determine which contrast(s) is/are significant. For this purpose we compute a POST HOC TEST, which compares all combinations of pairs of means. The alternative to conducting post hoc tests after obtaining a significant OMNIBUS F TEST is to plan your study to conduct only specific comparisons (referred to as PLANNED COMPARISONs). For example, in an experimental study with five different interventions we may want to know whether intervention A is superior to each of the other interventions. In that situation, we may not be interested in comparing all the possible combinations of groups. If we are interested in only a subset of the possible comparisons, it makes sense to use planned comparisons, rather than post hoc tests, because of POWER issues. The choice of whether to use planned comparisons versus post hoc tests must be made before you begin your analysis.

The striking advantage of one-way ANOVA is that it can be applied when there are more than two groups in the IV so that the means of three, four, or even more groups on a DV can be tested simultaneously for significant differences. The nonparametric alternative to a one-way ANOVA is the KRUSKALL-WALLIS TEST.

see also ONE-WAY REPEATED MEASURES ANOVA

📖 Brown 1988; Dörnyei 2007; Ho 2006; Larson-Hall 2010; Pallant 2010; Salkind 2007; Urdan 2010

one-way between-subjects ANOVA
another term for ONE-WAY ANOVA

one-way between-subjects design
see BETWEEN-SUBJECTS DESIGN

one-way chi-square test
another term for CHI-SQUARE GOODNESS-OF-FIT TEST

one-way goodness-of-fit chi-square test
another term for CHI-SQUARE GOODNESS-OF-FIT TEST

one-way hypothesis
another term for DIRECTIONAL HYPOTHESIS

one-way independent ANOVA
another term for ONE-WAY ANOVA

one-way MANCOVA
see MULTIVARIATE ANALYSIS OF COVARIANCE

one-way MANOVA
see MULTIVARIATE ANALYSIS OF VARIANCE

one-way repeated measures ANOVA
also **one-way within-subjects ANOVA, single-factor within-subjects ANOVA, one-factor within-subjects ANOVA**
a REPEATED-MEASURES ANOVA with a single WITHIN-SUBJECTS FACTOR in which all subjects are exposed to two or more different TREATMENT conditions, or measured on two or more occasions. That is, the same subjects are measured on all levels of the repeated measures INDEPENDENT VARIABLE (IV) or at different points in time. More specifically, one-way repeated measures ANOVA involves two variables: one *categorical* IV with two or more levels (e.g., Time 1, Time 2, Time 3, or Condition A, Condition B, Condition C); and one *continuous* DEPENDENT VARIABLE (e.g., scores on an achievement test). It can also be used to compare respondents' responses to two or more different questions or items. These questions, however, must be measured using the same scale (e.g. 1 = strongly disagree, to 5 = strongly agree).

For example, Table O.1 shows the representation of five subjects (S1, S2, S3, S4, S5) in a design with three time points (T1, T2, T3). Each participant produces three scores, one in each of the three occasions. The one-way repeated measures ANOVA makes it possible to make a direct comparison between each participant's three scores in all the occasions to see if there is a significant difference somewhere among the obtained sets of scores.

Time		
Time 1	Time 2	Time 3
subject 1	subject 1	subject 1
subject 2	subject 2	subject 2
subject 3	subject 3	subject 3
subject 4	subject 4	subject 4
subject 5	subject 5	subject 5

Table O.1. One-Way Repeated Measures ANOVA

This procedure is also sometimes called a **treatment × subjects design** because all of the levels of the IV are crossed with all of the subjects in the study.

📖 Gamst et al. 2008; Pallant 2010; Salkind 2007

one-way within-subjects ANOVA
another term for ONE-WAY REPEATED MEASURES ANOVA

one-way within-subjects design
see WITHIN-SUBJECTS DESIGN

on-line outlier
see OUTLIER

ontology
a theory which derives from the Greek words for *thing* and *rational account*. Ontology refers to the study of being or reality. In classical and speculative philosophy, ontology was the philosophical science of being. Its general aim was to provide reasoned, deductive accounts of the fundamental sorts of things that existed. It was not concerned with the specific nature of empirical entities, but rather with more basic questions of the universal forms of existence. Examples of classical ontological questions are as follows: 'Are bodies the only things that exist, or are immaterial forms real? Is there a supreme intelligence in the universe, or is all activity reducible to mechanical motion? Are individuals alone real, or are collectivities independently real? Are there real objects of universal terms, or are universals simply names that humans give to mental abstractions?' The very generality of these questions means that they will always have some connection to the investigation of natural and social phenomena. In the contemporary era, however, it would be wrong to continue to think of ontology as a fundamental science given that hypothetical-empirical methods of research have permanently displaced the deductive-rationalist methods of classical philosophy.
see also EPISTEMOLOGY
📖 Given 2008

open coding
see CODING

open-ended item
another term for OPEN-FORM ITEM

open-ended question
another term for OPEN-FORM ITEM

open-ended response
another term for OPEN-FORM ITEM

open-form item
also **open-ended response, open-response item, open-ended question, open question, open-form question, open-response question, free response item, unrestricted question, non-directive question, open-ended item**

a type of item or question which allows participants to give their own answers without restrictions. In open-form items, the actual question is not followed by response options for the respondent to choose from but rather by some blank space (e.g., dotted lines) for the respondent to fill. Open-form items provide participants of research with the opportunity to choose the terms with which to construct their descriptions and highlight the topics that are meaningful to them. The freedom on the part of research participants to elaborate on self-selected aspects related to the researcher's topic of examination in response to open-form items contrasts with the kind of responses called for by CLOSED-FORM ITEMS. They enable respondents to answer as much as they wish, and are particularly suitable for investigating complex issues, to which simple answers cannot be provided. Open-form items may be useful for generating items that will subsequently become the stuff of closed-form items.

Open-form items provide a way to find out, in an unstructured manner, what people are thinking about a particular topic or issue. As such, they often serve as the basis for further, more structured research. Since open-form items are primarily exploratory, they are commonly associated with QUALITATIVE RESEARCH, particularly CASE STUDY, ETHNOGRAPHY, ACTION RESEARCH, and MIXED METHODS RESEARCH, and often complement OBSERVATION, INTERVIEW, and DIARY STUDY.

Open-response items can take many forms in applied linguistics studies because such items are often: (a) used for a variety of purposes (e.g., research, curriculum development, course evaluation); (b) applied at various levels (e.g., classroom, institutional, provincial, state, national, international); and (c) administered to various groups of people (e.g., students, teachers, administrators, parents). The most common types of open-response items are FILL-IN and SHORT-ANSWER ITEMS.

It is also important to understand what open-form items are not. They are not tests; they do not have good or bad answers. They seek information about respondents in a nonevaluative manner, without gauging their performance against a set of criteria or against the performance of a norm group. Open-form items are also not DISCOURSE COMPLETION TASKs that require the informant to produce some form of authentic language for pragmatic or grammatical analysis. Thus, in qualitative research, open-form items are used to collect data that will be analyzed for its content (see CONTENT ANALYSIS) and not for its language (or language analysis). Open-form items, however, can lead to irrelevant and redundant information; they may be too open-ended for the respondent to know what

kind of information is being sought; they may require much more time from the respondent to enter a response (thereby leading to refusal to complete the item), and they may make the measure appear long and discouraging. With regard to analysis, the data are not easily compared across participants, and the responses are difficult to code and to classify. Here is an example of an open-response item: 'What types of classroom activities do you think are best for effective language learning?' (followed by a three-line blank). Such items explore an issue deeply by not restricting the respondents to a set of answers but asking them to express their own ideas more fully or inviting them to elaborate or explain their answers to closed-response items in their own words.
📖 Best & Kahn 2006; Dörnyei 2003; Given 2008; Perry 2011

open-form question
another term for OPEN-FORM ITEM

open question
another term for OPEN-FORM ITEM

open-response item
another term for OPEN-FORM ITEM

open-response question
another term for OPEN-FORM ITEM

operational definition
defining a CONSTRUCT by specifying precisely how it is measured or manipulated in a particular study. An operational definition describes or defines a VARIABLE in terms of the operations or techniques used to make it happen or measure it. When researchers describe the variables in their study, they specify what they mean by demonstrating how they measured the variable. Such an operational definition should take a variable out of the realm of theory and plant it squarely in concrete reality. Basically, it must be a definition that is based on observable, testable, or quantifiable characteristics. Demographic variables like age, gender, or ethnic group are usually measured simply by asking the participant to choose the appropriate category from a list. Likewise, abstract concepts like language proficiency, self-concept, intelligence, or motivation need to be defined operationally by spelling out in some detail how they were measured in a particular study.
Operational definition is an important aspect of measurement. Researchers define key concepts and terms in the context of their research studies by using operational definitions. That is, researchers ensure that everyone is talking about the same phenomenon. For example, if a researcher

wants to study the effects of exercise on stress levels, it would be necessary for the researcher to define what exercise is. 'Does exercise refer to jogging, weight lifting, swimming, jumping rope, or all of the above?' By defining exercise for the purposes of the study, the researcher makes sure that everyone is referring to the same thing. Clearly, the definition of exercise can differ from one study to another, so it is crucial that the researcher define exercise in a precise manner in the context of his/her study. Having a clear definition of terms also ensures that the researchers' study can be replicated by other researchers.

Although researchers can certainly use the same operational definitions in different studies (which facilitates replication of the study results), different studies can operationally define the same terms and concepts in different ways. For example, in one study, a researcher may define gifted children as those children who are in advanced classes. In another study, however, gifted children may be defined as children with IQs of 130 or higher. There is no one correct definition of gifted children, but providing an operational definition reduces confusion by specifying what is being studied.

Operational definition is contrasted with **conceptual definition** (also called **theoretical definition, nominal definition, constitutive definition)**, which is an abstract, dictionary-type definition. A conceptual definition is more or less like the definition we might find in a dictionary.

For example, intelligence may be defined as the ability to think abstractly or the capacity to acquire knowledge. This type of definition helps convey the general meaning of a construct, but it is not precise enough for research purposes. The researcher needs to define constructs so that readers know exactly what is meant by the term and so that other investigators can replicate the research. Although conceptual definitions are necessary, they are seldom specific enough for research purposes.

 Brown 1988; Marczyk et al. 2005; Morgan et al. 2004

opportunistic sampling
also accidental sampling, haphazard sampling, incidental sampling

a type of NON-PROBABILITY SAMPLING which involves the researcher taking advantage of unforeseen opportunities as they arise during the course of fieldwork, adopting a flexible approach to meld the sample around the fieldwork context as it unfolds. Opportunistic sampling is, indeed, an unplanned and potentially haphazard procedure in the sense that it is followed on the spur of the moment. While working in the field, the researcher sometimes comes across respondents who are too good to miss and a decision to include them on the spot. The problem is that they are not always exactly what is needed, yet their selection is very much in line with the emergent nature of the QUALITATIVE RESEARCH.

see also CONVENIENCE SAMPLING, QUOTA SAMPLING, DIMENSIONAL SAMPLING, PURPOSIVE SAMPLING, SNOWBALL SAMPLING, SEQUENTIAL SAMPLING, VOLUNTEER SAMPLING
 Dörnyei 2003; Ritchie & Lewis 2003

OR
an abbreviation for ODDS RATIO

order effect
also **multiple treatment interference, sequencing effect, carryover effect, accumulative treatment effect**
a source of threat to EXTERNAL VALIDITY which is the result of the accumulative effect due to the particular order in which TREATMENTs are presented. An order effect is where an obtained difference on the DEPENDENT VARIABLE is a direct result of the order of presentation of the experimental conditions, rather than being due to the INDEPENDENT VARIABLE manipulated by the experimenter. For example, participants may become less interested the more tasks they carry out or they may become more experienced in what they have to do. When requiring participants to conduct more than one task, it may be important to determine whether the order in which they carry out the tasks has any effect on their performance. The most common ways to control for the order effect are LATIN SQUARE DESIGN and COUNTER BALANCED DESIGN. If the number of tasks is very small, it is possible to have each task carried out in all possible orders. For example, with three tasks, A, B and C, there are six different orders: ABC, ACB, BAC, BCA, CAB and CBA. It assumes that by varying the order in such a systematic fashion, order effects are systematically cancelled out. If there are a large number of tasks, it may be useful to select a few of these either at random or on some theoretical basis to determine if order effects exist. Assessing order effects essentially requires that comparisons are made according to the order of carrying out the tasks, not according to type of task.
 Cramer & Howitt 2004; Perry 2011; Sheskin 2011

ordinal data
see ORDINAL SCALE

ordinal level of measurement
another term for ORDINAL SCALE

ordinal scale
also **ordinal level of measurement, rank-order scale**
a type of MEASUREMENT SCALE which, unlike the NOMINAL SCALE, is characterized by the ability to measure a VARIABLE in terms of both

identity and *magnitude*. Ordinal data indicate order ('high to low', 'first to last', 'smallest to largest', 'strongly disagree to strongly agree', 'not at all to a very great deal'). This makes it a higher level of measurement than the nominal scale because the ordinal scale allows for the categorization of a variable and its relative magnitude in relation to other variables. In other words, ordinal data answer two questions: 'are they different?' and 'which is larger?' For example, a researcher might want to use a scale that orders language learners from least to most proficient in their overall English. To do this, the investigator could use proficiency test scores to arrange the learners from low to high and then assign each a rank using simple ordinal numbers. The highest learner would be 'first', followed by the 'second' student, and so forth. Other examples of potential ordinal scales in language research may include the rankings of students' performances in a particular class, the ordering of teachers' abilities in a language program, and the achievement rankings of various sections of a course. Data which are obtained by using an ordinal level of measurement are called **ordinal data**. In addition, a variable which is measured on an ordinal scale is called **ordinal variable**.

The important point is that ordinal scales rank people, objects, or concepts, with each point on the scale being 'more than' and 'less than' the other points on the scale. But there is still an absence of a metric—a measure using calibrated or equal intervals (see INTERVAL SCALE). Therefore one cannot assume that the distance between each point of the scale is equal, i.e. the distance between 'very little' and 'a little' may not be the same as the distance between 'a lot' and 'a very great deal' on a RATING SCALE. One could not say, for example, that, in a 5-point rating scale (see LIKERT SCALE) (1 = strongly disagree; 2 = disagree; 3 = neither agree nor disagree; 4 = agree; 5 = strongly agree) point 4 is in twice as much agreement as point 2, or that point 1 is in five times more disagreement than point 5. However, one could place them in an order: 'not at all', 'very little', 'a little', 'quite a lot', 'a very great deal', or 'strongly disagree', 'disagree', 'neither agree nor disagree', 'agree', 'strongly agree', i.e., it is possible to rank the data according to rules of 'lesser than' of 'greater than', in relation to whatever the value is included on the rating scale.

see also RATIO SCALE

📖 Bachman 2004; Brown 1992; Cohen et al. 2011; Dörnyei 2007

ordinal variable
see ORDINAL SCALE

ordinary least squares
see LEAST SQUARES METHOD OF ANALYSIS

ordinate
  another term for VERTICAL AXIS

orthogonal data
  another term for BALANCED DATA

orthogonal design
  another term for BALANCED DESIGN

orthogonality
  a perfect nonassociation (no CORRELATION) between VARIABLEs. If two variables are orthogonal, knowing the value of one variable gives no clue as to the value of the other; the CORRELATION between them is zero.
  📖 Tabachnick & Fidell 2007

outcome evaluation
  another term for SUMMATIVE EVALUATION

outcome variable
  another term for DEPENDENT VARIABLE

outlier
  extreme scores that are so obviously deviant from the remainder of the data that one can question whether they belong in the data set at al. Many researchers consider a score to be an outlier if it is farther than three STANDARD DEVIATIONs from the mean of the data. Figure O.3 shows two kinds of outliers. Figure O.3a shows two **on-line outlier**s. Two participants' scores, although falling in the same pattern as the rest of the data, are extreme on both variables. On-line outliers tend to artificially inflate CORRELATION COEFFICIENTs, making them larger than is warranted by the rest of the data. Figure O.3b shows two **off-line outlier**s. Off-line outliers tend to artificially deflate the value of r. The presence of even a few off-line outliers will cause r to be smaller than indicated by most of the data.
  The existence of such cases can have important repercussions on certain statistical tests and distort the interpretation of the data. There are basically two strategies that can be used in dealing with outliers. One strategy is to develop and employ procedures for identifying outliers. Within the framework of this strategy, criteria should be established for determining under what conditions one or more scores that are identified as outliers should be deleted from a set of data. A second approach in dealing with outliers is to develop statistical procedures that are not influenced (or only minimally affected) by the presence of outliers (see ROBUST).

see also ACCOMMODATION, DATA TRANSFORMATION, INTERQUARTILE RANGE, BOX-AND-WHISKER PLOT
📖 Leary 2011; Porte 2010; Sheskin 2011; Urdan 2010

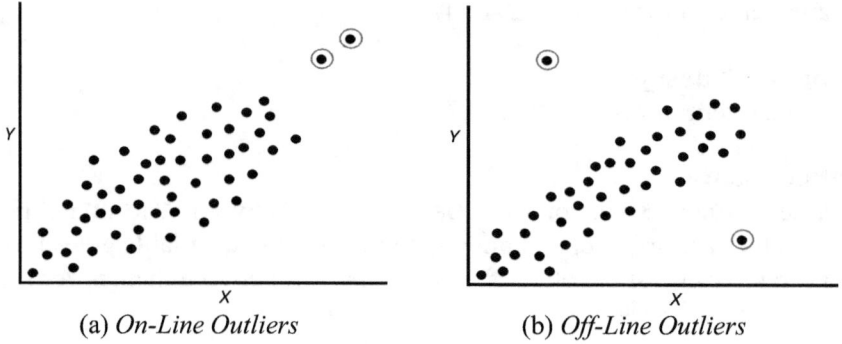

Figure O.3. Schematic Representation of Outliers

overall F test
another term for OMNIBUS F TEST

P

p
an abbreviation for PROBABILITY

paired groups
another term for DEPENDENT SAMPLES

paired samples
another term for DEPENDENT SAMPLES

paired-samples *t*-test
also **repeated measures *t*-test, matched-samples *t*-test, matched *t*-test, matched-pairs *t*-test, dependent samples *t*-test, correlated *t*-test, related-samples *t*-test, within-subjects *t*-test, pairs *t*-test, related *t*-test**
a type of *t*-TEST used when we have only one group of participants and we collect data from them on two different occasions (e.g., Time A, Time B) or under two different conditions (e.g., Condition A, Condition B). A typical example is a comparison of pretest and posttest scores obtained from one group of subjects. We assess each person on some *continuous* measure at Time A, and then again at Time B, after exposing them to some experimental manipulation or intervention. This approach is also used when we have matched pairs of subjects (i.e., each person is matched with another on specific criteria, such as age, sex, IQ, grades). One of the pair is exposed to intervention A and the other is exposed to Intervention B. Scores on a continuous measure are then compared for each pair. Paired-samples *t*-tests can also be used when we measure the same person in terms of his/her response to two different questions or items. Both questions, however, must be measured using the same scale (e.g., 1 = strongly disagree, to 5 = strongly agree).

The most important requirement for conducting this *t*-test is that the two sets of scores are paired. It is also assumed that the samples were randomly selected; the two sets of scores are normally distributed (see NORMALITY); and the two samples have equal population variances (see HOMOGENEITY OF VARIANCE). Like the INDEPENDENT *t*-TEST, the dependent t-test is quite ROBUST to violation of the normality assumption. As the SAMPLE SIZE must be equal for the two samples due to the pairing of scores, the dependent *t*-test is also quite robust to violation of the homogeneity of variance assumption. With sample sizes of 30+, violation of normality is unlikely to cause any serious problems.

The nonparametric alternative to a paired-sample *t*-test is the WILCOXON MATCHED-PAIRS SIGNED-RANKS TEST.

see also INDEPENDENT SAMPLES *t*-TEST, PARAMETRIC TEST(S), NONPARAMETRIC TEST(S)
📖 Dörnyei 2007; Larson-Hall 2010; Lomax 2007; Mackey & Gass 2005; Pallant 2010; Peers 1996; Ravid 2011

pairs *t*-test
another term for PAIRED-SAMPLES *t*-TEST

pairwise comparison
see NONPAIRWISE COMPARISON

panel conditioning
see PANEL STUDY

panel design
another term for PANEL STUDY

panel study
also **prospective longitudinal study, follow up study, panel design**
a type of LONGITUDINAL RESEARCH in which successive measures are taken at different points in time from the *same* respondents. In other words, the researcher observes exactly the same people, group, or organization periodically (across multiple time points). For example, researchers have studied how age affects IQ by measuring the same individuals as adolescents and when they were college-aged, middle-aged, and older. Because the same subjects are studied over time, researchers can see the changes in the individuals' behavior and investigate the reasons for the changes.

The main reason for the popularity of the panel study is the fact that it allows us to collect information about change at micro level as it really happens. Panel studies offer a powerful nonexprimental method for examining development and causality. However, they are rather expensive and time consuming to run, and they also require a committed research team maintained over years. In addition, these designs also suffer from two serious problems to their validity: attrition (see MORTALITY) and **panel conditioning**. The usual pattern of participation in a long-term panel study is that an increasing number of participants drop out of the panel in the successive waves. There are multiple reasons for this attrition; there may be, e.g., logistic ones (non-availability, changing address or telephone number, etc.), or panel members may become ill or simply unwilling to continue because of a lack of time or loss of interest. The second problem concerns the fact that when a group of people take part in a longitudinal study, there is a real danger that the regular meetings that the participants involves and the knowledge of being part of the

study can alter the panel members behavior and responses. They may also behave differently because they want to please the researcher whom they are getting to know better and better. Thus, the resulting panel conditioning effect can be seen as a combination of PRACTICE EFFECT and the HAWTHORNE EFFECT.
see also TREND STUDY, RETROSPECTIVE LONGITUDINAL STUDY
📖 Dörnyei 2007; Neuman 2007

paper-and-pencil test
see PERFORMANCE ASSESSMENT

paradigm
a term used very widely and loosely to refer to a conceptual framework of beliefs, theoretical assumptions, accepted research methods, and standards that define legitimate work in a particular science or discipline. Paradigms function as maps or guides for scientific communities, determining important problems or issues for its members to address and defining acceptable theories or explanations, methods and techniques to solve defined problems.
Researchers, explicitly and implicitly, develop conceptual frameworks which fashion how they carry out their research. These frameworks are shaped by each researcher's view of the world, and are also informed by how other academics conceptualize research. In the social sciences, a number of generally accepted models have been developed that articulate these conceptual frameworks and they are called paradigms. They are often distinguished by their beliefs about ONTOLOGY ('What is reality?'), epistemology ('What is knowledge?') and AXIOLOGY (Is truth value-free or value-laden?). POSITIVISM and CONSTRUCTIVISM are two examples of paradigms.
📖 Heigham & Croker 2009; O'Donoghue 2007; Richards & Schmidt 2010

parallel-form reliability
also **equivalent-form reliability, alternate-form reliability, alternative-form reliability**
an approach to estimating the RELIABILITY of a measuring instrument (e.g., a test). In this approach, two or more forms of a test (e.g., Form A and Form B) that are different but equivalent in content and difficulty are administered to the same group of test takers at essentially the same time (in immediate succession). Then a CORRELATION COEFFICIENT between the total scores of the alternate forms of the test is calculated. The resulting correlation coefficient is interpreted as a numerical index of the extent to which the alternate forms are equivalent to each other or consistent in measuring test takers abilities. This measure reflects variations in performance from one specific set of items to another. It indicates

whether you can generalize a subject's score to what the subject would receive if another form of the same test had been given. If subjects are tested with one form on one occasion and with an equivalent form on a second occasion and their scores on the two forms are correlated, the resulting coefficient is called the coefficient of stability and equivalence. This coefficient reflects two aspects of test reliability: variations in performance from one time to another and variations from one form of the test to another. A high coefficient of stability and equivalence indicates that the two forms are measuring the same construct and measuring consistently over time.

One major problem with this approach is that you have to be able to generate lots of items that reflect the same construct, which is often no easy feat. Furthermore, this approach makes the assumption that the randomly divided halves are parallel or equivalent. Even by chance, this will sometimes not be the case. In addition, since administering two alternate forms to the same group of individuals will necessarily involve giving one form first and the other second, there is a possibility that individuals may perform differently because of the order in which they take the two forms. That is, they may do better on the second form they take because of the PRACTICE EFFECT of having taken the first, thus confounding the relative equivalence of the forms with the test-retest effect. One way to minimize the possibility of an ordering effect is to use a COUNTER BALANCED DESIGN, in which half of the individuals take one form first and the other half take the other form first. The MEANs and STANDARD DEVIATIONs for each of the two forms can then be computed and compared to determine their equivalence, after which the correlation between the two sets of scores (Form A and Form B) can be computed. This correlation is then interpreted as indicator of the equivalence of the two tests, or as an estimate of the reliability of either one.

The parallel-forms approach is similar to the SPLIT-HALF RELIABILITY. The major difference is that parallel forms are constructed so that the two forms can be used independently of each other and considered equivalent measures. For practical reasons, however, this method of assessing test reliability is used less frequently than an INTERNAL CONSISTENCY RELIABILITY approach.

📖 Ary et al. 2010; Richards & Schmidt 2010; Trochim & Donnelly 2007

parameter

see STATISTIC

parametric design

a TRUE EXPERIMENTAL DESIGN in which participants are randomly assigned to groups whose parameters are fixed in terms of the LEVELs of the INDEPENDENT VARIABLE (IV) that each receives. For example, imagine that an experiment is conducted to improve the reading abilities of poor, average, good, and outstanding readers (four levels of the IV 'reading ability'). Four experimental groups are set up to receive the intervention (i.e., the IV or TREATMENT), thus: EXPERIMENTAL GROUP one (poor readers); experimental group two (average readers), experimental group three (good readers and experimental group four (outstanding readers). The CONTROL GROUP (group five) would receive no intervention. The researcher could chart the differential effects of the intervention on the groups, and thus have a more sensitive indication of its effects than if there was only one experimental group containing a wide range of reading abilities; the researcher would know which group was most and least affected by the intervention.

Parametric designs are useful if an IV is considered to have different levels or a range of values which may have a bearing on the outcome or if the researcher wishes to discover whether different levels of an IV have an effect on the outcome.

📖 Cohen et al. 2011

parametric procedure(s)

another term for PARAMETRIC TEST(S)

parametric statistic(s)

another term for PARAMETRIC TEST(S)

parametric test(s)

also parametric statistic(s), parametric procedure(s)

a group of statistical procedures that should be used if their basic ASSUMPTIONS can be met. The word parametric comes from PARAMETER, or characteristic of a POPULATION. The parametric tests (e.g., t-TEST, ANALYSIS OF VARIANCE, and PEARSON-PRODUCT-MOMENT CORRELATION COEFFICIENT) make assumptions about the population from which the sample has been drawn. These assumptions are based on the nature of the population distribution and on the way the type of SCALE is used to quantify the data. For example, for most parametric statistics the observations should be independent; that is, the scores on one measure do not influence scores on another measure, e.g., a score on an oral test at Time A does not bias the score on an oral test at time B; the data should be normally distributed (see NORMALITY); and the data are measured on an INTERVAL or RATIO SCALE. Nominal and ordinal measures do not quantify for parametric treatment.

Parametric tests are, as a general rule, more powerful than NONPARAMETRIC TESTs when assumptions underlying the procedures are met. In part this is because they are tests which utilize the most information. Also, tests which require NORMAL DISTRIBUTION are more powerful be-

cause characteristics of the normal distribution are known. Therefore, parametric tests should be the first choice if the assumptions of the particular procedure are met and if we feel confident about the measurement of the variables and if we have overcome the many threats to the validity of the study so that we can generalize our findings. In practice, however, the data collected may violate one or some of these assumptions. Yet, because parametric inference tests are thought to be ROBUST with regard to violations of underlying assumptions, researchers may use these tests even if the assumptions are not met. An alternative is to transform variables if their distribution is not normal (see DATA TRANSFORMATION). When the data collected flagrantly violate these assumptions, the researcher must select an appropriate nonparametric test. Nonparametric inference tests have fewer requirements or assumptions about population characteristics.
 Dörnyei 2007; Mackey & Gass 2005; Hatch & Lazaraton 1991

Pareto chart
also **Pareto diagram, Pareto graph**
a graph that combines the properties of a BAR GRAPH, displaying FREQUENCY and RELATIVE FREQUENCY, with a line displaying CUMULATIVE FREQUENCY. As shown in Figure P.1, the bar chart portion displays the number and percentage of cases, ordered in descending frequency from left to right (so the most common cause is the furthest to the left and the least common the furthest to the right). A cumulative frequency line is superimposed over the bars.
 Boslaugh & Watters 2008

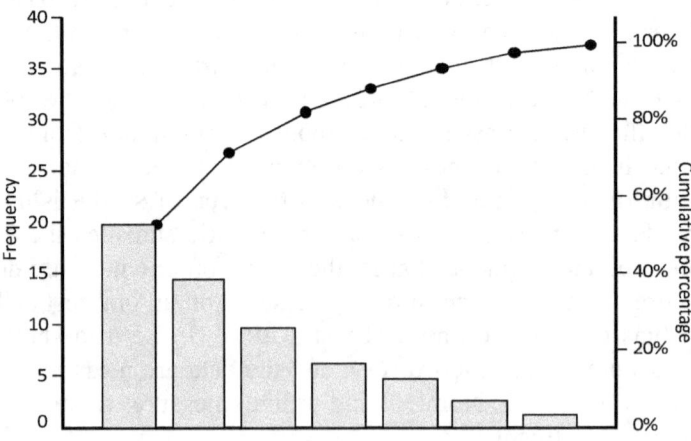

Figure P.1. An Example of Pareto Chart

Pareto diagram
another term for PARETO CHART

Pareto graph
another term for PARETO CHART

part correlation
a value that measures the strength of the relationship between a DEPENDENT VARIABLE and a single INDEPENDENT VARIABLE (IV) when the predictive effects of the other IVs in the regression model are removed. The objective is to portray the unique predictive effect due to a single IV among a set of IVs. Part correlation differs from the PARTIAL CORRELATION coefficient, which is concerned with incremental predictive effect.
📖 Hair et al. 2010

partial autocorrelation
see AUTOCORRELATION

partial correlation
a type of CORRELATION which aims at establishing the degree of *association* between two VARIABLEs (e.g., variable A and variable B) after the influence of a third variable (i.e., COVARIATE, e.g., variable C) has been controlled for or partialled out (see Figure P.2). By statistically removing the influence of this CONFOUNDING VARIABLE, you can get a clearer and more accurate indication of the relationship between your two variables. This relationship can be represented graphically as:

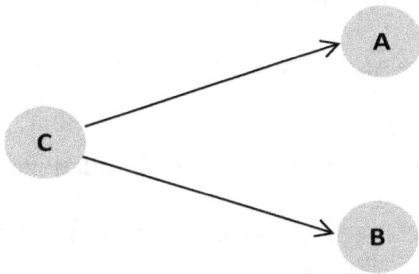

*P.2. Schematic Representation
of Partial Correlation*

In this case, variable A and variable B may look as if they are related, but in fact their apparent relationship is due, to a large extent, to the influence of C. If you were to statistically control for the variable C, then the correlation between variable A and variable B is likely to be reduced, resulting in a smaller correlation coefficient. For example, you may have noticed while administering a timed vocabulary test that your older students struggled more with this than your younger students. You are actually interested in the relationship between amount of vocabulary knowledge and scores on a reading test, but you decide you need to factor the effect of age out of the relationship to get an accurate view of it. For this you would use a partial correlation. Consider, too, the relationship between success in basketball and previous experience in the game. Suppose, also, that the presence of a third factor, the height of the players was known to have an important influence on the other two factors. The use of partial correlation techniques would enable a measure of the two primary variables to be achieved, freed from the influence of the secondary variable. The remaining correlation between two variables when their correlation with a third variable is removed is called a **first-order partial correlation**. Partial correlation may be used to remove the effect of more than one variable. However, because of the difficulty of interpretation, partial correlation involving the elimination of more than one variable is not often used.

A partial correlation has the following attributes:

- There are three or more variables, i.e., two variables that we wish to explore the relationship between and one or more variables that we wish to control for.
- These variables do not have any LEVELs within them.
- If you took averages of the variables, you would have three or more averages.
- All variables are *continuous* (measured on INTERVAL or RATIO SCALEs).
- The variables cannot necessarily be defined as independent and dependent (having a cause-and-effect structure), although they might be.

Partial correlation is, in a way, the correlational counterpart of ANCOVA.

see also MULTIPLE CORRELATION, PART CORRELATION
📖 Larson-Hall 2010; Pallant 2010

partial eta squared

an EFFECT SIZE statistics which indicates the proportion of VARIANCE of the DEPENDENT VARIABLE that is explained by the INDEPENDENT VARIABLE. It is partial because it eliminates the influence of other factors in the design. Values can range from 0 to 1.

see also ETA-SQUARED, OMEGA-SQUARED, PARTIAL OMEGA-SQUARED
📖 Dörnyei 2007; Larson-Hall 2010; Pallant 2010

partial gamma

a measure of PARTIAL ASSOCIATION between two ordinal variables controlling for the influence of a third ordinal variable. Partial gamma is the number of concordant pairs minus the number of discordant pairs for the two variables summed across the different LEVELs of the third variable divided by the number of concordant and discordant pairs summed across the different levels of the third variable. A concordant pair is one in which the first case is ranked higher than the second case, while a discordant pair is the reverse, in which the first case is ranked lower than the second case.
📖 Cramer & Howitt 2004

partial omega-squared

an EFFECT SIZE statistics which indicates the proportion of VARIANCE of the DEPENDENT VARIABLE that is explained by the INDEPENDENT VARIABLE. Like PARTIAL ETA SQUARED, it removes the variance of other factors which are not currently of interest from the calculation. Values can range from 0 to 1.
see also ETA-SQUARED, OMEGA-SQUARED
📖 Larson-Hall 2010

participant-as-observer

a type of PARTICIPANT OBSERVATION which involves a researcher to be a part of the social life of participants and documents and records what is happening for research purposes. The researcher is more observer than participant and actively participates and becomes an insider in the event being observed so that s/he experiences events in the same way as the participants. The researcher's role is known to the people being observed. Anthropologists often are participant observers when they conduct a study of a particular culture. In applied linguistics research, however, it is difficult for the investigator to pretend to be a member of a group and play the same role as the subjects who are being studied. It might be possible for a young researcher to be accepted in a group of college freshman in order to gather data on the freshman experience but not to become a participating member of a junior high school club.
see also COMPLETE OBSERVER, OBSERVER AS PARTICIPANT, COMPLETE PARTICIPANT
📖 Ary et al. 2010; Given 2008

participant feedback

another name for MEMBER CHECKS

participant mortality

another term for MORTALITY

participant observation

a method of data collection in which the researcher takes part in everyday activities related to an area of social life in order to study an aspect of that life through the OBSERVATION of events in their natural contexts. The purpose of participant observation is to gain a deep understanding of a particular topic or situation through the meanings ascribed to it by the individuals who live and experience it. Participant observation is regarded as being especially appropriate for studying social phenomena about which little is known and where the behavior of interest is not readily available to public view. Through its emphasis on firsthand access to the real world and its meanings it is effective in allowing understanding of the way of life of others. Participant observation is characterized by emergent design involving a variety of methods including direct observation of human behavior and the physical features of settings, informal interviewing, and document analysis. Researchers adopt roles that have been described as varying along a continuum of participation ranging from COMPLETE OBSERVER, through PARTICIPANT AS OBSERVER, and OBSERVER AS PARTICIPANT, to a COMPLETE PARTICIPANT. The move is from complete detachment to complete participation. The mid-points of this continuum strive to balance involvement with detachment, closeness with distance, familiarity with strangeness. The observer must decide what degree of participation will provide the most appropriate data.

It is easier to ask questions and record observations if members of the group know your purpose; furthermore, it may be more ethical to make people aware of what is going on. Being open, however, may present problems. Knowing they are being observed, group members may behave differently from the way they usually do, or they may not be truthful when answering questions. This impact of the observer on the participants being studied is called **observer effect** and can result in an inaccurate picture of the group and its interactions. There is a risk that the observer will destroy the very naturalness of the setting that s/he wants. Observer expectation may occur when the researcher knows the participants are associated with certain characteristics and may expect certain behaviors. In other words, expectations may cause you to see or interpret actions or events in a particular way. Another problem with observation as a data-gathering tool is the possible effect that the observer him- or herself might have on the results. **Observer bias** occurs when the observer's personal attitudes and values affect the observation and/or the interpretation of the observation. In participant observation, there may be a problem of the observer's getting emotionally involved in the group and hence losing objectivity. Furthermore, it is not well suited to the study of large groups or populations. Gaining access to social contexts of interest—in other words, obtaining permission to collect data, establishing CREDIBILITY, and earning the trust of those being observed—can be very challenging.

In participant observation data are typically recorded in the form of FIELDNOTES that, in order for the investigator to remain as unobtrusive as possible, are written up from memory either in secluded areas or at the end of the day. Participant observation usually entails prolonged engagement in the field that allows for gathering more detailed and accurate information. For example, a researcher who observes a setting for several months can identify discrepancies between what people say and what they actually do.

see also PARTICIPANTS AS CO-RESEARCHERS, INTERVIEW

📖 Given 2008

participants
also **subjects**

people from whom data are gathered. In the METHOD section of a RESEARCH REPORT, the characteristics of the subjects or participants should be described. Appropriate identification of research participants is critical to the science and practice of applied linguistics research, particularly for generalizing (see GENERALIZABILITY) the findings, making comparisons across replications, and using the evidence in research syntheses and secondary data analyses. If humans participated in the study, report the eligibility and exclusion criteria, including any restrictions based on demographic characteristics. You should describe the SAMPLE adequately. Detail the sample's major demographic characteristics, such as age; sex; ethnic and/or racial group; level of education; native language; level of proficiency, nationality; socioeconomic, generational, or immigrant status; disability status; gender identity; and language preference as well as important topic-specific characteristics. As a rule, you should describe the groups as specifically as possible, with particular emphasis on characteristics that may have bearing on the interpretation of results. Often, participant characteristics can be important for understanding the nature of the sample and the degree to which results can be generalized.

You should also describe the procedures for selecting participants, including (a) the SAMPLING method, if a systematic sampling plan was used; (b) the percentage of the sample approached that participated; and (c) the number of participants who selected themselves into the sample. Describe the settings and locations in which the data were collected as well as any agreements and payments made to participants, agreements with the institutional review board, ethical standards met, and safety monitoring procedures.

Along with the description of subjects, give the intended size of the sample and number of individuals meant to be in each CONDITION, if separate conditions were used. You should state whether the achieved sample differed in known ways from the target POPULATION. Conclusions and interpretations should not go beyond what the sample would warrant. State how this intended SAMPLE SIZE was determined. If interim analysis and stopping rules were used to modify the desired sample size, describe the methodology and results.

see also MATERIALS, PROCEDURES, ANALYSES

 American Psychological Association 2010

participants as co-researchers

a participatory method of research that situates participants as joint contributors and investigators to the findings of a research project. This QUALITATIVE RESEARCH approach validates and privileges the experiences of participants, making them experts and therefore co-researchers and collaborators in the process of gathering and interpreting data. Participants have the opportunity to tell their own stories and give an insider perspective to the process of being the object or subject of research. Participants are also able to offer their own interpretation of the researcher's findings, voicing their opinion in response to the researcher, thereby giving voice to the community or group that is being researched. Together, the researcher and participant work to come to conclusions, engaging in dialogue and offering each other feedback. Additionally, utilizing participants as coresearchers gives researchers the opportunity to use the experiences and knowledge of participants to learn about and discuss the research. Co-researchers contribute to the research by offering credibility to the findings and credibility to the researcher (within the community or organization). The involvement of an active participant encourages other participants to join the conversation and respond with their own interpretations. This encouragement allows the researcher to take on the role of student, allowing the research process to be a learning event.

The insider status of participants in research projects contributes to the benefit of *insider* status and, more generally, to the information gathered in the study. When participants are co-researchers, they share knowledge, access, and responsibility, which offers a perspective that would usually be unavailable to an outside researcher. Additionally, when participants take on a valid role in the research, they are further motivated to cooperate; that prompts others to become active participants as well. When participants are invited to be co-researchers in the process, they become equally invested in the success of the project. Participants become involved in the process of research from the initial inquiries of the investigation to findings and conclusions. Their feedback offers an opportunity to consider the perspective of the people being represented in the research. This method merges the experience of the participants with the research skills of the researcher. Participants as co-researchers transition from a role of being asked questions and being observed, to asking questions and observing. Co-researchers, however, are not necessarily credited as co-authors but rather as collaborators in the writing process.

The original researcher remains individually responsible and accountable for the technical responsibilities of the research because participants turned co-researchers often are not familiar or comfortable with the concept of fieldnotes, formal interviewing, transcribing, or writing, but they can offer their opinions, observations, and expertise, being involved in varying degrees over the course of the project. The theory development remains the responsibility of the first researcher, who is more familiar with the process of research; co-researchers contribute alternatives to the theory and responses and interpretations of events in their own words.

In addition to the benefits of utilizing participants as co-researchers, there are also some disadvantages. Although inviting participants as co-researchers allows the researcher the benefit of access and credibility, there is still a risk of misrepresentation. Researchers are likely able to invite only one person or a small group of participants to be co-researchers, a restriction that means that only a limited perspective is being represented or considered in the research while many others remain marginalized.

Co-researchers as participants as a method of participatory research offers the opportunity for otherwise unidentifiable or unavailable themes and conclusions to be drawn; however, there is also the chance that more observable conclusions will be over-looked. The view of participants as co-researchers is limited to their perspective as insiders, a limitation that means that they may ignore important data that they have grown accustomed to as participants.

📖 Given 2008

participatory action research
also collaborative research

a type of ACTION RESEARCH which is a collaborative approach to research that provides people with the means to take systematic action in an effort to resolve specific problems. Participatory action research encourages consensual, democratic, and participatory strategies to encourage people to examine reflectively problems affecting them. Further, it encourages people to formulate accounts and explanations of their situation, and to develop plans that may resolve these problems.

Participatory action research, while sharing the focus on a specific local issue and on using the findings to implement action, differs in important ways from PRACTICAL ACTION RESEARCH. The first difference is that it has two additional purposes: to empower individuals and groups to improve their lives and to bring about social change at some level—school, university, community, or society. Accordingly, it deliberately involves a sizable group of people representing diverse experiences and viewpoints, all of whom are focused on the same problem. The intent is to have intensive involvement of all these STAKEHOLDERS, who function as equal partners. Achieving this goal requires that the stakeholders, although they may not all be involved at the outset, become active early in the process and jointly plan the study. This includes not only clarifying purposes but also agreeing on other aspects, including data collection and analysis, interpretation of data, and resulting actions. For this reason, participatory action research is often referred to as *collaborative research*.

Sometimes a trained researcher identifies a problem and brings it to the attention of the stakeholders. But it is essential that the researcher realize that the problem to be studied must be a problem that is important to the stakeholders, and not simply of interest to the researcher. The researcher and the stakeholders jointly formulate the research problem (often through brainstorming or by conducting focus groups). This approach contrasts with many of the more traditional investigations, in which the researchers formulate the problem by themselves.

see also PRACTICAL ACTION RESEARCH
📖 Fraenkel & Wallen 2009

participatory pedagogy
see CRITICAL PEDAGOGY

path analysis
also **path modeling**

an analysis in which three or more VARIABLEs are ordered by the researcher in terms of their presumed CAUSAL RELATIONSHIPs. Path analysis allows researchers to look at the relationships between variables both directly and indirectly. Path analysis is not a statistical procedure in and of itself. Rather, it is an application of MULTIPLE REGRESSION techniques to the testing of **causal model**s (i.e., a mathematical model describing causal relations among sets of *exogenous* and *endogenous* variables, defined below). It allows you to test a model specifying the causal links among variables by applying simple multiple regression techniques. Whereas multiple regression looks at how well a set of INDEPENDENT VARIABLEs (IVs) can be used to predict a single DEPENDENT VARIABLE (DV), path analysis can have the same variable acting as a DV at one stage in the model and as an IV in another part of the model.

There are a number of general assumptions in path analysis:

1) The variables are linear, additive, and causal. This means that the data cannot be curvilinear (see CURVILINEARITY). Additivity means that the variables cannot be interactive (i.e., they should be independent of

each other). And finally, logic should argue that there is a causal direction to the relationship.
2) The data are normally distributed (see NORMALITY) and the variances are equal (see HOMOGENEITY OF VARIANCE). You know that one method of obtaining a normal distribution with equal variances is to increase the SAMPLE SIZE. This is not a small-sample technique.
3) The RESIDUALs are not correlated with variables preceding them in the model nor among themselves. This implies that all relevant variables are included in the system.
4) There is a one-way casual flow in the system. That is, the final goal (DV) cannot be seen as causal for the preceding IVs.
5) The data are *continuous*. That is, the procedure is not appropriate for NOMINAL VARIABLEs.

The heart of path analysis is developing a causal model and identifying causal relationships. A diagram which shows the presumed causal relationships between the variables is called a **path diagram**. Causal relationships among variables can take many forms. The simplest of these is shown in panel (a) of Figure P.3, where variable A (IV) causes changes in variable B (dependent variable). Another possible causal relationship is shown in panel (b). Here, two variables impinge on variable B. This model suggests that variation in the DV has multiple causes. These causal variables can be uncorrelated as shown in panel (b). Panel (c) shows a situation in which two variables believed to cause changes in the DV are correlated. In Figure P.3 (and in path analysis, in general), straight arrows denote causal relationships and are called *paths*. Curved, double-headed arrows denote correlational relationships.

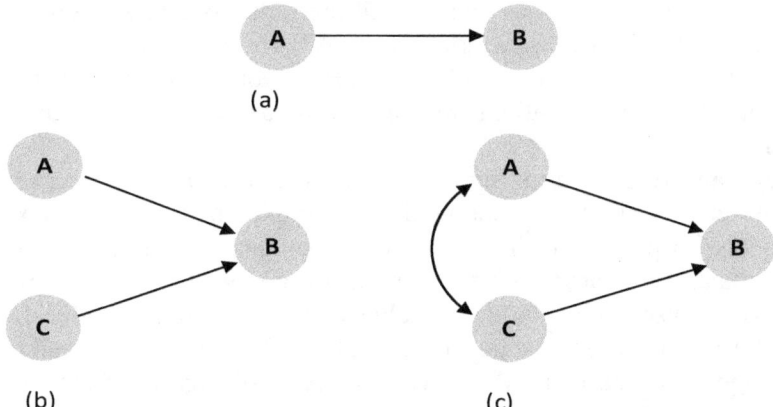

Figure P.3. Three Possible Causal Relationships. (a) Variable A Causes Changes in B; (b) Uncorrelated Variables A and C Contribute to Changes in the Value of B; (c) Correlated Variables A and C Cause Changes in the Value of B.

The simple causal relationships just described can be combined to form more complex causal models. One such model is the causal chain in which a sequence of events leads ultimately to variation in the DV. To illustrate a simple causal chain, consider an example in which you were trying to determine what variables correlated with second language acquisition (SLA). Suppose you believe that parental education (PE) and student motivation (SM) relate to variation in SLA. You have reason to believe that a causal relationship exists. So you develop a causal model like the one illustrated in panel (a) of Figure P.4. Your model suggests that PE causes changes in SM, which then causes changes in SLA. Notice that you are proposing that PE does not directly cause changes in SLA but rather operates through SM.

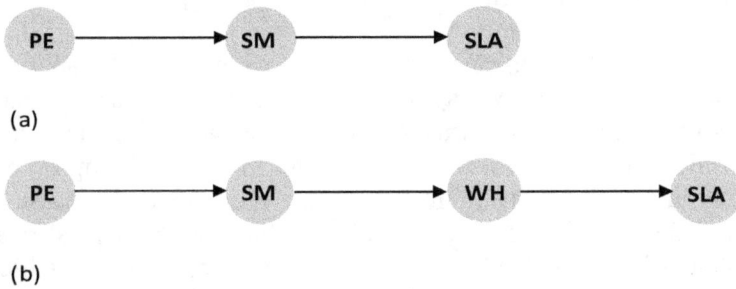

Figure P.4. (a) Three-Variable Causal Chain and (b) Four-Variable Causal Chain

When developing simple causal chains (and more complex causal models), note that the VALIDITY of your causal model depends on how well you have conceptualized your model. Perhaps SM does not directly cause changes in SLA as conjectured but rather operates through yet another variable, such as working hard (WH) in class. Panel (b) of Figure P.4 shows a causal chain including WH. If you excluded WH from your model, the causal relationships and the model you develop may not be valid.

You can progress from simple causal chains to more complex models quite easily. Figure P.5 shows three examples of more complex causal models. In panel (a), the causal model suggests variables A and B are correlated (indicated with the curved arrow). Variable A is believed to exert a causal influence on Variable C, and B on D. Variable D is hypothesized to cause changes in C, and both D and C are believed to cause changes in E. Variables A and B in panel (a) of Figure P.5 are called **exogenous variable**s which are assumed to begin the causal sequence and the correlation between them is depicted by a curved line with two-headed arrows. An exogenous variable is not explained by any other variables in the analysis but which explains one or more other variables. As a consequence, it has one or more arrows leading from it but none leading to it. Note that no causal paths lead to variable A or B. All the other variables in the model shown in panel (a) are **endogenous variables**. These DVs are internal to the model, and changes in them are believed to be caused or explained by other variables (i.e., exogenous variables) in the analysis. As a consequence they have one or more arrows leading either directly or indirectly to them from other variables. Variables C, D, and E are all endogenous variables. Panel (b) of Figure P.5 shows essentially the same model as panel (a), except that the two exogenous variables are not correlated in panel (b).

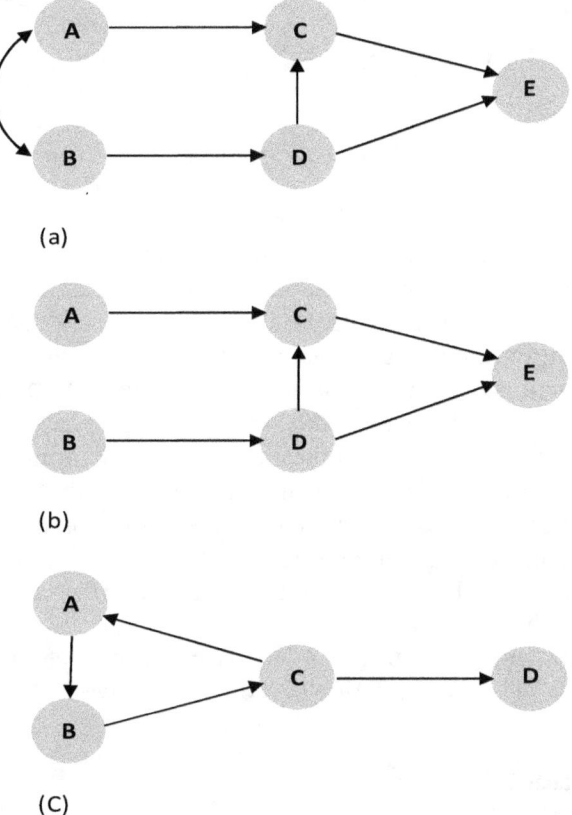

Figure P.5. Three Complex Causal Models

The models in panels (a) and (b) are both known as **recursive models**. Notice that there are no loops of variables. That is, causal relationships run in only one direction (e.g., D causes C, but C does not cause D). In contrast, panel (c) of Figure P.5 shows a **nonrecursive model**, which has a causal loop. In this case, variable A is believed to be a cause of C (operating through B), but C also can cause A. In general, recursive models are much easier to deal with conceptually and statistically.

After you have developed your causal models and measured your variables, you then obtain estimates of the causal relationships among your variables. These estimates are called **path coefficient**s. Figure P.6 shows a causal model with the path coefficients indicated for each causal path.

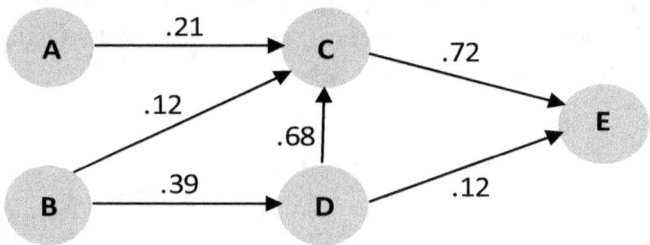

Figure P.6. Path Diagram Showing Path Coefficients

Path coefficients are determined by using a series of multiple regression analyses. Each endogenous variable is used as a DV in the regression analysis. All the variables in the model that are assumed to impinge on the DV are used as predictors. For example, the path coefficients for A-C and D-C, in Figure P.6, are obtained by using C as the DV and A, B, and D as predictors. The path coefficients are the STANDARDIZED REGRESSION COEFFICIENTs (beta weights) from these analyses.

A danger of path analysis is that researchers will forget what they have been told about correlational techniques, namely, that we cannot identify cause-and-effect relationships. There is a temptation to see the arrow in a path diagram as suggesting a direction of cause. As with regression, it is only telling you about the degree to which one variable can be used to predict another.

see also MANIFEST VARIABLE, STRUCTURAL EQUATION MODELING

📖 Bachman 2004; Bordens & Abbott 2011; Cramer & Howitt 2004; Hatch & Lazaraton 1991

path coefficient
see PATH ANALYSIS

path diagram
see PATH ANALYSIS

path modeling
another term for PATH ANALYSIS

PCA
an abbreviation for PRINCIPLE COMPONENTS ANALYSIS

Pearson correlation coefficient
another term for PEARSON PRODUCT-MOMENT CORRELATION COEFFICIENT

Pearson product-moment correlation coefficient
also **product moment correlation, Pearson correlation coefficient, Pearson r, r**
the most widely used measure of CORRELATION or association. It is a PARAMETRIC STATISTIC which indicates the strength and direction of the relationship between two CONTINUOUS VARIABLEs (i.e., measured on INTERVAL or RATIO SCALEs). In evaluating the extent to which two variables covary (i.e., vary in relationship to one another), the Pearson product-moment correlation coefficient (often referred to as *Pearson r*) determines the degree to which a linear relationship exists between the variables. One variable (usually designated as the X variable) is referred to as the INDEPENDENT VARIABLE or predictor and another variable, which is referred to as the DEPENDENT VARIABLE or criterion, is usually designated as the Y variable. The degree of accuracy with which a researcher will be able to predict a subject's score on the criterion variable from the subject's score on the predictor variable will depend upon the strength of the linear relationship between the two variables. The use of correlational data for predictive purposes is summarized under the general subject of REGRESSION.

In order to appropriately use and interpret the Pearson product-moment correlation coefficient (r), the following ASSUMPTIONs need to be made about the data:

1) for each subject in the study, there must be related pairs of scores, i.e., if a subject has a score on variable X, then the same subject must also have a score on variable Y;
2) the relationship between the two variables is linear (the relationship can be characterized by a straight line);
3) both variables are continuous (measured on interval or ratio scales);
4) The variability of scores on the Y variable should remain constant at all values of the X variable (also referred to as HOMOSCEDASTICITY);
5) both variables are normally distributed (i.e., a BIVARIATE NORMAL DISTRIBUTION); and
6) each pair of scores is independent from all other pairs.

If these assumptions are not met, or are violated in the data, then it is likely that the correlation coefficient we obtain will not give us an unbiased estimate of the relationship between the two variables (see BIAS). Pearson correlation can be strongly affected by extreme scores or OUTLIERS. Consequently, if the scores are not normally distributed, the scores can be ranked and the SPEARMAN RANK ORDER CORRELATION COEFFICIENT (the *nonparametric* alternative to Pearson correlation coefficient) is used.

see also NONPARAMETRIC TEST(S)

📖 Brown 1988; Richards & Schmidt 2010; Sheskin 2011; Urdan 2010

Pearson *r*

another term for PEARSON PRODUCT-MOMENT CORRELATION COEFFICIENT

Pearson's chi-square

another term for CHI-SQUARE TEST

peer debriefing

another term for PEER REVIEW

peer review

also **expert review, peer debriefing, independent scientific review, auditing**

a method used by administrators, funding officials, journal editors, and researchers to inform decision making and to improve the research process and outcomes by engaging independent and qualified experts to provide critical and consultative evaluation of the merits of a research project or product, proposal. Depending on its environment, peer reviewing can differ as to its purposes, participants, process, and product. For example, peer review may be used to improve a research proposal or project's trustworthiness. Researchers may call upon peers with relevant methodological and content area expertise and experience to scrutinize and critique a study's procedures and outcomes. This type of peer review (sometimes called INVESTIGATOR TRIANGULATION) provides researchers with an objective source familiar with the research or the phenomenon being explored to review the study's methodology, to analyze portions of data, and to critique findings. This peer reviewer can provide support and guidance, challenge researchers' assumptions and findings, and help improve the study's rigor or trustworthiness. This support can be provided via formal, written reports or through informal conversations and emails. Peer reviewers can also improve data analysis and interpretation credibility by seeking the assistance of peer debriefers and using the feedback to reach consensus on the findings' coherence and agreement as to the find-

ings' credibility or to generate additional reflections. Peer debriefing can also help prevent researchers from becoming overly intrusive in their research participants' lives, from going native, or becoming overly connected with the research site and its inhabitants. The goal is to help researchers become more aware of their work's impact on themselves and other study participants.
📖 Given 2008

percentage
see PROPORTION

percentage of the total frequency
see MODE

percentage variance effect size
see EFFECT SIZE

percentage agreement
another term for AGREEMENT COEFFICIENT

percentile
also percentile rank, percentile score
a DISTRIBUTION which is divided into 100 equal parts, each of which contains 1% of total observations (see Table P.1). The MEDIAN is the 50th percentile, the first quartile is the 25th percentile, and the third quartile is the 75th percentile. A specific percentile value corresponds to the point in a distribution at which a given percentage of scores falls at or below. For example, if a given student's score is at the 90th percentile, this means that 90 per cent of the students in the reference group scored equal or below her/his score. The term percentile rank is also employed to mean the same thing as a percentile; in other words, we can say that a score has a percentile rank of 84%. At times, a percentile rank is used to indicate the percentage of examinees that scored below that score (omitting the word '*at*'). In practice, a percentile rank of 100 is not reported. We cannot say that a person with a certain raw score did better than 100 percent of the people in the group, because that person has to be included in the group. Instead, 99 percent (or in some cases, 99.9 percent) is considered the highest percentile rank. A **percentile band** is also often used to provide an estimated range of the true percentile rank. The bands are used due to the fact that the tests are not completely reliable and include a certain level of error.

The NORMAL CURVE can be used to calculate percentiles, assuming that the distribution of scores is normally distributed. For example, a Z SCORE of +1 corresponds to a percentile rank of 84.13 (or 84). We find that percentile rank by adding up the percent of scores between the MEAN and a z score of +1 on the normal curve (it is 34.13 percent) to the percent of scores below the mean (50 percent). A z score of -2 corresponds to a percentile rank of 2 (the percent of area under the normal curve below a z score of -2).

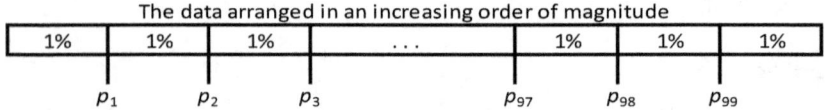

Table P.1. Schematic Representation of Percentiles of a Data Set

A number of considerations must be kept in mind when using percentile ranks. First, percentile ranks are specific to a particular level and form of a test or subtest. Second, percentile ranks, can be interpreted only with respect to the reference group or groups on which they are based. Finally, the primary limitation in percentile ranks is that they provide only an ORDINAL SCALE, so that a difference in one percentile at different points in the scale may not correspond to the same difference in levels of ability. Specifically for percentile ranks, a difference of one percentile between scores in the middle of the distribution is much smaller than it is between scores at the extremes of the distribution. For this reason, differences in percentile ranks at the ends of the score distribution are more likely to be meaningful than similar differences in the middle of the score distribution. Furthermore, because percentile ranks constitute an ordinal scale, they should not be averaged arithmetically to obtain a mean; the median, or the 50th percentile, is the appropriate indicator of CENTRAL TENDENCY for percentile ranks.

see also DECILE, QUARTILE QUINTILE

📖 Bachman 2004; Sahai & Khurshid 2001; Sheskin 2011

percentile band
see PERCENTILE

percentile rank
another term for PERCENTILE

percentile score
another term for PERCENTILE

per-comparison error rate
another term for COMPARISONWISE ERROR RATE

per-experiment error rate
another term for EXPERIMENTWISE ERROR RATE

performance assessment
also **authentic assessment**
a popular alternative to traditional **paper-and-pencil test**s among educators, usually administered individually. The most common achievement tests are paper-and-pencil tests measuring cognitive objectives. This familiar format, usually administered to groups, requires individuals to compose answers or choose responses on a printed sheet. In some cases, however, a researcher may want to measure performance—what an individual can do rather than what s/he knows. A performance test is a technique in which a researcher directly observes and assesses an individual's performance of a certain task and/or judges the finished product of that performance. The test taker is asked to carry out a process such as producing a product such as a written essay. The performance or product is judged against established criteria. An everyday example of a performance test is the behind-the-wheel examination taken when applying for a driver's license. A paper-and-pencil test covering knowledge of signs and rules for driving is not sufficient to measure driving skill. In investigating a new method of teaching, for example, you would want to know the effect of the method not only on students' cognitive behavior but also on their learning of various procedures and techniques teaching. In this case, the researcher's test would require the students to perform a real teaching. **Portfolio**s that contain a collection of student work such as poetry, essays, sketches, audiotapes of speeches, and diaries are popular in performance assessments. They provide an opportunity for teachers and researchers to gain a more holistic view of changes in students' performance over time. However, fewer tasks can be included given time constraints, creating agreed-upon criteria for scoring is time-consuming, and judgment of students' work is highly subjective, all of which make performance assessment expensive and open to bias.
📖 Ary et al. 2010; Fernandez-Ballesteros 2003

permutation
a sequence of events in PROBABILITY. A permutation is all the possible ways elements in a set can be arranged. For instance, if a set consists of the elements (a, b, c), then the permutations of this set are (a, b, c), (a, c, b), (b, a, c), (b, c, a), (c, a, b), and (c, b, a). Note that the order of elements is important in permutations: (a, b, c) is a different permutation than (a, c, b). If we ignore sequence, then the different possibilities are known as combinations. **Combination**s are similar to permutations, with the difference that the order of elements is not significant in combina-

tions: (a, b, c) is the same combination as (b, a, c). For this reason there is only one combination of the set (a, b, c).

Permutations of outcomes such as taking a name from a hat containing initially six names can be calculated by multiplying the possibilities at each selection. So if we take out a name three times the number of different combinations is $6 \times 5 \times 4 = 120$. This is because for the first selection there are six different names to choose from, then at the second selection there are five different names (we have already taken one name out) and at the third selection there are four different names. Had we replaced the name into the hat then the permutations would be $6 \times 6 \times 6$. Combinations and permutations are used in statistics to calculate the number of ways a subset of specified size can be drawn from a set, which allows the calculation of the probability of drawing any particular subset.
📖 Boslaugh & Watters 2008; Cramer & Howitt 2004

personal interview
another term for FACE-TO-FACE INTERVIEW

phenomenology
a school of thought and approach to QUALITATIVE RESEARCH which emphasizes a focus on people's subjective experiences and interpretations of the world. That is, the phenomenologist wants to understand how the world appears to others. Phenomenology is the reflective study of prereflective or lived experience. A main characteristic of the phenomenological tradition is that it is the study of the lifeworld as we immediately experience it, prereflectively, rather than as we conceptualize, theorize, categorize, or reflect on it. Indeed, it is the study of lived or experiential meaning and attempts to describe and interpret these meanings in the ways that they emerge and are shaped by consciousness, language, our cognitive and noncognitive sensibilities, and by our preunderstandings and presuppositions. It is a reaction against the empiricist conception (see EMPIRICISM) of the world as an objective universe of facts. Phenomenological studies attempt to capture the essence of the human experience. Like other qualitative researchers, phenomenologists are interested in recording the individual perspectives of the participants in the study. However, phenomenology stresses the importance of each individual and his/her respective view of reality. To encourage these perspectives to emerge, phenomenologists use open-ended INTERVIEWs as their primary data collection tool. The phenomenologist's role is to give voice to those perspectives. Consider the following: Take a look at the person sitting next to you in class. You both are sitting in the same course, at the same college, with the same professor; yet, the way you perceive the reality of this graduate experience is quite different. You each bring a history of

personal experiences, attitudes, behaviors, and emotions, all of which will influence how you view this shared experience.

Originally, phenomenology was the name for the major movement in philosophy and the humanities in continental Europe in the 20th century. More recently, the term has acquired a broader meaning as phenomenology has been developed as a human science that is employed in professional disciplines such as education and applied linguistics. Phenomenology may explore the unique meanings of any human experience or phenomenon. For example, it may study what it is like to have a conversation, how students experience difficulty in learning something, how pain is experienced in childbirth, what it is like to experience obsessive compulsions, how young people begin to experience secrecy and inwardness, and so forth. For example, a TESOL research project in this tradition might seek to understand the experience of being forced to learn a new language when the learner has strong negative feelings about this. The first step would be to identify a group of perhaps 10 to 20 students who have had this experience and to set up a series of IN-DEPTH INTERVIEWs, perhaps beginning with the general question, 'What is it like having to start learning a language when you feel a strong antipathy to this?' The aim would then be to follow the procedures outlined above in order to understand the essence of this particular language-learning experience. There are two terms of fundamental importance in phenomenology, both related to the avoidance of contamination by outside prejudices and presuppositions. The process of removing these from the research process, or setting them aside, in order to penetrate to the essence of the phenomenon, is known as **bracketing**. It involves the researcher intentionally setting aside his/her own experiences, suspending his/her own beliefs in order to take a fresh perspective based on data collected from persons who have experienced the phenomenon. The resulting suspension of such elements and uncontaminated access to the essence of the phenomenon is known as **epoche**. A related concept sometimes referred to is **ideation**, where we try to go from the particular to the general: starting from what appears to consciousness; we try to acquire an understanding of the idea that determines its meaningfulness.

see also ETHNOMETHODOLOGY, SYMBOLIC INTERACTIONISM

Given 2008; Keith Richards 2003; Ridenour & Newman 2008

phi (φ)

an abbreviation for PHI CORRELATION COEFFICIENT

phi correlation coefficient
also **phi (φ)**

a measure of *association* between two genuinely dichotomous variables. The most common applications of phi correlation coefficient are in cor-

relating two items on a QUESTIONNAIRE, for example, where the answers are coded *yes* or *no* (or as some other binary alternatives), and in circumstances in which a 2 × 2 (two-by-two) CONTINGENCY TABLE would alternatively be employed. For example, phi (φ) would be used to describe the relationship between the gender of high school students and whether they are counseled to take college preparatory courses or not. Gender is dichotomized as male = 0, female = 1. Being counseled to take college preparatory courses is scored 1, and not being so counseled is scored 0. The degree of relationship between the two dichotomous can be determined by using the phi coefficient. While there is a distinct formula for the phi coefficient, it is simply a special case of PEARSON PRODUCT-MOMENT CORRELATION COEFFICIENT. The value of phi correlation coefficient can be between 0 and 1. A coefficient of 0 indicates that the variables are perfectly independent. The larger the coefficient, the closer the variables are to forming a pattern that is perfectly dependent.
 Brown 1988; Cramer & Howitt 2004; Heiman 2011; Urdan 2010

pictogram

a form of BAR GRAPH in which the rectangular bars are replaced by a pictorial representation appropriate to the measures being summarized. For example, the frequencies of males and females in a SAMPLE could be represented by male and female figures of heights which correspond to the frequencies. This is illustrated in the Figure P.7.
 Cramer & Howitt 2004

Figure P.7. A Pictogram Indicating Relative Frequencies of Males and Females

pie chart
another term for PIE GRAPH

pie diagram
another term for PIE GRAPH

pie graph
also pie chart, pie diagram
a common way of presenting frequencies of categories of a VARIABLE. Pie graph looks like a circle that is divided into *wedges*, or *segments*. Each wedge represents a category or subgroup within that distribution. The size of each wedge indicates the percent of cases represented by that wedge. By inspecting the pie graph, we can readily see the proportion of each wedge to the total pie as well as the relationships among the different wedges. The percentages represented by the different-sized wedge should add up to 100 percent (see Figure P.8).

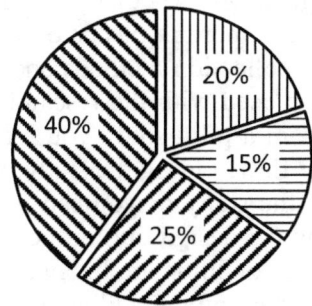

Figure P.8. An Example of Pie Chart

When drawing a pie graph, the different wedges of the pie should be identified, and numerical information, such as percentages, should be included. This would allow easy and accurate interpretation of the graph. There should not be too many wedges in the pie circle. It is not uncommon to see reports that include pie graphs with more than five wedges.
 Ravid 2011

Pillai-Bartlett trace
another term for PILLAI'S CRITERION

Pillai's criterion
also Pillai-Bartlett trace, V
a test used in *multivariate* statistical procedures such as CANONICAL CORRELATION, DISCRIMINANT FUNCTION ANALYSIS, and MULTIVARIATE ANALYSIS OF VARIANCE to determine whether the means of the groups differ. This test is said to be more ROBUST than WILKS' LAMBDA, HOTELLING'S TRACE CRITERION, and ROY'S GCR CRITERION. As sample size decreases and the assumption of HOMOGENEITY OF VARIANCE-COVARIANCE MATRICES is violated, the advantage of Pillai's criterion in

terms of robustness is more important. When the research design is less than ideal, then Pillai's criterion is the criterion of choice.
📖 Cramer & Howitt 2004; Tabachnick & Fidell 2007

pilot study
a small-scale trial of the proposed procedures, materials, and methods, and sometimes also includes coding sheets and analytic choices. The point of carrying out a pilot study is to test—often to revise—and then finalizes the materials and the methods. Pilot study is carried out to uncover any problems, and to address them before the main study is carried out. For example, you want to know whether participants understand the instructions they are given and whether your measures have FACE VALIDITY. A pilot study is an important means of assessing the feasibility and usefulness of the data collection methods and making any necessary revisions before they are used with the research participants. Without the information gained from a pilot study you may be presented with a dilemma if you discover flaws during the study: you can either alter the design midway through the study or you can plough on regardless with a poor design. Changing the design during the study obviously means that participants in the same condition are likely not to have been treated similarly. This will mean that you are adding an extra source of variation in the results, which can be a problem for their interpretation. On the other hand, to continue with a design that you know is flawed is simply a waste of both your time and that of your participants.
📖 Clark-Carter 2010; Mackey & Gass 2005

planned comparison
another term for A PRIORI TEST

planned test
another term for A PRIORI TEST

planning-evaluation cycle
see EVALUATION RESEARCH

platykurtic
see KURTOSIS

point-biserial correlation coefficient
also r_{pbis}, r_{pbi}, r_{pb}
a variant of the PEARSON PRODUCT MOMENT CORRELATION which is used as a measure of *association* between a CONTINUOUS VARIABLE and a genuinely dichotomous variable. For example, a researcher might want to investigate the degree of relationship between being male or female (a

naturally occurring dichotomy, or a *true* dichotomy) and achievement in Farsi (a *continuous* variable). The CATEGORICAL VARIABLE does not have to be normally distributed. For example, the number of male vs. female or foreign students vs. native speakers can have quite a SKEWED DISTRIBUTION.

Point biserial correlations are frequently used in the area of test evaluation, where answers are scored as either correct or incorrect. For example, answers to a single test item are either right or wrong. This is a dichotomy where 1 might = wrong and 2 might = right. Thus, it is possible to run a correlation of the performance on a single test item with the total test score (minus that one item, of course). If there are several subtests within the test for, say, reading, grammar, vocabulary, listening comprehension, and so forth, it would be possible to correlate the single test item with each subtest score. The single test item should correlate most with the subtest in which it appears. In addition, those students who do well on the subtest should pass the item and those who fail the item should have lower subtest scores. If not, then it is probably a poor item to use to test that particular skill. That is, the point biserial correlation will tell you how well single items are related to, or fit with, other items which purport to test the same thing.

In using the point-biserial correlation coefficient, it is assumed that the dichotomous variable is not based on an underlying continuous distribution. In fact, if the dichotomous variable is based on the latter type of distribution, the BISERIAL CORRELATION COEFFICIENT is the appropriate measure to employ.

📖 Brown 1988; Hatch & Farhady 1982; Hatch & Lazaraton 1991; Richards & Schmidt 2010; Sheskin 2011

point estimate

a single numerical value that describes SAMPLE DATA used as an estimate of the value of a POPULATION PARAMETER. Put simply, when we calculate a single statistic, such as the MEAN, to describe a SAMPLE, that is referred to as calculating a point estimate because the number represents a single point on the number line. The sample mean is a point estimate, and is a useful statistic as the best estimate of the population mean. The process of estimation of a parameter in terms of a single numerical value is called a **point estimation** and the method of calculating a point estimate from the sample data is known as a **point estimator**. However, we know that the sample mean is only an estimate and that if we drew a different sample, the mean of the sample would probably be different. We do not expect that every possible sample we could draw will have the same sample mean. It is reasonable to ask how much the point estimate is likely to vary by chance if we had chosen a different sample, and it has be-

come common practice to report both point estimates and INTERVAL ES-TIMATEs, which specifies a range of values.
see also CONFIDENCE INTERVAL
📖 Boslaugh & Watters 2008

point estimation
see POINT ESTIMATE

point estimator
see POINT ESTIMATE

polychomous variable
another term for MULTINOMIAL VARIABLE

polynomial relationship
see CURVILINEARITY

polytomous variable
another term for MULTINOMIAL VARIABLE

pooled variances
combined or averaged variances. Variances are pooled to provide a better population estimate in the INDEPENDENT SAMPLES t-TEST where the variances are equal but the number of cases is unequal in the two groups.
📖 Cramer & Howitt 2004

population
a group you wish to generalize to in your study. This is the group you would like to sample from because this is the group you are interested in generalizing to (see Figure P.9). Let's imagine that you want to generalize all second language (L2) learners between the ages of 15 and 18 in the United States. If that is the population of interest, you must develop a **sampling plan**. You are probably not going to find an accurate listing of this population, and even if you did, you would almost certainly not be able to mount a national sample across thousands L2 language learners. So you probably should make a distinction between the population you would like to generalize to, and the population that is accessible to you. The former is called the **theoretical population** and the latter the **accessible population**. In this example, the accessible population might be L2 language learners between the ages of 15 and 18 in six selected areas across the United States.
After you identify the theoretical and accessible populations, you have to do one more thing before you can actually draw a sample: get a list of the members of the accessible population. The listing of the accessible popu-

lation from which you will draw your sample is your SAMPLING FRAME. If you were doing a phone survey (see TELEPHONE INTERVIEW) and selecting names from the telephone book, the phone book would be your sampling frame. That would not be a great way to sample because significant subportions of the population either do not have a phone or have moved in or out of the area since the last phone book was printed. Notice that in this case, you might identify the area code and all three-digit prefixes within that area code and draw a sample simply by randomly dialing numbers (known as **random-digit-dialing**). In this case, the sampling frame is not a list per se, but is rather a procedure that you follow as the actual basis for sampling.

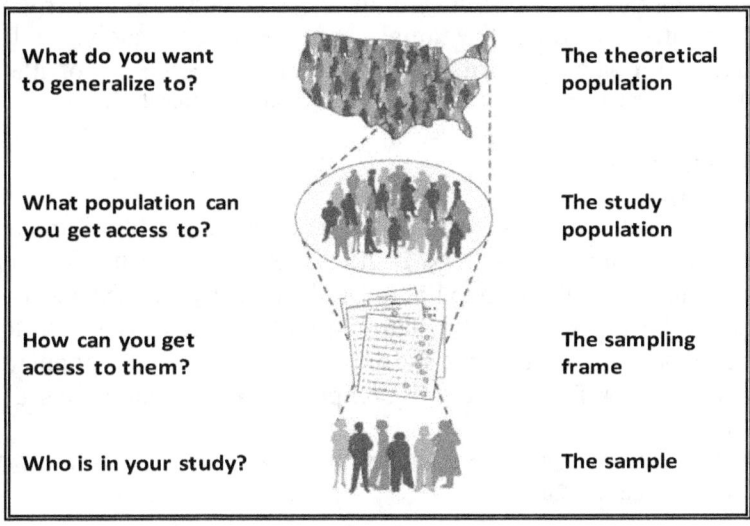

Figure P.9. The Different Groups in the Sampling Model

Finally, you actually draw your sample—using one of the sampling procedures (see PROBABILITY SAMPLING and NON-PROBABILITY SAMPLING). In most case, it is not possible for us to measure every individual in a population, and so we must rely on obtaining information from a smaller group of individuals who are similar to, or representative of, the individuals in the population. This smaller group which is a portion of a population is called **sample**, and if the individuals in the sample are representative of those in the population, we can use the scores from the sample to estimate the scores for the population. The individuals measured in a sample are called the participants (or sometimes, the subjects) and it is the scores from the sample(s) that constitute our data. The data obtained from a SAMPLE rather than from the entire population are called **sample data** (also called **sample observations, sample values**).

Notice that sample was not the group of people who are actually in your study. You may not be able to contact or recruit all of the people you actually sample, or some could drop out (see MORTALITY) over the course of the study. The group that actually completes your study is a subsample of the sample; it does not include nonrespondents or dropouts.

At this point, you should appreciate that sampling is a difficult multistep process and that you can go wrong in many places. In fact, as you move from each step to the next in identifying a sample, there is the possibility of introducing error (see SAMPLING ERROR). For instance, even if you are able to identify perfectly the population of interest, you may not have access to all of it. Even if you do, you may not have a complete and accurate enumeration or sampling frame from which to select. Even if you do, you may not draw the sample correctly or accurately. And, even if you do, your participants may not all come and they may not all stay.

📖 Bachman 2004; Fraenkel & Wallen 2009; Trochim & Donnelly 2007

population mean
also **mu (μ)**

the MEAN value of some VARIABLE that is measured for all members of a possibly infinite POPULATION. If the value of the variable for a randomly chosen member of the population is denoted by X, then the population mean is the expectation of X and is usually denoted by μ (the lowercase Greek letter *mu*). If the data constitute a SAMPLE from a population, then mean may be referred to as the **sample mean**. It is an unbiased estimate of the population mean.

see also POPULATION STANDARD DEVIATION, POPULATION VARIANCE

📖 Sahai & Khurshid 2001

population parameter
see STATISTIC

population standard deviation
also **sigma (σ)**

the most commonly used measure of DISPERSION or variability of a POPULATION.

see also VARIANCE, STANDARD DEVIATION

📖 Sahai & Khurshid 2001

population variance
also **sigma (σ²)**

a PARAMETER that measures the DISPERSION or variability of the characteristics of a POPULATION (denoted σ^2, lowercase Greek letter sigma squared). It is equal to the square of the POPULATION STANDARD DEVIATION.

see also VARIANCE, STANDARD DEVIATION
📖 Sahai & Khurshid 2001

portfolio
see PERFORMANCE ASSESSMENT

portraiture
a form of QUALITATIVE RESEARCH that seeks to join science and art in an attempt to describe complex human experiences within an organizational culture. The *portrait* is shaped by the dialogue between the researcher (portraitist) and the subject and attempts to reveal the essence of the subject and to tell the central story. Portraiture is a method framed by the traditions and values of the phenomenological paradigm, sharing many of the techniques, standards, and goals of ethnography. But it pushes against the constraints of those traditions and practices in its explicit effort to combine empirical and aesthetic description, in its focus on the convergence of narrative and analysis, in its goal of speaking to broader audiences beyond the academy. The goal of portraiture is to paint a vivid portrait or story that reflects meaning from the perspectives of both the participants and the researcher. Data can be collected using in-depth interviews and observations over a period of time, which typically result in a personal relationship between the researcher and participants.
📖 Ary et al. 2010; Lawrence-Lightfoot & Davis 1997

positive correlation
see CORRELATION COEFFICIENT

positively skewed distribution
see SKEWED DISTRIBUTION

positivism
a hugely influential philosophy of science associated with a 19th-century model of the physical sciences. Positivism asserts that the world exists of observables that are knowable through sensory experience, aspires to the discovery of universal causal laws through the identification of statistical regularities, and commits to value neutrality. It includes any philosophical system that confines itself to the data of experience, excludes a priori or metaphysical speculations, and emphasizes the achievements of science. It is the codeword for a package of philosophical ideas that most likely no one has ever accepted in its entirety. These ideas include a distrust of abstraction, a preference for observation unencumbered by too much theory, a commitment to the idea of a social science that is not vastly different from natural science, and a profound respect for quantification. Like EMPIRICISM, to which it is closely related and with which it

overlaps to a considerable degree, positivism is the label for a series of claims rather than any single claim. Like empiricism, then, positivism is a family of claims and concepts. It shares with empiricism a commitment to making experience the test of all knowledge and is skeptical about the idea of an unobservable reality that includes entities and forces not discoverable in experience, a skepticism that extends even to laws of nature. In its later forms, positivism adds to empiricism an enthusiasm for statistics—indeed, for quantification in general—and the assumption that if a statement is meaningful, then it can, by definition, be subject to scientific testing and verification. This specific type of positivism that rejects as meaningless all statements that cannot be empirically verified is called **logical positivism**. It is a system of philosophy that excludes everything from its consideration except natural phenomena and their interrelations. One of the major principles of logical positivism is the verifiability principle, which states that something is meaningful if and only if it can be observed by human senses. This implies that what is claimed through human knowledge will not be meaningful unless it can be verified through direct observation of the world. According to the logical positivists, all statements were of one of three types, *synthetic*, *analytic*, or *nonsense*. Synthetic statements are empirical ones such as *grass is green*; analytic statements are logical ones that are true by definition such as 'all bachelors are unmarried'. Statements that are neither analytic nor synthetic are nonsense. The nonsense category would include metaphysical statements and all others that were not verifiable empirically or demonstrable logically.

However, if there is an overlap with empiricism, there is also common ground with American PRAGMATISM, which had a similar preference for experience, verifiability, antirealism, and operationalism. It is noticeable, though, that the resonances of positivism, as well as its variety, are now often ignored. The term frequently signifies what is regarded as an exaggerated respect for the natural sciences and is inevitably associated with quantification. Moreover, it is usually assumed that positivists believed in a determinate reality and in the possibility of a correspondence between that reality and representations of it. This image of positivism, approaching a caricature, has been boosted by POSTMODERNISM, which portrays it as a reactionary force, committed to oppressive universal truths, a chimerical objectivity, and foundational narratives.

Since positivists believe that there is only one, fixed, agreed-upon reality, research must strive to find a singular, universal truth. They see the world as real, as something that exists independently of themselves. They believe that this reality can be quantified, and that the purpose of research is to measure it as precisely as possible. They also presume that any truths they discover about that reality are equally applicable to other groups or situations, regardless of the context. For researchers who take a positivist approach, one of the primary aims of investigation is therefore to formulate hypotheses that will allow them to make predictions about what will happen in the future, or inferences about other contexts. The purpose of research is to produce knowledge not contingent on the researcher's beliefs, desires, or biases According to the positivist school of thought, the role of the researcher is to be detached and objective both in the gathering of data and the interpretation of the findings.

see also OBJECTIVISM, SUBJECTIVISM, CONSTRUCTIVISM, POSTPOSITIVISM

 Farhady 1995; Given 2008; Heigham & Croker 2009; O'Leary 2004; Richards & Schmidt 2010; Ridenour & Newman 2008

postal survey
also **mail survey**
a type of QUESTIONNAIRE administration in which the researcher has no contact with the respondents except for a COVER LETTER s/he has written to accompany the questionnaire. Postal surveys can reach a large number of people, gather data at comparatively low cost and quite quickly, and can give assurances of CONFIDENTIALITY. Similarly they can be completed at the respondents' own convenience and in their preferred surroundings and own time; this will enable them to check information if necessary (e.g., personal documents) and think about the responses. As standardized wording is used, there is a useful degree of comparability across the responses, and, as no interviewer is present, there is no risk of **interviewer bias** (which occurs when the interviewer's own feelings and attitudes or the interviewer's gender, race, age, and other characteristics influence the way questions are asked or interpreted). Further, postal questionnaires enable widely scattered populations to be reached.

On the other hand, postal surveys typically suffer from a poor RESPONSE RATE, and, because one does not have any information about the nonrespondents, one does not know whether the sample is representative of the wider population. In addition, respondents may not take the care required to complete the survey carefully and, indeed, may misunderstand the questions. There is no way of checking this.

see also ONE-TO-ONE ADMINISTRATION, GROUP ADMINISTRATION
 Cohen et al. 2011; Dörnyei 2003

post hoc comparison
another term for POST HOC TEST

post hoc contrast
another term for POST HOC TEST

post hoc fallacy
see EX POST FACTO RESEARCH

post hoc test
also **a posteriori test, unplanned test, post hoc contrast, post hoc comparison, unplanned comparison, follow-up test, multiple comparison test**

a test, comparison, or contrast which is used after the data have been analyzed and examined, and the researcher simply looks at any or all combination of MEANs in order to compare them. More specifically, a post hoc test is a follow-up statistical test which is performed after a comparison of more than two groups (e.g., ANOVA) shows a significant F RATIO (indicating that there are differences among your groups), without a priori hypotheses about which group differences might be causing that effect. If an ANOVA reveals a significant effect for an INDEPENDENT VARIABLE (IV) that has only two LEVELs, no further statistical tests are necessary. The significant F ratio tells us that the two means differ significantly, and we can inspect the means to understand the direction and magnitude of the difference between them. However, If your overall F ratio is significant for an IV that has more than two levels, you can then go on and perform additional tests to identify where these differences occur. Suppose an ANOVA reveals a significant MAIN EFFECT that involves an IV that has three levels. The significant main effect indicates that a difference exists between at least two of the three groups means, but it does not indicate which means differ from which. To identify which means differ significantly, researchers use post hoc tests (e.g., does Group 1 differ from Group 2 or Group 3, do Group 2 and Group 3 differ). Thus, the post hoc test is a way of pinpointing where between which groups or tests, the significant difference lies. Note that post hoc is conducted if and only if the initial F ratio for the ANOVA was statistically significant. There is a variety of post hoc tests which is rather bewildering. They are designed to control the FAMILYWISE ERROR RATE due to the large number of different comparisons being made. However, they differ in how much control they put over the familywise error rate. There is a lack of consensus about where and when to apply the different measures. A reasonable recommendation is to do a range of post hoc tests. Where they all indicate the same conclusions then clearly there is no problem. If they indicate very different conclusions for a particular set of data, then the reasons and importance of this have to be assessed. Some most commonly used post hoc tests are FISHER'S LEAST SIGNIFICANT DIFFERENCE, BONFERRONI ADJUSTMENT, NEWMAN-KEULS TEST, DUNCAN'S NEW MULTIPLE RANGE TEST, TUKEY'S TEST, DUNNETT'S TEST, and SCHEFFÉ TEST.

📖 Cramer & Howitt 2004; Dörnyei 2007; Heiman 2011; Kirk 1995; Larson-Hall 2010; Mackey & Gass 2005; Pallant 2010

postmodernism
an ideological perspective that questions the early twentieth-century emphasis on science and technology, rationality, reason, and POSITIVISM. In this postmodern world, everything is contested. Multiple interpretations of the same phenomenon are possible, depending upon where one is standing. There are no absolutes, and no single theoretical framework for examining social and political issues; rather, diversity and plurality should be celebrated, and no one element privileged or considered more powerful than another. Postmodernism is a view whose ideas are included under the umbrella of QUALITATIVE RESEARCH, yet its basic assumptions are significantly different from the CONSTRUCTIVISM.
Most postmodernists do not talk about methodology and the literature provides only the vaguest indication of what ideals of multiple voices mean concretely in empirical studies. Indeed, it would be congruent with this worldview to not come up with a singular approach to doing research. Instead, postmodern research is highly experimental, playful, creative, and no two postmodern studies look alike. The broad topic of the hegemony of English as a world language provides a rich environment for postmodern researchers in applied linguistics.
📖 Heigham & Croker 2009

postpositivism
an approach to knowledge and an assessment of the nature of reality. Postpositivism is both an epistemological (see EPISTEMOLOGY) and an ontological (see ONTOLOGY) position. It may be simplistically defined postpositivism as those approaches that historically succeeded positivism, but more rigorously, it may be understood as a critique of positivist epistemology and ontology in which positivist claims concerning both the objective nature of reality and the ability of science to discern that reality are rejected. Postpositivists believe that the world may not be knowable. They see the world as infinitely complex and open to interpretation. Postpositivists see the world as: ambiguous—science may help us to someday explain what we do not know, but there are many things that we have gotten wrong in the past and many things that we may never be able to understand in all their complexity; variable—the world is not fixed, truth can depend on the limits of our ability to define shifting phenomena; and multiple in its realities—what might be truth for one person or cultural group may not be truth for another.
For postpositivists, reflexive research demands that understandings of the scientific endeavor begin to shift. While research can be based on the senses, it can also be: intuitive—hunches, metaphorical understandings,

and the creative are all legitimized as appropriate ways of knowing and exploring the world; and holistic—research needs to explore systems because the whole is often seen as more than the sum of the parts.

Postpositivists believe that the traditional gap between the researcher and the researched is one that can (and should) be diminished. Postpositivists researchers can act in ways that are: *participatory* and *collaborative*—rather than research focusing solely on a particular group, postpositivist researchers can also work both for and with participants; and *subjective*—researchers acknowledge being value-bound. They admit to biases that can affect their studies. The question for postpositivist researchers is how to recognize and manage, and in some situations, even-value and use subjectivities endemic to the research process.

For postpositivists, methods often reject or expand upon the rules of SCIENTIFIC METHOD. Methods are often: *inductive*—the process moves from specific observations to broader generalizations and theories; *dependable*—while RELIABILITY in method may not be possible, postpositivists attempt to use systematic and rigorous approaches to research; and *auditable*—the context-specific nature of researching may not lend itself to reproducibility, but research should be verifiable through full and transparent explication of method.

Postpositivists recognize the uniqueness of situations and/or cultural groups, but can still seek broader value in their findings. They seek findings that are: idiographic—(unique) may not be able to be generalized, yet have their own intrinsic worth—or are transferable—the lessons learned from one context are applicable to other contexts; valuable—postpositivist researchers are often interested in both the production of social knowledge and contributions to change; and qualitative—findings are often represented through imagery.

see also REALISM, RELATIVISM, SUBTLE REALISM, ANALYTIC REALISM, CRITICAL REALISM, STRUCTURALISM, CONSTRUCTIVISM, POSTSTRUCTURALISM

📖 Given 2008; O'Leary 2004

poststructuralism

a range of theoretical perspectives that can be seen to move away from the tenets of STRUCTURALISM. Poststructuralism is a broad term, but generally focuses on exploring concepts such as relativity, plurality, fragmentation, and **anti-foundationalism** (i.e., any philosophy which does not believe that there is some fundamental belief or principle being the basic ground or foundation of inquiry and knowledge). Comprehensive and prescriptive ideological frames or meta-narratives that clearly define and place boundaries around certain forms of knowledge are rejected. Poststructuralist perspectives tend to concentrate on the operation of language, the production of meaning, and the ways in which knowledge and power combine to create accepted or taken-for-granted forms of knowledge and social practices. Meaning can be produced only by the ongoing juxtaposition of the signified (meaning) and signifier (sound or written image) in discursive contexts. This concept has influenced poststructuralist perspectives in that meaning can never be regarded as being fixed or stable, but has always to be seen as ever changing and fluid. Meaning can be produced and temporarily fixed only in specific contexts. In relation to research, words and temporary meanings acquire a particular significance and are open to constant and continuing interrogation and analysis.

Poststructuralist analyses are used to critique notions of experience where experience is viewed in an essentialist manner and where experience is associated with individuals accessing the truth of a situation. Poststructural analysts are concerned with the detailed examination of texts, with a very broad definition being given to what is meant by a text. As high-lighted, particular attention is paid to language, meaning, power-knowledge frames, discursive interplays, and constructions of self, although other areas can also be the subject of detailed interrogation. Different researchers place emphasis on different areas. However, the integral association of linguistic practices with social practices can be seen to be a common feature, with the study of these connections facilitating the mapping out of interpretative repertoires or discourses. Meanings are also related to specific contexts. However, one area of difference is that for some researchers linguistic form would have a greater relevance than linguistic context. For other researchers this ordering would be reversed and for others still, both areas would be emphasized. Linguistic form concentrates on aspects such as grammar, cohesions, style(s), and the linguistic resources utilized. Rhetorical devices and the ways in which particular constructions have been used to create legitimacy are also attended to. Analyses that focus on content and form rather than on form and content pay attention to language to the extent that the significance given within the text to experiences and events within the text are socially and culturally available linguistic resources and practices. However, the main aspect of the analysis is not to concentrate on a repertoire, CONVERSATION ANALYSIS, or the operation of discourse in grammar, but to critically interrogate social relationships and social practices.

The use of poststructuralist analytical processes and techniques will produce many different readings of the texts. These readings will variously concentrate on recurring themes, contradictions, and the identification of patterns in the ways in which participant experiences are articulated. Readings will also place emphasis on absences, avoidances, inconsistencies, and contradictions. Some readings will demonstrate a concern with function and consequence and will focus on formulating hypotheses about the function and effect of what has been said in the text. Such hypotheses will then be tested by searching for further textual material. If supported, these hypotheses will continue to be built upon; if not supported, they will be disregarded.

In any research project, the question of SAMPLE SIZE has to be carefully considered. RESEARCH DESIGNs utilizing quantitative orientations and SURVEY or experimental research approaches rely for their RELIABILITY, VALIDITY, and GENERALIZABILITY on the statistically amenable way in which the sample has been formed. However, the situation with regard to poststructuralist forms of deconstructive textual or discourse analysis is somewhat different. The aim is to generate enough texts to address the research question or the area of focus, and emphasis may be placed on a poststructuralist deconstructive interrogation of just one text. Methodological rigor is attended to by considering the positioning of the researcher, the provision of ongoing detail about the analytical process, and the posing of different textual readings. In relation to matters concerned with representativeness, it has to be borne in mind that the site of the analytical investigation is the textual frame within which the participants speak, rather than the participants themselves.

📖 Given 2008

posttest
see PRETEST

posttest-comparison-group design
another term for STATIC-GROUP COMPARISON DESIGN

posttest control and experimental group design
another term for POSTTEST-ONLY CONTROL GROUP DESIGN

posttest-only control group design
also **two-group posttest-only design, randomized two-group posttest only design, posttest control and experimental group design, posttest-only equivalent-groups design, randomized subjects posttest-only control group design, two-group posttest-only randomized experimental design**

a TRUE EXPERIMENTAL DESIGN in which there are two groups: an EXPERIMENTAL GROUP which receives the special TREATMENT (denoted by X), and a CONTROL GROUP which does not. In this design, initial differences between the groups are controlled for by the RANDOM SELECTION and RANDOM ASSIGNMENT of the subjects (symbolized by R). Posttests (labeled O) are also administered for final measurement of groups. Thus, the design can be diagramed as follows:

Experimental Group (*R*)   X   O
Control Group (*R*)   O

The students are randomly assigned to one or other group, and the decision as to which group will be the experimental group is also decided randomly. In this design, initial differences between the groups are controlled for by the random selection and random assignment of the subjects. Because individual characteristics are assumed to be equally distributed through randomization, there is theoretically no real need for a pretest to assess the comparability of the groups prior to the intervention or treatment. In this design, random assignment ensures, to some degree, that the two groups are equivalent before treatment so that any post-treatment differences can be attributed to the treatment.

The focus of study is usually performance and not developmental. This design encompasses all the necessary elements of a true randomized experiment: (1) random assignment, to distribute extraneous differences across groups; (2) intervention and control groups, to determine whether the treatment had an effect; and (3) observations following the treatment. If the obtained means of the two groups differ significantly (i.e., more than would be expected on the basis of chance alone), the experimenter can be reasonably confident that the experimental treatment is responsible for the observed result.

This design controls for the main effects of HISTORY, MATURATION, STATISTICAL REGRESSION, and pretesting; because no pretest is used, there can be no interaction effect of pretest and treatment. Thus, this design is especially recommended for research on changing attitudes. It is also useful in studies in which a pretest is either not available or not appropriate, such as in studies with, for example, primary grades, where it is impossible to administer a pretest because the learning is not yet manifest. Another advantage of this design is that it can be extended to include more than two groups if necessary. Possible threats to INTERNAL VALIDITY are *subject effects* (e.g., HAWTHORNE EFFECT, JOHN HENRY EFFECT, DEMORALIZATION) and RESEARCHER EFFECT.

The posttest-only control group design does not permit the investigator to assess change. If such an assessment is desired, then a design that uses both a pretest and a posttest should be chosen (e.g., PRETEST-POSTTEST CONTROL GROUP DESIGN). Because of the lack of a pretest, MORTALITY could be a threat. Without having pretest information, preferably on the same DEPENDENT VARIABLE used as the posttest, the researcher has no way of knowing if those who dropped out of the study were different from those who continued.

📖 Ary et al. 2010; Hatch & Farhady 1982; Neuman 2007; Shadish et al.2002

posttest-only equivalent-groups design
another term for POSTTEST-ONLY CONTROL GROUP DESIGN

posttest-only nonequivalent group design
another term for STATIC-GROUP COMPARISON DESIGN

posttest two experimental groups design
also **posttest two treatment design**
a TRUE EXPERIMENTAL DESIGN in which participants are randomly assigned to each of two EXPERIMENTAL GROUPs. As shown in the following notation, in this design, experimental group 1 receives TREATMENT 1 (labeled X_1) and experimental group 2 receives treatment 2 (labeled X_2). As shown below, only posttests (O) are conducted on the two groups for final measurement.
 Cohen et al. 2011

$$\text{Experimental Group}_1 (R) \quad X_1 \quad O$$
$$\text{Experimental Group}_2 (R) \quad X_2 \quad O$$

posttest two treatment design
another term for POSTTEST TWO EXPERIMENTAL GROUPS DESIGN

power
the number of times that a quantity or number is multiplied by itself. It is usually written as an EXPONENT. For example, the exponent 2 in the expression 3^2 indicates that the quantity 3 is raised or multiplied to the second power or the power of 2, which is 3×3. The exponent 3 in the expression 3^3 indicates that the quantity 3 is raised to the third power or the power of 3, which is $3 \times 3 \times 3$. The number which is raised by the exponent is called the **base**. So 3 is the base in 3^2 and 5 is the base in 5^2.
 Cramer & Howitt 2004

power
another term for STATISTICAL POWER

power of a test
another term for STATISTICAL POWER

power test
see SPEED TEST

practical action research
a type of ACTION RESEARCH which is intended to address a specific problem within a classroom, school, university, or other community. Practical

action research can be carried out in a variety of settings, such as educational, social service, or business locations. Its primary purpose is to improve practice in the short term as well as to inform larger issues. It can be carried out by individuals, teams, or even larger groups, provided the focus remains clear and specific. To be maximally successful, practical action research should result in an action plan that, ideally, will be implemented and further evaluated.
 Fraenkel & Wallen 2009

practical significance
a term which is used in contrast to STATISTICAL SIGNIFICANCE to emphasize the fact that the observed difference is something meaningful in the context of the subject matter under investigation and not simply that it is unlikely to be due to chance alone. In other words, practical significance is a means of assessing *multivariate* analysis results based on their substantive findings rather than their statistical significance. Whereas statistical significance determines whether the result is attributable to chance, practical significance assesses whether the result is useful (i.e., substantial enough to warrant action) in achieving the research objectives. For example, with a large SAMPLE very small differences with no practical importance whatsoever may turn out to be statistically significant. The practical significance implies importance of research finding for theory, policy, or explanation. The use of CONFIDENCE INTERVALs can often help to assess the practical significance of study results.
 Hair et al. 2010; Sahai & Khurshid 2001

practice effect
the effect of previous practice on later performance. For example, in testing how much grammar improvement had occurred in students after a grammar course, if the same items appeared on a pretest and a posttest (see PRETEST), students might perform better on the posttest simply because they had already had practice on the items during the pretest, rather than because of what they had learned from the course.
 Richards & Schmidt 2010

practitioner research
another term for ACTION RESEARCH

pragmatism
a philosophy that insists on an intimate connection between theory and practice, and in which the meaning of a concept is best articulated as its conceivable practical consequences. For some this is a theory of meaning, and for others a theory of truth. Whichever line is taken, pragmatists are generally empiricists (see EMPIRICISM) who believe that there is no

division between the mind and the world, and that the meaning (or truth) of a claim lies in its utility in getting along with the world. Data from the world, and our perceptions of it in theory, are therefore interconnected and real, and essential to our understanding of any reality—including the VALIDITY of a test.

Pragmatism is a perspective in social research that encompasses both QUALITATIVE and QUANTITATIVE RESEARCH. It is not concerned with whether research is describing either a real or socially constructed world. Instead, for pragmatists, research simply helps us to identify what works. Of course, we might ask our pragmatists what they mean by what works. They are likely to reply that knowledge arises from examining problems and determining what works in a particular situation. It does not matter if there is a single reality or multiple realities as long as we discover answers that help us do things that we want to do. A pragmatist might insist that a good theory is one that helps us accomplish a specific goal (or set of goals) or one that reduces our doubt about the outcome of a given action. Most pragmatic researchers use a mixed-methods approach to research (see MIXED METHODS RESEARCH); for example, they use both qualitative and quantitative methods to answer their research questions. Pragmatic researchers propose that even within the same study, quantitative and qualitative methods can be combined in creative ways to more fully answer research questions. Pragmatic frameworks are used by both professional researchers and researchers who are primarily practitioners (e.g., teachers, counselors, administrators, school psychologists).

📖 Fulcher & Davidson 2007; Lodico et al. 2010

prediction matrix
another term for CLASSIFICATION MATRIX

predictive discriminative analysis
see DISCRIMINANT ANALYSIS

predictive validity
see CRITERION-RELATED VALIDITY

predictor variable
another term for INDEPENDENT VARIABLE

pre-experimental design
the least effective of EXPERIMENTAL RESEARCH design which provides either no CONTROL GROUP or no way of equating the groups that are used. Put simply, studies using pre-experimental designs either do not use control groups or, when such groups are used, no pretest is administered. Thus, researchers cannot confirm that changes observed on the

posttest are truly due to the INTERVENTION. Pre-experimental designs are not really considered model experiments because they do not account for EXTRANEOUS VARIABLEs which may have influenced the results. Thus, the INTERNAL VALIDITY of such a design is also questionable. However, they are easy, useful ways of getting introductory information on research questions. They are often used in preliminary research to provide direction and focus for further research using experimental designs, or when circumstances exclude more controlled research design.

There are a few pre-experimental methods which are common in applied linguistics, especially in language research. The three most commonly used pre-experimental designs are the ONE-SHOT DESIGN, ONE-GROUP PRETEST-POSTTEST DESIGN, and STATIC-GROUP COMPARISON DESIGN.

see also EX POST FACTO DESIGN, QUASI-EXPERIMENTAL DESIGN

📖 Best & Kahn 2006; Campbell & Stanley 1963; Hatch & Farhady 1982; Porte 2010

prestige bias
another term for SOCIAL DESIRABILITY BIAS

prestige question
see SOCIAL DESIRABILITY BIAS

pretest
a measurement stage preceding the administration of the EXPERIMENTAL TREATMENT. Pretest provides a BASELINE MEASUREMENT against which change due to the experimental treatment can be assessed. Without a pretest, it is not possible to know whether scores have increased, stayed the same or reduced. It also shows whether the MEANs of the groups are similar prior to the subsequent measurement. If the pretest means differ significantly and if the pretest is correlated with the **posttest** (the measurement made immediately after the experimental treatment or the control for the experimental treatment has been made), these pretest differences need to be taken into account when examining the posttest differences. The recommended statistical test for doing this is ANALYSIS OF COVARIANCE.

Research designs involving pretests are not without their problems. For one thing, the pretest may sensitize the participants and affect the degree of influence of the experimental treatment. For example, if the study is about changing attitudes, forewarning participants by giving them a pretest measure of their attitudes may make them realize that their susceptibility to influence is being assessed. Consequently, they may try their hardest not to change their attitude under the experimental treatment. Hence, sometimes a pretest design also includes additional groups which are not pretested to see whether the pretest may have had an influence.

📖 Cramer & Howitt 2004

pretest-posttest control and experimental group design
another term for PRETEST-POSTTEST CONTROL GROUP DESIGN

pretest-posttest control group design
also **randomized two-group pretest-posttest design, pretest-posttest control and experimental group design, pretest-posttest equivalent-groups design, randomized subjects pretest-posttest control group design**
a TRUE EXPERIMENTAL DESIGN type which is the same as the POSTTEST-ONLY CONTROL GROUP DESIGN except that a pretest is administered before the TREATMENT (labeled X). In this design, like posttest only control group, initial differences between the groups are controlled for by the RANDOM SELECTION and RANDOM ASSIGNMENT of the subjects (labeled R). In the following notation, O denotes pretests and posttests:

$$\begin{array}{lccc} \text{Experimental Group } (R) & O & X & O \\ \text{Control Group } (R) & O & & O \end{array}$$

The addition of a pretest has several important benefits. First, it allows the researcher to compare the groups on several measures following randomization to determine whether the groups are truly equivalent. Although it is likely that randomization distributed most differences equally across the groups, it is possible that some differences still exist (see RANDOMIZATION CHECK). The second major benefit of a pretest is that it provides baseline information that allows researchers to compare the participants who completed the posttest to those who did not. Accordingly, researchers can determine whether any between-group differences found at the end of the study are due to the treatment (i.e., the INDEPENDENT VARIABLE). This design, thus, controls most of the extraneous variables that pose a threat to INTERNAL VALIDITY. For example, the effects of HISTORY and MATURATION are experienced in both groups; therefore, any difference between the groups on the posttest measure could probably not be attributed to these factors. Differential selection of subjects and statistical regression are also controlled through the randomization procedure. There is one internal validity issue, however. Although both groups take the pretest and may experience the sensitizing effect, the pretest can cause the experimental subjects to respond to the treatment in a particular way just because of their increased sensitivity. The result is a difference on the posttest that could mistakenly be attributed to the effect of the treatment alone.

The main concern in using this design is EXTERNAL VALIDITY. Ironically, the problem stems from the use of the pretest, an essential feature of the design. There may be, however, an interaction between the pretest and the treatment so that the results are generalizable (see GENERALIZABILITY) only to other pretested groups. The responses to the posttest may not be representative of how individuals would respond if they had not been given a pretest. If the pretest influences the posttests of both the experimental and control groups, it becomes a threat to the external validity or generalizability of a study's findings. This is because the posttest will no longer reflect how participants would respond if they had not received a pretest.

The recommended statistical procedure to use with the pretest-posttest control group design is an ANALYSIS OF COVARIANCE with posttest scores as the dependent variable and pretest scores as the COVARIATE to control for initial differences on the pretest.

📖 Ary et al. 2010; Cohen et al. 2011; Hatch & Lazaraton 1991

pretest-posttest equivalent-groups design
another term for PRETEST-POSTTEST CONTROL GROUP DESIGN

pretest-posttest two experimental groups design
also **pretest-posttest two treatment design**

a TRUE EXPERIMENTAL DESIGN in which participants are randomly assigned (labeled R) to each of two EXPERIMENTAL GROUPs. Experimental group 1 receives TREATMENT 1 (labeled X_1) and experimental group 2 receives treatment 2 (labeled X_2). Pretests and posttests (labeled O) are also conducted to measure changes in individuals in the two groups.

$$\text{Experimental Group}_1 (R) \quad O \quad X_1 \quad O$$
$$\text{Experimental Group}_2 (R) \quad O \quad X_2 \quad O$$

The true experiment can also be conducted with one CONTROL GROUP and two or more experimental groups. So, for example, the design might be:

$$\text{Experimental Group}_1 (R) \quad O \quad X_1 \quad O$$
$$\text{Experimental Group}_2 (R) \quad O \quad X_2 \quad O$$
$$\text{Control Group} (R) \qquad\quad O \qquad\quad O$$

This can be extended to the posttest control and experimental group design and the posttest two experimental groups design, and the pretest-posttest two treatment design.

📖 Cohen et al. 2011

pretest-posttest two treatment design
another name for PRETEST-POSTTEST TWO EXPERIMENTAL GROUPS DESIGN

pretest-treatment interaction
a threat to EXTERNAL VALIDITY which is a problem only when a pretest is used in a study. Using a pretest may increase or decrease the experimental subjects' sensitivity or responsiveness to the experimental variable and thus make the results obtained for this pretested population unrepresentative of effects of the experimental variable on the unpretested population from which the experimental subjects are selected. In this case, you could generalize to pretested groups but not to unpretested ones. Consider the following: You are conducting a study where the experimental treatment is a workshop designed to improve students' sensitivity toward diversity. Your pretest is a measure of student awareness of their personal attitudes toward diversity. The pretest itself may make them more aware of the issues of diversity and its importance in their lives. If at the end of the study the EXPERIMENTAL GROUP is more sensitive to issues of diversity, could your results be generalizable to all other groups receiving the training, or would the findings be generalizable only to groups that received the pretest on attitudes toward diversity? One way to control for pretest treatment interaction is to use a pretest that does not increase participants' awareness of what behaviors you are trying to change. Some researchers use designs that include treatment groups that are not pretested to control for pretest-treatment interaction.
see also MULTIPLE-TREATMENT INTERACTION, SPECIFICITY OF VARIABLES, TREATMENT DIFFUSION, RESEARCHER EFFECT, HALO EFFECT, HAWTHORNE EFFECT, NOVELTY EFFECT
📖 Ary et al. 2010; Lodico et al. 2010

primary research
see SECONDARY RESEARCH

primary variance
another term for SYSTEMATIC VARIANCE

principle components analysis
also **PCA, component analysis**
a *multivariate* analysis which allows you to explore the interrelationships between a number of VARIABLEs to see whether there are a smaller number of higher-order factors (or components) that account for the pattern of intercorrelations between a set of OBSERVED VARIABLEs. In other words, principle components analysis (PCA) allows you to see whether the pattern of responses of participants suggests that certain variables are

measuring a similar factor or LATENT VARIABLE, while other variables are measuring other factors.

There are at least two uses of PCA, both of which involve explaining the variance among a set of observed variables. One use is to produce a set of components (or latent or unobserved variables) which can account for all the variance in the set of observed variables. The advantage of using the components over the original variables is that the components will be orthogonal (not correlated) and so will not produce a problem of MULTI-COLLINEARITY if used in analyses such as MULTIPLE REGRESSION. For all the variance in the original set of variables to be accounted for by the set of components, there will need to be as many components as there were observed variables.

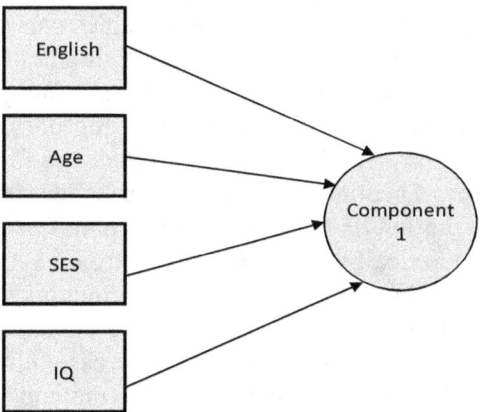

Figure P.10. Principle Components Analysis

As an example, if we conducted a PCA on the data where there were four PREDICTOR VARIABLEs—ability in English, age, socio-economic status (SES) and IQ—we would produce the relationship shown in Figure P.10 between the first component and the observed variables. Thus, we have a regression with the first component as the CRITERION VARIABLE and the observed variables as the predictors. Just as with regression, the PCA will provide coefficients which could be used to find an individual's score on a given component, if we knew his/her English ability, age, SES and IQ. Each observed variable will contribute to predicting the value of each component, using a different set of coefficients for the relationship between the observed variables and each component. In the current example, the four components could now be entered as predictor variables in a multiple regression with mathematical ability as the criterion variable and there would be no problem of multicollinearity among the set of predictor variables.

A more frequent use of PCA can be to produce a smaller set of components which accounts for most of the variance in the original set of observed variables. If we had a large set of variables and PCA showed that most of the variance in the set could be accounted for by a small set of components, then the components could be used in a multiple regression and increase the POWER of the test by having reduced the number of predictor variables.

Like FACTOR ANALYSIS (FA), the specific goals of PCA are to summarize patterns of CORRELATIONs among observed variables, to reduce a large number of observed variables to a smaller number of factors, to provide an OPERATIONAL DEFINITION for an underlying process by using observed variables, or to test a theory about the nature of underlying processes. However, PCA, unlike FA, maintains the information such that the correlations between the original variables can be completely reconstructed from the interrelationships among the factors. It includes all the variance in the scores, including that which is unique to a variable and ERROR VARIANCE. As such, it is summarizing the variance in the variables into a (possibly smaller) set of components. FA, on the other hand, only attempts to account for variance that is shared between variables, under the assumption that such variables are indicators of latent variables or factors. Theoretically, the difference between FA and PCA lies in the reason that variables are associated with a factor or component. PCA is more mathematically precise. FA is more conceptually realistic. Both PCA and FA solutions can be rotated to increase interpretability.

PCA and FA differ from most multivariate methods in that only a single set of measured variables is analyzed. PCA and FA are similar to other correlation methods that focus on the nature of the relationship among variables [e.g., MULTIPLE REGRESSION (MR), CANONICAL CORRELATION (CC)]. In contrast to group-difference methods (e.g., ANALYSIS OF COVARIANCE, MULTIVARIATE ANALYSIS OF VARIANCE), PCA and FA do not focus on the MEANs for a set of variables. With PCA and FA, as with several other methods (e.g., MR, DISCRIMINANT FUNCTION ANALYSIS, LOGISTIC REGRESSION, CC), we are much more interested in interpretable weights that link variables to underlying dimensions or linear combinations.

see also MULTIDIMENSIONAL SCALING

📖 Clark-Carter 2010; Harlow 2005

probability
also *p*

the mathematical chance or likelihood that a particular outcome will occur. Probability is expressed in terms of the ratio of a particular outcome to all possible outcomes. Thus, the probability of a coin landing heads is 1 divided by 2 (the possible outcomes are heads or tails). If the probability of an event is 0, that means there is no chance that it will occur, while if the probability of an event is 1, that means it is certain to occur. It is conventional in mathematics to specify probability using decimals, so we say that the probability of an event is between 0 and 1, but it is equally acceptable (and more common in everyday speech) to speak in terms of percentages, so it is equally correct to say that the probability of an event is always between 0% and 100%. To move from decimals to percent, multiply by 100 (per cent = per 100), so a probability of .4 is also a probability of 40% (.4 × 100 = 40) and a probability of .85 may also be stated as 85% probability.

The commonest use of probabilities is in significance testing. In research, when a HYPOTHESIS is offered for testing, an educated guess is being made about what is or is not probable. A hypothesis is tested by finding out the PROBABILITY VALUE of the result which is, once calculated, the proportion of times a particular outcome would happen if the research were repeated ad infinitum.

see also PROBABILITY SAMPLING, NONPROBABILITY SAMPLING

📖 Boslaugh & Watters 2008; Cramer & Howitt 2004; Porte 2010

probability density curve
see PROBABILITY DISTRIBUTION

probability distribution
a description of the possible values of a VARIABLE, and of the probabilities of occurrence of these values. For a discrete RANDOM VARIABLE, probability distribution is a mathematical formula that gives the PROBABILITY of each value of the variable. BINOMIAL DISTRIBUTION is an example. For a *continuous* random variable, it is a curve described by a mathematical formula which specifies, by way of areas under the curve, the probability that the variable falls within a particular interval. An example is the NORMAL DISTRIBUTION. A curve describing a continuous probability distribution is called **probability density curve** (also called **density curve**), which includes a finite area between itself and the HORIZONTAL AXIS.

see also CONTINUOUS VARIABLE, CATEGORICAL VARIABLE

📖 Everitt 2001; Everitt & Skrondal 2010; Sahai & Khurshid 2001; Upton & Cook 2008

probability sample
see PROBABILITY SAMPLING

probability sampling
also **random sampling**
a SAMPLING procedure wherein every member of the overall POPULATION has a fixed and known PROBABILITY or chance of being included in

the sample. A sample obtained in such a manner is called a **probability sample** (also called a **random sample**). Because probability sampling draws randomly from the wider population, it will be useful if the researcher wishes to make generalizations. Probability sampling, unlike NON-PROBABILITY SAMPLING, also permits TWO-TAILED TESTs to be administered in statistical analysis of quantitative data. For QUANTITATIVE RESEARCH, probability samples have two main advantages. First, they allow statistical statements about the accuracy of the sample's numerical results. Second, they are necessary for tests of STATISTICAL SIGNIFICANCE. For example, the results from a SURVEY may show that the scores for men and women are so far apart that there is only a 5% chance that the difference is due to having drawn an unusual sample. These statements about a 5% chance of error or 95% degree of confidence explicitly recognize that probability samples are not always accurate. Instead, they make it possible to say precisely how likely it is that the sample does accurately represent the population. The results are thus generalizable within statistically well-defined limits.

For QUALITATIVE RESEARCH, probability samples typically require information that is not likely to be available in most studies. In particular, if there is no way to count all the members of the original population, then there is no way to know what proportion of the total population is represented by any given sample. And even if the population size is known, there may not be any realistic way to give every member of that population a known probability of being included in the sample. As a further limitation, an accurate probability sampling requires a relatively large SAMPLE SIZE, and the accuracy of generalizations from probability samples declines rapidly for small samples.

For quantitative research, the statistical analyses that are possible only with probability samples justify the demands of knowing the population size, determining the probability of selection for each sample member, and gathering large samples. In contrast, for qualitative research, statistical analyses are not only of little interest but also are largely impractical due to the small sample sizes in those studies. Instead, most qualitative research concentrates on pairing purposive selection procedures (see PURPOSIVE SAMPLING) to define the population of interest with nonprobability techniques to select the actual data sources for any given study.

There are several types of probability samples: SIMPLE RANDOM SAMPLING, SYSTEMATIC SAMPLING, STRATIFIED SAMPLING, CLUSTER SAMPLING, AREA SAMPLING, MULTI-PHASE SAMPLING, and MULTISTAGE SAMPLING. They all have a measure of randomness built into them and therefore have a degree of GENERALIZABILITY.

Cohen et al. 2011; Dörnyei 2007; Everitt & Skrondal 2010; Given 2008; Sahai & Khurshid 2001

probability value
also *p*-value, significance probability, observed significance level
a statistic which is used in QUANTITATIVE RESEARCH to determine whether the result found was due to chance or due to a true relationship or difference in groups. Statistical tests provide probabilities or *p*-values for test statistics. These probabilities indicate the likelihood that obtained results are chance differences or are significant differences. In the majority of tests, the *p*-value is compared with the ALPHA LEVEL (represented as α) of significance, chosen by the researcher before the statistical HYPOTHESIS is tested. If the obtained *p*-value for the statistical test is less than or equal to the chosen alpha level then the NULL HYPOTHESIS is rejected and the results are said to be statistically significant at the chosen alpha level. That is, if the null hypothesis were to be rejected at the .05 alpha level, this would be reported as $p < .05$. Small *p*-values suggest that the null hypothesis is unlikely to be true. The smaller it is, the more convincing is the rejection of the null hypothesis in favor of the ALTERNATIVE HYPOTHESIS.

p-values often are reported in the literature for ANALYSIS OF VARIANCE, REGRESSION and CORRELATION COEFFICIENTs, among other statistical techniques.
 Lavrakas 2008; Peers 1996; Porte 2010

probe
a technique employed in interviewing to solicit a more complete answer to a question. Probe is a non-directive phrase or question used to encourage a respondent to elaborate on an answer. Examples include 'Anything more?' and 'How is that?' The aim of probe is always to obtain greater clarity, detail or depth of understanding—for instance to elicit further description, an example, an explanation, and so on. Its key feature is that it relates directly to what has already been said by the interviewee, often referring to the exact phrase or term that they have used. Probes are a crucial element of any IN-DEPTH INTERVIEW.
 Babbie 2011; Ritchie & Lewis 2003

procedures
a subsection in the METHOD section of a RESEARCH REPORT which tells you exactly how the materials and instruments were used. What did the subjects do in the study, or what was done to them? In detail, how were the materials prepared, administered, and scored? What were the environmental conditions like during the experiment? Were they the same for all the subjects involved? How long did the process take? Did any of the subjects drop out? The answers to these questions and many other potential questions should make it possible for the reader to understand exactly how the study was conducted.

see also PARTICIPANTS, MATERIALS, ANALYSES
📖 Brown 1988

process evaluation
another term for FORMATIVE EVALUATION

productive response item
another term for CONSTRUCTED-RESPONSE ITEM

product moment correlation
another term for PEARSON PRODUCT-MOMENT CORRELATION COEFFICIENT

proficiency test
a test that measures how much of a language someone has learned. Proficiency test assess the general knowledge or skills commonly required or prerequisite to entry into (or exemption from) a group of similar institutions. One example is the Test of English as a foreign language (TOEFL), which is used by many American universities that have English language proficiency prerequisite in common. Understandably, such tests are very general in nature and cannot be related to the goals and objectives of any particular language program.
see also ACHIEVEMENT TEST
📖 Brown 2005; Richards & Schmidt 2010

profile analysis
also **repeated-measures MANOVA**
a *multivariate* approach to REPEATED MEASURES DESIGNs. Profile analysis is a special application of MULTIVARIATE ANALYSIS OF VARIANCE (MANOVA) to a situation where there are several DEPENDENT VARIABLEs (DVs), all measured on the same SCALE. The set of DVs can either come from one DV measured several different times, or several different DVs all measured at one time. There is also a popular extension of the analysis where several different DVs are measured at several different times, called the **doubly-multivariate design**. The more common application is in research where subjects are measured repeatedly on the same DV. For example, second language (L2) achievement tests are given at various points during a semester to test the effects of alternative educational programs such as traditional classroom vs. computer-assisted instruction. Used this way, profile analysis offers a multivariate alternative to the univariate F VALUE for the within-subjects effect and its interactions. The choice between profile analysis and univariate REPEATED-MEASURES ANOVA depends on SAMPLE SIZE, STATISTICAL POWER, and whether statistical ASSUMPTIONS of repeated-measured ANOVA are met.

Rapidly growing in popularity is use of repeated-measures MANOVA for doubly-multivariate designs where several DVs, not all measured on the same scale, are measured repeatedly. For example, L2 language competence is measured several times during a semester, each time by both a grade on a language test (one DV) and a scale of language anxiety (a second DV).
The term profile analysis is also applied to techniques for measuring resemblance among profile patterns through CLUSTER ANALYSIS.
 Tabachnick & Fidell 2007

projective hypothesis
the thesis that an individual supplies structure to unstructured stimuli in a manner consistent with the individual's own unique pattern of conscious and unconscious needs, fears, desires, impulses, conflicts, and ways of perceiving and responding.
see PROJECTIVE TECHNIQUES
 Cohen & Swerdlik 2010

projective techniques
measures in which an individual is asked to respond to an ambiguous or unstructured stimulus. They are called projective because a person is expected to project into the stimulus his/her own needs, wants, fears, intentions, motives, urges, beliefs, anxieties, and experiences. In projective techniques the respondent in supplying information tends unconsciously to project his/her own attitudes or feelings on the subject under study. Projective techniques play an important role in motivational researches or in attitude SURVEYs. The use of these techniques requires intensive specialized training. In such techniques, the individual's responses to the stimulus-situation are not taken at their face value. The stimuli may arouse many different kinds of reactions. The nature of the stimuli and the way in which they are presented under these techniques do not clearly indicate the way in which the response is to be interpreted. The stimulus may be a photograph, a picture, an inkblot and so on. Responses to these stimuli are interpreted as indicating the individual's own view, his/her personality structure, his/her needs, tensions, etc. in the context of some pre-established psychological conceptualization of what the individuals responses to the stimulus mean.
Some important projective techniques are as follows:

1) *Word association tests*: These tests are used to extract information regarding such words which have maximum association. In this sort of test the respondent is asked to mention the first word that comes to mind, ostensibly without thinking, as the interviewer reads out each word from a list. If the interviewer says cold, the respondent may say

hot and the like. The general technique is to use a list of as many as 50 to 100 words. Analysis of the matching words supplied by the respondents indicates whether the given word should be used for the contemplated purpose. This technique is quick and easy to use, but yields reliable results when applied to words that are widely known and which possess essentially one type of meaning.

2) *Sentence completion tests*: These tests happen to be an extension of the technique of word association tests. This technique permits the testing not only of words (as in case of word association tests), but of ideas as well and thus, helps in developing hypotheses and in the construction of QUESTIONNAIREs. This technique is also quick and easy to use, but it often leads to analytical problems, particularly when the response happens to be multidimensional.

3) *Story completion tests*: Such tests are a step further wherein the researcher may contrive stories instead of sentences and ask the informants to complete them. The respondent is given just enough of story to focus his/her attention on a given subject and s/he is asked to supply a conclusion to the story.

4) *verbal projection tests*: These are the tests wherein the respondent is asked to comment on or to explain what other people do. For example, 'Why do some people tend to learn an additional language?' Answers may reveal the respondent's own motivations.

5) *quizzes, tests, and examinations*: This is also a technique of extracting information regarding specific ability of candidates indirectly. In this procedure both long and short questions are framed to test through them the memorizing and analytical ability of candidates.

6) SOCIOMETRY

7) *pictorial techniques*: There are several pictorial techniques. The important ones are: THEMATIC APPERCEPTION TEST, ROSENZWEIG TEST, RORSCHACH TEST, HOLTZMAN INKBLOT TEST, and TOMKINS-HORN PICTURE ARRANGEMENT TEST.

☐ Ary et al. 2010; Kothari 2008

prompt

any material presented to respondents which is designed to stimulate response (such as a piece of writing or oral production). A prompt may consist of a set of instructions and a text, a title, a picture or a set of pictures, diagrams, table, chart, or other data, and may be presented orally or in graphic form. The information provided on the purpose of the response or the intended audience may also be considered to be part of the prompt, although this is more properly termed TEST RUBRIC.

see also ITEM SPECIFICATIONS, ELICITATION, PROBE, OPEN-FORM ITEM, INTERVIEW

☐ Mousavi 2012

proportion

the FREQUENCY of cases in a category divided by the total number of cases. A proportion is a decimal number between 0 and 1 that indicates a fraction of the total. To transform a number to a proportion, simply divide the number by the total. If 4 out of 10 people pass an exam, then the proportion of people passing the exam is 4/10, which equals .4. Or, if you score 6 correct on a test out of a possible 12, the proportion you have corrected is 6/12, which is .5. We can also work in the opposite direction from a known proportion to find the number out of the total it represents. Here, multiply the proportion times the total. Thus, to find how many questions out of 12 you must answer correctly to get .5 correct, multiply .5 times 12, and the answer is 6. We can also transform a proportion into a percent or **percentage**. A percent is a proportion multiplied by 100. Above, your proportion correct was .5, so you had (.5) (100) or 50% correct. Altogether, to transform the original test score of 6 out of 12 to a percent, first divide the score by the total to find the proportion and then multiply by 100. Thus, (6/12) (100) equals 50%. To transform a percent back into a proportion, divide the percent by 100 (above, 50/100 equals .5). Altogether, to find the test score that corresponds to a certain percent, transform the percent to a proportion and then multiply the proportion times the total number possible. Thus, to find the score that corresponds to 50% of 12, transform 50% to the proportion, which is .5, and then multiply .5 times 12. Thus, 50% of 12 is equal to (50/100)(12), which is 6.

Heiman 2011

proportional quota sampling

see QUOTA SAMPLING

proportional stratified sampling

see STRATIFIED SAMPLING

prospective cohort study

see COHORT STUDY

prospective longitudinal study

another term for PANEL STUDY

protected *t*-test

another term for FISHER'S LEAST SIGNIFICANT DIFFERENCE

proximal similarity model

an approach to GENERALIZABILITY. Proximal similarity model was suggested as an appropriate relabeling of the term EXTERNAL VALIDITY.

With proximal similarity, you begin by thinking about different generalizability contexts and developing a theory about which contexts are more like your study and which are less so. For instance, you might imagine several settings that have people who are more similar to the people in your study or people who are less similar. This process also holds for times and places. When you place different contexts in terms of their relative similarities, you can call this implicit theoretical dimension a gradient of similarity. After you develop this proximal similarity framework, you can generalize. You can generalize the results of your study to other persons, places, or times that are more like (i.e., more proximally similar to) your study. Notice that here, you can never generalize with certainty; these generalizations are always a question of more or less similar.
📖 Trochim & Donnelly 2007

proxy respondent
a respondent's report on the properties or activities of another person or group of persons. Proxy responses are used only when there is a particular reason that the targeted person cannot report. Since a proxy response is treated the same as a self-reported response, an obvious benefit of allowing proxy responses is to increase the RESPONSE RATE. Some SURVEY items do not lend themselves to proxy responding because MEASUREMENT ERROR is apt to be particularly great. A noteworthy case is attitudinal items. Even if the proxy respondent knows the targeted person extremely well, the attitudes of the proxy respondent will likely be confounded with the attitudes of the targeted person in the responses.
📖 Lavrakas 2008

pseudo *R* square
a value of overall model fit that can be calculated for LOGISTIC REGRESSION. It is comparable to the *R* SQUARE (R^2) measure used in MULTIPLE REGRESSION.
📖 Hair et al. 2010

psychological constructivism
a theory which addresses the epistemological (see EPISTEMOLOGY) questions of CONSTRUCTIVISM and is especially relevant to education as it deals with how people learn and, thereby, how instruction should be carried out. Essentially, knowledge is not acquired but rather is made or constructed. The learner is an active participant in building knowledge, not a passive recipient of information.
📖 Given 2008

psychometrics
the science of measuring psychological abilities, attributes, and

characteristics. Modern psychometrics is embodied by standardized psychological tests. However, psychometrics has come to mean more than just the tests themselves; it also encompasses the mathematical, statistical, and professional protocols that underpin tests—how tests are constructed, used, scored, and indeed, how they are evaluated.

With the onset of the **psychometric-structuralist movement** of language testing, tests typically set out to measure the discrete structural points (see DISCRETE-POINT TEST) being taught in the audio-lingual and related teaching methods of the time. Like the language teaching methods, these tests were influenced by behavioral psychology. The psychometric-structuralist movement saw the rise of the first carefully designed and standardized tests like the *Test of English as a Foreign Language*, the *Michigan Test of English Language Proficiency: Form A*, *Modern Language Association Foreign Language Proficiency Tests for Teachers and Advanced Students* (ETS), *Comprehensive English Language Test for Speakers of English as a Second Language*, and others. Such tests, usually in MULTIPLE-CHOICE ITEM format, are easy to administer and score and are carefully constructed to be objective, reliable (see RELIABILITY), and valid (see VALIDITY). Thus, they were felt to be an improvement on the test design and scoring practices of the *prescientific movement* (characterized by translation and essay tests).

The psychometric-structuralist movement is important because, for the first time, language test development follows scientific principles. In addition, psychometric-structuralist test development is squarely in hands of trained linguists and language testes. As a result, statistical analyses are used for the first time. Psychometric-structuralist tests are still very much in evidence around the world, but have been supplemented by what labeled integrative tests.

📖 Brown 2005; Everitt & Howell; Fulcher & Davidson 2007

psychometric-structuralist movement
   see PSYCHOMETRICS

pure research
   another term for BASIC RESEARCH

purposeful sampling
   another term for PURPOSIVE SAMPLING

purposive sampling
   also **purposeful sampling, judgmental sampling, deliberate sampling, criterion-based sampling**
   a type of NON-PROBABILITY SAMPLING and a feature of QUALITATIVE RESEARCH in which researchers handpick the cases to be included in the

sample on the basis of their judgment of their typicality (see Figure P.11). Purposive sampling is different from convenience sampling in that researchers do not simply study whoever is available but rather use their judgment to select a sample that they believe, based on prior information, will provide the data they need. In this way, they build up a sample that is satisfactory to their specific needs. For example, a group of disaffected second language (L2) students may be selected because they might indicate most distinctly the factors which contribute to L2 students disaffection; or, one class of L2 students may be selected to be tracked throughout a week in order to report on the curricular and pedagogic diet which is offered to them so that other teachers in the school might compare their own teaching to that reported. Whilst it may satisfy the researchers' needs to take this type of sample, it does not pretend to represent the wider POPULATION; it is deliberately and unashamedly selective and biased.

There are a range of different approaches to purposive sampling, designed to yield different types of sample composition depending on the study's aims and coverage. These have been described as follows:

- **Comprehensive sampling**. In comprehensive sampling, every unit is included in the sample. For example, a study of physically disabled students in a high school would include all such students in the school. Comprehensive sampling is used when the number of units is small.
- **Homogeneous sampling**. This method of sampling is chosen to give a detailed picture of a particular phenomenon, for example, individuals who belong to the same subculture or have the same characteristics. This allows for detailed investigation of social processes in a specified context.
- **Maximum variation sampling** (also called **heterogeneous sampling**). In maximum variation sampling there is a deliberate strategy to include phenomena which vary widely from each other; the researcher selects cases with markedly different forms of experience. For example, a study of U.S. high school students might include students from schools that differ in location, student characteristics, parental involvement, and other factors. This process will allow the researchers to explore the variation within the respondents and it will also underscore any commonalities that they find; if a pattern holds across the sampled diversity, the researchers can assume that it is reasonably stable.
- **Extreme (deviant, or unique) case sampling**. In extreme case sampling, units or cases are chosen because they are unusual or special and therefore potentially enlightening. The researcher selects the most extreme cases (e.g., the most motivated and demotivated learners). On the one hand, this allows the researchers to find the limits of the experi-

ence; on the other hand, if even such cases share common elements, they are likely to be real core components of the experience.
- **Intensity sampling**. Intensity sampling employs similar logic to extreme or deviant case sampling but focuses on cases which strongly represent the phenomena of interest rather than unusual cases. The researcher would select several cases at each of several levels of variation of the phenomenon. For example, the researcher may select some high-achieving, average-achieving, and low-achieving students.
- **Negative (discrepant) case sampling**. This method of sampling selects units that are examples of exceptions to expectations. The researcher would intentionally look for examples that appear not to confirm the theory being developed. This strategy is also called **confirming and disconfirming sampling**.
- **Typical case sampling**. In this method of sampling, the researcher selects participants whose experience is typical with regard to the research focus (e.g., they all study a foreign language as a school subject at an intermediate level with moderate success). This strategy assumes that the researcher has a profile of the targeted attributes possessed by an average learner. Although the researcher cannot generalize from the results because s/he cannot claim that everybody will have the same experience, s/he can list the typical or normal features of the experience. This approach highlights what is normal or average.
- **Criterion sampling**. A sampling strategy through which the researcher selects participants who meet some specific predetermined criteria, e.g., company executives who failed an important language exam.
- **Stratified purposive sampling**. A hybrid approach in which the aim is to select groups that display variation on a particular phenomenon but each of which is fairly homogeneous, so that subgroups can be compared.
- **Random purposeful sampling**. When the potential purposeful sample is too large (e.g., when resources are limited), the credibility of the study can be enhanced by randomly selecting participants or sites from the larger group.
- **Critical case sampling**. A sampling strategy through which the researcher deliberately targets cases which offer a dramatic or full representation of the phenomenon, either by their intensity or by their uniqueness (e.g., in a language attrition study examining people who have completely forgotten an L2 they used to speak). Their case may be taken as the most salient or comprehensive manifestation of the phenomenon under scrutiny; in such situations researchers are not only interested in what they find but also in what they do not, because something that does not occur in such salient cases is unlikely to happen elsewhere.

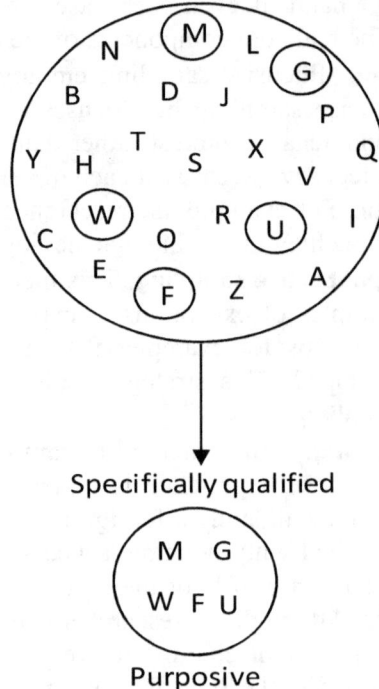

Figure P.11. Schematic Representation of Purposive Sampling

see also CONVENIENCE SAMPLING, QUOTA SAMPLING, DIMENSIONAL SAMPLING, SNOWBALL SAMPLING, SEQUENTIAL SAMPLING, VOLUNTEER SAMPLING, OPPORTUNISTIC SAMPLING

📖 Ary et al. 2010; Cohen et al. 2011; Dörnyei 2007; Mackey & Gass 2005; Ritchie & Lewis 2003

PV

an abbreviation for PERCENTAGE VARIANCE EFFECT SIZE

p-value

another term for PROBABILITY VALUE

Pygmalion effect

another term for EXPERIMENTER BIAS

Q

q
an abbreviation for STUDENTIZED RANGE TEST

Q
an abbreviation for TUKEY'S TEST

q index
see EFFECT SIZE

Q methodology
a technique for investigating individuals' subjective attitudes and beliefs on a topic for the purpose of identifying differing perspectives; it can be used to identify both what discourses exist within a community and who subscribes to or rejects these discourses.
📖 Kalof et al. 2008

Q-Q plot
an abbreviation for QUANTILE-QUANTILE PLOT

qualitative research
a RESEARCH METHODOLOGY that places primary importance on studying small samples of purposely chosen individuals; not attempting to control contextual factors, but rather seeking, through a variety of methods, to understand things from the informants' points of view; and creating a rich and in-depth picture of the phenomena under investigation. There is less of an emphasis on statistics (and concomitant attempts to generalize the results to wider populations) and more of an interest in the individual and his/her immediate context. By definition, qualitative research is *synthetic* or *holistic* (i.e., views the separate parts as a coherent whole), *heuristic* (i.e., discovers or describes the patterns or relationships), with little or no control and manipulation of the research context, and uses data collection procedures with *low explicitness*.
Qualitative research has roots in a number of different disciplines, principally ANTHROPOLOGY, sociology, and philosophy, and is now used in almost all fields of social science inquiry, including applied linguistics. Qualitative research is the primary example of HYPOTHESIS-GENERATING RESEARCH. That is, once all the data are collected, hypothesis may be derived from those data. The ultimate goal of qualitative research is to discover phenomena such as patterns of behavior not previously described and to understand them from the perspective of participants in the activi-

ty. Detailed definitions of qualitative research usually include the following characteristics:

1) *Rich description*: The aims of qualitative researchers often involve the provision of careful and detailed descriptions as opposed to the quantification of data through measurements, frequencies, scores, and ratings;
2) *Natural and holistic representation*: Qualitative researches aim to study individuals and events in their natural settings, i.e., rather than attempting to control and manipulate contextual factors through the use of laboratories or other artificial environments, qualitative researchers tend to be more interested in presenting a natural and holistic picture of the phenomena being studied. In order to capture a sufficient level of detail about the natural context, such investigations are usually conducted through an intense and prolonged contact with, or immersion in, the research setting;
3) *Few participants*: Qualitative researchers tend to work more intensively with fewer participants, and are less concerned about issues of GENERALIZABILITY. Qualitative research focuses on describing, understanding, and clarifying a human experience and therefore qualitative studies are directed at describing the aspects that make up an idiosyncratic experiences rather than determining the most likely, or mean experience, within a group. Accordingly, at least in theory, qualitative inquiry is not concerned with how representative the respondent sample is or how the experience is distributed in the population. Instead, the main goal of sampling is to find individuals who can provide rich and varied insights into the phenomenon under investigation. This goal is best achieved by means of some sort of PURPOSIVE SAMPLING;
4) **Emic perspective** (or participant or insider point of view): Qualitative researchers aim to interpret phenomena in terms of the meanings people attach to them, i.e., to adopt an emic perspective, or the use of categories that are meaningful to members of the speech community under study. An emic perspective requires one to recognize and accept the idea of multiple realities. Documenting multiple perspectives of reality in a given study is crucial to an understanding of why people think and act in the different ways they do. Emic perspectives can be distinguished from the use of **etic perspective** (or researcher or outsider point of view), which is an outsider's understanding of a culture or group that is not their own. Etic perspectives are more common in QUANTITATIVE RESEARCH;
5) *Cyclical and open-ended processes*: Qualitative research is often process-oriented or open ended, with categories that emerge. The re-

search often follows an inductive path that beings with few perceived notions, followed by a gradual fine tuning and narrowing of focus. Ideally, qualitative researchers enter the research process with a completely open mind and without setting out to test preconceived hypotheses. This means that the research focus is narrowed down only gradually and the analytic categories and concepts are defined during, rather than prior to, the process of the research. Thus, qualitative researchers tend to approach the research context with the purpose of observing whatever may be present there, and letting further questions emerge from the context;

6) *Possible ideological orientations*: Whereas most quantitative researchers consider impartiality to be a goal of their research, some qualitative researchers may consciously take ideological positions. This sort of research is sometimes described as *critical*, meaning that the researcher may have particular social or political goals, e.g., CRITICAL DISCOURSE ANALYSIS, a form of qualitative research, is a program of social analysis that critically analyzes discourse, (i.e., language in use), as a means of addressing social change;

7) *Interpretive analysis*: Qualitative research is fundamentally interpretive, which means that the research outcome is ultimately the product of the researcher's subjective interpretation of the data. Several alternative interpretations are possible for each data set, and because qualitative studies utilize relatively limited standardized instrumentation or analytical procedures, in the end it is the researcher who will choose from them. The researcher is essentially the main measurement device in the study. Accordingly, in qualitative research, the researcher's own values, personal history, and position on characteristics such as gender, culture, class, and age become integral part of the inquiry; and

8) *The nature of qualitative data*: Qualitative research works with a wide range of data including recorded INTERVIEWs, various types of texts (e.g., FIELDNOTES, JOURNAL and diary entries (see DIARY STUDY), DOCUMENTs, and images (photos or videos). During data processing most data are transformed into a textual form (e.g., interview recordings are transcribed) because most qualitative data analysis is done with words.

While the description of qualitative research stands in contrast with that presented for quantitative research (with its emphasis on RANDOMIZATION, STATISTICS, and generalizability), it should be understood that quantitative and qualitative approaches are not polar opposites (as the traditional labels of positivistic (see POSITIVISM) and interpretivist (see INTERPRETIVE PARADIGM) for quantitative and qualitative research, respectively, sometimes imply. It should also be kept in mind that, as it is not the case that certain methods (e.g., QUESTIONNAIREs, interviews, TESTs) are inherently either qualitative or quantitative. Questionnaire results, for example, can be analyzed quantitatively by determining what percentage of respondents answered in a particular manner, or qualitatively, by examining in detail the exact responses individuals provided and using them to triangulate (see TRIANGULATION) other data from those same participants. It is the researcher's approach to the data collection and analysis task that may be considered qualitative or quantitative—not the methods themselves.

A plethora of research designs has been developed within qualitative research, including NATURALISTIC INQUIRY, NARRATIVE INQUIRY, CASE STUDY, ETHNOGRAPHY, ACTION RESEARCH, PHENOMENOLOGY, CONVERSATION ANALYSIS, LIFE HISTORY RESEARCH, and GROUNDED THEORY. These approaches use a wide variety of data collection methods, such as OBSERVATION, interview, open-response questionnaire items, VERBAL REPORT, diary study, and DISCOURSE ANALYSIS. And within each of these research approaches and methods, a number of research techniques and strategies have been developed to help qualitative researchers do their day-to-day work—conceptualizing the research project, collecting and analyzing data, and writing up findings.

📖 Brown 2003; Dörnyei 2007; King & Hornberger 2008; Mackey & Gass 2005; Perry 2011; Seliger & Shohamy 1989

qualitative variable
see CATEGORICAL VARIABLE

quantile
also fractile
a general term for the $n - 1$ partitions that divide a FREQUENCY or PROBABILITY DISTRIBUTION into n equal parts. In a probability distribution, the term is also used to indicate the value of the RANDOM VARIABLE that yields a particular PROBABILITY. PERCENTILE, QUARTILE, QUINTILE, and DECILE are the most common examples of quantile.

📖 Howell 2010; Sheskin 2011

quantile-quantile plot
also Q-Q plot
a SCATTERPLOT that plots the QUANTILEs of the data under consideration against the quantiles of the NORMAL DISTRIBUTION. If a MEDIAN divides the distribution up at its halfway point, a quantile divides the data up the same way at a variety of points. For example, the 25th quantile notes the point at which 25% of the data are below it and 75% are above it. To plot two sets of quantiles against each other we put the expected quantiles on

the *Y* axis and the obtained quantiles on the *X* axis. If the distribution is normal the plot should form a straight line running at a 45 degree angle. These plots are illustrated in Figure Q.1 for a set of data drawn from a normal distribution and in Figure Q.2 for a set drawn from a decidedly *nonnormal* distribution. In Figure Q.1 you can see that for normal data the Q-Q plot shows that most of the points fall nicely on a straight line. They depart from the line a bit at each end, but that commonly happens unless you have very large SAMPLE SIZEs.

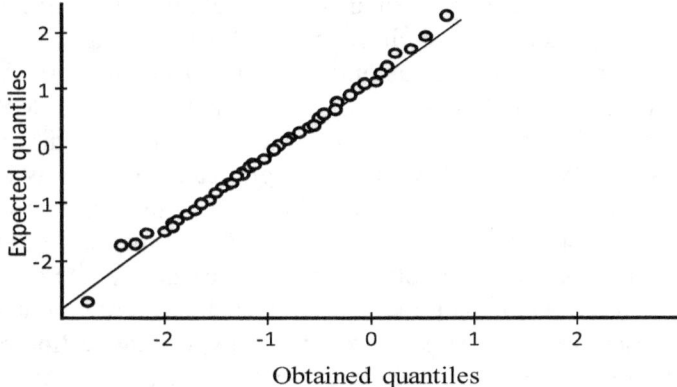

Figure Q.1. Q-Q Plot for Normal Sample

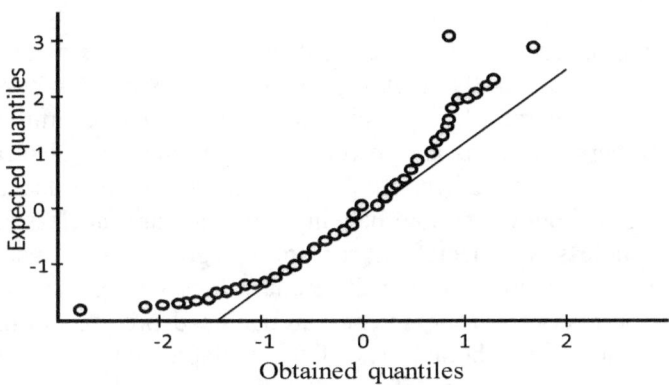

Figure Q.2. Q-Q Plot for Nonnormal Sample

For the nonnormal data, as shown in Figure Q.2, however, the plotted points depart drastically from a straight line. At the lower end where we would expect quantiles of around -1, the lowest obtained quantile was actually about -2. In other words the distribution was truncated on the left. At the upper right of the Q-Q plot where we obtained quantiles of around 2, the expected value was at least 3. In other words the obtained

data did not depart enough from the mean at the lower end and departed too much from the mean at the upper end.
📖 Howell 2010; Larson-Hall 2010

quantitative reductionism
see REDUCTIONISM

quantitative research
a RESEARCH METHODOLOGY that stresses the importance of large groups of randomly selected participants, manipulating VARIABLEs within the participants' immediate environment, and determining whether there is a relationship between the manipulated (independent) variable and some characteristic or behavior of the participants (the DEPENDENT VARIABLE). Statistical procedures are used to determine whether the relationship is significant—and when it is significant, the results are typically generalized to a larger population beyond the immediate group of participants. At best, the quantitative research is systematic, rigorous, focused, and tightly controlled, involving precise measurement and producing reliable and replicable data that is generalizable to other contexts. Quantitative research is the primary example of hypothesis-testing research (see HYPOTHESIS TESTING), which begins with a question or hypothesis to be investigated through data quantification and numerical analyses.
Main characteristics of quantitative research are listed as follows:

1) *Using numbers*: the single most important feature of quantitative research is, naturally, that it is centered around numbers. This both opens up a range of possibilities and sets some limitations for researchers. Numbers are powerful. Yet numbers are also rather powerless in themselves because in research context they do not mean anything without contextual backing, i.e., they are faceless and meaningless unless we specify exactly the category that we use the specific number for, and also the different values within the variable. Thus, for numbers to work, the researcher need precise definitions of the content and the boundaries of the variables s/he uses and exact descriptors for the range of values that are allowed within the variable;
2) *A priori categorization*: because the use of numbers already dominates the data collection phase, the work requires specifying the categories and values needed to be done prior to the actual study. If, e.g., respondents are asked to encircle figures in a questionnaire item, they have to know exactly what those figures represent, and in order to make sure that each respondent gives their numerical answer based on the same understanding, the definitions and value descriptors need to be unambiguous;

3) *Variables rather than cases*: quantitative researchers are less interested in individuals than in the common features of groups of people. Therefore, it is centered around the study of variables that capture these common features and which are quantified by counting, scaling, or by assigning values to CATEGORICAL DATA. All the various quantitative methods are aimed at identifying the relationships between variables by measuring them and often also manipulating them. Therefore, specifying the relationships amongst variables as the defining feature of quantitative social research;
4) *Statistics and the language of statistics*: this is undoubtedly the most salient quantitative feature statistical analyses can range from calculating the average (the MEAN) of several figures on a pocket calculator to running complex *multivariate* analyses on a computer. Because of the close link of quantitative research and statistics, much of the statistical terminology has become part of the quantitative vocabulary, and the resulting unique quantitative language adds further power to the quantitative paradigm;
5) *Standardized procedures to assess objective reality*: the general quantitative aspiration is to eliminate any individual-based subjectivity from the various phases of the research process by developing systematic canons and rules for every facet of data collection and analysis. Quantitative methodology has indeed gone a long way towards standardizing research procedures to ensure that they remain stable across investigators and subjects. This independence of idiosyncratic human variability and bias has been equated with OBJECTIVITY by quantitative researchers;
6) *Quest for* GENERALIZABILITY *and universal laws*: numbers, variables, standardized procedures, statistics, and scientific reasoning are all part of the ultimate quantitative quest for facts that are generalizable beyond the particular and add up to wide-ranging, ideally universal, laws. However, QUALITATIVE RESEARCHers often view quantitative research as overly simplistic, decontextualized, reductionist in terms of its generalizations, and failing to capture the meanings that actors attach to their lives and circumstances.

The difference between quantitative and qualitative research is often seen as quite fundamental, leading people to talk about paradigm wars in which quantitative and qualitative research are seen as belligerent and incompatible factions. Many researchers define themselves as either quantitative or qualitative. This idea is linked to what are seen as the different underlying philosophies and worldviews of researchers in the two paradigms. According to this view, two fundamentally different worldviews underlie quantitative and qualitative research. The quantitative view is described as being realist (see REALISM) or sometimes positivist (see POSITIVISM), while the worldview underlying qualitative research is viewed as being subjectivist (see INTERPRETIVE PARADIGM).

The term qualitative and quantitative were originally introduced to denote in antagonistic standpoint and this initial conflicting stance was given substance by the contrasting patterns of the two research paradigms in: (a) categorizing the world (quantitative: predetermined numerical category system; qualitative: emergent, flexible verbal coding); (b) perceiving individual diversity (quantitative: using large samples to iron out any individual idiosyncrasies; qualitative: focusing on the unique meaning carried by individual organisms); and (c) analytical data (quantitative: relying on the formalized system of statistics; qualitative: relying on the researcher's individual sensitivity.

In short, quantitative research was seen to offer a structured and highly regulated way of achieving a macro-perspective of the overarching trends in the world, whereas qualitative research was perceived to represent a flexible and highly context-sensitive micro-perspective of the everyday realities of the world. Although the two paradigms represent two different approaches to EMPIRICAL RESEARCH, they are not necessarily exclusive. They are not extremes but rather form a continuum that has led to an emerging third research approach, i.e., MIXED METHODS RESEARCH.

Quantitative research can be classified into one of the two broad research categories: EXPERIMENTAL RESEARCH, and NONEXPERIMENTAL RESEARCH.

📖 Dörnyei 2007; King & Hornberger 2008; Lavrakas 2008; Mackey & Gass 2005; Muijs 2004

quantitative variable

see CONTINUOUS VARIABLE

quartile

a DISTRIBUTION which is divided into four quarter or blocks, each of which contains 25 per cent of the observed values. The 25th percentile, 50th percentile, and 75th percentile are the same as the first, second, and third quartiles, respectively (see Table Q.1) More specifically, the first quartile (denoted by Q_1) is the point below which 25 per cent of the scores occur; the second quartile (denoted by Q_2) is the point below which 50 per cent of the scores occur; and the third quartile (denoted by Q_3) is the point below which 75 per cent of the scores occur. The first and third quartiles are often called the *lower* and the *upper* quartiles and the second quartile is known as MEDIAN. Thus, a score that corresponds to the 25th percentile falls at the upper limit of the first quartile of the

distribution. A score that corresponds to the 50th percentile falls at the upper limit of the second quartile of the distribution, and so on.
see also INTERQUARTILE RANGE, DECILE, PERCENTILE, QUINTILE
📖 Sahai & Khurshid 2001; Sheskin 2011

The data arranged in an increasing order of magnitude			
25%	25%	25%	25%
Q_1	Q_2	Q_3	

Table Q.1. Schematic Representation of Quartiles of a Data Set

quartile deviation
another term for SEMI-INTERQUARTILE RANGE

quasi-experimental design
also **naturally occurring group design**
an EXPERIMENTAL RESEARCH design in which the researcher cannot assign participants randomly to conditions and/or manipulate the INDEPENDENT VARIABLE (IV); instead, comparisons are made between groups that already exist or within a single group before and after a quasi-experimental TREATMENT has occurred. Quasi-experimental designs are practical compromise designs that are recommended where better designs, (e.g., TRUE EXPERIMENTAL DESIGNs) are not feasible. In quasi-experimental design an IV is manipulated like in an experiment (it may look as if it is an experiment but it is not a true experimental design, only a variant on it), but the CONTROL and EXPERIMENTAL GROUPs are not equivalent. That is, subjects have not normally been randomly selected nor randomly assigned to these groups; individuals naturally belong to one group or the other. Instead the comparisons depend on non-equivalent groups that differ from each other in many ways other than the presence of a treatment whose effects are being tested. This would be the case, for example, in comparing the performance of students in naturally occurring classrooms.
While quasi-experimental research is subject to threats of INTERNAL VALIDITY, it is more likely to have EXTERNAL VALIDITY because it is conducted closer to those normally found in educational contexts. Furthermore, since these designs are less intrusive and disruptive than others, it is easier to gain access to subject populations and thus easier to conduct such research. For these reasons, quasi-experimental designs are also ideal for teacher-conducted research and for pilot studies, in which the exploration of a research idea is the primary goal.
At best, quasi-experimental designs may be able to employ something approaching a true experimental design in which they have control over

what researchers refer to as 'the who and to whom of measurement' but lack control over 'the when and to whom of exposure', or the randomization of exposures. These situations are quasi-experimental and the methodologies employed by researchers are termed quasi-experimental designs.

Quasi-experimental designs can be divided into several major categories as follows: NONEQUIVALENT CONTROL GROUP DESIGN, TIME-SERIES DESIGN, EQUIVALENT MATERIAL DESIGN, COUNTERBALANCED DESIGN, RECURRENT INSTITUTIONAL CYCLE DESIGN, SEPARATE-SAMPLE PRETEST-POSTTEST CONTROL GROUP DESIGN, and SEPARATE-SAMPLE PRETEST-POSTTEST DESIGN.

📖 Best & Kahn 2006; Brown 1988; Campbell & Stanley 1963; Cohen et al. 2011; Cook & Campbell 1966; Leary 2011; Marczyk et al. 2005; Seliger & Shohamy 1989

questionnaire

a research instrument that presents respondents with a series of questions or statements to which they are to react either by writing out their answers or selecting them among existing answers. Questionnaires are used primarily in SURVEY RESEARCH but also in experiments, FIELD RESEARCH, and other modes of observation. The popularity of questionnaires is due to the fact that they are easy to construct, extremely versatile, and uniquely capable of gathering a large amount of information quickly in a form that is readily processable. Broadly speaking, questionnaires can yield three types of data about the respondent: factual, behavioral, and attitudinal. (1) **Factual question**s (also called **classification question**s or **subject descriptor**s) are used to find out about who the respondents are. They typically cover demographic characteristics (e.g., age, gender, and race), residential location, marital and socioeconomic status, level of education, religion, occupation, as well as any other background information that may be relevant to interpreting the findings of the survey. Such additional data in second language (L2) studies, for example, often include facts about the learner's language learning history, amount of time spent in an L2 environment, level of parents L2 proficiency, or the L2 coursebook used. (2) **Behavioral question**s are used to find out what the respondents are doing or have done in the past. They typically ask about people's actions, life-styles, habits, and personal history. Perhaps the most well-known questions of this type in L2 studies are the items in language learning strategy inventories that ask about the frequency one has used a particular strategy in the past. (3) **Attitudinal question**s are used to find out what people think. This is a broad category that concerns attitudes, opinions, beliefs, interests, and values.

The main attraction of questionnaires is their unprecedented efficiency in terms of (a) researcher time, (b) researcher effort, and (c) financial resources. By administering a questionnaire to a group of people, one can collect a huge amount of information in less than an hour, and the personal investment required will be a fraction of what would have been needed for, say, interviewing the same number of people. Furthermore, if the questionnaire is well constructed, processing the data can also be fast and relatively straightforward, especially by using some modern computer software. These cost benefit considerations are very important, particularly for all those who are doing research in addition to having a full-time job. Cost-effectiveness is not the only advantage of questionnaires. They are also very versatile, which means that they can be used successfully with a variety of people in a variety of situations targeting a variety of topics.

However, questionnaires have some serious limitations and some of these have led certain researchers to claim that questionnaire data are not reliable (see RELIABILITY) or valid (see VALIDITY). But there is no doubt that it is very easy to produce unreliable and invalid data by means of ill-constructed questionnaires. Some major problem sources include: simplicity and superficiality of answers, respondent literacy problems, little or no opportunity to correct the respondents' mistakes, SOCIAL DESIRABILITY BIAS, SELF-DECEPTION, ACQUIESCENCE BIAS, FATIGUE EFFECT, and HALO EFFECT.

Although questionnaires are often very similar to written TESTs, there is a basic difference between the two instruments types. A test takes a sample of the respondent's behavior/knowledge for the purpose of *evaluating* the individual's more general underlying competence/abilities/skills (e.g., overall L2 proficiency). Thus, a test measures how well someone can do something. In contrast, questionnaire items do not have good or bad answers; they elicit information about the respondents in a *non-evaluative* manner, without gauging their performance against a set of criteria.

With regard to the items (i.e., questions or statements) in a questionnaire, there are two broad types: OPEN-FORM ITEMs and CLOSED-FORM ITEMs.

see also POSTAL SURVEY, ONE-TO-ONE ADMINISTRATION, GROUP ADMINISTRATION, SELF-ADMINISTERED QUESTIONNAIRE, DISCOURSE COMPLETION TASK

Brown 2001; Dörnyei 2003, 2007; Dörnyei & Taguchi 2010; Heigham & Croker 2009

quintile

a DISTRIBUTION which is divided into five equal parts, each of which contains 20% of the total observations. As shown in Table Q.2, the percentile points at the 20th, 40th, 60th, and 80th intervals are the same as the first quintile, second quintile, third quintile, and fourth quintile respectively.

see also DECILE, PERCENTILE, QUARTILE

Sahai & Khurshid 2001

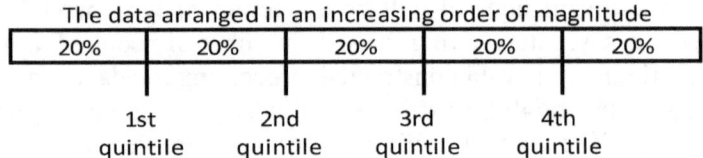

Table Q.2. Schematic Representation of Quintiles of a Data Set

quota sampling

a type of SAMPLING in which you select people nonrandomly according to some fixed quota. Quota sampling is a type of NON-PROBABILITY SAMPLING in which a specific number of cases (the quota) is selected from each stratum. Like a STRATIFIED SAMPLING, a quota sampling strives to represent significant characteristics (strata) of the wider POPULATION; unlike stratified sampling, it sets out to represent these in the proportions in which they can be found in the wider population. The two types of quota sampling are proportional and nonproportional. In **proportional quota sampling**, you want to represent the major characteristics of the population by sampling a proportional amount of each. For instance, if you know the population has 40 percent women and 60 percent men, and that you want a total SAMPLE SIZE of 100, you should continue sampling until you get those percentages and then stop. So, if you already have the 40 women for your sample, but not the 60 men, you would continue to sample men but even if legitimate women respondents come along, you would not sample them because you have already met your quota. The problem here (as in much PURPOSIVE SAMPLING) is that you have to decide the specific characteristics on which you will base the quota. 'Will it be by gender, age, education, race, or religion, etc.?'

Nonproportional quota sampling is less restrictive. In this method, you specify the minimum number of sampled units you want in each category. Here, you are not concerned with having numbers that match the proportions in the population. Instead, you simply want to have enough to assure that you will be able to talk about even small groups in the population.

This method is the nonprobabilistic analogue of stratified sampling in that it is typically used to assure that smaller groups are adequately represented in your sample.

see also CONVENIENCE SAMPLING, QUOTA SAMPLING, DIMENSIONAL SAMPLING, PURPOSIVE SAMPLING, SEQUENTIAL SAMPLING, VOLUNTEER SAMPLING, and SNOWBALL SAMPLING

📖 Cohen et al. 2011; Trochim & Donnelly 2007

R

r
    an abbreviation for PEARSON PRODUCT-MOMENT CORRELATION COEFFICIENT

r^2
    an abbreviation for COEFFICIENT OF DETERMINATION

r_b
    an abbreviation for BISERIAL CORRELATION COEFFICIENT

r_{bis}
    an abbreviation for BISERIAL CORRELATION COEFFICIENT

r_{pbi}
    an abbreviation for POINT-BISERIAL CORRELATION COEFFICIENT

r_{pbis}
    an abbreviation for POINT-BISERIAL CORRELATION COEFFICIENT

r_s
    another term for SPEARMAN RANK ORDER CORRELATION COEFFICIENT

r_{tet}
    an abbreviation for TETRACHORIC CORRELATION COEFFICIENT

r_{xx}
    an abbreviation for RELIABILITY COEFFICIENT

R
    an abbreviation for MULTIPLE CORRELATION COEFFICIENT

R^2
    an abbreviation for COEFFICIENT OF MULTIPLE DETERMINATION

r × c contingency table
    another term for CONTINGENCY TABLE

r × c table
    another term for CONTINGENCY TABLE

random allocation
another term for RANDOM ASSIGNMENT

random assignment
also **random allocation, randomization**
the most effective method of assigning participants to groups within a research study. The philosophy underlying random assignment is similar to the philosophy underlying RANDOM SELECTION. Random assignment involves assigning participants to groups within a research study in such a way that each participant has an equal probability of being assigned to any of the groups within the study. It ensures that, within the limits of chance variation, the EXPERIMENTAL and CONTROL GROUPs are similar at the beginning of the investigation. It randomization eliminates bias in the assignment of TREATMENTs and provides the sound basis for statistical analysis. Although there are several accepted methods that can be used to effectively implement random assignment, it is typically accomplished by using a TABLE OF RANDOM NUMBERS that determines the group assignment for each of the participants. By using a table of random numbers, participants are assigned to groups within the study according to a predetermined schedule. In fact, group assignment is determined for each participant prior to his/her entrance into the study. More specifically, random assignment is a dependable procedure for producing equivalent groups because it evenly distributes characteristics of the SAMPLE among all of the groups within the study. For example, rather than placing all of the participants over age 20 into one group, random assignment would, theoretically at least, evenly distribute all of the participants over age 20 among all of the groups within the research study. This would produce equivalent groups within the study, at least with respect to age. By using random assignment, the researcher distributes EXTRANEOUS VARIABLEs unsystematically across all of the groups.

When subjects have been randomly assigned to groups, the groups can be considered statistically equivalent. **Statistical equivalence** does not mean the groups are absolutely equal, but it does mean that any difference between the groups is a function of chance alone and not a function of experimenter bias, subjects' choices, or any other factor. A subject with high aptitude is as likely to be assigned to treatment A as to treatment B. The same is true for a subject with low aptitude. For the entire sample, the effects of aptitude on the dependent variable will tend to balance or randomize out. In the same manner, subjects' differences in viewpoints, temperament, achievement motivation, socioeconomic level, and other characteristics will tend to be approximately equally distributed between the two groups. The more subjects in the original sample, the more likely that random assignment will result in approximately equivalent groups. When random assignment has been employed, any pretreat-

ment differences between groups are nonsystematic—that is, a function of chance alone. Because these differences fall within the field of expected statistical variation, the researcher can use INFERENTIAL STATISTICS to determine how likely it is that posttreatment differences are due to chance alone.
see also RANDOMIZED MATCHING, HOMOGENEOUS SELECTION
📖 Ary et al. 2010; Cramer & Howitt 2004; Kazdin1992; Marczyk et al. 2005

random-digit-dialing
see POPULATION

random effects
those effects where you want to generalize beyond the parameters that constitute the VARIABLE. Random effects do not have informative FACTOR levels, and the factor LEVELs do not exhaust the possibilities. You want to generalize beyond the levels in your study if you have a random effect. A subject term is clearly a random effect, because you want to generalize the results of your study beyond those particular individuals who took the test. Other examples of random effects are the particular words or sentences used in a study, the classroom, or the school test.
see also FIXED EFFECT
📖 Larson-Hall 2010

random error
see MEASUREMENT ERROR

randomization
another term for RANDOM ASSIGNMENT

randomization check
the process of examining the overall effectiveness of RANDOM ASSIGNMENT. The goal of this process is to determine whether random assignment resulted in nonequivalent groups. In performing randomization checks, researchers compare study groups or conditions on a number of pretest variables. These typically include demographic variables such as age, gender, level of education, and any other variables that are measured or available prior to the INTERVENTION. Importantly, randomization checks should look for between-group differences on the BASELINE MEASUREMENTs of the DEPENDENT VARIABLEs because they are likely to have the most impact on outcomes. Generally, randomization checks involve the use of statistical analyses that can examine differences between groups. If differences are found on certain variables, the researcher should determine whether they are correlated with the outcomes. Any

such, variables that are correlated with outcomes should be controlled for in the final analyses.
📖 Marczyk et al. 2005

randomized block design

a TRUE EXPERIMENTAL DESIGN which is constructed to reduce the effects of ERROR VARIANCE in the data. Randomized block design requires you to divide the SAMPLE into relatively homogeneous subgroups or blocks (analogous to strata in STRATIFIED SAMPLING). Typically, you divide the pool of subjects into blocks on the basis of some VARIABLE whose effects are not of primary interest to you, such as gender or ability level. Then, the design you want to apply is implemented within each block or homogeneous subgroup. The key idea is that the VARIABILITY within each block is less than the variability of the entire sample. Thus each estimate of the treatment effect within a block is more efficient than estimates across the entire sample. When you pool these more efficient estimates across blocks, you should get a more efficient estimate overall than you would without blocking.

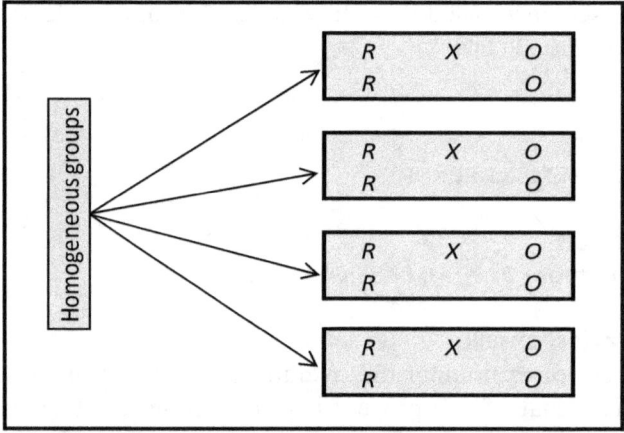

Figure R.1. A Randomized Block Design

Figure R.1 shows a simple example, where R = randomly assigned group, X = treatment, and O = posttest. Suppose that you originally intended to conduct a simple TWO-GROUP POSTTEST-ONLY RANDOMIZED EXPERIMENTAL DESIGN; but you recognized that your sample has several intact or homogeneous subgroups. For instance, in a study of second language college students, you might expect that students are relatively homogeneous with respect to class or year. So, you decide to block the sample into four groups: freshman, sophomore, junior, and senior. If your hunch is correct—that the variability within class is less man the variability for the entire sample—you will probably get more powerful estimates of the treatment effect within each block. Within each of your four blocks, you would implement the simple post-only randomized experiment.

A MATCHED SUBJECTS DESIGN and a WITHIN-SUBJECTS DESIGN are sometimes categorized as a randomized-blocks design.
📖 Sheskin 2011; Trochim & Donnelly 2007

randomized experimental design
another term for TRUE EXPERIMENTAL DESIGN

randomized-groups design
another term for BETWEEN-SUBJECTS DESIGN

randomized matched subjects posttest-only control group design
another term for MATCHED SUBJECTS DESIGN

randomized matching
also **matching**
when RANDOM ASSIGNMENT is not feasible, researchers sometimes select pairs of individuals with identical or almost identical characteristics and randomly assign one member of the matched pair to TREATMENT A and the other to treatment B. This procedure is called randomized matching. Note that randomized matching requires that the subjects be matched on relevant VARIABLEs first and then randomly assigned to treatments. The researcher first decides what variables to use for matching. These may be IQ, mental age, socioeconomic status, age, gender, reading, pretest score, or other variables known to be related to the DEPENDENT VARIABLE of the study. If the groups are adequately matched on the selected variable(s), the resulting groups are reasonably equivalent. The major limitation of matching is that it is almost impossible to find subjects who match on more than one variable. Subjects are lost to the experiment when no match can be found for them. This loss, of course, reduces the SAMPLE SIZE and introduces SAMPLING BIAS into the study. Subjects for whom matches cannot be found are usually those with high or low scores. Therefore, these subjects would be underrepresented.
see also HOMOGENEOUS SELECTION
📖 Ary et al. 2010

randomized subjects pretest-posttest control group design
another term for PRETEST-POSTTEST CONTROL GROUP DESIGN

randomized subjects posttest-only control group design
another term for POSTTEST-ONLY CONTROL GROUP DESIGN

randomized two-group posttest only design
another term for POSTTEST-ONLY CONTROL GROUP DESIGN

randomized two-group pretest-posttest design
another term for PRETEST-POSTTEST CONTROL GROUP DESIGN

random-numbers table
another term for TABLE OF RANDOM NUMBERS

random purposeful sampling
see PURPOSIVE SAMPLING

random sample
another term for PROBABILITY SAMPLE

random sampling
another term for PROBABILITY SAMPLING

random score
see ERROR SCORE

random selection
a method of selecting a SAMPLE wherein each element of the POPULATION has the equal PROBABILITY or chance of selection for constituting a sample independent of any other element in the selection process, i.e., the choice of one individual is in no way tied with other. Random selection is free from subjective factor or personal error or bias and prejudices or imagination of the investigator. It ensures that the sample formed by this method may be representative of the population. PROBABILITY SAMPLING enhances the likelihood of accomplishing this aim and also provides methods for estimating the degree of probable success.
Flipping a coin is the most frequently cited example: Provided that the coin is perfect (that is, not biased in terms of coming up heads or tails), the selection of a head or a tail is independent of previous selections of heads or tails. No matter how many heads turn up in a row, the chance that the next flip will produce heads is exactly 50-50. Rolling a perfect set of dice is another example.
see also RANDOM ASSIGNMENT, NON-PROBABILITY SAMPLING
📖 Babbie 2011; Sahai & Khurshid 2001

random variable
a VARIABLE where the researcher has randomly selected the LEVELs of that variable from a larger set of possible levels. Thus, if you had a complete list of all the possible methods for teaching reading and had picked

three randomly from the list to include in your study, teaching method would now be a random variable. Or, age is a random variable if you simply select people regardless of what age they are. The opposite of a random variable is a **fixed variable** for which particular values have been chosen. For example, we may select people of particular ages who lie within particular age ranges.

Another meaning of the term is that it is a variable with a specified PROBABILITY DISTRIBUTION, i.e., the values of which occur according to some specified probability distribution. In this sense, the value of a random variable is determined by a random experiment and thus depends on chance or RANDOM ERROR and cannot be predicted with certainty. It is also called a **chance variable** or **stochastic variable**.

The decision as to whether to use fixed or random variables has two consequences. Firstly, the use of a fixed variable prevents researchers from trying to generalize to other possible levels of the INDEPENDENT VARIABLE, while the use of a random variable allows more generalization. Secondly, the statistical analysis can be affected by whether a fixed or a random variable was used.

Clark-Carter 2010; Cramer & Howitt 2004; Everitt & Skrondal 2010; Sahai & Khurshid 2001

random variation
another term for RANDOM ERROR

range
the simplest possible MEASURE OF VARIABILITY or dispersion and is defined as the difference between the highest and lowest scores of a DISTRIBUTION. To determine the range, simply subtract the lowest score from the highest score:

Range = highest score - lowest score

For example, the scores of 0, 2, 6, 10, 12 have a range of 12 - 0 = 12. The less variable scores of 4, 5, 6, 7, 8 have a range of 8 - 4 = 4. The perfectly consistent sample of 6, 6, 6, 6, 6 has a range of 6 - 6 = 0.

For GROUPED DATA (see also GROUPED FREQUENCY DISTRIBUTION), because we do not know the individual measurements, the range is taken to be the difference between the upper limit of the last interval and the lower limit of the first interval. Range gives researchers a quick sense of how spread out the scores of a distribution are, but it is not a particularly useful statistic because it can be quite misleading. A great deal of information is ignored, since only the largest and the smallest data values are considered. It also follows that the range will be greatly influenced by the presence of just one unusually large or small value in the sample (i.e.,

OUTLIER). Researchers tend to look at the range when they want a quick snapshot of a distribution, such as when they want to know whether all of the response categories on a survey question have been used (i.e., 'Did people use all 5 points on the 5-point LIKERT SCALE?') or they want a sense of the overall balance of scores in the distribution. As such, range is mostly used as a rough measure of variability and is not considered as an appropriate measure in serious research studies.

see also VARIANCE, STANDARD DEVIATION

Ott & Longnecker 2010; Porte 2010

rank correlation
another term for RANK CORRELATION COEFFICIENT

rank correlation coefficient
also rank correlation
a *nonparametric* method for assessing *association* between two ORDINAL VARIABLEs. A rank correlation is interpreted the same way as the PEARSON PRODUCT-MOMENT CORRELATION COEFFICIENT. However, a rank correlation measures the association between the ranks rather than the original values. Two of the most commonly used methods of rank correlation are KENDALL'S RANK-ORDER CORRELATION COEFFICIENT and SPEARMAN RANK ORDER CORRELATION COEFFICIENT.

Sahai & Khurshid 2001

ranking question
another term for RANK ORDER QUESTION

ranking test(s)
another term for NONPARAMETRIC TEST(S)

rank order question
also ranking question
a CLOSED-FORM ITEM which is akin to the MULTIPLE-CHOICE ITEM in that it identifies options from which respondents can choose, yet it moves beyond multiple choice items in that it asks respondents to identify priorities. This enables a relative degree of preference, priority, intensity etc. to be charted. In the rank ordering exercise a list of factors is set out and the respondent is required to place them in a rank order. The following is an example:

Instructions: Please place these in rank order of the most to the least important, by putting the position (1-5) against each of the following statements, number 1 being the most important and number 5 being the least important.

Students should enjoy school [ ]
Teachers should set less homework [ ]
Students should have more choice of subjects in school [ ]
Teachers should use more collaborative methods [ ]
Students should be tested more, so that they work harder [ ]

Rankings are useful in indicating degrees of response. They are treated as ORDINAL DATA.

see also DICHOTOMOUS QUESTION, RATIO DATA QUESTION, MATRIX QUESTIONS, CONSTANT SUM QUESTIONS, CONTINGENCY QUESTION, CHECKLIST, NUMERIC ITEM

📖 Cohen et al. 2011

rank-order scale
another term for ORDINAL SCALE

rank sums test
another term for MANN-WHITNEY U TEST

Rasch model
also **one-parameter model**

the most popular of a family of ITEM RESPONSE THEORY models. Rasch model assumes that a response to a test item is a function of just two variables: the *difficulty* of the test item and the *ability* of the test taker. ITEM DIFFICULTY and test taker ability can be calculated on a single scale of measurement, so that when a test taker's ability is the same as the difficulty of the item, the probability of getting the item correct will be 50 per cent. Thus, the model is based only on the difficulty of a set of items.

📖 Bachman 2004; Fulcher & Davidson 2007

rating error
a judgment that results from the intentional or unintentional misuse of a RATING SCALE. Two types of rating error are **generosity error** (also called **leniency error**) and **severity error**. A generosity error is an error by a rater due to that rater's general tendency to be lenient or insufficiently critical. When raters are not sure, they tend to rate people favorably. In fact they give subjects the benefit of any doubt. In contrast, the severity error is a tendency to rate all individuals too low on all characteristics. The tendency to avoid either extreme and to rate all individuals in the middle of the scale is referred to as the **error of central tendency**. For example, the ratings that teachers of English give their students have been found to cluster around the mean, whereas mathematics teachers' ratings of students show greater variation.

see also HALO EFFECT

📖 Ary et al. 2010; Cohen & Swerdlik 2010

rating scale

a scale which is used for qualitative description of a limited number of aspects of a thing or of traits of a person. When we use rating scales, we judge an object in absolute terms against some specified criteria i.e., we judge properties of objects without reference to other similar objects. These ratings may be in such forms as 'like-dislike', 'above average, average, below average', or other classifications with more categories such as 'like very much—like somewhat—neutral—dislike somewhat—dislike very much'; 'excellent—good—average—below average—poor', 'always—often—occasionally—rarely—never', and so on. There is no specific rule whether to use a two-point scale, three-point scale or scale with still more points. In practice, three to seven points scales are generally used for the simple reason that more points on a scale provide an opportunity for greater sensitivity of measurement. Rating scale may be either graphic or itemized. The **graphic rating scale** (see Figure R.2) is quite simple and is commonly used in practice. Under it the various points are usually put along the line to form a continuum and the respondent indicates his/her rating by simply making a mark (such as ✓) at the appropriate point on a line that runs from one extreme to the other. Scale-points with brief descriptions may be indicated along the line, their function being to assist the respondent in performing his/her job. The following is an example of five-points graphic rating scale when we wish to ascertain people's likes or dislikes:

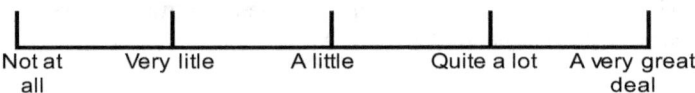

Figure R.2. An Example of a Graphic Rating Scale

This type of scale has several limitations. The respondents may check at almost any position along the line which fact may increase the difficulty of analysis. The meanings of the terms like 'very much' and 'somewhat' may depend upon respondent's frame of reference so much so that the statement might be challenged in terms of its equivalency. Several other rating scale variants (e.g., boxes replacing line) may also be used.

The **itemized rating scale** (also called **numerical scale**) presents a series of statements from which a respondent selects one as best reflecting his/her evaluation. These statements are ordered progressively in terms of more or less of some property. An example of itemized scale can be given to illustrate it. Suppose we wish to inquire as how well does a student get along with his/her fellow students? In such a situation, we may ask the respondent to select one, to express his/her opinion, from the following:

- He is almost always involved in some friction with a fellow student.
- He is often at odds with one or more of his/her fellow students.
- He sometimes gets involved in friction.
- He infrequently becomes involved in friction with others.
- He almost never gets involved in friction with fellow students.

The chief merit of this type of scale is that it provides more information and meaning to the rater, and thereby increases RELIABILITY. This form is relatively difficult to develop and the statements may not say exactly what the respondent would like to express.
The most commonly used rating scales are LIKERT SCALE, SEMANTIC DIFFERENTIAL SCALE, DIFFERENTIAL SCALE, CUMULATIVE SCALE, and ARBITRARY SCALE.
 Dörnyei 2003; Kothari 2008

ratio
a value which is obtained by dividing one quantity by another. It is used to show the magnitude of one quantity relative to the magnitude of another. It is calculated by an expression of the form a/b in which the NUMERATOR is not a component of the DENOMINATOR. Thus, in a ratio, the numerator and the denominator usually are separate and distinct quantities. The dimensions of the numerator and denominator may be different so that the ratio has dimensions.
 Sahai & Khurshid 2001

ratio data
see RATIO SCALE

ratio data question
a CLOSED-FORM ITEM which deals with CONTINUOUS VARIABLEs where there is a true zero, for example:

- How much money do you have in the bank? ....
- How many times have you been late for your classes? ....
- How many marks did you score in the grammar test? ....
- How old are you (in years)? ....

Here no fixed answer or category is provided, and the respondent puts in the numerical answer that fits his/her exact figure, i.e., the accuracy is higher, much higher than in categories of data. This enables MEANs, STANDARD DEVIATIONs, RANGE, and high-level statistics to be calculated, e.g., REGRESSION, FACTOR ANALYSIS, and STRUCTURAL EQUATION

MODELING. An alternative form of ratio scaling (Table R.1) is where the respondent has to award marks out of, say, ten, for a particular item

Please give a mark from 1 to 10 for the following statements, with 10 being excellent and 1 being very poor. Please circle the appropriate number for each statement.		
Teaching and learning	Very poor	Excellent
1 The attention given to teaching and learning at the school	1 2 3 4 5 6 7 8 9 10	
2 The quality of the lesson preparation	1 2 3 4 5 6 7 8 9 10	
3 How well learners are cared for, guided and	1 2 3 4 5 6 7 8 9 10	
4 How effectively teachers challenge and engage learners	1 2 3 4 5 6 7 8 9 10	
5 The educators' use of assessment for maximizing learners' learning	1 2 3 4 5 6 7 8 9 10	
6 How well students apply themselves to learning	1 2 3 4 5 6 7 8 9 10	
7 Discussion and review by educators of the quality of teaching and learning	1 2 3 4 5 6 7 8 9 10	

Table R.1. A 10-Point Marking Scale in a Questionnaire

This kind of question is often used in TELEPHONE INTERVIEWs, as it is easy for respondents to understand.
see also DICHOTOMOUS QUESTION, MULTIPLE-ITEMS, MATRIX QUESTIONS, CONSTANT SUM QUESTIONS, RANK ORDER QUESTION, CONTINGENCY QUESTION
📖 Cohen et al. 2011

ratio level of measurement
another term for RATIO SCALE

rationalism
see EMPIRICISM

ratio scale
also **ratio level of measurement**
a type of MEASUREMENT SCALE whose characteristics are identical to those of the INTERVAL SCALE, but in addition, ratio scale has an absolute or true zero, rather than arbitrary zero and the points on the scale are precise multiples, or ratios, of other points on the scale. Comparing two people in terms of a ratio scale, then, allows us to determine (1) that they are different (or the same), (2) that one is more than the other, (3) how much they differ, and (4) the ratio of one to another.
Ratio scale is the highest level of measurement and allows for the use of sophisticated statistical techniques. Because there is an absolute zero, all of the arithmetical processes of addition, subtraction, multiplication, and division are possible. Numerous examples of ratio scale data exist in our daily lives. Money is a pertinent example. It is possible to have no (or zero) money—a zero balance in a checking account, for example. Or, the zero point on a centimeter scale indicates the complete absence of length or height. Other examples include things like subjects' ages, the number of pages per book in a library, and the number of students enrolled in a language program. These are ratio scales because it makes sense to refer

to zero (i.e., zero years, zero pages, or zero students) and because ratios on the scales make sense (i.e., 20 years old is twice as old as 10; 300 pages is three times as many as 100; and 400 students is two times as many as 200; ten dollars is 10 times more than 1 dollar, and 20 dollars is twice as much as 10 dollars. If we have 100 dollars and give away half, we are left with 50 dollars, which is 50 times more than 1 dollar.). In contrast, an interval scale like TOEFL scores has no true zero (the score obtained by guessing is 200), and ratios between points on the scale are not exact (Is a student with 600 on the TOEFL exactly twice as proficient as one with 300?).

Data which are obtained using ratio scale of measurement are called **ratio data**. Likewise, a CONTINUOUS VARIABLE measured on a ratio scale is called a **ratio variable**.

see also NOMINAL SCALE, ORDINAL SCALE

Babbie 2011; Bachman 2004; Brown 1992; Marczyk et al. 2005

ratio variable

see RATIO SCALE

raw data

another term for RAW SCORE

raw score

also **crude score, raw data**

a score that is presented in terms of its original numerical value, not converted into some other value. It may be the total number of items an individual gets correct or answers in a certain way on a test, the number of times a certain behavior is tallied, the rating given by a teacher, and so forth. Taken by itself, an individual raw score is difficult to interpret, since it has little meaning. What, for example, does it mean to say a student received a score of 62 on a test if that is all the information you have? Even if you know that there were 100 questions on the test, you don't know whether 62 is an extremely high (or extremely low) score, since the test may have been easy or difficult. We often want to know how one individual's raw score compares to those of other individuals taking the same test, and (perhaps) how s/he has scored on similar tests taken at other times. This is true whenever we want to interpret an individual score. Because raw scores by themselves are difficult to interpret, they often are converted to what are called **derived score**s in order to make them more comparable and easier to interpret. Derived scores are obtained by taking raw scores and converting them into more useful scores on some type of standardized basis. They indicate where a particular individual's raw score falls in relation to all other raw scores in the same distribution. They enable a researcher to say how well the indi-

vidual has performed compared to all others taking the same test. Examples of derived scores are PERCENTAGES, PERCENTILES, ranks, and STANDARD SCORES.
see also CLASSICAL TEST THEORY, ERROR SCORE
📖 Fraenkel & Wallen 2009; Richards & Schmidt 2010

realism
an overarching philosophical doctrine which accords to the objects of human knowledge an existence that is independent of whether they are being perceived or thought about. Realism refers to a range of ontological (see ONTOLOGY) and epistemological (see EPISTEMOLOGY) positions within which research may be conducted. Realist ontologies (assumptions about the nature of reality) range from the view that the world of objects and social structures exists independent of human experience to the idea that, although the world exists independent of any one person, human perception is such that our reality is a preinterpreted one. Realist epistemologies (theories about what counts as knowledge) range from the view that the world can be known directly through the senses to the idea that internally consistent interpretations of reality can count as knowledge if bounded by, and revisable in light of, interactions with the world. Holding a realist ontology does not always commit a researcher to a realist epistemology. Realism has often been associated with quantification, but it is compatible with many QUALITATIVE RESEARCH methods and is the position of choice of many qualitative researchers.
NAIVE REALISM, SCIENTIFIC REALISM, SUBTLE REALISM, ANALYTIC REALISM, and CRITICAL REALISM are different forms of realism.
📖 Given 2008

realist ethnography
see ETHNOGRAPHY

recall bias
see RETROSPECTIVE LONGITUDINAL STUDY

receptive response item
another term for SELECTED-RESPONSE ITEM

reciprocal suppression
see SUPPRESSOR VARIABLE

reciprocal transformation
also **inverse transformation**
a DATA TRANSFORMATION method which may be useful when the square of the mean is proportional to the STANDARD DEVIATION (i.e., the pro-

portion between the square of the MEAN of a TREATMENT and the standard deviation of a treatment is approximately the same for all of the treatments). Under such circumstances the reciprocal transformation can be effective in normalizing distributions (see NORMALITY) that have a moderate positive skew (see SKEWED DISTRIBUTION), as well as making the treatment variances more homogeneous. Reciprocal transformation may result in a reversal in the direction of the scores. In other words, if we have two scores 'a' and 'b' with a > b, if we obtain the reciprocal of both, the reciprocal of 'b' will be greater than the reciprocal of 'a'. The process of reversing the direction to restore the original ordinal relationship between the scores is called **reflection**. Reflection can also be used to convert negatively skewed data into positively skewed data.
see also SQUARE ROOT TRANSFORMATION, LOG TRANSFORMATION
📖 Marczyk et al. 2005; Sheskin 2011

recruitment log
one of the key elements of the data tracking system. The recruitment log is a comprehensive record of all individuals approached about participation in a study. The log can also serve to record the dates and times that potential participants were approached, whether they met eligibility criteria, and whether they agreed and provided INFORMED CONSENT to participate in the study. Importantly, for ethical reasons (see ETHICS), no identifying information should be recorded for individuals who do not consent to participate in the research study. The primary purpose of the recruitment log is to keep track of participant enrollment and to determine how representative the resulting COHORT of study participants is of the POPULATION that the researcher is attempting to examine.
📖 Marczyk et al. 2005

rectangular distribution
another term for FLAT DISTRIBUTION

recurrent institutional cycle design
a QUASI-EXPERIMENTAL DESIGN which is actually more of a concept than a specific design. Recurrent institutional cycle design is appropriate in situations where a TREATMENT is repeatedly being applied, on a cyclical basis, to a new group of respondents. What you basically do is finetune the design on subsequent cycles to investigate questions raised on previous cycles. Here are three examples: In design A, the experimental treatment is applied to an incoming class (Class A). The posttest is administered at the same time a pretest is administered to the next incoming class (Class B). Class B then receives the experimental treatment and then a posttest. Comparing O_1 and O_2 is similar to comparing a treated population with an untreated population (though not as confidently).

Comparing O_2 with O_3 helps to answer questions about gain or loss due to the experimental treatment, and comparing O_3 to O_1 provides information about the possible effect of the pretest on posttest scores.

In the following notations, NR = nonrandom assignment, R = random assignment, X = treatment, and O = pretest and posttest.

Class A (NR)	X	O_1		
Class B (NR)		O_2	X	O_3

(Design A)

Class A (NR)	X	O_1		
Class B_1 (R)		O_2	X	O_3
Class B_2 (R)			X	O_4
Class C (NR)			O_5	X

(Design B)

Class A (NR)	X	O_1		
Class B_1 (R)		O_2	X	O_3
Class B_2 (R)			X	O_4
Class C (NR)				O_5 X

(Design C)

Designs B and C may be useful if you have the luxury of being able to randomize a group into two groups, one pretested and one not. Note that the only difference in these two designs is that:

- O_1 and O_2 occur at the same time in design B but at different times in design C (and on a different group of participants).
- O_3, O_4, and O_5 occur at the same time in design B, but in design C O_5 occurs in a subsequent cycle (and on a different group of participants).

see also NONEQUIVALENT CONTROL GROUP DESIGN, TIME-SERIES DESIGN, EQUIVALENT MATERIAL DESIGN, COUNTERBALANCED DESIGN, SEPARATE-SAMPLE PRETEST-POSTTEST CONTROL GROUP DESIGN, SEPARATE-SAMPLE PRETEST-POSTTEST DESIGN

📖 Campbell & Stanley 1963; Cook & Campbell 1966

recursive model
see PATH ANALYSIS

reductionism
a viewpoint that regards one phenomenon as entirely explainable by the properties of another phenomenon. The first can be said to be reducible to the second. It is a mere epiphenomenon of the second. It is really just another name for the second. Reductionism has no distinctive properties that require a distinctive theory or methodology.

For example, **biological reductionism** claims that the mind is explained entirely by physical properties of the brain, that the mind is physical, that what we call mental is really just another term for the brain, that mental/mind is actually only an epiphenomenon of the brain, that it can and should be studied by neurophysiologists, that there is nothing distinctively psychological about the mind, and that treating the mind as having properties distinct from those of the brain is an illusion.

An opposite form of reductionism is **sociological reductionism**. This reduces psychological phenomena to epiphenomena of social factors. In this view, psychology is determined entirely by nationality or social class. There is nothing to psychology besides the properties it acquires from ones nationhood or class. In this view, one may speak of U.S. psychology as a homogeneous phenomenon or lower-class psychology as a homogeneous phenomenon because no other factors determine psychology; it is reducible to social state or social class.

Another form of reductionism that bears directly on qualitative methodology is **quantitative reductionism**. The claim here is that qualitative characteristics of personality, emotions, and reasoning are entirely expressible in quantitative terms. An example is the notion of intelligence. IQ is construed as an entirely quantitative dimension. IQ can range from low to high. The only meaningful way to discuss IQ is in terms of its quantitative amount. IQ is reducible to quantity. Psychologists are concerned with operationalizing intelligence and measuring it, not with discussing theories about what it is.

Reductionism denies complex multiplicity and heterogeneity in favor of a single kind of phenomenon or factor. For example, biological reductionism construes the mind as continuous with the single realm of neurophysiology. It does not recognize the mind as a complication of neurophysiology that introduces a new kind of phenomenon. Quantitative reductionism similarly simplifies psychology by recognizing only one order of reality, the quantitative order. Qualitative complexity and multiplicity is reduced to simple quantitative differences.

There are two alternatives to reductionism. Both of them emphasize that there is more than one order of phenomena. **Dualism** postulates separate orders of phenomena. The postulating of a mind that is separate from the body is the classic dualistic alternative to reductionism. In this case, a separate realm of the mental stands apart from the physical body. In this view, the mind cannot be reduced to the body or be explained in physical terms. Studying the mind requires special theories and methodologies that are different from those that are applicable to physical phenomena.

Dialectical emergence is a second alternative to reductionism. It also recognizes that phenomena are complex, multifaceted, and heterogeneous. They are not reducible to single properties and processes. However, it postulates that these distinctive characteristics are related to others. They are not independent as in dualism. The classic example of emergence is the relation of water to its elements, oxygen and hydrogen. Water is composed of these elements; it is not independent of them. Yet oxygen and hydrogen are gaseous molecules, whereas water is a liquid. Although water depends on its constituents, it has a qualitatively new property—liquid—that cannot be understood in terms of its gaseous components. A new field of study is necessary to study the distinctive emergent liquid quality of water.

In analogous fashion, an emergent conception of the mind argues that it is grounded in neurophysiological processes; however, it emerges from them and is a distinctive form of them with distinctive properties. The mind is capable of willing action, thinking, predicting, comprehending, and even controlling the brain and the body. These are acts that are qualitatively different from their constituent neurons, just as water is qualitatively different from hydrogen and oxygen. A special field of psychology to study these emergent, distinctive mental qualities is warranted.

Qualitative research overcomes the simplification of POSITIVISM by acknowledging that psychological phenomena are qualitatively different in different individuals and cultures. Shame, introversion, attachment, intelligence, depression, love, memory, self-concept, and reasoning are not single, simple, invariant quantitative dimensions.
📖 Given 2008

references

a section of a RESEARCH REPORT which is used for citing all the books, journal articles, reports, websites, etc., used in the study. Only those sources that are actually referenced in the report should be cited, not all those that you read but did not necessarily use. If you want to refer to documents that you are not referencing but which readers might find useful, then place these in a **bibliography** section.

see also TITLE, ABSTRACT, INTRODUCTION, METHOD, RESULTS, DISCUSSION, APPENDIXes
📖 Gray 2009

reflection
see RECIPROCAL TRANSFORMATION

refusal rate
the extent to which participants may refuse to take part in a research study at all or refuse to take part in aspects of the research (e.g., they may be happy to answer any question but the one to do with their age). Researchers should keep a record of the persons approached and as much information as possible about their characteristics. Rates of refusal should be presented and any comparisons possible between participants and refusers identified. Some forms of research have notoriously high refusal rates such as telephone interviews and QUESTIONNAIREs sent out by post. RESPONSE RATEs as low as 15% or 20% would not be unusual. Refusal rates are a problem because of the (unknown) likelihood that they are different for different groupings of the sample. Research is particularly vulnerable to refusal rates if its purpose is to obtain estimates of POPULATION PARAMETERs from a sample. High refusal rates are less problematic when one is not trying to obtain precise population estimates. Experiments, for example, may be less affected than some other forms of research such as SURVEYs. Refusal rates are an issue in interpreting the outcomes of any research and should be presented when reporting findings.
see also MORTALITY, MISSING VALUES
📖 Cramer & Howitt 2004

region of acceptance
the range of possible values of the area in the SAMPLING DISTRIBUTION of a test statistic that does not lead to rejection of the NULL HYPOTHESIS. In other words, it is the region comprising the set of values of a test statistic for which the null hypothesis is accepted.
see also REJECTION REGION
📖 Sahai & Khurshid 2001; Upton & Cook 2008

regression
another term for REGRESSION ANALYSIS

regression analysis
also **regression**
a statistical technique for estimating or predicting a value for a single DEPENDENT VARIABLE or criterion from one or a set of INDEPENDENT VARIABLEs or predictors. Regression analysis can be described as a form of modeling because a mathematical model of the relationship between variables is created.

A regression analysis has the following attributes:
- It has two or more variables.
- For each subject in the study, there must be related pairs of scores, i.e., if a subject has a score on variable X, then the same subject must also have a score on variable Y.
- These variables do not have any LEVELs within them.
- If you took averages of the variables, you would have three or more averages.
- All variables are *continuous* (measured on INTERVAL or RATIO SCALEs).
- The relationship between the two variables must be linear (i.e., the relationship can be most accurately represented by a straight line).
- The variability of scores on the Y variable should remain constant at all values of the X variable (This assumption is called HOMOSCEDASTICITY).

Regression and CORRELATION are closely related. Both techniques involve the relationship between two variables, and they both utilize the same set of paired scores taken from the same subjects. However, whereas correlation is concerned with the magnitude and direction of the relationship, regression focuses on using the relationship for prediction. In terms of prediction, if two variables were correlated perfectly, then knowing the value of one score permits a perfect prediction of the score on the second variable. Generally, whenever two variables are significantly correlated, the researcher may use the score on one variable to predict the score on the second. For example, if a student scored 60% on a test of reading comprehension and 70% in a grammar test (the independent variables), regression analysis could be used to predict his/her likely score on a test of language proficiency (the dependent variable).
There are two basic types of regression analysis: SIMPLE REGRESSION and MULTIPLE REGRESSION.
📖 Cohen et al. 2011; Cramer & Howitt 2004; Ho 2006; Larson-Hall 2010; Marczyk et al. 2005; Perry 2011; Richards & Schmidt 2010; Walliman 2006; Urdan 2010

regression coefficient
also regression weight
a measure of the relationship between each INDEPENDENT VARIABLE or predictor and the DEPENDENT VARIABLE or criterion. No sign means that the association is positive with higher scores on the predictor being associated with higher scores on the criterion. A negative sign shows that the association is negative with higher scores on the predictor being associated with lower scores on the criterion. In SIMPLE REGRESSION, this is also the SLOPE of the regression line. In MULTIPLE REGRESSION, the various regression coefficients combine to create the slope of the re-

gression line. Regression coefficients are reported in a standardized and unstandardized beta forms (i.e., β and B) (see STANDARDIZED PARTIAL REGRESSION COEFFICIENT)
📖 Cramer & Howitt 2004; Larson-Hall 2010; Urdan 2010

regression equation
an algebraic equation relating the INDEPENDENT VARIABLE(s) or predictor(s) to the expected value of the DEPENDENT VARIABLE or criterion. A regression equation summarizes the relationship between a response variable and one or more predictor variables. The regression equation allows you to draw a REGRESSION LINE through the SCATTERPLOT and to use the relationship with X to predict any individual's Y score. The position of the line is determined by the SLOPE (the angle) and the INTERCEPT (the point where the line intersects the vertical axis, Y). The slope is represented by the letter 'b', and the intercept is represented by the letter 'a'. The slope may also be referred to as the *coefficient*, and the intercept may be referred to as the *constant*. When inspecting regression lines, we can see that the higher the value of b, the steeper the line, and the lower the value of b, the flatter the line.
📖 Heiman 2011; Ravid 2011; Sahai & Khurshid 2001

regression line
see SIMPLE REGRESSION

regression sum of squares
another term for SUM OF SQUARES REGRESSION

regression toward the mean
another term for STATISTICAL REGRESSION

regression weight
another term for REGRESSION COEFFICIENT

rejection level
another term for SIGNIFICANCE LEVEL

rejection region
also **region of rejection, critical region**
the range of possible values of the area in the SAMPLING DISTRIBUTION of a TEST STATISTIC that lead to rejection of NULL HYPOTHESIS. The value of the test statistic must fall in this region in order for the null hypothesis to be rejected. The size of the critical region is determined by the desired SIGNIFICANCE LEVEL of the test, often denoted by ALPHA (α). The smaller

the significance level, the smaller the critical region.
see also REGION OF ACCEPTANCE
📖 Sahai & Khurshid 2001; Upton & Cook 2008

related design
another term for WITHIN-SUBJECTS DESIGN

related groups
another term for DEPENDENT SAMPLES

related samples
another term for DEPENDENT SAMPLES

related-samples *t*-test
another term for PAIRED-SAMPLES *t*-TEST

related subjects design
another term for WITHIN-SUBJECTS DESIGN

related *t*-test
another term for paired-samples *t*-tests

relationship index
see EFFECT SIZE

relative frequency
also *rel.f*
the proportion of time a value or a score occurs. To compute relative frequency (*rel.f*), we divide the frequency (*f*) by the total number of scores (*N*) (see Table R.2). For example, if a score occurred four times (*f*) in a SAMPLE of 10 scores (*N*), then the score has a relative frequency of .40, meaning that the score occurred .40 of the time in the sample.

Score	*f*	*rel.f*
6	1	.05
5	0	.00
4	2	.10
3	3	.15
2	10	.50
1	4	.20
Total: 20		1.00 = 100%

Table R.2. An Example of Relative Frequency Distribution

Sometimes we transform relative frequency to percent. Converting relative frequency to percent gives the percent of the time that a score occurred. To transform relative frequency to percent or percentage, multiply the *rel.f* times 100. Above, the *rel.f* was .40, so $(.40)(100) = 40\%$. Thus, 40% of the sample had this score. A distribution showing the relative frequency of all scores is called a **relative frequency distribution**. It can be presented in a table or graph.
 Heiman 2011

relative frequency distribution
see RELATIVE FREQUENCY

relativism
any view that maintains that the truth or falsity of statements of a certain class depends on the person making the statement or upon his/her circumstances or society. Relativism does not refer to a unitary doctrine but rather announces a cluster of viewpoints. There are, however, two deeply interrelated points central to all discussions of relativism. The first is the claim that our experiences, moral judgments, claims to knowledge, and so on can be understood only relative to something else such as particular languages and particular social and cultural practices. The second is the denial that there can be any universal or apodictic truths. In the philosophical literature on relativism, various terms are used to broadly denote two different types or categories of relativism. The first type is most commonly described using the paired terms descriptive-normative, cognitive-ethical, and epistemological-moral, all of which refer to basically the same differentiation. Normative, ethical, and moral relativism state that what we accept as morally correct or incorrect varies from society to society and even within different segments of a society. There are no moral/ethical principles that are accepted by all people across societies or even by all members of any particular society. The validity and force of ethical and moral injunctions are context dependent, and there are not, and cannot be, any enduring universal ethical and moral strictures. This form of relativism does not allow for the possibility of an objectivist basis for moral/ethical judgment. Moreover, moral relativism obviously stands in conflict with the moral absolutes associated with religious doctrines.
The second type of relativism, cognitive or epistemological relativism, holds that there are no universal truths or truths about the world that stand outside our use of language; that is, there are no extra-linguistic truths. This claim is based on the idea that although we may accept that there is a world out there independent of our interests and purposes, as per common sense, the languages we use to depict that world are not out there independent of us. Relativists argue that because truth can be un-

derstood only within a language, there are no inherent or given characteristics of the world and, as such, there can be no ultimate fact of the matter. All that can be said about the world is that there are different ways of interpreting it—interpretations that are time and place contingent or, put differently, are relative to time and place. Although epistemological relativism is less widely held than is moral relativism, it recently has gained increased attention from, most especially, social researchers. As the implications of the idea of no theory-free knowledge have been more fully realized, arguments over epistemological relativism have become far more common in the philosophy of social research literature.

The most important issue that discussions of relativism have brought to the forefront for social researchers, most especially QUALITATIVE RESEARCHErs, is that of how to judge the quality of research and how to adjudicate among different claims to knowledge. For quantitative researchers, given their empiricist (see EMPIRICISM) and realist (see REALISM) philosophical dispositions, there has been a general agreement that there is a two-stage process appropriate for judging the quality of research. Judgments about good versus bad research are based on whether or not the researcher employed the proper methods; this judgment is then followed by a judgment as to the value of the findings in a practical and/or theoretical sense. Relativists argue that although judgments cannot be grounded extra-linguistically, this does not allow that researchers are exempt from engaging each other in open and unconstrained conversation in the attempt to justify claims to knowledge. They add that researchers have a moral obligation, in their attempts to persuade others to accept their knowledge claims and define the quality of research the way they do, to be open to having themselves persuaded by others. The idea that researchers must learn to live with uncertainty and the absence of the possibility for final vindications does not mean that judgment is to be abandoned.

📖 Given 2008

rel.f

an abbreviation for RELATIVE FREQUENCY

reliability

the consistency of data, scores, or observations obtained using measurement instruments, which can include a range of tools from standardized tests to tasks completed by participants in a research study. In other words, reliability indicates the extent to which measurement methods and procedures yield consistent results in a given POPULATION in different circumstances. For example, if a person takes an intelligence test several times, and each time the test produces a similar intelligence test score, that intelligence test has high reliability. Contrary to much of the usage in the methodological literature, it is not the test or the measuring instrument that is reliable. Reliability is a property of the scores on a test for a particular population of test-takers. The most common index used to indicate reliability is referred to as RELIABILITY COEFFICIENT.

When talking about measurement in the context of research, there is an important distinction between being valid (see VALIDITY) and being reliable. Validity refers to whether the measurement is correct; whereas reliability refers to whether the measurement is consistent. Validity is a more important and comprehensive characteristic than reliability. Validity is not obtained as directly as reliability. Assessing validity involves accumulating a great deal of evidence to support the proposed interpretations of scores. The conceptual framework indicates the kinds of evidence that you need to collect to support the meaning and interpretation of test scores. You must answer questions about the appropriateness of test content, the adequacy of criteria, the definitions of human traits, the specification of the behavioral domain, the theory behind the test content, and so forth. All these matters involve judgment and the gathering of data from many sources.

Reliability, in contrast, can be investigated directly from the test data; no data external to the measure are required. The basic issues of reliability lend themselves easily to mathematical analysis, and reasonable conclusions about the amount of error can be stated in mathematical terms. If a measure is to yield valid score-based interpretations, it must first be reliable. The reliability of an instrument determines the upper limit of its validity. Scores on a test with zero reliability are entirely random and therefore cannot correlate with any criterion. The possible correlation of an instrument with a criterion (i.e., VALIDITY COEFFICIENT) increases as the reliability of the instrument increases.

As shown in Figure R.3, when throwing darts at a dart board, validity refers to whether the darts are hitting the bull's eye (an valid dart thrower will throw darts that hit the bull's eye). Reliability, on the other hand, refers to whether the darts are hitting the same spot (a reliable dart thrower will throw darts that hit the same spot), regardless of where the darts hit. Therefore, an valid and reliable dart thrower will consistently throw the darts in the bull's eye—as shown in target (e). As may be evident, however, it is possible for the dart thrower to be reliable, but not valid—as shown in target (d). For example, the dart thrower may throw all of the darts in the same spot (which demonstrates high reliability), but that spot may not be the bull's eye (which demonstrates low validity). If the data are unreliable, they cannot lead to valid (legitimate) inferences—as shown in target (a). As reliability improves, validity may improve, as shown in target (b), or it may not, as shown in target (c). In QUALITATIVE RESEARCH, reliability depends on what is termed DEPENDABILITY.

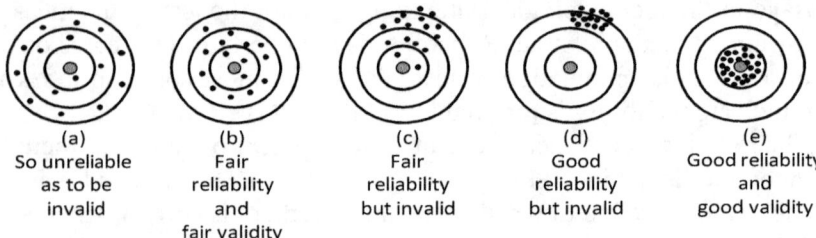

(a)	(b)	(c)	(d)	(e)
So unreliable as to be invalid	Fair reliability and fair validity	Fair reliability but invalid	Good reliability but invalid	Good reliability and good validity

Figure R.3. Schematic Representation of the Relationship between Reliability and Validity

There are two major ways of estimating reliability: *rater reliability* and *instrument reliability*. Not only do we have to make sure that our raters are judging what they believe they are judging in a consistent manner, but also we need to ensure that our measurement instrument is reliable. The methods of estimating rater reliability are INTERRATER and INTRARATER RELIABILITY and methods of estimating instrument reliability are TEST-RETEST, PARALLEL-FORM, and INTERNAL CONSISTENCY RELIABILITY.

📖 Ary et al. 2010; Cohen et al. 2011; Fraenkel & Wallen 2009; Marczyk et al. 2005; McKay 2006; Perry 2011; VanderStoep & Johnston 2009

reliability coefficient
also r_{xx}

a CORRELATION COEFFICIENT which is used to indicate RELIABILITY. Reliability coefficients range between 0 and +1. A coefficient of 0 means there is no reliability in the measurement. That is, if we were to make multiple measurements of a particular VARIABLE, a coefficient of 0 would mean that the measurements were inconsistent. Conversely, a coefficient of 1 indicates that there is perfect reliability or consistency. This means that the measurement procedure gives the same results regardless of who or what makes the measurement. Seldom, if ever, do reliability coefficients occur at the extreme ends of the continuum (i.e., 0 or 1). The higher the better, but better depends on the nature of the measurement procedure being used. Researchers using observation techniques are happy with reliability coefficients anywhere from .80 on up. Yet ACHIEVEMENT and APTITUDE TESTS should have reliabilities in the .90s. Other instruments such as interest inventories and attitude scales tend to be lower than achievement or aptitude tests. Generally speaking, reliabilities falling below 60 are considered low no matter what type of procedure is being used.

The interpretation of a reliability coefficient should be based on a number of considerations. Certain factors affect reliability coefficients, and unless these factors are taken into account, any interpretation of reliability will be superficial:

1) The reliability of a measuring instrument such as a test is in part a function of the length of the test. Other things being equal, the longer the test, the greater its reliability. A test usually consists of a number of sample items that are, theoretically, drawn from a universe of test items. Like SAMPLING that the greater the SAMPLE SIZE, the more representative it is expected to be of the POPULATION from which it is drawn, the greater the number of items included in the test, the more representative it should be of the TRUE SCOREs of the people who take it. Because reliability is the extent to which a test represents the true scores of individuals, the longer the test, the greater its reliability, provided that all the items in the test belong in the universe of items.
2) Reliability is in part a function of group heterogeneity. The reliability coefficient increases as the spread, or heterogeneity, of the subjects who take the test increases. Conversely, the more homogeneous the group is with respect to the trait being measured, the lower will be the reliability coefficient. One explanation of reliability is that it is the extent to which researchers can place individuals, relative to others in their groups, according to certain traits. Such placement is easier when you are dealing with individuals who are more heterogeneous than homogeneous on the trait being measured. Thus, the heterogeneity of the group with whom a measuring instrument is used is a factor that affects the reliability of that instrument. The more heterogeneous the group used in the reliability study, the higher the reliability coefficient.
3) The reliability of a test is in part a function of the ability of the individuals who take that test. A test may be reliable at one level of ability but unreliable at another level. The questions in a test may be difficult and beyond the ability level of those who take it—or the questions may be easy for the majority of the subjects. This difficulty level affects the reliability of the test. When a test is difficult, the subjects are guessing on most of the questions and a low reliability coefficient will result. When it is easy, all subjects have correct responses on most of the items, and only a few difficult items are discriminating among subjects. Again, we would expect a low reliability.
4) Reliability is in part a function of the specific technique used for its estimation. Different procedures for estimating the reliability of tests result in different reliability coefficients. The PARALLEL-FORM RELIABILITY with time lapse technique gives a lower estimation of reliability than either TEST-RETEST or SPLIT-HALF RELIABILITY estimates because in this technique form-to-form as well as time-to-time fluctu-

ation is present. The split-half method, in contrast, results in higher reliability coefficients than do its alternatives because of the speed element in most tests.
5) Reliability is in part a function of the nature of the variable being measured. Some variables of interest to researchers yield consistent measures more often than do other variables. For instance, because academic achievement is relatively easy to measure, most established tests of academic achievement have quite high reliability (coefficients of .90 or higher). Aptitude tests that are designed to predict future behavior—a more difficult task—have somewhat lower reliability (.80 or lower). Reliable measures of personality variables are most difficult to obtain; thus, these measures typically have only moderate reliability (.60 to .70)
6) Reliability is influenced by the objectivity of the scoring. Inconsistent scoring introduces error that reduces the reliability of a test. The potential unreliability of the scoring of essay tests, for example, means that essay tests are generally considered to be not as reliable as multiple-choice and other types of selected-response tests.

The degree of reliability you need in a measure depends to a great extent on the use you will make of the results. The need for accurate measurement increases as the consequences of decisions and interpretation become more important. If the measurement results are to be used for making a decision about a group or for research purposes, or if an erroneous initial decision can be easily corrected, scores with modest reliability (coefficients in the range of .50 to .60) may be acceptable. However, if the results are to be used as a basis for making decisions about individuals, especially important or irreversible decisions (e.g., rejection or admission of candidates to a professional school/university or the placement of children in special education classes), only instruments with the highest reliability are acceptable. Measurement experts state that in such situations a reliability of .90 is the minimum that should be tolerated, and a reliability of .95 should be the desired standard.
see also STANDARD ERROR OF MEASUREMENT
📖 Ary et al. 2010

repeated cross-sectional study
another term for TREND STUDY

repeated-measures ANCOVA
also **within-subjects ANCOVA, RM ANCOVA, within-groups ANCOVA**
an extension of REPEATED-MEASURES ANOVA with the COVARIATE(s). In this way, the researcher can examine the effects of the desired variables and their interaction knowing that the effects of the covariates have been

mathematically factored out. For example, we may want to investigate whether learners of Japanese progress more in their reading development in a situation of intensive immersion (where they do not leave the country where their first language (L1) is spoken) or in a study abroad context living in Japan, over the course of a semester. Each of the two groups will be tested at two times, necessitating a repeated-measures ANOVA. In addition, because previous studies have shown that L1 and second language (L2) reading ability affect reading development, measures of these constructs will be also included in the analysis as covariates. We want to know whether two groups differ in their scores over time on a self-assessment task when two variables shown to affect reading development are factored out (the covariates). This is a 2 (context) × 2 (time of test) repeated-measures ANCOVA, controlling for reading ability in L1 and L2 (i.e., L1 and L2 are partialled out).
 Larson-Hall 2010

repeated-measures ANOVA
also RM ANOVA, within-subjects ANOVA, within-groups ANOVA

a PARAMETRIC TEST for designs in which the same participants are tested on more than one occasion (e.g., Time 1, Time 2, Time 3), or participated in more than one experimental condition (e.g., Condition 1, Condition 2, Condition 3). In other words, we cannot assume the independence of scores in the design because the same people were tested more than once. The ASSUMPTIONS for a repeated-measures ANOVA test are similar to those of other parametric tests (e.g., NORMALITY, HOMOGENEITY OF VARIANCE), but also include the assumption of SPHERICITY.

Like an ANOVA design, a repeated-measures (RM) ANOVA has one *continuous* DEPENDENT VARIABLE (i.e., measured on INTERVAL or RATIO SCALEs) and at least one *categorical* INDEPENDENT VARIABLE (IV) with two or more LEVELs. The difference with RM ANOVA is that one or more of the IVs must be a WITHIN-GROUPS FACTOR. If it is a within-groups IV, then each participant will be included in all of the levels of the variable. For example, in a pretest/posttest situation the same person will have both a pretest and a posttest score.

The variation in any ANOVA can be divided into variation between groups (explained by the IV) and variation within groups (cannot be explained by the IV). With FACTORIAL ANOVA, we account only for BETWEEN-GROUP VARIABILITY. There is an ERROR TERM into which we sweep all of the variance that we cannot explain. A lot of this variance is due to the fact that people are just different, and so may respond differently. However, with RM ANOVA, because it looks at the same individuals with at least two different measures, we can account for some of the WITHIN-GROUP VARIABILITY as well. This reduces the amount of error, and thus increases POWER OF A TEST.

RM ANOVAs, like ANOVA, may be called ONE-WAY REPEATED MEASURES ANOVA, TWO-WAY REPEATED MEASURES ANOVA, THREE-WAY REPEATED MEASURES ANOVA, or higher depending on how many IVs are included. RM ANOVAs, with two or more IVs are called **repeated-measures factorial ANOVA** (also called **within-subjects factorial ANOVA**).
📖 Greene & Oliveira 2005; Larson-Hall 2010; Mackey & Gass 2005; Porte 2010

repeated-measures design
another term for WITHIN-SUBJECTS DESIGN

repeated-measures factor
another term for WITHIN-GROUPS FACTOR

repeated-measures factorial ANOVA
see REPEATED-MEASURES ANOVA

repeated-measures MANOVA
another term for PROFILE ANALYSIS

repeated measures *t*-test
another term for PAIRED-SAMPLES *t*-TEST

replication
repetition of an experiment with different subjects, and frequently with a different experimenter and different location. There are three types of replications: **Literal replication** (also called **exact replication**) is the exact duplication of a previous methodologically sound study whereby the methods and conditions are repeated to confirm the original findings; **approximate replication** (also called **systematic replication**) involves the duplication of the methods of the original study as closely as possible but altering some non-major variable; and **constructive replication** (or **conceptual replication**) means beginning with a similar problem statement as the original study but creating a new means or design to verify the original findings.
📖 Hinkel 2011

representative sample
a SAMPLE that is similar in terms of characteristics of the POPULATION to which the findings of a study are being generalized. A representative sample is not biased and therefore does not display any patterns or trends that are different from those displayed by the population from which it is drawn. It is rather difficult and often impossible to obtain a representative

sample. NONRANDOM SAMPLEs usually tend to have some kind of bias. The use of a RANDOM SAMPLE usually leads to a representative sample.
📖 Sahai & Khurshid 2001

reputational sampling
another term for SNOWBALL SAMPLING

resampling
the technique of selecting a SAMPLE many times and computing the statistic of interest with reweighted sample observations. To put it another way, resampling is the use of the scores obtained in a study to produce a SAMPLING DISTRIBUTION of the possible outcomes of the study based on that data. Take the simple example of a study comparing two groups (A and B) on the variable C. If the NULL HYPOTHESIS were true (that there is no difference between group A and group B), then the distribution of scores between group A and group B is just haphazard. If this is so, then what we can do is to collect together the scores for group A and group B and then randomly allocate each score to either group A or group B. This will produce two samples which can be compared. Repeating the process will produce increasing numbers of pairs of samples each of which are easily compared. So, based on the data above, it is possible to produce a sampling difference between all of the possible combinations of scores in the table. This, in fact, is like any other sampling distribution except that it is rigidly limited by the scores in the data. They are the same scores but resampling assigns them to group A and group B differently. There are a number of statistical techniques which employ such procedures. Their major difficulty is that they require computer software capable of generating the random sampling distribution.
There are a number of statistical techniques which employ such procedures. Their major difficulty is that they require computer software capable of generating the random sampling distribution. Some commonly used resampling techniques include BOOTSTRAP, JACKKNIFE, and their variants.
📖 Cramer & Howitt 2004; Upton & Cook 2008

research
a systematic process of collecting and analyzing data that will investigate a research problem or question, or help researchers obtain a more complete understanding of a situation. The goal of research is to describe, explain, or predict present or future phenomena.
More specifically, research should be:

1) *Systematic*: A study has a clear structure with definite procedural rules that must be followed. There are rules for designing a study, for

controlling different problems that may adversely influence the study, and for choosing and applying statistics (if necessary). It is these rules that make such studies systematic and that can help us read, interpret, and critique studies. It is these rules that underlie the logic of research.
2) *Logical research*: The rules and procedures underlying these studies form a straightforward, logical pattern—a step-by-step progression of building blocks, each of which is necessary for the logic to succeed. If the procedures are violated, one or more building blocks may be missing and the logic will break down like any other logic.
3) *Tangible research*: Research is tangible in that it is based on the collection (and sometimes manipulation) of data from the real world. The set of data may take the form of scores, subjects' ranks on course grades, the number of language learners who have certain characteristics, and so forth. It is the manipulation, or processing, of these data that links the study to the real world.
4) *Research should also be replicable*: The researcher's proper presentation and explanation of the system, logic, data collection, and data manipulation in a study should make it possible for the reader to replicate the study (see REPLICATION). If the study is clearly explained and if we can understand it well enough to replicate it, then we probably have enough information to judge its quality. Perhaps then, we should consider replicability to be one of the first yardstick when critiquing any such article.
5) *Reductive research*: Research can reduce the confusion of facts that language and language teaching, for example, frequently present, sometimes on a daily basis. Through doing or reading such studies, we may discover new patterns in the facts. Or through these investigations and the eventual agreement among many researchers, general patterns and relationships may emerge that clarify the field as a whole.

see also QUALITATIVE RESEARCH, QUANTITATIVE RESEARCH
 Brown 1988

research design
also **study design**
the architectural plan of a research project. Decisions regarding what, where, when, how much, by what means concerning an inquiry or a research study constitute a research design. A research design is the arrangement of conditions for collection and analysis of data in a manner that aims to combine relevance to the research purpose. In fact, the research design is the conceptual structure within which research is conducted; it constitutes the blueprint for the collection, measurement, and analysis of data. As such, the design includes an outline of what the

researcher will do from the formulation of the research questions and hypotheses to reporting the research findings. In designing any research study, the researcher should be familiar with the basic steps of the research process that guide all types of research designs. Also, the researcher should be familiar with a wide range of research designs in order to choose the most appropriate design to answer the research questions and hypotheses of interest. QUANTITATIVE RESEARCHers maintain that once the research plan is set forth, it must be followed. Unhypothesized observed relationships among variables may be reported and proposed as topics for future research, but they should not replace the original intent of the study. In qualitative research, the design is flexible and may change during the investigation if appropriate. The design of QUALITATIVE RESEARCH is thus often described as emergent.

Generally, the research designs can be classified into three broad research categories: (1) QUANTITATIVE RESEARCH designs, (2) QUALITATIVE research designs, and (3) MIXED METHODS RESEARCH designs.

see also EXPERIMENTAL DESIGN

📖 Ary et al. 2010; Kothari 2008; Lavrakas 2008

researcher bias
see RESEARCHER EFFECT

researcher effect
also **experimenter effect**
a source for data distortion which in turn weakens the EXTERNAL VALIDITY of the results. Researcher effect occurs when data are distorted by some characteristic of the researcher either in administering the TREATMENT or collecting the data. Good experimental researchers are careful about their own influence on the research they are conducting. Note that in QUANTITATIVE RESEARCH, the researcher maintains an independent and separate role. However, there are times when the researcher may exert unintentional influence on the outcome of the study. These influences can be the result of the personal attributes of the researcher or may occur because the researcher's expectations affect his/her behavior and the performance of the participants. Personal attributes include gender, race, age, or emotional disposition. Researcher influence due to expectations that affect the behavior of research participants (sometimes called **experimenter bias**, **researcher bias**, **Pygmalion effect**) can occur if the researcher, hoping to obtain a difference between the experimental and control groups, gives the experimental group any unintended advantage (more testing time, slower instructions, more attention, positive feedback for correct responses, etc.). Note that bias can occur unintentionally and even unconsciously, especially if researchers have strong expectations regarding which group will do better. For instance, if the data collector

thinks that the participants they are observing are high-ability students, they might be more lenient (or demanding) in their observations than if they thought the participants were low ability. Any time participants have been divided into ability groups such as high/middle/low second language language proficiency and the data collector is aware of this, there is a danger of this effect. The danger is even greater if the type of data collected requires any form of qualitative judgment on the part of the data collector. The researcher needs to take precautions that the data collectors are unaware of the ability level of the participants they are observing and clearly state what precautions s/he has taken in his/her report. When bias is present, GENERALIZABILITY is limited because other researchers may not obtain similar results.

Perhaps the most effective way to eliminate experimenter effects is to use a **double-blind technique**. With a double-blind procedure, neither the participants nor the experimenters (hence the term double) who interact with them know which experimental condition a participant is in at the time the study is conducted. The experiment is supervised by another researcher, who assigns participants to conditions and keeps other experimenters in the dark. This procedure ensures that the experimenters who interact with the participants will not subtly and unintentionally influence participants to respond in a particular way.

see also HALO EFFECT, HAWTHORNE EFFECT, NOVELTY EFFECT, PRE-TEST-TREATMENT INTERACTION, MULTIPLE-TREATMENT INTERACTION, SPECIFICITY OF VARIABLES, TREATMENT DIFFUSION
📖 Leary 2011; Lodico et al. 2010; Perry 2011

research method
a systematic and rigorous way of collecting and analyzing information. QUANTITATIVE RESEARCHers use a wide variety of instruments to gather data, including TEST, QUESTIONNAIRE, and RATING SCALE. In QUALITATIVE RESEARCH this includes, for example, PARTICIPANT OBSERVATION, INTERVIEW, VERBAL REPORT, DIARY STUDY, and DISCOURSE ANALYSIS.
📖 Heigham & Croker 2009

research methodology
a theory of how inquiry should occur. Research methodology defines the kinds of problems that are worth investigating and frames them, determines what research approaches and research methods to use, and also how to understand what constitutes a legitimate and warranted explanation. Research methodology involves such general activities as identifying problems, review of the literature, formulating hypotheses, procedure for testing hypotheses, measurement, data collection analysis of data, interpreting results, and drawing conclusions. Researchers need to understand the assumptions underlying various techniques and they need to

know the criteria by which they can decide that certain techniques and procedures will be applicable to certain problems and others will not. For example, an architect, who designs a building, has to consciously evaluate the basis of his/her decisions, i.e., s/he has to evaluate why and on what basis s/he selects particular size, number and location of doors, windows and ventilators, uses particular materials and not others and the like. Similarly, in research you have to expose the research decisions to evaluation before they are implemented. You have to specify very clearly and precisely what decisions you select and why you select them so that they can be evaluated by others too.

Research methodology has many dimensions and RESEARCH METHODs do constitute a part of the research methodology. The scope of research methodology is wider than that of research methods. Thus, when we talk of research methodology we not only talk of the research methods but also consider the logic behind the methods we use in the context of our research study and explain why we are using a particular method or technique and why we are not using others so that research results are capable of being evaluated either by the researcher himself or by others. Why a research study has been undertaken, how the research problem has been defined, in what way and why the HYPOTHESIS has been formulated, what data have been collected and what particular method has been adopted, why particular technique of analyzing data has been used and a host of similar other questions are usually answered when we talk of research methodology concerning a research problem or study. Thus, research methodology consists of all general and specific activities of research.

📖 Heigham & Croker 2009; Kothari 2008

research problem

a problem that someone would like to research. A problem can be anything that a person finds unsatisfactory or unsettling, a difficulty of some sort, a state of affairs that needs to be changed, anything that is not working as well as it might. Problems involve areas of concern to researchers, conditions they want to improve, difficulties they want to eliminate, questions for which they seek answers.

📖 Porte 2010

research question

a specific question asked in the course of investigation to which a specific answer or set of answers is sought. Very often the researcher's prior study of the field and REVIEW OF THE LITERATURE will have exposed a need to explore, describe, or explain further a particular phenomenon through research questions, before arriving at possible hypotheses (see HYPOTHESIS). It will be useful for the reader to predict the nature of the

study suggested by the particular research question as part of the valuable practice of progressively building up a critical response to what s/he is being told. In this way, we can begin to envisage outcomes and perhaps already consider possible problems or drawbacks in the RESEARCH DESIGN.
see also HYPOTHESIS
📖 Porte 2010

research report
a formal report in which the findings from research are presented. Whether the research is *quantitative* or *qualitative* in nature, the research report needs to consist of a number of sections which deal with the different stages of, and rationale behind, the research process. Journal articles or theses may have a predetermined list of headings which have to be adhered to, but regardless of the precise wording of the headings, the same elements will need to be included. A research report normally consists of the following sections:

- TITLE
- ABSTRACT
- INTRODUCTION
- METHOD
- RESULTS
- DISCUSSION
- REFERENCES
- APPENDIXES

This is the basic, standard structure which underlies the majority of research reports. However, sometimes other sections are included where appropriate. Similarly, sometimes sections of the report are merged.
📖 Howitt & Cramer 2011

resentful demoralization
another term for DEMORALIZATION

residual
also **residual effect, residual error term**
an error in prediction. Residual is the difference between the actual value of a DEPENDENT VARIABLE or criterion and its predicted value. Put differently, residual is the portion of the score on the dependent variable which is not explained by INDEPENDENT VARIABLEs. Larger differences or residuals imply that the predictions are less accurate. The concept is commonly used to indicate the disparity between the data and the statis-

tical model for that data. It has the big advantage of simplicity. Careful scrutiny of the residuals will help a researcher identify where the model or statistic is especially poor at predicting the data. The variance of the residual (scores) is quite simply the **residual variance**.
see also SIMPLE REGRESSION, HOMOSCEDASTICITY
📖 Cramer & Howitt 2004; Sahai & Khurshid 2001; Urdan 2010

residual effect
another name for RESIDUAL

residual error
another name for ERROR TERM

residual error term
another name for RESIDUAL

residual sum of squares
another name for ERROR SUM OF SQUARES

residual variable
in PATH ANALYSIS, an unmeasured VARIABLE that is posited to cause the VARIANCE in the DEPENDENT VARIABLE not explained by the path model.
📖 Sahai & Khurshid 2001

residual variance
see RESIDUAL

respondent fatigue
a well-documented phenomenon that occurs when SURVEY participants become tired of the survey task and the quality of the data they provide begins to deteriorate. Respondent fatigue occurs when survey participants' attention and motivation drop toward later sections of a QUESTIONNAIRE. Tired or bored respondents may more often answer 'don't know,' engage in 'straight-line' responding (i.e., choosing answers down the same column on a page), give more perfunctory answers, or give up answering the questionnaire altogether. Thus, the causes for, and consequences of, respondent fatigue, and possible ways of measuring and controlling for it, should be taken into account when deciding on the length of the questionnaire, question ordering, survey design, and interviewer training. Generally speaking, as (a) the survey is more time consuming, (b) the questions are boring and complicated, (c) more OPEN-ENDED QUESTIONs are asked, (d) the interviewer does not motivate adequate answers, and (e) the issue of the survey is mundane or repetitive, respond-

ents' motivation may decrease and fatigue effects may arise.
📖 Lavrakas 2008

respondent validation
another name for MEMBER CHECKS

response rate
the proportion of the selected sample that agrees to be interviewed or returns a completed QUESTIONNAIRE. With INTERVIEWs, response rates are very high—perhaps 90 percent or better. Personal contact increases the likelihood that the individual will participate and will provide the desired information. With mailed questionnaires, the personal contact is missing, and people are more likely to refuse to cooperate. This results in many nonreturns (people who do not complete and return the questionnaire). The proportion of individuals that fail to provide the relevant information being sought by the investigator is referred to as **nonresponse rate**. The low response rate typical for a mailed questionnaire (less than 30 percent is common) not only reduces the SAMPLE SIZE but also may bias the results. However, an interviewer can get an answer to all or most of the questions. Missing data represent a serious problem for the mailed questionnaire.
see also REFUSAL RATE
📖 Ary et al. 2010; Sahai & Khurshid 2001

response variable
another term for DEPENDENT VARIABLE

restricted question
another term for CLOSED-FORM ITEM

restricted range
confining scores to a narrow range of possible scores. The restricted range weakens the scores which may cause the researcher to misinterpret the data. More specifically, a common problem concerns restrictions on the range over which X and Y vary. The effect of such range restrictions is to alter the CORRELATION between X and Y from what it would have been if the range had not been so restricted. Depending on the nature of the data, the correlation may either rise or fall as a result of such restriction, although most commonly correlation is reduced. With the exception of very unusual circumstances, restricting the range of X will increase correlation only when the restriction results in eliminating some curvilinear relationship (see CURVILINEARITY). For example, if we correlated reading ability with age, where age ran from 0 to 70 years, the data would be decidedly curvilinear (flat to about age 4, rising to about 17 years of age and then

leveling off) and the correlation, which measures linear relationships (see LINEARITY), would be relatively low. If, however, we restricted the range of ages to 5 to 17 years, the correlation would be quite high, since we would have eliminated those values of Y that were not varying linearly as a function of X. The more usual effect of restricting the range of X or Y is to reduce the correlation. This problem is especially pertinent in the area of test construction, since here criterion measures (Y) may be available for only the higher values of X.

We must take into account the effect of range restrictions whenever we see a CORRELATION COEFFICIENT based on a restricted SAMPLE. The coefficient might be inappropriate for the question at hand. Essentially, what we have done is to ask how well a standardized test predicts a person's suitability for college, but we have answered that question by referring only to those people who were actually admitted to college.
 Howell 2010

results
also **findings**
a section of a RESEARCH REPORT which contains summaries of the data that focus on the main findings of the research. For clarity, it helps if data can be presented in the form of tables or graphs. Note that the results section should concentrate precisely on this and not discuss the findings (see DISCUSSION).

see also TITLE, ABSTRACT, INTRODUCTION, METHOD, REFERENCES, APPENDIXES
 Gray 2009; Perry 2011

résumé
a document used by individuals to present their background and skills. It usually includes one's educational background, work experience, and references. Résumés can be used for a variety of reasons but most often to secure new employment. A typical résumé contains a summary of relevant job experience and education. In many contexts, a résumé is short (usually one to three pages), and directs a reader's attention to the aspects of a person's background that are directly relevant to a particular position.

While formats vary considerably, all follow one of three patterns:

- *Chronological organization*: Experiences are listed beginning with the earliest; the most recent experiences appear last.
- *Reverse chronological organization*: The most recent experiences appear first.
- *Experiences grouped in relation to the job currently sought*: Little effort is made to show time relationships, but dates are included.

No matter its format, a resume will include these common characteristics:

- One's name, mailing address, e-mail address, phone numbers, and fax number, if you have one,
- the position for which a person is applying,
- One's experience, including places, dates of employment, and responsibilities or duties held,
- One's education and special training,
- References

It is important to know the difference between a **Curriculum Vitae** (CV), and résumé. A résumé generally outlines a person's key qualifications (including education, work experience, and skills) in one to three pages. A curriculum vitae is a form of résumé; however, it is much more exhaustive and can encompass many pages. CVs are generally used in academic settings and include degrees earned, teaching and research experience, publications, and presentations.

The following is an example of résumé:

Jenifer Roberts
1320 Forest Drive
Palo Alto, CA94309
Email: Jeniffer@mailbox.com
Telephone: (650) 498-129

Objectives:	To obtain a position as a full-time Persian-English translator, in which I can contribute my skills and many years of experience to the success of ABC Company
Education	
2000-2002	Master of Arts in Translation, Stanford University
1994-1998	Bachelor of Arts in English language teaching, Georgetown University
Experience	
2002-present	Freelance technical translator, Persian-English, mostly for hi-tech industries in California
2000-2002	Teaching assistant (Persian), Standford University
1998-2000	English teacher, Cambridge Institute, Heidelberg, Germany
Languages	Fluent English, Conversational Spanish
Personal	Interests include Ping-Pong, playing the guitar, cooking
References	Dr. M Rosen, Chair, Dep. of Modern Language, Standford University, Palo Alto, CA94305

 Sorenson 2010

retrospective cohort study
see COHORT STUDY

retrospective longitudinal study
a type of LONGITUDINAL RESEARCH which differs from PANEL STUDY and TREND STUDY in that the data are gathered during a single investigation in which respondents are asked to think *back* and answer questions about the past. A major deterrent of both panel and trend studies is the fact that the researchers have to wait a considerable period of time before they can see the results. Retrospective longitudinal studies offer a way around this delay, although not without a cost. This may sound like a straightforward idea that can save us a lot of time and money but past retrospective research has revealed that the quality of the recollected data can be very uneven: as much 50 per cent of the responses may be incorrect or inaccurate in some way; the retrospective accounts can be simplified or selective, with some important details omitted, suppressed, or simply wrong. Furthermore, by looking at the past through tinted glass the reconstruction of the participants' experiences might be distorted and past feelings and events might be reinterpreted to match subsequent events or the respondents' current perception, or simply to fit some coherent storyline. If there is a long gap in time between the study and the events in question, then **recall bias** may influence the results. On the other hand, if the study focuses on a relatively short period (two weeks or months rather than years), a retrospective design may be appropriate, especially if the data concerns primarily events or behavior rather than attitudes or beliefs.
see also SIMULTANEOUS CROSS-SECTIONAL STUDY
 Dörnyei 2007; Ruspini 2002

retrospective protocol
see VERBAL REPORT

reversal time-series design
another term for EQUIVALENT TIME-SAMPLES DESIGN

reverse causality
see EX POST FACTO RESEARCH

reverse scoring
a process of reversing the scores of a VARIABLE, while retaining the distributional characteristics, to change the relationships (CORRELATIONs) between two variables. Reverse scoring is used in SUMMATED SCALE construction to avoid a canceling out between variables with positive and

negative FACTOR LOADINGs on the same factor.
 Hair et al. 2010

reversion line
another term for REGRESSION LINE

review of the literature
another term for LITERATURE REVIEW

r family of effect size
another term for RELATIONSHIP INDEX

rho (ρ)
an abbreviation FOR SPEARMAN RANK ORDER CORRELATION COEFFICIENT

RM ANCOVA
an abbreviation for REPEATED-MEASURES ANCOVA

RM ANOVA
an abbreviation for REPEATED-MEASURES ANOVA

robust
a property which refers to some statistical procedures which are not overly dependent on critical ASSUMPTIONS regarding an underlying POPULATION distribution. A robust statistics provides reliable information in spite of the fact that one or more of its assumptions have been violated. It means that a significant relationship will be found to be statistically significant when there is such a relationship even when the assumptions underlying the test about the distribution of the data are not met. It does not mean robust ESTIMATORs are totally immune to such violations, but merely that they are less sensitive to deviations from the assumptions. For example, one assumption of the t-TEST and ANOVA is that the DEPENDENT VARIABLE is normally distributed for each group (see NORMALITY). Statisticians who have studied these statistics have found that even when data are not normally distributed (e.g., skewed a lot), they still can be used under many circumstances.
Robust methods were developed in response to the realization that even small deviations from a normal distribution could cause the classical PARAMETRIC STATISTICs to fail. In other words, classical procedures were not robust (did not perform well) in the face of some kinds of violations of assumptions. Robust methods will result in the objective elimination of OUTLIERs. Robust methods are a more principled and powerful way to both identify and eliminate outliers. These statistics will be more powerful (i.e., they will be more likely to find differences if they exist)

and more accurate (i.e., they will estimate more precise confidence intervals) than parametric statistics if the data is not normally distributed.
One strategy within the context of employing a robust statistical procedure is described as ACCOMMODATION.
 Cramer & Howitt 2004; Larson-Hall 2010; Marczyk et al. 2005; Morgan et al. 2004

rorschach test
a PROJECTIVE TECHNIQUE which consists of ten cards having prints of inkblots. The design happens to be symmetrical but meaningless. The respondents are asked to describe what they perceive in such symmetrical inkblots and the responses are interpreted on the basis of some predetermined psychological framework. This test is frequently used but the problem of VALIDITY still remains a major problem of this test.
see also SOCIOMETRY, THEMATIC APPERCEPTION TEST, ROSENZWEIG TEST, HOLTZMAN INKBLOT TEST, TOMKINS-HORN PICTURE ARRANGEMENT TEST
 Kothari 2008

rosenzweig test
a PROJECTIVE TECHNIQUE which uses a cartoon format wherein we have a series of cartoons with words inserted in balloons above. The respondent is asked to put his/her own words in an empty balloon space provided for the purpose in the picture. From what the respondents write in this fashion, the study of their attitudes can be made.
see also SOCIOMETRY, THEMATIC APPERCEPTION TEST, RORSCHACH TEST, HOLTZMAN INKBLOT TEST, TOMKINS-HORN PICTURE ARRANGEMENT TEST
 Kothari 2008

rotating panels
a type of LONGITUDINAL MIXED DESIGN in which a new group of individuals chosen via PROBABILITY is added to the SAMPLE at each successive wave to correct distortions due to ATTRITION or to match the sample to the changing POPULATION. The idea is to keep samples of changing populations up-to-date. SAMPLE SIZE is controlled by stipulating the period of time any subject will be included in the survey, i.e. there is a limit on the time each subject will participate in the panel (e.g., two years). Such rotation serves both as a good method for maintaining the original characteristics of the sample and reduces the distortion which would otherwise be created by natural loss of subjects. This refreshing of the sample has the advantage that subjects will develop survey boredom less easily, that there will be fewer testing and learning effects, and that there will be less panel mortality. Thus, rotating panel surveys combine the features of both PANEL STUDY and TREND STUDY.

see also SPLIT PANELS, LINKED PANELS, COHORT STUDY, ACCELERATED LONGITUDINAL DESIGN, DIARY STUDY
📖 Ruspini 2002

rotation experiment
another term for COUNTER BALANCED DESIGN

rounding decimal places
the process by which long strings of decimals are shortened. To avoid systematic biases in reporting findings (albeit very small ones in most terms), there are rules in terms of how decimals are shortened. These involve checking the decimal place after the final decimal place to be reported. If that extra decimal place has a numerical value between 0 and 4 then we simply report the shortened number by deleting the extra decimals. Thus:

17.632 = 17.63 (to two decimal places)
103.790 = 103.79 (to two decimal places)
12.5731 = 12.573 (to three decimal places)

However, if the additional decimal place is between 5 and 9 then the last figure reported in the decimal is increased by 1. For example,

17.639 is reported as 17.64 (to two decimal places)
103.797 is reported as 103.80 (to two decimal places)
12.5738 is reported as 12.574 (to three decimal places

We add zeroes to the right of the decimal point to indicate the level of precision we are using. For example, rounding 4.996 to two decimal places produces 5, but to show we used the precision of two decimal places, we report it as 5.
📖 Cramer & Howitt 2004; Heiman 2011

Roy's gcr criterion
also **Roy's largest root criterion, Roy's greatest characteristic root criterion**
a test used in *multivariate* statistical procedures such as CANONICAL CORRELATION, DISCRIMINANT FUNCTION ANALYSIS, and MULTIVARIATE ANALYSIS OF VARIANCE to determine whether the MEANs of the groups differ. As the name implies, it only measures differences on the greatest or the first canonical root or discriminant function (i.e., a function of a set of variables used to classify an object or event).

see also WILKS' LAMBDA, HOTELLING'S TRACE CRITERION, PILLAI'S CRITERION
📖 Cramer & Howitt 2004; Tabachnick & Fidell 2007

Roy's greatest characteristic root criterion
another term for ROY'S GCR CRITERION

Roy's largest root criterion
another term for ROY'S GCR CRITERION

row sum of squares
another term for SUM OF SQUARES FOR ROWS

r square
another term for COEFFICIENT OF DETERMINATION

R square
another term for COEFFICIENT OF MULTIPLE DETERMINATION

runs test
a NONPARAMETRIC TEST which is designed to test whether a *categorical* LEVEL of your VARIABLE (with only two levels) is randomly distributed in your data. For example, you could use the runs test to see whether males and females were randomly distributed in your SAMPLE.
📖 Larson-Hall 2010

S

s
    an abbreviation for SAMPLE STANDARD DEVIATION

s²
    an abbreviation for SAMPLE VARIANCE

SD
    an abbreviation for STANDARD DEVIATION

SE
    an abbreviation for STANDARD ERROR

SEM
    an abbreviation for STANDARD ERROR OF MEASUREMENT. Also an abbreviation for STRUCTURAL EQUATION MODELING

SS
    an abbreviation for SUM OF SQUARES

SS$_{BG}$
    an abbreviation for SUM OF SQUARES BETWEEN GROUPS

SS$_{R}$
    an abbreviation for REGRESSION SUM OF SQUARES

SS$_{res}$
    an abbreviation for RESIDUAL SUM OF SQUARES

SS$_{T}$
    an abbreviation for SUM OF SQUARES FOR TOTAL

SS$_{WG}$
    an abbreviation for SUM OF SQUARES WITHIN GROUPS

sample
    see POPULATION

sample data
    see POPULATION

sample mean
see POPULATION MEAN

sample observations
another term for SAMPLE DATA

sample size
the number of subjects to be selected from the POPULATION to constitute a SAMPLE. Sample size is usually denoted by the letter n. The size of sample should neither be excessively large, nor too small. It should be optimum. An optimum sample is one which fulfills the requirements of *efficiency*, *representativeness*, RELIABILITY, and *flexibility*. While deciding the size of sample, researcher must determine the desired precision as also an acceptable confidence level for the estimate. The importance of sample size in determining the accuracy of the results is the reason that larger samples generate more precise estimates and smaller samples produce less accurate estimates—regardless of the size of the larger population.

There are a number of issues that need to be taken into account in determining sample size:

- *The heterogeneity of the population*—if the population is known to be very diverse in nature in relation to the subject of enquiry, then this is likely to increase the required sample size. Conversely if the population is reasonably homogeneous, then a smaller sample will include all the internal diversity that is needed.
- *The number of selection criteria*—the number of criteria that are felt to be important in designing the sample will influence the sample size—the more there are, the larger the sample.
- *The extent to which nesting of criteria is needed*—if criteria need to be interlocked or nested (that is, controlling the representation of one criterion within another) for reasons of interdependency or because of the requirement for diversity, then this will increase the sample size.
- *Groups of special interest that require intensive study*—if groups within the study population require intensive study, they will need to be included with sufficient symbolic representation and diversity. This will require a larger overall sample.
- *Multiple samples within one study*—it is sometimes necessary to have more than one sample within a study for reasons of comparison or control, and this will have a significant impact on the number of cases that need to be covered.
- *Type of data collection methods*—the overall sample size will be increased depending on whether the methods of data collection involve

(roughly in ascending order) single interviews, paired interviews, small or average size group discussions.
- *The budget and resources available*—each sample unit will need intensive resources for data collection and analysis. The scale of the budget available will therefore place some limits on sample size. This may mean that the scope and focus of the study needs to be reviewed.

📖 Given 2008; Kothari 2008; Ritchie & Lewis 2003

sample standard deviation
also **estimated standard deviation**

the most commonly used estimate of the POPULATION STANDARD DEVIATION. When the standard deviation of a SAMPLE (denoted by s) is being used to estimate the standard deviation of the POPULATION, the sum of squared deviations is divided by the number of cases minus one: $(N - 1)$. In tests of statistical inference, the estimated standard deviation rather than the standard deviation is used.

see also STANDARD DEVIATION

📖 Cramer & Howitt 2004; Sahai & Khurshid 2001

sample statistic
see STATISTIC

sample values
another term for SAMPLE DATA

sample variance
also **variance estimate, estimated variance, s^2**

the most commonly used estimate of the POPULATION VARIANCE. Sample variance or variance estimate (symbolized by s^2) is equal to the square of the SAMPLE STANDARD DEVIATION. The larger the VARIANCE is, the more the scores differ from the MEAN. The sample variance is the sum of the squared difference or deviation between the mean score and each individual score which is divided by the number of scores minus one. The variance estimate differs from the VARIANCE in that the sum is divided by one less than the number of scores rather than the number of scores. This is done because the variance of a sample is usually less than that of the population from which it is drawn. In other words, dividing the sum by one less than the number of scores provides a less biased estimate of the population variance. The variance estimate rather than variance is used in many PARAMETRIC STATISTICS as these tests are designed to make inferences about the population of scores from which the samples have been drawn.

see also STANDARD DEVIATION

📖 Cramer & Howitt 2004; Sahai & Khurshid 2001

sampling
the process of choosing actual data sources from a larger set of possibilities. This overall process actually consists of two related elements: (1) defining the full set of possible data sources—which is generally termed the POPULATION, and (2) selecting a specific SAMPLE of data sources from that population. In other words, it is the procedure through which the researcher picks out, from a set of units that make up the object of study (the population), a limited number of cases (sample) chosen according to criteria that enable the results obtained by studying the sample to be extrapolated to the whole population. The QUANTITATIVE and QUALITATIVE RESEARCH differ greatly in how they approach participant sampling. In quantitative studies the principle is straightforward: The researchers need a sizeable sample to be able to iron out idiosyncratic individual differences. Qualitative research, on the other hand, focuses on describing, understanding, and clarifying a human experience and therefore qualitative studies are directed at describing the aspects that make up an experience, within a group. Accordingly, at least in theory, qualitative inquiry is not concerned with how representative the respondent sample is or how the experience is distributed in the population. Instead the main goal of sampling is to find individuals who can provide rich and varied insights into phenomenon under investigation so as to maximize what the researchers can learn. The goal is best achieved by means of some sort of PURPOSIVE SAMPLING.

Broadly speaking, sampling procedures can be divided into two groups: (1) scientifically sound PROBABILITY SAMPLING, which involves complex and expensive procedures that are usually well beyond the means of applied linguists, and (2) NON-PROBABILITY SAMPLING, which consists of a number of strategies that try to achieve a tradeoff, that is, a reasonably representative sample using resources that are within the means of the ordinary researcher.

📖 Best & Kahn 2006; Dörnyei 2007; Given 2008; Mackey & Gass 2005

sampling bias
another term for SAMPLING ERROR

sampling distribution
a theoretical PROBABILITY DISTRIBUTION of a STATISTIC which is calculated from a RANDOM SAMPLE of a particular size from a POPULATION. It is a distribution that describes the variation in the values of a statistic over all possible samples. Different SAMPLE SIZEs will produce different distributions (see STANDARD ERROR OF THE MEAN). Different population distributions will also produce different sampling distributions. The distribution of the MEANs of samples, for example, can be plotted on a HISTOGRAM. This distribution in the histogram illustrates the sampling dis-

tribution of the mean. Sampling distribution is most usually associated with testing the NULL HYPOTHESIS.

📖 Cramer & Howitt 2004; Everitt & Skrondal 2010; Sahai & Khurshid 2001; Upton & Cook 2008

sampling error
also **sampling variability, sampling uncertainty, sampling bias**

the VARIABILITY of SAMPLEs from the characteristics of the POPULATION from which they come. Sampling error is the difference between the data obtained on a specific sample selected for a study and the data that would have been obtained if the entire population had been studied. When we use information from a sample to make inferences or estimates about a population PARAMETER, we lose accuracy. This is because we are estimating the value for the entire population on the basis of incomplete information from a sample, and the accuracy of our estimate will depend upon which particular sample we base our estimates on. If many samples are taken from the same population, it is unlikely that they will all have characteristics identical with each other or with the population. Sample statistics, therefore, will vary from one sample to another, simply as a matter of chance differences in the characteristics of individuals in the different samples. For example, if we take a large number of samples from the population and measure the MEAN value of each sample, then the sample means will not be identical. Some will be relatively high, some relatively low, and many will cluster around an average or mean value of the samples. This is true even if we follow careful sampling procedures to assure that our samples are representative of the population. However, the more representative the samples are of the population, the smaller the chance differences are likely to be.

The amount of sampling error in sample statistics will depend upon not only the representativeness of our samples, but also their size (see SAMPLE SIZE). As the size of a RANDOM SAMPLE increases, there is less fluctuation from one sample to another in the value of the mean. In other words, as the size of a sample increases, the expected sampling error decreases. Small samples produce more sampling error than large ones. You would expect the means based on samples of 10 to fluctuate a great deal more than the means based on samples of 100. Intuitively, it is clear that the average score of a single classroom would be a better estimate of the average of the school to which it belongs than of all the fourth graders in the district, or of all the fourth graders in an entire country. This is partly because we would expect to find lots of variation in performance from school to school in a district and from district to district within a country. This is also due to fact that a single class is a much larger sample, relative to its population, from a single school, where it might represent twenty per cent of the population, if there were five fourth grade classes, than it is from an entire district or country, where it might represent less than one per cent of the total population of fourth graders. For these reasons, sampling errors are likely to be relatively large when our estimates, or INFERENTIAL STATISTICS, are based on small samples. To put it another way, we are likely to obtain more accurate estimates of population parameters when these are based on relatively large and representative samples of the populations from which they are taken.

Sampling error is also a direct function of the STANDARD DEVIATION of the population. The more spread, or variation, there is among members of a population, the more spread there will be in sample means.

see also COVERAGE ERROR, NONRESPONSE ERROR, MARGIN OF ERROR, STANDARD ERROR OF THE MEAN

📖 Ary et al. 2010; Bachman 2004; Cohen et al. 2011; Richards & Schmidt 2010

sampling frame
also **source list**

a list of the POPULATION from which the SAMPLE will be drawn—in the sense of drawing a boundary or frame around those cases that are acceptable for inclusion in the sample. Sampling frame is usually defined by geographic listings, maps, directories, administrative records, membership lists or from telephone or other electronic formats. If the sampling frame is not available, researcher has to prepare it. Such a list should be comprehensive, correct, reliable, and appropriate. It is extremely important for the sampling frame to be as representative of the population as possible. This terminology is most common in survey SAMPLING, where it is associated with a countable listing of all the data sources in the population that are accessible for sampling. For example, a sampling frame might be all the public schools in a city. The actual sample would then be drawn from the population defined by this frame.

📖 Given 2008; Kothari 2008; Ritchie & Lewis 2003

sampling plan
see POPULATION

sampling statistics
another term for INFERENTIAL STATISTICS

sampling uncertainty
another term for SAMPLING ERROR

sampling unit
a unit that is included in, or excluded from, an analysis. Sampling units are units of selection. It is not necessarily the unit of observation or

study. A decision has to be taken concerning a sampling unit before selecting SAMPLE. There are five kinds of sampling units:

- *physical units* (e.g., time, place, size);
- *syntactical units* (words, grammar, sentences, paragraphs, chapters, series etc.);
- *categorical units* (members of a category have something in common);
- *propositional units* (delineating particular constructions or propositions);
- *thematic units* (putting texts into themes and combinations of categories).

The researcher will have to decide one or more of such units that s/he has to select for his/her study.
 Cohen et al. 2011

sampling variability
another term for SAMPLING ERROR

sampling without replacement
another term for SIMPLE RANDOM SAMPLING

sampling with replacement
another term for SIMPLE RANDOM SAMPLING

SAQ
an abbreviation for SELF-ADMINISTERED QUESTIONNAIRE

SAS
an abbreviation for 'Statistical Analysis Software'. It is one of several widely used statistical packages for manipulating and analyzing data.
see also SPSS
 Cramer & Howitt 2004

satisficing
a term that is a blend of *satisfy* and *suffice*. In SURVEY RESEARCH respondents must execute four stages of cognitive processing to answer survey questions optimally. Respondents must (1) interpret the intended meaning of the question, (2) retrieve relevant information from memory, (3) integrate the information into a summary judgment, and (4) map the judgment onto the response options offered. When respondents diligently perform each of these four steps, they are said to be optimizing. However, instead of seeking to optimize, respondents may choose to perform one or

more of the steps in a cursory fashion, or they may skip one or more steps altogether.

Respondents who devote less-than-optimal effort to the task of answering questions can engage in weak or strong satisficing. Weak satisficing occurs when a respondent performs all four cognitive steps but performs one or more of these less carefully or attentively than is needed to optimize. A respondent implementing weak satisficing may be less thoughtful in inferring the intended meaning of a question, less thorough in searching memory for all relevant information, less balanced in integrating the retrieved information into a summary judgment, and more haphazard in selecting the appropriate response option from the list offered. Strong satisficing occurs when a respondent skips the retrieval and judgment steps altogether and seeks merely to identify a plausible answer based on cues provided by the question, without reference to any internal psychological cues directly relevant to the attitude, belief, or event of interest to the researcher. If no cues pointing to such an answer are immediately evident in a question, a satisficing respondent may choose a response at random. Strong satisficing allows a respondent to provide a reasonable and seemingly defensible answer while applying very little effort. An individual's response to any given question can fall somewhere along a continuum ranging from optimizing at one end to strong satisficing at the other.

The likelihood a survey respondent will satisfice is a function of the respondent's ability to perform the cognitive tasks of optimizing, the respondent's motivation to perform the tasks, and the difficulty of the tasks. Satisficing should be more common when the respondent has less ability to optimize, when the respondent is less motivated to optimize, and when the tasks are more difficult.

📖 Lavrakas 2008

saturation

(in QUALITATIVE RESEARCH) the point when additional data do not seem to develop the concepts any further but simply repeat what previous information have already revealed. In other words, saturation is the point when the researcher becomes empirically confident that s/he has all the data needed to answer the research question. In practice, however, researchers usually decide when to stop adding cases to a study based on a combination of theoretical saturation and pragmatic considerations such as available time and money.

see also ITERATION

📖 Dörnyei 2007

scale

another term for MEASUREMENT SCALE

scale analysis
see CUMULATIVE SCALE

scale of measurement
another term for MEASUREMENT SCALE

scalogram analysis
see CUMULATIVE SCALE

scatter diagram
another term for SCATTERPLOT

scattergram
another term for SCATTERPLOT

scatterplot
also **scattergram, scatter diagram, bivariate distribution**
a graphic representation of the data along two dimensions in which the values of one VARIABLE are represented on the vertical axis (sometimes called Y axis) and the values of the other are represented on the horizontal axis (sometimes called X axis). In fact, the scores on one variable are plotted against scores on a second variable. Each value computed contributes one point to the scatterplot, on which points are plotted but not joined. The resulting pattern indicates the type and strength of the relationship between the two variables. The scatterplot will give you an indication of whether your variables are related in a linear (straight-line) (see LINEARITY) or curvilinear (see CURVILINEARITY) fashion. Only linear relationships are suitable for CORRELATION analyses. If the resulting plotted points appear in a scattered and random arrangement, then no association is indicated. If, however, they fall into a linear arrangement, a relationship can be assumed, either positive or negative. The closer the points are to a perfect line, the stronger the association. When the relationship can be characterized by a straight line (REGRESSION LINE), it is called a **linear correlation** or **relationship**. Whereas the SLOPE of the regression line indicates whether a computed r value is a positive or negative number, the magnitude of r reflects how close the data points (i.e., dots on the graph) fall in relation to the regression line. When $r = +1$ or $r = -1$, all of the data points fall on the regression line. As the value of r deviates from 1 and moves toward 0, the data points deviate further and further from the regression line. Figure S.1 depicts a variety of hypothetical regression lines, which are presented to illustrate the relationship between the sign and value of r and the regression line. In Figure S.1 the regression lines (a), (b), (c), and (d) are positively sloped, and are thus associated with a positive correlation. Lines (e), (f), (g), and (h), on the

other hand, are negatively sloped, and are associated with a negative correlation. Note that in each graph, the closer the data points are to the regression line, the closer the value of r is to one. Thus, in graphs (a)-(h), the strength of the correlation (i.e., maximum, strong, moderate, weak) is a function of how close the data points are to the regression line. Graphs (i) and (j) in Figure S.1 depict data which result in a correlation of zero, since in both instances the distribution of data points is random and, consequently, a straight line cannot be used to describe the relationship between the two variables with any degree of accuracy. Whenever the r equals zero, the regression line will be parallel to either the X axis (as in Graph (i)) or the Y axis (as in Graph (j)), depending upon which regression line is drawn. Two other instances in which the regression line is parallel to the X axis or the Y axis are depicted in Graphs (k) and l). Both of these graphs depict data for which a value of r cannot be computed. The data depicted in graphs (k) and l) illustrate that in order to compute a coefficient of correlation, there must be variability on both the X and the Y variables. Specifically, in Graph (k) the regression line is parallel to the X axis. The configuration of the data upon which this graph is based indicates that, although there is variability with respect to subjects' scores on the X variable, there is no variability with respect to their scores on the Y variable—i.e., all of the subjects obtain the identical score on the Y variable. As a result of the latter, the computed value for the estimated population variance for the Y variable will equal zero.

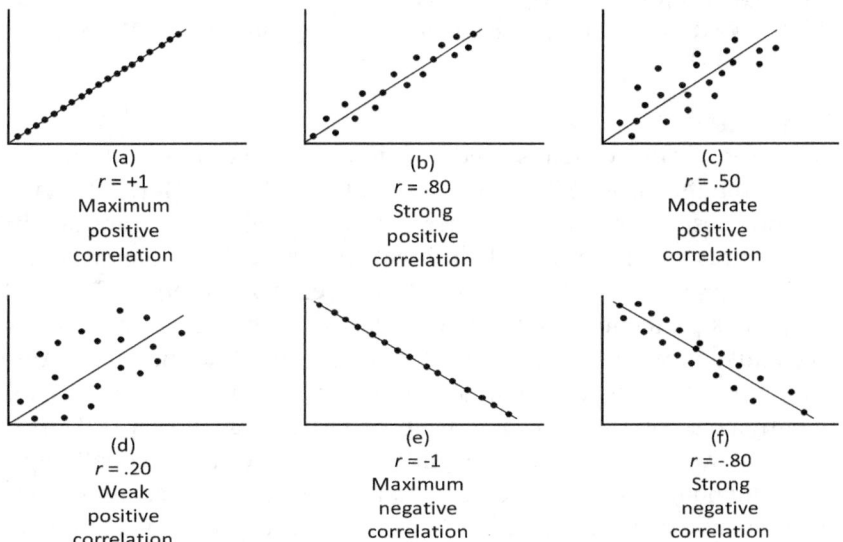

(a)
$r = +1$
Maximum
positive
correlation

(b)
$r = .80$
Strong
positive
correlation

(c)
$r = .50$
Moderate
positive
correlation

(d)
$r = .20$
Weak
positive
correlation

(e)
$r = -1$
Maximum
negative
correlation

(f)
$r = -.80$
Strong
negative
correlation

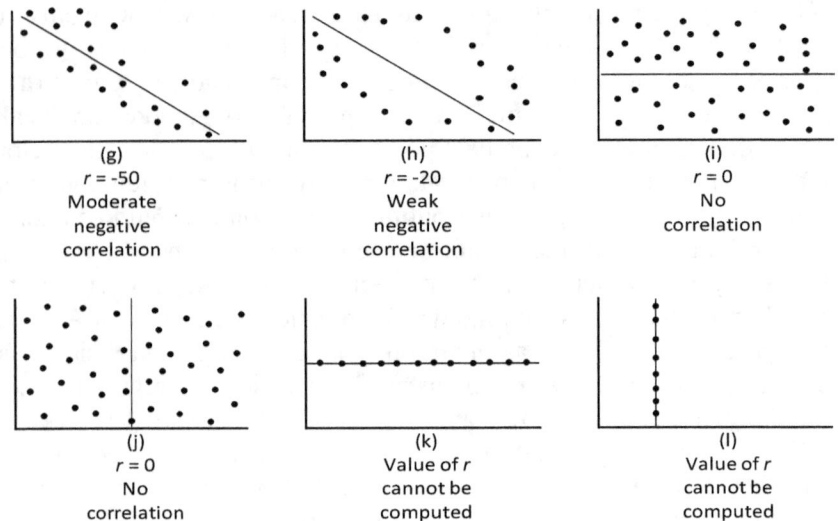

Figure S.1. Scatterplots and Correlations

Since a scatterplot is a useful summary of a set of data from two variables, it gives a good visual picture of the relationship, and aids the interpretation of the CORRELATION COEFFICIENT or REGRESSION model. Scatterplots should be presented when the relationship between two variables is of interest.

see also LINEARITY, CORRELATION

📖 Cramer & Howitt 2004; Larson-Hall 2010; Leary 2011; Porte 2010; Sheskin 2011; Walliman 2006

Scheffé test

a POST HOC TEST which is used to compare three or more MEANs following a significant F TEST in an ANALYSIS OF VARIANCE (ANOVA). The Scheffé test helps the researcher identify whether there are significant differences in the means of different groups and pinpoint where those differences are really located. The test is very *conservative*. That is, it has enormous protection against TYPE I ERRORs, because it was designed for the situation where the researcher wishes to make all possible PAIRWISE COMPARISONs plus all possible NONPAIRWISE COMPARISONs. It is sufficiently conservative that there is no point in conducting it if the original F RATIO was not statistically significant. Scheffé test is equally applicable with both equal and unequal SAMPLE SIZEs. It can accommodate unequal sample sizes and is quite ROBUST with respect to violations of the ASSUMPTIONS underlying the ANOVA (i.e., HOMOGENEITY OF VARIANCE and NORMALITY of the underlying POPULATION distributions).

📖 Huck 2012; Porte 2010

school survey

an assessment and evaluation study which is used to gather detailed information for judging the effectiveness of instructional facilities, curriculum, learning process, teaching and supervisory personnel, and financial resources in terms of best practices and standards in education. Some SURVEYs are concerned with legal, administrative, social, or physical settings for learning. Information can be obtained around the characteristics of teachers, supervisors, administrators, and students. Factors such as motivation, attitude, educational background, socio-economic status, and life conditions can be included in school surveys. Furthermore, the characteristics of the educational process including curriculum planning, methods and strategies of teaching, materials development, and textbook evaluation can be researched through school surveys.

 Best & Kahn 2006; Farhady 1995

scientific method

a methodological and systematic approach to the acquisition of new knowledge. The scientific method is founded on direct observation and driven by the formulation of research questions, the collection of data, and the analysis and interpretation of data within a theoretical framework. In other words, scientific method is based on objective data that were reliably and validly obtained in the context of a carefully designed research study. Some versions of the scientific method include prediction in the form of a research HYPOTHESIS which is put to a test through prediction and experimentation. Others explore some phenomena prior to the development of any hypothesis and seek to answer research questions without testing any hypothesis.

see also INDUCTIVE REASONING, DEDUCTIVE REASONING, QUALITATIVE RESEARCH, QUANTITATIVE RESEARCH

 Richards & Schmidt 2010; Ridenour & Newman 2008

scientific realism

a term applied to the framework used by most researchers who take a purely quantitative approach to research (see QUANTITATIVE RESEARCH). Scientific realists strive to establish cause-and-effect relationships where possible, using data collection methods such as QUESTIONNAIREs, TESTs, and observational CHECKLISTs to produce quantitative data. The philosophical underpinnings of the scientific realism approach can be found in the positivist arguments (see POSITIVISM) developed primarily to describe knowledge generation in the physical sciences. The first assumption made by scientific realists is that there is a real social and psychological world that can be accurately captured through research. Put another way, there is an objective reality that research aims to describe. Scientific realists further assume that the social and psychological world can be studied in much the same way as the natural world by breaking complex phenomena and problems into smaller parts (CONSTRUCTs and VARIABLEs). The major job for the researcher is to identify the most important parts or variables and accurately describe how these are related to each other in the real world.

However, because humans are fallible and social scientists study human characteristics, reporting that reality must be done with a certain degree of probability. Scientific realists see knowledge as conjectural and therefore subject to possible revision. All hypotheses are tested using statistical tests that establish the level of confidence that one can have in the results obtained. Scientific realists do recognize that because educators study human behaviors and characteristics, research may be influenced by the investigator. For an investigator to maintain clear objectivity, s/he must play a detached role, where there is little opportunity for interaction with the participants under study. Scientific realists believe that inquiry can be value-free and that a researcher who strives to eliminate any personal bias can reliably determine findings. Although they borrow rigorous scientific techniques from the natural sciences, they recognize that in education and psychology, true scientific experiments are not always possible. Scientific realists concede that different persons might have different perceptions of reality; however, they assume that experiences overlap to a large degree and that a good researcher can take these different perceptions into account in providing the best possible explanation of reality.

see also SUBTLE REALISM, ANALYTIC REALISM, CRITICAL REALISM, NAIVE REALISM

📖 Lodico et al. 2010

scree diagram
also scree plot

a diagram (see Figure S.2) which is used in the PRINCIPAL COMPONENTS ANALYSIS to provide a visual aid for determining the number of factors that explain most of the variability in the data set. The following diagram shows the percentage of total variance which is accounted for by each of nine successively extracted factors.

📖 Sahai & Khurshid 2001

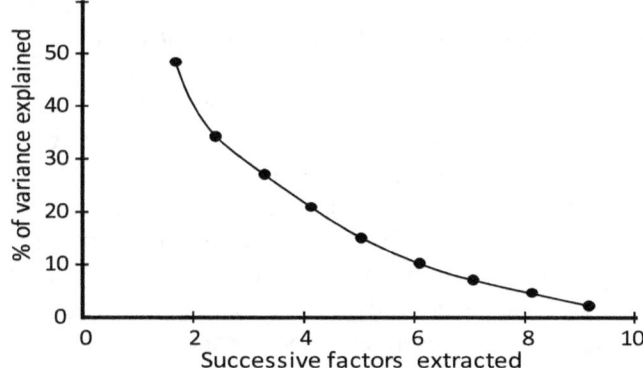

Figure S.2. An Example of a Scree Diagram

scree plot
  another term for SCREE DIAGRAM

secondary research
  also **library research**
a type of research which is based on sources or data that are one step removed from the original information, i.e., they refer to the sources and data which have already been collected and analyzed by someone else. When the researcher utilizes secondary data, then s/he has to look into various sources from where s/he can obtain data. Secondary data may either be published data or unpublished them. Usually published data are available in: (a) various publications of the central, state are local governments; (b) various publications of foreign governments or of international bodies and their subsidiary organizations; (c) technical and trade journals; (d) books, magazines and newspapers; (e) reports and publications of various associations connected with business and industry, banks, stock exchanges, etc.; (f) reports prepared by research scholars, universities, economists, etc. in different fields; and (g) public records and statistics, historical documents, and other sources of published information. The sources of unpublished data are many; they may be found in diaries, letters, unpublished biographies and autobiographies and also may be available with scholars and research workers, trade associations, labor bureaus and other public/private individuals and organizations.
By way of caution, the researcher, before using secondary data, must see that they possess following characteristics:

1) *Reliability of data*: The reliability can be tested by finding out such things about the said data: (a) Who collected the data? (b) What were the sources of data? (c) Were they collected by using proper methods

(d) At what time were they collected? (e) Was there any bias of the compiler? (f) What level of accuracy was desired? Was it achieved?
2) *Suitability of data*: The data that are suitable for one enquiry may not necessarily be found suitable in another enquiry. Hence, if the available data are found to be unsuitable, they should not be used by the researcher. In this context, the researcher must very carefully scrutinize the definition of various terms and units of collection used at the time of collecting the data from the primary source originally. Similarly, the object, scope and nature of the original enquiry must also be studied. If the researcher finds differences in these, the data will remain unsuitable for the present enquiry and should not be used.
3) *Adequacy of data*: If the level of accuracy achieved in data is found inadequate for the purpose of the present enquiry, they will be considered as inadequate and should not be used by the researcher. The data will also be considered inadequate, if they are related to an area which may be either narrower or wider than the area of the present enquiry.

Secondary research is often contrasted with **primary research**, which is a type of research in which researchers gather original data (primary data) to answer a particular research question. When researchers gather firsthand data, the outcome is knowledge nobody had before.
see also PRIMARY RESEARCH
 Dörnyei 2007; Kothari 2008; Mckay 2006; Trochim & Donnelly 2007

secondary variance
another term for ERROR VARIANCE

selected-response item
also receptive response item
a type of test item or test task that requires test takers to choose answers from a ready-made list rather than providing an answer. The most commonly used types of selected-response items include MULTIPLE-CHOICE ITEMS, TRUE/FALSE ITEMs, and MATCHING ITEMs.
see also CONSTRUCTED-RESPONSE ITEM
 Brown 2005; Cohen & Swerdlik 2010; Richards & Schmidt 2010

selection bias
another term for DIFFERENTIAL SELECTION

selection error
an error that arises when the research is carried out on a SAMPLE of subjects rather than an entire POPULATION. Three types of selection error can

be distinguished: COVERAGE ERROR, SAMPLING ERROR, and NONRESPONSE ERROR.
 Corbetta 2003; O'Leary 2004

selection-maturation interaction
a threat to INTERNAL VALIDITY which is the result of some of the threats that may interact to affect internal validity. For example, DIFFERENTIAL SELECTION and MATURATION may interact in such a way that the combination results in an effect on the DEPENDENT VARIABLE that is mistakenly attributed to the effect of the experimental treatment. Such interaction may occur in a QUASI-EXPERIMENTAL DESIGN in which the EXPERIMENTAL and CONTROL GROUPs are not randomly selected but instead are preexisting INTACT GROUPs, such as classrooms. Although a pretest may indicate that the groups are equivalent at the beginning of the experiment, the experimental group may have a higher rate of maturation than the control group, and the increased rate of maturation accounts for the observed effect. If more rapidly maturing students are selected into the experimental group, the selection-maturation interaction may be mistaken for the effect of the experimental variable.
Selection-maturation interaction can be a particularly difficult problem when volunteers are compared with nonvolunteers. For example, suppose you offer an after-school reading improvement program to those who wish it. Reading pretest means show no difference between those who volunteer for the after-school program and those who do not. If the posttreatment scores show greater gain for the treatment group than for the control group, you cannot confidently attribute the greater gain to the treatment. It is quite possible that students who were willing to participate in the after-school program were more concerned about their reading or their parents were more concerned about their reading and they were therefore more likely to show greater gain in reading whether they received treatment or not.
 Ary et al. 2010; Cook & Campbell 1979

selection-treatment interaction
a major threat to EXTERNAL VALIDITY of experiments is the possibility of interaction between subject characteristics and TREATMENT so that the results found for certain kinds of subjects may not hold for different subjects. This interaction occurs when the subjects in a study are not representative of the larger POPULATION to which one may want to generalize. When two experimentally accessible populations are not representative of the same target population, seemingly similar studies can lead to entirely different results. For example, teaching method A may produce better results than method B in inner-city high schools, whereas method B is superior in affluent suburban high schools. Or, the best method for teaching

second language vocabulary among fourth-graders may be the worst method among first-graders. As the old saying goes, 'One man's meat is another man's poison.' Again, a thorough description of the accessible population will help other researchers judge whether a particular treatment is likely to be 'meat or poison' for their populations of interest.
📖 Ary et al. 2010; Cook & Campbell 1979

selective coding
see CODING

self-administered questionnaire
also SAQ
a QUESTIONNAIRE that has been designed specifically to be completed by a respondent without intervention of the researchers collecting the data. A self-administered questionnaire (SAQ) is usually a stand-alone questionnaire though it can also be used in conjunction with other data collection modalities directed by a trained interviewer. Traditionally the SAQ has been distributed by mail (see MAIL SURVEY) or in person to large groups, but now SAQs are being used extensively for WEB SURVEYs. Because the SAQ is completed without ongoing feedback from a trained interviewer, special care must be taken in how the questions are worded as well as how the questionnaire is formatted in order to avoid measurement error.
📖 Lavrakas 2008

self-deception
a problem to QUESTIONNAIRE which is related to SOCIAL DESIRABILITY BIAS but in this case respondents do not deviate from the truth consciously but rather because they also deceive themselves (and not just the researcher). Human defense mechanisms cushion failures, minimize faults, and maximize virtues so that we maintain a sense of personal worth. People with personality problems might simply be unable to give an accurate self-description, but the problem of self-delusion may be present on a more general scale, though to a lesser degree, affecting many other people.
📖 Dörnyei 2003

semantic differential scale
also SD scale, bipolar scale
a variation of a RATING SCALE which asks respondents to choose between two opposite positions. Semantic differential (SD) scale operates by putting an adjective at one end of a scale and its opposite at the other (Table. S.1). For example, for the following item respondents indicate their opinion by putting a mark on that position on the scale which most represents what they feel.

Research methodology texts are:

	Very Much	Somewhat	Neither	Somewhat	very much	
Teacher-centered	☐	☐	☐	☐	☐	Learner-centerd
Informative	☐	☐	☐	☐	☐	Uninformative
Traditional	☐	☐	☐	☐	☐	Modern
Enjoyable	☐	☐	☐	☐	☐	Unenjoyable
Cheap	☐	☐	☐	☐	☐	Expensive
Simple	☐	☐	☐	☐	☐	Complex
Useful	☐	☐	☐	☐	☐	Useless

Table S.1. An Example of Semantic Differential Scale

The SD scale is an attempt to measure the psychological meanings of an object to an individual. This scale is based on the presumption that an object can have different dimensions of connotative meanings which can be located in multidimensional property space, or what can be called the semantic space in the context of SD scale. These are very useful in that by using them we can avoid writing statements (which is not always easy); instead, respondents are asked to indicate their answers by marking a continuum between two bipolar adjectives on the extremes. These scales are based on the recognition that most adjectives have logical opposites and where an opposing adjective is not obviously available, one can easily be generated with 'in-' or 'un-' or by simply writing 'not'. Although the scope of SD scales is more limited than that of LIKERT SCALEs, the ease of their construction and the fact that the method is easily adaptable to study virtually any concept, activity, or person, may compensate for this. By their more imaginative approach, such scales can be used to cover aspects that respondents can hardly put into words, though they do reflect an attitude or feeling. An additional bonus of SD scales is that because they involve little reading, very little testing time is required.

SD scales are similar to Likert scales in that several items are used to evaluate the same target, and multi-item scores are computed by summing up the individual item scores. An important technical point concerning the construction of such bipolar scales is that the position of the negative and positive poles, if they can be designated as such, should be varied (i.e., the positive pole should alternate between being on the right and the left sides) to avoid superficial responding or a position response set.

The general conclusion is that there are three major factors of meaning involved in SD scales:

• evaluation, referring to the overall positive meaning associated with the target (e.g., good-bad, wise-foolish, honest-dishonest);

- potency, referring to the targets overall strength or importance (e.g., strong-weak, hard-soft, useful-useless); and
- activity, referring to the extent to which the target is associated with action (active-passive, tense-relaxed, quick-slow).

The SD scale has a number of specific advantages. It is an efficient and easy way to secure attitudes from a large sample. These attitudes may be measured in both direction and intensity. The total set of responses provides a comprehensive picture of the meaning of an object, as well as a measure of the subject doing the rating. It is a standardized technique that is easily repeated, but escapes many of the problems of response distortion found with more direct methods.
see DIFFERENTIAL SCALE, CUMULATIVE SCALE, ARBITRARY SCALE
📖 Dörnyei 2003; Kothari 2008

semi-interquartile range
see INTERQUARTILE RANGE

semi-partial correlation coefficient
a CORRELATION COEFFICIENT similar to the PARTIAL CORRELATION but with the difference that the effect of the third VARIABLE is only removed from the DEPENDENT VARIABLE (DV). The INDEPENDENT VARIABLE (IV) would not be adjusted. Normally, the influence of the third variable is removed from both the IV and the DV in partial correlation. For example, imagine we find that there is a relationship between intelligence and second language (L2) proficiency of .50. Intelligence is our IV and L2 proficiency our DV for the present purpose. We then find out that social class is correlated with L2 proficiency at a level .30. In other words, some of the variation in L2 proficiency is due to social class. If we remove the variation due to social class from the variable L2 proficiency, we have left L2 proficiency without the influence of social class. So the correlation of intelligence with L2 proficiency adjusted for social class is the semi-partial correlation. But there is also a correlation of social class with our IV intelligence—say that this is the higher the intelligence, the higher the social class. Partial correlation would take off this shared variation between intelligence and social class from the intelligence scores. By not doing this, semi-partial correlation leaves the variation of intelligence associated with social class still in the intelligence scores. Hence, we end up with a semi-partial correlation in which intelligence is exactly the variable it was when we measured it and unadjusted any way. However, L2 proficiency has been adjusted for social class and is different from the original measure of L2 proficiency.

Semi-partial correlation coefficients are rarely presented in reports of statistical analyses but they are an important component of MULTIPLE REGRESSION.
 Cramer & Howitt 2004

semi-structured interview
an INTERVIEW in which the researcher has a clearer idea about the questions that are to be asked but is not necessarily concerned about the exact wording, or the order in which they are to be asked. It is likely that the interviewer will have a list of questions to be asked in the course of the interview. It incorporates elements of both quantifiable, fixed-choice responding and the facility to explore, and probe in more depth, certain areas of interest. The interviewer will allow the conversation to flow comparatively freely but will tend to steer it in such a way that s/he can introduce specific questions when the opportunity arises. The order in which the various topics are dealt with and the wording of the questions are left to the interviewer's discretion. Within each topic, the interviewer is free to conduct the conversation as s/he thinks fit, to ask the questions s/he deems appropriate in the words s/he considers best, to give explanations and ask for clarification if the answer is not clear, to prompt the respondent to elucidate further if necessary, and to establish his/her own style of conversation. The interviewers outline may contain varying degrees of specification and detail. It may simply be a CHECKLIST of the topics to be dealt with, or a list of questions (usually of a general nature) having the goal of supplying the interviewer with guidelines.
In applied linguistics research most interviews conducted belong to the semi-structured interview type, which offers a compromise between the STRUCTURED and UNSTRUCTURED INTERVIEWS. Therefore, this type of interview carries with it the advantages of both approaches (generally easy to analyze, quantify and compare, but allowing interviewees to explain their responses and to provide more in-depth information where necessary) as well as the disadvantages (the temptation to spend too long on peripheral subjects, the danger of losing control to the interviewee, and the reduction in reliability when using non-standardized approaches to interview each respondent).
see also ETHNOGRAPHIC INTERVIEW, NON-DIRECTIVE INTERVIEW, STRUCTURED INTERVIEW, INTERVIEW GUIDE, INFORMAL INTERVIEW, TELEPHONE INTERVIEW, FOCUS GROUP
 Brewerton & Millward 2001; Corbetta 2003; Dörnyei 2007; Mackey & Gass 2005; Perry 2011

semi-structured observation
see OBSERVATION

sentence completion item
see FILL-IN ITEM

separate-sample pretest-posttest control group design
a QUASI-EXPERIMENTAL DESIGN which is used in those settings in which the TREATMENT (denoted by X), if presented at all, must be presented to the group as a whole. If there are comparable (if not equivalent) groups from which X can be withheld, then a CONTROL GROUP can be added to SEPARATE-SAMPLE PRETEST-POSTTEST DESIGN, as represented below (where O denotes pretest and posttest):

$$O\ (X)$$
$$\underline{\quad\quad X\ O\quad}$$
$$O$$
$$\quad\quad O$$

The weakness of the design for INTERNAL VALIDITY comes from the possibility of mistaking for an effect of X a specific local trend in the experimental group which is, in fact, unrelated. By increasing the number of the units involved (e.g., schools) and by assigning them in some number and with RANDOMIZATION to the experimental and control treatments, the one source of invalidity can be removed, and a true experiment, like PRETEST-POSTTEST CONTROL GROUP DESIGN except for avoiding the retesting of specific individuals, can be achieved.
see also NONEQUIVALENT CONTROL GROUP DESIGN, TIME-SERIES DESIGN, EQUIVALENT MATERIAL DESIGN, COUNTERBALANCED DESIGN, RECURRENT INSTITUTIONAL CYCLE DESIGN
📖 Campbell & Stanley 1963

separate-sample pretest-posttest design
also **split subjects pretest posttest, simulated before-and-after design**
a QUASI-EXPERIMENTAL DESIGN which used for large POPULATIONs, such as schools where although one cannot randomly segregate subgroups for differential experimental TREATMENTs, one can exercise something like full experimental control over the when and to whom of the measurement (O), employing RANDOM ASSIGNMENT procedures. Such control makes possible this design:

$$\underline{\quad O\ (X)\quad\quad}$$
$$\quad\quad X\quad O$$

In this diagram, rows represent randomly equivalent subgroups, the parenthetical X standing for a presentation of the treatment irrelevant to the argument. One sample is measured prior to the treatment (*X*), an equivalent one subsequent to *X*. While it has been called the simulated before-and-after design, it is well to note its superiority over the ordinary before-and-after design, through its control of both the main effect of *testing* and the interaction of testing with *X*. The main weakness of the design is its failure to control for HISTORY.

see also NONEQUIVALENT CONTROL GROUP DESIGN, TIME-SERIES DESIGN, EQUIVALENT MATERIAL DESIGN, COUNTERBALANCED DESIGN, RECURRENT INSTITUTIONAL CYCLE DESIGN, SEPARATE-SAMPLE PRETEST-POSTTEST CONTROL GROUP DESIGN, TESTING EFFECT

📖 Campbell & Stanley 1963

sequencing effect
another term for ORDER EFFECT

sequential multiple regression
also hierarchical multiple regression

a type of MULTIPLE REGRESSION where all of the areas of the INDEPENDENT VARIABLEs or predictors that overlap with the DEPENDENT VARIABLE or criterion will be counted, but the way that they will be included depends on the order in which the researcher enters the variables into the equation. This means that the researcher will be entering the variables in steps or blocks in a predetermined order (not letting the computer decide, as would be the case for STEPWISE REGRESSION). Each predictor variable is assessed at its own point of entry in terms of the additional explanatory power it contributes to the equation. The order in which variables are entered into the model is normally dictated by logical or theoretical considerations. The order of entry can often make a difference as to whether they will be found to be statistical predictors. Therefore, the importance of hours of study (in the example given under the entry for STANDARD MULTIPLE REGRESSION) will increase with sequential regression if it is entered first, because it will account for both areas *a* and *b* (as shown in Figure S.3). If Modern Language Aptitude Test (MLAT) score is added second, it will account for even more of the VARIANCE than it did in standard regression because it will be able to claim areas *c* and *d*.

The importance of any variable, therefore, can be emphasized in sequential regression, depending on the order in which it is entered. If two variables overlap to a large degree, then entering one of them first will leave little room for explanation for the second variable. Therefore researchers are advised to assign the order of variables depending on a theoretical or logical reason.

📖 Ho 2006; Larson-Hall 2010

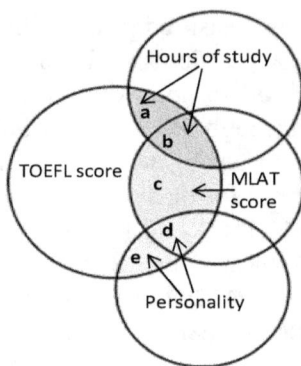

Figure S.3 Schematic Representation of a Sequential Regression Design

sequential sampling
 also theoretical sampling
a type of NON-PROBABILITY SAMPLING in which the researcher samples incidents, people or units on the basis of their potential contribution to the development and testing of theoretical constructs. The process is *iterative*: the researcher picks an initial SAMPLE in a given time interval, conducts his/her study, analyzes the data, and then selects a further sample in order to refine his/her emerging categories and theories. This process is continued until the researcher reaches data SATURATION or a point when no new insights would be obtained from expanding the sample further. Sequential sampling is similar to PURPOSIVE SAMPLING with one difference. In purposive sampling, the researcher tries to find as many relevant cases as possible, until time, financial resources, or his/her energy is exhausted. The goal is to get every possible case. In sequential sampling, however, a researcher continues to gather cases until the amount of new information or diversity of cases is filled. This sampling technique gives the researcher limitless chances of fine tuning his/her research methods and gaining a vital insight into the study that s/he is currently pursuing. The ultimate SAMPLE SIZE under this technique is thus not fixed in advance, but depends on the actual observations and varies from one sample to another.

This sampling method is hardly representative of the entire population. Further, the sampling technique is also hardly randomized. This contributes to the very little degree representativeness of the sampling technique. In addition, this kind of sampling often results in much fewer observations than would be required if the sample size were fixed in order to provide the same control over TYPE I and TYPE II ERRORS. Due to such disadvantages, results from this sampling technique cannot be used to create conclusions and interpretations pertaining to the entire population.

Sequential sampling is mainly associated with the development of GROUNDED THEORY.

see also CONVENIENCE SAMPLING, QUOTA SAMPLING, DIMENSIONAL SAMPLING, PURPOSIVE SAMPLING, SNOWBALL SAMPLING, VOLUNTEER SAMPLING, OPPORTUNISTIC SAMPLING

📖 Cohen et al. 2011; Dörnyei 2007; Kothari 2008; Neuman 2007; Ridenour & Newman 2008; Ritchie & Lewis 2003; Sahai & Khurshid 2001; Upton & Cook 2008

serial correlation

the term is used to describe the CORRELATION between pairs of measurements on the same subject in a LONGITUDINAL STUDY. The magnitude of such correlation usually depends on the time lag between the measurements; as the time lag increases, the correlation usually becomes weaker. In a TIME-SERIES DESIGN analysis, the term is used to refer to the correlation between observations that either lead or lag by a specified time interval.

see also AUTOCORRELATION

📖 Everitt & Skrondal 2010; Sahai & Khurshid 2001; Upton & Cook 2008

severity error

see RATING ERROR

Shapiro-Wilk test

see NORMALITY

short-answer item

an OPEN-FORM ITEM that, unlike FILL-IN ITEM, requires responses that may be a few phrases or sentences long, and there is no PROMPT. There are two types of short-answer questions: **specific open question**s and **broad open question**s. First, specific open questions ask about particular pieces of information and can usually be answered in one or two lines, often explicitly marked on the QUESTIONNAIRE with dots or lines. Below is an example of a specific open question:

What type of English activities are your students most receptive to?
....
....

Second, broad open questions allow for a deeper exploration of one (and preferably only one) issue and they generate more expansive, and often unpredicted, responses. Effective broad open questions prompt the respondent to write a succinct answer of more than a phrase and up to a paragraph (or two at the most). These questions should not require the respondent to write too lengthy a response—most respondents do not have the time to do so, and may object to such an expectation. Broad open questions are followed by a blank space where respondents can write their ideas in their own words. Examples of broad open questions could include the following:

Why do you use communicative activities in your class?
What do your students find most challenging in preparing for the university entrance English examinations?

📖 Best & Kahn 2006; Dörnyei 2003; Given 2008; Perry 2011

SI
an abbreviation for SYMBOLIC INTERACTIONISM

Siegel-Tukey test
a NONPARAMETRIC TEST for testing the EQUALITY OF VARIANCEs of two POPULATIONs having the common MEDIAN. The Siegel-Tukey test is based on the following ASSUMPTIONS:

a) Each SAMPLE has been randomly selected from the population it represents;
b) The two samples are independent of one another;
c) The level of measurement the data represent is at least ordinal; and
d) The two populations from which the samples are derived have equal medians.

If the latter assumption is violated, but the researcher does know the values of the population medians, the scores in the groups can be adjusted so as to allow the use of the Siegel-Tukey test. When, however, the population medians are unknown, and one is unwilling to assume they are equal, the Siegel-Tukey test is not the appropriate nonparametric test of dispersion to employ
see also MOSES TEST, KLOTZ TEST, ANSARI-BRADLEY TEST, CONOVER TEST
📖 Everitt & Skrondal 2010; Sahai & Khurshid 2001; Sheskin 2011

sigma (σ)
an abbreviation for POPULATION STANDARD DEVIATION

sigma squared (σ^2)
an abbreviation for POPULATION VARIANCE

sigma (Σ)
a summation sign

signal-contingent design
see DIARY STUDY

signed-ranks test
another term for WILCOXON MATCHED-PAIRS SIGNED-RANKS TEST

significance level
also **level of significance, alpha (α) level, alpha (α), rejection level**
a predetermined value which is chosen by the researcher and used to judge whether a test statistic is statistically significant. Significance level is traditionally symbolized by 'α' (the lowercase Greek letter alpha). Alpha represents an acceptable PROBABILITY of making a TYPE I ERROR in a statistical test. It is set at the beginning of an experiment and limits the probability of making a Type I error. In other words, it is the probability of a Type I error that an investigator is willing to risk in rejecting a NULL HYPOTHESIS. Because alpha corresponds to a probability, it can range from 0 to 1. In practice, .01 and .05 are the most commonly used values for alpha which represent a 1% and 5% chance of a Type I error occurring, depending on whether the researcher is willing to accept only one percent of error (99 per cent confidence level) or tolerate up to 5 percent error (95 per cent confidence level), respectively. If the *P*-VALUE of a test is equal to or less than the chosen level of alpha, it is deemed statistically significant; otherwise it is not.
Sometimes alpha levels of .1 are used, which is a more lenient standard; alpha levels greater than .1 are rarely if ever used. All things being equal, **standard error**s will be larger in smaller data sets, so it may make sense to choose .1 for alpha in a smaller data set. Similarly, in large data sets (hundreds of thousands of observations or more), it is not uncommon for nearly every test to be significant at the alpha .05 level; therefore the more stringent level of .01 is often used (or even .001 in some instances). When multiple tests are performed, investigators sometimes use corrections, such as the BONFERRONI CORRECTION, to adjust for this. In and of itself, specifying a stringent alpha (e.g., .01 or .001) is not a guarantee of anything. In particular, if a statistical model is misspecified, alpha does not change that. In tabular presentation of results, different symbols are often used to denote significance at different values of alpha (e.g., one asterisk for .05, two asterisks for .01, three asterisks for .001). When *p*-values of tests are reported, it is redundant also to state significance at a given alpha.
Best practice is to specify alpha before analyzing data. Specifying alpha after performing an analysis opens one up to the temptation to tailor significance levels to fit the results. For example, if a test has a *p*-value of .07, this is not significant at the customary .05 level but it meets what sometimes is referred to as *marginal significance* at the .1 level. If one

chooses a level of alpha after running the model, nothing would prevent, in this example, an investigator from choosing .1 simply because it achieves significance. On the other hand, if alpha is specified a priori, then the investigator would have to justify choosing .1 as alpha for reasons other than simply *moving the goalpost*. Another reason to specify alpha in advance is that SAMPLE SIZE calculations require a value for alpha (or for the CONFIDENCE LEVEL).
 Brown 1988; Lavrakas 2008; Richards & Schmidt 2010

significance probability
 another term for PROBABILITY VALUE

significance test
 another term for STATISTICAL TEST

sign test
 a very simple NONPARAMETRIC TEST procedure for detecting differences in *related* or *matched* data. The sign test requires that the researcher do nothing more than classify the participants of the study into two categories. Each of the participants put into one of these categories receives a plus sign (i.e., a +); in contrast, a minus sign (i.e., -) is given to each participant who falls into the other category. The HYPOTHESIS TESTING procedure is then used to evaluate the NULL HYPOTHESIS that says the full SAMPLE of participants comes from a population in which there are as many pluses as minuses. If the sample is quite lopsided with far more pluses than minuses (or far more minuses than pluses), the sign test's H_0 is rejected. However, if the frequencies of pluses and minuses in the sample are equal or nearly equal, the null hypothesis of the sign test is retained.

The sign test can be used in any of three situations. In one situation, there is a single group of people, with each person in the group evaluated as to some characteristic (e.g., handedness) and then given or depending on his/her status on that characteristic. In the second situation, there are two matched groups; here, the two members of each pair are compared, with given to one member of each dyad (and given to his/her mate) depending on which one has more of the characteristic being considered. In the third situation, a single group is measured twice, with or given to each person depending on whether his/her second score is larger or smaller than his/her first score.

Despite its simplicity, generally the loss of information from the scores (the size of the differences being ignored) makes it a poor choice in anything other than the most exceptional circumstances.

see also WILCOXON SIGNED-RANKS TEST
 Cramer & Howitt 2004; Huck 2012

simple ANOVA
another term for ONE-WAY ANOVA

simple comparison
another term for PAIRWISE COMPARISON

simple effect
also **simple main effect**
an analysis which allows the nature of an INTERACTION between two INDEPENDENT VARIABLES (IVs) to be explored further. When there is a statistically significant interaction between two IVs, it is worth attempting to explore the nature of that interaction further. It isolates one LEVEL of one IV at a time to see how the levels of the other IV vary. Simple main effect is, in essence, a MAIN EFFECT of the variable, but one that occurs under only one level of the other variable.

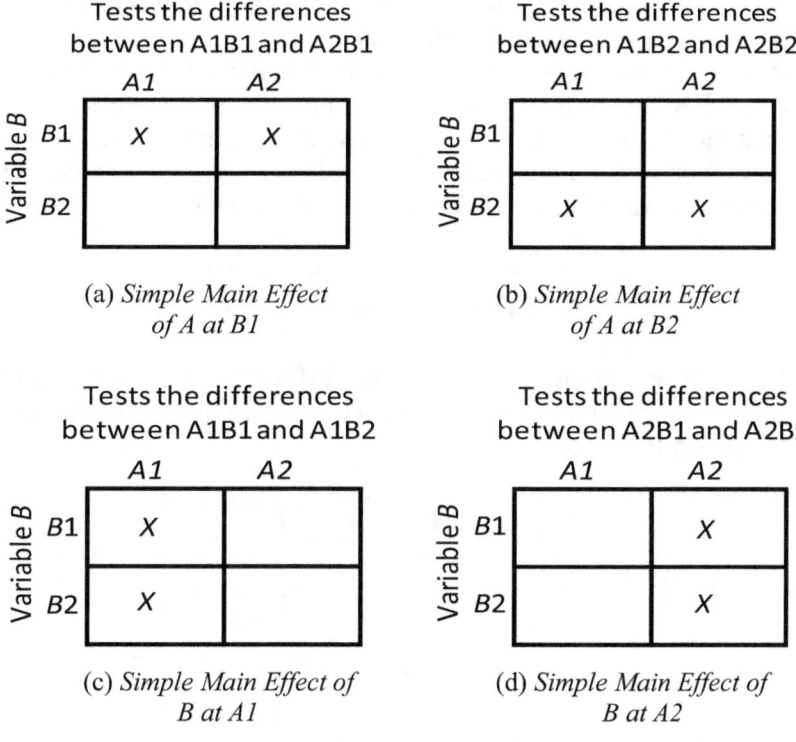

Figure S.4. Schematic Representation of Simple Effect

As shown in Figure S.4, if we obtained a significant A × B interaction, we could examine four simple main effects:

1) The simple main effect of A at $B1$. (Do the means of Conditions $A1$ and $A2$ differ for participants who received Condition $B1$?)—See Figure S.4a.
2) The simple main effect of A at $B2$ (Do the means of Conditions $A1$ and $A2$ differ for participants who received Condition $B2$?)—See Figure S.4b.
3) The simple main effect of B at $A1$. (Do the means of Conditions $B1$ and $B2$ differ for participants who received Condition $A1$?)—See Figure S.4c.
4) The simple main effect of B at A2. (Do the means of Conditions $B1$ and $B2$ differ for participants who received Condition $A2$?)—See Figure S.4d.

 Clark-Carter 2010; Leary 2011; Urdan 2010

simple frequency distribution
also regular frequency distribution

the most common way to organize scores. A simple frequency distribution shows the number of times each score occurs in a set of data. The symbol for a score's simple frequency is simply f. To find f for a score, count how many times the score occurs. If three participants scored 6, then the frequency of 6 (its f) is 3. Creating a simple frequency distribution involves counting the frequency of every score in the data. One way to see a distribution is in a table. Take the following raw scores:

14 14 13 15 11 15 13 10 12
13 14 13 14 15 17 14 14 15

In this disorganized arrangement, it is difficult to make sense out of these scores. See what happens, though, when we arrange them into the simple frequency table shown in Table S.2.

Score	f
17	1
16	0
15	4
14	6
13	4
12	1
11	1
10	1

Table S.2. Simple Frequency

Thus, the highest score is 17, the lowest score is 10, and although no one obtained a score of 16, we still include it. Opposite each score in the column is the score's frequency: In this sample there is one 17, zero 16s, four 15s, and so on. Not only can we easily see the frequency of each score, but we can also determine the combined frequency of several scores by adding together their individual fs. For example, the score of 13 has an f of 4, and the score of 14 has an f of 6, so their combined frequency is 10.

Notice that, although there are 8 scores in the score column, N is not 8. There are 18 scores in the original sample, so N is 18. You can see this by adding together the frequencies in the f column: The 1 person scoring 17 plus the 4 people scoring 15 and so on adds up to the 18 people in the sample. In a frequency distribution, the sum of the frequencies always equals N.

📖 Heiman 2011

simple interrupted time-series design
also one-group time-series design

a variation of TIME-SERIES DESIGN and a WITHIN-GROUPS DESIGN in which periodic observations (i.e., pretests) are made on a single group in an effort to establish a baseline. At some point in time, the INDEPENDENT VARIABLE (i.e., TREATMENT) is introduced, and it is followed by additional periodic measurements (i.e., posttests) to determine whether a change in the DEPENDENT VARIABLE (DV) occurs. The more immediate the change in the DV, the more likely that the change is due to the influence of the independent variable. This design can be represented graphically as follows (where O_1, O_2, O_3, O_4 = pretest, O_5, O_6, O_7, O_8 = posttest, and X = treatment):

$O_1 \quad O_2 \quad O_3 \quad O_4 \quad X \quad O_5 \quad O_6 \quad O_7 \quad O_8$

A simple interrupted time-series design might be used in a school or university setting to study the effects of a major change in administrative policy on disciplinary incidents. Or, a study might involve repeated measurements of students' attitudes and the effect produced by introducing a documentary film designed to change attitudes. Figure S.5 illustrates some possible patterns from time-series studies into which an experimental treatment is introduced. It shows the series of measurements O_1 through O_8, with the introduction of the experimental treatment at point X. You can assess the effect of the X by examining the stability of the repeated measurements.

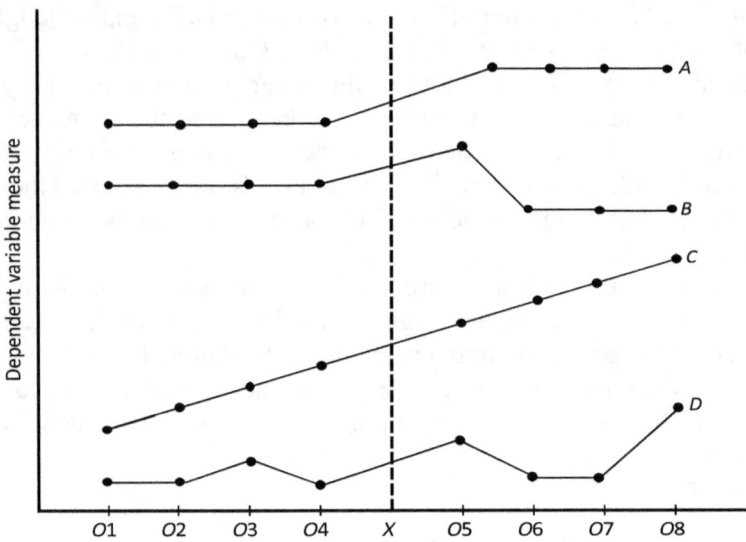

Figure S.5. Simple Interrupted Time-Series Design

From examining the difference between O_4 and O_5 in pattern A in Figure S.5, perhaps you would be justified in assuming that X affects the DV. Pattern B suggests the possibility of a temporary experimental effect of X. However, you could not assume that X produces the change in either pattern C or pattern D. Pattern C appears to result from MATURATION or a similar influence. The erratic nature of pattern D suggests the operation of EXTRANEOUS VARIABLEs.

The major weakness of this design is its failure to control HISTORY; that is, you cannot rule out the possibility that it is not X but, rather, some simultaneous event that produces the observed change. You must also consider the EXTERNAL VALIDITY of the time design. Because there are repeated tests, perhaps there is a kind of interaction of TESTING EFFECT that would restrict the findings to those populations subject to repeated testing. However, as long as the measurements are of a typical, routine type used in school settings, this is not likely to be a serious limitation. Furthermore, a SELECTION-TREATMENT INTERACTION may occur, especially if you select some particular group that may not be typical.

📖 Ary et al. 2010; Cook & Campbell 1966; Marczyk et al. 2005; Seliger & Shohamy 1989

simple linear regression
another term for SIMPLE REGRESSION

simple mixed design
see MIXED DESIGN

simple random sampling
also **chance sampling**

a type of PROBABILITY SAMPLING in which each member of the POPULATION under study has an equal chance of being selected and the probability of a member of the population being selected is unaffected by the selection of other members of the population, i.e., each selection is entirely independent of the next. As shown in Figure S.6, the method involves selecting at random from a list of the population (i.e., SAMPLING FRAME). One common approach is to write the name of each case in the population on a slip of paper, shuffle the slips of paper, then pull slips out until a sample of the desired size is obtained. For example, we could type each of the 1000 students' names on cards, shuffle the cards, then randomly pick 200. This can also be done by tossing a coin, throwing a dice, or by using a TABLE OF RANDOM NUMBERS.

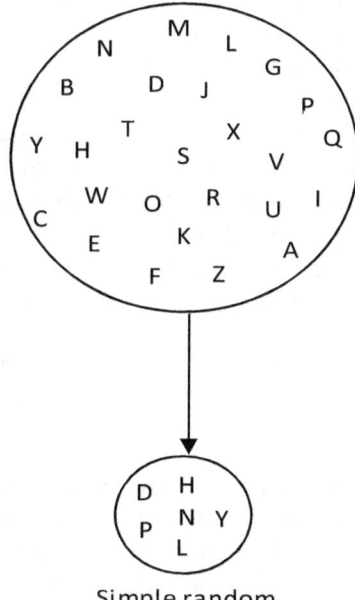

Figure S.6. Schematic Representation of Simple Random Sampling

There are two specific types of simple random sampling: **sampling with replacement** and **sampling without replacement**. To illustrate the difference between these two methods of sampling, let's assume we wish to form a sample of two scores from a population composed of the scores 4, 5, 8, and 10. One way would be to randomly draw one score from the population, record its value, and then place it back in the population before drawing the second score. Thus, the first score would be eligible for selection again on the second draw. This method of sampling is called sampling with replacement. A second method would be to randomly draw one score from the population and not replace it before drawing the second one. Thus, the same member of the population could appear in the sample only once. This method of sampling is called sampling without replacement. When subjects are being selected to participate in an experiment, sampling without replacement must be used because the same individual cannot be in the sample more than once. Sampling with replacement forms the mathematical basis for many of the inference tests. Although the two methods do not yield identical results, when sample size is small relative to population size, the differences are negligible and with-replacement techniques are much easier to use in providing the mathematical basis for inference.

Because of probability and chance, the sample should contain subjects with characteristics similar to the population as a whole; some old, some young, some tall, some short, some fit, some unfit, some rich, some poor etc. One problem associated with simple random sampling is that a complete list of the population is needed and this is not always readily available. As a result the representativeness of a sample cannot be ensured by this method. Furthermore, simple random sampling is not used if researchers wish to ensure that certain subgroups are present in the sample in the same proportion as they are in the population. To do this, researchers must engage in what is known as STRATIFIED SAMPLING.

see also SYSTEMATIC SAMPLING, CLUSTER SAMPLING, AREA SAMPLING, MULTI-PHASE SAMPLING

📖 Glass & Hopkins 1996; Cohen et al. 2011; Dörnyei 2007; Leary 2011; Lomax 2007; Pagano 2009

simple regression
also **simple linear regression, bivariate regression**
a statistical technique for estimating or predicting a value for one DEPENDENT VARIABLE or criterion from one INDEPENDENT VARIABLE or predictor measured on INTERVAL or RATIO SCALEs. Simple regression analysis involves a single predictor variable and a single criterion variable. For example, we may wish to see the effect of hours of study on levels of achievement in an examination, to be able to see how much improvement will be made to an examination mark by a given number of hours of study. 'Hours of study' is the predictor variable and 'level of achievement' is the criterion variable. Conventionally, as shown in the Figure S.7, one places the predictor variable in the VERTICAL AXIS and the criterion variable in the HORIZONTAL AXIS. There is also a **regression line** (also called **correlation line**, **reversion line**) which is an imaginary line drawn through the plotted points on the scatterplot of the values of the criterion and predictor variables so that it best describes the linear re-

lationship between these variables. If these values are standardized scores the regression line is the same as the correlation line. This line is sometimes also called the **line of best fit** or **best-fit line**. It indicates the relationship between the two variables. This line is the closest straight line that can be constructed to take account of variance in the scores, and strives to have the same number of cases above it and below it and making each point as close to the line as possible.

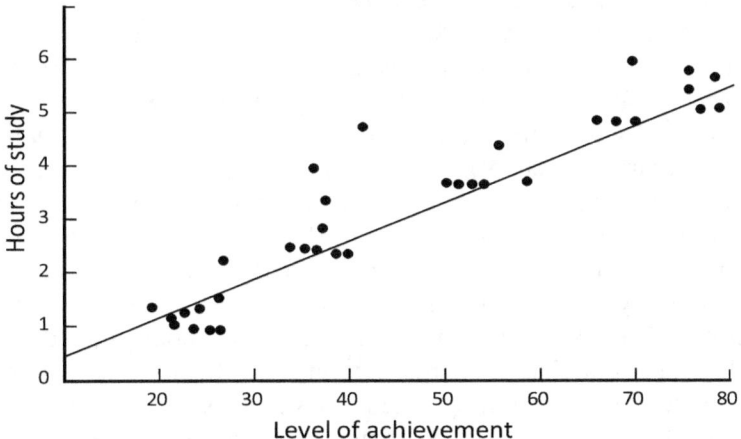

Figure S.7. Plotted Points in Simple Regression

For example, one can see that some scores are very close to the line and others are some distance away. One can observe that the greater the number of hours spent in studying, generally the greater is the level of achievement. This is akin to CORRELATION. The line of best fit indicates not only that there is a positive relationship, but also that the relationship is strong, i.e., the SLOPE of the line is quite steep (see SCATTERPLOT). When it slopes down (from top left to bottom right), there is evidence for a negative or inverse relationship between the variables; when it slopes up, a positive or direct relationship is indicated. A horizontal line indicates no relationship at all between the variables. The position of the line is determined by the slope (the angle) and the INTERCEPT (the point where the line intersects the vertical axis).

However, where regression departs from correlation is that regression provides an exact prediction of the value—the amount—of one variable when one knows the value of the other. Yet, one has to be cautious to predict outside the limits of the line; simple regression is to be used only to calculate values within the limits of the actual line, and not beyond it. One can observe, also, that though it is possible to construct a straight line of best fit, some of the data points lie close to the line and some lie a long way from the line; the distance of the data points from the line is

termed the RESIDUAL and where the line strikes the vertical axis is named the **intercept**.
📖 Cohen et al. 2011; Larson-Hall 2010; Mackey & Gass 2005; Porte 2010; Ravid 2011; Urdan 2010

simulated before-and-after design
another term for SEPARATE-SAMPLE PRETEST-POSTTEST DESIGN

simultaneous cross-sectional study
a type of LONGITUDINAL RESEARCH which is only partially longitudinal because it does not involve the examination of change over time but rather across age groups. Within this design a CROSS-SECTIONAL SURVEY is conducted with different age groups sampled (e.g., investigating four different years in a school). In effect, most SURVEYs might be considered an example of this design since nearly all investigations gather some information about the respondents' age. However, in a simultaneous cross-sectional study the respondents' age is the key sampling variable, whereas in ordinary cross-sectional design age is just another variable to be controlled. This design is straightforward and economical, and because it yields data about changes across age groups, it can be used to examine developmental issues. One problem, however, is that it measures different COHORTs, and the observed changes may not be due to the age difference but to the special experiences of a cohort (which are usually referred to as the *cohort effects*). Further, similar to TREND STUDY, the researchers need to administer the same QUESTIONNAIRE to all the different subgroups, which may mean that they have to devise generic items that cannot be too age-specific.
📖 Dörnyei 2007

simultaneous multiple regression
another term for STANDARD MULTIPLE REGRESSION

single-case design
another term for SINGLE-SUBJECT EXPERIMENTAL DESIGN

single-case experimental design
another term for SINGLE-SUBJECT EXPERIMENTAL DESIGN

single-factor ANOVA
another term for ONE-WAY ANOVA

single-factor between-subjects ANOVA
another term for ONE-WAY ANOVA

single-factor within-subjects ANOVA
another term for ONE-WAY REPEATED MEASURES ANOVA

single-participant experimental design
another term for SINGLE-SUBJECT EXPERIMENTAL DESIGN

single-sample *t*-test
another term for ONE-SAMPLE *t*-TEST

single-sample *z* test
another term for ONE-SAMPLE Z TEST

single-subject design
another term for SINGLE-SUBJECT EXPERIMENTAL DESIGN

single-subject experimental design
also **single-case experimental design, single-subject design, single-participant experimental design, single-case design**
a type of EXPERIMENTAL DESIGN in which the SAMPLE SIZE is limited to one participant or a few participants who are treated as one group. In single-subject designs, there can be no RANDOM ASSIGNMENT or use of CONTROL GROUPs. Obviously, the participant serves as both the TREATMENT GROUP and the control group. The researcher measures participant's behavior repeatedly during at least two different points in time, when a TREATMENT is not present and again when a treatment is present. The periods during which the treatment is not present are called baseline periods, and the periods during which the treatment is given are called treatment periods. For example, a teacher might want to know the effect of a certain reward (INDEPENDENT VARIABLE) (IV) on the time-on-task behavior (DEPENDENT VARIABLE) (DV) of a child with attention deficit/hyperactivity disorder. The child's behavior would be measured before the treatment (baseline), during the treatment, and after the treatment. The data for the baseline phase would serve as the control group data and would be the point of comparison with the behavior exhibited during the treatment and posttreatment phases of the study. In addition, all single-subject designs include continuous measurement of behavior throughout all of the phases.
Single-subject design's distinguished feature is the rigorous study of the effect of interventions on an individual. Although the focus of this type of study is the individual subject, most of these studies include more than one subject. When there are multiple subjects, the data are still analyzed separately for each subject rather than as a group. Single-participant researchers emphasize the importance of studying intraparticipant variance—variability in an individual's behavior when s/he is in the same

situation. Because averages are not used, the data from single-participant experiments cannot be analyzed using INFERENTIAL STATISTICS such as *t*-TESTs and ANOVAs. Moreover, since data are not aggregated across participants in single-participant research, individual differences do not contribute to ERROR VARIANCE. Each individual serves as his/her own control, so comparability is not a problem.

Single-subject experiments can be seen as *true* experiments because they can demonstrate CAUSAL RELATIONSHIPs and can rule out or make implausible threats to INTERNAL VALIDITY with the same elegance of group research. Similar to other experimental designs, the single-subject design seeks to establish that changes in the DV occur following introduction of the IV and identify differences between study conditions. The one way that single-subject designs differ from other experimental designs is in how they establish control, and thereby demonstrate that changes in a DV are not due to EXTRANEOUS VARIABLEs. For example, TRUE EXPERIMENTAL DESIGNs rely on RANDOMIZATION to equally distribute extraneous variables and on statistical techniques to control for such factors if they are found. Alternatively, single-subject designs eliminate between-subject variables by using only one participant, and they control for relevant environmental factors by establishing a stable baseline of the DV. If change occurs following the introduction of the IV, the researcher can reasonably assume that the change was due to the intervention (i.e., the IV or treatment) and not to extraneous factors. However, many critics of single-subject research question its EXTERNAL VALIDITY, in particular its ability to generalize to other subjects.

Single-case designs that use quantitative data are different from case studies that are used extensively in qualitative research. In the CASE STUDY, one or several individuals or cases (such as a student, a classroom, or a school) are studied in-depth, usually over an extended period of time. Researchers employing a qualitative case study approach typically use a number of data collection methods (such as INTERVIEWs and OBSERVATIONs) and collect data from multiple data sources. They study people in their natural environment and try not to interfere or alter the daily routine. Data collected from these nonexperimental studies are usually in a narrative form. Case studies are, in fact, qualitative in nature and describe the case, as it exists, in detail. In contrast, single-case studies, which use an experimental approach, collect mostly numerical data and focus on the effect of a single IV on the DV. In other words, single-subject research has all of the attributes of experimental research (e.g., hypotheses, control of variables, intervention).

Single-subject designs are also similar to QUASI-EXPERIMENTAL DESIGNs. The major difference between these designs is that the quasi-experimental designs are used with a group of subjects and data are analyzed accordingly, whereas single-subject research is concerned with individuals.

Well-designed single-subject research can meet the criteria for internal validity. However, the question of external validity—the GENERALIZABILITY of experimental findings—is not as easily answered by designs that use only one or a few subjects. Although any one particular single-subject study will be low in external validity, a number of similar studies that carefully describe subjects, settings, and treatments will build the case for wide application of particular treatment effects.

The most commonly used single-subject research designs are SINGLE-SUBJECT REVERSAL DESIGN, MULTIPLE-I DESIGN, and SINGLE-SUBJECT MULTIPLE-BASELINE DESIGN.

📖 Ary et al. 2010; Best & Kahn 2006; Kennedy 2005; Lodico et al. 2010; Marczyk et al. 2005; Ravid 2011

single-subject multiple-baseline design
also **multiple baseline design**
a variation of SINGLE-SUBJECT EXPERIMENTAL DESIGN in which observations are made on several participants, different target behaviors of one or more subjects, or different situations. Thus, there are three basic designs: *multiple-baseline across-participants design*, *multiple-baseline across-behaviors design*, and *multiple-baseline across-settings design*. In a **multiple-baseline across-behaviors design**, the same TREATMENT or intervention is applied to similar behaviors to the same individual in the same setting. For example, the researcher might record the number of times a student talked in class without permission, the number of times a student got out of his/her seat without permission, and the number of times a student hit another student. In a **multiple-baseline across-participants design**, the same intervention is applied to the same or similar behaviors of different individuals in the same setting. For example, the same behavior of several clients, such as amount of eye contact with the teacher, could be recorded for two or more subjects in a preschool class during the baseline phase. In both cases, the treatment is the same across all conditions or students. In a **multiple-baseline across-settings design**, the same intervention is applied to the same behavior to the same individual in different settings. For example, one might want to know if a type of reinforcement is as effective with an individual in a math class as it is in a reading class.

Experimental control in the multiple baseline results from starting the treatment at a different point in time for each behavior and/or person involved rather than from returning to baseline. Thus, after the baseline is established, treatment for behavior 1 is instituted and the baseline is continued for behaviors 2 and 3. When treatment for behavior 2 is instituted, treatment for behavior 1 and baseline for behavior 3 are continued. Finally, treatment for behavior 3 is instituted. It is expected that each behavior will change in the desired direction at the point at which treatment is begun, not before or after. If this happens, we have confidence that the treatment effected the change.

Thus, the multiple-baseline design uses two or more basic AB units. If some outside event other than the treatment was the actual cause of the changes, it should affect all subjects or all behaviors at the same point in time. One assumption of this design is that treatment affects different behaviors specifically. Reinforcing one behavior (completing assignments on time) is not expected to increase another response (reading rate). The behaviors, or situations, must be independent (uncorrelated) for the multiple-baseline study to show interpretable effects. In actuality, independence of behavior may be difficult to attain. Modifying one behavior (such as talking in class) may influence other targeted behaviors (completing assignments on time).

Overall, single-subject designs may be an important and logical alternative to RANDOMIZED EXPERIMENTAL DESIGNs. Importantly, because of their focus on single-subject behavior, these designs may be particularly suited for researchers who want to determine whether certain treatments are working for specific students.

see also SINGLE-SUBJECT REVERSAL DESIGN

 Ary et al. 2010; Evans & Rooney 2008; Marczyk et al. 2005

single-subject reversal design

a variation of SINGLE-SUBJECT EXPERIMENTAL DESIGN which measures behavior during three phases: before the TREATMENT or INDEPENDENT VARIABLE (IV) is introduced (labeled A), after introducing the treatment (labeled B), and again after withdrawing the treatment (labeled A). In this design, the participant is first observed in the absence of the IV (the baseline or control condition). The target behavior is measured many times during this phase to establish an adequate baseline for comparison. Then, after the target behavior is seen to be relatively stable, the IV is introduced and the behavior is observed again. If the IV influences behavior, we should see a change in behavior from the baseline to the treatment period. So, an **ABA design** involves a baseline period (A), followed by introduction of the IV (B), followed by the reversal period in which the IV is removed (A).

To rule out the possibility that apparent effects might be due to a certain cyclical pattern involving either MATURATION or PRACTICE EFFECT, the researcher may decide to introduce the same LEVEL of the IV (i.e., treatment) a second time. This design would be labeled an **ABAB design**. To rule out even more complicated maturation or practice effects, the researcher could extend the design even further to an **ABABA design**. Logically, a researcher could reintroduce then remove a level of the IV again and again, as in an ABABAB or ABABABA design. Obviously, the more measurements that are made, the less likely it is that measured change is due to anything other than the intervention, or IV.

The primary goal of single-subject reversal design is, first, to determine whether there is a change in the DEPENDENT VARIABLE (DV) following the introduction of the IV; and second, to determine whether the DV reverses or returns to baseline once the IV is withdrawn. This design, however, has the same limitations as its time-series counterpart (i.e., REVERSAL TIME-SERIES DESIGN). First, and most obviously, not all behaviors are reversible. Certain behaviors, such as reading, riding a bike, or learning a language, are somewhat permanent. Second, withdrawal of certain useful interventions or curative treatments may be unethical. To address this issue, many studies opt for the ABAB variant, in which the intervention is repeated and is designated as the final condition.

Leary 2011; Lodico et al. 2010; Marczyk et al. 2005

singularity

the extreme case of MULTICOLLINEARITY in which an INDEPENDENT VARIABLE (IV) is perfectly predicted (a CORRELATION of ±1) by one or more IVs. REGRESSION models cannot be estimated when a singularity exists. The researcher must omit one or more of the IVs involved to remove the singularity.

Hair et al. 2010

SIQR

an abbreviation for SEMI-INTERQUARTILE RANGE

situational ethnomethodology

see ETHNOMETHODOLOGY

skewed distribution

a measure of the lack of symmetry of a DISTRIBUTION. A skewed distribution, unlike a NORMAL DISTRIBUTION, is asymmetrical since the shapes of the upper and lower portions of the distributions are not mirror images of each other. Skewed distributions are characterized by having a peak toward one end of the distribution and a longer tail toward the other. In a **positively skewed distribution** such as Figure S.8, there are more low scores than high scores in the data; if data are positively skewed, one observes a clustering of scores toward the lower, left-hand end of the scale, with the tail of the distribution extending to the right.

600 skewed distribution

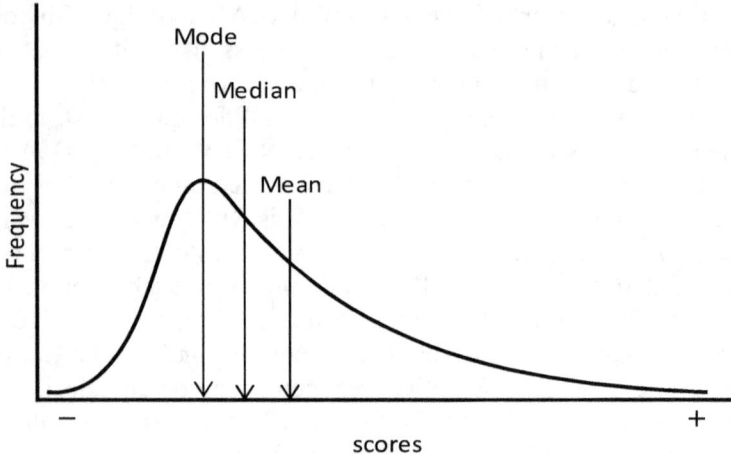

Figure S.8. A Positively Skewed Distribution

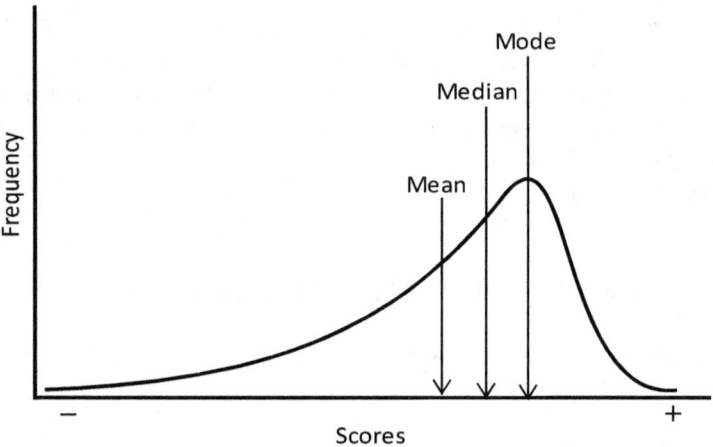

Figure S.9. A Negatively Skewed Distribution

In a **negatively skewed distribution** such as Figure S.9, there are more high scores than low scores; the hump is to the right of the graph, and the tail of the distribution extends to the left. Distributions obtained with CRITERION-REFERENCED TESTS are typically, but not necessarily, peaked and negatively skewed. Figure S.9 also shows the relative positions of the MEAN, MEDIAN, and MODE in skewed distributions. In both graphs, the mean is pulled toward the extreme tail and is not where most scores are located. Since the mean is most affected by extreme scores, it will have a value closer to the extreme scores than will the median. Thus, with a negatively skewed distribution, the mean will be lower than the median. With a positively skewed distribution, the mean will be larger

than the median. The mode is toward the side away from the extreme tail. Thus, of the three measures, the median most accurately reflects the central tendency of a skewed distribution.
📖 Heiman 2011; Pagano 2009; Porte 2010

slope

an angle or steepness of a REGRESSION LINE. The slope is a number that indicates how slanted the regression line is and the direction in which it slants. Graphically, it is measured as the change in Y axis values associated with a change of one unit on X axis values. Lines with positive slopes are slanted up toward the right (small values on the X axis align with small values on the Y axis; large values on the X axis align with large values on the Y axis), while negative value slopes are slanted up toward the left. Figure S.10 shows examples of regression lines having different slopes. When no relationship is present, the regression line is horizontal, such as line A, and the slope is zero. A positive linear relationship produces regression lines such as B and C; each of these has a slope that is a positive number. Because line C is steeper, its slope is a larger positive number. A negative linear relationship, such as line D, yields a slope that is a negative number.

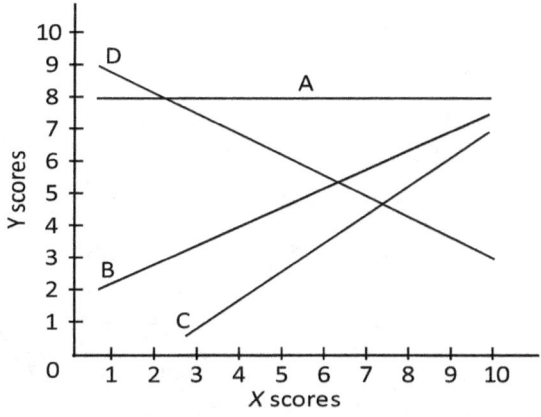

Figure S.10. Examples of Slope

It is important to keep in mind that although the slope of the regression line plays a role in determining the specific value of Y that is predicted from the value of X, the magnitude of the slope is not related to the magnitude of the absolute value of the coefficient of correlation. A regression line with a large slope can be associated with a CORRELATION COEFFICIENT that has a large, moderate, or small absolute value. In the same respect, a regression line with a small slope can be associated with a correlation coefficient that has a large, moderate, or small absolute value.

602 SNK test

Thus, the accuracy of a prediction is not a function of the slope of the regression line. Instead, it is a function of how far removed the data points or values (i.e., dots on the graph) are from the regression line. Consequently, for any of the regression lines depicted in Figure S.10, the data points can fall on, close to, or be far removed from the regression line.
see also INTERCEPT

📖 Heiman 2011; Porte 2010; Sheskin 2011

SNK test
an abbreviation for STUDENT-NEWMAN-KEULS TEST

snowball sampling
also **chain sampling, network sampling, chain referral sampling, reputational sampling**

a type of NON-PROBABILITY SAMPLING in which researchers identify a small number of individuals who have the characteristics in which they are interested. These people are then used as informants to identify, or put the researchers in touch with, others who qualify for inclusion and these, in turn, identify yet others—hence the term snowball sampling. Snowball sampling is, in fact, a multistage technique. It begins with one or a few people or cases and spreads out on the basis of links to the initial case.

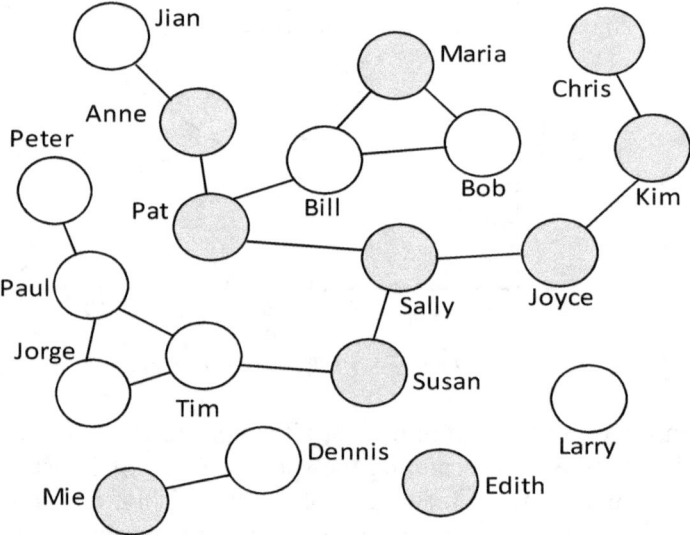

Figure S.11. Sociogram of Friendship Relations

One use of snowball sampling is to sample a network. Social researchers are often interested in an interconnected network of people or organizations. The crucial feature is that each person or unit is connected with another through a direct or indirect linkage. This does not mean that each person directly knows, interacts with, or is influenced by every other person in the network. Rather, it means that, taken as a whole, with direct and indirect links, they are within an interconnected web of linkage. Researchers represent such a network by drawing a sociogram—a diagram of circles connected with lines (see Figure S.11). For example, Sally and Tim do not know each other directly, but each has a good friend, Susan, so they have an indirect connection. All three are part of the same friendship network. The circles represent each person or case, and the lines represent friendship or other linkages.

This method is also useful for sampling a POPULATION where access is difficult, maybe because it is a sensitive topic or where communication networks are undeveloped (e.g., where a researcher wishes to interview stand-in supply teachers—teachers who are brought in on an ad hoc basis to cover for absent regular members of a schools teaching staff—but finds it difficult to acquire a list of these stand-in teachers, or where a researcher wishes to contact curriculum coordinators who have attended a range of in-service courses and built up an informal network of inter-school communication). The task for the researcher is to establish who are the critical or key informants with whom initial contact must be made.

see also CONVENIENCE SAMPLING, QUOTA SAMPLING, DIMENSIONAL SAMPLING, PURPOSIVE SAMPLING, SEQUENTIAL SAMPLING, VOLUNTEER SAMPLING, OPPORTUNISTIC SAMPLING

📖 Cohen et al. 2011; Dörnyei 2007; Neuman 2007

SOC

an abbreviation for SUPPLIANCE IN OBLIGATORY CONTEXTS

social constructivism

a theory which addresses the ontological (see ONTOLOGY) and epistemological (see EPISTEMOLOGY) questions of CONSTRUCTIVISM in describing the bodies of knowledge developed over human history as social constructs that do not reflect an objective external world. Everything we know has been determined by the intersection of politics, values, ideologies, religious beliefs, language, and so on. Social constructivists challenge the scientific realist assumption that reality can be reduced to its component parts. Instead, they argue that phenomena must be understood as complex wholes that are inextricably bound up with the historical, socioeconomic, and cultural contexts in which they are embedded. Therefore, they attempt to understand social phenomena from a context-specific perspective. Social constructivists view scientific inquiry as value-bound and not value-free. This means that the process of inquiry is in-

fluenced by the researcher and by the context under study. This philosophical perspective argues that reality is socially constructed by individuals and this social construction leads to multiple meanings. Different persons may bring different conceptual frameworks to a situation based on their experiences, and this will influence what they perceive in a particular situation. In other words, there is no one true reality, nor can one assume that the experiences that people have had will overlap to a large degree. Rather, we construct reality in accord with the concepts most appropriate to our personal experiences. Thus, the researcher must attempt to understand the complex and often multiple realities from the perspectives of the participants. The acceptance of the existence of multiple realities leads social constructivists to insist that a set of initial questions asked in a study will likely change or be modified as these multiple realities are uncovered or reconstructed during the process of conducting research. The only true way to accomplish this understanding is for the researcher to become involved in the reality of the participants and interact with them in deeply meaningful ways. This provides an opportunity for mutual influence and allows the researcher to see the world through the eyes of the participants. The inquirer and the object of inquiry interact to influence one another; knower and known are inseparable. This approach, then, requires that researchers use data collection methods that bring them closer to the participants using techniques such as in-depth observations, life histories, interviews, videos, and pictures.
 Given 2008; Lodico et al. 2010

social desirability bias
also **prestige bias**
the tendency of respondents to answer questions in a manner that will be viewed favorably by others. social desirability bias can take the form of over-reporting good behavior or under-reporting bad behavior. The tendency poses a serious problem with conducting research with self-reports, especially QUESTIONNAIREs. This bias interferes with the interpretation of interpreting average tendencies as well as individual differences. Questionnaire items are often transparent, that is, respondents can have a fairly good guess about what the desirable/acceptable/expected answer is, and some of them will provide this response even if it is not true. Questionnaire items that people are likely to answer one way or another because they think that it will make them look better are called **prestige question**s.
see also ACQUIESCENCE BIAS
 Dörnyei 2003; Heigham & Croker 2009

sociological reductionism
see REDUCTIONISM

sociometry

a PROJECTIVE TECHNIQUE for describing the social relationships among individuals in a group. In an indirect way, sociometry attempts to describe attractions or repulsions between individuals by asking them to indicate whom they would choose or reject in various situations. Thus, sociometry is a new technique of studying the underlying motives of respondents. Under this an attempt is made to trace the flow of information amongst groups and then examine the ways in which new ideas are diffused. Sociograms (i.e., charts) are constructed to identify leaders and followers.

see also THEMATIC APPERCEPTION TEST, ROSENZWEIG TEST, RORSCHACH TEST, HOLTZMAN INKBLOT TEST, TOMKINS-HORN PICTURE ARRANGEMENT TEST

📖 Best & Kahn 2006; Kothari 2008

Solomon four-group design

a true EXPERIMENTAL DESIGN type which is a combination of the POSTTEST ONLY CONTROL GROUP DESIGN and PRETEST-POSTTEST CONTROL GROUP DESIGN. In this design, two of the groups receive the TREATMENT and two do not. Furthermore, two of the groups receive a pretest and two do not. This design can be diagramed as follows (where R = randomly assigned group, O = pretest and posttest, and X = TREATMENT):

Experimental Group (R)	O	X	O
Control Group$_1$ (R)	O		O
Control Group$_2$ (R)		X	O
Control Group$_3$ (R)			O

This design with its four groups has strength because it incorporates the advantages of several other designs. It provides good control of the threats to INTERNAL VALIDITY. It has two pretested groups and two without a pretest; one of the pretested groups and one of the nonpretested groups receive the experimental treatment, and then all four groups take the posttest. The first two lines control EXTRANEOUS VARIABLEs such as HISTORY and MATURATION, and the third line controls the pretest-treatment interaction effect. When the fourth line is added, you have control over any possible contemporary effects that may occur between pretest and posttest.

In Solomon four-group design, you can make several comparisons to determine the effect of the experimental treatment. If the posttest mean of the experimental group (E) is significantly greater than the mean of the first control group (C_1) and if the second control group (C_2) posttest mean is significantly greater than that of third control group (C_3), you have evidence for the effectiveness of the experimental treatment. You can determine the influence of the experimental conditions on a pretested group by comparing the posttests of E and C_1, or the pre-post changes of E and C_1. You can find the effect of the experiment on an unpretested group by comparing C_2 and C_3. If the average differences between posttest scores, E-C_1 and C_2-C_3, are approximately the same, then the experiment must have had a comparable effect on pretested and unpretested groups.

The main disadvantage of this design is the difficulty involved in carrying it out in a practical situation. More time and effort are required to conduct two experiments simultaneously, and there is the problem of locating the increased number of subjects of the same kind that would be needed for the four groups. Another difficulty is with the statistical analysis. There are not four complete sets of measures for the four groups. As noted, you can compare E and C_1, and C_2 and C_3, but no single statistical procedure would use the six available measures simultaneously. It is suggested working only with posttest scores in a TWO-WAY ANOVA design. The pretest is considered as a second INDEPENDENT VARIABLE (IV), along with X. Therefore, the Solomon four-group design can be viewed as a very basic example of a FACTORIAL DESIGN, as it examines the separate effect and combined effect of more than one IV.

see also SOLOMON THREE-GROUP DESIGN

Ary et al. 2010; Campbell & Stanley 1963; Marczyk et al. 2005

Solomon three-group design

a TRUE EXPERIMENTAL DESIGN which uses three groups, with RANDOM ASSIGNMENT of subjects to groups. The Solomon three-group design has the advantage of employing a second CONTROL GROUP that is not pretested but is exposed to both the TREATMENT and posttest. This group, despite receiving the experimental treatment, is functioning as a control and is thus labeled control group. This design can be represented as follows (where R = randomly assigned group, O = pretest and posttest, and X = treatment):

Experimental Group (R)	O	X	O
Control Group$_1$ (R)	O		O
Control Group$_2$ (R)		X	O

If the experimental group has a significantly higher mean on the posttest than does the first control group (C_1), the researcher cannot be confident that this difference is caused by X. It might have occurred because of the subjects' increased sensitization after the pretest and the interaction of their sensitization and X. However, if the posttest mean of the second control group (C_2) is also significantly higher than that of the first control group, then one can conclude that the experimental treatment, rather than the pretest-X interaction effect, has produced the difference because the second control group is not pretested.

This design overcomes the difficulty inherent in PRETEST-POSTTEST CONTROL GROUP DESIGN—namely, the interactive effect of pretesting and the experimental treatment. The posttest scores for the three groups are compared to assess the interaction effect.

see SOLOMON FOUR-GROUP DESIGN

📖 Ary et al. 2010

somer's *d*
also **somer's delta**
an asymmetric measure of *association* in a CONTINGENCY TABLE where row and column variables are measured on an ORDINAL SCALE. The measure is appropriate when one VARIABLE is considered dependent and the other independent.

📖 Everitt & Skrondal 2010; Sahai & Khurshid 2001

somer's delta
another term for SOMER'S *d*

source list
another term for SAMPLING FRAME

space triangulation
see DATA TRIANGULATION

spatial autocorrelation
see AUTOCORRELATION

Spearman-brown prophecy formula
see SPLIT-HALF RELIABILITY

Spearman rank order correlation coefficient
also **Spearman rho correlation coefficient, Spearman rho (ρ), rho (ρ), r_s**
a *nonparametric* bivariate measure of *association* between two ORDINAL VARIABLEs (e.g., ranked data). The Spearman rank-order correlation coefficient, a specialized form of the PEARSON PRODUCT-MOMENT CORRELATION COEFFICIENT, is usually represented by the symbol ρ, (the lower-case Greek letter rho). In computing Spearman rank-order correlation coefficient, one of the following is true with regard to the rank-order data that are evaluated: a) The data for both variables are in a rank-order for-

mat, since it is the only format for which data are available; b) The original data are in a rank-order format for one variable and in an *interval/ratio* format for the second variable. In such an instance, data on the second variable are converted to a rank-order format in order that both sets of data represent the same level of measurement; and c) The data for both variables have been transformed into a rank order-format from an interval/ratio format, since the researcher has reason to believe that one or more of the assumptions underlying the Pearson product-moment correlation coefficient (which is the analogous parametric correlational procedure employed for INTERVAL/RATIO DATA) have been violated. It should be noted that since information is sacrificed when interval/ratio data are transformed into a rank-order format, some researchers may elect to employ the Pearson product-moment correlation coefficient rather than Spearman rank-order correlation coefficient, even when there is reason to believe that one or more of the assumptions of the former measure have been violated.

Spearman rank-order correlation coefficient determines the degree to which a **monotonic relationship** exists between two variables. A monotonic relationship can be described as monotonic increasing (which is associated with a positive correlation) or monotonic decreasing (which is associated with a negative correlation). A relationship between two variables is monotonic increasing, if an increase in the value of one variable is always accompanied by an increase in the value of the other variable. A relationship between two variables is monotonic decreasing, if an increase in the value of one variable is always accompanied by a decrease in the value of the other variable. Based on the above definitions, a positively sloped straight line represents an example of a monotonic increasing function, while a negatively sloped straight line represents an example of a monotonic decreasing function (see SCATTERPLOT). In addition to the aforementioned linear functions, curvilinear functions can also be monotonic. It should be noted that when the interval/ratio scores on two variables are monotonically related to one another, a linear function can be employed to describe the relationship between the rank-orderings of the two variables.

To do the correlation, we arrange the scores on the two variables in a rank order from high to low and then, through computation, obtain a coefficient which tells us how the rankings of scores on the two variables are related.

The interpretation of Spearman rho (ρ) is the same as the pearson product-moment correlation coefficient. When used appropriately, they can be interpreted in essentially the same way, as indicators of the strength and directionality of the relationship between two variables. The Pearson r can be used appropriately with large SAMPLEs where we can assume

NORMAL DISTRIBUTIONs. The Spearman rho, on the other hand, does not assume that variables are normally distributed, and should thus be used to investigate relationships among variables with small SAMPLE SIZEs. Because ρ is a special case of the product-moment correlation coefficient, as the size of the sample increases, the value of ρ will approach that of r. There are other differences between ρ and r. Rank-order correlations have to do with place in a rank order, and we assume that those ranks are real even if not strictly equal interval in nature. If the distances between ranks is radically uneven (e.g., if ranks 1 and 2 are extremely close and ranks 2, 3, and 5 widely spaced), then the ranks, and the order itself, may be meaningless. A second difference between the two types of correlation coefficients is that the Spearman rank-order correlation coefficient should not be squared to be interpreted as the amount of VARIANCE accounted for by either variable.

📖 Bachman 2004; Cramer & Howitt 2004; Hatch & Farhady 1982; Ho 2006; Sheskin 2011; Urdan 2010

Spearman rho (ρ)

another term for SPEARMAN RANK ORDER CORRELATION COEFFICIENT

Spearman rho correlation coefficient

another term for SPEARMAN RANK ORDER CORRELATION COEFFICIENT

specificity of variables

a threat to EXTERNAL VALIDITY. All experimental research is conducted in a specific location, at a specific time, with a specific POPULATION, with variables measured with a certain instrument and under a specific set of circumstances. The more specific the conditions are, the more limited the GENERALIZABILITY of the study. A study that is conducted with fourth graders in an inner-city school district, using a specific instructional approach, during the first hour of school, with a specific teacher, and with reading achievement measured with the ABC achievement test may be applicable only to a similar setting. This is one reason why often the purpose of research studies is to replicate previous studies with different groups in different settings using different measures. Any single study has limited generalizability, so it is often useful to replicate studies. However, the criticism of specificity of variables can be avoided by randomly selecting persons and schools that are diverse, using measures that are widely regarded as reliable and valid, and using treatments that can be easily replicated in other settings without specialized resources or circumstances.

see also TREATMENT DIFFUSION, RESEARCHER EFFECT, HALO EFFECT, HAWTHORNE EFFECT, NOVELTY EFFECT, PRETEST-TREATMENT INTERAC-

TION, MULTIPLE-TREATMENT INTERACTION
📖 Lodico et al. 2010

specific open question
see SHORT-ANSWER ITEM

speed test
also timed test
a test in which the examinees compete against the available time. In speed test, examinees are instructed to work within a limited amount of time. Even if they know the answers to the test items, they may not have enough time to attempt all items. By contrast, in a **power test**, the examinees concentrate on the content of the test. In a power test, the time factor is eliminated and the examinees are given a chance to try all the items. To the extent a test is speed, ERROR SCOREs creep into testees' performance because time limitation will make the testees rush through the items. Consequently, most of them will not get to all items in a relaxed environment. Of course, an unlimited time allocation will negatively influence test results as well because the testees will work luxuriously and thus lose their concentration. Therefore, there should be a balance between the time allowed and the number of items.
📖 Farhady et al. 1995

sphericity
also circularity
an ASSUMPTION for REPEATED-MEASURES ANOVA. Sphericity refers to the need for repeated-measures ANOVAs to have HOMOGENEITY OF VARIANCE among difference scores. When a repeated-measures ANOVA is used, the assumption of *independence* is violated, giving rise to an additional assumption of sphericity. This assumption requires that the variances of difference scores between conditions be roughly equal. That is, it measures whether differences between the variances of a single participant's data are equal. In fact, sphericity is like homogeneity of variances assumption for the same person when we have repeated measures.
More specifically, the F TEST of repeated measures ANOVA is not ROBUST to violations of the sphericity assumption. If this assumption is violated, the F VALUE from this ANOVA is positively biased (i.e., too liberal); this means that the calculated value will be larger than it should be, thus increasing the probability of a TYPE I ERROR above the nominal alpha level. If we were to find, for each participant, the difference between his/her score on two of the LEVELs of an INDEPENDENT VARIABLE (IV), then we would have a set of difference scores. We could then calculate the variance of those difference scores. If we found the difference

scores for each pair of levels of the IV and calculated the variance for each set of difference scores we would be in a position to check whether sphericity was present in the data. It would be present if the variances of the difference scores were homogeneous. When an IV only has two levels, and therefore DEGREES OF FREEDOM (df) = 1, there is only one set of difference scores and so sphericity is not an issue. When sphericity is not present, there are at least two possible ways around the problem. One is to use a MULTIVARIATE ANALYSIS OF VARIANCE. An alternative approach comes from the finding that even when sphericity is not present, the F RATIO calculated from a REPEATED-MEASURES ANOVA still conforms to the F DISTRIBUTION. However, it is necessary to adjust the df to allow for the lack of sphericity. Tests such as GREENHOUSE-GEISSER CORRECTION, HUYNH-FELDT CORRECTION, and MAUCHLY'S TEST, are used to compensate for possible lack of sphericity.

 Clark-Carter 2010; Larson-Hall 2010; Salkind 2007; Tabachnick & Fidell 2007

split-half reliability

an approach to estimating the INTERNAL CONSISTENCY RELIABILITY based on the CORRELATION COEFFICINT between two halves of a measuring instrument test (e.g., a test), which are assumed to be parallel (see Figure S.12). The method requires only one form of a test, there is no time lag involved, and the same physical and mental influences will be operating on the subjects as they take the two halves.

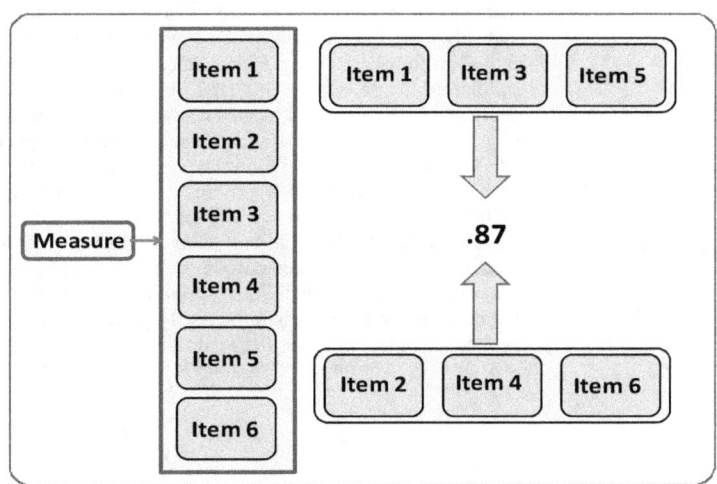

Figure S.12. An Example of Split-Half Reliability

A problem with this method is in splitting the test to obtain two comparable halves. If, through ITEM ANALYSIS, you establish the difficulty level of each item, you can place each item into one of the two halves on the basis of equivalent difficulty and similarity of content. The most common procedure, however, is to correlate the scores on the odd-numbered items of the test with the scores on the even-numbered items. However, the correlation coefficient computed between the two halves systematically underestimates the RELIABILITY of the entire test because the correlation between the 50 odd-numbered and 50 even-numbered items on a 100-item test is a reliability estimate for a 50-item test, not a 100-item test.

Usually the **Spearman-brown prophecy formula** is applied to the resulting split-half reliability estimate in order to estimate the reliability of the full-length test rather than its separate halves because with all other factors being equal, the longer the test the higher the reliability. In using the spearman-brown split-half approach, it is assumed that the two halves are equivalent and independent of each other. Because this assumption is seldom exactly correct, in practice, the split-half technique with the Spearman-Brown correction tends to overestimate the reliability that would be obtained with test-retest or equivalent-forms procedures.

Another approach to estimating reliability from spilt-halves is **Guttman split-half method** which does not assume equivalence of the halves, and which does not require computing a correlation between them. This split-half reliability coefficient is based on the ratio of the sum of the variances of the two halves to the variance of the whole test. Since this estimate of reliability is based on the variance of the total of test, it provides a direct estimate of the reliability of the whole test. Therefore, unlike the correlation between the halves that is the basis for the spearman-brown reliability coefficient, the Guttman split-half estimate does not require an additional correction for length.

Split-half reliability is an appropriate technique to use when time-to-time fluctuation in estimating reliability is to be avoided and when the test is relatively long. For short tests the other techniques, such as test-retest or equivalent-forms, are more appropriate. The split-half procedure is not appropriate to use with SPEED TESTs because it yields spuriously high coefficients of equivalence in such tests. A speed test is one that purposefully includes easy items so that the scores mainly depend on the speed with which subjects can respond. Errors are minor, and most of the items are correct up to the point where time is called. If a subject responds to 50 items, his/her split-half score is likely to be 25-25; if another subject marks 60 items, his/her split-half score is likely to be 30-30, and so on. Because individuals' scores on odd- and even-numbered items are very nearly identical, within-individual variation is minimized and the correlation between the halves would be nearly perfect. Thus, other procedures are recommended for use with speed tests.

Ary et al. 2010; Bachman 1990; Richards & Schmidt 2010; Trochim & Donnelly 2007

split panels
a type of LONGITUDINAL MIXED DESIGN which combines LONGITUDINAL and CROSS-SECTIONAL DESIGNs by including a classic panel which is accompanied by an additional rotating sample interviewed alongside another sample of the long-term panel members who are being followed over time. The rotating sample is interviewed once only and never again and serves as a CONTROL GROUP as they are not exposed to MORTALITY and PANEL CONDITIONING.
see also ROTATING PANELS, LINKED PANELS, COHORT STUDY, ACCELERATED LONGITUDINAL DESIGN, DIARY STUDY
 Dörnyei 2007; Ruspini 2002

split-plot design
another term for MIXED DESIGN

split subjects pretest posttest
another term for SEPARATE-SAMPLE PRETEST-POSTTEST DESIGN

SPSS
an abbreviation for 'Statistical Product and Service Solutions' (formerly 'Statistical Package for the Social Sciences'). SPSS is one of several widely used statistical packages for manipulating and analyzing data. It is an integrated system of computer programs designed for the analysis of social sciences data. It is one of the most popular of the many statistical packages currently available for statistical analysis.
 Cramer & Howitt 2004; Ho 2006

spurious variable
another term for CONFOUNDING VARIABLE

squared
also **squaring**
multiplying a number by itself. It is normally written as 2^2 or 3^2 or 3.2^2 indicating 2 squared, 3 squared and 3.2 squared respectively. This is simply another way of writing 2×2, 3×3 and 3.2×3.2. Another way of saying the same thing is to say two to the POWER of two, three to the power of two, and three point two to the power of two. It is very commonly used in statistics.
 Cramer & Howitt 2004

squared multiple correlation
another term for COEFFICIENT OF MULTIPLE DETERMINATION

square root
of a number is another number which when squared gives the first number. Thus, the square root number of 9 is 3 since 3 multiplied by itself equals 9. The sign $\sqrt{}$ is an instruction to find the square root of what follows. It is sometimes written as $^2\sqrt{}$ and as the EXPONENT 1/2. Square roots are not easy to calculate by hand but are a regular feature of even the most basic hand-held calculators.
📖 Cramer & Howitt 2004

square root transformation
a type of DATA TRANSFORMATION which involves taking the SQUARE ROOT of each value within a certain VARIABLE. The one caveat is that you cannot take a square root of a negative number. Fortunately, this can be easily remedied by adding a constant, such as 1, to each item before computing the square root.
see also LOG TRANSFORMATION, INVERSE TRANSFORMATION
📖 Marczyk et al. 2005

squaring
another name for SQUARED

stacked bar chart
see COMPOUND HISTOGRAM

stakeholders
any persons (or groups) who have an interest in your project and can be affected by it or who can influence its outcome. Stakeholders can therefore be sponsors of the project, providing the vital resources to undertake the work. They may be policy makers or practitioners, or the end users of the research findings who have an interest in the outcome and its implications. Stakeholders can be the gatekeepers to the data or facilitators to the research subjects and thereby vital to the viability of the project. They may be the subjects of the research who will participate but who might ultimately be the beneficiaries of the research if it leads to developments in policy and practice that affects their lives. The general public (and the media as communicators of the findings to them) may also have an interest in the research and, of course, there will be other researchers or the academic community in general that will be keen to learn from the research. Last, but by no means least, those working on the project (the research team or other partners) will have a stake in the project. Obviously any one person or group of persons or organizations can be a stakeholder in more than one of the ways described above. Similarly their position may change throughout the life of a project. It is also important to be aware that stakeholders can adopt different stances to the research or

may have different attitudes towards it. Some may be enthusiastic supporters or champions keen to promote the research while others may feel threatened by the research as it may be perceived as enquiring critically into their practices or the quality of the service they provide. Some who might be asked to assemble information for the researchers (get out files, produce databases and so on) may have little interest but just see the research as leading to additional burdens and additional demands on their time. While some will accord the research high priority others will see it as low priority, to be involved with only if time permits. To the researchers the project is perhaps the most salient aspect of their working lives on which their careers are built.

see also INVESTIGATOR TRIANGULATION, PEER REVIEW

📖 Tarling 2006

standard deviation
also *SD*

the most widely used MEASURE OF VARIABILITY of a set of data in inferential statistical procedures. The best way to understand a standard deviation *(SD)* is to consider what the two words mean. *Deviation*, in this case, refers to the difference between an individual score in a DISTRIBUTION and the average score for the distribution. The other word in the term *SD* is *standard*. In this case, standard means typical, or average. Therefore, a *SD* is the typical, or average, deviation between individual scores in a distribution and the MEAN for the distribution. The distance between each score in a distribution and the mean of that distribution $(X - \bar{X})$ is called the **deviation score**, indicating the amount the score deviates from the mean—hence the label standard deviation. Thus, if the SAMPLE MEAN is 47, a score of 50 deviates by +3 (47 - 50 = 3).

The *SD* is calculated by taking the square root of the VARIANCE. That is, the square root of the sum of the squared deviations from the mean divided by the total number of scores *(N)* if the data set is a POPULATION or by $N - 1$ if the data set is from a SAMPLE. This is done because the variance of a sample is usually less than that of the population from which it is drawn. In other words, dividing the sum by one less than the number of scores provides a less biased estimate of the population variance. Thus, the formula for *population standard deviation* (represented by σ, the lowercase Greek letter sigma) is:

$$\sigma = \sqrt{\frac{\Sigma(X - \bar{X})^2}{N}}$$

and for *sample standard deviation* (represented by *s*) is:

standard deviation

$$\sigma = \sqrt{\frac{\Sigma(X - \bar{X})^2}{N-1}}$$

Where
X = scores
$\bar{X}$ = mean
N = number of scores
Σ = sum (or add)

For an illustration, consider the Table S.3. It shows the distribution of a set of scores. The mean of this distribution is 69. Using the same scores and mean, the table shows the steps required to calculate the standard deviation: we (a) line up each score with the mean, (b) subtract the mean from each score, (c) square each of the deviations (differences) from the mean, (d) add up all the squared values, (e) and put the values into the formula and calculate the result. In the example, after applying the first formula, the square root is around 3.87 which is the standard deviation of the population. We can also apply the second formula to compute the sample standard deviation which is 4.

X	$-$	$\bar{X}$	$=$	$(X - \bar{X})$	$(X - \bar{X})^2$
77	$-$	69	$=$	8	64
75	$-$	69	$=$	6	36
72	$-$	69	$=$	3	9
72	$-$	69	$=$	3	9
70	$-$	69	$=$	1	1
70	$-$	69	$=$	1	1
69	$-$	69	$=$	0	0
69	$-$	69	$=$	0	0
69	$-$	69	$=$	0	0
69	$-$	69	$=$	0	0
68	$-$	69	$=$	-1	1
68	$-$	69	$=$	-1	1
67	$-$	69	$=$	-2	4
64	$-$	69	$=$	-5	25
64	$-$	69	$=$	-5	25
61	$-$	69	$=$	-8	64
$N = 16$		$\bar{X} = 69$		$\Sigma(X - \bar{X}) = 0$	$\Sigma(X - \bar{X})^2 = 240$

Table S.3. Calculation of Standard Deviation

As shown in the Table S.3, adding up the deviations including both the positive and negative values will yield zero. Such a result will usually be obtained because typically about half of the deviations will be positive (above the mean) and half will be negative (below the mean). Thus, they will usually add to zero or a value very close to zero. To get around this problem each value is squared as shown in the table under $(X - \bar{X})^2$. Then the resulting numbers can be added with a result other than zero. After the sum of these numbers is devided by N in the averaging process the result is brought back down to a score value by taking its square root. In other words, the square root is taken to counteract the squaring process that wen on earlier.

It is clear that, if the scores are more tightly clustered around the mean, the *SD* will be smaller (Figure S.13b), while, if they are spread out further from the mean, the *SD* will be larger (Figure S.13a).

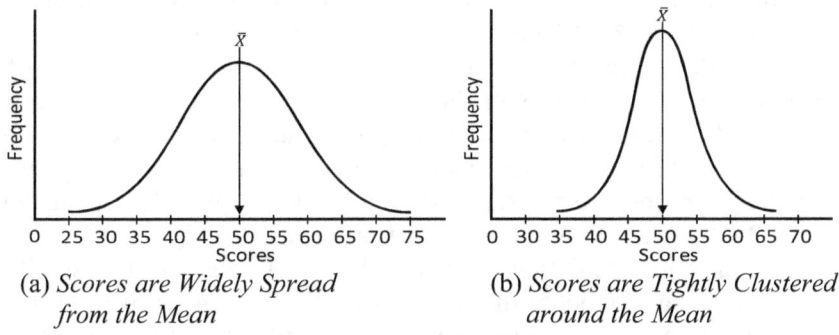

(a) *Scores are Widely Spread from the Mean*

(b) *Scores are Tightly Clustered around the Mean*

Figure S.13. *Two Graphs Showing Distributions with the same Means but Different Standard Deviations*

The *SD* is the appropriate indicator of variability for scores that are intervally scaled. In NORM-REFERENCED TESTs with large numbers of test scores and symmetric distributions, we will typically find that about two-thirds of the scores occur within one *SD* of the mean. When we divide the *SD* by the arithmetic average of the distribution, the resulting quantity is known as **coefficient of standard deviation** which happens to be a relative measure and is often used for comparing with similar measure of other distributions.

The *SD* is used mostly in research studies and is regarded as a very satisfactory measure of dispersion in a distribution. It has many important characteristics. First, the *SD* gives us a measure of dispersion relative to the mean. This differs from the range, which gives us an absolute measure of the spread between the two most extreme scores (OUTLIERs). Second, the *SD* is sensitive to each score in the distribution. If a score is moved closer to the mean, then the *SD* will become smaller. Conversely, if a score shifts away from the mean, then the *SD* will increase. Third, like the mean, the *SD* is stable with regard to sampling fluctuations. If

samples were taken repeatedly from populations, the *SD* of the samples would vary much less from sample to sample than the range. This property is one of the main reasons why the *SD* is used so much more often than the range for reporting variability. Finally, the *SD* can be manipulated algebraically. This allows mathematics to be done with it for use in INFERENTIAL STATISTICS. These advantages make *SD* and its coefficient a very popular measure of the scatteredness of a distribution. It is popularly used in the context of estimation and HYPOTHESIS TESTING.
 Bachman 2004; Brown 2005; Kothari 2008; Larson-Hall 2010; Pagano 2009; Porte 2010; Ravid 2011; Urdan 2010

standard error
also SE
a statistic used for determining the degree to which the estimate of a POPULATION PARAMETER is likely to differ from the computed SAMPLE STATISTIC. The standard error of a statistic provides an indication of how accurate an estimate it is of the POPULATION PARAMETER. It can be interpreted as a measure of variation that might be expected to occur merely by chance in the various characteristics of samples drawn equally randomly from one and the same population. Its magnitude depends on the SAMPLE SIZE and variability of measurements. It indicates the degree of uncertainty in calculating an estimate from a data set. The smaller the standard error, the better the sample statistic is as an estimate of the population parameter. One commonly used standard error is the STANDARD ERROR OF THE MEAN, which indicates how close the MEAN of the observed sample is to the mean of the entire population.
see also POPULATION, SAMPLE, STATISTIC
 Sahai & Khurshid 2001; Richards & Schmidt 2010

standard error of measurement
also SEM
an estimate of the range of scores wherein a test taker's true score lies. The standard error of measurement (SEM) decreases as the RELIABILITY of a test increases. In practice, you usually do not have repeated measures for an individual but you can get an estimate of the SEM from one group administration of a test.

The formula for SEM is:

$$\text{SEM} = SD\sqrt{1-r}$$

where
SD = the STANDARD DEVIATION of test scores
r = the reliability estimate of a test

Thus, using the standard deviation of the obtained scores and the reliability of the test, we can estimate the amount of error in individual scores. If the aptitude test has a reliability coefficient of .96 and a standard deviation of 15, then

$$\text{SEM} = 15\sqrt{1-.96} = 15\sqrt{.04} = 3$$

SEM tells us something about how accurate an individual's score is on a test. We can use a NORMAL DISTRIBUTION to make statements about the percentage of scores that fall between different points in a distribution. Given a student's obtained score, you use the SEM to determine the range of score values that will, with a given probability, include the individual's true score. This range of scores is referred to as a CONFIDENCE BAND. Assuming that the errors of measurement are normally distributed about a given score and equally distributed throughout the score range, you could be 68 percent confident that a person's true score (the score if there were no errors of measurement) lies within one SEM on either side of the observed score. For example, if a subject has an observed score of 105 on an aptitude test where the SEM is 3, you could infer at the 68 percent confidence level that the subject's true score lies somewhere between 102 and 108. Or, you can state at the 95 percent confidence level that the true score will fall within 1.96 (or rounded to 2) SEM of the obtained score (between 99 and 111). You can also use the SEM to determine how much variability could be expected on retesting the individual. If the subject could be retested on the same aptitude test a number of times, you could expect that in approximately two-thirds of the retests the scores would fall within a range of 6 points of the observed score, and in 95 percent of retests the scores would fall within a range of 12 points. Figure S.14 shows the distribution of error scores (SEM of the test) and Figure S.15 the distribution of errors around an obtained score of 105 with SEM = 3.

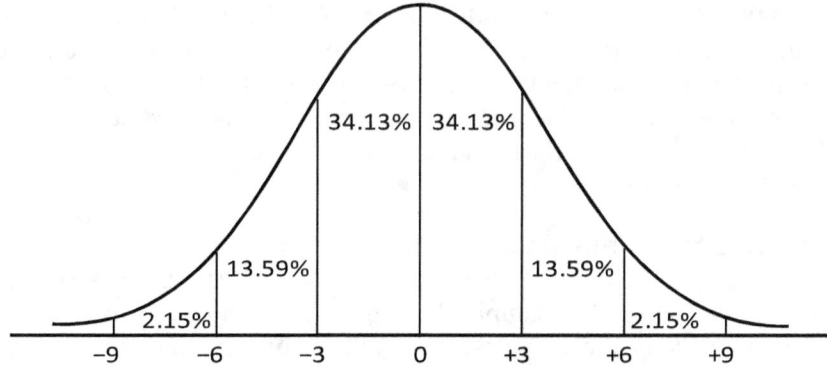

Figure S.14. The Distribution of Error Scores When SEM = 3

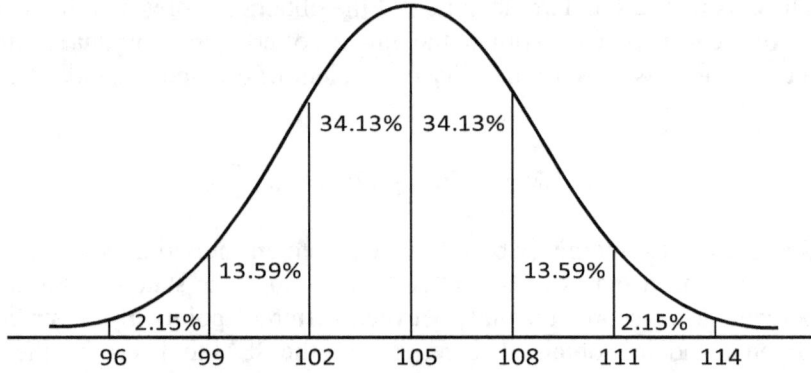

Figure S.15. The Distribution around an Obtained Score of 105 with SEM = 3

The SEM and the reliability coefficient are alternative ways of expressing how much confidence we can place in an observed score. The reliability coefficients provide an indicator of the consistency of a group of scores or items making up a test. The SEM provides an estimate of the consistency of an individual's performance on a test. How accurate or precise an estimate of the true score any observed score will provide is indicated by the size of these two indexes of reliability. As the reliability coefficient increases, the SEM decreases; as reliability decreases, the SEM increases. No one method of estimating reliability is optimal in all situations. The SEM is recommended for use when interpreting individual scores, and the reliability coefficient is recommended for use when comparing the consistency of different tests. You always want scores that are sufficiently consistent to justify anticipated uses and interpretations.
 Ary et al. 2010; Richards & Schmidt 2010

standard error of the estimate

a measure of the extent to which the estimate in a SIMPLE or MULTIPLE REGRESSION varies from SAMPLE to sample. The standard error of the estimate is a measure of how accurate the observed score of the criterion is from the score predicted by one or more PREDICTOR VARIABLEs. The bigger the difference between the observed and the predicted scores, the bigger the standard error is and the less accurate the estimate is.
 Cramer & Howitt 2004

standard error of the mean

a measure of the extent to which the MEAN of a POPULATION is likely to differ from SAMPLE to sample. The bigger the standard error of the mean, the more likely the mean is to vary from one sample to another. The standard error of the mean takes account of the size of the sample (see

SAMPLE SIZE) as the smaller the sample, the more likely it is that the sample mean will differ from the population mean. The STANDARD ERROR is used to provide an estimate of the probability of the difference between the population and the sample mean falling within a specified interval of values called the CONFIDENCE INTERVAL of the difference. Suppose, for example, that the difference between the population and the sample mean is 1.20, the standard error of the mean is .20 and the size of the sample is 50. To work out the 95% probability that this difference will fall within certain limits of a difference of 1.20, we look up the critical value of the 95% or .05 two-tailed level of t for 48 DEGREES OF FREEDOM (50 - 2 = 48), which is 2.011. We multiply this t-VALUE by the standard error of the mean to give the interval that this difference can fall on either side of the difference. This interval is .4022 (2.011 × .20 = .4022). To find the lower limit or boundary of the 95% confidence interval of the difference we subtract .4022 from 1.20 which gives about .80 (1.20 - .4022 = .7978). To work out the upper limit we add .4022 to 1.20 which gives about 1.60 (1.20 + .4022 = 1.6022). In other words, there is a 95% probability that the difference will fall between .80 and 1.60. If the standard error was bigger than .20, the confidence interval would be bigger.
📖 Cramer & Howitt 2004

standardization
see STANDARD SCORE

standardized beta (β) coefficient
another term for STANDARDIZED PARTIAL REGRESSION COEFFICIENT

standardized open-ended interview
another term for STRUCTURED INTERVIEW

standardized partial regression coefficient
also **standardized regression coefficient, standardized beta (β) coefficient**
a statistic in a MULTIPLE REGRESSION which describes the strength and the direction of the linear *association* between an INDEPENDENT VARIABLE or predictor and a DEPENDENT VARIABLE or criterion. Standardized partial regression coefficient provides a measure of the unique association between that predictor and criterion, controlling for or partialling out any association between that predictor, the other predictors in that step of the multiple regression and the criterion. In multiple regression output, the strength of the association is expressed in terms of the size of the standardized partial regression coefficient (symbolized by the lowercase Greek letter β (**beta**) and sometimes called a **beta coefficient**, or **beta**

weight) and the **unstandardized partial regression coefficient** (symbolized by its upper case equivalent **B**). They are partial because the effects of all other variables are held constant when examining beta for a given variable. The direction of the association is indicated by the sign of the REGRESSION COEFFICIENT as it is with CORRELATION COEFFICIENTs. No sign means that the association is positive with higher scores on the predictor being associated with higher scores on the criterion. A negative sign shows that the association is negative with higher scores on the predictor being associated with lower scores on the criterion. The term partial is often omitted when referring to partial regression coefficients. The standardized regression coefficient is standardized so that it can vary from -1 to 1 whereas the **unstandardized regression coefficient** can be greater than ±1. One advantage of the standardized coefficient is that it enables the size of the association between the criterion and the predictors to be compared on the same scale as this scale has been standardized to ±1. Unstandardized coefficients enable the value of the criterion to be predicted if we know the values of the predictors. Unstandardized regression coefficients are used to predict what the likely value of the criterion will be (e.g., second langauge proficiency) when we know the values of the predictors for a particular case (e.g., their years in education, age, gender, and so on). These two coefficients can be calculated from each other if the STANDARD DEVIATION of the criterion and the predictor are known. A standardized regression coefficient can be converted into its unstandardized coefficient by multiplying the standardized regression coefficient by the standard deviation of the criterion and dividing it by the standard deviation of the predictor. An unstandardized regression coefficient can be converted into its standardized coefficient by multiplying the unstandardized regression coefficient by the standard deviation of the predictor and dividing it by the standard deviation of the criterion.
📖 Cramer & Howitt 2004; Larson-Hall 2010

standardized regression coefficient
another term for STANDARDIZED PARTIAL REGRESSION COEFFICIENT

standardized score
another term for STANDARD SCORE

standard normal distribution
see NORMAL DISTRIBUTION

standard multiple regression
also **simultaneous multiple regression**
a type of MULTIPLE REGRESSION which involves simply putting all the

INDEPENDENT VARIABLEs or predictors into the model simultaneously. In fact, there is no ORDER EFFECT for the order in which variables are entered; all the study's predictor variables are entered into the REGRESSION EQUATION at once; each predictor variable is then assessed in terms of the unique amount of VARIANCE it accounts for. This method is useful for ascertaining which variables are most strongly related to the DEPENDENT VARIABLE or criterion taking into account their association with the other predictors. If standard multiple regression is used, the importance of the predictor variable depends on how much it uniquely overlaps with the criterion variable.

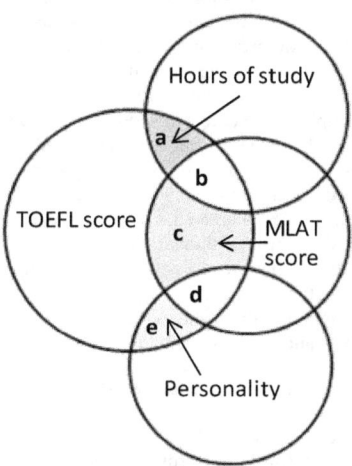

Figure S.16. Schematic Representation of Standard Multiple Regression

In Figure S.16, Modern Language Aptitude Test (MLAT) score has the largest unique contribution to the variance of the TOEFL score (the area in *c*), because it overlaps most with the TOEFL score only and not with any of the other explanatory variables. Thus, in standard regression only the areas of each predictor variable that overlap with the criterion variable, but not with any other variables, contribute to the overall estimation of how much the variables predict the response. In other words, each variable is evaluated as if it had entered the regression after all other predictor variables had entered.

If one of the predictor variables is very highly correlated with another predictor variable, it may appear to contribute very little to the overall regression equation in spite of being highly correlated with the criterion variable. For this reason, you should consider both the CANONICAL CORRELATION of the variables and the information about the unique contribution made by the predictor variable from the regression analysis.

The disadvantage of the standard regression model is that it is possible for a predictor variable to be strongly related to the criterion variable, and yet be considered an unimportant predictor, if its unique contribution in explaining the criterion variable is small.
see also SEQUENTIAL REGRESSION
📖 Ho 2006; Larson-Hall 2010; Pallant 2010

standard score
also **standardized score**

a transformed score that expresses how far a score is from the MEAN of DISTRIBUTION in terms of STANDARD DEVIATION units. The process of converting individual RAW SCOREs in a distribution to a standard score is called **standardization**. Through a process of standardization, researchers are able to generate a standard score to help them understand where an individual score falls in relation to other scores in the distribution. For example, a standardized score of .75 is a score that is .75 standard deviations above the mean; a standardized score of -2.43 is a score that is -2.43 standard deviations below the mean. Because standard scores are based on the standard deviation, the NORMAL CURVE can be used to determine the PERCENTILE RANK or relative standing of a person's score based on his/her standard score. Therefore, a standard score shows immediately how well a person did in comparison with the rest of the group taking that measure.
Commonly used standard scores are the T SCORE and Z SCORE. STANINE, CEEB, and WECHSLER SCALES subtests are also other types of standard scores.
📖 Lodico et al. 2010; Richards & Schmidt 2010; Urdan 2010

stanine

(derived from the words *standard* and *nine*) a type of STANDARD SCORE that divides a distribution into nine parts, each of which includes about one half of a STANDARD DEVIATION. Stanines comprise a scale with nine points, a mean of 5, and a standard deviation of 2. In a BELL-SHAPED DISTRIBUTION, stanines allow the conversion of PERCENTILE ranks into nine larger units. Subjects are assigned scores ranging from 1 through 9 based on their performance. All subjects within a given stanine are considered to be equal in performance. Thus, stanine 5 includes the middle 20 percent of the distribution; stanines 4 and 6 each include 17 percent; stanines 3 and 7 each include 12 percent; stanines 2 and 8 each include 7 percent; and stanines 1 and 9 each include 4 percent of the distribution. Approximately one-fourth of the scores in the distribution (23 percent, to be exact) are in stanines 1-3, and 23 percent of the scores are in stanines 7-9. Approximately one-half (54 percent) of the scores in the distribution

are contained in 4-6, the middle stanines (see Figure N.1 under the *entry* of NORMAL DISTRIBUTION).
📖 Ravid 2011

statement of purpose
a subsection (usually untitled) in a RESEARCH REPORT which follows the LITERATURE REVIEW and further narrows the INTRODUCTION to the exact topic under investigation. It does so by (1) stating the purpose in such a way that you know precisely what the author was looking for in the study, (2) presenting precise research questions that clarify what was being investigated, or (3) including specific research hypotheses that are stated in such a way that you know exactly what was being tested or studied.
📖 Brown 1988

static-group comparison design
also **posttest-comparison-group design, posttest-only nonequivalent group design, intact group design**
a PRE-EXPERIMENTAL DESIGN which uses two or more preexisting or intact (static) groups, only one of which is exposed to the EXPERIMENTAL TREATMENT. Put differently, this design compares the status of a group that has received an experimental treatment with one that has not. There is no provision for establishing the equivalence of the EXPERIMENTAL and CONTROL GROUPs. To attempt to assess the effects of the treatment, the researcher compares the groups on the DEPENDENT VARIABLE (DV) measure. This design can be represented as follows (where NR = nonrandom assignment, X = treatment, and O = posttest):

$$\begin{array}{ll} \text{Experimental Group } (NR) & X \quad O \\ \text{Control Group } (NR) & \quad O \end{array}$$

For example, if you are working with a class and there are students in other sections of that same course, it is possible to establish a control group for the research. Students have not been randomly selected for the course nor randomly assigned to sections of the course. However, you could randomly assign the special treatment to the sections by the flip of a coin. Although this design uses two groups for comparison, it is flawed because the subjects are not randomly assigned to the groups and no pretest is used. The researcher makes the assumption that the groups are equivalent in all relevant aspects before the study begins and that they differ only in their exposure to treatment.

This design may be most appealing for language experiments conducted in environments such as schools because it requires the least amount of disruption of school routines. It involves the use of intact groups. However, the researchers have to be cautious about the generalizing (see GENERALIZABILITY) the results of the study beyond their experiment because the subjects in the study have not been randomly assigned to the two groups. Besides, there is a problem of INTERNAL VALIDITY because the groups may not have been equivalent to start with. There is a low probability that any resulting between-group differences on the DV could be attributed to the INDEPENDENT VARIABLE. That is, differences in performance on the DV may be due to intrinsic group differences such as first language background, sex, exposure to the second language, the time of the day during which instruction takes place, the level of motivation of the groups, and the effects of different teachers on group response. In addition to SELECTION BIAS, MATURATION and MORTALITY are threats to the internal validity of this design.

One way to avoid some of these problems when using a static design is for the researcher to match subjects (see MATCHING) in the two groups for various characteristics such as placement test scores, sex, first language, and teacher rankings to make the groups more comparable. In this approach, each individual in one sample is matched with an individual in the other sample. The matching is done so that the two individuals are equivalent (or nearly equivalent) with respect to a specific variable that the researcher would like to control.

see also MATCHED SUBJECTS DESIGN

📖 Ary et al. 2010; Best & Kahn 2006; Cohen et al. 2011; Hatch & Farhady 1982; Hatch & Lazaraton 1991; Seliger & Shohamy 1989; Ravid 2011

statistic

a numerical value which is based on observations of the characteristics of a SAMPLE. A statistic computed from a sample may be used to estimate a **parameter**, the corresponding value in the POPULATION from which the sample is selected. **Sample statistic**s are usually represented by letters of Roman alphabet such as s^2 for the SAMPLE VARIANCE and s for the STANDARD DEVIATION of a sample. **Population parameter**s, on the other hand, are usually represented by letters of the Greek alphabet such as POPULATION MEAN (μ, the lowercase Greek letter mu), POPULATION VARIANCE (σ^2, read as sigma squared), and POPULATION STANDARD DEVIATION (σ, the lowercase Greek letter sigma).

The distinction between population parameters or characteristics and sample statistics is an important one because, while we can actually measure the attributes of individuals in a sample, and hence can actually calculate sample statistics, we seldom are able to measure the attributes of all the individuals in a population, and hence can seldom calculate population parameters. Rather, we typically use the procedures of INFER-

ENTIAL STATISTICS to estimate population parameters from sample statistics.

When choosing a statistic as an ESTIMATOR of a parameter four properties are desirable:

- *The statistic should be unbiased.* An unbiased statistic is an estimator that has an expected value equal to the parameter to be estimated. The sample mean is an unbiased estimator of the corresponding population parameter.
- *The statistic should be efficient.* An efficient statistic is one that is a better estimator in all respects than any other statistic. Both the MEDIAN and the mean are unbiased estimators of the population parameter μ, but the mean is more efficient. If we select repeated random samples of equal size from a defined population and plot the averages of each sample and the medians of each sample we would find that the averages cluster closer around the population mean than do the medians. The sample average is therefore more efficient because any average is, in the long run, more likely to be closer to the population mean than a sample median.
- *The statistic should be sufficient.* A sufficient statistic is one which uses the maximum amount of relevant sample information. The sample RANGE uses only two values in a distribution whereas the variance and standard deviation uses all the values. Similarly the mean uses all the values but the MODE uses only the most common observations. The mean and variance are more sufficient statistics than the mode and range.
- *The statistic should be resistant.* A resistant statistic is the degree to which a statistic is influenced by OUTLIERs (extreme values) in a distribution. As we have mentioned the mean is greatly influenced by extreme values whereas the median is relatively uninfluenced. The median is more resistant than the mean.

📖 Bachman 2004; Peers 1996; Porte 2010; Richards & Schmidt 2010

statistical conclusion validity

another term for STATISTICAL VALIDITY

statistical equivalence

see RANDOM ASSIGNMENT

statistical multiple regression

a type of MULTIPLE REGRESSION model in which the order of entry of INDEPENDENT VARIABLEs or predictors is based solely on statistical criteria. The meaning or interpretation of the variables is not relevant. Decisions about which variables are included and which omitted from the equation are based solely on statistics computed from the particular SAMPLE drawn; minor differences in these statistics can have a profound effect on the apparent importance of an predictor variable. Variables that correlate most strongly with the DEPENDENT VARIABLE or criterion will be afforded priority of entry, with no reference to theoretical considerations. The disadvantage of this type of regression is that the statistical criteria used for determining priority of entry may be specific to the sample at hand. For another sample, the computed statistical criteria may be different, resulting in a different order of entry for the same variables. The statistical regression model is used primarily in exploratory work, in which the researcher is unsure about the relative predictive power of the study's predictor variables.

Statistical regression can be accomplished through one of three methods: *forward selection, backward deletion,* and *stepwise regression*. In **forward selection**, the variables are evaluated against a set of statistical criteria, and if they meet these criteria, are afforded priority of entry based on their relative correlations with the criterion variable. The variable that correlates most strongly with the criterion variable gets entered into the equation first, and once in the equation, it remains in the equation. In **backward deletion**, the researcher starts with a large pool of predictor variables. Each variable is then evaluated one at a time, in terms of its contribution to the REGRESSION EQUATION. Those variables that do not contribute significantly are deleted. In **stepwise regression**, variables are evaluated for entry into the equation under both forward selection and backward deletion criteria. That is, variables are entered one at a time if they meet the statistical criteria, but they may also be deleted at any step where they no longer contribute significantly to the regression model. Stepwise regression is considered the safest procedure of the three.
 Ho 2006; Tabachnick & Fidell 2007

statistical notation
the standardized code for symbolizing the mathematical operations performed in the formulas and for symbolizing the answers we obtain.
 Heiman 2011

statistical power
also **power of a test, power**
the PROBABILITY that a study will correctly reject the NULL HYPOTHESIS (H_0) when it is actually false. Statistical power refers to the ability of a statistical test to detect a significant relationship with a specified number of participants. In other words, it is the probability of not making a TYPE II ERROR. Therefore, the power of a test is $1 - \beta$ (the lowercase Greek letter beta, representing Type II error). Low statistical power is the most

common threat to STATISTICAL VALIDITY. The presence of this threat produces a low probability of detecting a difference between experimental and control conditions even when a difference truly exists. You may think of power in terms of looking through a microscope; if it has sufficient power to see the details, you will be able to see the true situation, but if the power is too low you will not be able to find out any useful information.

Statistical power depends on different factors. First, power is determined by the LEVEL OF SIGNIFICANCE (α). As α increases, power increases. Thus, if α increases from .05 to .10, then power will increase. This factor is under the control of the researcher. Second, power is determined by SAMPLE SIZE. As sample size n increases, power increases. Thus, if sample size increases, meaning we have a SAMPLE that consists of a larger proportion of the population, this will cause the STANDARD ERROR OF THE MEAN to decrease, as there is less SAMPLING ERROR with larger samples. This factor is also under the control of the researcher. In addition, because a larger sample yields a smaller STANDARD ERROR, it will be easier to reject H_0 (all else being equal), and the CONFIDENCE INTERVALs generated will also be narrower. Third, power is determined by the size of the POPULATION STANDARD DEVIATION (σ). Although not under the researcher's control, as σ increases, power decreases. Thus if σ increases meaning the variability in the population is larger, this will cause the standard error of the mean to increase as there is more sampling error with larger variability. Fourth, power is determined by the difference between the true POPULATION MEAN (μ) and the hypothesized mean value. Although not always under the researcher's control, as the difference between the true population mean and the hypothesized mean value increases, power increases. Thus if the difference between the true population mean and the hypothesized mean value is large, it will be easier to correctly reject H_0. This would result in greater separation between the two SAMPLING DISTRIBUTIONs. Finally, power is determined by whether we are conducting a ONE- or a TWO-TAILED TEST. There is greater power in a one-tailed test, such as when $\mu > 100$, than in a two-tailed test. This factor is under the researcher's control.

Power analysis can be used in two ways. It can be used prospectively during the design stage to decide on the sample size required to achieve a given level of power. It can also be used retrospectively once the data have been collected, to ascertain what power the test had. The more useful approach is prospective power analysis. Once the design, α level, and tail of test have been decided, researchers can calculate the sample size they require. However, they still have the problem of arriving at an indication of the EFFECT SIZE before they can do the power calculations. It is important to consider power in the plan of a QUASI-EXPERIMENTAL or

TRUE EXPERIMENTAL DESIGN. If the power of an experiment is low, there is then a good chance that the experiment will be inconclusive.
📖 Clark-Carter 2010; Larson-Hall 2010; Lomax 2007; Perry 2011; Porte 2010

statistical regression
also regression toward the mean

a threat to INTERNAL VALIDITY where the difference between scores on the pretest and posttest is due to the natural tendency for initial extreme scores to move toward the average on subsequent-testing. Statistical regression is a fancy name for a phenomenon found in research where participants chosen from two opposite ends of an ability continuum, usually based on performance on some test, have a high probability of scoring closer to the middle of the continuum on the second testing without any outside help. This movement of scores toward the middle is referred to as regression toward the mean or statistical regression. For example, suppose an IQ test is administered to a group of students. A few weeks later, the same students are tested again, using the same test. If we examine the scores of those who scored at the extreme (either very high or very low) when the test was administered the first time, we would probably discover that many low-scoring students score higher the second time around, while many high-scoring students score lower.

see also MORTALITY, TESTING EFFECT, INSTRUMENTATION, DIFFERENTIAL SELECTION, HISTORY, MATURATION
📖 Perry 2011; Ravid 2011

statistical significance

a criterion used when testing a statistical HYPOTHESIS which refers to the likelihood that an obtained effect, such as a difference or CORRELATION, could have occurred by chance alone. First, the difference between the results of the experiment and the NULL HYPOTHESIS is determined. Then, proceeding with the assumption that the null hypothesis is true, the PROBABILITY VALUE (p-value) of a difference that large or larger is computed. Finally, this probability is compared to the SIGNIFICANCE LEVEL (also called *alpha* (α) *level*). If this probability is sufficiently low (i.e., less than or equal to the significance level), then the null hypothesis is rejected and the outcome is said to be statistically significant. If the p-value is greater than alpha level, we fail to reject the null hypothesis and the result is said to be not statistically significant. The researcher would want to make the significance level as small as possible in order to protect the null hypothesis and to avoid inadvertently making false claims. An alpha of .01 (compared with .05 or .10) means that the researcher is being relatively careful. S/he is only willing to risk being wrong 1 in a 100 times in rejecting the null hypothesis when it is true (i.e., saying there is an effect or relationship when there really is not).

see also PRACTICAL SIGNIFICANCE
📖 Porte 2010

statistical table
presentation of numerical facts usually arranged in the form of columns and rows. A statistical table either summarizes or displays the results of a statistical analysis.
📖 Sahai & Khurshid 2001

statistical test
also **test of significance, significance test**
a statistical procedure or any of several tests of STATISTICAL SIGNIFICANCE used to test a NULL HYPOTHESIS. The test assesses the compatibility of the experimental data with the null hypothesis. The procedure rejects the null hypothesis if an observed difference (or a more extreme one) would have a small PROBABILITY if the null hypothesis were true. Some examples of statistical tests are t-TEST, CHI-SQUARE TEST, and F TEST.
📖 Sahai & Khurshid 2001

statistical validity
also **statistical conclusion validity, conclusion validity**
a type of VALIDITY which refers to aspects of quantitative evaluation that affect the accuracy of the conclusions drawn from the results of a study. Put differently, statistical conclusion validity refers to the appropriate use of statistics to infer whether an observed relationship between the INDEPENDENT VARIABLEs and DEPENDENT VARIABLEs in a study is a true cause-effect relationship or whether it is just due to chance. Any inappropriate use of statistics is thus a threat because it may result in an erroneous conclusion about the effect of the independent variable on the dependent variable. Threats to statistical conclusion validity include using tests with low STATISTICAL POWER, which may fail to detect a relationship between variables; violating the ASSUMPTIONS of STATISTICAL TESTs, which can lead to over- or underestimating the size and significance of an effect; using measures with low RELIABILITY or with RESTRICTED RANGE of scores, both of which lessen the probability of detecting a relationship; and using statistical tests that result in over- or underestimations of the size of an effect. Such problems with statistical analysis may lead researchers to report incorrectly that a treatment has no effect. In that case, a difference that is real but small may be lost in the statistical noise.
Statistical conclusion validity and INTERNAL VALIDITY are related because both are concerned with the relationship between treatment and outcome. A study may be very carefully designed and well controlled

(internal validity), but a statistical error can occur and lead to incorrect conclusions about STATISTICAL SIGNIFICANCE and EFFECT SIZEs. Thus, in quantitative experiments, internal validity depends substantially on statistical conclusion validity.
 Ary et al. 2010

statistics
a body of mathematical techniques or procedures for gathering, organizing, analyzing, interpreting, and displaying numerical data, and making decisions based on data. Statistics is a basic tool for measurement, evaluation, and research.
see also DESCRIPTIVE STATISTICS, INFERENTIAL STATISTICS
 Walliman 2006

stem-and-leaf plot
a method of displaying data in which each observation is split into two parts labeled the *stem* and the *leaf*. Stem-and-leaf plot presents raw data in a HISTOGRAM-like display and combines features of both a frequency table and a histogram. Histograms display data using somewhat arbitrarily defined slices of the data to create the bins of the plot. Individual data points or values (i.e., dots on the graph) cannot clearly be seen. Stem and leaf plots basically display the same kind of information as a histogram that uses frequency counts, but use the data itself to show the distribution, and thus retain all of the data points. The method is illustrated with measures taken from a hypothetical study aimed at understanding how children acquire reading skills. A portion of the study was based on a measure that reflects the ability of children to identify words.

58	58	58	58	58	64	64	68	72	72	72	75	75	77	77	79	80
82	82	82	82	82	84	84	85	85	90	91	91	92	93	93	93	95
95	95	95	95	95	95	95	98	98	99	101	101	101	102	102	102	102
102	103	104	104	104	104	104	105	105	105	105	105	107	108	108	110	111
112	114	119	122	122	125	125	125	127	129	129	132	134				

Table S.4. Word Identification Scores

Table S.4 lists the observed scores in ascending order. The construction of a stem-and-leaf display begins by separating each value into two components. The first is the leaf, which in this example is the number in the 1s position (the single digit just to the left of the decimal place). For example, the leaf corresponding to the value 58 is 8. The leaf for the value 64 is 4, and the leaf for 125 is 5. The digits to the left of the leaf are called the stem. Here the stem of 58 is 5, the number to the left of 8. Similarly, 64 has a stem of 6 and 125 has a stem of 12. We can display the results for all 81 children in the Table S.5.

Srems	Leaves
5	88888
6	448
7	22255779
8	0222224455
9	0112333555555889
10	1112222234444455555788
11	01249
12	22555799
13	24

Table S.5. Stem-and-Leaf Plot

There are five children who have the score 58, so there are five scores with a leaf of 8, and this is reflected by the five 8s displayed to the right of the stem 5, in the Leaves column. Two children got the score 64, and one child got the score 68. That is, for the stem 6, there are two leaves equal to 4 and one equal to 8, as indicated by the list of leaves in the display. Now look at the third row of numbers, where the stem is 7. The leaves listed are 2, 2, 2, 5, 5, 7, 7, and 9. This indicates that the value 72 occurred three times, the value 75 occurred two times, as did the value 77, and the value 79 occurred once. Notice that the display of the leaves gives us some indication of the values that occur most frequently and which are relatively rare. Like the histogram, the stem-and-leaf display gives us an overall sense of what the values are like. The choice of which digit is to be used as the leaf depends in part on which digit provides a useful graphical summary of the data.
 Larson-Hall 2010; Wilcox 2003

stimulated recall
another term for RETROSPECTIVE PROTOCOL

stochastic variable
another term for CHANCE VARIABLE

strata
see STRATIFIED SAMPLING

stratified purposive sampling
see PURPOSIVE SAMPLING

stratified random sampling
another term for STRATIFIED SAMPLING

stratified sample

see STRATIFIED SAMPLING

stratified sampling
also stratified random sampling

a type of PROBABILITY SAMPLING which involves dividing the POPULATION into two or more homogenous groups, known as **strata**, each group containing subjects with similar characteristics. A stratum is a subset of the population that shares a particular characteristic. If the population from which a SAMPLE is to be drawn does not constitute a homogeneous group, then stratified sampling technique is applied so as to obtain a representative sample. In this technique, the population is stratified into a number of non-overlapping subpopulations or strata and sample items are selected from each stratum. The procedure gives every individual in a stratum an equal and independent chance of appearing in the sample. The strata are formed such that they are internally homogenous, but differ from one another with respect to some characteristics of interest.

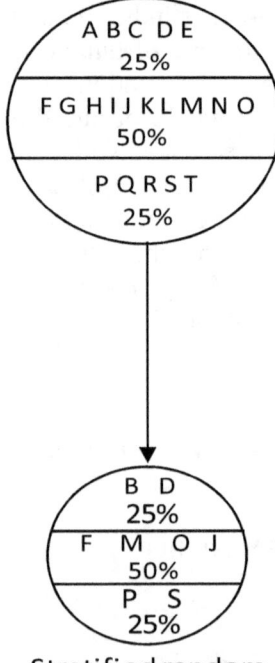

Figure S.17. Schematic Representation of a Proportional Stratified Sampling

A sample consisting of random samples selected from each stratum or subpopulation of a population is called a **stratified sample**. It is used to ensure that each subpopulation of a large heterogeneous population is appropriately represented in the sample.

There are two main ways in which stratified sampling can be conducted: proportionately and disproportionately. As shown in Figure S.17, **proportional stratified sampling** attempts to choose cases that represent the proportion of each of the subgroups. For example, if you wanted to sample 100 second language learners and the population consisted of 25% Japanese, 50% Iranian, and 25% Chinese, a proportionate stratified sample would be 25 Japanese, 25 Chinese, and 50 Iranian. In a **disproportionate stratified sampling** you would use a different ratio. Note that stratification can be used in conjunction with *systematic* as well as *simple random* sampling.

A stratified random sample is a useful blend of *randomization* and *categorization*, thereby enabling both a quantitative and qualitative piece of research to be undertaken. A quantitative piece of research will be able to use analytical and INFERENTIAL STATISTICS, whilst a qualitative piece of research will be able to target those groups in institutions or clusters of participants who will be able to be approached to participate in the research.

see also SIMPLE RANDOM SAMPLING, SYSTEMATIC SAMPLING, CLUSTER SAMPLING, AREA SAMPLING, MULTI-PHASE SAMPLING

📖 Cohen et al. 2011; Dörnyei 2007; O'Leary 2004; Perry 2011

structural equation modeling
also covariance structure analysis, SEM

a sophisticated and complex set of *multivariate* statistical procedures which can be used to carry out FACTOR ANALYSIS and PATH ANALYSIS to test a researcher's theoretical model that involves both a manifest (observed) and latent (unobserved) variables. Structural equation modeling (SEM) is a powerful analytic procedure that combines the capability of path analysis to investigate relationships among multiple INDEPENDENT and DEPENDENT (observed) VARIABLEs with the capability of factor analysis to investigate relationships between observed and unobserved variables, or factors, and the relationships among factors. SEM is theory driven; that is, when a researcher employs SEM to test a theory, there is a strong need for justification for the specification of the dependence relationships; theory provides this justification.

In its most general form, SEM consists of two parts: the 'measurement model' and the 'structural equation model'. The *measurement model* which specifies the rules governing how the latent variables are measured in terms of the observed variables, and it describes the measurement properties of the observed variables. That is, measurement models are concerned with the relations between observed and latent variables. Such models specify hypotheses about the relations between a set of observed variables, such as ratings or QUESTIONNAIRE items, and the unobserved variables or constructs they were designed to measure.

The *structural equation model* is a flexible, comprehensive model that specifies the pattern of relationships among independent and dependent variables, either observed or latent. It incorporates the strengths of MULTIPLE REGRESSION analysis, factor analysis, and MULTIVARIATE ANOVA in a single model that can be evaluated statistically. Moreover, it permits directional predictions among a set of independent or a set of dependent variables, and it permits modeling of indirect effects.

Of the two models, the structural model is of greater interest to the researcher, because it offers a direct test of the theory of interest. The measurement model is important as it provides a test for the reliability of the observed variables employed to measure the latent variables. A measurement model that offers a poor fit to the data suggests that at least some of the observed indicator variables are unreliable, and precludes the researcher from moving to the analysis of the structural model.

The usefulness of SEM in research is distinguished by three following characteristics:

1) It provides a method of dealing with multiple relationships simultaneously. Model testing via path analysis can be carried out with the conventional multiple regression technique. That is, PATH COEFFICIENTs can be estimated by regressing the ENDOGENOUS VARIABLE on to the EXOGENOUS VARIABLEs, and then repeating the procedure by treating the exogenous variables as endogenous variables. Such a method, however, is typically piecemeal in nature and does not provide information regarding the hypothesized model's goodness-of-fit (see GOODNESS-OF-FIT TEST). Without information about the model's goodness-of-fit, it is difficult to assess the adequacy of the theory underlying the hypothesized model. SEM, on the other hand, is able to estimate the multiple and interrelated dependence relationships simultaneously. Because it tests the model as a whole, rather than in a piecemeal fashion, statistics can be calculated to show the goodness-of-fit of the data to the hypothesized model.

2) It is able to represent unobserved concepts in the analysis of dependence relationships. Although multiple regression can be used to analyze relationships between variables, its use is limited to the analysis of those variables that can only be directly observed (or measured). SEM, on the other hand, has the ability to incorporate latent variables in the analysis. For example, a researcher wants to investigate the pattern of relationships between three psychological constructs: aggression, authoritarianism, and intelligence. All three constructs cannot be directly observed and, therefore, cannot be directly measured. They

are measured indirectly using various types of scale items, from questionnaires and inventories. Based on the responses to these scale items, the magnitude of these latent variables can be estimated. This is similar to factor analysis, in which highly interrelated clusters of scale items are identified as latent factors. SEM can then be used to estimate paths between latent factors rather than between variables.

3) It improves statistical estimation by accounting for MEASUREMENT ERROR in the estimation process. The univariate and multivariate techniques all assume that there is no error associated with the measurement of variables. That is, these techniques assume that variables in the analyses are error-free. Although this is an unrealistic assumption, many if not most researchers, regrettably, act as if this is indeed the case for their data. We know from both theoretical and practical perspectives that concepts can seldom be measured perfectly, either because of inaccurate responses by the respondents, or because of problems associated with the operationalization of the concepts. Consequently, measured variables usually contain at least moderate amounts of error, and when such measures are used in univariate and multivariate models (e.g., ANOVA, ANCOVA, MANOVA, and multiple regression), the coefficients obtained will be biased, most often in unknown degree and direction. SEM, on the other hand, uses scores on the measured or MANIFEST VARIABLEs to develop estimates of the individual's scores on the underlying construct, or latent variables. As these estimates are derived on the basis of the common or shared variance among the measured variables, scores on the latent variables are unaffected by random measurement error. Thus, when these variables are used in SEM analysis, the potentially biasing effects of random measurement error on the results are removed. The net result is that the statistical estimation process is improved, because the structural paths between latent variables are relatively free of the unreliabilities of their measurement indicators.

📖 Bachman 2004; Clark-Carter 2010; Ho 2006; Leary 2011

structuralism

a theoretical concept that has been interpreted in a number of different ways, but a common theme is the prioritization of the explanatory power of linguistic, social, and economic structures over individual AGENCY and meaning. Emphasis is also placed on underlying processes and systems that determine individual action. In relation to the practice of research, structuralism can be associated with POSITIVISM, which focuses on the methodology utilized by physical science applied to the social field, and to CRITICAL REALISM, which concentrates on a more qualitative engagement between conceptual DECONSTRUCTION and reconstruction in the social arena. Associations between structuralism and positiv-

ism can take a number of different forms, but commonalities include an emphasis on rational inquiry and on uncovering cause and effect, the achievement of OBJECTIVITY, and the production of value-free knowledge, which is regarded as factual and incontrovertible. Structuralist and positivist research methodologies predominantly utilize quantitative orientations. These orientations clearly have a different emphasis on qualitative approaches, but they can be used alongside qualitative data collection methods and data analysis techniques to interrogate research questions in different ways.
📖 Given 2008

structured interview
also **standardized open-ended interview**
an INTERVIEW in which the organization and procedure of the interview, as well as the topics to be asked about, the questions, and the order in which they will be presented, have all been determined in advance. Structured interview involves a prescribed set of questions which the researcher asks in a fixed order, and which generally require the interviewee to respond by selection of one or more fixed options. This means that the sequence and wording of the questions are determined by means of a pre-prepared elaborate INTERVIEW GUIDE and the interviewer is left little freedom to make modifications. All respondents are asked the same questions with the same wording and in the same sequence. The stimulus is therefore the same for all respondents. Such tightly controlled interviews ensure that the interviewee focuses on the target topic area and that the interview covers a well-defined domain, which makes the answers comparable across different respondents. This method ensures rapid data coding and analysis, easy quantification of data and consequent comparability of responses and guaranteed coverage of the area of interest to the research.

However, in a structured interview there is generally little room for variation or spontaneity in the responses because the interviewer is to record the responses according to a coding scheme. There is also very little flexibility in the way questions are asked because by adopting a standardized format it is hoped that nothing will be left to chance. Structured interviews are used in situations where a QUESTIONNAIRE would in theory be adequate except that for some reason the written format is not feasible (e.g., because of the low level of literacy amongst the participants).

see also ETHNOGRAPHIC INTERVIEW, NON-DIRECTIVE INTERVIEW, UNSTRUCTURED INTERVIEW, SEMI-STRUCTURED INTERVIEW, INTERVIEW GUIDE, INFORMAL INTERVIEW, TELEPHONE INTERVIEW, FOCUS GROUP
📖 Brewerton & Millward 2001; Cohen et al. 2011; Corbetta 2003; Dörnyei 2007; Mackey & Gass 2005

structured observation
see OBSERVATION

structured questionnaire
a type of QUESTIONNAIRE which is used when researchers have a clear idea about the range of possible answers they wish to elicit. Structured questionnaire will involve precise wording of questions, which are asked in a fixed order and each one of which is likely to require respondents to answer one of a number of alternatives that are presented to them. There are a number of advantages of this approach to asking questions. Firstly, respondents could fill in the questionnaire themselves, which means that it could save the researcher's time both in interviewing and in travelling to where the respondent lives. Secondly, a standard format can minimize the effect of the way in which a question is asked of the respondent and on his/her response. Without this check any differences that are found between people's responses could be due to the way the question was asked rather than any inherent differences between the respondents. A third advantage of this technique is that the responses are more immediately quantifiable. For example, respondents can be said to have scored 1 if they said that they strongly agreed with the statement and 5 if they strongly disagreed.
 Clark-Carter 2010

studentized maximum modulus
see STUDENTIZED RANGE TEST

Studentized range
another term for STUDENTIZED RANGE TEST

studentized range statistic
another term for STUDENTIZED RANGE TEST

studentized range test
also **studentized range statistic, studentized range, q**
a statistic which is used in some MULTIPLE COMPARISON TESTs (e.g., TUKEY'S TEST, NEWMAN-KEULS TEST, GAMES-HOWELL MULTIPLE COMPARISON). Studentized range statistic is the difference or range between the smallest and the largest mean divided by the standard error of the range of means which is the SQUARE ROOT of the division of the ERROR MEAN SQUARE by the number of cases in a group.

$$q = \frac{\text{largest mean} - \text{smallest mean}}{\sqrt{\text{error mean square/number of cases in a group}}}$$

The distribution of this statistic depends on two sets of DEGREES OF FREEDOM, one for the number of means being compared, and the other for the error mean square. With four groups of three cases each, the degrees of freedom for the number of groups being compared are 4 and for the error mean square is the number of cases minus the number of groups, which is 8 (12 - 4 = 8). Studentized range test is contrasted with the **studentized maximum modulus,** which is the maximum absolute value of the group means divided by the standard error of the means.
see also STANDARD ERROR OF THE MEAN
📖 Cramer & Howitt 2004; Everitt & Skrondal 2010

Student-Newman-Keuls test
another term for NEWMAN-KEULS TEST

Student's *t* distribution
another term for *t* DISTRIBUTION

Student's *t* statistic
another term for *t* STATISTIC

Student's *t*-test
another term for *t*-TEST

study design
another term for RESEARCH DESIGN

subject attrition
another term for MORTALITY

subject descriptor
another term for FACTUAL QUESTION

subjectivism
a certain way of conceptualizing subjectivity. Subjectivity is what makes us subjects rather than objects. Subjectivism includes processes denoted by the terms mental, mind, conscious, experience, will, intentionality, thinking, feeling, remembering, interpreting, understanding, learning, and psyche. These subjective processes comprise the activity of subjects. Without subjectivity, we would only be physical objects devoid of activity. Subjectivism dominates qualitative methodology. It construes interactions between researcher and subjects (through INTERVIEWs in particular) and the active interpretation of data—which are central features of QUALITATIVE RESEARCH—as a license for the free exercise of subjective processes. The subject is free to express whatever subjective idea s/he de-

sires, and the researcher is free to subjectively interpret data. The subjectivistic tendency in qualitative research (which is contradicted by OBJECTIVISM) claims that the world, including the psychological world of subjects, is unknowable. Consequently, the researcher constructs an impression of the world as s/he sees it, without regard for whether this subjective impression corresponds to any reality beyond.

In qualitative research, one way of dealing with subjectivity is through multiplicity of approach (see TRIANGULATION).
 Davies & Elder 2004; Given 2008

subject variable
a term which is sometimes used to describe the characteristics of subjects or participants which are not manipulated such as their gender, age, socio-economic status, abilities and personality characteristics. A distinction may be made between subject variables, which have not been manipulated, and INDEPENDENT VARIABLEs, which have been manipulated.
 Cramer & Howitt 2004

subtle realism
a middle ground between the NAIVE REALISM and the RELATIVISM. Subtle realism shares the naive realist ONTOLOGY that the world consists of independent phenomena but argues that we do not have direct access to them. In terms of EPISTEMOLOGY, subtle realism agrees with naive realism that the world is knowable but adds that our understanding always relies on cultural assumptions and is, at best, a selective representation; that is, one of many possible valid accounts. This is a correspondence theory of truth but one that allows that, because we have no direct access to reality, we can never have absolutely certain knowledge. Hence, subtle realism requires that researchers make explicit the relevances on which their accounts are based. For example, accounts must be plausible given our existing knowledge, have credibility as the kinds of accounts that might reasonably be expected given the conditions of the research, and have relevance to issues of human concern.
see also SCIENTIFIC REALISM, ANALYTIC REALISM, CRITICAL REALISM
 Given 2008

summated scale
another term for LIKERT SCALE

summative evaluation
also **outcome evaluation**
a type of EVALUATION RESEARCH which focuses on gathering specific kinds of outcome data, such as test scores and final results to determine whether the program has met its overall goals, and might also assess the

overall effects of the program both intended and unintended. The goal is to provide information that can assess the effectiveness, efficiency, and ethicality of the change strategy in question. Summative evaluations summarize it by describing what happens subsequent to delivery of the program or technology; assessing whether the object can be said to have caused the outcome; determining the overall impact of the causal factor beyond only the immediate target outcomes; and estimating the relative costs associated with the object. Examples of summative evaluations are changes in second language students reading scores, number of people served by the program, and job satisfaction ratings.
 Lodico et al. 2010; O'Leary 2004; Richards & Schmidt 2010; Trochim & Donnelly 2007

sum of squares
also *SS*
the sum of squared deviations around a particular MEAN, i.e., either the GRAND MEAN or the individual group mean.
 Sahai & Khurshid 2001

sum of squares between groups
also **between-groups sum of squares,** SS_{BG}
the sum of the squared deviations of the group MEANs (the mean of all the scores in a particular group) from the GRAND MEAN. It is calculated by subtracting each group mean from the grand mean, squaring these differences for all items, and then summing them. The between-groups sum of squares is the numerator of the equation that represents BETWEEN-GROUPS VARIABILITY (i.e., the equation that represents the amount of variability between the means of the k groups)
 Sahai & Khurshid 2001; Sheskin 2011

sum of squares for columns
also **column sum of squares**
the variability between TREATMENTs, which are represented in the columns, calculated as the sum of the squared deviations of the column MEANs from the GRAND MEAN, weighted by the number of cases in the column.
 Sahai & Khurshid 2001

sum of squares for error
the variability due to individual differences between subjects, MEASUREMENT ERRORs, uncontrolled variations in experimental procedures, and so on, calculated by subtracting the SUM OF SQUARES FOR ROWS, COLUMNS, and INTERACTION from the TOTAL SUM OF SQUARES.
 Sahai & Khurshid 2001

sum of squares for interaction
also **interaction sum of squares**
the variability due to the INTERACTION between the two experimental FACTORs.
📖 Sahai & Khurshid 2001

sum of squares for rows
also **row sum of squares**
the variability between blocks of subjects, which are represented in the rows, calculated as the sum of the squared deviations of the row MEANs from the GRAND MEAN, weighted by the number of cases in the row.
📖 Sahai & Khurshid 2001

sum of squares for total
also **total sum of squares, SS_T**
the overall sum of squared deviations within all the groups. Total sum of squares is obtained by subtracting each individual value from the MEAN of all values, squaring, and summing these values.
📖 Sahai & Khurshid 2001; Sheskin 2011

sum of squares for treatment
also **treatment sum of squares**
the sum of the squared deviations between each treatment MEAN and the GRAND MEAN. It is the component of the TOTAL SUM OF SQUARES that can be attributed to possible differences among the treatments.
📖 Sahai & Khurshid 2001

sum of squares regression
also **regression sum of squares (SS_R)**
sum of the squared differences between the MEAN and predicted values of the DEPENDENT VARIABLE for all observations. It represents the amount of improvement in explanation of the dependent variable attributable to the INDEPENDENT VARIABLE(s).
📖 Hair et al. 2011

sum of squares within groups
also **within-groups sum of squares, SS_{WG}**
the overall sum of squared deviations within all the groups. It is obtained by subtracting each score from its group MEAN (the mean of all the scores in a particular group), squaring these differences, and then summing them. The within-groups sum of squares is the numerator of the equation that represents WITHIN-GROUPS VARIABILITY (i.e., the equation that represents the average amount of variability within each of the k groups, which represents error variability).
📖 Sahai & Khurshid 2001; Sheskin 2011

suppliance in obligatory contexts
also SOC
a coding unit for oral and written data. Some language acquisition studies have focused on grammatical accuracy with respect to specified linguistic features. A researcher may be interested in whether a learner has acquired a particular grammatical form such as the simple past tense, the progressive *-ing*, or the third person singular *s*. The learner's level of acquisition can be measured in terms of how often these features are supplied where they are required. For example, in the sentence 'He is singing right now', the *-ing* is required because this is a context in which the progressive form is obligatory. Suppliance in obligatory contexts was first used in early studies of the acquisition of grammatical morphemes by children acquiring English as their first language, but it has also been applied in second language studies.
see also T-UNITS, CHAT
 Mackey & Gass 2005

suppressor variable
also masking variable
a VARIABLE in a REGRESSION ANALYSIS that is not correlated with the DEPENDENT VARIABLE or criterion, but that is still useful for increasing the size of the MULTIPLE CORRELATION COEFFICIENT by virtue of its correlations with other INDEPENDENT VARIABLEs or predictors. This predictor variable is called a suppressor variable because it suppresses variance that is irrelevant to prediction of the criterion variable. Thus, a suppressor variable is defined not by its own REGRESSION WEIGHT, but by its enhancement of the effects of other variables in the set of predictor variables. It is a suppressor only for those variables whose regression weights are increased. Another type of suppression is **reciprocal suppression** (also called **cooperative suppression**), in which predictor variables correlate positively with the criterion variable and correlate negatively with each other (or vice versa). Both predictor variables end up with higher CORRELATIONs with the criterion variable after each predictor variable is adjusted for the other.

A third type of suppression occurs when the sign of a regression weight of a predictor variable is the opposite of what would be expected on the basis of its correlation with the criterion variable. This is **negative suppression** (also called **net suppression**). Prediction still is enhanced because the magnitude of the effect of the predictor variable is greater (although the sign is opposite) in the presence of the suppressor.

In output, the presence of a suppressor variable is identified by the pattern of REGRESSION COEFFICIENTs and correlations of each predictor variable with the criterion variable. Compare the simple correlation between each predictor variable and the criterion variable in the CORRELATION MATRIX with the STANDARDIZED REGRESSION COEFFICIENT (beta weight) for the predictor variable. If the beta weight is significantly different from zero, either one of the following two conditions signals the presence of a suppressor variable: (1) the absolute value of the simple correlation between predictor variable and criterion variable is substantially smaller than the beta weight for the predictor variable, or (2) the simple correlation and beta weight have opposite signs. There is as yet no STATISTICAL TEST available to assess how different a regression weight and a simple correlation need to be to identify suppression.

It is often difficult to identify which variable is doing the suppression if there are more than two or three predictor variables. If you know that a suppressor variable is present, you need to search for it among the regression coefficients and correlations of the predictor variables. The suppressor is among the ones that are congruent, where the correlation with the criterion variable and the regression coefficients are consistent in size and direction. One strategy is to systematically leave each congruent predictor variable out of the equation and examine the changes in regression coefficients for the predictor variable(s) with inconsistent regression coefficients and correlations in the original equation.

If a suppressor variable is identified, it is properly interpreted as a variable that enhances the importance of other predictor variables by virtue of suppression of irrelevant variance in them.

📖 Everitt & Skrondal 2010; Howitt & Cramer 2011; Tabachnick & Fidell 2007

survey
another term for SURVEY RESEARCH

survey research
also **survey**
a set of methods used to gather data in a systematic way from a range of individuals, organizations, or other units of interest. Specific methods may include QUESTIONNAIRE, INTERVIEW, FOCUS GROUP, or OBSERVATION. Many studies using more than one data collection method will include a survey method. For example, a quantitatively oriented questionnaire could be used to generate general understanding of a set of related questions, to identify interview questions for deeper qualitative investigation, and to identify possible interview participants. Alternatively, a questionnaire could be used to confirm the GENERALIZABILITY of results from a small interview study to a larger, more statistically representative SAMPLE. Surveys can be *exploratory*, in which no assumptions or models are postulated, and in which relationships and patterns are explored (e.g., through CORRELATION, REGRESSION, and FACTOR ANALYSIS). They can also be *confirmatory*, in which a model, CAUSAL RELATIONSHIP or HYPOTHESIS is tested. Surveys can be *descriptive* or *analytic*. Descriptive

surveys simply describe data on variables of interest, while analytic surveys operate with hypothesized predictor variables that are tested for their influence on DEPENDENT VARIABLEs.

Survey research is common because it is so flexible, open to researchers taking quantitative as well as qualitative approaches. Survey methods can answer a wide range of research questions, from the 'who' and 'what' to the 'how' and 'why'. Because of this flexibility, survey research is appealing to inexperienced researchers and is, therefore, open to careless design and data collection practices. However, trustworthy survey research requires careful consideration of design and research conduct.

Although some researchers believe survey research to be a wholly quantitative approach, this opinion is not universally shared. Data gathered from any survey method may be entirely quantitative, may be largely qualitative, or may be a mixture. For example, OPEN-ENDED QUESTIONs on a questionnaire or asked in an interview will produce text that may be analyzed qualitatively. Qualitative data gathered in survey methods tends to be in text form, such as narrative responses to open-ended questions posed in an interview or written responses to a comments item on a questionnaire.

Generally, surveys are also classified according to the time of data collection: LONGITUDINAL SURVEYs, which study changes across time, and CROSS-SECTIONAL SURVEYs, which focus on a single point in time.

see also DESCRIPTIVE RESEARCH

Brown 2001; Dörnyei 2003; Given 2008; McKay 2006

switching-replications design

one of the strongest of the TRUE EXPERIMENTAL DESIGNS. When the circumstances are right for this design, it addresses one of the major problems in experimental designs: the need to deny the TREATMENT to some participants through RANDOM ASSIGNMENT. The design notation indicates that this is a two-group design with three waves of measurement. You might think of this as two pre-post, treatment-control designs grafted together. That is, the implementation of the treatment is repeated or replicated. In the repetition of the treatment, the two groups switch roles; the original CONTROL GROUP becomes the TREATMENT GROUP in phase two; whereas the original treatment acts as the control. By the end of the study, all participants have received the treatment.

This design can be diagramed as follows (where R = random assignments of subjects, X = treatment, and O = pretest and posttest):

```
Experimental Group (R)    O  X  O        O
Control Group (R)         O        O  X  O
```

The switching-replications design is most feasible in organizational contexts where treatment is repeated at regular intervals. For instance, it works especially well in schools that are on a semester system. All students are pretested at the beginning of the school year. During the first semester, Group A receives the treatment, and during the second semester, Group B gets it.
📖 Trochim & Donnelly 2007

switch-over design
another term for COUNTER BALANCED DESIGN

symbolic interactionism
also **SI**
a sociological and social-psychological perspective grounded in the study of the meanings that people learn and assign to the objects and actions that surround their everyday experiences. The term symbolic interactionism is comprised of two concepts: *symbol* and *interaction*. Symbol refers to any social object (e.g., a physical object, a gesture, or a word) that stands in place of or represents something else. Symbols are a uniquely human creation. Interaction highlights the significance of interpersonal communication in transmitting the meaning of symbols. Through interaction, culture arises. Central to social behavior is the notion of meaning. Human interaction with the world is mediated through the process of meaning-making and interpretation. For interactionists, humans are pragmatic actors who continually adjust their behavior to the actions and reactions of other actors. People can adjust to these actions only because humans are able to interpret the actions of others; that is, humans are capable of denoting actions symbolically and treating these actions, and those who perform them, as symbolic objects. This process of adjustment is aided by human's ability to imaginatively rehearse alternative lines of action before acting—as if performing before an imaginary audience. The process is further aided by the ability to think about and to react to one's own actions and even oneself as a symbolic object. Thus, the interactionist sees humans as active, creative participants who construct their social world, not as passive, conforming objects of socialization.
The essential tenets of symbolic interactionism are that:

- People interpret the meaning of objects and actions in the world and then act upon those interpretations.
- Meanings arise from the process of social interaction.
- Meanings are handled in, and are modified by, an interactive process used by people in dealing with the phenomena that are encountered.

Therefore, meanings are not fixed or stable but are revised on the basis of experience. This includes the definition of self and of who we are. For example, if someone is promoted from supervisor to manager their perception of themselves and the company may change, which in turn leads to changes in the meaning of objects, and thereby to changes in behavior. In order to understand this process, researchers have to study a subject's actions, objects, and society from the perspective of the subject themselves. In practice, this can mean entering the field setting and observing at first-hand what is happening. The kinds of research methodologies that are often associated with symbolic interactionism include ETHNOGRAPHY and the use of PARTICIPATIVE OBSERVATION methods.

see also ETHNOMETHODOLOGY, PHENOMENOLOGY

📖 Given 2008; Gray 2009

symmetric distribution
see NORMAL DISTRIBUTION

synthesis
the process of blending **external criticism** and **internal criticism** in HISTORICAL RESEARCH. Two ideas that have proved useful in evaluating historical sources are the concepts of external (or lower) criticism and internal (or higher) criticism. Basically, external criticism asks if the evidence under consideration is genuine and authentic. Several questions come to mind in evaluating the genuineness of a historical source: 'Who wrote this document? Was the author living at that time? For what purpose was the document written? For whom was it intended? And why? When was the document written? Is the date on the document accurate? Could the details described have actually happened during this time? Where was the document written? Could the details described have occurred in this location? Under what conditions was the document written? Is there any possibility that what was written might have been directly or subtly coerced? Do different forms or versions of the document exist?' The important thing to remember with regard to external criticism is that researchers should do their best to ensure that the documents they are using are genuine. The above questions (and others like them) are directed toward this end.

Once researchers have satisfied themselves that a source document is genuine, they need to determine if the contents of the document are accurate. This involves what is known as internal criticism. Both the accuracy of the information contained in a document and the truthfulness of the author need to be evaluated. Whereas external criticism has to do with the nature or authenticity of the document itself, internal criticism has to do with what the document says. 'Is it likely that what the author says happened really did happen? Would people at that time have behaved as they are portrayed? Could events have occurred this way? Are the data presented (attendance records, budget figures, test scores, and so on) reasonable?' Note, however, that researchers should not dismiss a statement as inaccurate just because it is unlikely—unlikely events do occur. What researchers must determine is whether a particular event might have occurred, even if it is unlikely. As with external criticism, several questions need to be asked in attempting to evaluate the accuracy of a document and the truthfulness of its author. With regard to the author of the document: 'Was the author present at the event s/he is describing? In other words, is the document a primary or a secondary source? Was the author a participant in or an observer of the event? Was the author competent to describe the event? Was s/he an expert on whatever is being described or discussed? An interested observer? A passerby? Was the author emotionally involved in the event? Did the author have any vested interest in the outcomes of the event?'

With regard to the contents of the document: 'Do the contents make sense (i.e., given the nature of the events described, does it seem reasonable that they could have happened as portrayed)? Could the event described have occurred at that time? Would people have behaved as described? Does the language of the document suggest a bias of any sort? Is it emotionally charged, intemperate, or otherwise slanted in a particular way? Might the ethnicity, gender, religion, political party, socioeconomic status, or position of the author suggest a particular orientation? Do other versions of the event exist? Do they present a different description or interpretation of what happened?'

Ary et al. 2010; Fraenkel & Wallen 2009; Ridenour & Newman 2008

systematic error
see ERROR SCORE

systematic replication
another term for APPROXIMATE REPLICATION

systematic sample
see SYSTEMATIC SAMPLING

systematic sampling
a type of PROBABILITY SAMPLING which is a modified form of SIMPLE RANDOM SAMPLING. Systematic sampling involves selecting subjects from a POPULATION list in a systematic rather than a random fashion. In systematic sampling, every nth individual is selected within a defined population for inclusion in the SAMPLE. Usually the interval between names on the list is determined by dividing the number of persons desired in the sample into the full population.

systematic sampling

1	26	51	76	
2	27	52	77	
3	28	53	78	
4	29	54	79	determine the number of units. $N = 100$
5	30	55	80	
6	31	56	81	
7	32	57	82	
8	33	58	83	Determine the sample size. e.g., $n = 20$
9	34	59	84	
10	35	60	85	
11	36	61	86	
12	37	62	87	
13	38	63	88	The interval size is $K = N/n$ $100/20 = 5$ $k = 5$
14	39	64	89	
15	40	65	90	
16	41	66	91	
17	42	67	92	Select a random integer from 1 to k: e.g., 4
18	43	68	93	
19	44	69	94	
20	45	70	95	
21	46	71	96	
22	47	72	97	Select every kth (5th) unit
23	48	73	98	
24	49	74	99	
25	50	75	100	

Figure S.18. An Example of Systematic Sampling

For example imagine, as shown in Figure S.18, that you have a population that only has $N = 100$ people in it and that you want to take a sample of $n = 20$. To use systematic sampling, the population must be listed in a random order. The sampling fraction (ratio) would be $f = 20/100 = 20\%$. In this case, the interval size, k, is equal to $N/n = 100/20 = 5$. Now, select a random integer from 1 to 5. (**integer** is a whole number such as 1, 50, or 209. Fractions and decimals, then, are not integers.) In this example, imagine that you chose 4. Now, to select the sample, start with the 4th unit in the list and take every kth unit (every 5th, because $k = 5$). You would be sampling units 4, 9, 14, 19, and so on to 100 and you would wind up with 20 units in your sample. A sample obtained by using a systematic method of sampling is called a **systematic sample**.

When planning to select a sample from a list of some sort researchers should carefully examine the list to make sure there is no cyclical pattern present. If the list has been arranged in a particular order, researchers should make sure the arrangement will not bias the sample in some way that could distort the results. If such seems to be the case, steps should be taken to ensure representativeness—for example, by randomly selecting individuals from each of the cyclical portions. In fact, if the elements of a

population are distributed in a random order, then systematic sampling gives results that are equivalent to SIMPLE RANDOM SAMPLING.
Systematic sampling provides a useful alternative to simple random sampling because it is easier to perform in the field and can provide greater information per unit cost than simple random sampling.
see also STRATIFIED SAMPLING, CLUSTER SAMPLING, AREA SAMPLING, MULTI-PHASE SAMPLING
📖 Berg 20001; Cohen et al. 2011; Dörnyei 2007; Fraenkel & Wallen 2009

systematic variance
see ERROR VARIANCE

systemic functional linguistics
also **systemic functional theory**
an approach to linguistics that sees language as a resource used for communication in social contexts, rather than as an abstract formal system. Systemic functional linguistics contrasts with traditional grammar, which is formal; rigid; based on the notion of 'rule'; syntactic in focus, and oriented to the sentence. According to systemic functional linguistics, what is needed is a grammar that is functional; flexible; based on the notion of 'resource'; semantic in focus, and oriented towards the text. Within systemic functional linguistics, three macrofunctions of language are emphasized: *textual*, *interpersonal*, and *ideational*. The textual function deals with the phonological, syntactic, and semantic signals that enable language users to understand and transmit messages. The interpersonal function deals with sociolinguistic features of language required to establish roles, relationships, and responsibilities in a communicative situation. The ideational function deals with the concepts and processes underlying natural, physical, and social phenomena.
As applied to research, a systemic functional linguistics approach enables the researchers to track the development of new social practices, of new registers, and of functional recasts. By extension, it enables them to track a rich variety of possible developments at the social practice, discourse, and sentence levels
see also CRITICAL DISCOURSE ANALYSIS
📖 Egbert & Petrie 2005; Kumaravadivelu 2006; Richards & Schmidt 2010

systemic functional theory
another term for SYSTEMIC FUNCTIONAL LINGUISTICS

T

t

an abbreviation for STUDENT'S *t* DISTRIBUTION

*T*²

an abbreviation for HOTELLING'S TRACE CRITERION

table of random numbers
  also random-numbers table
  a table used when researchers want to obtain a RANDOM SAMPLE from a larger POPULATION. The numbers on such a table are generated in a random order. A small portion of a table of random numbers is shown below (Table T.1) for demonstrational purposes.

54	83	80	53	90	50	90	46	47	12	62	68	30	91	21	01	37	36	20
36	85	49	83	47	89	46	28	54	02	87	98	10	47	22	67	27	33	13
60	98	76	53	02	01	82	77	45	12	68	13	09	20	73	07	92	53	45
62	79	39	83	88	02	60	92	82	00	76	30	77	98	45	00	97	78	16
31	21	10	50	42	16	85	20	74	29	64	72	59	58	09	30	73	43	32

Table T.1. An Example of Random Numbers

You will note that the table consists of two-digit numbers (54, 83, 80 ...). These are arranged in columns to make them easier to read and use. In practice, you should disregard the two-digit numbers and columns and think of the table as a very long list of single-digit numbers (5, 4, 8, 3, 8, 0, 5, 3 ,9 ,0 ...). To use the table, you first number the cases in your population. For example, if the school system from which you were sampling had 5,000 students, you would number the students from 0001 to 5000. Then, beginning anywhere in the table, you would take 200 sets of four-digit numbers. For example, let's say you randomly entered the table at the fifth digit in the second row:

| 36 | 85 | 49 | 83 | 47 | 89 | 46 | 28 | 54 | 02 | 87 | 98 | 10 | 47 | 22 | 67 | 27 | 33 | 13 |

Imagine you selected 49 as your starting point. Starting with this number, you would take the next four digits, which are 4983. Thus, the first participant you would select for your sample would be the student who was number 4983 in your list of 5000. The next four digits are 4789, so you would take student number 4789 for your sample. The third participant to be selected would be number 4628 because the next four digits on the table are 4628. The next four digits are 5402. However, there were only 5,000 students in the population, so student number 5402 does not exist.

Similarly, the next four digits, 8798, are out of the range of your population size. You would ignore numbers on the table that exceed the size of the population, such as 5402 and 8798. However, the next four digits, 1047, do represent a student in the population—number 1047—and this student would be included in the sample. Continue this process until you reach your desired SAMPLE SIZE. In our example, in which we wanted a sample of 200, we would continue until we obtained 200 four-digit random numbers between 0001 and 5000, inclusive. (Obviously, to draw a sample of 200, you would need to use the full table rather than the small portion of the table shown here). The cases in the population that correspond to these numbers would then be used in the sample.

Tables of random numbers are used for purposes other than selecting samples. For example, when using an experimental design, researchers usually want to assign in a random fashion participants to the various experimental conditions. Thus, a random numbers table can be used to ensure that the manner in which participants are assigned to conditions is truly random.
📖 Leary 2011

table of specifications
see CONTENT VALIDITY

tabulation
a procedure by which the researcher uses tables to arrange a mass of assembled data in some kind of concise and logical order. Put another way, tabulation is the process of summarizing raw data and displaying the same in compact form (i.e., in the form of statistical tables) for further analysis. In a broader sense, tabulation is an orderly arrangement of data in columns and rows. Tabulation is essential because of the following reasons:

1) It conserves space and reduces explanatory and descriptive statement to a minimum.
2) It facilitates the process of comparison.
3) It facilitates the summation of items and the detection of errors and omissions.
4) It provides a basis for various statistical computations.

For many kinds of studies, using tables to summarize the findings is an effective strategy. If the study is SURVEY RESEARCH, tables can be used to summarize the answers given on the survey. If the study analyzed some type of discourse such as VERBAL PROTOCOLs or teacher student

conferences, tables can be used to summarize the number of occurrences of particular categories of the coding system.
📖 Kothari 2008; McKay 2006

TAT
an abbreviation for THEMATIC APPERCEPTION TEST

tau (τ)
an abbreviation for KENDALL'S RANK-ORDER CORRELATION COEFFICIENT

t distribution
also **Student's t distribution, t sampling distribution, t**
a PROBABILITY DISTRIBUTION that is used to calculate the PROBABILITY of two MEAN scores being statistically different from one another. The t distribution varies according to the number of cases in a SAMPLE. It becomes increasingly similar to a Z or NORMAL DISTRIBUTION the bigger the sample. The smaller the sample, the flatter the distribution becomes. The t distribution is used to determine the CRITICAL VALUE that t has to be, or to exceed, in order for it to achieve statistical significance (see Table T.2). The larger this value, the more likely it is to be statistically significant. The sign of this value is ignored. For large samples, t has to be about 1.96 or more to be statistically significant at the 95% or .05 TWO-TAILED TEST. The smaller the sample, the larger t has to be statistically significant at this level.

df	Critical value
1	12.706
5	2.571
10	2.228
20	2.086
50	2.009
100	1.984
1000	1.962
∞	1.960

Table. T.2. The .05 Two-Tailed Critical Value

The critical value that t has to be, or to be bigger than, to be significant at the .05 two-tailed level is shown in Table T.2 for selected samples increasing in size. SAMPLE SIZE is expressed in terms of DEGREES OF FREEDOM (abbreviated df), rather than number of cases because the way in which the degrees of freedom are calculated varies slightly according

to the *t*-TEST used for determining STATISTICAL SIGNIFICANCE. For samples of 20 or more this critical value is close to 2.
 Cramer & Howitt 2004; Larson-Hall 2010

teacher research
another term for ACTION RESEARCH

telephone interview
a method of data collection and a common practice in SURVEY RESEARCH. Telephone interviews were first used in large-scale quantitative surveys. More recently the method has been applied to qualitative interviewing. As with any method, the use of telephone interviews is determined by the practical advantages and pitfalls associated with the method and with regard to the research topics and participants involved. Free flowing conversations can be held and rich data obtained from telephone interviews. However, participants tend to answer briefly compared with FACE-TO-FACE INTERVIEWs. Researchers, therefore, need to probe to ensure questions and topics are fully addressed. There is an important and unresolved issue about SOCIAL DESIRABILITY BIAS generated through telephone interviews. On the one hand, use of the telephone can offer anonymity to participants, enabling them to talk freely, openly, and honestly. On the other hand, during interviews on the telephone it can be difficult to build up trust and rapport, as well as gain the full attention of the participant.
Several attractions to telephone interviewing are suggested:

- It is sometimes cheaper than FACE-TO-FACE INTERVIEWing.
- It enables researchers to select respondents from a much more dispersed POPULATION than if they have to travel to meet the interviewees.
- It is useful for gaining rapid responses to a STRUCTURED QUESTIONNAIRE.
- Monitoring and quality control are undertaken more easily since interviews are undertaken and administered centrally, indeed there are greater guarantees that the researcher actually carries out the interview as required.
- Call-back costs are so slight as to enable frequent call-backs possible, enhancing reliability and contact.
- Many groups, particularly of busy people, can be reached at times more convenient to them than if a visit were to be made.
- They are safer to undertake than, for example, having to visit dangerous neighborhoods.

- They can be used to collect sensitive data, as possible feelings of threat of face to-face questions about awkward, embarrassing or difficult matters is absent.
- Response rate is higher than, for example, questionnaires.

Clearly this issue is not as cut-and-dried as the claims made for it, as there are several potential problems with telephone interviewing, for example:

- It is very easy for respondents simply to hang up on the caller.
- There is a chance of skewed sampling, as not all of the population have a telephone or can hear (e.g., the old and second language speakers in addition to those with hearing difficulties).
- There is a lower response rate at weekends.
- Some people have a deep dislike of telephones, that sometimes extends to a phobia, and this inhibits their responses or willingness to participate.
- Respondents may not disclose information because of uncertainty about actual (even though promised) confidentiality.
- Many respondents (up to 25 per cent, will be ex-directory and so their numbers will not be available in telephone directories.
- Respondents may withhold important information or tell lies, as the non-verbal behavior that frequently accompanies this is not witnessed by the interviewer.
- It is often more difficult for complete strangers to communicate by telephone than face-to-face, particularly as non-verbal cues are absent.
- Respondents are naturally suspicious.
- One telephone might be shared by several people.
- Responses are difficult to write down or record during the interview.

Because telephone interviews lack the sensory stimulation of visual or face to-face interviews or written instructions and presentation, it is unwise to plan a long telephone survey call. Ten to fifteen minutes is often the maximum time tolerable to most respondents and, indeed, fifteen minutes for many may be too long. This means that careful piloting will need to take place in order to include those items, and only those items, that are necessary for the research. The risk to RELIABILITY and VALIDITY is considerable, as the number of items may be fewer than in other forms of data collection.

see also ETHNOGRAPHIC INTERVIEW, NON-DIRECTIVE INTERVIEW, UNSTRUCTURED INTERVIEW, SEMI-STRUCTURED INTERVIEW, STRUCTURED INTERVIEW, INTERVIEW GUIDE, INFORMAL INTERVIEW, FOCUS GROUP

 Cohen et al. 2011; Given 2008

telescoping

a term that describes a phenomenon that threatens the VALIDITY of self-reported dates, durations, and frequencies of events. Respondents often are asked to retrospectively report when something occurred, how long something lasted, or how often something happened within a certain time period. Answering such question requires the respondent to remember exact dates and temporal sequences and to determine whether an event happened within a certain time period. At this stage of the response process, dates or events can be forgotten entirely or *telescoped* forward or backward. While forgetting describes not remembering an event at all, telescoping focuses on errors made by incorrectly dating events that were recalled.

Researchers distinguish between two types of telescoping: forward and backward. Forward telescoping occurs when an event is erroneously remembered as having occurred more recently than it actually did. A backward telescoped event is erroneously remembered as having occurred earlier than its actual date. In general, empirical data show that forward telescoping is more likely to occur than backward telescoping.

Why telescoping occurs is not fully understood. Two main theories have emerged in the literature: the time compression and variance theories. However these theories explain only parts of the phenomenon. The time compression theory focuses only on explaining forward telescoping, arguing that telescoping occurs because of a subjective distortion of the time line. Time is compressed when respondents perceive that events happened more recently than they actually did or a time period seems shorter than the true length of time. This theory also hypothesizes that forward telescoping decreases as the length of the reference period increases. Empirical findings testing this HYPOTHESIS, however, have been mixed. Variance theory uses the uncertainty in one's memory about the time of an event as an explanation for telescoping. The theory argues that uncertainty about the timing of an event increases as the elapsed time from the event to when the question is asked expands, explaining both forward and backward telescoping.
📖 Lavrakas 2008

temporal reliability

another term for TEST-RETEST RELIABILITY

test

any procedure for measuring ability, knowledge, or performance. It is a set of stimuli presented to an individual in order to elicit responses on the basis of which a numerical score can be assigned. This score, based on a representative sample of the individual's behavior, is an indicator of the extent to which the subject has the characteristic being measured. The utility of these scores as indicators of the construct of interest is in large part a function of the *validity, reliability, authenticity,* and *practicality* of the tests. Test validity refers to the extent to which inferences made from assessment results are appropriate, meaningful, and useful in terms of the purpose of the assessment. A valid test of reading validity actually measures reading ability not writing ability, for example. A reliable test is consistent and dependable. A test is said to be reliable if it gives the same results when it is given on different occasions or when it is used by different people. In addition, an effective test is practical. This means that it (1) is not excessively expensive, (2) stays within appropriate time constraints, (3) is relatively easy to administer, and (4) has a scoring/evaluation procedure that is specific and time-efficient. A fourth major principle is authenticity, a concept that is the degree of correspondence of characteristics of a given test to the features of a target task. In a test, authenticity may be present if (a) the test is as natural as possible, (2) items are contextualized rather than isolated, (3) topics are meaningful (relevant, interesting) for the respondent, (4) some thematic organization to items is provided, such as through a story line or episode, and (5) tasks represent, or closely approximate, real-world tasks.

Test items can assess, for example, language abilities through observing outward behavior, as when testing oral proficiency via an oral INTERVIEW, or they can assess cognitive outcomes through responses on paper or a computer screen. Test items differ by making different cognitive demands on participants. Some items require participants to recall information (e.g., FILL-IN ITEMs). Other items require participants to recall and integrate information, such as a test of writing ability where they must compose an essay. Other test items require participants to recognize from a set of alternatives which is the most appropriate answer (e.g., MULTIPLE-CHOICE ITEMs).

📖 Ary et al. 2010; Bachman & Palmer 1996; Brown 2004; Cohen et al. 2011; Perry 2011; Richards & Schmidt 2010

test battery

a selection of tests and assessment procedures typically composed of tests designed to measure different VARIABLEs but having a common objective; for example, an intelligence test, a personality test, and a neuropsychological test might be used to obtain a general psychological profile of an individual.

📖 Cohen & Swerdlik 2010

test bias

the characteristic of a measure that is not equally valid for different groups of subjects. That is, if test scores more accurately reflect the true ability or characteristics of one group than another, the test is biased.

Identifying test bias is difficult. Simply showing that a certain gender, cultural, racial, or ethnic group performs worse on a test than other groups does not necessarily indicate that the test is unfair. The observed difference in scores may reflect a true difference between the groups in the attribute being measured. Bias exists only if groups that do not differ on the attribute or ability being measured obtain different scores on the test. Bias can creep into measures in very subtle ways. For example, test questions sometimes refer to objects or experiences that are more familiar to members of one group than to those of another. If those objects or experiences are not relevant to the attribute being measured, some individuals may be unfairly disadvantaged. Test bias is hard to demonstrate because it is often difficult to determine whether the groups truly differ on the attribute in question. One way to document the presence of bias is to examine the PREDICTIVE VALIDITY of a measure separately for different groups. A biased test will predict future outcomes better for one group than another.
 Leary 2011

testing effect
also **measurement effect**
a threat to INTERNAL VALIDITY which refers to the effects that taking a test on one occasion may have on subsequent administrations of the same test. For example, in a study designed to test a new spelling method, students are asked to spell the same twenty-five words before and after the new instructional method is used. If they score higher on the posttest, it may be simply because they were exposed to the same words before rather than due to the effectiveness of the new method. In essence, when participants in a study are measured several times on the same variable (e.g., with the same instrument or test), their performance might be affected by factors such as PRACTICE EFFECT, memory, sensitization, and participant and researcher expectancies. This threat to internal validity is most often encountered in LONGITUDINAL RESEARCH where participants are repeatedly measured on the same variables over time. The ultimate concern with this threat to internal validity is that the results of the study might be related to the repeated testing or evaluation and not the INDEPENDENT VARIABLE itself.
see INSTRUMENTATION, DIFFERENTIAL SELECTION, HISTORY, MATURATION, STATISTICAL REGRESSION, MORTALITY
 Perry 2011; Ravid 2011

test of significance
another term for STATISTICAL TEST

test-retest reliability
also **multiple-occasions reliability, temporal reliability**
a measure of consistency over time. Test-retest reliability is estimated when you administer the same measuring instrument (e.g., a TEST) to the same group of individuals on two or more different occasions (see Figure T.1). This approach assumes that there is no substantial change in the construct being measured between the two occasions. A common technique for assessing test-retest reliability is to compute the CORRELATION COEFFICIENT between the scores from each occasion of testing. The correlation coefficient obtained by this procedure is called a **test-retest reliability coefficient**. The test-retest reliability coefficient, because it indicates consistency or stability of subjects' scores over time, is sometimes referred to as a **coefficient of stability**. A high coefficient tells you that you can generalize from the score a person receives on one occasion to a score that person would receive if the test had been given at a different time.

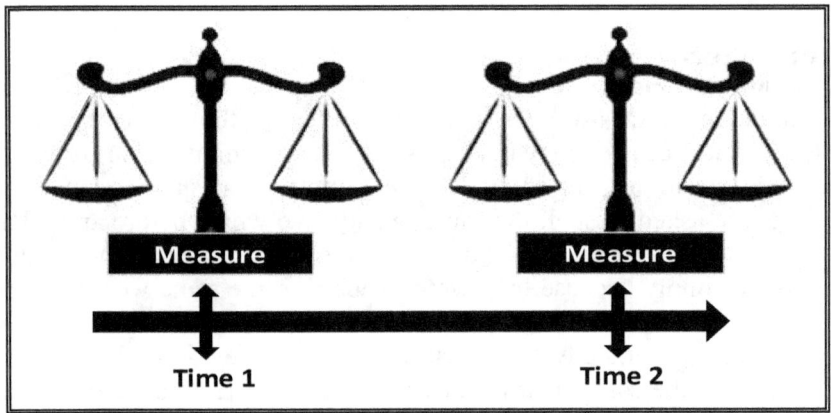

Figure T.1. Schematic Representation of Test-Retest Reliability

A test-retest coefficient assumes that the characteristic being measured by the test is stable over time, so any change in scores from one time to another is caused by RANDOM ERROR. The error may be caused by the condition of the participants themselves or by testing conditions. The test-retest coefficient also assumes there is no PRACTICE EFFECT or memory effect. For example, subjects may learn something just from taking a test and thus will react differently on the second taking of the test. These practice effects from the first testing will not likely be the same across all participants, thus lowering the reliability estimate. The amount of time allowed between measures is critical. The researcher has to decide what an appropriate length of time is; too short a time and respondents may remember what they said or did in the first test situation;

too long a time and there may be extraneous effects operating to distort the data (e.g., MATURATION in subjects, outside influences on the subjects). If the researcher is assessing, for example, participants' second language pronunciation abilities, administering the instrument two weeks later should produce similar results if it is reliable. However, if there is a month or two between testing sessions, any training on pronunciation may create differences between the two sets of scores that would depress the reliability coefficient. If the time between the two administrations is too little, memory of the test from the first session could help the participants give the same responses, which would inflate the reliability coefficient. A researcher seeking to demonstrate this type of reliability will have to choose an appropriate time scale between the test and retest. In effect, this procedure can only work if the trait being measured can be assumed to remain stable over the time between the two measurements.

In addition to stability over time, reliability as stability can also be stability over a similar sample. For example, we would assume that if we were to administer a test or a QUESTIONNAIRE simultaneously to two groups of participants who were very closely matched on significant characteristics (e.g., age, gender, ability, etc.), then similar results (on a test) or responses (to a questionnaire) would be obtained. The correlation coefficient on this form of the test/retest method can be calculated either for the whole test or for sections of the questionnaire. This form of reliability over a sample is particularly useful in piloting tests and questionnaires.

 Ary et al. 2010; Cohen et al. 2011; Perry 2011; Trochim & Donnelly 2007; VanderStoep & Johnston 2009

test-retest reliability coefficient
see TEST-RETEST RELIABILITY

test rubric
the facets that specify how test takers are expected to proceed in taking the test. These include the *test organization*, *time allocation*, and *instructions*.
 Bachman 1990

test statistic
a function of sample observations (data obtained from a SAMPLE rather than from the entire POPULATION) that provides a basis for testing a statistical HYPOTHESIS. In order to be useful, a test statistic must have a known distribution when the NULL HYPOTHESIS is true. A comparison of the calculated value of the test statistic to the theoretical or CRITICAL VALUE provides the basis for decision whether to accept or reject a given

hypothesis. The *t* STATISTIC, chi square (χ^2), and *F* STATISTIC are examples of some test statistics.
 Sahai & Khurshid 2001

testwiseness
the ability to easily comprehend almost any test directions, knowledge of guessing, or strategies for maximizing the speed of task performance.
 Brown 2005

tetrachoric correlation coefficient
also r_{tet}
a measure of *association* between two *artificially* dichotomized VARIABLES (i.e., both variables that are continuously measurable have been reduced to two categories). The tetrachoric correlation coefficient is based on the assumption that the underlying distribution for both of the variables is *continuous* and *normal* (see NORMALITY). For example, if a researcher were interested in the degree of relationship between passing a grammar course and having been absent 10 or more times from class, the tetrachoric correlation coefficient would be appropriate. Each of the variables (grade A-F and the number of absences) was originally an INTERVAL SCALE. However, they have been converted to artificial dichotomies: passing versus not passing and 1-9 absences versus 10 or more absences. The resulting coefficient is an approximate estimate of PEARSON *R*.
 Brown 1988; Richards & Schmidt 2010; Sheskin 2011

thematic apperception test
also **TAT**
a PROJECTIVE TECHNIQUE which consists of a set of pictures (some of the pictures deal with the ordinary day-to-day events while others may be ambiguous pictures of unusual situations) that are shown to respondents who are asked to describe what they think the pictures represent. The replies of respondents constitute the basis for the investigator to draw inferences about their personality structure, attitudes, etc.
see also SOCIOMETRY, ROSENZWEIG TEST, RORSCHACH TEST, HOLTZMAN INKBLOT TEST, TOMKINS-HORN PICTURE ARRANGEMENT TEST
 Kothari 2008

theoretical definition
another term for CONCEPTUAL DEFINITION

theoretical population
see POPULATION

theoretical sampling
another term for SEQUENTIAL SAMPLING

theoretical triangulation
a type of TRIANGULATION which draws upon alternative or competing theories in preference to utilizing one viewpoint only. Examining the research findings using different theoretical lenses can also aid researchers in overcoming their own personal biases or ideological blinders. Different facets of the research problem can be explored by examining research results using analytical frameworks related to different theories. This kind of triangulation does not normally allow for any kind of integration of results and would not be used to make claims of increased VALIDITY: this method of triangulation suggests that different theoretical approaches will undermine the credibility of competing research findings. However, exploring research data using a different theoretical lens can be a particularly useful way to examine dissonant or anomalous data. Theoretical triangulation can enable a deeper understanding of the research as investigators can explore different ways to make sense of the data. Tensions that might arise between theoretical explanations of the same data may yield new insights into the aspects of the research problem. However, many qualitative researchers disagree with the notion that researchers can stand outside of the epistemological perspectives that they bring to any project, claiming that it is not logical to compare analyses of data that are informed by different theoretical concepts.
see also DATA TRIANGULATION, INVESTIGATOR TRIANGULATION, METHODOLOGICAL TRIANGULATION
📖 Cohen et al. 2011; Given 2008; Ridenour & Newman 2008

theoretical validity
(in QUALITATIVE RESEARCH) a type of VALIDITY which corresponds to some extent to the INTERNAL VALIDITY of the research as it concerns whether the researcher's account includes an appropriate level of theoretical abstraction and how well this theory explains or describes the phenomenon in question.
see also DESCRIPTIVE VALIDITY, INTERPRETIVE VALIDITY, EVALUATIVE VALIDITY
📖 Dörnyei 2007

theory
a system of ideas based on interrelated concepts, definitions, and propositions with the purpose of explaining or predicting phenomena. The term theory is widely used in both everyday language and academic discourse, but its precise meaning is vague and contested. A theory, in both everyday and scientific use, is normally used to denote a model or set of concepts and propositions that pertains to some actual phenomena; a theory can provide understanding of these phenomena or form the basis for action with respect to them.

Researchers have generally accepted the view that all observation is theory-laden—that our understanding of the world is inherently shaped by our prior ideas and assumptions about the world and that there is no possibility of purely objective or theory-neutral description independent of some particular perspective. Thus, theory is an inescapable component of all research, whether or not it is explicitly acknowledged. While *quantitative* researchers usually design their research primarily to apply or test formally constructed theories about the topics and settings they study, *qualitative* researchers normally seek to better understand these topics and settings through their investigations and to inductively (rather than deductively) develop theory about these from their data. Unlike quantitative researchers, qualitative researchers generally acknowledge, and often explicitly analyze, the influence of their prior assumptions about these topics and settings, and they typically use insights or concepts taken from existing theories and relate their findings to these theories, but their research normally draws on these theories selectively and eclectically, rather than deliberately seeking to contribute to a particular theory.
see also QUALITATIVE RESEARCH, QUANTITATIVE RESEARCH, NORMATIVE PARADIGM, ABDUCTION, INDUCTIVE REASONING, DEDUCTIVE REASONING
📖 Given 2008

theta (θ)
an abbreviation for *ability* (see ITEM CHARACTERISTIC CURVE)

thick description
using multiple perspectives to explain the insights gleaned from a study, and taking into account the participants interpretations of their actions and speech. It also involves the presentation of representative examples and patterns in data, along with interpretive commentary.
📖 Mackey & Gass 2005

think-aloud protocol
see VERBAL REPORT

three-way ANCOVA
an ANCOVA which involves three *categorical* INDEPENDENT VARIABLEs (each with two or more LEVELs), one *continuous* DEPENDENT VARIABLE, and one or more continuous COVARIATEs.
📖 Pallant 2010

three-way ANOVA
see FACTORIAL ANOVA

three-way between-subjects design
see BETWEEN-SUBJECTS DESIGN

three-way factorial design
see FACTORIAL DESIGN

three-way repeated measures ANOVA
a REPEATED MEASURES FACTORIAL ANOVA performed when three FACTORs are WITHIN-SUBJECTS FACTORs. Because each participant produces scores on all the CONDITIONs or occasions, the scores for each participant are related.
 Greene & Oliveira 2005

three-way within-subjects design
see WITHIN-SUBJECTS DESIGN

Thurstone scale
another term for DIFFERENTIAL SCALE

tied scores
two or more scores which have the same value on a VARIABLE. When we rank these scores we need to give all of the tied scores the same rank. This is calculated as being the average rank which would have been allocated had we arbitrarily ranked the tied scores. For example, if we had the five scores of 5, 7, 7, 7 and 9, 5 would be given a rank of 1, 7 a rank of 3 [(2 + 3 + 4)/3 = 3] and 9 a rank of 5.
 Cramer & Howitt 2004

timed test
another term for SPEED TEST

time-sampling design
another term for TIME-SERIES DESIGN

time-series design
also **interrupted time-series design, ITS design, time-sampling design**
a type of QUASI-EXPERIMENTAL DESIGN and an extension of a ONE-GROUP PRETEST-POSTTEST DESIGN which is extended by the use of numerous pretests and posttests over a period of time. Because of the problems involved with RANDOM ASSIGNMENT and the difficulties in finding CONTROL GROUPs that match the EXPERIMENTAL GROUP in many ways, researchers often turn to time-series designs. While the subjects selected for such studies are not usually randomly selected, these designs solve the control group problem in interesting ways. In this type design, peri-

odic observations or measurements are made on a group prior to the presentation of the TREATMENT to establish a stable baseline and then, following the treatment, further observations are made to ascertain the effects of the treatment. If there is a treatment effect, it will be reflected by differing patterns of the pretests versus posttest responses. This discontinuity could be manifested by a change in the level of the pretest and posttest responses (e.g., a change in the slope or direction of the evolving scores). Observing and establishing the normal fluctuation of the DEPENDENT VARIABLE over time allows the researcher to more accurately interpret the impact of the INDEPENDENT VARIABLE.

There are four reasons for utilizing this deign type: (1) it is practical, i.e., it can be used with small numbers of participants; (2) it reduces HAWTHORNE EFFECT because many instances of data collection are used; (3) it can be used as a means of exploration and hypothesis-generation; and (4) given LONGITUDINAL DESIGN and many instances of measurement, it provides a richer picture of development.

Time-series designs can be distinguished from non-experimental longitudinal designs because they have a controlled treatment (X) inserted after a number of observations or measurement.

There are three basic variations of this design: the SIMPLE INTERRUPTED TIME-SERIES DESIGN, the EQUIVALENT TIME-SAMPLES DESIGN, and the CONTROL GROUP TIME SERIES DESIGN.

see also NONEQUIVALENT CONTROL GROUP DESIGN, EQUIVALENT MATERIAL DESIGN, COUNTERBALANCED DESIGN, RECURRENT INSTITUTIONAL CYCLE DESIGN, SEPARATE-SAMPLE PRETEST-POSTTEST CONTROL GROUP DESIGN, SEPARATE-SAMPLE PRETEST-POSTTEST DESIGN

📖 Dörnyei 2007; Hatch & Lazaraton 1991; Mackey & Gass 2005; Marczyk et al. 2005

time triangulation
see DATA TRIANGULATION

title
a section of RESEARCH REPORT which summarizes the main idea of the research study. A title should be a concise statement of the main topic and should identify the VARIABLEs or theoretical issues under investigation and the relationship between them. A title should be fully explanatory when standing alone. Titles are commonly indexed and compiled in numerous reference works. Therefore, you should avoid words that serve no useful purpose; they increase length and can mislead indexers.

see also ABSTRACT, INTRODUCTION, METHOD, RESULTS, DISCUSSION, REFERENCES, APPENDIXES

📖 American Psychological Association 2010

tobit analysis
see CENSORED REGRESSION ANALYSIS

tolerance
see MULTICOLLINEARITY

Tomkins-horn picture arrangement test
a PROJECTIVE TECHNIQUE which is designed for GROUP ADMINISTRATION. It consists of twenty-five plates, each containing three sketches that may be arranged in different ways to portray sequence of events. The respondent is asked to arrange them in a sequence which s/he considers as reasonable. The responses are interpreted as providing evidence confirming certain norms, respondent's attitudes, etc.
see also SOCIOMETRY, THEMATIC APPERCEPTION TEST, ROSENZWEIG TEST, RORSCHACH TEST, HOLTZMAN INKBLOT TEST
📖 Kothari 2008

topic guide
another term for INTERVIEW GUIDE

total sum of squares
another term for SUM OF SQUARES FOR TOTAL

total variance
see ERROR VARIANCE

trait
another term for CONSTRUCT

trait accuracy
the facet of VALIDITY that indicates how accurately a procedure measures the TRAIT under investigation. However, accuracy depends on the definition of the construct being measured or observed. Language proficiency, for example, is a trait that is often measured in research. Nevertheless, how this trait is measured should be determined by how it is defined (see OPERATIONAL DEFINITION). If language proficiency is defined as the summation of grammar and vocabulary knowledge, plus reading and listening comprehension, then an approach needs to be used that measures all of these components to accurately measure the trait as defined. However, if other researchers define language proficiency as oral and writing proficiency, they would have to use procedures to directly assess speaking and writing ability. In other words, the degree to which a procedure is valid for trait accuracy is determined by the degree

to which the procedure corresponds to the definition of the trait.
📖 Perry 2011

transferability
the degree to which the findings of QUALITATIVE RESEARCH can be applied or generalized to other contexts or to other groups. In QUANTITATIVE RESEARCH, the term EXTERNAL VALIDITY is used to refer to the generalizability of the findings. A qualitative researcher should provide sufficiently rich, detailed, THICK DESCRIPTIONs of the context so that potential users can make the necessary comparisons and judgments about similarity and hence transferability. This is referred to as *descriptive adequacy*. The researcher must strive to provide accurate, detailed, and complete descriptions of the context and participants to assist the reader in determining transferability.

There are a range of studies that do not have the SAMPLE SIZE necessary to ensure generalizability. These may be case studies, ACTION RESEARCH projects, or studies focused on the collection of qualitative data. Nevertheless, illustrating the significance of findings to larger populations or within other contexts is still often a goal. For research of this nature, transferability can be a useful indicator of applicability. Rather than make claims about populations, transferability highlights that lessons learned are likely to be applicable in alternative settings or across populations. For example, the results of an in-depth CASE STUDY of university second language English students in Iran may not be generalizable to university English students worldwide, but there are likely to be lessons learned that could illuminate relevant issues within other cultures. The degree of transferability depends to a large degree on the similarity of the learning contexts being examined. The indicator of transferability suggests that researchers have provided a highly detailed description of the research context and methods so that readers can determine to what extent the findings might be applicable to other contexts.

One strategy to enhance transferability is to include cross-case comparisons. The researcher may investigate more than one case. If findings are similar, this would increase the possibility of transferability of findings to other settings or contexts. In some cases, even a single case can be compared with other cases in the published literature that might demonstrate transferability.

There are also threats to transferability, such as selection effects (the fact that the constructs being investigated are unique to a single group), setting effects (the fact that results may be a function of the specific context under investigation), and history effects (the fact that unique historical experiences of the participants may militate against comparisons). The researcher should recognize limitations of the study in the description.

Detailing of circumstances helps the reader to understand the nature of the data and what might be peculiar to your particular study.

Reactivity (the effect of the research itself) might also limit transferability. Although eliminating the influence of the researcher may be impossible in a qualitative study because the researcher is the key data collection instrument, the researcher can help the reader understand the potential influence by describing his/her own biases through a reflective statement and providing detailed descriptions of such things as observation strategies and INTERVIEW questions. Reactivity is a more serious threat in studies using interview techniques.

📖 Ary et al. 2010; Clark-Carter 2010; Lodico et al. 2010; McKay 2006

treatment
also **intervention, experimental treatment, experimental manipulation**
anything done to groups in order to measure its effect. The treatment is not a random experience which the groups might have, but a controlled and intentional experience, such as exposure to a language teaching method specially constructed for the experiment, or materials presented under controlled circumstances, say, in a language laboratory. Treatments are the INDEPENDENT VARIABLE in the research.

📖 Seliger & Shohamy 1989

treatment × subjects design
see ONE-WAY REPEATED MEASURES ANOVA

treatment diffusion
also **imitation of the treatment**
a threat to EXTERNAL VALIDITY which occurs when the CONTROL GROUP learn about and adopt the same TREATMENT that is given to the experimental participants. Put differently, diffusion occurs when participants in one group (typically the experimental group) communicate information about the treatment to subjects in the control group in such a way as to influence the latter's behavior on the dependent variable. Anytime you conduct a study with an experimental and a control group, you run the risk of the two groups communicating with each other, thereby diffusing or making the treatment less distinct. The EXTRANEOUS VARIABLE here is not competition but rather the inclusion of the treatment factors in the control group due to knowledge about what constituted the treatment. This often happens when the control and treatment groups are in close proximity and have time to get to know what the other is doing. Care should be taken to reduce the possibility of participants from the two groups discussing what the other is doing. Deemphasizing the fact that an experiment is going on can lessen the likelihood of diffusion problems.

see also RESEARCHER EFFECT, HALO EFFECT, HAWTHORNE EFFECT, NOVELTY EFFECT, PRETEST-TREATMENT INTERACTION, MULTIPLE-TREATMENT INTERACTION, SPECIFICITY OF VARIABLES
📖 Ary et al. 2010; Perry 2011

treatment effect
another term for EFFECT SIZE

treatment group
see CONTROL GROUP

treatment sum of squares
another term for SUM OF SQUARES FOR TREATMENT

treatment variability
another term for SYSTEMATIC VARIANCE

treatment variance
another term for SYSTEMATIC VARIANCE

trend analysis
a statistical procedure performed to evaluate hypothesized linear and nonlinear relationships between two QUANTITATIVE VARIABLEs. Trend analysis is commonly used in situations when data have been collected over time or at different LEVELs of a variable; especially when a single FACTOR [i.e., INDEPENDENT VARIABLE (IV)] has been manipulated to observe its effects on a DEPENDENT VARIABLE (DV). In particular, the MEANs of a DV are observed across conditions, levels, or points of the manipulated IV to statistically determine the form, shape, or trend of such relationship. Trend analysis may be used in ANALYSIS OF VARIANCE to determine the shape of the relationship between the DV and an IV which is quantitative in that it represents increasing or decreasing levels of that variable. Examples of such a quantitative IV include increasing levels of a state such as sleep deprivation or increasing intensity of a variable such as noise. If the F RATIO of the ANOVA is statistically significant, we may use trend analysis to find out if the relationship between the DV and the IV is a linear or non-linear one and, if it is non-linear, what kind of non-linear relationship it is.
The shape of the relationship between two variables can be described in terms of a *polynomial* equation. A first-degree or linear polynomial represents a linear or straight line relationship between two variables where the values of one variable either increase or decrease as the values of the other variable increase. For example, performance may decrease as sleep deprivation increases. A minimum of two groups or levels is necessary to

define a linear trend. A second-order or *quadratic* relationship (see Figure T.2) represents a curvilinear relationship in which the values of one variable increase (or decrease) and then decrease (or increase) as the values of the other variable increase. For instance, performance may increase as background noise increases and then decrease as it becomes too loud. A minimum of three groups or levels is necessary to define a quadratic trend.

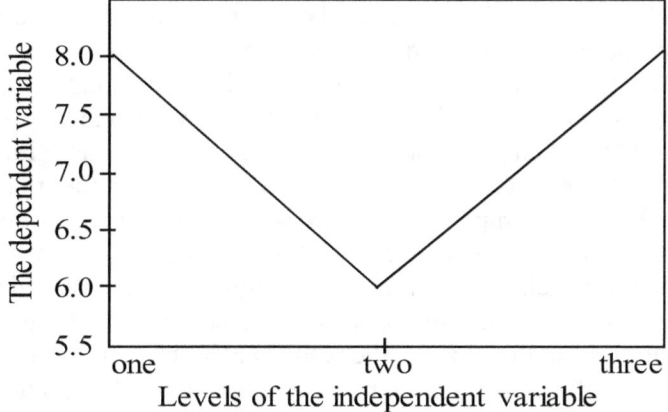

Figure T.2. An Illustration of a Quadratic Trend

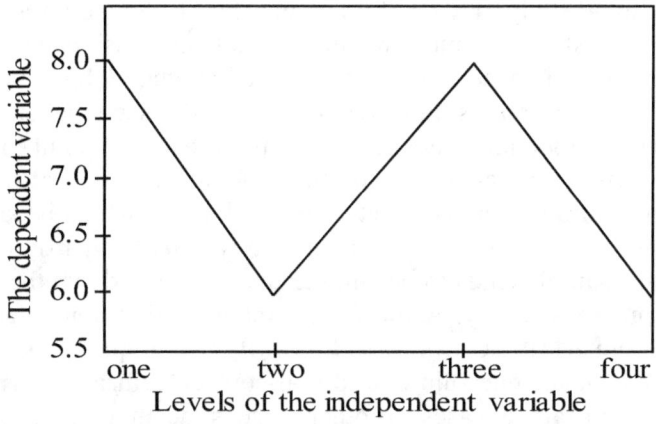

Figure T.3. An Illustration of a Cubic Trend

A third-order or *cubic* relationship (see Figure T.3.) represents a curvilinear relationship in which the values of one variable first increase (or decrease), then decrease (or increase) and then increase again (or decrease). A minimum of four groups or levels is necessary to define a cubic trend. A fourth-order or *quartic* relationship represents a curvilinear relationship in which the values of one variable first increase (or decrease), then

decrease (or increase), then increase again (or decrease) and then finally decrease again (or increase). A minimum of five groups or levels are necessary to define a quartic trend.
 Clark-Carter 2010; Cramer & Howitt 2004; Lavrakas 2008

trend study
also repeated cross-sectional study
a type of LONGITUDINAL RESEARCH which analyzes different subjects at intervals over a period of time. Trend study refers to obtaining information about change by administering repeated *questionnaire* SURVEYs to different SAMPLEs of respondents at different points in time. If the subsequent waves examine samples that are representative of the same POPULATION, then the results can be seen to carry longitudinal information at the macro level (i.e., for the whole group rather than for the individuals). For example, researchers who have studied national trends in vocabulary development sample high school students at various intervals and measure their achievement. Although the same individuals are not tested each time, if the samples from the population of high school students are selected randomly, the results each time can be considered representative of the high school population from which the student samples were drawn. Test scores from year to year are compared to determine if any trends are evident.

Trend study has certain advantages over PANEL STUDY. Like COHORT STUDY, trend study may be of relatively short or long duration. Essentially, the trend study examines recorded data to establish patterns of change that have already occurred in order to predict what will be likely to occur in the future. In trend studies two or more cross-sectional studies are undertaken with identical age groups at more than one point in time in order to make comparisons over time. Trend study is also easier and cheaper to arrange and conduct over panel study, which is partly due the fact that the respondents can remain anonymous and partly that organizing a new sample tends to be simpler than tracking down the participants of the previous survey. A further advantage is that trend study does not suffer from ATTRITION or PANEL CONDITIONING problems (i.e., subsequent loss of membership due to non-contact, refusal to answer, failure to follow-up sample cases for other reasons, death, emigration) and each wave can be made representative of the population. A major difficulty researchers face in conducting trend analyses is the intrusion of unpredictable factors that invalidate forecasts formulated on past data. For this reason, short-term trend studies tend to be more accurate than long-term analyses.
 Dörnyei 2007; Ruspini 2002

triangulation
a procedure which refers to the generation of multiple perspectives on a phenomenon by using a variety of data sources, investigators, theories, or research methods with the purpose of corroborating an overall interpretation. The name triangulation comes from the same term used in surveying and in ship navigation in which multiple measurements are used to provide the best estimate of the location at a specific, like the point at the top of a triangle. Triangulation has been considered as an effective strategy to ensure research VALIDITY by cross-checking the validity of findings. If a finding survives a series of tests with different methods, it can be regarded as more valid than a HYPOTHESIS tested only with the help of a single method. As in the law courts, one witness is not enough. The more independent witnesses, the stronger the case. The same holds true for QUALITATIVE RESEARCH: qualitative researchers may increase the CREDIBILITY of their research findings by drawing from evidence taken from a variety of data sources. To name just a few common sources of data, researchers may gather evidence from INTERVIEWs, PARTICIPANT OBSERVATION, written documents, archival and historical documents, public records, personal papers, and photographs. For example, in studying a particular group of second language learners, a researcher might observe the students in the classroom, with their peers outside the classroom, and at home with their families. They might also conduct IN-DEPTH INTERVIEWs with them as well as with their teachers, parents, and peers. All of this would be done in order to have multiple sources on which to build an interpretation of what is being studied. Each type of source of data will yield different evidence that in turns provides different insights regarding the phenomena under study.

Triangulation can be impractical for some qualitative research projects due to the inflation of research costs related to multiple methods of inquiry and team investigations. Researchers using strategies of triangulation need increased amounts of time to collect and analyze data. The amount of data collected can pose its own problems as triangulation can result in vast amounts of evidence. Although there is general consensus among qualitative research commentators that triangulation enables researchers to deepen their understanding of either a single phenomenon or of a contextual set of interrelated phenomena, there is some disagreement as to the epistemological (see EPISTEMOLOGY) foundations of such a research strategy. For example, some commentators suggest that one research method comes with its own assumptions about reality, about what is knowable, and about what counts as evidence such that it is incommensurate with another research method that carries its own epistemological concepts and array of ontological evidence. There also continues to be debate among qualitative researchers regarding the degree to which triangulation strategies allow for comparison and integration of evidence from multiple methods of data collection and multiple analytical perspectives. Furthermore, the tension between notions of verification and the enrichment of understanding is not resolved; qualitative researchers continue to use methods of triangulation to render a fuller picture of research phenomena as well as to verify and validate the consistency and integrity of research findings.

There are four basic types of triangulation including: DATA TRIANGULATION, INVESTIGATOR TRIANGULATION, THEORETICAL TRIANGULATION, and METHODOLOGICAL TRIANGULATION.

see also TRIANGULATION DESIGN, DESCRIPTIVE VALIDITY

📖 Cohen et al. 2011; Dörnyei 2007; Perry 2011

triangulation design

the most common MIXED METHODS RESEARCH design. The EXPLANATORY and the EXPLORATORY DESIGNs are straightforward to implement because of the sequential order of each data collection and analysis phase. However in the triangulation design, quantitative and qualitative data are collected simultaneously. For instance, both QUESTIONNAIREs and FOCUS GROUPs are conducted at the same time with the same participants, and then a researcher compares the quantitative and qualitative results. Often quantitative and qualitative data are collected using a questionnaire that contains closed-ended (quantitative) and open-ended (qualitative) response items. Triangulation design is best suited when a researcher wants to collect both types of data at the same time about a single phenomenon, in order to compare and contrast the different findings to produce well-validated conclusions. For example, the triangulation design was designed to investigate the effects of two types of bilingual programs (two-way and transitional) on the academic performance and attitudes of fifth grade students who entered kindergarten or first grade with different levels of English proficiency. The researchers collected both quantitative data, such as students' academic achievement scores, Spanish reading skills, and attitudes toward bilingualism, and qualitative data, including interviews with the randomly selected subsample of 32 students. Both quantitative and qualitative data were collected, analyzed, and reported separately. Quantitative data analysis revealed no significant differences in standardized measures of English achievement between the two programs, although significant differences were found among students in oral language acquisition in English, Spanish-reading ability, their attitudes, and perceived levels of proficiency in English and Spanish. Qualitative data indicated that students in the two-way bilingual education program had more positive attitudes toward bilingualism. Based on the quantitative and qualitative results of the study it was concluded that despite some similarities in the outcomes, each bilingual education program also has its unique effects. Figure T.4 presents the visual diagram of the triangulation design procedures in this study.

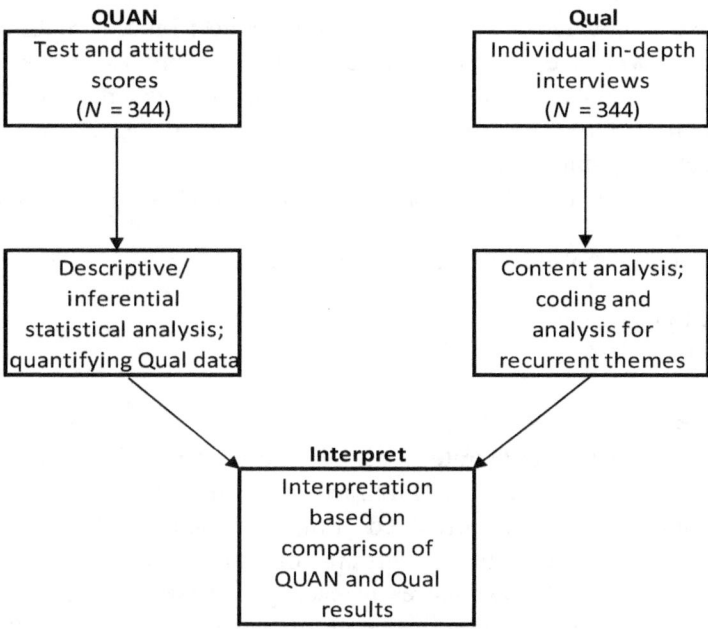

Figure T.4. A Visual Diagram of Triangulation Design

The *weight* in this design can be given to either quantitative or qualitative data, or equally to both. The *mixing* of the two methods occurs either at the data analysis stage or during the interpretation of the results from the two components of the study. As for data analysis, there are a lot of options. The most popular approach is to compare the quantitative results and qualitative findings to confirm or cross-validate the findings from the entire study. Another commonly used strategy is to transform qualitative data into quantitative data by counting codes, categories, and themes (called quantifying), or quantitative data into qualitative data through cluster or FACTOR ANALYSIS (called qualifying) in order to compare it directly with another data set or include it in the overall analysis. The reporting structure of the triangulation design differs from the sequential explanatory and exploratory designs. A researcher presents the quantitative and qualitative data collection and analysis in separate sections, but combines the interpretation of the quantitative and qualitative findings into the same section, to discuss whether the results from both study components converge or show divergence.

An advantage of the triangulation design is that it typically takes less time to complete than the sequential explanatory and exploratory designs. It can also result in well-validated and substantiated findings because it offsets the weaknesses of one method with the strengths of another method.

There are, however, two significant challenges: First, it requires a lot of effort, as well as expertise, to collect and analyze two separate sets of data simultaneously; and second, it is sometimes technically difficult to compare different quantitative and qualitative data sets, especially if the two sets of results do not converge.

see also QUANTITATIVE RESEARCH, QUALITATIVE RESEARCH, EMBEDDED DESIGN

📖 Heigham & Croker 2009; Lopez & Tashakkori 2006

trimmed mean
    see TRIMMING

trimming

an ACCOMMODATION strategy which involves removing a fixed percentage of extreme scores (OUTLIERs) from each of the tails of any of the DISTRIBUTIONs that are involved in the data analysis. As an example, in an experiment involving two groups, one might decide to omit the two highest and two lowest scores in each group (since by doing this, any outliers in either group would be eliminated). Common trimming levels are the top and bottom DECILEs (i.e., the extreme 10% from each tail of the distribution) and the first and fourth QUARTILEs (i.e., the extreme 25% from each tail). The latter **trimmed mean** (i.e., the MEAN computed by only taking into account scores that fall in the middle 50% of the distribution) is often referred to as the **interquartile mean**. Sometimes the bottom and top 5 per cent of values are removed and the mean is calculated on the remaining 90 per cent of values. Similarly, a 10% trimmed mean drops the highest and the lowest 10% of the measurements and averages the rest.

The trimmed mean may be used with large samples and is similar to the ARITHMETIC MEAN but has some of the smallest and largest scores removed before calculation. In addition to using trimming for reducing the impact of outliers, it is also employed when a distribution has heavy or long tails (i.e., a relatively SKEWED DISTRIBUTION with a disproportionate number of observations falling in the tails). This will be particularly important when the SAMPLE mean is used to predict the corresponding POPULATION central value.

see also WINSORIZATION

📖 Peers 1996; Sheskin 2011; Wilcox 2003

true experimental design
also randomized experimental design
an EXPERIMENTAL RESEARCH design that involves manipulating the INDEPENDENT VARIABLE(s) and observing the change in the DEPENDENT VARIABLE(s) on a randomly chosen SAMPLE. A typical true experimental design would be an intervention study which contains at least two groups: a TREATMENT GROUP and a CONTROL GROUP. The treatment group receives the TREATMENT or which is exposed to some special conditions, and the control group provides a baseline for comparison. From a theoretical perspective, the ultimate challenge is to find a way of making the control group as similar to the treatment group as possible. So, true experimental studies require RANDOM SELECTION of subjects and RANDOM ASSIGNMENT of subjects to control and experimental groups. The assignment of control and experimental status is also done randomly. This means that all subjects of an identified group have an equal chance of being selected to participate in the experiment.

One of the great breakthroughs in true experimental design is the realization that with sufficient participants the RANDOM ASSIGNMENT of the participants to experimental and control groups can provide a way of making the average participant in one group comparable to the average participant in the other group before the treatment is applied. The goal of this genre of design is that researchers try to control changes in the VARIANCE of the independent variable(s) without allowing the intervention of other unwanted variables. Attempts are made by the researcher to keep constant all variables with the exception of the independent variable(s). EXTRANEOUS VARIABLEs must be controlled so that the researcher will be able to determine to what degree the IV(s) is/are related to the dependent variable.

PRETEST-POSTTEST CONTROL GROUP DESIGN, POSTTEST-ONLY CONTROL GROUP DESIGN, POSTTEST TWO EXPERIMENTAL GROUPS DESIGN, PRETEST-POSTTEST TWO EXPERIMENTAL GROUPS DESIGN, MATCHED SUBJECTS DESIGN, SWITCHING-REPLICATIONS DESIGN, PARAMETRIC DESIGN, SOLOMON THREE-GROUP DESIGN, and SOLOMON FOUR-GROUP DESIGN are considered as true experimental designs.

Hatch & Farhady 1982; Mackey & Gass 2005; Perry 2011; Seliger & Shohamy 1989; Tailor 2005

true/false item
a type of test item or test task that requires test takers to decide whether a given statement is either *true* or *false*, which is a dichotomous choice, as the answer or response. Frequently used variations of the words true and false are yes/no or right/wrong, and correct/incorrect.

see also SELECTED-RESPONSE ITEM

Richards & Schmidt 2010

true score
see CLASSICAL TEST THEORY

true score theory
another term for CLASSICAL TEST THEORY

***t* sampling distribution**
another term for *t* DISTRIBUTION

***T* score**
a STANDARD SCORE measured on a scale with a MEAN of 50 and a STANDARD DEVIATION of 10 (see Figure T.5). In order to calculate *T* scores, Z SCOREs have to be calculated first. Unlike Z SCOREs, all the scores on the *T* score scale are positive and range from 10 to 90. Additionally, they can be reported in whole numbers instead of decimal points. In order to convert scores from *z* to *T*, we multiply each *z* score by 10 and add a constant of 50 to that product. The formula to convert from a *z* score to a *T* score is:

$$T = 10(z) + 50$$

Thus, a *z* score of +1 equals a *T* score of 60 (1 × 10 = 10; 10 + 50 = 60). A *z* score of zero (which is the equivalent of the mean of the raw scores) equals a *T* score of 50.
see also NORMAL DISTRIBUTION
📖 Hatch & Lazaraton 1991; Ravid 2011

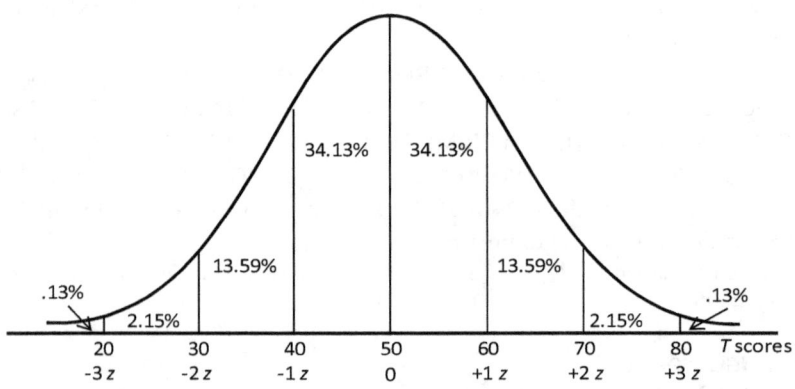

Figure T.5. *T* Scores Associated with the Normal Curve

***t* statistic**
also **Student's *t* statistic**
any statistic that has a *t* DISTRIBUTION. It assesses the STATISTICAL SIG-

NIFICANCE between two groups on a single DEPENDENT VARIABLE (see *t*-TEST). There are many statistical applications of the *t* statistic. One of the most common situations involves making inferences about the unknown population mean.
📖 Sahai & Khurshid 2001

t-test
also **Student's *t*-test**
a PARAMETRIC TEST which is used to discover whether there are statistically significant differences between the MEANs of two groups (e.g., men and women). The results of applying the *t*-test provide the researcher with a ***t*-value** (i.e., the score obtained when we perform a *t*-test). That *t*-value is then entered in a special table of *t* values which indicates whether, given the size of the SAMPLE in the research, the *t*-valu e is statistically significant. When the obtained *t*-test exceeds its appropriate CRITICAL VALUE, the null HYPOTHESIS is rejected. This allows us to conclude that there is a high level of PROBABILITY that the difference between the means is notably greater than zero and that a difference of this magnitude is unlikely to have occurred by chance alone. When the obtained *t*-test does not exceed the critical value, the null hypothesis is retained.

The *t*-test has one distinct advantage over the Z STATISTIC. Using the *z* statistic requires large samples, while the *t*-test does not. If you use the *t*-test with large-size samples, the values of *t* critical and *z* critical will be almost identical. As the sample size increases, the values of *t* and *z* become very close (the value of *t* will always be somewhat larger than the *z* value). Since the values are so close, many researchers use the *t*-test regardless of the size of the two samples and is, therefore, much more commonly in applied linguistics.

A *t*-test is used to compare two means in three different situations: INDEPENDENT-SAMPLES *t*-TEST (e.g., the comparison of experimental and control groups) and PAIRED-SAMPLES *t*-TEST (e.g., the comparison of pretest and posttest scores obtained from one group of people), and SINGLE SAMPLE *t*-TEST. The two main types of *t*-tests (independent-samples *t*-test and paired-samples *t*-test) share two things in common. First, they both test the equality of means. Second, they both rely on the *t* DISTRIBUTION to produce the probabilities used to test statistical significance. However, these two types of *t*-tests are really quite different. The independent samples *t*-test is used to examine the equality of means from two INDEPENDENT GROUPS. In contrast, the dependent samples *t*-test is used to examine whether the means of RELATED GROUPS, or of two variables examined within the same group, are equal.

In much applied linguistics research, however, we may wish to investigate differences between more than two groups. For example, we may wish to look at the examination results of four regions or four kinds of universities. In this case the *t*-test will not suit our purposes, and we must turn to ANALYSIS OF VARIANCE.

see also WELCH'S TEST

📖 Cohen et al. 2011; Dörnyei 2007; Larson-Hall 2010; Mackey & Gass 2005; Seliger & Shohamy 1989; Urdan 2010

Tukey-Kramer test
a POST HOC TEST which is used to determine whether three or more MEANs differ significantly in an ANALYSIS OF VARIANCE. Tukey-Kramer test which is a modification of the TUKEY'S TEST assumes EQUAL VARIANCE for the three or more means. It uses the STUDENTIZED RANGE STATISTIC to determine the critical difference two means have to exceed to be significantly different.

📖 Cramer & Howitt 2004; Lomax 2007

Tukey's honestly significant difference test
another term for TUKEY'S TEST

Tukey's HSD multiple comparisons test
another term for TUKEY'S TEST

Tukey's HSD test
another term for TUKEY'S TEST

Tukey's test
also **Tukey's honestly significant difference test, Tukey's HSD test, *Q*, Tukey's HSD multiple comparisons test, HSD test**
a POST HOC TEST which is used when the group sizes are the same. The Tukey's test is generally recommended when a researcher wants to make all possible PAIRWISE COMPARISONs in a set of data. It controls the FAMILYWISE ERROR RATE so that it will not exceed the prespecified ALPHA (α) LEVEL employed in the analysis. The test is one of a number of comparison procedures that are based on the STUDENTIZED RANGE TEST instead of the *F* VALUE to test all possible MEAN differences (i.e., all pairwise comparisons). The Tukey's test is more *conservative* than the NEWMAN-KEULS TEST, in that it has a lower family-wise TYPE I ERROR rate, a higher TYPE II ERROR rate, and therefore less STATISTICAL POWER. It is more powerful (i.e., liberal) than the DUNN and SCHEFFÉ TESTs for testing all possible pairwise contrasts, but for less than all possible pairwise contrasts the Dunn test is more powerful than the Tukey's or Scheffé tests. This method is less conservative than the scheffé test, as it assumes that not all possible types of comparison between the means are going to be made. The Tukey's test provides better control over the Type I error rate than the Dunn test as the family-wise error rate is exactly held

at alpha (α). The Tukey's test is reasonably ROBUST to *nonnormality* (see NORMALITY), but not in extreme cases and not as robust as the Scheffé test.

see also LIBERAL TEST, CONSERVATIVE TEST

📖 Cohen et al. 2011; Lomax 2007; Mackey & Gass 2005; Page et al. 2003; Sheskin 2011

T-unit
also **minimal terminable unit**
a measure of the linguistic complexity and accuracy of sentences, defined as the shortest unit (the terminable unit, minimal terminable unit, or T-unit) which a sentence can be reduced to, and consisting of one main clause with all subordinate clauses attached to it. T-units were originally used to measure syntactic development in children's first language writing. However, they have become a common measurement in second language study as well, and have served as the basis for several ratio units, such as number of words per T-unit, words per error-free T-unit, and clauses per T-unit. An example of a T-unit is the utterance 'After she had eaten, Sally went to the park'. This T-unit is error-free; that is, it contains no nontargetlike language. An alternative T-unit 'After eat, Peter go to bed' would be coded as a T-unit containing errors. To code using T-units, a researcher may, for example, go through an essay or a transcription and count the total number of T-units; from this number, the researcher could count all the T-units not containing any errors and then present a ratio. For instance, the researcher could say that of 100 T-units used by a learner, 33 contained no errors.

Although commonly employed and sometimes held up as useful because of comparability between studies, the use of T-units has been criticized. For example, it has been argued that the error-free T-unit measure is not always able to take into account the linguistic complexity of the writing or speech or the severity of the errors. In addition, the definitions and types of error and the methods of counting errors have varied considerably from one researcher to the next. Nevertheless, T-units remain popular in second language studies, in part because they are easy to identify and are relatively low-inference categories.

see also SUPPLIANCE IN OBLIGATORY CONTEXTS, CHAT

📖 Mackey & Gass 2005

t-value
see *t*-TEST

two-factor between-subjects ANOVA
another term for two-way anova

two-factor within-groups ANOVA
another term for TWO-WAY REPEATED MEASURES ANOVA

two-factor within-subjects ANOVA
another term for TWO-WAY REPEATED MEASURES ANOVA

two-group discriminant analysis
see DISCRIMINANT FUNCTION ANALYSIS

two-group posttest-only design
another term for POSTTEST-ONLY CONTROL GROUP DESIGN

two-group posttest-only randomized experimental design
another term for POSTTEST-ONLY CONTROL GROUP DESIGN

two-sample Kolmogorov-Smirnov test
another term for KOLMOGOROV-SMIRNOV TEST FOR TWO INDEPENDENT SAMPLES

two-sample *t*-test
another term for INDEPENDENT SAMPLES *t*-TEST

two-sided test
another term for TWO-TAILED TEST

two-tailed hypothesis
another term for NONDIRECTIONAL HYPOTHESIS

two-tailed test
also **two-sided test, nondirectional test**
a SIGNIFICANCE TEST for which the ALTERNATIVE HYPOTHESIS is nondirectional. Put differently, a two-tailed test, unlike ONE-TAILED TEST, takes into account deviations in both directions from the value stated in the NULL HYPOTHESIS, those that are greater than it and those that are less than it. In a two-tailed test, the rejection of the null hypothesis occurs in either tail of the SAMPLING DISTRIBUTION, and thus the CRITICAL REGION consists of both extremes of the sampling distribution of the TEST STATISTIC. As shown in Figure T.6, we usually split the PROBABILITY of .05 into .025 on one side of the distribution and .025 in the other tail. In other words, 2.5% of possible occurrences are in one rejection region and 2.5% of them are in the other rejection region.
see also DIRECTIONAL HYPOTHESIS, NONDIRECTIONAL HYPOTHESIS
📖 Ary et al. 2010; Brown 1988; Clark-Carter 2010; Everitt & Skrondal 2010; Lavrakas 2008; Sahai & Khurshid 2001

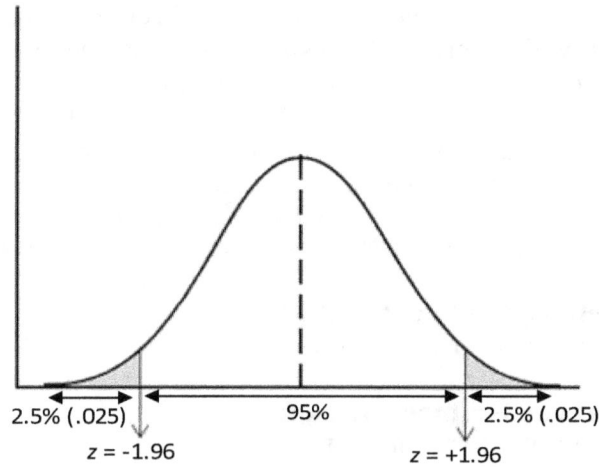

Figure T.6. An Example of a Two-Tailed Test

two-variable chi-square test
another term for CHI-SQUARE TEST OF INDEPENDENCE

two-way ANCOVA
an ANCOVA which involves two *categorical* INDEPENDENT VARIABLEs (IVs) (each with two or more LEVELs), one *continuous* DEPENDENT VARIABLE, and one or more continuous COVARIATEs. ANCOVA will control for scores on your covariate(s) and then perform a normal TWO-WAY ANOVA. This will tell you if there is:

- a significant MAIN EFFECT for your first IV (group);
- a main effect for your second IV; and
- a significant INTERACTION EFFECT between the two.

All two-way ANOVA and ONE-WAY ANCOVA *ASSUMPTIONS* apply (e.g., NORMALITY, HOMOGENEITY OF VARIANCE).
📖 Pallant 2010

two-way ANOVA
also **two-way factorial ANOVA, two-factor ANOVA, two-way between-subjects ANOVA, two-factor between-subjects ANOVA, two-way independent ANOVA**
a FACTORIAL ANOVA which estimates the effect of two *categorical* INDEPENDENT VARIABLEs (IV) (each with two or more LEVELs) on a single *continuous* DEPENDENT VARIABLE and the INTERACTION between them. There are many situations in which we would like to include more than one IV in our study. When there is more than one IV, the results will show MAIN EFFECT (which is the influence of a variable acting on its

own or independently) and an interaction effect (which is the conjoint influence of two or more IVs). This interaction may not be apparent when a series of ONE-WAY ANOVA tests is conducted.

Mathematically, the two-way ANOVA is more complex than its one-way counterpart, because here instead of one F score three are needed: one for each of the IVs and one for their interaction.

There is no *nonparametric* alternative to two-way ANOVA.

📖 Cohen et al. 2011; Dörnyei 2007; Greene & Oliveira 2005; Mackey & Gass 2005

two-way between-subjects ANOVA
another term for TWO-WAY ANOVA

two-way between-subjects design
see BETWEEN-SUBJECTS DESIGN

two-way chi-square test
another term for CHI-SQUARE TEST OF INDEPENDENCE

two-way factorial ANOVA
another term for TWO-WAY ANOVA

two-way factorial design
also **simple factorial design, 2 × 2 factorial design**
the simplest factorial design which has two FACTORs, and each factor has two LEVELs. As shown in Table T.3, a two-way factorial design can be represented as follows:

Variable 2 (X_2)	Variable 1 (X_1)	
	Treatment A	Treatment B
Level 1	Cell 1	Cell 3
Level 2	Cell 2	Cell 4

Table T.3. Schematic Representation of a Simple Factorial Design

To illustrate, assume that an experimenter is interested in comparing the effectiveness of two types of teaching methods—methods A and B—on the achievement of second language university students, believing that there may be a differential effect of these methods based on the students' level of aptitude. Table T.4 shows the 2 × 2 (two-by-two) factorial design. The aptitude factor has two levels—high and low; the other factor (teaching method) also has two levels (A and B). The researcher randomly selects 60 subjects from the high-aptitude group and randomly assigns 30 subjects to method A and 30 subjects to method B. This process is repeated for the low-aptitude group. Teachers are also randomly assigned to the groups. Note that a 2 × 2 design requires four groups of subjects; each group represents a combination of a level of one factor and a level of the other factor.

	Teaching method X_1		
Aptitude (X_2)	Method A	Method B	Mean
High	75	73	74
Low	60	64	62
Mean	67.5	68.5	

Table T.4. *An Example of a Factorial Design*

In this example, we want to investigate whether there is any difference in achievement among the following groups after the TREATMENT:

Group 1   Method A, High Aptitude
Group 2   Method A, Low Aptitude
Group 3   Method B, High Aptitude
Group 4   Method B, Low Aptitude

The scores in the four cells represent the MEAN scores of the four groups on the DEPENDENT VARIABLE, the achievement test. In addition to the four cell scores representing the various combinations of treatments and levels, there are four marginal mean scores: two for the columns and two for the rows. The marginal column means are for the two methods, or treatments, and the marginal row means are for the two levels of aptitude. From the data given, you can first determine the MAIN EFFECTs for the two INDEPENDENT VARIABLEs (IVs). The main effect for treatments refers to the treatment mean scores without regard to aptitude level. If you compare the mean score of the two method *A* groups, 67.5, with that of the two method *B* groups, 68.5, you find that the difference between these means is only 1 point. Therefore, you might be tempted to conclude that the method used has little effect on the achievement scores, the dependent variable.

Now examine the mean scores for the levels to determine the main effect of aptitude level on achievement scores. The main effect for levels does not take into account any differential effect caused by treatments. The mean score for the two high-aptitude groups is 74, and the mean score for the two low-aptitude groups is 62; this difference, 12 points, is the effect attributable to aptitude level. The high-aptitude group has a markedly higher mean score; thus, regardless of treatment, the high-aptitude groups perform better than the low-aptitude groups. Note that the term main effects does not mean the most important effect but, rather, the effect of one IV (factor) ignoring the other factor. In the example, main effect for teaching method refers to the difference between method *A* and method *B* (column means) for all students regardless of aptitude. The main effect for aptitude is the difference between all high-and low-aptitude students (row means) regardless of teaching method.

A factorial design also permits the investigator to assess the INTERACTION between the two IVs—that is, the different effects of one of them at different levels of the other. If there is an interaction, the effect that the treatment has on learning will differ for the two aptitude levels. If there is no interaction, the effect of the treatment will be the same for both levels of aptitude. Looking at Table T.4, you can see that the method *A* mean is higher than the method *B* mean for the high-aptitude group, and the method *B* mean is higher for the low-aptitude group. Thus, some particular combinations of treatment and level of aptitude interact to produce greater gains than do some other combinations. This interaction effect between method and aptitude levels is shown graphically in Figure T.7. If this interaction is statistically significant, you conclude that the effectiveness of the method depends on aptitude. Method *A* is more effective with the high-aptitude students; method *B* is more effective with the low-aptitude group.

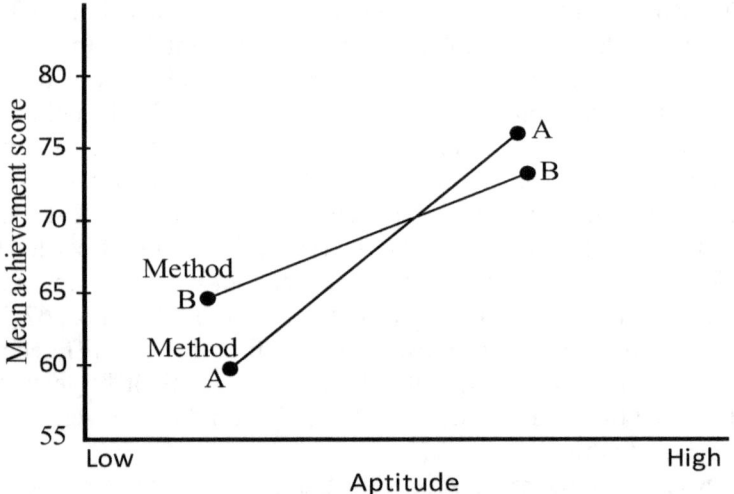

Figure T.7. Interaction between Method and Aptitude

Now examine another set of data obtained in a hypothetical 2 × 2 factorial study. Table T.5 shows the results of a study designed to investigate the effect of two methods of instruction on achievement. Because the investigator anticipates that the method may be differentially effective depending on the aptitude of the subject, the first step is to use an aptitude measure and place participants into one of two levels: high aptitude or low aptitude. The researcher randomly assigns subjects within each aptitude level to one of the two methods.

Aptitude (X_2)	Treatment (X_1)		Mean
	Method A	Method B	
High	50	58	54
Low	40	48	44
Mean	45	53	

Table T.5. An Example of a Factorial Design

After the experiment, the researcher administers achievement tests and records the scores for every subject. If you compare the mean score of the two groups taught by method B, 53, with that of the two groups taught by method A, 45, the former is somewhat higher and method B appears to be more effective than method A. The difference between the means for the two aptitude levels, or the main effects for aptitude, is 10 (54 - 44). Regardless of treatment, the high-aptitude group performs better than the low-aptitude group. The data reveal no interaction between treatment and levels. Method B appears to be more effective regardless of the aptitude level. In other words, treatments and levels are independent of each other. It would not be possible to demonstrate either the presence or the absence of interaction without using a factorial design. The lack of interaction is illustrated graphically in Figure T.8.

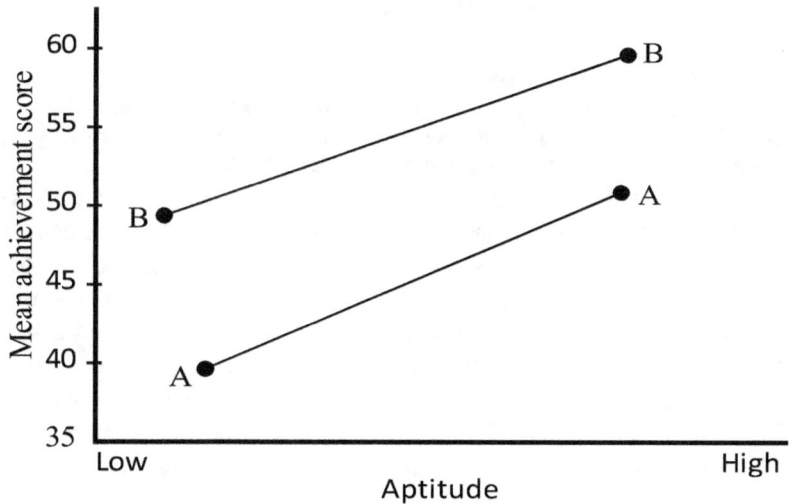

Figure T.8. Lack of Interaction between Method and Aptitude Level

The 2 × 2 factorial design can be extended to include more than two levels within each IV, such as a 2 × 3, 3 × 3, 2 × 4, 4 × 3, etc. The factorial design can be also extended to more complex experiments in which there are a number of IVs; the numeric values of the digits indicate the number of levels for the specific IVs. For instance, in a 2 × 3 × 4 factorial design, there are three IVs with two, three, and four levels, respectively. Such an experiment might use two teaching methods, three ability levels, and four grades. Theoretically, a factorial design may include any number of IVs with any number of levels of each. However, when too many factors are manipulated or controlled simultaneously, the study and the statistical analysis become unwieldy and some of the combinations may be artificial. The number of groups required for a factorial design is the product of the digits that indicate the factorial design. In the 2 × 3 × 4 design, 24 groups would be required to represent all combinations of the different levels of the multiple IVs.
 Ary et al. 2010

two-way group-independence chi-square test
another term for CHI-SQUARE TEST OF INDEPENDENCE

two-way hypothesis
another term for NONDIRECTIONAL HYPOTHESIS

two-way independent ANOVA
another term for TWO-WAY ANOVA

two-way mixed design
another term for SIMPLE MIXED DESIGN

two-way repeated measures ANOVA
also **two-way repeated measures factorial ANOVA, two-way within-subjects ANOVA, two-factor within-subjects ANOVA, two-way within-groups ANOVA, two-factor within- groups ANOVA**
a *parametric* inferential procedure performed when both FACTORs (i.e., INDEPENDENT VARIABLE) are WITHIN-SUBJECTS FACTORs. Because each participant produces scores on all the CONDITIONs, the scores for each participant are related. In two-way repeated measures ANOVA the same participants do the two or more conditions on one factor and also do the two or more conditions on the other factor. An example would be an experiment in which the first factor is a comparison between learning lists of long or short words. The second factor is a comparison between fast and slow rates of presenting the lists of words, as shown below:

Variable A (length of words)
Condition A_1 (short words)
Condition A_2 (long words)
Variable B (presentation rates)
Condition B_1 (fast rate)
Condition B_2 (slow rate)

In two-way repeated measures ANOVA the same participants will be doing the two conditions on variable *A* and also the two conditions on variable *B*. The same participants will be doing all four conditions listed in Table T.6.
📖 Greene & Oliveira 2005

Condition 1	Short words (A_1) presented at a fast rate (B_1)
Condition 2	Short words (A_1) presented at a slow rate (B_2)
Condition 3	Long words (A_2) presented at a fast rate (B_1)
Condition 4	Long words (A_2) presented at a slow rate (B_2)

Table T.6. Same Participants Doing all Four Conditions

two-way repeated measures factorial ANOVA
another term for TWO-WAY REPEATED MEASURES ANOVA

two-way table
see CONTINGENCY TABLE

two-way within-groups ANOVA
another term for TWO-WAY REPEATED MEASURES ANOVA

two-way within-subjects ANOVA
another term for TWO-WAY REPEATED MEASURES ANOVA

two-way within-subjects design
see WITHIN-SUBJECTS DESIGN

Type I error
also **alpha (α) error, false positive, false alarm**
an error in decision making or HYPOTHESIS TESTING that results from rejecting a NULL HYPOTHESIS (H_0) when, in fact, it is true. Type I error occurs when there is really no difference between the POPULATION PARAMETERs being tested, but the researcher is misled by chance differences in the SAMPLE DATA. In other words, it occurs when a researcher erroneously concludes that there is a difference between the groups being stud-

ied when, in fact, there is no difference and, thus, concludes that a false ALTERNATIVE HYPOTHESIS is true.

Consider the first row of the Table T.7 where H_0 is in actuality true. First, if H_0 is true and we fail to reject H_0, then we have made a correct decision; that is, we have correctly failed to reject a true H_0. The PROBABILITY of this first outcome (i.e., correct acceptance) is known as (denoted by) 1 - ALPHA (α). Second, if H_0 is true and we reject H_0, then we have made a Type I error. That is, we have incorrectly rejected a true H_0. Our sample data has led us to a different conclusion than the population data would have. The probability of this second outcome (making a Type I error) is known as α. Therefore, if H_0 is actually true, then our sample data lead us to one of two conclusions: Either we correctly fail to reject H_0, or we incorrectly reject H_0. The sum of the probabilities for these two outcomes when H_0 is true is equal to 1, i.e., $(1 - \alpha) + \alpha = 1$. The more concerned a researcher is with committing a Type I error, the lower the value of alpha the researcher should employ. A Type I error is therefore a **false positive** judgment concerning the validity of the mean difference obtained.

(a) For General case

state of nature (reality)	decision	
	fail to reject H_0	reject H_0
H_0 is true	correct decision $(1-\alpha)$	Type I error (α)
H_0 is false	Type II error (β)	correct decision $(1-\beta)$ = power

(b) For example umbrella/rain case

state of nature (reality)	decision	
	fail to reject H_0 do not carry umbrella	reject H_0 carry umbrella
H_0 is true, no rain	correct decision no umbrella needed $(1-\alpha)$	Type I error look silly (α)
H_0 is false, rains	Type II error get wet (β)	correct decision stay dry $(1-\beta)$ = power

Table T.7. Statistical Decision Table

By contrast, a **Type II** error (also called **beta (β) error, false negative**) occurs when the researcher fails to reject H_0 when it is, in fact, false (i.e., one concludes that a true alternative hypothesis is false). In this case, the researcher concludes that the TREATMENT or INDEPENDENT VARIABLE does not have an effect when, in fact, it does. That is, the researcher concludes that there is not a difference between the two groups being studied when, in fact, there is a difference.

Consider the second row of the Table T.7 where H_0 is in actuality false. First, if H_0 is really false and we fail to reject H_0, then we have made a Type II error. That is, we have incorrectly failed to reject a false H_0. Our sample data has led us to a different conclusion than the population data would have. The probability of this outcome—accepting the null hypothesis when the alternative hypothesis is true—is known as **β (beta)**. Second, if H_0 is really false and we reject H_0, then we have made a correct decision; that is, we have correctly rejected a false H_0. The probability of this second outcome (i.e., correct rejection) is known as 1 - β (also referred to as POWER). Thus, if H_0 is actually false, then our sample data lead us to one of two conclusions: Either we incorrectly fail to reject H_0, or we correctly reject H_0. The sum of the probabilities for these two outcomes when H_0 is false is equal to 1, i.e., β + (1 - β) = 1. A Type II error is therefore a **false negative** judgment concerning the validation of the mean difference obtained.

Consider the following example, as shown in part (b) of Table T.7. We wish to test the following hypotheses about whether or not it will rain tomorrow. Again there are four potential outcomes. First, if H_0 is really true (no rain) and we do not carry an umbrella, then we have made a correct decision as no umbrella is necessary (probability = 1 - α). Second, if H_0 is really true (no rain) and we carry an umbrella, then we have made a Type I error as we look silly carrying that umbrella around all day (probability = β). Third, if H_0 is really false (rains) and we do not carry an umbrella, then we have made a Type II error and we get wet (probability = α). Fourth, if H_0 is really false (rains) and we carry an umbrella, then we have made the correct decision as the umbrella keeps us dry (probability = 1 - β).

One can totally eliminate the possibility of a Type I error by deciding to never reject H_0. That is, if we always fail to reject H_0, then we can never make a Type I error. One can totally eliminate the possibility of a Type II error by deciding to always reject H_0. That is, if we always reject H_0, then we can never make a Type II error. With these strategies we do not even need to collect any sample data as we have already decided to never/always reject H_0. Taken together, one can never totally eliminate the possibility of both a Type I and a Type II error. No matter what decision we make, there is always some possibility of making a Type I and/or Type II error.

In qualitative data a Type I error is committed when a statement is believed when it is, in fact, not true, and a Type II error is committed when a statement is rejected when it is, in fact, true.

see also CONFIDENCE INTERVAL
📖 Clark-Carter 2010; Cohen et al. 2011; Kirk 2008; Leary 2011; Marczyk et al. 2005; Porte 2010; Sahai & Khurshid 2001; Sheskin 2011; Upton & Cook 2008

Type-token ratio
a measure of lexical diversity which involves dividing the number of types by the number of tokens, e.g., types can refer to the different words that are used in one data set, and tokens can refer to the number of repetitions of those words.
📖 Mackey & Gass 2005

Type II error
see TYPE I ERROR

typical case sampling
see PURPOSIVE SAMPLING

U

U
    an abbreviation for MANN-WHITNEY *U* TEST

unbalanced design
    also **nonorthogonal design**
    a term which is used to denote a FACTORIAL DESIGN with two or more FACTORs having unequal numbers of observations or values in each cell or LEVEL of a factor. There are at least three situations in which you might have an unbalanced design. One is if the SAMPLEs are proportional and reflect an imbalance in the POPULATION from which the sample came. Thus, if we knew that two-thirds of second language (L2) students were female and one-third male, we might have a sample of L2 students with a 2:1 ratio of females to males. For example, we might look at the way male and female L2 students differ in their exam performance after receiving two teaching techniques—seminars or lectures. With such proportional data it is legitimate to use the WEIGHTED MEANs analysis.
    A second possible reason for an unbalanced design is that participants were not available for particular TREATMENTs but there was no systematic reason for their unavailability; that is, there is no connection between the treatment to which they were assigned and the lack of data for them. Under these circumstances it is legitimate to use the UNWEIGHTED MEANS ANALYSIS or the LEAST SQUARES METHOD OF ANALYSIS.
    A third possible reason for an unbalanced design would be if there were a systematic link between the treatment group and the failure to have data for such participants; this is more likely in a quasi-experiment.
    Given the difficulties with unbalanced designs, unless you are dealing with proportional samples, some people recommend randomly removing data points from the treatments that have more than the others. Alternatively, it is possible to replace missing data with the mean for the group, or even the overall mean. If you put in the group mean you may artificially enhance any differences between conditions, and if you use the overall mean to replace missing data you may obscure any genuine differences between groups. If either of these methods is used then the total degrees of freedom should be reduced by one for each data point estimated.
    📖 Clark-Carter 2010; Hatch & Lazaraton 1991; Sahai & Khurshid 2001

uncorrelated design
    another term for BETWEEN-SUBJECTS DESIGN

uncorrelated *t*-test
another term for INDEPENDENT SAMPLES *t*-TEST

unequal variance *t*-test
another term for WELCH'S TEST

ungrouped variable
another term for CONTINUOUS VARIABLE

unidimensional scale
see CUMULATIVE SCALE

unidirectional hypothesis
another term for DIRECTIONAL HYPOTHESIS

unimodal distribution
see MODE

unique variance
see MULTIVARIATE ANALYSIS OF VARIANCE

unitary trait hypothesis
see INTEGRATIVE TEST

univariate analysis
the analysis of single VARIABLEs without reference to other variables. The commonest univariate statistics are DESCRIPTIVE STATISTICS such as the MEAN and VARIANCE. When a data distribution for one DEPENDENT VARIABLE (DV) of interest is displayed this is called a **univariate distribution**; the BAR CHART and HISTOGRAM are examples of univariate graphic displays. Univariate statistical analysis does not imply analysis involving only one variable, there may be one or more INDEPENDENT VARIABLEs. For example, a researcher may want to investigate differences, in final examinations performance, among different groups of students. The DV, performance in final examinations, may be explained by a student's age (classified as mature candidate, not mature) and gender. ANALYSIS OF VARIANCE, which is a classical example of a univariate statistical analysis, may well be an appropriate statistical procedure to use. This would still be a univariate analysis because the research question relates to whether there are any differences between groups with respect to a single DV.
Univariate analysis is used in contrast to BIVARIATE and MULTIVARIATE

ANALYSIS involving measurements on two or more variables simultaneously.
 Cramer & Howitt 2004; Peers 1996

univariate distribution
see UNIVARIATE ANALYSIS

universe score
see GENERALIZABILITY THEORY

unobserved variable
another term for LATENT VARIABLE

unobtrusive measure
see HAWTHORNE EFFECT

unplanned comparison
another term for POST HOC TEST

unrelated design
another term for BETWEEN-SUBJECTS DESIGN

unrelated samples
another term for INDEPENDENT SAMPLES

unrelated t-test
another term for INDEPENDENT SAMPLES t-TEST

unrestricted question
another term for OPEN-FORM ITEM

unstandardized partial regression coefficient
see STANDARDIZED PARTIAL REGRESSION COEFFICIENT

unstandardized regression coefficient
another term for UNSTANDARDIZED PARTIAL REGRESSION COEFFICIENT

unstructured interview
a conversational type of INTERVIEW in which the questions arise from the situation. Unstructured interview involves a particular topic or topics to be discussed but the interviewer has no fixed wording in mind and is happy to let the conversation deviate from the original topic if potentially interesting material is touched upon; the participant is free to talk about what s/he deems important, with little directional influence from the re-

searcher. The intention is to create a relaxed atmosphere in which respondents may reveal more than they would in formal contexts, with the interviewer assuming a listening role. The respondents will be allowed to develop the chosen theme as they wish and to maintain the initiative in the conversation, while the interviewer will restrict himself/herself to encouraging the respondents to elucidate further whenever they touch upon a topic that seems interesting. Naturally, the interviewer will also have to exercise a degree of control by leading the respondents back to the point if they begin to digress towards subjects that have nothing to do with the issue under examination. Should the respondents go off at a tangent, the interviewer will bring them back to the main theme. Though the basic theme of the conversation has been chosen beforehand, unforeseen sub-themes may nevertheless arise during the interview. If these are seen to be relevant and important, they will be developed further. Thus, different interviews might emphasize different topics. Moreover, some respondents have more to say than others; some are more outgoing, while others are more reserved. In addition, the empathetic relationship that is built up during the course of the interview varies from case to case; some interviewees will get on the same wavelength as the interviewer, develop a relationship of trust with him/her and reveal their innermost feelings and personal reflections, while in other cases this mechanism is not triggered. It, thus, follows that the interviews will have an extremely individual character and will differ widely in terms of both the topics discussed and the length of the interview itself. Such a technique could be used when a researcher is initially exploring an area with a view to designing a more structured format for subsequent use. In addition, this technique can be used to produce the data for a CONTENT ANALYSIS or even for a qualitative method such as DISCOURSE ANALYSIS.

see also ETHNOGRAPHIC INTERVIEW, NON-DIRECTIVE INTERVIEW, SEMI-STRUCTURED INTERVIEW, STRUCTURED INTERVIEW, INTERVIEW GUIDE, INFORMAL INTERVIEW, TELEPHONE INTERVIEW, FOCUS GROUP

 Clark-Carter 2010; Corbetta 2003; Dörnyei 2007; Heigham & Croker 2009

unstructured observation
see OBSERVATION

unsystematic error
another term for RANDOM ERROR

unsystematic variance
another term for ERROR VARIANCE

unweighted mean
see WEIGHTED MEAN

unweighted means analysis

a method of analysis in two-way and higher-order FACTORIAL DESIGNs containing unequal numbers of observations or values in each cell. The procedure consists of calculating the cell means and then carrying out a balanced data analysis by assuming that the cell means constitute a single observation in each cell

see also UNBALANCED DESIGN

📖 Sahai & Khurshid 2001

U-shaped distribution

an asymmetrical FREQUENCY DISTRIBUTION having general resemblance to the shape of the letter U. As shown in Figure U.1, the distribution has maximum frequencies at both ends of the distribution, which decline rapidly at first and then more slowly, reaching a minimum between them.

📖 Sahai & Khurshid 2001

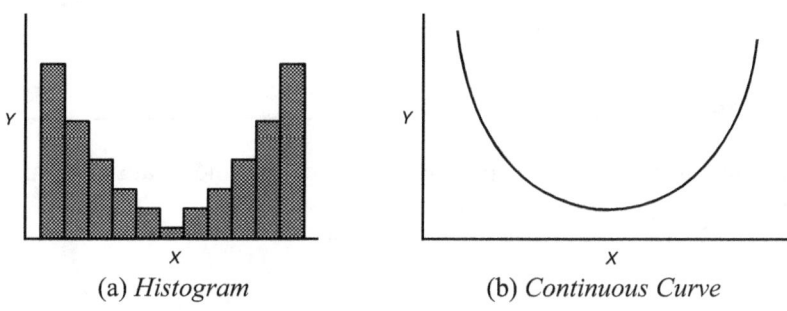

(a) *Histogram* (b) *Continuous Curve*

Figure U.1. Two U-Shaped Distributions

U test

an abbreviation for MANN-WHITNEY *U* TEST

utility

the facet of VALIDITY that is concerned with whether measurement or observational procedures are used for the correct purposes. If a procedure is not used for what it was originally intended for, there might be a question as to whether it is a valid procedure for obtaining the data needed in a particular study. If it is used for something other than what it was originally designed to do, the researcher must provide additional evidence that the procedure is valid for the purpose of his/her study. For example, if you wanted to use the results from the TOEFL to measure the effects of a treatment over a two-week training period, this would be invalid. To reiterate, the reason is that the TOEFL was designed to measure language proficiency, which develops over long periods of time. It was not

designed to measure the specific outcomes that the treatment was targeting.
📖 Perry 2011

V

V
an abbreviation for CRAMER'S V. Also an abbreviation for PILLAI'S CRITERION

validity
the degree to which a study and its results correctly lead to, or support, exactly what is claimed. Generally, validity refers to the appropriateness, meaningfulness, correctness, and usefulness of the inferences a researcher makes. Validation is the process of collecting and analyzing evidence to support such inferences. Validity is a requirement for both QUANTITATIVE and QUALITATIVE RESEARCH. In qualitative data validity might be addressed through the honesty, depth, richness and scope of the data achieved, the participants approached, the extent of TRIANGULATION and the disinterestedness (see CONFIRMABILITY) of the researcher. In quantitative research validity might be improved through careful SAMPLING, appropriate instrumentation and appropriate statistical treatments of the data. Quantitative research possesses a measure of STANDARD ERROR which is inbuilt and which has to be acknowledged. In qualitative data the subjectivity of respondents, their opinions, attitudes, and perspectives together contribute to a degree of BIAS. Validity, then, should be seen as a matter of degree rather than as an absolute state.
There are several different kinds of validity: CONTENT VALIDITY, CRITERION-RELATED VALIDITY, CONSTRUCT VALIDITY, INTERNAL VALIDITY, EXTERNAL VALIDITY, FACE VALIDITY, CONSEQUENTIAL VALIDITY, CATALYTIC VALIDITY, ECOLOGICAL VALIDITY, CULTURAL VALIDITY, DESCRIPTIVE VALIDITY, INTERPRETIVE VALIDITY, THEORETICAL VALIDITY, and EVALUATIVE VALIDITY.
📖 Cohen et al. 2011; Dörnyei 2007; Fraenkel & Wallen 2009

validity coefficient
see CRITERION-RELATED VALIDITY

VARBRUL
a statistical package for DATA ANALYSIS often used in sociolinguistic research.
📖 Mackey & Gass 2005

variability
also **dispersion**
the amount of spread among the scores in a group. For example, if the scores of participants on a test were widely spread from low, middle to

high, the scores would be said to have a large dispersion. To examine the extent to which scores in a distribution vary from one another, researchers use measures of variability, i.e., descriptive statistics that convey information about the spread or variability of a set of data. The common statistical **measures of variability** (also called **measures of dispersion**) are VARIANCE, STANDARD DEVIATION, RANGE, and INTER-QUARTILE RANGE. Less common is the COEFFICIENT OF VARIATION. Variability is the complementary quality to the CENTRAL TENDENCY of a distribution. Various data sets may have the same center but different amount of spreads.
 Richards & Schmidt 2010

variable

any characteristics or attributes of an object or of a person that can have different values from one time to the next or from one individual to another. Variable is something that may vary, or differ from person to person or from object to object. For example, you may be left-handed. That is an attribute, and it varies from person to person. There are also right-handed people. Height, sex, nationality, and language group membership are all variables commonly assigned to people. Variables often attributed to objects include temperature, weight, size, shape, and color. A person's proficiency in English as a foreign language may differ over time as the person learns more and more English. Thus, proficiency in English can be considered a variable because it may change over time or differ among individuals. Variables can be quantified on different MEASUREMENT SCALEs depending on whether we want to know how much of the variable a person has or only about the presence or absence of the variable.

The opposite notion to a variable is a **constant**, which is simply a condition or quality that does not vary between cases. It is a construct that has only one value (e.g., if every member of a sample was 10 years old, the *age* construct would be a constant). The number of cents in a United States dollar is a constant: every dollar note will always exchange for 100 cents; or, the number of hours in a day—twenty-four—is also a constant. Adding a constant to every score in a distribution does not affect the outcome of the statistical calculations.

In REGRESSION ANALYSIS, constant is the point where the REGRESSION LINE intersects the vertical axis.

see also LEVEL, INDEPENDENT VARIABLE, DEPENDENT VARIABLE, MODERATOR VARIABLE, INTERVENING VARIABLE, CATEGORICAL VARIABLE, CONTINUOUS VARIABLE
 Brown 1988, 1992; Hatch & Farhady 1982; Porte 2010

variance
a statistical MEASURE OF VARIABILITY of a set of data around the MEAN. Variance is calculated by summing the squared deviations of the data values about the mean and then dividing the total by N if the data set is a POPULATION or by $N - 1$ if the data set is from a SAMPLE. Variance is, in fact, the squared value of the STANDARD DEVIATION. It is calculated from the average squared deviation of each number from its mean. The larger the variance, the more scattered are the observations on average. Because of the mathematical manipulation needed to produce a variance statistic variance is not often used by researchers to gain a sense of a distribution. In general, variance is used more as a step in the calculation of other statistics (e.g., t-TEST, ANALYSIS OF VARIANCE) than as a stand-alone statistic. But with a simple manipulation, the variance can be transformed into the standard deviation.
see also SAMPLE VARIANCE, POPULATION VARIANCE
📖 Porte 2010; Urdan 2010

variance estimate
another term for SAMPLE VARIANCE

variance inflation factor
see MULTICOLLINEARITY

variate
see DISCRIMINANT FUNCTION ANALYSIS

Venn diagram
a graphical representation of the extent to which two or more quantities or concepts are mutually inclusive and mutually exclusive. Venn diagram is a system of representing the relationship between subsets of information. Usually the totality is represented by a rectangle. Within that rectangle are to be found circles which enclose particular subsets. The circles may not overlap, in which case there is no overlap between the subsets. Alternatively, they may overlap totally or partially. The amount of overlap is the amount of overlap between subsets. Figure V.1 shows examples of Venn diagrams.

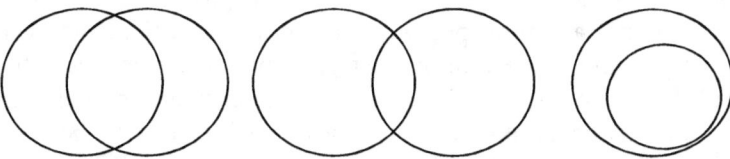

Figure V.1. Examples of Venn Diagrams

see also COEFFICIENT OF DETERMINATION
📖 Cramer & Howitt 2004; Sahai & Khurshid 2001

verbal protocol
another term for VERBAL REPORT

verbal report
  also **verbal protocol, verbal reporting**
an introspective qualitative data collection method which consists of oral records of an individual's thought processes, provided by the individual when thinking aloud either *during* or immediately *after* completing a task. These tasks are usually relatively specific and bounded, e.g., reading a short text. The verbalized thoughts of the participants are usually free-form, since participants are not provided with preformatted choices of answers. It is important to understand that verbal reports do not mirror the thought processes. Verbal reports are not immediate revelations of thought processes. They represent (a subset of) the information currently available in short-term memory rather than the processes producing the information. Cognitive processes are not directly manifest in protocols but have to be inferred, just as in the case of other types of data.
Typically when researchers talk about verbal reporting they usually imply two specific techniques: **think-aloud protocol** and **retrospective protocol** (sometimes called **stimulated recall**), differentiated by *when* the data is collected. In a think-aloud protocol, the participants are given a task to perform and *during* the performance of that task they are asked to verbalize (i.e., to articulate) what their thought processes are. The researcher's role is merely to encourage that verbalization through prompting the participants with utterances such as 'please keep telling me what you are thinking'; 'please keep thinking aloud if you can'. Think-aloud implies no direct inspection of the mental state, but merely reportage. It involves the concurrent vocalization of one's inner speech without offering any analysis or explanation. Thus, respondents are asked to verbalize only the thoughts that enter their attention while still in the respondents' short-term memory. In this way, the procedure does not alter the sequence of thoughts mediating the completion of a task and can therefore be accepted as valid data on thinking. The resulting verbal protocol is recorded and then analyzed. It is clear that providing think-aloud commentary is not a natural process and therefore participants need precise instructions and some training before they can be expected to produce useful data. They need to be told to focus on their task performance rather than on the think-aloud and they usually need to be reminded to keep on talking while carrying out an activity (e.g., 'What made you do that?', or 'What are you thinking about now?').

The second type is a retrospective protocol or a stimulated recall in which learners verbalize their thought processes immediately *after* they have performed a task or mental operation. In such cases, the relevant information needs to be retrieved from long-term memory and thus the validity of retrospective protocols depends on the time interval between the occurrence of a thought and its verbal report. For tasks with relatively short response latencies (less than 5-10 seconds), subjects are able to produce accurate recollections, but for cognitive processes of longer duration, the difficulty of accurate recall of prior thoughts increases. In order to help the respondents retrieve their relevant thoughts, some sort of stimulus is used as a support for the recall (hence the term *stimulated recall*), such as watching the respondent's own task performance on video, listening to a recording of what the person has said, or showing the person a written work that s/he has produced. Thus, the underlying idea is that some tangible (visual or aural) reminder of an event will stimulate recall to an extent that the respondents can retrieve and then verbalize what was going on in their minds during the event.

There are several principles that should be adhered to in conducting verbal reports. These principles include the following:

1) time intervening between mental operations and report is critical and should be minimized as much as possible;
2) verbalization places additional cognitive demands on mental processing that requires care in order to achieve insightful results;
3) verbal reports of mental processes should avoid the usual social conventions of talking to someone;
4) there is a lot of information in introspective reports aside from the words themselves. Researchers need to be aware of these parallel signal systems and be prepared to include them in their analyses;
5) verbal reports of automatic processes are not possible. Such processes include visual and motor processes and low-attention, automatized linguistic processes such as the social chat of native speakers.

Many criticisms have been leveled against verbal reports, the major one being that it is highly unnatural and obtrusive to verbalize ones thoughts. In addition, verbal reports do not elicit all of the cognitive processes involved in an activity and thus are incomplete. Furthermore, the analysis of verbal report data is subject to the idiosyncratic interpretations of the researcher and hence may not be valid. For example, for second language learners there is also the problem that students are asked to report on their thought processes in a second language. Although few dispute the limitations of verbal reports, at this point, the method is one of the few

available means for finding out more about the thought processes of the participants.
📖 Brown & Rodgers 2002; Cohen & Macaro 2010; Dörnyei 2007; Gass & Mackey 2000; Heigham & Croker 2009; Mckay 2006; Perry 2011; Nunan 1992

verbal reporting
another term for VERBAL REPORT

verificationalism
a view that a claim or belief is meaningful only if we can state the conditions under which it could be verified or falsified. That is, we need to state what EMPIRICAL RESEARCH would need to be done to show that the claim or belief was true, or false. Verifiability and falsifiability are associated with LOGICAL POSITIVISM.
📖 Fulcher & Davidson 2007

vertical axis
see BAR GRAPH

VIF
an abbreviation for VARIANCE INFLATION FACTOR

vignettes
a technique, used in STRUCTURED and IN-DEPTH INTERVIEWs as well as FOCUS GROUPs, providing sketches of fictional (or fictionalized) scenarios. The respondent is then invited to imagine, drawing on his/her own experience, and how the central character in the scenario will behave. Vignettes thus collect situated data on group values, group beliefs, and group norms of behavior. While in structured interviews respondents must choose from a multiple-choice menu of possible answers to a vignette, as used in-depth interviews and focus groups, vignettes act as stimulus to extended discussion of the scenario in question.
📖 Bloor & Wood 2006

volunteer sampling
a type of NON-PROBABILITY SAMPLING used when the researchers ask people to volunteer to take part in their research. In cases where access is difficult, the researcher may have to rely on volunteers, for example, personal friends, or friends of friends, or participants who reply to a newspaper advertisement, or those who happen to be interested from a particular school, or those attending courses. This method has the obvious advantage of being easy and cheap but is highly problematic from the point of view of obtaining an unbiased sample (see SAMPLING ERROR). Closely related to CONVENIENCE SAMPLING is the use of volunteers as a sampling

strategy. They differ from a convenience sampling in that they are not under any obligation to participate in the study, whereas the former usually consists of students who are required to be participants of a research study as partial fulfillment of their courses. Volunteers are often paid for their services, whereas participants in convenience samples are not. When all attempts fail to find participants using other strategies, using volunteers is often the only way researchers can go. However, research has shown that using volunteers frequently leads to a sample that is not representative of a target POPULATION. Findings have shown that in the West, volunteers tend to be better educated, more motivated, more outgoing, higher in need achievement, and from a higher socioeconomic level. It is pointed out that if any of these qualities could possibly impact the variable(s) under investigation, you would have to treat the findings of the study with some reservation.

see also QUOTA SAMPLING, DIMENSIONAL SAMPLING, PURPOSIVE SAMPLING, SNOWBALL SAMPLING, SEQUENTIAL SAMPLING, OPPORTUNISTIC SAMPLING

📖 Cohen et al. 2011; Perry 2011

W

W
an abbreviation for KENDALL'S COEFFICIENT OF CONCORDANCE

Waller-Duncan *t*-test
a POST HOC TEST used for determining which of three or more MEANs differ significantly in an ANALYSIS OF VARIANCE (ANOVA). This test is based on the **Bayesian *t*-value** (also called **Bayes' Theorem**) which depends on the *F* RATIO for a ONE-WAY ANOVA, its DEGREES OF FREEDOM and a measure of the relative seriousness of making a TYPE I ERROR versus a TYPE II ERROR. It can be used for groups of equal or unequal size.
📖 Cramer & Howitt 2004

web survey
another term for INTERNET SURVEY

Wechsler scales
a group of intelligence tests, including the *Wechsler Adult Intelligence Scale* (WAIS), later revised (WAIS-R); the *Wechsler Intelligence Scale for Children* (WISC), later revised (WISC-R); the *Wechsler Preschool and Primary Scale of Intelligence* (WPPSI); and the *Wechsler-Bellevue Scale*, no longer used, all of which emphasize performance and verbal skills and give separate scores for subtests in vocabulary, arithmetic, memory span, assembly of objects, and other abilities.
📖 Ary et al. 2010; Coaley 2010

weighted least squares
see LEAST SQUARES METHOD OF ANALYSIS

weighted mean
the MEAN of two or more groups which takes account of or weights the size of the groups when the sizes of one or more of the groups differ. If you end up with unequal sample sizes for reasons not related to the effects of your TREATMENTs, one solution is to equalize the groups by randomly discarding the excess data from the larger groups. In a weighted means analysis, each group mean is weighted according to the number of subjects in the group. As a result, means with higher weightings (those from larger groups) contribute more to the analysis than do means with lower weights. When the size of the groups is the same, there is no need to weight the group mean for size and the mean is simply the sum of the means divided by the number of groups. When the size of the groups differs, the mean of each group is multiplied by its size to give the total or

sum for that group. The sum of each group is added together to give the overall or grand sum.

Groups	Means	Size	Sum
1	4	10	40
2	5	20	100
3	9	40	360
Sum	18		500
Number	3	60	60
Mean	6		8.33

Table W.1. Weighted and Unweighted Mean of Three Groups

This grand sum is then divided by the total number of cases to give the weighted mean. Take the means of the three groups in Table W.1. The **unweighted mean** (an ARITHMETIC MEAN of a set of observations in which no weights are assigned to them) of the three groups is 6, $(4 + 5 + 9)/3 = 6$). If the three groups were of the same size (say, 10 each), there would be no need to weight them as size is a constant and the mean is 6, $(40 + 50 + 90)/30 = 6$). If the sizes of the groups differ, as they do here, the weighted mean is higher at 8.33 than the unweighted mean of 6 because the largest group has the highest mean.
📖 Bordens & Abbott 2011; Cramer & Howitt 2004

Welch's analysis of variance test
another term for WELCH'S TEST

Welch's statistic
another term for WELCH'S TEST

Welch's test
also **Welch's *t*-test, Welch's statistic, unequal variance *t*-test, Welch's analysis of variance test**
a modified version of the INDEPENDENT SAMPLES *t*-TEST for which EQUAL VARIANCEs are not assumed. The *t*-test assume that the underlying population variances of the two groups are equal (since the variances are pooled as part of the test); if they are not, then the Welch's test should be used, since this provides a direct means to adjust for the inequality. In other words, when homogeneity of variance is not present but the other requirements of an independent samples *t*-test are fulfilled then Welch's test is used. It should be also used whenever the SAMPLE SIZE is small, or you wish to be conservative in the inferences that you draw. If you wish to use the two-sample *t*-test, the best approach is to calculate

the homogeneity of variance prior to any *t*-testing, and then decide whether to use the two-sample *t*-test or the unequal variance *t*-test. When the data are *ordinal*, none of these procedures as such are recommended, as they have been specifically designed for *interval*- or *ratio*-level DEPENDENT VARIABLES (see MANN-WHITNEY *U* TEST).
📖 Boslaugh & Watters 2008; Clark-Carter 2010; Lomax 2007

Welch's *t*-test
another term for WELCH'S TEST

Wilcoxon-Mann-Whitney test
another term for MANN-WHITNEY *U* TEST

Wilcoxon matched-pairs signed-ranks test
also **Wilcoxon signed-ranks test, signed-ranks test, Wilcoxon *T* test**
a *nonparametric* alternative to the PAIRED-SAMPLES *t*-TEST which is used with ordinal data. Wilcoxon matched-pairs signed-ranks test is used to determine whether the two sets of data or scores obtained from the same individuals (as in a pretest /posttest situation) are significantly different from each other. It is used when you have one *categorical* INDEPENDENT VARIABLE with two LEVELs (the same participants are measured two times, e.g., Time 1, Time 2, or under two different conditions) and one ordinal DEPENDENT VARIABLE. The differences between pairs of scores are ranked in order of size, ignoring the sign or direction of those differences. The ranks of the differences with the same sign are added together. If there are no differences between the scores of the two samples, the sum of positive ranked differences should be similar to the sum of negative ranked difference. The bigger the differences between the positive and negative ranked differences, the more likely the two sets of scores differ significantly from each other.
The Wilcoxon signed ranks test considers both the magnitude of the difference scores and their direction, which makes it more powerful (i.e., lower risk of TYPE II ERROR) than the SIGN TEST. The Wilcoxon can also be used in situations involving a MATCHED SUBJECT DESIGN, where subjects are matched on specific criteria.
see also CONSERVATIVE TEST, LIBERAL TEST
📖 Cohen et al. 2011; Cramer & Howitt 2004; Hatch & Lazaraton 1991; Mackey & Gass 2005; Pagano 2009; Sheskin 2011

Wilcoxon rank-sums test
another term for MANN-WHITNEY *U* TEST

Wilcoxon signed-ranks test
another term for WILCOXON MATCHED-PAIRS SIGNED-RANKS TEST

Wilcoxon test
another term for MANN-WHITNEY U TEST

Wilcoxon T test
another term for WILCOXON MATCHED-PAIRS SIGNED-RANKS TEST

Wilks' Lambda
also **lambda (λ), multivariate F**
a test used in multivariate statistical procedures such as CANONICAL CORRELATION, DISCRIMINANT FUNCTION ANALYSIS, and MULTIVARIATE ANALYSIS OF VARIANCE to determine whether the MEANs of the groups differ. Wilks' lambda is a likelihood ratio statistic that tests the likelihood of the data under the assumption of equal population mean vectors for all groups against the likelihood under the assumption that population mean vectors are identical to those of the sample mean vectors for the different groups. It varies from 0 to 1. A lambda of 1 indicates that the means of all the groups have the same value and so do not differ. Lambdas close to 0 signify that the means of the groups differ. It can be transformed as a CHI-SQUARE or an F RATIO. It is the most widely used of several such tests which include HOTELLING'S TRACE CRITERION, PILLAI'S CRITERION and ROY'S GCR CRITERION.
When there are only two groups, the F ratios for Wilks' lambda, Hotelling's trace, Pillai's criterion and Roy's gcr criterion are the same. When there are more than two groups, the F ratios for Wilks' lambda, Hotelling's trace, and Pillai's criterion may differ slightly. Pillai's criterion is said to be the most ROBUST when the assumption of the HOMOGENEITY OF VARIANCE-COVARIANCE MATRIX is violated. In terms of availability Wilks' lambda is the criterion of choice unless there is reason to use Pillai's criterion.
📖 Cramer & Howitt 2004; Hair et al. 2010; Tabachnick & Fidell 2007

willful bias
see BIAS

***w* index**
see EFFECT SIZE

Winsorization
a strategy which involves replacing a fixed number of OUTLIERs (i.e., extreme scores) with the score that is closest to them in the tail of the DISTRIBUTION in which they occur. The rationale underlying Winsorization is that the outliers may provide some useful information concerning the magnitude of scores in the distribution, but at the same time may unduly influence the results of the analysis unless some adjustment is made. For

example, Winsorization, involves replacing a fixed number of extreme scores with the score that is closest to them in the tail of the distribution in which they occur. As an example, in the distribution 0, 1, 18, 19, 23, 26, 26, 28, 33, 35, 98, 654 (which has a mean value of 80.08), one can substitute a score of 18 for both the 0 and 1 (which are the two lowest scores), and a score of 35 for the 98 and 654 (which are the two highest scores). Thus, the Winsorized distribution will be: 18,18,18,19, 23, 26, 26, 28, 33, 35, 35, 35. The **Winsorized mean** of this distribution will be 26.17. If the number of scores to be trimmed or Winsorized in the right tail is the same as the number of scores to be trimmed or Winsorized in the left tail then the TRIMMING or Winsorization process is considered symmetric; otherwise the process is considered asymmetric.
 Sheskin 2011

Winsorized mean
see WINSORIZATION

Winsorized variance
the SAMPLE VARIANCE of the Winsorized values (see WINSORIZATION). To compute the Winsorized variance, simply Winsorize the observations as was done when computing the Winsorized mean. For example, when computing a 20% Winsorized sample variance, more than 20% of the observations must be changed in order to make the sample Winsorized variance arbitrarily large.
 Wilcox 2003

within-groups ANCOVA
another term for REPEATED-MEASURES ANCOVA

within-groups ANOVA
another term for REPEATED-MEASURES ANOVA

within-groups design
another term for WITHIN-SUBJECTS DESIGN

within-groups factor
see BETWEEN-GROUPS FACTOR

within-groups independent variable
another term for WITHIN-GROUPS FACTOR

within-groups sum of squares
another term for SUM OF SQUARES WITHIN GROUPS

within-groups variability
another term for ERROR VARIANCE

within-groups variance
another term for ERROR VARIANCE

within-participants factor
another term for WITHIN-GROUPS FACTOR

within-subjects ANCOVA
another term for REPEATED-MEASURES ANCOVA

within-subjects ANOVA
another term for REPEATED-MEASURES ANOVA

within-subjects design
also **within-groups design, repeated-measures design, related design, related subjects design, correlated subjects design, correlated samples design, correlated measures design, dependent samples design**
an EXPERIMENTAL DESIGN in which the same participants in the research receive or experience all of the LEVELs or conditions of the INDEPENDENT VARIABLE (IV) (i.e., TREATMENT). Generally, there are two structural forms that this repeated measurement can take: (a) it can mark the passage of time, or (b) it can be unrelated to the time of the measurement but simply indicate the conditions under which participants were measured (e.g., Condition 1, Condition 2, Condition 3). Although these two forms of within-subjects designs do not affect either the fundamental nature of the design or the data analysis, they do imply different research data collection procedures to create the measurement opportunities. A within-subjects variable marking the passage of time is one in which the first level of the variable is measured at one point in time, the next level of the variable is measured at a later point in time, the third level of the variable is assessed at a still later period of time, and so on. The most commonly cited example of a time-related within-subjects design is ONE-GROUP PRETEST-POSTTEST DESIGN.

A within-subjects variable does not have to be time related to measure participants under all of the research conditions. For example, if the subjects receive instruction in the three different teaching methods and scores are recorded after each type of instruction, this is a within-groups variable since the same subjects' scores are in all levels of the variable.

The main advantage of a within-subjects design is that it eliminates the problem of differences in the groups that can confound the findings in BETWEEN-SUBJECTS DESIGNs. Another advantage of within-subjects designs is that they can be conducted with fewer subjects. Further, since the same individual is measured repeatedly, many EXTRANEOUS VARIABLEs can be held constant. However, because each participant receives all levels of the IV, the possibility arises that the order in which the levels are received affects participants' behavior. To guard against the possibility of ORDER EFFECTs, researchers use COUNTERBALANCED DESIGN. Alternatively, a LATIN SQUARE DESIGN may be used to control for order effects, thus making it easier to reduce the effects of ERROR VARIANCE.

Within-subjects designs can theoretically contain any number of within-subjects IVs. Thus, a **one-way within-subjects design** contains only *a single* IV, a **two-way within-subjects design** contains *two* IVs, a **three-way within-subjects design** contains *three* IVs, and so on. A within-subjects design with more than one IV is called a **within-subjects factorial design**. The most appropriate statistical analysis for a within-subjects design is a **repeated-measures ANOVA**, which takes into account the fact that the measures are related.

A within-subjects design is sometimes categorized as a RANDOMIZED-BLOCKS DESIGN because within each block the same subject is matched with himself by virtue of serving under all of the experimental conditions. Within-subjects designs are still *univariate* studies in that there is only one DV in the design.

📖 Cramer & Howitt 2004; Leary 2011; Sheskin 2011

within-subjects factor
see BETWEEN-GROUPS FACTOR

within-subjects factorial ANOVA
another term for REPEATED-MEASURES FACTORIAL ANOVA

within-subjects factorial design
see WITHIN-SUBJECTS DESIGN

within-subjects independent variable
another term for WITHIN-GROUPS FACTOR

within-subjects *t*-test
another term for PAIRED-SAMPLES *t*-TEST

within-subjects variability
another term for ERROR VARIANCE

within-subjects variance
another term for ERROR VARIANCE

WMW test
    an abbreviation for MANN-WHITNEY U TEST

WWW survey
    another term for INTERNET SURVEY

X

X axis
another term for HORIZONTAL AXIS

$\bar{X}$
an abbreviation for MEAN

x intercept
see INTERCEPT

X variable
another term for INDEPENDENT VARIABLE

Y

Y axis
>another term for VERTICAL AXIS

Yule's Q
>a measure of association for a 2 × 2 (two-by-two) CONTINGENCY TABLE. Yule's Q is actually a special case of GOODMAN-KRUSKAL'S GAMMA which can be used for both ordered and unordered tables.
>📖 Sahai & Khurshid 2001

Y variable
>another term for DEPENDENT VARIABLE

Z

z distribution
a DISTRIBUTION produced by transforming all RAW SCOREs in the data into Z SCOREs. By envisioning such a *z* distribution, you can see how *z* scores form a standard way to communicate relative standing. The *z* score of 0 indicates that the raw score equals the MEAN. A '+' indicates that the *z* score (and raw score) is above and graphed to the right of the mean. Positive *z* scores become increasingly larger as we proceed farther to the right. Larger positive *z* scores (and their corresponding raw scores) occur less frequently. Conversely, a '-' indicates that the *z* score (and raw score) is below and graphed to the left of the mean. Negative *z* scores become increasingly larger as we proceed farther to the left. Larger negative *z* scores (and their corresponding raw scores) occur less frequently. However, most of the *z* scores are between +3 and -3.

Three important characteristics of any *z* distribution are the following:

1) A *z* distribution has the same shape as the raw score distribution. Only when the underlying raw score distribution is normal will its *z* distribution be normal.
2) The mean of any *z* distribution is 0. Whatever the mean of the raw scores is, it transforms into a *z* score of 0.
3) The STANDARD DEVIATION of any *z* distribution is 1. Whether the standard deviation in the raw scores is 10 or 100, it is still one standard deviation, which transforms into an amount in *z* scores of 1.

📖 Heiman 2011

zero hypothesis
another term for NULL HYPOTHESIS

z score
also *z* value, *z* statistics
a type of STANDARD SCORE that indicates how many STANDARD DEVIATION units a given score is above or below the MEAN for that group. The *z* scores create a scale with a mean of zero and a standard deviation of one. The shape of the *z* score distribution is the same as that of the RAW SCOREs used to calculate the *z* scores. The theoretical range of the *z* scores is $\pm\infty$ (i.e., plus/minus infinity). Since the area above a *z* score of +3 or below a *z* score of -3 includes only .13 percent of the cases, for practical purposes most people only use the scale of -3 to +3. To convert a raw score to a *z* score, the raw score as well as the group mean and standard deviation are used. The conversion formula is:

$$z \text{ score} = (\text{score} - \text{mean})/\text{standard deviation}$$

Any raw score can be converted to a *z* score if the mean of a distribution and the standard deviation are known. If Bill got a score of 75 on a test with a mean of 65 and a standard deviation of 5, his *z* score would be as follows:

$$z \text{ score} = (75 - 65)/5 = 10/5 = +2$$

The *z* score is used to describe a particular participant's score relative to the rest of the data. A participant's *z* score indicates how far from the mean in terms of standard deviations the participant's score varies. With *z* scores we can easily determine the underlying raw score's location in a distribution, its relative and simple frequency, and its PERCENTILE. All of this helps us to know whether the individual's raw score was relatively good, bad, or in-between. As shown in Figure Z.1, a *z* score always has two components: (1) either a positive or negative sign which indicates whether the raw score is above or below the mean, and (2) the absolute value of the *z* score which indicates how far the score lies from the mean when measured in standard deviations.

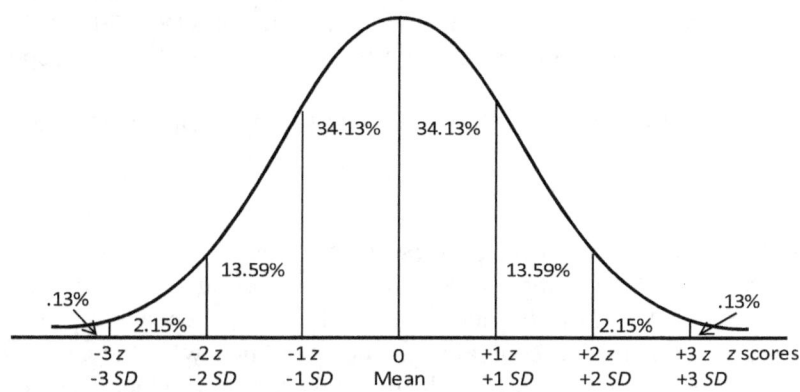

Figure Z.1. Scores Associated with the Normal Curve

For example, if we find that a participant has a *z* score of -1, we know that his/her score is 1 standard deviation below the mean. By referring to Figure Z.1, we can see that only about 16% of the other participants scored lower than this person. Similarly, a *z* score of +2.9 indicates a score nearly 3 standard deviations above the mean—one that is in the uppermost ranges of the distribution. Sometimes we know a *z* score and want to find the corresponding raw score. We multiplied the *z* score times standard deviation and then added the mean.

As stated above, z scores may be either positive or negative numbers. (If you add all the z scores in a distribution, the answer will be zero). In addition, they often contain decimal points (a z score might be 1.8 standard deviations from the mean rather than just 1 or 2). This makes for error in reporting. T SCOREs seem easier to interpret since they are always positive numbers and contain no fractions.
see NORMAL DISTRIBUTION
📖 Hatch & Lazaraton 1991; Heiman 2011; Leary 2011; Ravid 2011; Urdan 2010

z statistics
another term for Z SCORE

z test for two dependent samples
a statistical test used when a researcher wants to compare the MEANs of two DEPENDENT SAMPLES, and happens to know the VARIANCEs of the two underlying POPULATIONs. In such a case, the z test for two dependent samples should be employed to evaluate the data instead of the *t*-TEST for two dependent samples. The z test for two dependent samples assumes that the two samples are randomly selected from populations that have NORMAL DISTRIBUTIONs. The effect of violation of the NORMALITY assumption on the test statistic decreases as the size of the sample employed in an experiment increases. The HOMOGENEITY OF VARIANCE assumption is not an assumption of the z test for two dependent samples.
see also ONE-SAMPLE Z TEST, Z TEST FOR TWO INDEPENDENT PROPORTIONS
📖 Sheskin 2011

z test for two independent proportions
an alternative large sample procedure for evaluating a 2 × 2 (two-by-two) CONTINGENCY TABLE. In fact, the z test for two independent proportions yields a result that is equivalent to that obtained with the CHI-SQUARE TEST OF INDEPENDENCE. If both the z test for two independent proportions (which is based on the NORMAL DISTRIBUTION) and chi-square test of independence are applied to the same set of data, the square of the z value obtained for the former test will equal the chi-square value obtained for the latter test.
see also ONE-SAMPLE Z TEST, Z TEST FOR TWO DEPENDENT SAMPLES
📖 Sheskin 2011

z value
another term for Z SCORE

Bibliography

Adair, G. (1984). The Hawthorne effect: A reconsideration of the methodological artifact. *Journal of Applied Psychology, 69* (2), 334-345.
Airasian, P. W. (2001). *Classroom assessment: Concepts and applications* (4th ed.). New York: McGraw-Hill.
Alastair, P. (2001). *Critical applied linguistics: A critical introduction.* Lawrence Erlbaum Associates.
Alaszewski, A. (2006). *Using diaries for social research.* London: Sage.
Allison, D. (2002). *Approaching English language research.* Singapore: Singapore University Press.
Allwright, D. (1988). *Observation in the language classroom.* New York: Longman.
Allwright, D. (2003). Exploratory practice: Rethinking practitioner research in language teaching. *Language Teaching Research, 7,* 113–141.
Allwright, D. (2005). Developing principles for practitioner research: The case for exploratory practice. *The Modern Language Journal, 89*(3), 353–366.
Allwright, D., & Bailey, K. M. (1991). *Focus on the language classroom: An introduction to classroom research for language researchers.* Cambridge, UK: Cambridge University Press.
Allwright, D., & Hanks, J. (2009). *The developing language learner.* Basingstoke: Palgrave Macmillan.
Altrichter, H., Feldman, A., Posch, P., & Somekh, B. (2007). *Teachers investigate their work.* London: Routledge.
American Educational Research Association. (2004). *Encyclopedia of educational research* (7th ed.). New York: Macmillan.
American Psychological Association (APA). (2010). *Publication manual of the American Psychological Association* (6th ed.). Washington, DC: Author.
Anderson, G. & Arsenault, N. (2001). *Fundamentals of educational research.* London: Routledge.
Andrews, M., Squire, C., & Tamboukou, M. (Eds.). (2008). *Doing narrative research in the social sciences.* London: Sage.
Anfara, V. A., & Mertz, N. T. (2006). *Theoretical frameworks in qualitative research.* Thousand Oaks, CA: Sage.
Aron, A., & Aron, E. (1999). *Statistics for psychology.* Upper Saddle River, NJ: Prentice Hall.
Aronson, E., P. Ellsworth, J. Carlsmith, & M. Gonzales. (1990). *Methods of research in social psychology.* New York: McGraw Hill.

Ary, D., Jacobs, L. C., Sorensen, C. K. (2010). *Introduction to research in education* (8th ed.). Belmont, CA: Wadsworth.
Atkinson, R. (1998). *The life story interview*. Thousand Oaks, CA: Sage.
Baayen, R. H. (2008). *Analyzing linguistic data: A practical introduction to statistics using R*. Cambridge, UK: Cambridge University Press.
Babbie, E. (2011). *The basics of social research* (5th ed.). Belmont, CA: Wadsworth.
Bachman, L. F. (1990). *Fundamental considerations in language testing*. Oxford, UK: Oxford University Press.
Bachman, L. F., & Palmer, A. S. (1996). *Language testing in practice: Designing and developing useful language test*s. Oxford, UK: Oxford University Press.
Bachman, L. F. (2004). *Statistical analyses for language assessment*. Cambridge, UK: Cambridge University Press.
Bailey, K. M. (1991). Diary studies of classroom language learning: The doubting game and the believing game. In E. Sadtono (Ed.), *Language acquisition and the second/foreign language classroom* (pp. 60-102). RELC Anthology Series 28, Singapore: RELC.
Bailey, K. M. (1998). *Learning about language assessment: Dilemmas, decisions, and directions*. Boston, MA: Heinle & Heinle.
Bailey, K. M. (2001). Observation. In R. Carter & D. Nunan (Eds.), *The Cambridge guide to teaching English to speakers of other languages* (pp. 114-119). Cambridge, UK: Cambridge University Press.
Bailey, K. M., & Ochsner, R. (1983). A methodological review of the diary studies: Windmill tilting or social science? In K. M. Bailey, M. H. Long & S. Peck (Eds.), *Second language acquisition studies* (pp. 188-198). Rowley, Mass.: Newbury House.
Bakeman, R. & Robinson, B. F. (2005). *Understanding statistics in the behavioral sciences*. Mahwah, NJ: Lawrence Erlbaum Associates.
Baker, C. (1997). Survey methods in researching language and education. In N. H. Hornberger & D. Corson (Eds.), *Research methods in language and education* (pp. 35-46). Encyclopedia of Language and Education. (Vol. 8). Dordrecht: Kluwer.
Baker, P. (2006). *Using corpora in discourse analysis*. London: Continuum.
Bartels, N. (2005). *Applied linguistics and language teacher education*. New York: Springer.
Bassey, M. (1999). *Case study research in educational settings*. Buckingham, UK: Open University Press.
Bell, J. S. (2002). Narrative inquiry: More than just telling stories. *TESOL Quarterly, 36*, 207-218.
Benson, P. (2004). (Auto)biography and learner diversity. In P. Benson & D. Nunan (Eds*.), Learners' stories: Difference and diversity in language learning* (pp. 4-21). Cambridge, UK: Cambridge University Press.

Benson, P, Chik, A., Gao, X., Huang, J. & Wang, W. (2009). Qualitative research in language teaching and learning journals, 1997–2006. *The Modern Language Journal, 93*(1), 79–90.
Benton, T., & Craib, I. (2001). *Philosophy of social science: The philosophical foundations of social thought.* London: Palgrave.
Beretta, A. (1991). Theory construction in SLA: Complementarity and opposition. *Studies in Second Language Acquisition, 13*, 493-511.
Berg, B. L. (2009). *Qualitative research methods for the social sciences* (7th ed.). Boston: Allyn & Bacon.
Bernard, H. R. (1995). *Research methods in anthropology: Qualitative and quantitative approaches.* Walnut Creek, CA: AltaMira.
Berns, P. M. (2010). *Concise encyclopedia of applied linguistics.* Elsevier Ltd.
Bertaux, D. (Ed.). (1981). *Biography and society: The life history approach in the social sciences.* Beverley Hills, CA: Sage.
Best, J. W. & Kahn, J. V. (2006). *Research in education* (10th ed.). New York: Pearson Education Inc.
Bhatia, V. K., Flowerdew, J. & Jones, R. H. (Eds.). (2008). *Advances in discourse studies.* London: Routledge.
Biber, D., & Conrad, S. (2001). Quantitative corpus-based research: Much more than bean counting. *TESOL Quarterly, 35* (2), 331-336.
Biber, D., Conrad, S., & Reppen, R. (1998). *Corpus linguistics: Investigating language structure and use.* Cambridge, UK: Cambridge University Press.
Bickman, L & Rog, D. J. (Eds.). (1998). *Handbook of applied social research methods.* Thousand Oaks, CA: Sage.
Black, T. R. (1999). *Doing quantitative in the social sciences.* London: Sage.
Bliss, J., Monk, M. & Ogborn, J. (1983). *Qualitative data analysis for educational research.* London: Croom Helm.
Blaxter, L., C. Hughes, & M. Tight. (1996). *How to research.* Buckingham, UK: Open University Press.
Block, D. (1995). Social constraints on interviews. *Prospect, 10* (3), 35-48.
Block, D. (1996). Not so fast: Some thoughts on theory culling, relativism, accepted findings and the heart and soul of SLA. *Applied Linguistics, 17* (1), 63-83.
Block, D. (2000). Problematizing interview data: Voices in the mind's machine? *TESOL Quarterly, 34*, 757-763.
Block, D. (2003). *The social turn in second language acquisition.* Edinburgh: Edinburgh University Press.
Bloor, M. & Wood, F. (2006). *Keywords in qualitative methods.* Thousand Oaks, CA: Sage.

Blot, R. K. (1991). The role of hypothesis testing in qualitative research: A second researcher comments. *TESOL Quarterly, 25* (1), 202-205.
Bogdan, R. C., & Biklen, S. (2007). *Qualitative research for education: An introduction to theories and methods.* Boston: Allyn & Bacon.
Bordens, K. S. & Abbott, B. B. (2011). *Research design and methods: A process approach* (8th ed.). New York: McGraw-Hill.
Borenstein M., Hedges, L. V., Higgins, J.P.T., & Rothstein, H.R. (2009). *Introduction to meta-analysis.* UK: John Wiley & Sons.
Borg, I. Groenen, P. J. F. (2005). *Modern multidimensional scaling: Theory and applications* (2nd ed.). New York: Springer.
Borg, S. (1998). Teachers' pedagogical systems and grammar teaching: A qualitative study. *TESOL Quarterly, 32*(1), 9–38.
Borg, S. (2006a). *Classroom research in English language teaching in Oman.* Muscat: Sultanate of Oman, Ministry of Education.
Borg, S. (Ed.) (2006b). *Language teacher research in Europe.* Alexandria, VA: TESOL.
Borg, W. R. (1989). *Educational research: an introduction.* New York: Addison Wesley Longman.
Boslaugh, S. & Watters, P. A. (2008). *Statistics in a Nutshell.* CA: O'Reilly Media.
Bowles, H., & Seedhouse, P., (2007a). *Conversation analysis and LSP.* Berlin: Peter Lang.
Box, G. E. P., Hunter, J. S. & Hunter, W. G. (2005). *Statistics for experimenters: Design, innovation, and discovery* (2nd ed.). NJ: John Wiley & Sons.
Brace, N., Kemp, R., & Snelgar, R. (2003). *SPSS for psychologists: A guide to data analysis using SPSS for Windows.* Mahwah, NJ: Lawrence Erlbaum Associates.
Bracht, G. H., & Glass, G. V. (1998). The external validity of experiments. *American Educational Research Journal, 5,* 437-474.
Brewerton, P. & Millward, L. (2001). *Organizational research methods.* Thousand Oaks, CA: Sage.
Brown, D. B. (2007). *Principles of language learning and teaching* (5th ed.). New York: Pearson Education.
Brown, D. B. (2010). *Language assessment: Principles and classroom practices* (2nd ed.). New York: Pearson Education.
Brown, J. D. (1988). *Understanding research in second Language learning.* Cambridge, UK: Cambridge University Press.
Brown, J. D. (1990). The use of multiple t-tests in language research. *TESOL Quarterly, 24* (24), 770-773.
Brown, J. D. (1991). Statistics as a foreign language—Part 1: What to look for in reading statistical language studies. *TESOL Quarterly, 25* (4), 569-585.

Brown, J. D. (1992). Statistics as a foreign language—Part 2: More things to consider in reading statistical language studies. *TESOL Quarterly, 26* (4), 629-664.
Brown, J. D. (2001). *Using surveys in language programs*. Cambridge, UK: Cambridge University Press.
Brown, J. D., & Rodgers, T. S. (2002). *Doing second language research*. Oxford, UK: Oxford University Press.
Brown, J. D. (2004a). Research methods for applied linguistics: Scope, characteristics, and standards. In A. Davis & C. Elder (Eds.), *The handbook of applied linguistics*. Oxford, UK: Blackwell.
Brown, J. D. (2004b). Resources on quantitative/statistical research for applied linguists. *Second Language Research, 20* (4), 372-393.
Brown, J. D. (2005). *Testing in language programs: A comprehensive guide to English Language Assessment*. New York: McGraw Hill.
Brown, J. D. (2009). Open-Response Items in Questionnaires. In Juanita Heigham & Robert A. Croker (Eds.), *Qualitative research in applied linguistics* (pp. 200-219). New York: Palgrave Macmillan.
Bruner, J. (1991). The narrative construction of reality. *Critical Inquiry, 8*, 1-21.
Bryant, A., & Charmaz, K. (Eds.). (2007). *The Sage handbook of grounded theory*. London: Sage.
Bryman, A. & Cramer, D. (1994). *Quantitative data analysis for social scientists*. London: Routledge.
Bryant, M. T. (2004). *The portable dissertation advisor*. Thousand Oaks, CA: Corwin.
Buchanan, D. & Bryman, A. (2009).*The SAGE handbook of organizational research methods*. London: Sage.
Burns, A. (2010). *Doing action research in English language teaching: A guide for practitioners*. New York: Routledge
Butler, C. (1985). *Statistics in linguistics*. Oxford, UK: Basil Blackwell.
Button, G. (Ed.). (1991*). Ethnomethodology and the human sciences*. New York: Cambridge University Press.
Byram, M. (Ed.). (2000). *Routledge encyclopedia of language teaching and learning*. London: Routledge.
Cameron, D. (2000). Difficult subjects. *Critical Quarterly, 42* (4), 89-94.
Cameron, D. (2001). *Working with spoken discourse*. Thousand Oaks, CA: Sage.
Cameron, D., Frazer, E., Harvey, P., Rampton, M. B. H., & Richardson, K. (Eds.). (1992). *Researching language: Issues of power and method*. London: Routledge.
Campbell, D., & J. Stanley. (1963). *Experimental and quasi-experimental designs for research*. Chicago: Rand McNally.

Campbell, D. T., Stanley, J. C., & Gage, N. L. (1981). *Experimental and quasi-experimental designs for research*. Boston: Houghton Mifflin.

Canagarajah, A. S. (1996). From critical research practice to critical research reporting. *TESOL Quarterly, 30* (3), 321-330.

Carmines, E., & Zeller, R. (1979). *Reliability and validity assessment*. Beverly Hills, CA: Sage.

Carspecken, P. F. & Apple, M. (1992).Critical qualitative research: theory, methodology, and practice. In M. LeCompte, W. L. Millroy & J. Preissle (Eds.), *The handbook of wualitative research in education*. London: Academic Press, 507-53.

Carter, R., & Nunan. D. (Eds.). (2001). *The Cambridge guide to teaching English to speakers of other languages*. Cambridge, UK: Cambridge University Press.

Catford, J. C. (1998). Language Learning and applied linguistics: A historical sketch. *Language Learning, 48* (4), 465-496.

Cazden, C. B. (2001). *Classroom discourse: The language of teaching and learning*. Portsmouth, NH: Heinemann.

Cazden, C. B., & Beck, S.W. (2003). Classroom Discourse. In A.C. Graesser, M.A. Gernsbacher, S. Goldman (Eds.), *Handbook of discourse processes* (p. 165-198). Mahwah, NJ: Lawrence Erlbaum Associates.

Celce-Murcia, M., & Olshtain, E. (2000). *Discourse and context in language teaching: A guide for language teachers*. Cambridge, UK: Cambridge University Press.

Chamberlayne, P., Bornat, J., & Wengraf, T. (Eds.). (2000). *The turn to biographical methods in social science: Comparative issues and examples*. London: Routledge.

Charmaz, K. (2006). *Constructing grounded theory: A practical guide through qualitative analysis*. London: Sage.

Chaudron, C. (1988). *Second language classrooms: Research on teaching and learning*. Cambridge, UK: Cambridge University Press.

Cho, J., & Trent, A. (2006). Validity in qualitative research revisited. *Qualitative Research, 6*, 319-340.

Charmaz, K. (2006). *Constructing grounded theory: A practical guide through qualitative analysis*. London: Sage.

Christ, T. (2007). A recursive approach to mixed methods research in a longitudinal study of postsecondary education disability support services. Journal of *Mixed Methods Research, 1*(3), 226-241.

Christie, F. (2002). *Classroom discourse analysis: A functional perspective*. London: Continuum.

Clandinin, D. J. (Ed.). (2006). *Handbook of narrative inquiry: Mapping a methodology*. Thousand Oaks, CA: Sage.

Clark-Carter, D. (2010). *Quantitative psychological research: The complete student's companion* (3rd). New York: Psychology Press.

Coaley, K. (2010). *An introduction to psychological assessment and psychometrics*. London: Sage.
Cochran,W. (1981). *Statistical analysis in psychology and education*. New York:McGraw Hill.
Coffey, A., & Atkinson, P. (1996). *Making sense of qualitative data: Complementary research strategies*. Thousand Oaks, CA: Sage.
Cohen, A. D. & Macaro, E. (2010). Research methods in second language acquisition. In E. Macaro (Ed.), *Continuum companion to second language acquisition* (pp. 107-133). London: Continuum.
Cohen, J. (1988). *Statistical power and analysis for the behavioral sciences* (2nd ed.). Hillsdale, NJ: Lawrence Erlbaum Associates.
Cohen, J., Cohen, P., West, S. G., & Aiken, L. S. (2003). *Applied multiple regression/correlation analysis for the behavioral sciences*. Mahwah, NJ: Lawrence Erlbaum Associates.
Cohen, L., Manion, L., & Morrison, K. (2011). *Research methods in education* (7th ed.). London: Routledge.
Cohen, R. J., & Swerdlik, M. E. (2010). *Psychological testing and assessment: An introduction to tests and measures* (7th ed.). Boston: McGraw-Hill.
Connolly, P. (2007). *Quantitative data analysis in education: A critical introduction using SPSS*. London: Routledge.
Connor, U. (1994). Text Analysis. *TESOL Quarterly, 28* (4), 682-684.
Conover, W. J. (1980). *Practical nonparametric statistics* (2nd ed.). New York: Wiley.
Conrad, S. (1999). The importance of corpus-based research for language teachers. *System, 27*, 1-18.
Cook, G. (2003). Applied Linguistics. Oxford, UK: Oxford University Press.
Cook, T. D., & Campbell, D. T. (1979). *Quasi-experimental: Design and analysis issues for field settings*. Chicago: Rand McNally.
Coolican, H. (2009). *Research methods and statistics in psychology* (5th ed.). London: Hodder Education.
Cooper, H. M. (1998). *Synthesizing research: A guide for literature reviews* (3rd ed.). Thousand Oaks, CA: Sage.
Cooper, H. M. (2006). Research questions and research designs. In P. Alexander & P. Winne (Eds.), *Handbook of educational psychology* (2nd ed.). Mahwah, NJ: Lawrence Erlbaum Associates.
Corbin, J., & Strauss, A. (2008). *Basics of qualitative research* (3rd ed.). Thousand Oaks, CA: Sage.
Corson, D. (1997). Critical realism: An emancipatory philosophy for applied linguistics? *Applied Linguistics, 18*, 166-168.
Corson, D. (Ed.). (1997). *Encyclopedia of language and education* (vols. 1-8). Amsterdam: Kluwer.

Cortazzi, M. (1993). *Narrative analysis*. London: Falmer Press.
Coulon, A. (2000). *Ethnomethodology*. London: Sage.
Cox, T. F. & Cox. M.A.A. (2001). *Multidimensional scaling*. Boca Raton, FL: Chapman & Hall/CRC.
Cramer, D. & Howitt, D. (2004). *The SAGE dictionary of statistics: A practical resource for students in the social sciences*. Thousand Oaks, CA: Sage.
Crano, W. D. & M. B. Brewer (2002). *Principles and methods of social research*. Mahwah, NJ: Lawrence Erlbaum Associates.
Creswell, J. W. (2007). *Qualitative inquiry and research design: Choosing among five approaches* (2nd ed.). Thousand Oaks, CA: Sage.
Creswell, J. W. (2008). *Educational research: Planning, conducting, and evaluating quantitative and qualitative approaches to research* (3rd ed.). Upper Saddle River, NJ: Merrill/Pearson Education.
Creswell, J. W. (2009). *Research design: Qualitative, quantitative, and mixed method approaches*. (3rd ed.). Thousand Oaks, CA: Sage.
Creswell, J. W., & Plano Clark, V. L. (2007). *Designing and conducting mixed methods research*. Thousand Oaks, CA: Sage.
Crookes, G. (1993). Action research for second language instructors: Going beyond instructor research. *Applied Linguistics, 14* (2), 130-144.
Cumming, A. (Ed.). (1994). Alternatives in TESOL research: Descriptive, interpretive, and ideological orientations. *TESOL Quarterly, 28* (4), 673-703.
Cummins, J., & Davison, C. (Eds.). (2007). *The international handbook of English language teaching* (Vol. 1 & 2). Norwell, MA: Springer.
Dalgaard, P. (2002). *Introductory statistics with R*. New York: Springer-Verlag.
Dana, N. F., & Yendol-Silva, D. (2003). *The reflective educator's guide to classroom research: Learning to teach and teaching to learn through practitioner inquiry*. Thousand Oaks, CA: Corwin.
Davies, A., & Elder, C. (Eds.). (2004). *The handbook of applied linguistics*. Oxford, UK: Blackwell.
Davis, K. A. (1992). Validity and reliability in qualitative research: Another researcher comments. *TESOL Quarterly, 26* (3), 605-608.
Davis, K. A. (1995). Qualitative theory and methods in applied linguistics research. *TESOL Quarterly, 29*, 427-453.
Davis, K. A., & Henze, R. C. (1998). Applying ethnographic perspectives to issues in cross-cultural pragmatics. *Journal of Pragmatics, 30*, 399-419.
Davis, S. F. (2003). *Handbook of research methods in experimental psychology*. Oxford, UK: Blackwell.
Dawson, C. (2007). *Practical research methods: A user-friendly guide to mastering research techniques and projects*. UK: HowtoBooks.

deMarrais, K. & Lapan, S.D. (Eds.). (2004). *Foundations for research: Methods of inquiry in education and the social sciences*. Mahwah, NJ: Lawrence Erlbaum Associates.

Denzin, N. K. (1970a). Strategies of multiple triangulation. In N. Denzin (Ed.), *The research act in sociology: A theoretical introduction to sociological method*. London: Butterworth, 297-313.

Denzin, N. K. (1970b). *The research act in sociology: A theoretical introduction to sociological methods*. London: Butterworth.

Denzin, N. K. (1989a). *Interpretive biography*. Newbury Park, CA: Sage.

Denzin, N. K. (1989b). *The research act* (3rd ed.). Englewood Cliffs, NJ: Prentice Hall.

Denzin, N. K. (1997). Triangulation in educational research. In J. P. Keeves (Ed.), *Educational research, methodology and measurement: An international handbook* (2nd ed.). Oxford, UK: Elsevier Science, 318-22.

Denzin, N. K. (1999). Biographical research methods. In J. P. Keeves & G. Lakomski (Eds.), *Issues in educational research*. Oxford, UK: Elsevier Science, 92-102.

Denzin, N. K., & Lincoln, Y. S. (2008*). Strategies of qualitative inquiry* (3rd ed.). Thousand Oaks, CA: Sage.

Denzin, N. K., & Lincoln, Y. S. (Eds.). (2011). *The Sage handbook of qualitative research* (4th ed.). Thousand Oaks, CA: Sage.

DeVaus, D. (2002). *Conducting surveys using the Internet*. Thousand Oaks, CA: Sage.

Dey, I. (1993). *Grounding grounded theory*. San Diego, CA: Academic Press.

Deyle, D. L., Hess, G. & LeCompte, M. L. (1992). Approaching ethical issues for qualitative researchers in education. In M. LeCompte, W. L. Millroy & J. Preissle (Eds.), *The handbook of qualitative research in education*. London: Academic Press, 597-642.

Dickinson Gibbons. J. (1994). *Non-parametric statistics: An introduction*. Thousand Oaks: Sage.

Dillman, D. A. (2000). *Mail and Internet surveys: The tailored design method* (2nd ed.). New York: Wiley.

Dobbert, M. L. & Kurth-Schai, R. (1992). Systematic ethnography: toward an evolutionary science of education and culture. In M. LeCompte, W. L. Millroy and J. Preissle (Eds.), *The handbook of qualitative research in education*. London: Academic Press, 93-160.

Dochartaigh, N. O. (2002). *The internet research handbook*. London: Sage.

Dooley, D. (2001). *Social research methods* (4th ed.). Englewood Cliffs, NJ: Prentice Hall.

Dörnyei, Z. (2001). *Teaching and researching motivation*. Harlow: Longman.

Dörnyei, Z. (2003). *Questionnaires in second language research: Constructing, administering, and processing*. Mahwah, NJ: Lawrence Erlbaum Associates.

Dörnyei, Z. (2007). *Research in applied linguistics: Quantitative, qualitative, and mixed methodologies*. Oxford, UK: Oxford University Press.

Dörnyei, Z. & Taguchi, T. (2010). *Questionnaires in second language research: Constructing, administering, and processing*. London: Routledge.

Doughty, C. J., & Long, M. H. (Eds.). (2003). *The handbook of second language acquisition*. Oxford, UK: Blackwell.

Duff, P. A. (1995). An ethnography of communication in immersion classrooms in Hungary. *TESOL Quarterly, 29* (3), 505-536.

Duff, P. A. (2002). Research approaches in applied linguistics. In R. Kaplan (Ed.), *The Oxford handbook of applied linguistics* (pp. 13-23). Oxford, UK: Oxford University Press.

Duff, P. A., & Bailey, K. M. (Eds.). (2001). Identifying research priorities: Themes and directions for the TESOL International Research Foundation. *TESOL Quarterly, 35* (4), 595-616.

Edge, J. (2001). *Action research*. Alexandria, VA: TESOL.

Edge, J., & Richards, K. (1998). May I see your warrant, please? Justifying outcomes in qualitative research. *Applied Linguistics, 19* (3), 334-356.

Egbert, J. L., & Petrie, G. M. (Eds.). (2005). *CALL research perspectives*. Mahwah, NJ: Lawrence Erlbaum Associates.

Eisenhart, M. A. & Howe, K. R. (1992). Validity in educational research. In M. D. LeCompte, W. L. Millroy & J. Preissle (Eds.), *The handbook of qualitative studies in education*. New York: Academic Press, 643-680.

Eisner, E. (1998). *The enlightened eye: Qualitative inquiry and the enhancement of educational practice*. New York: Macmillan.

Ericsson, K. A., & Simon, H. A. (1993). *Protocol analysis*. Cambridge, MA: The MIT Press.

Evans, A. N., & Rooney, B. F. (2008). *Methods in psychological research*. Thousand Oaks, CA: Sage.

Everitt, B. S (2001). *Statistics for psychologists: an intermediate course*. Mahwah, NJ: Lawrence Erlbaum Associates.

Everitt, B. S., & Dunn, G. (2001). *Applied multivariate data analysis* (2nd ed.). New York: Hodder Arnold.

Everitt, B. S. & Howell, D. C. (Eds.). (2005). *Encyclopedia of statistics in behavioral science*. NJ: John Wiley & Sons.

Everitt, B. S. & Skrondal, A. (2010). *The Cambridge dictionary of statistics*. (4th ed.). Cambridge, UK: Cambridge University Press.

Ezzy, D. (2002). *Qualitative analysis: Practice and innovation*. London: Routledge.

Fairclough, N. (1992). *Discourse and social change*. Cambridge: Polity Press.
Fairclough, N. (1995). *Critical discourse analysis: The critical study of language*. New York: Longman.
Faltis, C. (1997). Case study methods in researching language and education. In N. H. Hornberger & D. Corson (Eds.), *Research methods in language and education* (pp. 145-153). Encyclopedia of Language and Education. (Vol. 8). Dordrecht: Kluwer.
Farhady, H. (1995). *Research methods in applied linguistics*. Tehran: Payame Noor University.
Farhady, H., Jafarpur, A., & Birjandi, P. (1995). Testing language skills: From theory to practice (2nd ed.). Tehran: SAMT Publication.
Fernandez-Ballesteros, R. (2003). *Encyclopedia of psychological assessment*. (Vol. 1 & 2). Thousand Oaks, CA: Sage.
Fetterman, D. (1989). *Ethnography step by step*. Newbury Park, CA: Sage.
Field, A. (2005). *Discovering statistics using SPSS* (2nd ed.). London: Sage.
Firth, A., & Wagner, J. (1997). On discourse, communication and some fundamental concepts in SLA research. *Modern Language Journal, 81*, 285-300.
Fischer, C. T. (Ed.). (2006). *Qualitative research methods for psychologists: Introduction through empirical studies*. Boston: Academic Press.
Flick, U. (2004). Design and process in qualitative research. In U. Flick, E. von Kardoff & I. Steinke (Eds.), *A companion to qualitative research* (146-52). London: Sage.
Flick, U. (2006). *An introduction to qualitative research* (3rd ed.). Thousand Oaks, CA: Sage.
Flick, U., von Kardoff, E., & Steinke, I. (Eds.). (2004). *A companion to qualitative research*. Translated by B. Jenner. London: Sage.
Flood, J., Lapp, D., Squire, J. R., & Jensen, J. M. (Eds.). (2005). *Methods of research on teaching the English language arts: the methodology chapters from the Handbook of research on teaching the English language arts* (2nd ed.). Mahwah, NJ: Lawrence Erlbaum Associates.
Floud, R. (1979). *An introduction to quantitative methods for historians* (2nd ed.). London: Methuen.
Fosnot, C. T. (Ed.). (2005). *Constructivism: Theory, perspectives, and practice* (2nd ed.). New York: Teachers College Press.
Fotos, S., Browne, C. (Eds.). (2004). *New perspectives on CALL for second language classrooms*. Mahwah, NJ: Lawrence Erlbaum Associates.
Fowler, F. J. (2002). *Survey research methods* (3rd ed.). Thousand Oaks, CA: Sage.
Fraenkel, J. R., & Wallen, N. E. (2009). *How to design and evaluate research in education* (5th ed.). New York: McGraw-Hill.

Freeman, D. (1998). *Doing teacher research*. New York: Heinle & Heinle.
Frowley, W., & Lantolf, J. P. (1984). Speaking and self-order: A critique of orthodox L2 research. *Studies in Second Language Acquisition, 6* (2), 143-159.
Fulcher, G. and Davidson, F. (2007). *Language testing and assessment: An advanced resource book*. London: Routledge.
Gall, M. D., Borg, W. R., & Gall, J. P. (2006). *Educational research: An introduction* (8th ed.). Upper Saddle River, NJ: Pearson Education.
Gamst, G., Meyers, L. S., & Guarino, A. J. (2008). *Analysis of variance designs: A conceptual and computational approach with SPSS and SAS*. Cambridge, UK: Cambridge University Press.
Gao, Y. H., Li, L. C., & Lü, J. (2001). Trends in research methods in applied linguistics: China and the West. *English for Specific Purposes, 20*, 1-14.
Garcez, P. M. (1997). Microethnography. In N. H. Hornberger & D. Corson (Eds.), *Research methods in language and education* (pp. 187-198). Encyclopedia of Language and Education, Vol. 8. Dordrecht: Kluwer.
Garfinkel, H. (1967). *Studies in ethnomethodology*. Englewood Cliffs, NJ: Prentice-Hall.
Gass, S. M. (2001). Innovations in second language research methods. *Annual Review of Applied Linguistics, 21*, 221-232.
Gass, S. M., & Mackey A. (2000). *Stimulated recall methodology in second language research*. Mahwah, NJ: Lawrence Erlbaum Associates.
Gay, L.R., Mills, G., & Airasian, P. W. (2008). *Educational research: Competencies for analysis and applications* (9th ed.). Upper Saddle River, NJ: Prentice Hall.
Gee, J.P. (2005). *An introduction to discourse analysis: Theory and method*. New York: Routledge.
Geertz, C. (1973). *The interpretation of cultures*. New York: Basic Books.
Geisinger, K., Spies, R., Carlson, J., & Plake, B. (Eds.). (2007). *The seventeenth mental measurements yearbook*. Lincoln: University of Nebraska, Buros Institute of Mental Measurements.
George, A., & Bennett, A. (2005*). Case study and theory development in the social sciences*. Cambridge: MIT Press.
Gerring, J. (2007). *Case study research: Principles and practices*. Cambridge, UK: Cambridge University Press.
Gibbons, J. D. (1976). *Nonparametric methods for quantitative analysis*. New York: Holt, Rinehart & Winston.
Gibbons, P. (2006). *Bridging discourses in the ESL classroom: Students, teachers and researchers*. London: Continuum.
Giere, R. N. (2004). *Understanding scientific reasoning*. Graton, CA: Wadsworth.

Given, L. M. (2008). *The Sage encyclopedia of qualitative research methods*. Thousand Oaks, CA: Sage.
Glass, G. V., & Hopkins, K. D. (1996). *Statistical methods in education and psychology*. Englewood Cliffs, NJ: Prentice Hall.
Glass, G. V., McGaw, B., & Smith, M. L. (1981). *Meta-analysis in social research*. Beverly Hills, CA: Sage.
Glaser, B. G. (1992). *The basics of grounded theory analysis: Emergence vs. forcing*. Mill Valley, CA: Sociology Press.
Glaser, B. G. (2001). *The grounded theory perspective: Conceptualization contrasted with description*. Mill Valley, CA: Sociology Press.
Glaser, B. G., & Strauss, A. L. (1967). *The discovery of grounded theory: strategies for qualitative research*. Chicago: Aldine.
Glesne, C. (2006). *Becoming qualitative researchers: An introduction* (3rd ed.). Boston: Pearson Education.
GonzÁlez, J. M. (Ed.). (2008). *Encyclopedia of bilingual education* (Vol. 1 & 2). Thousand Oaks, CA: Sage.
Gorard, S. (2001). *Quantitative methods in educational research: The role of numbers made easy*. London: Continuum.
Gorard, S. (2003). *Quantitative methods in social science*. London: Continuum.
Golden-Biddle, K., & Locke, K. (1997). *Composing qualitative research*. Thousand Oaks, CA: Sage.
Goldstein, T. (1995). Interviewing in multicultural/multilingual settings. *TESOL Quarterly, 29* (3), 587-593.
Goldstein, T. (1997). Language research methods and critical pedagogy. In N. H. Hornberger & D. Corson (Eds.), *Research methods in language and education* (pp. 67-78). Encyclopedia of Language and Education, Vol. 8. Dordrecht: Kluwer.
Gomm, R., Hammersley, M., & Foster, P. (Eds.). (2000). *Case study method*. Thousand Oaks, CA: Sage.
Goodley, D., Lawthorn, R., Clough, P., & Moore, M. (2004). *Researching life stories: Method, theory, and analyses in a biographical age*. London: Routledge.
Goodson, I., & Sikes, P. 2001. *Life history research in educational settings: Learning from lives*. Buckingham, UK: Open University Press.
Gorard, S. & Taylor, C. (2004). *Combining methods in educational and social research*. Buckingham, UK: Open University Press.
Gravetter, F. J., & Wallnau, L. B. (2010). *Statistics for the behavioral sciences* (8th ed.). Belmont, CA: Wadsworth.
Gray, D. E. (2009). *Research in the real world*. (2nd ed.) Thousand Oaks, CA: Sage.

Green, J. L., & Nixon, C. N. (2002). Exploring differences in perspectives on microanalysis of classroom discourse: Contributions and concerns. *Applied Linguistics, 23*, 393-406.

Greene, J. (2007). *Mixed methods in social inquiry*. Hoboken, NJ: Wiley.

Greene, J. (2008). Is mixed methods social inquiry a distinctive methodology? *Journal of Mixed Methods Research, 2*(1), 7-22.

Greene, J., & M. D'Oliveira. (2005). *Learning to use statistical tests in psychology* (3rd ed.). Milton Keynes: Open University Press.

Grbich, C. (2004). *New approaches in social research*. London: Sage.

Gries, S. T. (2009). *Quantitative corpus linguistics with R: A practical introduction*. New York: Routledge.

Grills, S. (Ed.). (1998). *Doing ethnographic research*. London: Sage.

Grotjahn, R. (1987). On the methodological basis of introspective methods. In C. Faerch & G. Kasper (Eds.), *Introspection in second language research* (pp. 54-81). Clevedon: Multilingual Matters.

Grotjahn, R. (1991). The research program subjective theories: A new approach in second language research. *Studies in Second Language Acquisition, 13*, 187-214.

Guba, E. G. (Ed.). (1990). *The paradigm dialog*. Newbury Park, CA: Sage.

Guba, E. G., & Lincoln, Y. S. (1994). Competing paradigms in qualitative research. In N. K. Denzin & Y. S. Lincoln (Eds.), *Handbook of qualitative research* (2nd ed.). (pp. 105-117). Thousand Oaks, CA: Sage.

Guilford J., & Fruchter, B. (1973). *Fundamental statistics in psychology and education*. New York: McGraw Hill.

Gupta, A. (2006). *Empiricism and experience*. Oxford, UK: Oxford University Press.

Gwet, K. (2001). *Handbook of inter-rater reliability*. Gaithersburg, MD: Stataxis.

Hair, J. F., Black, W. C., Babin, B. J., & Anderson, R. E. (2010). *Multivariate data analysis* (7th ed.). Prentice Hall.

Haladyna, T. M. (2004). *Developing and validating multiple-choice test items*. Mahwah, NJ: Lawrence Erlbaum Associates.

Hammersley, M. (1990). *Classroom ethnography: Empirical and methodological essays*. Milton Keynes: Open University Press.

Hammersley, M., & Atkinson, P. (1995). *Ethnography*. London: Routledge.

Hancock, G. R. & Mueller, R. O. (2010). *The reviewer's guide to quantitative methods in the social sciences*. London: Routledge.

Harklau, L. (2005). Ethnography and ethnographic research on second language teaching and learning. In E. Hinkel (Ed.), *Handbook of research in second language learning* (pp. 179-194). Mahwah, NJ: Lawrence Erlbaum Associates.

Harlow, L. L. (2005). *The essence of multivariate thinking: basic themes and methods*. Mahwah, NJ: Lawrence Erlbaum Associates.

Harris, R. J. (2001). *A primer of multivariate statistics* (3rd ed.). Mahwah, NJ: Lawrence Erlbaum Associates.
Hart, C. (1998). *Doing a literature review*. London: Sage.
Hatch, E. M., & Farhady, H. (1982). *Research design and statistics for applied linguistics*. Rowley, Mass.: Newbury House.
Hatch, E. M., & Lazaraton, A. (1991). *The research manual: Design and statistics for applied linguistics*. New York: Newbury House.
Hatch, J. A. (2002). *Doing qualitative research in education settings*. State University of New York Press.
Have, P. (1999). *Doing conversation analysis*. London: Sage.
Healey, J., F. (2009). *Statistics: A tool for social research* (8th ed.). Belmont, CA: Wadsworth.
Heap, J. L. (1997). Conversation analysis methods in researching language and education. In N. H. Hornberger & D. Corson (Eds.), *Research methods in language and education* (pp. 217-226). Encyclopedia of Language and Education, Vol. 8. Dordrecht: Kluwer.
Heigham, J. & & Croker, R. A. (2009). *Qualitative research in applied linguistics*. New York: Palgrave Macmillan.
Heiman, G. W. (2011). *Basic statistics for the behavioral sciences*. Belmont, CA: Wadsworth.
Hendricks, C. (2009). *Improving schools through action research: A comprehensive guide for educators*. Upper Saddle River, NJ: Pearson.
Henn, M., Weinstein, M. & Foard, N. (2006). A short introduction to social research. London: Sage.
Henning, G. (1986). Quantitative methods in language acquisition research. *TESOL Quarterly, 20*, 701-708.
Hesse-Biber, S. N. (2010). *Mixed methods research: merging theory with practice*. New York: The Guilford Press.
Hewson, C., Yule, P., Laurent, D. & Vogel, C. (2003). *Internet research methods*. London: Sage.
Hildenbrand, B. (2004). Anselm Strauss. In U. Flick, E. von Kardoff & I. Steinke (Eds.), *A companion to qualitative research*. London: Sage, 17-23.
Hinkel, E. (Ed.). (2005*). Handbook of research in second language learning*. Mahwah, NJ: Lawrence Erlbaum Associates.
Hinkel, E. (Ed.). (2011). *Handbook of research in second language learning* (Vol. 2). Mahwah, NJ: Lawrence Erlbaum Associates.
Hinton, P. R. (2004*). Statistics explained* (2nd ed.). London: Routledge.
Ho, R. (2006). *Handbook of univariate and multivariate data analysis and interpretation with SPSS*. Chapman and Hall/CRC.
Hock, R. (2004*). Extreme searcher's Internet handbook*. Medford, NJ: Information Today.

Holliday, A. (1996). Developing a sociological imagination: Expanding ethnography in international English language education. *Applied Linguistics, 17* (2), 234-255.

Holliday, A. (2002). *Doing and writing qualitative research*. Thousand Oaks, CA: Sage.

Holliday, A. (2004). Issues of validity in progressive paradigms of qualitative research. *TESOL Quarterly, 38* (4), 731-734.

Hood, M. (2009). Case Study. In Juanita Heigham & Robert A. Croker (Eds.), *Qualitative research in applied linguistics* (pp. 66-90). New York: Palgrave Macmillan.

Hopkins, D. A. (2008). A *teacher's guide to classroom research* (4th ed.). Buckingham, UK: Open University Press.

Hopkins, K. D., & Glass, G. V. (1996). *Basic statistics for the behavioral sciences*. Englewood Cliffs, NJ: Prentice-Hall.

Hornberger, N. H. (2008). *Encyclopedia of language and education* (Vols 1-10). (2nd ed.). New York: Springer.

Hornberger, N. H. (1994). Ethnography. *TESOL Quarterly, 28* (4), 688-690.

Howell, D. C. (2010). *Statistical methods for psychology* (7th ed.). Pacific Grove, CA: Duxbury/Thomson Learning.

Howitt, D. (2010). *Introduction to qualitative research methods in psychology*. Harlow: Pearson Education.

Howitt, D. & Cramer, D. (2011). *Introduction to research methods in Psychology*. (3rd ed.). Harlow: Pearson.

Huber, P. J. & Ronchetti, E. M. (2009). *Robust statistics* (2nd ed.). NJ: John Wiley & Sons.

Huberty, C. (1994). *Applied discriminant analysis*. New York: Wiley.

Huck, S. W. (2012). *Reading statistics and research* (6th ed.). Boston: Pearson Education.

Hughes, A. (2003). *Testing for language teachers* (2nd ed.). Cambridge, UK: Cambridge University Press.

Hulstijn J. H. (1997). Second language acquisition research in the laboratory: Possibilities and limitations. *Studies in Second Language Acquisition, 19*, 131-143.

Hyland, K. (2002). *Teaching and researching writing*. London: Longman

Hyland, K. & Paltridge, B. (Eds.). (2011). *Continuum companion to discourse analysis*. London: Continuum.

Janke, S. J. & Tinsley, F. C. (2005). *Introduction to linear models and statistical inference*. NJ: John Wiley & Sons.

Jarvis, S. (2002a). Research in TESOL Part I. *TESOL Research Interest Section Newsletter*, 8(3), 1–2.

Jarvis, S. (2002b). *Research in TESOL Part II. TESOL Research Interest Section Newsletter*, 9(1), 1–2.

Johnson, A. P. (2008). *A short guide to action research* (3rd ed.). Boston: Pearson Education.
Johnston, B. (1997). Do EFL teachers have careers? *TOFEL Quarterly, 31* (4), 681-712.
Johnson, D. M. (1992). *Approaches to research in second language learning.* New York: Longman.
Johnson, D. M., & Saville-Troike, M. (1992). Validity and reliability in qualitative research: Two researchers comment. *TESOL Quarterly, 26* (3), 602-605.
Johnson, K. (1996). The role of theory in L2 teacher education. *TESOL Quarterly, 30* (4), 765-771.
Johnson, K. (2008). *Quantitative methods in linguistics.* Oxford, UK: Blackwell.
Johnson, R. B. & Christensen, L. B. (2010). *Educational research: Quantitative, qualitative, and mixed approaches* (4nd ed.). Thousand Oaks, CA: Sage.
Josselson, R. B., & Lieblich, A. (Eds.). (1993). *The narrative study of lives.* Newbury Park, CA: Sage.
Johnson, R. B., & Onwuegbuzie, A. J. (2004). Mixed methods research: A research paradigm whose time has come. *Educational Researcher, 33*(7), 14-26.
Johnson, R. B., Onwuegbuzie, A. J., & Turner, L. A. (2007). Toward a definition of mixed methods. *Journal of Mixed Methods Research, 1*(1), 112-133.
Kalof, L., Dan, A. & Dietz, T. (2008). *Essentials of social research.* Maidenhead, UK: Open University Press.
Kane, M., & Trochim, W. M. K. (2007*). Concept mapping for planning and evaluation.* Thousand Oaks, CA: Sage.
Kasper, G. (1998). Analyzing verbal protocols. *TESOL Quarterly, 32* (2), 358-362.
Kaplan, R. (Ed.). (2010*). The Oxford handbook of applied linguistics* (2nd ed.). Oxford, UK: Oxford University Press.
Keppel, G. & Wickens, T. D. (2004) (4th ed.). *Design and analysis: A researcher's handbook.* Upper Saddle River, NJ: Pearson/Merrill Prentice Hall.
Kiely, R. & Rea-Dickins, P. (2005). *Program evaluation in language education.* New York: Palgrave Macmillan.
King, K. & Hornberger, N. H. (2008). *Research methods in language and education: Encyclopedia of language and education* (Vol. 10). (2nd ed.). New York: Springer.
Kirk, R. E. (1982). *Experimental design: Procedures for the behavioral sciences* (2nd ed.). Monterey, CA: Brooks/Cole.

Kirk, R. E. (1995). *Experimental design: Procedures for the behavioral sciences* (3rd ed.). Pacific Grove, CA: Brooks/Cole.

Kirk, R. E. (1996). Practical significance: A concept whose time has come. *Educational and Psychological Measurement, 56*, 746-759.

Kirk, R. E. (2008). *Statistics: An introduction* (5th ed.). Belmont, CA: Wadsworth.

Kvale, S. (1996). *Interviews: An introduction to qualitative research interviewing.* London: Sage.

Kemmis, S., & McTaggart, R. (Eds.). (1992). *The action research planner.* Geeloong, Victoria, Australia: Deakin University Press.

Kennedy, G. (1998). *An introduction to corpus linguistics.* London: Longman.

Kennedy, C. H. (2005). *Single-case designs for educational research.* Boston: Pearson.

Kiel, L. D., & Elliot, E. (Eds.) (1996). *Chaos theory in the social sciences: Foundations and applications*. Ann Arbor: University of Michigan Press.

Kincheloe, J. L. (2003). *Teachers as researchers: Qualitative inquiry as a path to empowerment* (2nd ed.). London: Routledge.

Kline, R. (2004). *Beyond significance testing: Reforming data analysis methods in behavioral research.* Washington, DC: American Psychological Association.

Kothari, C. R. (2008). *Research methodology: Methods and techniques* (2nd ed.). New Delhi: New Age International Publishers.

Kouritzin, S. (2000). Bringing life to research: Life history research and ESL. *TESL Canada Journal, 17* (2), 1-35.

Krathwohl, D. R. (1998*). Methods of educational and social science research: An integrated approach* (2nd ed.). New York: Longman.

Krippendorp, K. (2004). *Content analysis: An introduction to its methodology.* Thousand Oaks, CA: Sage.

Kubiszyn, T., & Borich, G. (2006). *Educational testing and measurement.* New York: Wiley.

Kumaravadivelu, B. (1999). Critical classroom discourse analysis. *TESOL Quarterly, 33* (3), 453-484.

Kumaravadivelu, B. (2006a). *Understanding language teaching: From method to postmethod.* Mahwah, NJ: Lawrence Erlbaum.

Kumpulainen, K., & Wray, D. (Eds.). (2002). *Classroom interaction and social learning: From theory to practice.* London: Routledge.

Landau, S. & Everitt, B. (2004). *Handbook of statistical analysis using SPSS.* Boca Raton, FL: Chapman & Hall/CRC.

Lantolf, J. P. (1996). Second language acquisition theory-building: Letting all the flowers bloom! *Language Learning, 46* (4), 713-749.

Lapan, D. S. &_Quartaroli, M. T. (Eds.). (2009). *Research essentials: An introduction to designs and practices.* San Francisco: Jossey-Bass.

Lapp, D., & Fisher, D. (Eds.). (2011). *Handbook of research on teaching the English language arts* (3nd ed.). New York: Routledge.
Larsen-Freeman, D. (1997). Chaos/complexity science and second language acquisition. *Applied Linguistics, 18* (2), 141-165.
Larsen-Freeman, D., & Long, M. H. (1991). *An introduction to second language acquisition research.* New York: Longman.
Larson-Hall, J. (2010). *A guide to doing statistics in second language research using SPSS.* New York: Routledge.
Lavrakas, P. J. (2008). *Encyclopedia of survey research methods* (Vol. 1 & 2). Thousand Oaks, CA: Sage.
Lawrence-Lightfoot, S., & Davis, J. H. (1997). *The art and science of portraiture.* San Francisco: Jossey-Bass.
Lazaraton, A. (1991). *A computer supplement to the research manual.* New York: Newbury House.
Lazaraton, A. (1995). Qualitative research in TESOL: A progress report. *TESOL Quarterly, 29* (3), 455-472.
Lazaraton, A. (1998). Research methods in applied linguistics journal articles. *TESOL Research Interest Section Newsletter, 5* (2), 3.
Lazaraton, A. (2000). Current trends in research methodology and statistics in applied linguistics. *TESOL Quarterly, 34* (1), 175-181.
Lazaraton, A. (2002). Quantitative and qualitative approaches to discourse analysis. *Annual Review of Applied Linguistics, 22*, 32-51.
Lazaraton, A. (2003). Evaluative criteria for qualitative research in applied linguistics: Whose criteria and whose research? *Modern Language Journal, 87* (1), 1-12.
Lazaraton, A. (2005). Quantitative research methods. In E. Hinkel (Ed.), *Handbook of research in second language learning* (pp. 209-224). Mahwah, NJ: Lawrence Erlbaum Associates.
Lazaraton, A. (2009). Discourse analysis. In Juanita Heigham & Robert A. Croker (Eds.), *Qualitative research in applied linguistics* (pp. 242-259). New York: Palgrave Macmillan.
Leary, M. R. (2011). *Introduction to behavioral research methods* (6th ed.). Englewood Cliffs, NJ: Prentice-Hall.
LeCompte, M., Millroy, W. L. & Preissle, J. (Eds.). (1992). *The Handbook of qualitative research in education.* London: Academic Press.
LeCompte, M. & Preissle, J. (1993). *Ethnography and qualitative design in educational research* (2nd ed.). London: Academic Press.
Lee, E., & Simon-Maeda, A. (2006). Racialized research identities in ESL/EFL research. *TESOL Quarterly, 40* (3), 573-594.
Leech, N. A., Barrett, K. C., & Morgan, G. A. (2005). *SPSS for intermediate statistics: Use and interpretation* (2nd ed.). Mahwah, NJ: Lawrence Erlbaum Associates.

Leech, N. L., & Onwuegbuzie, A. J. (2007). An array of qualitative data analysis tools: A call for qualitative data analysis triangulation. *School Psychology Quarterly, 22* (4), 557-584.

Leow, R. P., & Morgan-Short, K. (2004). To think aloud or not to think aloud. *Studies in Second Language Acquisition, 26* (1), 35-57.

Levy, M. (1997). CALL: Context and Conceptualisation. Oxford, UK: Oxford University Press.

Levy, P. S. & Lemeshow, S. (1999). *Sampling of populations: Methods and applications.* New York: Wiley-Interscience.

Lewins, A., & Silver, C. (2007). *Using software in qualitative analysis.* Thousand Oaks, CA: Sage.

Lewis-Beck, M. (Ed.). (1993). *Experimental design and methods.* Thousand Oaks, CA: Sage.

Liamputtong, P., & Ezzy, D. (2005). *Qualitative research methods* (2nd ed.). Melbourne, Australia: Oxford University Press.

Lieblich, A., Tuval-Mashiach, R., & Zilber, T. (1998). *Narrative research: Reading, analysis and interpretation.* Thousand Oaks, CA: Sage.

Lincoln, Y. S., & Guba, E. G. (1985). *Naturalistic inquiry.* Beverley Hills: Sage.

Lipsey, M. W., & Wilson, D. B. (2000). *Practical meta-analysis.* Thousand Oaks, CA: Sage.

Litosseliti, L. (Ed.). (2010). *Research methods in linguistics.* London: Continuum.

Locke, L. F., Silverman, S. J., & Spirduso, W. W. (1998). *Reading and understanding research.* Thousand Oaks, CA: Sage.

Locke, L., Silverman, S., & Spirduso, W. (2007). *Proposals that work: A guide for planning dissertations and grant proposals.* Thousand Oaks, CA: Sage.

Lodico, M. G., Spaulding, D. T. & Voegtle, K. H. (2010). *Methods in educational research: From theory to practice* (2nd ed.). San Francisco: Jossey-Bass.

Loehlin, J. (2004). *Latent variable models: An introduction to factor, path, and structural equation analysis.* Mahwah, NJ: Lawrence Erlbaum Associates.

Lohr, S. L. (1998). *Sampling: design and analysis.* Pacific Grove, CA: Brooks/Cole.

Lomax, R. G. (2007). *An introduction to statistical concepts for education and behavioral sciences* (2nd ed.). Mahwah, NJ: Lawrence Erlbaum Associates.

Long, M. H. (1990). The least a second language acquisition theory needs to explain. *TESOL Quarterly, 24* (4), 649-666.

Long, M. H. (1997). Construct validity in SLA research: A response to Firth and Wagner. *Modern Language Journal, 81* (3), 318-323.

Lopez, M. G., & Tashakkori, A. (2006). Differential outcomes of two bilingual education programs on English language learners. *Bilingual Research Journal, 30* (1), 123-145.

Low, M. (1999). Exploring cross-cultural inscriptions and difference: The effects of researchers' positionalities on inquiry practices. *TESOL Quarterly, 33*, 292-298.

Mack, N., Woodsong, C., Macqueen, K. M., Guest, G., Namey, E. (2005). *Qualitative research methods: A data collector's field guide*. NC: Family Health International.

McKay, S. L. (2006). *Researching second language classrooms*. Mahwah, NJ: Lawrence Erlbaum Associates.

Mackey, A., & Gass, S. M. (2005). *Second language research. Methodology and design*. Mahwah, NJ: Lawrence Erlbaum Associates.

Madison, D. S. (2005). *Critical ethnography: Method, ethics, and performance*. Thousand Oaks, CA: Sage.

Marczyk, G., DeMatteo, D., & Festinger, D. (2005). *Essentials of research designs and methodology*. NJ: John Wiley & Sons.

Markee, N. (1997). Second language acquisition research: A resource for changing teachers' professional cultures? *Modern Language Journal, 81* (1), 80-93.

Markee, N. (2000). *Conversation analysis*. Mahwah, NJ: Lawrence Erlbaum Associates.

Marshall, C., & Rossman, G. B. (2006*). Designing qualitative research* (4th ed.). Thousand Oaks, CA: Sage.

Marton, F. (1981). Phenomenography-Describing conceptions of the world around us. *Instructional Science, 10*, 177-200.

Maso, I. (2001). Phenomenology and ethnography. In P. Atkinson, et al. (Eds.), *Handbook of ethnography* (pp. 136-144). Thousand Oaks, CA: Sage.

Mason, J. (2002). *Qualitative researching* (2nd ed.). London: Sage.

Mathison, S. (Ed.). (2005). *Encyclopedia of evaluation*. Thousand Oaks, CA: Sage.

Matsuda, T. K., & Silva, T. (Eds.). (2005). *Second language writing research: Perspectives on the process of knowledge construction*. Mahwah, NJ: Lawrence Erlbaum.

Mauch, J., & Birch, J. (1998). *Guide to the successful thesis and dissertation*. New York: Marcel Dekker.

Mauthner, M., Birch, M., Jessop, J. & Miller, T. (Eds.). (2002). *Ethics in qualitative research*. London: Sage.

Maxwell, J. A. (1992). Understanding and validity in qualitative research. Harvard *Educational Review, 62* (3), 279-300.

Maxwell, J. A. (2005). *Qualitative research design: An interactive approach* (2nd ed.). Thousand Oaks, CA: Sage.

Maykut, P., & Morehouse, R. (1994). *Beginning qualitative research: A philosophic and practical guide*. Washington, DC: Falmer.
May, S. A. (1997). Critical ethnography. In N. H. Hornberger & D. Corson (Eds.), *Research methods in language and education* (pp. 197-206). Encyclopedia of Language and Education, Vol. 8. Dordrecht: Kluwer.
Mayring, P. (2004). Qualitative content analysis. In U. Flick, E. von Kardoff & I. Steinke (Eds.), *A companion to qualitative research*. London: Sage.
McBurney, D. H., & White, T. L. (2004). *Research methods*. Belmont, CA: Thomson.
McCarthy, M. (1991). *Discourse analysis for language teachers*. Cambridge, UK: Cambridge University Press.
McCarthy, M., & Carter, R. (2001). Size isn't everything: Spoken English, corpus, and the classroom. *TESOL Quarterly, 35* (2), 337-340.
McDonough, J., & McDonough, S. (1990). What's the use of research? *ELT Journal, 44* (2), 102-109.
McDonough, J., & McDonough, S. (1997). *Research methods for English language instructors*. London: Edward Arnold.
McGroarty, M. E., & Zhu, W (1997). Triangulation in classroom research: A study of peer revision. *Language Learning, 47* (1), 1-43.
McKay, S. L. (2006*). Researching second language classrooms*. Mahwah, NJ: Lawrence Erlbaum Associates.
McNiff, J., & Whitehead, J. (2002). *Action research: Principles and practice* (2nd ed.). London: Routledge.
Meinefeld,W. (2004). Hypotheses and prior knowledge in qualitative research. In U. Flick, E. von Kardoff & I. Steinke (Eds.), *A companion to qualitative research*. London: Sage, 153-8.
Mellow, J. D., Reeder, K., & Forster, F. (1996). Using time-series research designs to investigate the effects of instruction on SLA. *Studies in Second Language Acquisition, 18*, 325-350.
Menard, S. (2008). *Handbook of longitudinal research: Design, measurement, and analysis*. Elsevier Inc
Merriam, S. B. (1998). *Qualitative research and case study application in education*. San Francisco: Jossey-Bass.
Merriam, S. B., & Associates. (2002*). Qualitative research in practice*. San Francisco: Jossey-Bass.
Mertens, D. M. (2010). *Research and evaluation in education and psychology: Integrating diversity with quantitative, qualitative, and mixed methods* (3rd ed.). Thousand Oaks, CA: Sage.
Mertler, C. A. (2009). *Action research: Teachers as researchers in the classroom* (2nd ed.). Thousand Oaks, CA: Sage.
Messick, S. (1995). Validity of psychological assessment. *American Psychologist, 50*(9), 741-749.

Miles, M. & Huberman, M. (1994). *Qualitative Data Analysis* (2nd ed.). Beverly Hills, CA: Sage.
Miles, J., & Shevlin, M. E. (2001). *Applying regression and correlation.* London: Sage.
Mills, G. E. (2003). *Action research: A guide for the teacher researcher* (2nd ed.). Upper Saddle River, NJ: Merrill Prentice Hall.
Mills, A. J., Durepos, G., & Wiebe, E. (Eds.). (2010). *Encyclopedia of case study research* (Vol. 1 & 2). Thousand Oaks, CA: Sage.
Miller, R. L. & Brewer J. D. (2003). *The A-Z of social research: A dictionary of key social science research concepts.* Thousand Oaks, CA: Sage.
Miller, S. (1984). *Experimental design and statistics* (2nd ed.). London: Routledge.
Milroy, L. & Gordon, M. (2003). *Sociolinguistics: methods and interpretation.* Oxford, UK: Blackwell.
Mishler, E. G. (1986). *Research interviewing: Context and narrative.* Cambridge, Mass.: Harvard University Press.
Montfort, K. V., Oud, J. H. L., & Satorra, A. (Eds.). (2010). Longitudinal research with latent variables. Springer-Verlag Berlin Heidelberg.
Moran, D. (2000). *Introduction to phenomenology.* London: Routledge.
Morgan, D. L. (1988). *Focus groups as qualitative research.* Beverly Hills, CA: Sage.
Morgan, G. A., Leech, N. L., Gloeckner, G. W., & Barrett, K.C. (2004). *SPSS for introductory statistics: Use and interpretation* (2nd ed.). Mahwah, New Jersey: Lawrence Erlbaum Associates.
Morgan, S. E., Reichart T., & Harrison T. R. (2002). *From numbers to words: Reporting statistical results for the social sciences.* Boston: Allyn & Bacon.
Morse, J. M. & Richards, L. (2002). *Readme first for a user's guide to qualitative research.* Thousand Oaks, CA: Sage.
Mouton, J. & Marais, HC. (1990). Basic concepts: The methodology of the social sciences. HSRC Press.
Mousavi, S. A. (2012). *An encyclopedic dictionary of language testing* (5th ed.). Tehran: Rahnama Publications.
Moustakas, K. (1994). *Phenomenological research methods.* Thousand Oaks, CA: Sage.
Muijs, D. (2004). *Doing quantitative research in education with SPSS.* London: Sage.
Murphy, K. R., & Myors, B. (2004). *Statistical power analysis.* Mahwah, NJ: Lawrence Erlbaum Associates.
Murphy, L., Plake, B., & Spies, R. (Eds.). (2006). *Tests in print VII: An index to tests, test reviews, and the literature on specific tests.* Lincoln: University of Nebraska, Buros Institute of Mental Measurements.

Myers, J. L. & Well, A, D. (2003). *Research design and statistical analysis* (2nd ed.). Mahwah, NJ: Lawrence Erlbaum Associates.

Myers, J. L., Well, A, D., & Lorch, R. F. (2011). *Research design and statistical analysis*. (3rd ed.). Mahwah, NJ: Lawrence Erlbaum Publishers.

Nataliya V. Ivankova & John W. Creswell (2009). Mixed methods. In Juanita Heigham & Robert A. Croker (Eds.), *Qualitative research in applied linguistics* (pp. 135-161). New York: Palgrave Macmillan.

Neuman W. L. (2007). *Social research: qualitative and quantitative approaches* (2nd ed.). Boston: Pearson Education.

Nitko, A. J. (2001). *Educational assessment of students* (3rd ed.). Upper Saddle River, NJ: Prentice-Hall.

Norris, J., & Ortega, L. (2000). Effectiveness of L2 instruction: A research synthesis and quantitative meta-analysis. *Language Learning, 50*, 417-528.

Norton, B. (1997). Critical discourse research. In N. H. Hornberger & D. Corson (Eds.), *Research methods in language and education* (pp. 207-216). Encyclopedia of Language and Education, Vol. 8. Dordrecht: Kluwer.

Norton, L. S. (2009). *Action research in teaching and learning: A practical guide to conducting pedagogical research in universities*. London: Routledge.

Norton Pierce, B. (1995). The theory of methodology in qualitative research. *TESOL Quarterly, 29* (3), 569-576.

Norusis, M. J. (2006). *SPSS 15.0 guide to data analysis*. Upper Saddle River, NJ: Prentice Hall.

Nunan, D. (1991). Methods in second language classroom-oriented research: A critical review. *Studies in Second Language Acquisition, 13*, 249-274.

Nunan, D. (1992). *Research methods in language learning*. Cambridge, UK: Cambridge University Press.

Nunan, D. (2000). Research methods. In M. Byram (Ed.), *Routledge encyclopedia of language teaching and learning* (pp. 501-505). London: Routledge.

O'Donoghue, T. (2007). *Planning your qualitative research project: An introduction to interpretivist research in education*. London: Routledge.

O'Keeffe, A. & McCarthy, M. (2010). *The Routledge handbook of corpus linguistics*. London: Routledge.

O'Leary, Z. (2004). *The essential guide to doing research*. Thousand Oaks, CA: Sage.

Onwuegbuzie, A., & Johnson, B. (2006). The validity issue in mixed research. *Research in the Schools, 13*(1), 48-63.

Orna, L. (1995). *Managing information for research*. Buckingham, UK: Open University Press.
Ortega, L., & Iberri-Shea, G. (2005). Longitudinal research in second language acquisition: Recent trends and future directions. *Annual Review of Applied Linguistics, 25*, 26-45.
Ott, R. L. & Longnecker, M. (2010). *An introduction to statistical methods and data analysis* (6th ed.). Pacific Grove, CA: Brooks/Cole, Cengage Learning.
Pagano, R. R. (2009). *Understanding statistics in the behavioral sciences* (9th ed.). Belmont, CA: Wadsworth.
Page, M. C., Braver, S. L. & Mackinnon D. P. (2003). *Levine's guide to SPSS for analysis of variance* (2nd ed.). Mahwah, NJ: Lawrence Erlbaum Associates.
Pallant, J. (2010). *SPSS survival manual* (4rd ed.). Maidenhead, England: Open University Press.
Paltridge, B., & Phakiti, A. (Eds.) (2010). *Continuum companion to research methods in applied linguistics*. London: Continuum.
Paltridge, B. & Starfield, S. (2007). *Thesis and dissertation writing in a second Language: A handbook for supervisors*. London: Routledge.
Panetta, C. G. (Ed.). (2001). *Contrastive rhetoric revisited and redefined*. Mahwah, NJ: Lawrence Erlbaum Associates.
Patton, M. Q. (2002). *Qualitative evaluation and research methods* (3rd ed.). Newbury Park, CA: Sage.
Pavlenko, A. (2001). Language learning memoirs as a gendered genre. *Applied Linguistics, 22* (2), 213-240.
Pavlenko, A. (2002). Narrative study: Whose story is it, anyway? *TESOL Quartely, 36*, 213-218.
Pedhazur, E. (2006). *Multiple regression in behavioral research: Explanation and prediction* (3rd ed.). Belmont, CA: Wadsworth.
Pedhazur, E., & Schmelkin, L. (1991). *Measurement, design, and analysis: An integrated approach*. Hillsdale, NJ: Lawrence Erlbaum Associates.
Peers, I. (1996). *Statistical analysis for education and psychology researchers*. London: Falmer Press.
Peirce, B. N. (1995b). The theory of methodology in qualitative research. *TESOL Quarterly, 29* (3), 569-576.
Pennycook, A. (1994). Critical pedagogical approaches to research. In A. Cumming (Ed.), *Alternatives in TESOL research: Descriptive, interpretive, and ideological orientations*. TESOL Quarterly, 28, 690-693.
Pennycook, A. (2001). *Critical applied linguistics: A critical introduction*. Mahwah, NJ: Lawrence Erlbaum Associates.
Perry, F. L. (2011). *Research in applied linguistics: Becoming a discerning consumer* (2nd ed.). London: Routledge.

Peters, M. A. & Burbules, N. C. (2004). *Poststructuralism and educational research*. Rowman & Littlefield Publishers.

Phelps, R., Fisher, K., & Ellis, A. (2007). *Organizing and managing your research*. London: Sage.

Polkinghorne, D. E. (1988). *Narrative knowing and the human sciences*. Albany, New York: State University of New York Press.

Pollo, H. R., Henley, T. B., & Thompson, C. J. (1997). *The phenomenology of everyday life*. Cambridge, UK: Cambridge University Press.

Popham, W. J. (2005*). Classroom assessment: What teachers need to know*. Boston: Allyn & Bacon.

Porte, G. K. (2010). *Appraising research in second language learning: A practical approach to critical analysis of quantitative research* (2nd ed.). Amsterdam: John Benjamins.

Prior, L. (2003). *Using documents in social research*. London: Sage.

Pring, R. (2004). *Philosophy of Educational Research*. London: Continuum.

Punch, K. F. (2003). *Survey research: The basics*. London: Sage.

Punch, K. F. (2005). *Introduction to social research* (2nd ed.). Thousand Oaks, CA: Sage.

Ragin, C. C., Nagel, J., & White, P. (2004). *Workshop on scientific foundations of qualitative research*. Washington, DC: National Science Foundation.

Ragin, C. C. & Becker, H. S. (1992). *What is a case? Exploring the foundations of social inquiry*. New York: Cambridge University Press.

Ramanathan,V, & Atkinson, D. (1999). Ethnographic approaches and methods in L2 writing research: A critical guide and review. *Applied Linguistics, 20* (1), 44-70.

Rampton, B. (1997). Second language research in late modernity: A response to Firth & Wagner. *Modern Language Journal, 81*, 329-333.

Rampton, B., Roberts, C., Leung, C., & Harris, R. (2002). Methodology in the analysis of classroom discourse. *Applied Linguistics, 23* (3), 373-392.

Rao, P. S. R. S., Rao, Poduri, S. R. S. & Miller, W. (2000). *Sampling methodologies with applications*. New York: Lewis Publishers.

Ravid, R. (2011). *Practical statistics for educators* (4th ed.). UK: Rowman & Littlefield Publishers.

Reason, P., & Bradbury, H. (Eds.). (2001). *Handbook of action research*. Thousand Oaks, CA: Sage.

Remler, D. K. & Van Ryzin, G.G. (2011). *Research methods in practice: strategies for description and causation*. Thousand Oaks, CA: Sage.

Richards, J. C. & Renandya, W. A. (Eds.). (2002). *Methodology in language teaching: An anthology of current practice*. Cambridge, UK: Cambridge University Press.

Richards, J. C. & Schmidt, R. W. (2002*). Longman dictionary of language teaching and applied linguistics* (3rd ed.). London: Longman Group.
Richards, J. C. & Schmidt, R. W. (2010). *Longman dictionary of language teaching and applied linguistics* (4rd ed.). Pearson Education.
Richards, K. (2003). *Qualitative inquiry in TESOL*. Basingstoke: Palgrave Macmillan.
Richards, L. (2005). *Handling qualitative data: A practical guide*. Thousand Oaks, CA: Sage.
Richards, L., & Morse, J. (2007). *Read me first for a user's guide to qualitative methods* (2nd ed.). Thousand Oaks, CA: Sage.
Richardson, V. (Ed.). (2001). *Handbook of research on teaching* (4th ed.). New York: Macmillan.
Ridenour, C. S., & Newman, I. (2008). *Mixed methods research: Exploring the interactive continuum* (2nd ed.). Southern Illinois University Press.
Riessman, C. K. (1993). *Narrative analysis*. Newbury Park, CA: Sage.
Riessman, C. K. (2007). *Narrative methods in the human sciences*. Thousand Oaks, CA: Sage.
Rietveld, T., & van Hout, R. (2005). *Statistics in language research: Analysis of variance*. New York: Mouton de Gruyter.
Riggenbach, H. (1999). *Discourse analysis in the language classroom (*Vol. 1). Ann Arbor, MI: University of Michigan Press.
Ritchie, J. & Lewis, J. (Eds.). (2003). *Qualitative research practice: A guide for social science students and researchers*. Thousand Oaks, CA: Sage.
Roberts, B. (2002). *Biographical research*. Buckingham, UK: Open University Press.
Robertson, R., & Combs, A., (Eds.). (1995). *Chaos theory in psychology and the life sciences*. Hillsdale, NJ: Lawrence Erlbaum Associates.
Robson, C. (2002). *Real world research: a resource for social scientists and practitioner-researcher* (2nd ed.). Oxford, UK: Blackwell.
Rogers, R. (Ed.). (2011). *An introduction to critical discourse analysis in education* (2nd ed.). New York: Routledge.
Rohwer, G. (2010). *Models in statistical social research*. London: Routledge.
Rosenthal, R., & DiMatteo, M. R. (2001). Meta-analysis: Recent developments in quantitative methods for literature reviews. *Annual Review of Psychology, 52* (1), 59-82.
Rossman, G. B., & Rallis, S. F. (2003). *Learning in the field: An introduction to qualitative research* (2nd ed.). Thousand Oaks, CA: Sage.
Rowntree, D. (2004). *Statistics without tears: A primer for non-mathematicians*. Boston: Pearson.
Ruane, J. M. (2005). *Essentials of research methods: A guide to social science research*. Oxford, UK: Blackwell

Rubin, H. J., & Rubin, I. (2005). *Qualitative interviewing: The art of hearing data* (2nd ed.). Thousand Oaks, CA: Sage.

Rubio, O. (1997). Ethnographic interview methods in researching language and education. In N. H. Hornberger & D. Corson (Eds.), *Research methods in language and education* (pp. 153-164). Encyclopedia of Language and Education, Vol. 8. Dordrecht: Kluwer.

Rugg, G. & Petre, M. (2007). *A gentle guide to research methods*. Buckingham, UK: Open University Press.

Ruiyang, Y., & Allison, D. (2003). Research articles in applied linguistics: Moving from results to conclusions. *English for Specific Purposes, 22*, 365-385.

Ruspini, E. (2002). *Introduction to longitudinal research*. London: Routledge.

Russo, R. (2003). *Statistics for the behavioral sciences: An introduction*. New York: Psychology Press.

Rust, R. T, & Cooil, B. (1994). Reliability measures for qualitative data: Theory and implications. *Journal of Marketing Research, 31*, 1-14.

Rustin, M. (2000). Reflections on the biographical turn in social science. In P. Chamberlayne, J. Bornat & T. Wengraf (Eds.), *The turn to biographical methods in social science: Comparative issues and examples* (pp. 33-52). London: Routledge.

Sacks, H. (1992). *Lectures on conversation*. Oxford, UK: Basil Blackwell.

Sagor, R. (2011). *The action research guidebook: A four-step process for educators and teams* (2nd ed.). CA: Corwin Press.

Sahai, H. & Khurshid, A. (2001). *Pocket dictionary of statistics*. McGraw-Hill/Irwin.

Saito, H., & Ebsworth, M. E. (2004). Seeing English language teaching and learning through the eyes of Japanese EFL and ESL students. *Foreign Language Annals, 37* (1), 111-124.

Salkind, N. J. (2007). *Encyclopedia of measurement and statistics*. (Vols. 1-3). Thousand Oaks, CA: Sage.

Salkind, N. J. (2010a). *Excel statistics: A quick guide*. Thousand Oaks, CA: Sage.

Salkind, N. J. (2010b). *Statistics for people who (think they) hate statistics* (4th ed.). Thousand Oaks, CA: Sage.

Sandelowski, M., & Barroso, J. (2007). *Handbook for synthesizing qualitative research*. New York: Springer.

Sapsford, R., & V. Jupp. (Eds.). (2006). *Data collection and analysis* (2nd ed.). Thousand Oaks, CA: Sage.

Sarantakos, S. (2005). *Social research* (3rd ed.). New York: Palgrave Macmillan.

Schachter, J., & Gass, S. (1996). *Second language classroom research: Issues and opportunities*. Mahwah, NJ: Lawrence Erlbaum Associates.

Schegloff, E. A. (1993). Reflections on quantification in the study of conversation. *Research on Language and Social Interaction, 26*, 99-128.

Schegloff, E. A., Koshik, I., Jacoby, S., & Olsher, D. (2002). Conversation analysis and applied linguistics. *Annual Review of Applied Linguistics, 22*, 3-31.

Schensul, J. & LeCompte, D. (eds). (1999). *The ethnographer's* toolkit (Vols. 1-7). London: Sage.

Schiffrin, D., Tannen, D., & Hamilton, H. (Eds.). (2001). The handbook of discourse analysis. Oxford, UK: Blackwell.

Scholfield, P. (1995). Quantifying Language: *A researcher's and teacher's guide to gathering language data and reducing it to figures.* Clevedon, UK: Multilingual Matters.

Schwandt, T. A. (2007). *The Sage dictionary of qualitative inquiry* (3rd ed.). Thousand Oaks, CA: Sage.

Scollen, R. (1995). From sentences to discourses, ethnography to ethnographic: conflicting trends in TESOL research. *TESOL Quarterly, 29*, 381-384.

Scott, D., & Morrison, M. (2005). *Key ideas in educational research.* London: Continuum.

Sealey, A., & Carter, B. (2004). *Applied linguistics as social science.* London: Continuum.

Seedhouse, P. (2004). *The interactional architecture of the language classroom: A conversation analysis perspective.* Malden, MA: Blackwell.

Seidman, I. (2006). *Interviewing as qualitative research: A guide for researchers in education and the social sciences* (3rd ed.). New York: Teachers College Press.

Seidman, I. (2006). *Interviewing as qualitative research* (3rd ed.). New York: Teachers College Press.

Seliger, H. W., & Shohamy, E. (1989). *Second language research methods.* Oxford, UK: Oxford University Press.

Shadish, W. R., Cook, T. D., & Campbell, D. T. (2002). *Experimental and quasi-experimental designs for generalized causal inference.* Boston, MA: Houghton Mifflin.

Shank, G. D. (2006). *Qualitative research: A personal skills approach* (2nd ed.). Upper Saddle River, NJ: Pearson Education.

Shaughnessy, J. J., E. Zechmeister, & J.S. Shaughnessy. (2011). *Research methods in psychology* (9th ed.). New York: McGraw Hill.

Sherman, R. R. & Webb, R. B. (Eds.). (2005). *Qualitative research in education: Focus and methods.* London: Routledge.

Sheskin, D. J. (2011). *Handbook of parametric and nonparametric statistical procedures* (5th ed.). Boca Raton, FL: Chapman & Hall/CRC.

Siegel, A. F. (1990). Multiple *t*-tests: Some practical considerations. *TESOL Quarterly, 24* (4), 773-775.

Silverman, D. (2005). *Doing qualitative research: A practical handbook* (2nd ed.). London: Sage.

Silverman, D. (2006). Interpreting qualitative data: Methods for analyzing talk, text and interaction (3rd ed.). London: Sage.

Simpson, J. (Ed.). (2011). *The Routledge handbook of applied linguistics.* London Routledge.

Singh, Y. K. (2006). *Fundamental of research methodology and statistics.* New Delhi: New Age International Publishers.

Skehan, P. (1998). *A cognitive approach to language learning.* Oxford, UK: Oxford University Press.

Slezak, P. (2002). Thinking about thinking: Language, thought, and introspection. *Language & Communication, 22,* 373-394.

Sokolowski, R. (2000). *Introduction to phenomenology.* Cambridge, UK: Cambridge University Press.

Somekh, B. (2006). *Action research: A methodology for change and development.* Maidenhead, UK: Open University Press.

Sorenson, S. (2010). *Webster's new world student writing handbook* (5th ed.). Hoboken, NJ: John Wiley & Sons.

Sowell, E. J. (2000). *Educational research: An integrative introduction.* New York: McGraw Hill.

Spada, N. (1994). Classroom interaction analysis. *TESOL Quarterly, 28* (4), 685-688.

Spector, P. E. (1994). *Research designs.* Thousand Oaks, CA: Sage.

Spicer, J. (2005). *Making sense of multivariate data analysis.* Thousand Oaks, CA: Sage.

Spielberg, H. (1982). *The phenomenological movement.* Dordrecht: Kluwer Academic Press.

Spradley, J. P. (1979). *The ethnographic interview.* New York: Holt, Rinehart and Winston.

Spradley, J. P. (1980). *Participation observation.* New York: Holt, Rinehart & Winston.

SPSS Inc. (2011). *SPSS base 20.0 for windows user's guide.* SPSS Inc., Chicago

Stake, R. E. (1995). *The art of case study research.* Thousand Oaks, CA: Sage.

Stake, R. E. (2000). Case studies. In N. K. Denzin & Y. S. Lincoln. (Eds.), *Handbook of qualitative research* (2nd ed.). (pp. 435-454). Thousand Oaks, CA: Sage.

Stebbins, R. (2001). *Exploratory research in the social sciences.* London: Sage.

Stephen, M. & Hornberger, N. H. (2008). *Encyclopedia of language and education.* (Vols. 1-10). (2nd ed.). New York: Springer.

Stevens, J. R. (2002). *Applied multivariate statistics for the social sciences.* Mahwah, NJ: Lawrence Erlbaum Associates.

Steven J. R., Paul S., & Keith R. (2011). *Research methods for applied language studies: An advanced resource book for students.* London: Routledge.

Stewart D., Shamdasani, P., & Rook, D. (2007). *Focus groups: Theory and practice* (2nd ed.). Thousand Oaks, CA: Sage.

Stewart, A. (2002). *Basic statistics and epidemiology: A practical guide.* UK: Radcliffe Medical Press Ltd.

Stewart, T. (2006). Teacher-researcher collaboration or teachers' research? *TESOL Quarterly, 40* (2), 421-430.

Strauss, A., & Corbin, J. (1994). Grounded Theory methodology. In N. K. Denzin & Y. S. Lincoln (Eds.), *Handbook of qualitative research* (pp. 273-85). Thousand Oaks, CA: Sage.

Strauss, A., & Corbin, J. (1998). *Basics of qualitative research: Techniques and procedures for developing Grounded Theory* (2nd ed.). Thousand Oaks, CA: Sage.

Stringer, E. (2008). *Action research in education* (2nd ed.). Upper Saddle River, NJ: Pearson/Merrill Prentice Hall.

Sue, V. M., & Ritter, V. A. (2007*). Conducting online surveys.* Thousand Oaks, CA: Sage.

Swales, J. M. (1990). *Genre analysis.* Cambridge, UK: Cambridge University Press.

Swales, J. M., & Feak, C. (2000). *English in today's research world.* Ann Arbor: University of Michigan Press.

Tabachnick, B. G. & Fidell, L.S (2000). *Computer-assisted research design and analysis.* Pearson Education.

Tabachnick, B. G., & Fidell, L. S. (Eds.). (2001). *Handbook of mixed methods in social and behavioral research.* Thousand Oaks, CA: Sage.

Tabachnick, B. G. & Fidell, L.S (2006). *Experimental designs using ANOVA.* Duxbury Press.

Tabachnick, B. G. & Fidell, L.S. (2007). *Using multivariate statistics* (5th ed.). Boston: Pearson Education.

Tailor, G., R. (Ed.). (2005). *Integrating qualitative and quantitative methods in research* (2nd ed.). Maryland: University Press of America.

Tarling, R. (2006). *Managing social research.* London: Routledge.

Tarone, E. S. (1994a). Analysis of learner language. In A. Cumming (Ed.), Alternatives in TESOL research: Descriptive, interpretive, and ideological orientations. *TESOL Quarterly, 28,* 676-678.

Tarone, E., S. Gass, & A. Cohen. (Eds.). (1994). *Research methodology in second language acquisition.* Hillsdale, NJ: Erlbaum.

Tashakkori, A., & Teddlie, C. (1998). *Mixed methodology: Combining qualitative and quantitative approaches.* Thousand Oaks, CA: Sage.
Tashakkori, A., & Teddlie, C. (Eds.). (2003). *Handbook on mixed methods in social and behavior science.* Thousand Oaks, CA: Sage.
Teddlie, C., & Tashakkori, A. (2006). A general typology of research designs featuring mixed methods. *Research in the Schools, 13*(1), 12-28.
Tesch, R. (1990). *Qualitative research: Analysis types and software tools.* London: Falmer.
Tetnowski, J., & Damico, J. (2001). A demonstration of the advantages of qualitative methodologies in stuttering research. *Journal of Fluency Disorders, 26*, 17-42.
Thieberger, N. (2012). *The Oxford handbook of linguistic fieldwork.* Oxford: Oxford University Press.
Thomas, R. M. (2005). *Teachers doing research: An introductory guidebook.* Boston: Pearson Education.
Thomas, M. (1994). Assessment of L2 proficiency in second language acquisition research. *Language Learning, 44*, 307-336.
Thompson, B. (1984). *Canonical correlation analysis: Uses and interpretation.* Beverly Hills, CA: Sage.
Thompson, B. (2004). *Exploratory and confirmatory factor analysis: Understanding concepts and applications.* Washington, DC: American Psychological Association.
Thompson, B. & Snyder, P. A. (1997). Statistical significance testing practices. *Journal of Experimental Education, 66*, 75-83.
Thompson, S. K. (2002). *Sampling.* New York: John Wiley & Sons.
Thorndike, R. M. (2005). *Measurement and evaluation in psychology and education.* Upper Saddle River, NJ: Pearson Education.
Todd, Z., Nerlich, B., McKeown, S., Clarke, D. D. (Eds.). (2004). *Mixing methods in psychology: The integration of qualitative and quantitative methods in theory and practice.* New York: Psychology Press.
Toohey, K. (1995). Qualitative research and teacher education: from the ethnography of communication to critical ethnography in ESL teacher education. *TESOL Quarterly, 29* (3), 576-581.
Tortu, S., Goldsamt, L. A. & Hamid, R. (Eds.). (2001). *A practical guide to research and services with hidden populations.* Boston, MA: Allyn and Bacon.
Trochim, W. M. K. & Donnelly, James P. (2007). *The research methods knowledge base* (3rd ed.). Cincinnati: Atomic Dog Publishing.
Trochim, W. M. K (2005). *Research methods: The concise knowledge base.* Cincinnati: Atomic Dog Publishing.

Tsui, A. (2001). Classroom interaction. In R. Carter & D. Nunan (Eds.), *The Cambridge guide to teaching English to speakers of other languages.* Cambridge, UK: Cambridge University Press.

Tuckman, B. (1994). *Conducting educational research.* New York: Harcourt Brace College.

Twisk, J. W. R. (2003). *Applied longitudinal data analysis for epidemiology: A practical guide.* Cambridge, UK: Cambridge University Press.

Ulichny, P. (1991). The role of hypothesis testing in qualitative research: A researcher comments. *TESOL Quarterly, 25* (1), 200-202.

Upton, G. & Cook, I. (2008). *A dictionary of statistics* (2nd ed.). New York: Oxford University Press.

Urdan, T. C. (2005). *Statistics in plain English* (2nd ed.). Mahwah, NJ: Lawrence Erlbaum Associates.

Urdan, T. C. (2010). *Statistics in plain English* (3rd ed.). Mahwah, NJ: Lawrence Erlbaum Associates.

Upton, T. C., & Connor, U. (2001). Using computerized corpus analysis to investigate the textlinguistic discourse moves of a genre. *English for Specific Purposes, 20* (4), 313-329.

VanderStoep, S. W., & Johnston, D. D. (2009). *Research methods for everyday life: blending qualitative and quantitative approaches.* CA: John Wiley & Sons.

Van Lier, L. (1988). *The classroom and the language learner: Ethnography and second language classroom research.* London: Longman.

Van Lier, L. (1994). Forks and hope: Pursuing understanding in different ways. *Applied Linguistics, 15* (3), 328-346.

Van Lier, L. (2005). Case study. In E. Hinkel (Ed.), *Handbook of research in second language learning* (pp. 195-208). Mahwah, NJ: Lawrence Erlbaum Associates.

Van Manen, M. (1990). *Researching lived experience: Human science for an action sensitive pedagogy.* New York: State University of New York Press.

Van Someren, M. W., Barnard, Y. F., & Sandberg, J. (1994). *The think aloud method: Apractical guide to modeling cognitive processes.* London: Academic Press.

Verhoeven, L. (1997). Experimental methods in researching language and education. In N. H. Hornberger & D. Corson (Eds.), *Research methods in language and education* (pp. 79-88). Encyclopedia of Language and Education, Vol. 8. Dordrecht: Kluwer.

Yin, R. K. (2003). *Case study research: Design and methods* (3rd ed.). Thousand Oaks, CA: Sage.

Vogt, W. P. (1999). *Dictionary of statistics and methodology* (2nd ed.). Newbury Park, CA: Sage.

Wajnryb, R. (1993). *Classroom observation tasks: A resource book for language teachers and trainers.* Cambridge, UK: Cambridge University Press.
Walford, G. (2001). *Doing qualitative educational research: A personal guide to the research process.* London: Continuum.
Wallace, M. J. (1998). *Action research for language instructors.* Cambridge, UK: Cambridge University Press.
Watson-Gegeo, K. A. (1988). Ethnography in ESL: Defining the essentials. *TESOL Quarterly, 22,* 575-592.
Watson-Gegeo, K. A. (1997). Classroom ethnography. In N. H. Hornberger & D. Corson (Eds.), *Research methods in language and education (pp.135-144). Encyclopedia of Language and Education,* Vol. 8. Dordrecht: Kluwer.
Wainer, H. (2000). *Drawing inferences from self-selected samples.* Mahwah, NJ: Lawrence Erlbaum Associates.
Wasserman, L. (2004). *All of statistics: A concise course in statistical inference.* New York: Springer.
Weinberg, S. L. (2008). *Statistics using SPSS: An integrative approach* (2nd ed.). Cambridge, UK: Cambridge University Press.
Weinberg, S. L., & Abramowitz, S. K. (2002). *Data analysis for the behavioral sciences using SPSS.* Cambridge, UK: Cambridge University Press.
Wengraf, P. (2001). *Qualitative research interviewing: Biographic narrative and semi-structured methods.* London: Sage.
Widdowson, H. (2000). On the limitations of linguistics applied. *Applied Linguistics, 21*(1), 3–25.
Wiersma, W. & Jurs, S. T. (2009). *Research methods in education: An introduction* (9th ed.). Pearson/Allyn and Bacon.
Wilcox, R. R. (2010). *Fundamentals of modern statistical methods: Substantially improving power and accuracy* (2nd ed.). New York: Springer.
Wilcox, R. R. (2003). *Applying contemporary statistical techniques.* San Diego, CA: Elsevier Science.
Willett, J. (1995). Becoming first graders in an L2: An ethnographic study of L2 socialization. *TESOL Quarterly, 29,* 473-503.
Williams, M. & May, T. (1996). *Introduction to the philosophy of social research.* London: Routledge.
Winer, B. J. (1971). *Statistical principles in experimental design* (2nd ed.). New York: McGraw-Hill.
Winer, B. J., Brown, D. R., & Michels, K. M. (1991). *Statistical principles in experimental design.* New York: McGraw-Hill.
Wolcott, H. F. (1994). *Transforming qualitative data: Description, analysis, and interpretation.* Thousand Oaks, CA: Sage.

Wolcott, H. F. (2001). *Writing up qualitative research*. Thousand Oaks, CA: Sage.
Wolf, F. M. (1986). *Meta-analysis: Quantitative methods for research synthesis*. Newbury Park, CA: Sage.
Woods, P. (1992). Symbolic interactionism: theory and method. In M. LeCompte, W. L. Millroy and J. Preissle (Eds.), *The Handbook of qualitative research in education*. London: Academic Press, 337-404.
Woods, A., Fletcher, P. & Hughes, A. (1986). *Statistics in language studies*. Cambridge, UK: Cambridge University Press.
Wooffitt, R. (2005). *Conversation analysis and discourse analysis: A comparative and critical introduction*. London: Sage.
Wray, A., Trott, K., & Bloomer, A. (2006). *Projects in linguistics: A practical guide to researching language* (2nd ed.). London: Edward Arnold.
Wright, D. B. (2003). Making friends with your data: improving how statistics are conducted and reported. *British Journal of Educational Psychology, 73*, 123-36.
Wright, D. (1996). *Understanding statistics*. Thousand Oaks, CA: Sage.
Yin, R. K. (2009). *Case study research: Design and methods*. Thousand Oaks, CA: Sage.

www.ingramcontent.com/pod-product-compliance
Lightning Source LLC
Chambersburg PA
CBHW052037290426
44111CB00011B/1534